EXCAVATIONS ALONG HADRIAN'S WALL 2019–2021

EXCAVATIONS ALONG HADRIAN'S WALL 2019–2021

STRUCTURES, THEIR USES, AND AFTERLIVES

ROB COLLINS & JANE HARRISON

OXBOW | books
Oxford & Philadelphia

Published in the United Kingdom in 2024 by
OXBOW BOOKS
The Old Music Hall, 106–108 Cowley Road, Oxford, OX4 1JE

and in the United States by
OXBOW BOOKS
1950 Lawrence Road, Havertown, PA 19083

Hardback Edition: ISBN 978-1-78925-944-5
Digital Edition: ISBN 978-1-78925-945-2 (epub)

A CIP record for this book is available from the British Library

Library of Congress Control Number: 2023949574

Printed in Malta by Melita Press

Typeset in India by Lapiz Digital Services, Chennai.

For a complete list of Oxbow titles, please contact:

UNITED KINGDOM
Oxbow Books
Telephone (0)1226 734350
Email: oxbow@oxbowbooks.com
www.oxbowbooks.com

UNITED STATES OF AMERICA
Oxbow Books
Telephone (610) 853-9131, Fax (610) 853-9146
Email: queries@casemateacademic.com
www.casemateacademic.com/oxbow

Oxbow Books is part of the Casemate Group

Front cover: A view of the WallCAP excavation at Walltown Crags, across the early 20th century remains of Walltown Quarry East (Pete Savin, used with permission)
Back cover: WallCAP's excavations at Walltown Crags (WallCAP)

Contents

List of figures	vi
List of tables	ix
Abbreviations	x
Preface	xi
Acknowledgements	xii
1. Introduction	1
2. The Vallum under pasture and under plough at Heddon	12
3. Geophysical survey of the curtain at Thirlwall and Drumburgh *Alex Turner*	24
4. The curtain at Port Carlisle: survey and excavation	33
5. The curtain at Walltown Crags: survey and excavation	43
6. The Wall-crossing at the Cam Beck: survey and excavation	56
7. Corbridge: survey and excavation	89
8. Conclusion	161
Appendix 1: Contexts	166
Appendix 2: Specialist report data	201
Cam Beck: Gorge Survey *(Rob Collins and Nicky Garland)*	201
Charred plant remains and wood charcoal assessment: Cam Beck, Corbridge, and Heddon-on-the-Wall *(Ellen Simmons)*	203
Corbridge: assessment of animal bone (COR21) *(Don O'Meara)*	210
Corbridge: burnt bone from structured deposit *(Lauren McIntyre)*	213
Corbridge: bulk finds *(Rob Collins)*	214
Corbridge: assessment of slag and related material *(David Dungworth)*	218
Corbridge: building materials and fired clay *(Amparo Valcarcel)*	218
Cat's Stairs: consolidation of collapsed fabric *(Jane Harrison)*	225
Port Carlisle: consolidation of collapsed fabric and insertion of new farm gate *(Jane Harrison and Kathryn Murphy)*	226
Steel Rigg: consolidation of collapsed fabric *(Jane Harrison)*	227
Turret 44b (Mucklebank), Walltown: consolidation of collapsed fabric *(Jane Harrison)*	228
Walltown Crags: reconditioning and consolidation of tumbled fabric *(Jane Harrison)*	228
Bibliography	229
Index	235

List of figures

Map 1	Hadrian's Wall	xiii
Figure 1.1	The stone curtain of Hadrian's Wall at Walltown Crags	1
Figure 1.2	WallCAP volunteers recording a trench section at Cam Beck	2
Figure 1.3	A map of Hadrian's Wall relative to contemporary settlement	3
Figure 1.4	Looking east along the Solway coast at Bowness	4
Figure 1.5	The Wall in Wall-mile 37, as viewed from the air and the ground	4
Figure 1.6	The gently rolling hills that flank the upland central sector	5
Figure 1.7	The A69 and West Road following the line of the Wall	5
Figure 1.8	The ditch and berm north of the Wall at Carvoran	5
Figure 1.9	The Vallum at Down Hill, looking east	6
Figure 1.10	Turret 7b at Denton	6
Figure 1.11	Milecastle 39, looking west	6
Figure 1.12	An aerial view of the fort at Housesteads	7
Figure 1.13	A map showing the extent of the Stone Wall and Turf Wall	8
Figure 1.14	A map showing the location of HAR sites	10
Figure 2.1	Location of the fieldwork area	13
Figure 2.2	A LiDAR model of the survey area	13
Figure 2.3	Location and results of gradiometry surveys across the Vallum	14
Figure 2.4	Location and results of resistivity surveys across the Vallum	15
Figure 2.5	Comparative profiles of topographic surface transects across the Vallum	15
Figure 2.6	The excavation trench across the Vallum	16
Figure 2.7	The full plan of the trench	16
Figure 2.8	The position of the Vallum north and south mounds and ditch coloured	17
Figure 2.9	The full profile of the trench	18
Figure 2.10	The Vallum ditch in profile, mid-excavation and post-excavation	19
Figure 2.11	Section drawing of the Vallum ditch, west section	20
Figure 2.12	Section drawing of the Vallum north mound, east section	20
Figure 2.13	The Vallum north mound, as revealed in the west section	21
Figure 2.14	Section drawing of the Vallum north mound, west section	22
Figure 2.15	Section drawing of the Vallum south mound, west section	22
Figure 2.16	Section drawing of the Vallum south mound, east section	22
Figure 2.17	The northern edge of the Vallum south mound	22
Figure 2.18	Interpretation of the excavation results	23
Figure 3.1	Location of the survey area	25
Figure 3.2	LiDAR model of the location	25
Figure 3.3	The north–south elevation profile across the survey area	26
Figure 3.4	Gradiometry survey results and interpretation	26
Figure 3.5	Resistivity survey results and interpretation	27
Figure 3.6	Location of the Drumburgh survey area	28

Figure 3.7	Richmond's 1947 plan of Drumburgh	29
Figure 3.8	LiDAR imaging showing Drumburgh's location at the top of a knoll	29
Figure 3.9	Overview of the gradiometer survey results	30
Figure 3.10	Interpretation of the gradiometer survey results, western part	31
Figure 3.11	Interpretation of the gradiometer survey results, eastern part	31
Figure 3.12	Resistivity survey results and interpretation	31
Figure 4.1	Location of the site	33
Figure 4.2	The portion of Wall curtain *in situ*, west of the existing field gate	34
Figure 4.3	Gradiometry survey results with trench positions	35
Figure 4.4	Resistivity survey results with trench positions	35
Figure 4.5	Elevation and section drawing of the curtain	36
Figure 4.6	A photogrammetric model of the existing fieldgate	36
Figure 4.7	Possible foundation stones of the Wall surviving at ground level	37
Figure 4.8	The line of the Wall curtain over a LiDAR model	38
Figure 4.9	Trench 1 south	39
Figure 4.10	Section drawing of Trench 1, south, west section	39
Figure 4.11	Trench 1, south	40
Figure 4.12	Trench 1, north	40
Figure 4.13	Trench 2 before excavation	41
Figure 4.14	Trench 2 after excavation	41
Figure 4.15	Section drawing of Trench 2, west section	41
Figure 4.16	Photograph of Trench 2, west section	42
Figure 5.1	The location of the site	43
Figure 5.2	The stone curtain looking east at Walltown	44
Figure 5.3	The locations of Trenches 1 and 2 and the line of the curtain, on LiDAR	45
Figure 5.4	Trench 1 from the south following removal of the turf	46
Figure 5.5	Trench 1, south, east section drawing and photograph	47
Figure 5.6	Trench 1, south, west section drawing and photograph	47
Figure 5.7	A section drawing and photograph of the north face of the Wall	48
Figure 5.8	A section drawing and photograph of the south face of the Wall	50
Figure 5.9	Trench 2 before and after excavation	51
Figure 5.10	Trench 2, east section and photograph	52
Figure 5.11	South face of the Wall curtain in Trench 2	53
Figure 5.12	A reconstruction of phases of ruin and collapse at Walltown	54
Figure 6.1	An aerial view of the Cam Beck looking northwest	56
Figure 6.2	The location of the site	57
Figure 6.3	The historic weir from the base of the gorge formed by the Cam Beck	59
Figure 6.4	The central and eastern portions of the historic weir	60
Figure 6.5	A U-shaped cut in the bedrock at the east end of the weir	60
Figure 6.6	Dressed stones, almost certainly re-used Roman stones, at the west end of the weir	61
Figure 6.7	Stones projecting from the east bank of the gorge	62
Figure 6.8	Results of the gradiometry survey east of the Cam Beck	63
Figure 6.9	Results of the resistivity survey east of the Cam Beck	63
Figure 6.10	Plan of Trench 3 and east section at Cam Beck	64
Figure 6.11	Plan of Trench 2 indicating key features and contexts	66
Figure 6.12	Plan of Trench 2 indicating identified structural features in discrete colours	67
Figure 6.13	West section of slot 3 located along the northwest edge of Trench 2	68
Figure 6.14	The west and east sections of the northern end of slot 3	68
Figure 6.15	Plan of the area in Trench 2 where Structure 1 was detected	69
Figure 6.16	The south and west sections across Structure 1	70
Figure 6.17	Plan of Trench 2	72
Figure 6.18	The area of Structure 2, looking west	73
Figure 6.19	Plan of the destruction deposits associated with Structure 2	74
Figure 6.20	Section drawing of sub-oval pit [2010]	75
Figure 6.21	A large stone associated with a levelling layer	75
Figure 6.22	An aerial photograph of the ploughed field west of the beck	77

Figure 6.23	Key objects in Trench 2	81
Figure 6.24	A cast-iron stake	84
Figure 6.25	A reconstruction of the Turf Wall phase at Cam Beck	86
Figure 6.26	A reconstruction of the Stone Wall phase at Cam Beck	87
Figure 7.1	Location of the excavation site at Corbridge	89
Figure 7.2	The extent of Roman Corbridge as revealed by gradiometry	91
Figure 7.3	Resistivity survey results and interpretation	92
Figure 7.4	Superimposition of 2019 features on a 2012 aerial photograph, Trench 4	96
Figure 7.5	The south section of pit [1018]	97
Figure 7.6	Superimposition of 2019 features on a 2021 aerial photograph, Trench 5	98
Figure 7.7	Plan of Trench 4 after removal of the top soil and initial subsoil	99
Figure 7.8	Plan of Trench 4, phases 1 and 2	100
Figure 7.9	Section drawing of various features from Trench 4, phase 1	101
Figure 7.10	Plan of the early road surface in Trench 4	102
Figure 7.11	Section drawings of foundations and roads from Trench 4, phases 1 and 2	103
Figure 7.12	Plan of the phase 2 road surface in Trench 4	105
Figure 7.13	Sections of the conduit associated with the phase 2 road in Trench 4	106
Figure 7.14	A plan of surviving flagging associated with the west wall	107
Figure 7.15	The remains of the phase 2 smithy	107
Figure 7.16	A plan of the pit [4045]	111
Figure 7.17	The plan of Trench 5	114
Figure 7.18	Sections through the walls of the building	115
Figure 7.19	A plan of the building in Trench 5, focusing on internal features	117
Figure 7.20	A section of the oven or hearth [5022]	118
Figure 7.21	Plan of a sub-circular pit cut into the remains of the oven or hearth [5022]	120
Figure 7.22	Decorated sherds of samian	123
Figure 7.23	A. Graphical breakdown of ceramics by fabric and function. B. Graphical breakdown of vessel form / function	131
Figure 7.24	A. Breakdown of fabric from Trenches 4 and 5. B. Breakdown of fabric from Trench 5	132
Figure 7.25	Illustration of vessels from fills in Trench 4	133
Figure 7.26	A–N. Artefacts from the Corbridge excavations	142
Figure 7.27	Reconstruction buildings at Corbridge	160

List of tables

Table 6.1	Quantification of the Roman ceramics	78
Table 6.2	Distribution of Roman ceramics	79
Table 6.3	Distribution and quantification of the post-Roman pottery	79
Table 6.4	Artefacts summarised by context	80
Table 7.1	Fabric codes and expansions with a list of relevant typologies	124
Table 7.2	Quantification of the Roman pottery	126
Table 7.3	Distribution and dating of the ceramics per context	129
Table 7.4	Quantification and distribution of the post-Roman ceramics	135
Table 7.5	Summary of artefacts and material culture by context	140
Table A2.1	Dislodged stonework along eastern base of the weir	201
Table A2.2	Dressed stones found at the western terminal of the weir	201
Table A2.3	Stones projecting out of the east bank of the gorge	202
Table A2.4	Dislodged stonework found approx. 100–150 m downstream of the weir	203
Table A2.5	Archaeobotanical sample assessment	206
Table A2.6	Animal bone summarised by context	211
Table A2.7	Summary of weights from the deposit	213
Table A2.8	Categories of slag and related materials identified from excavation	218
Table A2.9	Summary of slag and related materials	218
Table A2.10	Summary of metallic objects	219
Table A2.11	Summary of other objects	219
Table A2.12	Quantity and weight of the different types of stone identified	222
Table A2.13	Materials and fabrics by context	222
Table A2.14	Comparative table between the material found in both trenches	224

Abbreviations

CSIR *Corpus Signorum Imperii Romani: Great Britain, Vol. 1.x*, with the x indicating the specific fascicule of the series

RIB *Roman Inscriptions of Britain*, typically followed by a number referring to a specific stone. This is accessible online at https://romaninscriptionsofbritain.org

TV *Tabulae Vindolandenses*, typically followed by a number referring to a specific tablet. This is accessible online at https://romaninscriptionsofbritain.org/tabvindol

Preface

This monograph is the result of research and activity undertaken as part of the Hadrian's Wall Community Archaeology Project (WallCAP), funded by the UK National Lottery Heritage Fund. The funding from Lottery supported the salaries of project staff, paid for the expenses accrued by staff and project volunteers, and supported costs for training of volunteers and undertaking of fieldwork and subsequent analysis. The bespoke illustrations in this volume, too, were made possible with Lottery's support.

WallCAP was a complex project with many aims, and working with various audiences and stakeholders. Broadly speaking, the project sought to: increase our knowledge and understanding of Hadrian's Wall; better understand and reduce the risks facing various parts of Hadrian's Wall; and ensure that local communities and the public were more engaged with the monument. WallCAP organised and hosted more than 300 activities during the course of the project (2019–2022) to meet these aims, with two strands in particular contributing to this volume.

The Heritage At Risk (HAR) strand consisted of fieldwork undertaken with the primary aim of better understanding a known risk to one or more elements of the Wall monument, to investigate a part of the monument that was poorly understood, and/or to complete conservation or consolidation work that would better protect the monument in future years. That fieldwork is reported on in this volume.

The work of the Stone Sourcing & Dispersal (SSD) strand was focused on the geology of the Wall, its host region, and attempting to identify and/or confirm links between the Wall and post-Roman structures. This strand made use of data acquired during HAR fieldwork, but also fed into the results of the fieldwork, enhancing the geological understanding of each site.

Staffing changes during the course of the project should also be highlighted. The initial Community Archaeologist was Paul Frodsham, who was vital to initial completion of the heritage-at-risk survey along the Hadrian's Wall World Heritage Site (prior to WallCAP) and guided the design and initial implementation of fieldwork. Nicky Garland was the initial Project Support Officer, and was also fundamental to helping obtain statutory permissions and completion of early stages of fieldwork, including supporting mapping and archiving. Paul and Nicky left the project in March 2020, and were succeeded by Jane Harrison as Community Archaeologist and Kathryn Murphy as Project Support Officer in September 2020.

All information and data necessary to understanding the archaeological fieldwork from the project can be found in this volume. But further information about WallCAP and digital data from the project is also available in other sources. A synthetic report of WallCAP can be found in *Community Archaeology on Hadrian's Wall 2019–2022* (Collins *et al.* 2023a), which provides an overview of the project, its structure and aims, and a summary of results of both the HAR and SSD strands of work, as well as statistics on volunteer participation and community engagement. Detailed research and interpretation of the sourcing, use, and re-use of geological material pertaining to the Wall from the SSD strand of the project are reported in *Fabric of the Frontier: Prospection, Use and Re-Use of Stone from Hadrian's Wall* (Collins *et al.* 2023b).

Further archived data and reports can be found at data.Ncl, the official archive of Newcastle University, and also with the Archaeology Data Service (ADS).

- data.Ncl: https://doi.org/10.25405/data.ncl.c.4893762.v1
- ADS: https://doi.org/10.5284/1100068

Acknowledgements

This monograph and the research underpinning it was made possible through the generous support of the National Lottery Heritage Fund (NLHF). Throughout the course of the project, the NLHF was unwavering in their support and enthusiasm, not least as the project adjusted in response to the global pandemic of COVID-19.

Just as important as the Lottery, the many dozens of volunteers that participated in the training, data-gathering, data-entry, and interpretation that all make up a citizen-science project are to be thanked and congratulated. Thank you to everyone (listed below) that worked as part of the Heritage At Risk strand of the project, and which this monograph presents the results of.

In addition, we also wish to thank English Heritage, Historic England, the National Trust, and the Northumberland National Park Authority, and the many individual landowners that provided access to the sites and archives that allowed us to complete the research presented here.

Rob Collins would like to thank Jane for her exemplary work as the Community Archaeologist for WallCAP, leading on the vast majority of fieldwork, and Kathryn who also substantially contributed to the fieldwork before, during, and after the actual time in the field. The rest of the WallCAP team was also integral to the completion of this work, and I would like to thank them for their hard work and dedication to see this project to its fruition. This extends to Nicky Garland and Paul Frodsham, who were members of the team when WallCAP began its work. Sam Turner provided guidance and goodwill throughout the project, and Fiona Watson was an essential member of the team, liaising and assisting with Lottery when adjustments needed to be made. Lastly, I would like to thank my family, Sarah, Mara, and Hudson, who were occasionally drafted in or held as bored captives when I needed to quickly visit a site, ferry tools and materials between locations, and even providing an extra pair of hands for the odd day here and there.

Jane Harrison would like heartily to thank all the WallCAP team and especially Kathryn, who was key in the field. Under Covid restrictions Kathryn and I had to complete smaller excavations without volunteers: hard work but great fun. Rob, thank you for providing the essential humour, support, and Wall detail we needed throughout the project. I would like to add a personal thanks to the landowners and farmers who permitted the work and provided valuable local information, and to the volunteers whose dedication and hard work drove the two major excavations. Alison Wilkins did most of the digitising of site drawings and very sadly died shortly after completing them. I worked with Alison for many years on many sites and will greatly miss her professionalism and creativity. Matilde Grimaldi was exciting to work with in generating the reconstruction drawings and I hugely enjoyed collaborating with our geologist Ian Kille. Finally, thanks as ever to my wonderful family, Chris, Laura and the lads, Ewan and Alfie, who kept everything including me, together.

Finally, maps have been made (by Kathryn Murphy or Alex Turner) containing public sector information licensed under the Open Government Licence v3.0 (available at: https://www.nationalarchives.gov.uk/doc/open-government-licence/version/3/) and OpenStreetMap basemap for images containing LiDAR (https://www.openstreetmap.org/copyright). A minority of maps also make use of small amounts of OS data contributing to backdrop information, in compliance with rules about use of such data for academic publications (https://digimap.edina.ac.uk/help/copyright-and-licensing/os_eula/).

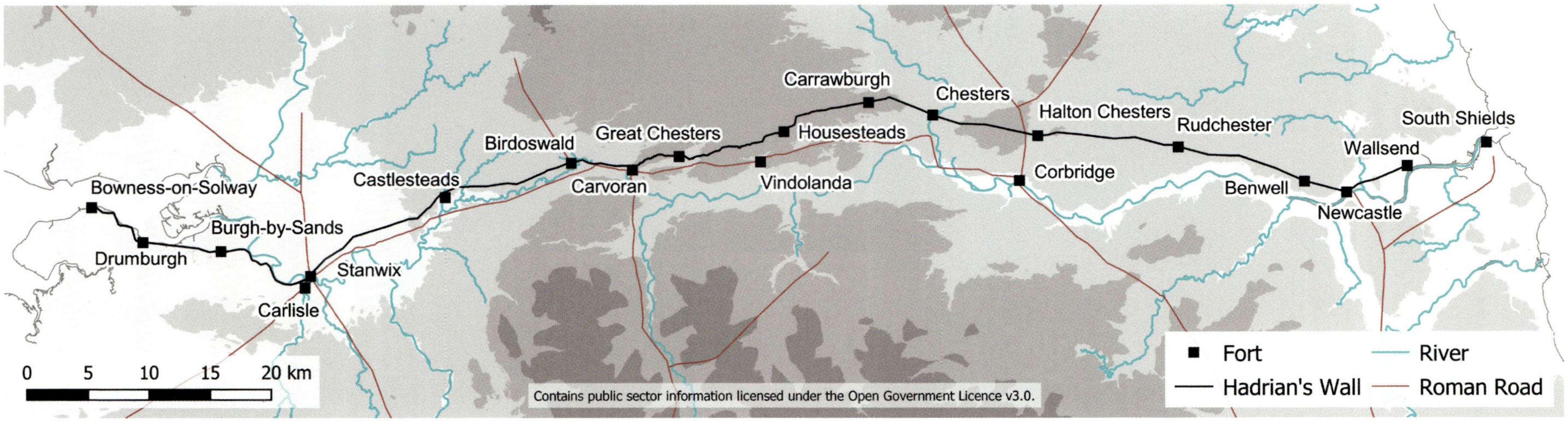

Map 1: Hadrian's Wall, locating the forts and towns along its length, Roman roads, and sites in its hinterland relative to topography.

1

Introduction

The history of Hadrian's Wall traditionally begins in AD 122, when the emperor Hadrian visited the province of *Britannia*, and it is assumed to have ended in AD 410, when Britain was permanently lost to the Roman Empire. At the time of its initial construction, the Roman army had been operating in the region of Central Britain, that is the lands north of Humber Estuary and south of the Firth of Forth, since *c*. AD 70 – a period of approximately 50 years. This knowledge of the landscape allowed the Roman army to plot the course of the Wall and implement its construction along the narrow isthmus of the Tyne-Solway gap, effectively raising a barrier between the North Sea in the east and the Irish Sea in the West studded with forts to house a multitude of soldiers (Map 1). While Roman politics and interest in northern Britain ebbed and flowed over the subsequent decades and centuries, the Wall remained a constant, retaining garrisons of various size until Roman rule ended in Britain, and perhaps even for some years beyond the formal end of empire.

This is a reasonable *precis* of the *Roman* history of the Wall, but the monument has a much longer and more complex life. The origins of the monument extend hundreds of millions of years into the past with the formation of the rock quarried and worked to build the Wall. And to date, the Wall has not 'ended'. Following its use as a Roman military work, sites along the Wall continued to provide homes and shelters to different communities through the ages, with houses and farms built directly on top of the Wall and occupied to this very day. Alternatively, the Wall was also a source of convenient stone, from which new structures were built. There are many locations where the Wall is no longer visible or has been entirely dismantled, but there are also substantial lengths where its survival attracts visitors, tourists, and researchers (Fig. 1.1). In short, the Wall has a rich and complex life beyond the 300 years it served as a Roman frontier monument (Hingley 2012), and this does not even account for the incredible details of daily life that have been unearthed from the Roman occupation of the monument and its sites (Collins *et al*. 2020).

There is a vast body of scholarship on Hadrian's Wall, with focused research and interpretation of its remains and ruins beginning in the 16th century, consisting largely of descriptions of sites, inscriptions, and objects. A narrative history of the monument emerged in the 18th century, and the advent of archaeology and the use of excavations to recover information in the 19th century resulted in a fundamental shift in the approach to the Wall and its understanding through the 20th century (Breeze 2014). Archaeological analysis has underpinned interpretation of the monument and its constituent elements, its

Figure 1.1: The stone curtain of Hadrian's Wall at Walltown Crags, looking west as the line of the Wall follows the forward line of the crags. This stretch of Wall survives in very good condition, often exceeding 2 m in height.

chronology, the operation and practices of the Roman army, and aspects of the daily lives of the people that lived along its length. Dozens of papers can be found in journals such as *Archaeologia Aeliana*, the *Transactions of the Cumberland and Westmorland Antiquarian and Archaeological Society*, and *Britannia*, supplemented by detailed excavation reports of specific sites. The first comprehensive synthesis and interpretation of the Wall appeared nearly 50 years ago (Breeze and Dobson 1976), and new discoveries have since refined understanding and sparked further debate as captured in the handbooks that have accompanied the decennial Pilgrimages along Hadrian's Wall (Bidwell 1999; Hodgson 2009; Collins and Symonds 2019).

Excellent recent syntheses (Hodgson 2017; Symonds 2020) are available that provide a good starting point for understanding the Roman history and archaeology of the Wall. More focused research has considered the conception of the Wall (Breeze 2009), its construction (Hill 2004; 2006), and its use in the final years of the Roman Empire in Britain (Collins 2012). Other studies have examined the way that the Wall has been physically incorporated into post-Roman structures (Whitworth 2000) and its reception and presentation in more recent centuries (Hingley 2012; Whitworth 2012). More recently, the Wall has contributed to research in the fields of heritage and management, as the complexities and priorities of managing a large World Heritage Site and its relationships with local communities and stakeholders have become more widely appreciated (Stone and Brough 2014; Alberti and Mountain 2022). All of these studies draw on a substantial amount of data accumulated through excavation and detailed research, as seen in the bibliographies of all the works referenced above and in the 14 editions of the *Handbook to the Roman Wall* (most recently Breeze 2006).

Figure 1.2: WallCAP volunteers learning to record a trench section at Cam Beck.

Despite the impressive quantity of data available for Hadrian's Wall, there is much that is still not known or understood about the Wall. A formal Research Framework for the Wall was published more than a decade ago, which assessed the current state of knowledge and identified gaps in data and understanding (Symonds and Mason 2009). In the intervening 14 years, an impressive amount of new investigations, initiatives, and publications have appeared that do much to redress the research gaps highlighted in the Hadrian's Wall Research Framework (summarised in Collins and Symonds 2019). Still, this knowledge is unequal in its spread, both in terms of geography and chronology, and many of the challenges in managing and preserving such a large monument and its World Heritage persist.

This volume reports on discrete site-based archaeological investigations along the Wall, which were undertaken to either resolve a threat to the monument, or where such threats cannot be removed to at least better understand the Wall and/or the relationship between the archaeology and the threat. In this regard, the work addressed the agenda and needs of heritage-at-risk as it pertains to Hadrian's Wall, in consultation with Historic England and their Heritage At Risk register. Fieldwork also incorporated research questions that linked back to agendas and priorities identified in the Hadrian's Wall Research Framework. This work was carried out as part of the Hadrian's Wall Community Archaeology Project (WallCAP), which ran between March 2018 and September 2022 and was funded by the National Lottery Heritage Fund. The project was large and multi-facetted, undertaking work with various stakeholders and audiences to better understand, interpret, and protect Hadrian's Wall. As such, much of the work of WallCAP was undertaken with volunteers and local communities. The aims and engagements undertaken by WallCAP are detailed elsewhere (Collins *et al.* 2023a), but the data contributing to this volume is derived from the Heritage at Risk (HAR) and Stone Sourcing and Dispersal (SSD) strands of the project. Across these two strands, fieldwork was undertaken by the project team and in collaboration with volunteers and local communities to collect data pertaining to geology, Roman archaeology, and post-Roman archaeology (Fig. 1.2). The results of the archaeological fieldwork are presented here. In that regard, this volume complements the existing scholarship associated with the Wall and provides further data to enhance our understanding not only of the monument in the Roman era, but also its post-Roman life.

The volume is organised thematically for each chapter, and within each chapter by site for smaller interventions. Larger fieldwork endeavours are reported by site, with each site receiving its own chapter. Notably, most of these discrete pieces of fieldwork deal with linear elements of the Wall complex, and this has allowed for more general observations to be made. Where data or detail is not directly pertinent to chapter content, but necessary for reference it is included in an appendix. Given that the focus of the volume is Hadrian's Wall, with its established traditions and lexicon, a good understanding of the so-called Wall basics is required.

Wall basics

There are a number of aspects of Hadrian's Wall that need to be understood to better appreciate the data and interpretations offered in this volume. Firstly, this includes an overview of the different landscapes the Wall ran through. Secondly, it is necessary to reiterate the basic terminology and anatomy of the Wall as a monument. Thirdly, the chronology and sequence of how the Wall was built in the 2nd century AD very directly relates to interpretations of the earliest phases of archaeological activity as some of the sites reported on here.

Landscapes of the Wall corridor

The Wall runs from Wallsend in the east, positioned on the north bank of the River Tyne, to Bowness-on-Solway in the west, positioned on the southern shore of the Solway Firth (Fig. 1.3). Between its eastern and western terminals, the specific local conditions and elevations vary considerably. For convenience, the Wall is often broken up into three discrete sectors, east, central, and west. The east and west sectors tend to be lowland, while the central sector lying between the North Tyne and Irthing rivers consists of uplands. Though broadly accurate, within each sector there is a regular changing of elevation along the Wall, and its position relative to slopes, crags, mossy moors, and boggy marshes lends a distinct local character to each and every location along thc Wall. For example, the western miles of the Wall sit atop relatively flat land averaging only 15–20 m above sea level; centuries of improvement have introduced good drainage and flood management to the area, but in the Roman era there would have been regular flooding and much of the land immediately north of the Wall could be fairly characterised as salt marsh (Fig. 1.4). In contrast, there are approximately 20 kms in the central sector where the Wall is built on the north face of a steep, rocky crag or cliff, with the natural topography 200–325 m above sea level (Fig. 1.5). Here the elevation and the crags expose the Wall to more wind and rain, and the lands around the Wall can be characterised as upland moor. Flanking the central sector, however, are picturesque wooded river valleys as at Cam Beck/Castlesteads and Chesters (Fig. 1.6). Recent history, too, has also dramatically changed the environment of the Wall,

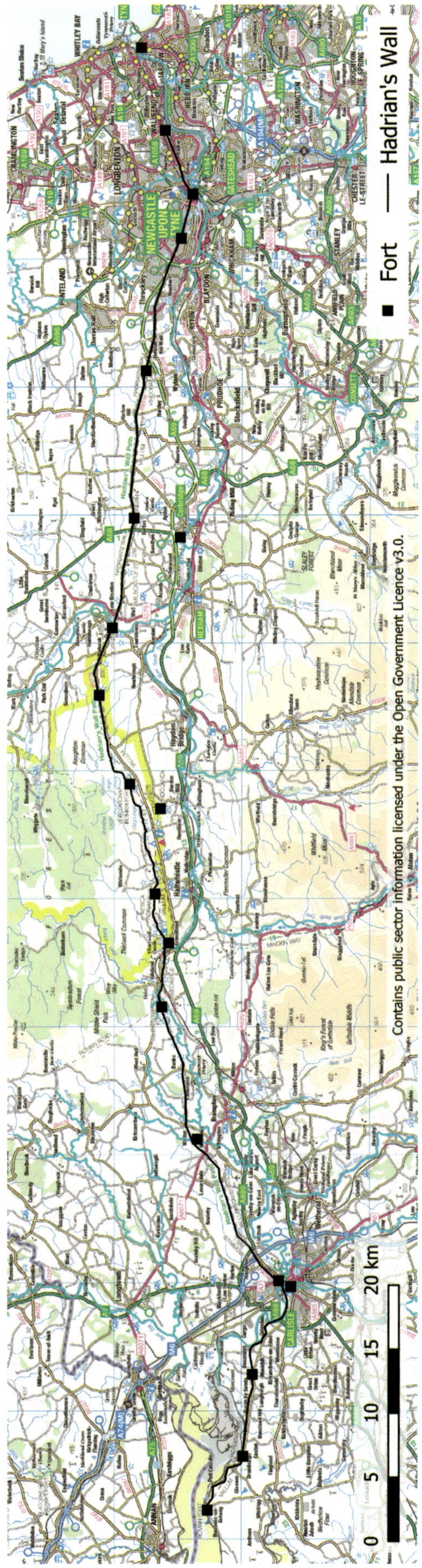

Figure 1.3: A map of Hadrian's Wall and its immediate vicinity, showing the line of the monument and the key Roman forts and sites along its length, relative to contemporary settlement.

Figure 1.4: Looking east along the Solway coast at Bowness, at the approximate location of the Wall's western terminus. Note the flat, low-lying, and marshy ground.

particularly at its east end where the urban conurbation of Newcastle (Tyneside) has expanded through the 19th and 20th centuries. The Wall in Tyneside is typically invisible, though some consolidated curtain can be seen at Wallsend and Denton; for those 'in the know', different pavements mark the course of the Wall, but the urban environment has almost completely destroyed or submerged the visible aspects of the Roman landscape (Fig. 1.7). Urban conurbation, though to a lesser extent, has also affected the Wall in Carlisle.

These different environments have had important impacts on the Wall, including not only the survival of the archaeology, but also on-going threats to its continued existence and preservation. Issues that relate to slope, flooding and/or draining, and weathering directly affect all locations with exposed and even buried features of the monument. Human activity, from development and expansion of the amenities and infrastructure of modern

Figure 1.5: (A) The Wall as it runs atop the crags in Wall-mile 37, west of Housesteads fort, as viewed from the air to the north. (B) The same stretch of Wall, looking west, from the ground. Note the changing elevation of the crags, which appear more uniform from the air.

Figure 1.6: The gently rolling hills that flank the upland central sector of the Wall are visible at Black Carts, looking east from the north side of the curtain.

life, to agricultural work, and also the leisure and tourism industry also impact the monument. The interaction of these different activities varies in scale and significance at any given location. For example, in the central sector, there is considerably less development and building activity, but the upland topography exposes the monument to weathering and erosion, exacerbated by the steep slopes along the Wall's course, and this is coupled with on-going agricultural needs in the form of pasture and also as the sector of the Wall with the highest levels of tourism.

Anatomy and terminology

Hadrian's Wall is more than a very high and very long wall; it should be understood as a monumental complex consisting of several discrete elements and/or features. These inter-related features can be framed as anatomical, with each constituent element clearly defined in its own terms but also fundamental to the make-up of the Wall as a whole. These are separated into linear features and site-based structures (Breeze 2006, 53–90 provides more extensive discussion of each element).

The central or most fundamental feature of the Wall monument is the element built as a wall, known as the curtain (as seen in Figs 1.1, 1.6). All other features relate to the curtain, either directly attached to it, or positioned and aligned to it. The curtain is a linear feature, built primarily of stone, but there was a phase in which a portion of the Wall curtain was built primarily in turf. This will be detailed below relative to the building sequence, but it introduces a distinction between the Stone Wall (SW) and Turf Wall (TW). Use of Stone Wall or Turf Wall is limited to the early phases of construction and occupation of the Wall, and applied either more generally or in conjunction with a specific site. The curtain always refers to the stone-built Wall, regardless of a specific date. In this way, it can be distinguished from the walls of other structures, like milecastles or turrets.

Figure 1.7: The Wall can be seen as a short consolidated stretch at Denton (right side of the image), with the A69 and West Road generally following the line of the Wall up the hill to Benwell and further east into Newcastle. Note all the urban development visible in the image.

Figure 1.8: The ditch and berm north of the Wall at Carvoran, looking east. Here the ditch has a V-shaped profile, with the base of the ditch indicated by the taller grasses and reeds. The land immediately to the right of the ditch formed the berm. The stone curtain is not visible to any surviving height at this location.

In addition to the curtain, there are three other linear features of the monument: the ditch, the berm, and the Vallum. The ditch and the berm are located to the north of the curtain. The berm is the strip of land 4–6 m wide that separates the curtain from the ditch. At locations in the eastern sector of Hadrian's Wall, between Wallsend and Heddon-on-the-Wall, evidence has been found along the berm for pits and postholes. This has been interpreted as evidence for a series of obstacles, such as upward-pointed sharpened stakes, located on the berm to increase the defensiveness of the curtain (Bidwell 2005). The ditch was typically dug by the Romans in a V-shape in clay and soil conditions, though when excavated from bedrock it takes on a U-shape (Fig. 1.8). Where the curtain runs along the forward edge of crags or cliff-faces, there is no ditch or well-defined berm. South of the curtain is the Vallum,

Figure 1.9: The Vallum at Down Hill, looking east. The V-shaped ditch of the Vallum has a mound to its north and south. The Vallum survives in variable condition, with it being completely destroyed at some locations.

Figure 1.10: Turret 48b, east of Willowford Farm, looking into the low surviving courses of the structure from the southeast.

a monumental feature in its own right consisting of a central ditch flanked by large earthen mounds (Fig. 1.9).

One further linear feature should be noted, the Military Way. This was a paved road that ran immediately south of the curtain. In the upland central sector, the Military Way is a visible feature of raised, flattened ground or a distinct and general level shelf of ground running across a slope; in more lowland locations the Military Way has been known to run along the top of the north mound of the Vallum. Its exact course is not fully known, and based on very limited evidence, it appears to have been built or at least paved in the later 2nd century. In other words, it does not appear to be part of the initial construction of the Wall, but was an important element for most of the Roman period.

Along the line of the curtain were a series of distinct structures: turrets, milecastles, and forts. Turrets are towers, built to a square or sub-square plan, and found every one-third of a Roman mile along the curtain (Fig. 1.10). Their function seems to have been simple – to

Figure 1.11: Milecastle 39, looking west. Note the breaks in the north and south walls of the structure, which provided gateway access through the line of the curtain.

act as elevated observation platforms for the immediate vicinity of the Wall (ideally for a *c.* 500–1000 m radius, depending on terrain), and possibly to also provide platforms for signalling (Woolliscroft 1989; Foglia 2014). Milecastles, as the name suggests, were small rectangular fortlets positioned every Roman mile along the curtain, consisting of an outer wall integrally joined to the curtain with a gate through the curtain surmounted by a tower; along with a south gate through its perimeter, a milecastle had the potential to provide access through the Wall every Roman mile, though the true extent of such accessibility is debated (Fig. 1.11; Symonds 2013). Forts are the largest of the structures found in the Wall corridor (Fig. 1.12). These were the primary bases for the units of the Roman army that garrisoned the Wall, and each fort consisted of a number of buildings to house and support the unit(s) in residence. All forts also had four primary gates and two secondary gates; the primary north gate provided access through the curtain. The use and accessibility of milecastle and fort gates changed over time.

There are other features that are also part of the Wall complex, though they are less numerous and/or not as well understood. There are, for example, at least three independent gates that provided access through the Wall curtain distinct from those at forts and milecastles. These have been found and excavated at Portgate, located where the Roman road known as Dere Street intersects with the Wall north of Corbridge, and at the Knag Burn, immediately east of Housesteads fort. A third gate is expected to be positioned on the Roman road running north of Carlisle and to the west of Stanwix, but to date it has not been found. There were also considerable bridgeworks that carried the Wall across major and minor rivers; these have been confirmed by excavation at Chesters across the North Tyne, at Willowford across the Irthing and (as reported in this volume) at Castlesteads across the Cam Beck.

Specific local placenames can be used to specify and locate sites along the Wall, such as Denton or Halton Chesters, but a simple scheme that makes use of the built features of the Wall also provides a framework for convenient location and discussion. Given that the Wall is

Figure 1.12: An aerial view of the fort at Housesteads, viewed from the south.

80 Roman miles in length, and a milecastle can be found each mile, the Wall is often discussed in detail in reference to Wall-miles, and this designation is also extended to the features within such a mile. For example, Poltross Burn is the local placename applied to a milecastle, which can also be named as milecastle 48. It is followed by turrets 48a and 48b, and the Wall-mile ends with milecastle 49 (Harrow's Scar).

When taken together, the terminology applied to the various elements and features of the Wall helps to communicate its monumentality and provide specificity. For example, the Wall's existence as a monumental complex is made abundantly clear if you consider approaching it from the north. First, one would encounter the ditch, then the berm (and possibly its obstacles), followed by the curtain, and subsequently the mound-ditch-mound construct known as the Vallum. When crossing the curtain, one would be observed from the top of a turret or the north tower of a milecastle, and may have required traversing through the internal walls of a fort, full of Roman soldiers.

The building sequence of the Wall

The Wall had a complex building sequence that began under the emperor Hadrian, and was not fully completed until later in the 2nd century, though the exact date of completion is unknown. The building sequence is particularly important to understand in reference to this volume, given that multiple pieces of fieldwork were focused on the Wall's linear elements. Therefore, understanding this process in the planning and building of the Wall frames the data and interpretations offered in subsequent chapters.

However, it is also important to remember that the Roman army had been operating in the regions of Central and Northern Britain for approximately 50 years prior to the construction of Hadrian's Wall. Indeed, following the withdrawal from highland Scotland (or Caledonia, as the Romans called it), a linear cordon of forts across the Tyne-Solway isthmus was established by Trajan, supplementing the existing forts at Corbridge, Vindolanda, and Carlisle, and subsequently connected by a paved road. This is known as the Stanegate system, and highlights that the Roman army had already identified the Tyne-Solway isthmus as a strategic east–west corridor in the landscape of Central Britain. In that regard, the landscape where the Wall was built was not 'new' to the Romans, but one in which they were already intimately familiar with the topography, which will have further informed and influenced the process of planning and constructing the Wall. Indeed, in addition to the permanent forts located on the Stanegate, there are numerous camps located in the Tyne-Solway isthmus positioned to access and presumably monitor key locations and routeways both east–west and north–south, for example the series of camps of varying size on Haltwhistle Common (Welfare and Swan 1995).

Highly detailed accounts of the interpretation and supporting evidence for the planning and building sequence of the Wall are available (most recently Poulter 2009; Graafstal 2012; 2018; Symonds and Breeze 2016; Hodgson 2017; Breeze 2018; Symonds 2019a; 2019b; 2020), but these can be summarised in brief. In essence, the building sequence consists of eight steps, though only the final steps (5–8) are attested archaeologically.

1. The initial conception of the Wall, perhaps by Hadrian himself.
2. Initial survey of the course of the Wall by army surveyors.
3. Planning the work and supporting logistics for construction.
4. Gathering the labour and necessary materials to begin construction.
5. Initial construction, including foundations and possible completion for some lengths of the curtain and some milecastles and turrets.
6. Alterations to the building plan, including:
    a. The decision to build forts on the line of the Wall;
    b. Construction of the Vallum;
    c. Narrowing the width (thickness) of the stone curtain.
7. Completion of the building work.
8. Replacement of the Turf Wall with stone.

The initial plan or concept for the Wall (step 1) seems to have consisted of a rather uniform monumental barrier consisting of the curtain with very regularly spaced milecastles and turrets, probably also consisting of the ditch in front of the curtain. There were no forts planned, as the Stanegate and its garrisons could act as the main bases for military units. Though it cannot be proven that the concept for the Wall originated with Hadrian (Breeze 2009), the monumentality of the project agrees with the known architectural interests of the emperor, and certainly the authority to implement the project and marshal the resources for its construction required imperial approval. Initial surveys for the course of the Wall and the planning of and assembly of soldiers and tools for construction (steps 2, 3, and 4) were undertaken to execute this initial plan (Hill 2004; Poulter 2009; Graafstal 2020). Though it cannot be proven, it seems likely that during these phases, identification of quarries for sourcing building stone (almost exclusively sandstones) was also undertaken, though at present there are no identified definite Hadrianic quarries (O'Donnell 2021; Collins *et al.* 2023b).

The initial construction of the Wall (step 5) was undertaken in stone at various locations between Newcastle and the River Irthing. West of the Irthing, construction of turrets was completed in stone but the curtain and milecastles were built in turf and timber (Fig. 1.13). This first-phase construction in stone is identifiable on the ground as any structures built to a 'Broad Wall' gauge or thickness of curtain, 2.7–3.2 m wide in the foundations and 2.7–3 m wide above the foundations. The presence of Broad Wall dimensions with associated wingwalls of turrets and milecastles, along with other morphological features have also allowed for identification of structures built first, for example at milecastles 47 and 48. These first-built structures have been argued to be priority constructions (Symonds 2005; 2019b; Graafstal 2012; Hunneysett 2017), highlighting the Roman army's sensitivity to local landscape issues. Priority construction will also have required associated quarrying. It is assumed that construction of the Turf Wall began at the same time, and it has been argued that the Turf Wall could have been completed in one season of building work (Graafstal 2012, 137–138; Hodgson 2017, 66–69).

At some point during the construction of the Wall, the initial plan was altered (step 6). Three important changes were introduced to the Wall, and are frequently clustered together under the notion of nominal 'fort decision'. First, it was decided that forts would now be built in the line of the Wall curtain. Second, after the positions of the forts were decided and laid out (though probably not built), the Vallum was constructed. Significantly, the Vallum seems to have been completed in its entirety before the rest of the Wall. Third, the thickness of the Stone Wall curtain was reduced from Broad Wall to Narrow Wall (2.4–2.7 m foundations, 2.1–2.4 m above the foundations). These decisions made and implemented, work was eventually completed on the Wall (step 7).

It is uncertain how long it took for the Wall to be built, or at exactly what date various changes were made. Graafstal (2012) resurrected a suggestion made some decades ago by Stevens (1966, 39) that building work for the Wall commenced *c.* AD 120, with the fort decision made or approved by Hadrian during his visit in 122, and with the entire building project completed by 127. Hodgson (2017, 63) notes the possibility that with enough labour and resource directed toward the project, the Wall complex could have been completely built in 4–5 years. There is evidence, however, for breaks in the building program, and RIB 1736 from Great Chesters names Hadrian as *Pater Patriae*, a title he did not take until 128 and indicating completion of the fort no earlier than that year. It is feasible that the Wall was not completed by the end of Hadrian's reign in 137 (Breeze 2019, 90), though there is no specific evidence that demonstrates this.

Subsequently, the Turf Wall and its milecastles were sleighted (destroyed), and then rebuilt in stone. From the River Irthing to Wall-mile 54, this replacement seems to have occurred in the AD 130s, during the final years of Hadrian's reign, and was built to a Narrow Wall gauge. The stone replacement of Wall-miles 54–80 was completed in a different fashion, the curtain being built to the Intermediate gauge (2.6–3.3 m at the foundations; 2.4–2.9 m above the foundations). The construction of the Intermediate Wall is often dated to the 160s on the basis of the small amount of pottery associated with the work, but the pottery could date from the 120s–190s.

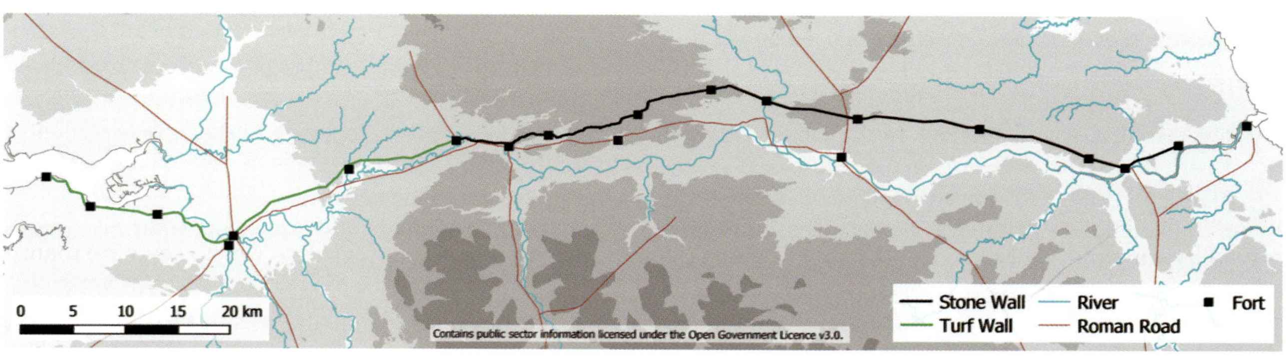

Figure 1.13: A map showing the extent of the Stone Wall and Turf Wall executed in the initial construction of Hadrian's Wall.

The building sequence is important as it provides a simple order for the events in the construction of the Wall. For the more general purposes of better interpreting the monument, this helps to elucidate how the Roman builders prioritised aspects of construction and infer significance of particular structures to localised aspects of the landscape or the otherwise unattested socio-political conditions of the frontier region. However, there are limits to the knowledge and insight the building sequence provides. First and foremost, it is a relative chronology. That is to say there are almost no unambiguous calendrical dates to correlate to particular events or activities; each step in the building sequence is positioned relative to the others, deduced through vertical and horizontal stratigraphic relationships. Second, the underlying motivation for much of the research on the building sequence has been focused on achieving a deeper understanding of the intended purpose and function of the Wall. Given the subsequent changes to the Wall and its long-term use and occupation by the Roman army, such insights are limited to a narrow chronological band, and it has been observed that more academic fixation on separating functional use of the Wall for defence or control is a false dichotomy (McCluskey 2018).

For the purposes of this volume, however, the building sequence and associated dating is useful in correlating changes in the building materials with different phases of activity.

Significant changes to the Wall after Hadrian

Further phases of change can be identified along the Wall after its Hadrianic construction, though the dating of these changes are rather general. For example, a number of turrets were blocked up and subsequently demolished in the later 2nd century, sometime after the recommissioning of Hadrian's Wall following its temporary abandonment during the construction and occupation of the Antonine Wall (Breeze 2006, 105–107). However, the full extent of turrets that were demolished is uncertain, given the number of turrets that remain unexcavated. It is presumed that the turrets that were abandoned and demolished were no longer deemed essential to the operation of the Wall. Given that turrets were observational platforms and their select demolition indicates that observation was no longer required, this underscores that changes to the monument were made in respect to changing socio-political circumstances on the ground.

Another major period of construction work is associated with ceramics of the very late 2nd–early 3rd century, in which substantial lengths of the Wall curtain were rebuilt using a very hard white mortar. These rebuilt lengths of curtain were reduced in thickness, given the name Extra-narrow Wall (1.5–1.9 m thick). This phase of rebuilding is typically correlated to direct imperial attention from Septimius Severus, either in advance of or concurrent with his British campaigns in the early 3rd century and appears to be the last Wall-wide construction programme. Significantly, a date for stone quarrying in 207 is provided by an inscription at the Written Rock of Gelt (RIB 1009). This quarry was located 6 km south of the Wall and produced a fine-grained red-brown sandstone, though there is no certain evidence that the stone was used in the Wall curtain. Further east, this period is likely to be the date that a new fort was added to the Wall at Newcastle (Snape and Bidwell 2002).

However, it should be noted that sites and discrete structures throughout the entire Wall corridor continued to be refurbished, demolished, replaced, or simply repaired throughout the Roman period. It can be difficult to archaeologically detect these changes. Even in its initial phases of construction, the Wall was a diverse monument when examined in detail. There is variation of the size of stones employed in building the Wall, further underscoring the variation observed along the Wall that relates not only to the builders and their skill, but also the attributes of the stones used (Breeze *et al.* 2020; Collins *et al.* 2023b). These variables also change across the *c.* 300 years of the Wall's occupation by the Roman army. Truncation or outright destruction of sites like turrets reduce prospects of identifying later modifications or repairs of built elements, even when stratigraphic layers demonstrate long-term occupation. Along the curtain or Turf Wall, this is even more difficult, as there are no associated layers of concentrated occupation. For example, the full extent of Extra-narrow Wall construction/repair is unknown due to the generally low or short height of surviving remains of the curtain in the eastern and central sectors. On occasion, the arrangement of surviving building fabric reveals refurbishment, along with a number of other features or indicators of rebuilding (Bidwell 2018; Collins *et al.* 2023b). However, the diminished remains of the stone curtain underscore the importance of understanding post-Roman activity along the Wall.

In the centuries following the end of the Roman Empire, its monuments, buildings, and structures became a convenient source of dressed stone for subsequent communities. The robbing and re-use of Roman fabric happened across the entirety of the former province of *Britannia*. The re-use of Roman fabric, rather than fresh quarrying and preparation of stone, could introduce a considerable saving in skilled labour and time for medieval and later builders (Eaton 2000), and integration of Roman stone or structures into buildings and communities often had ideological benefits (Fafinski 2021), though caution must be applied against projecting ideological motivations onto the past. The fact that in no location does Hadrian's Wall survive to its full height and that no fort or other settlement is perfectly preserved provides some indication not only of the extent of collapse and ruin of the Roman structures, but also the extent to which they were robbed for building materials and reworked to suit contemporary needs. Roman inscriptions and sculptures built into structures provide a direct testimony, whether it is the use of decorated stones from Corbridge integrated into the

7th century crypt at Hexham Abbey, or a centurial stone last seen in 1732 incorporated into a farmhouse doorjamb at Willowford (RIB 1864). The destruction of the Wall and plundering of its stone in varying quantities is a recurring theme at many of the sites reported in this volume.

Aims, objectives, and methods

An assessment conducted in 2016 revealed that 20 sites could be considered At Risk in the World Heritage Site of Hadrian's Wall (Frodsham 2016). The nature of these threats varied. Beckfoot, on the Cumbrian coast, is prone to coastal erosion that is destroying Roman mortuary deposits. Landslip of the plateau overlooking the Irthing west of Birdoswald similarly destroyed part of a Roman cemetery. In both cases, archaeological excavation was able to investigate the sites in advance of further destruction, following the principle of preservation by recording (Howard-Davis *et al.* 2017; Wilmott forthcoming). Other locations, however, have not had the benefit of attention. For example, a short length of curtain west of Port Carlisle had been prone to damage due to cattle and other agricultural activity. At Steel Rigg and other locations in the central sector, the pressure of visitors walking along the top of the curtain instigated collapse of the curtain face and the spilling of its core rubble. Elsewhere, different agricultural practices over decades and centuries have resulted in differential preservation of the Vallum. There are also locations where the absence of any firm knowledge of the monument means that appropriate measures for management or conservation cannot be followed. These problems – threats – endanger the monument and its future preservation. WallCAP, therefore, undertook fieldwork to address and where possible mitigate these threats.

The Heritage At Risk (HAR) strand of WallCAP was designed and implemented with a series of five objectives:

1. To investigate and understand factors adversely affecting the Wall, for example arable ploughing, visitor pressure, natural erosion, etc.
2. To target investigations at sites along the Wall on Historic England's Heritage At Risk register, or assess sites that could be deemed 'at risk'.
3. To undertake conservation or other activity to remove sites from the Heritage At Risk register.
4. To provide information to ensure better management of Wall sites going forward.
5. To use interventions as a further opportunity to address research questions in addition to conservation and management needs.

To this end, a range of archaeological methods and approaches were adopted to address research questions and management/conservation concerns at each site (Fig. 1.14). Work was undertaken along the Vallum at Heddon-on-the-Wall (Chapter 2). At Thirlwall and Drumburgh, geophysical survey was conducted to locate the traces of the curtain that is largely invisible, if not destroyed outright (Chapter 3). Survey, excavation, and consolidation was undertaken at Port Carlisle (Chapter 4) and Walltown Crags (Chapter 5). Larger scale survey and excavation was undertaken at Cam Beck (Chapter 6) and Corbridge (Chapter 7). The work undertaken at these sites has provided a wide-ranging assessment of the panoply of risks facing the Wall, as well as revealing exciting new information about the monument. Other sites were also included in WallCAP's Heritage At Risk work, such as vegetation clearance along the Vallum at Portgate, or consolidation of damaged fabric at turret 44b (Mucklebank), Steel Rigg, and the Cat's Stairs; however, these did not entail much, if any archaeological fieldwork and consequently no substantially new archaeological information. For these latter sites, any such information is captured in the Appendices, along with supplemental information pertaining to the archaeological fieldwork.

It should be noted that there were a number of further sites that were part of the original plan for WallCAP to investigate. Unfortunately, the COVID-19 pandemic impacted on the time and resources available to the project to conduct work at every site within the original project plan. In consultation with Historic England, the sites noted above were prioritised on the basis of either a pressing need and/or the feasibility of mitigating the risk.

While each intervention brought its own insights, the geographic spread of WallCAP's fieldwork has provided a rare opportunity for the Wall to be considered in its near

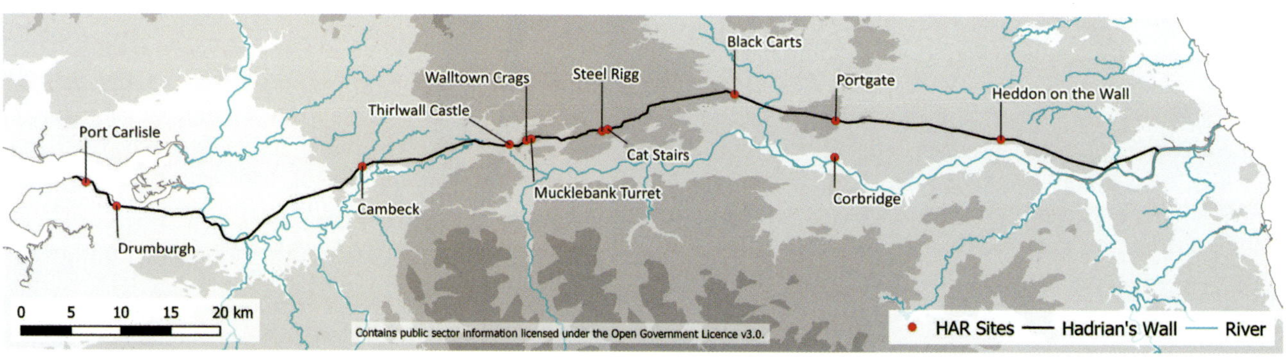

Figure 1.14: A map locating key sites of investigation by WallCAP within this study.

entirety within the scope of one project. Coupled with the data gathered and the results generated from WallCAP's Stone Sourcing and Dispersal (SSD) strand, the importance of local landscape conditions have taken on a new significance not only in understanding contemporary and future risks to the monument, but also the manner in which the Wall was built and maintained by the Roman army. The interventions at the sites in this volume have supported observations to be made about the linear elements of the Wall, with particular reference to its construction, and its destruction and/or ruination. The excavations at Cam Beck have provided the first evidence for the manner in which the Turf Wall and subsequent Stone Wall dealt with a 'minor' river crossing, while the excavations at Corbridge have provided the first modern assessment of site preservation at the fringe of the northernmost town of the Roman Empire. The cumulative insights from this fieldwork are considered in the Conclusion (Chapter 8).

2

The Vallum under pasture and under plough at Heddon

An almost entirely earthwork feature, the Vallum is a significant monumental element of the Wall complex in its own right, but one that has been vulnerable to modification and destruction in the centuries between its initial construction and the present. During the Roman period and after the initial construction of the Vallum, its preservation and survival was not guaranteed; local needs and pressures, particularly in the vicinity of forts could result in the infilling of the Vallum ditch and levelling of its mounds. In the centuries following the Roman occupation of the Wall, treatment of the Vallum was even more locally varied. Most destruction, however, has happened in the 20th century, as revealed by examining OS maps. The level of destruction ranges from complete annihilation and visual eradication of the Vallum, to partial destruction with the obliteration of only one or more aspects (*e.g.* a ditch or a mound). These processes can be natural, through landslips, erosion, or invasive vegetation, or anthropogenic, especially when land is 'reclaimed' for agriculture or the expansion of housing and/or industry.

Fields located between the villages of Throckley and Heddon-on-the-Wall, west of Newcastle, provided an opportunity to examine the variable survival of the Vallum in relation to historic and contemporary arable and pastoral regimes. The Vallum complex runs through three fields lying immediately south of the B6528 road, with Bank Top (merged with Throckley) at the east and Heddon at the west. The Wall curtain is buried beneath the road along this stretch but is then visible as a 250 m length of standing remains in a field on the eastern edge of Heddon-on-the-Wall (Fig. 2.1). The Vallum ditch and banks can still be discerned as earthworks in the most westerly of the three fields, which is in pasture. The middle field retains a very shallow preservation of the Vallum mounds and ditch, while the eastern field only retains the Vallum as soil marks, and in the gentle rise and dip of fencing on the field's western margin and as very slight earthworks (Fig. 2.2), with both these fields under plough. The Vallum is best preserved in the westernmost field (under pasture) and as the Vallum runs east through the arable central and eastern fields, it becomes increasingly shallow and almost invisible at ground surface. This variable condition of the Vallum is not only the result of recent agricultural activity, but also of a succession of agricultural and mining activities over the course of centuries. To explore this variable survival, topographic and geophysical surveys were undertaken, and one trench was placed across the entire width of the Vallum in the easternmost field. The fieldwork underscored the conclusion of visual examination – greater destruction of the Vallum as a result of ploughing – but significantly also provided insights into when destruction began and when acceleration could be detected.

Archaeological background

Within Wall-mile 11, the presumed site of turret 11b was excavated in 1919 but found no traces of the structure; the location of the turret was subsequently identified and excavated on Great Hill to the west of the site in 1928 with the discovery of ceramics and 'occupation earth', and survives as a buried feature below the B6528 (Fig. 1.1; Breeze 2006, 165). The location of turret 11a has not been confirmed, but is likely to be under the road in the vicinity of the small stand of trees and lane between the easternmost field and the central field. In 1879, a hoard of over 5000 silver Roman coins was found just south of the Wall and east of the likely location of turret 11a (Clayton 1879). In 1962, limited excavation just southwest of the exposed section of the curtain at Heddon found the south mound of the Vallum. Here the mound was *c.* 4.5 m wide, kerbed with large stones up to 0.5 m long, with a core of sand and stone (Tait 1962, 142–143).

Figure 2.1: Location of the fieldwork area, with the location of the excavation trench indicated by the red triangle. The three fields south of the road and between Throckley and Heddon were the focus of the surveys.

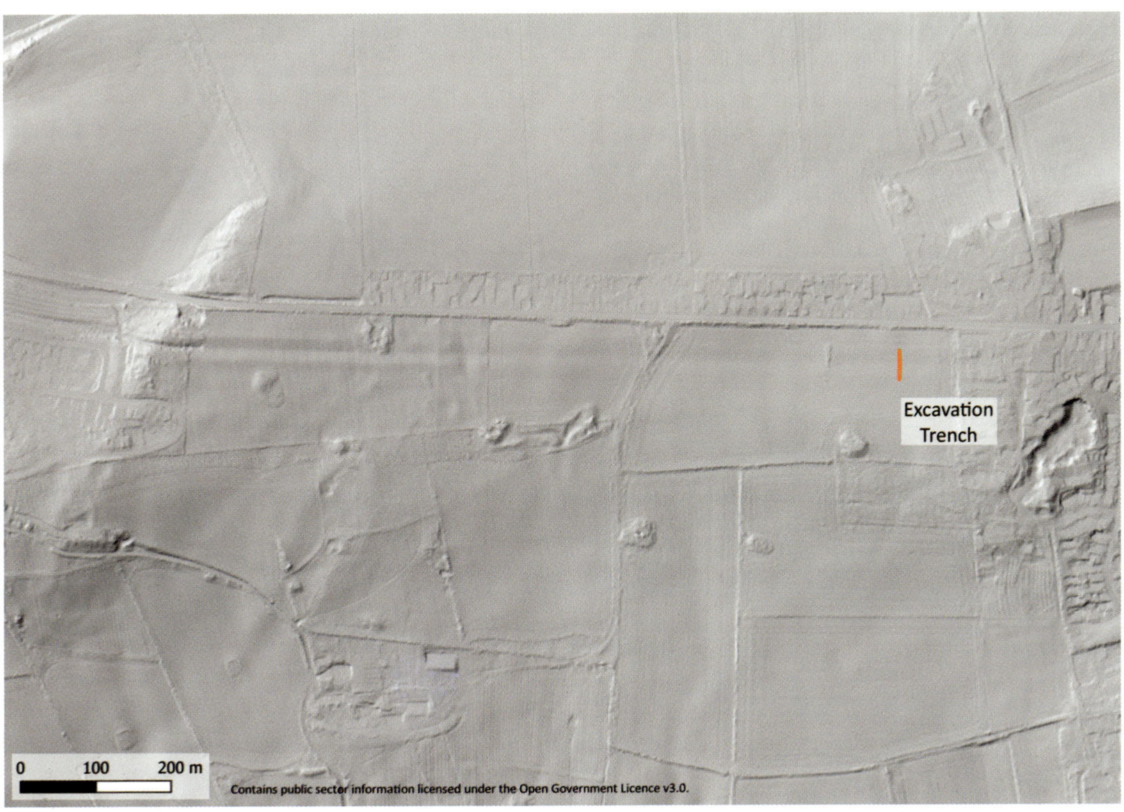

Figure 2.2: A LiDAR model of the survey area, with the location of the excavation trench. Note the decreasing topographic evidence of the Vallum moving from west to east, as well as the pits and quarries of historic mining.

Other excavations of the Vallum complex along the Wall are discussed below, including of the ditch at Throckley (Bennett 1983).

Excavations ahead of a new water main investigated a narrow, 2.2 km length of the northern carriageway of the B6528 at Throckley and included trenches at the presumed sites of milecastle MC11, turret 11a, and turret 11b; no structural evidence was found but between MC11 and turret 11b 145 pits, presumed to be for obstacles, were recorded on the berm north of the curtain Wall (Frain *et al.* 2005).

It is uncertain when the earliest pits were dug for mining or quarrying, but historic maps of different dates identify 'pits' and 'old workings'. However, their presence on the OS 1859 County Series maps provides a *terminus ante quem*. Trenches and survey blocks were located to avoid these features.

Geophysical and topographic survey

Alex Turner

Geophysical and topographical survey of six block transects in all three fields were completed to determine the extent to which subsoil survival of the Vallum could be detected relative to surface visibility. Gradiometry (Fig. 2.3) and resistivity results (Fig. 2.4) highlighted that the reduced surface visibility was due to destruction of the mounds and infilling of the ditch. Gradiometry was less successful in identifying Vallum features in those areas where it was much diminished or infilled, probably due to a general lack of magnetic materials in soils relating to the mounds or the ditch. Resistivity was more successful in sub-surface features of the Vallum, with the strength of signal and 'presence' of the Vallum directly relating to its visible condition on the surface. Nonetheless, these results remain valuable for comparative use in geophysical surveys of the Vallum at other locations, particularly where it is significantly less visible, though local soil and environmental conditions will also generate variation in results.

Six transects to generate a topographic profile further demonstrate the diminishing of the Vallum from west to east, as well as indicating the overall slope of the site relative to the Vallum. At the western end of the site there is an overall 11.5 m north–south slope (Fig. 2.5, transect 1). At the eastern end of the site, the north–south slope is even greater at 11.93 m (Fig. 2.5, transect 6). In the smaller field at the centre of the survey the north–south slope was 9.69 m (Fig. 2.5, transect 4). The maximum difference in height in an east–west direction is 24.97 m at the northern edge of the survey area and 25.38 m at the southern edge of the survey. The most noticeable change in topography, within individual survey areas, relates to the presence of the Vallum and shows a significantly greater earthwork at the western edge of the survey than at the eastern edge (Fig. 2.5, transect 1 and 6). The transition occurs from west–east and mirrors the change from pasture to arable, such that the profile of the Vallum is greater in transects 1–3 relative to transects 4–6.

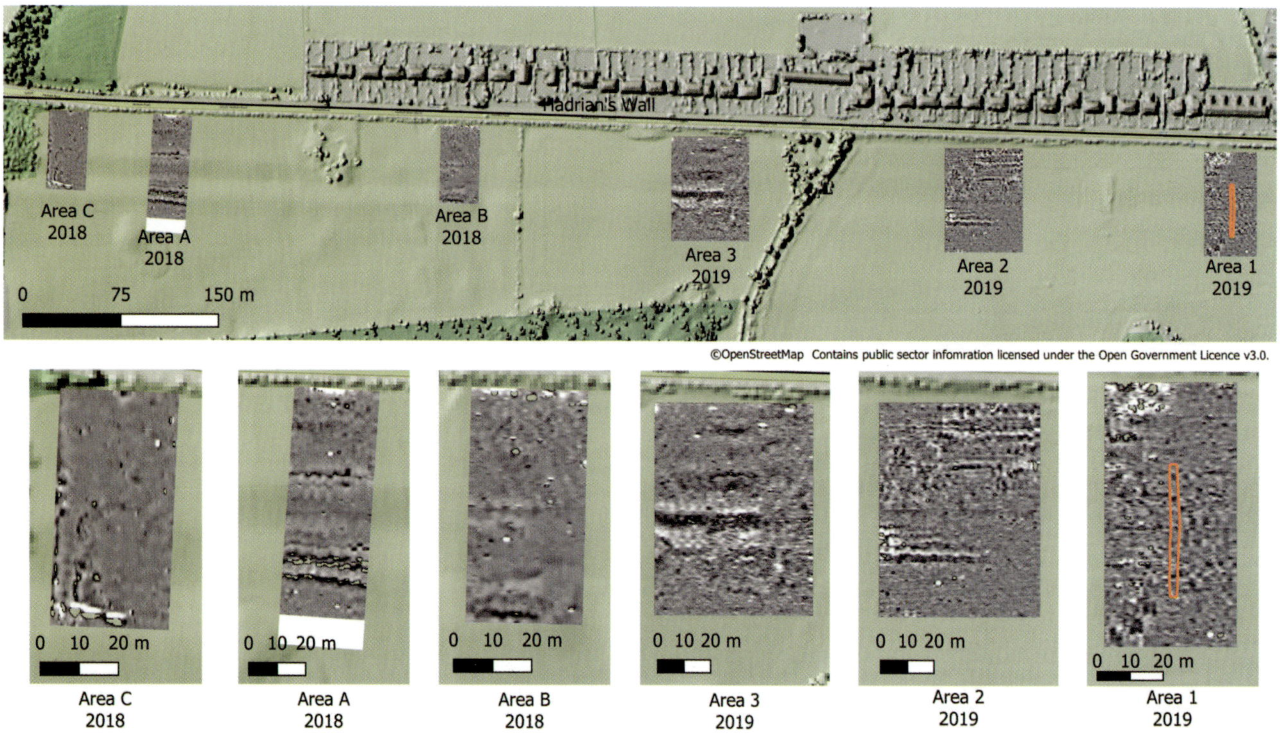

Figure 2.3: The location and results of six gradiometry surveys as transects across the Vallum. The location of the trench is indicated with the orange rectangle.

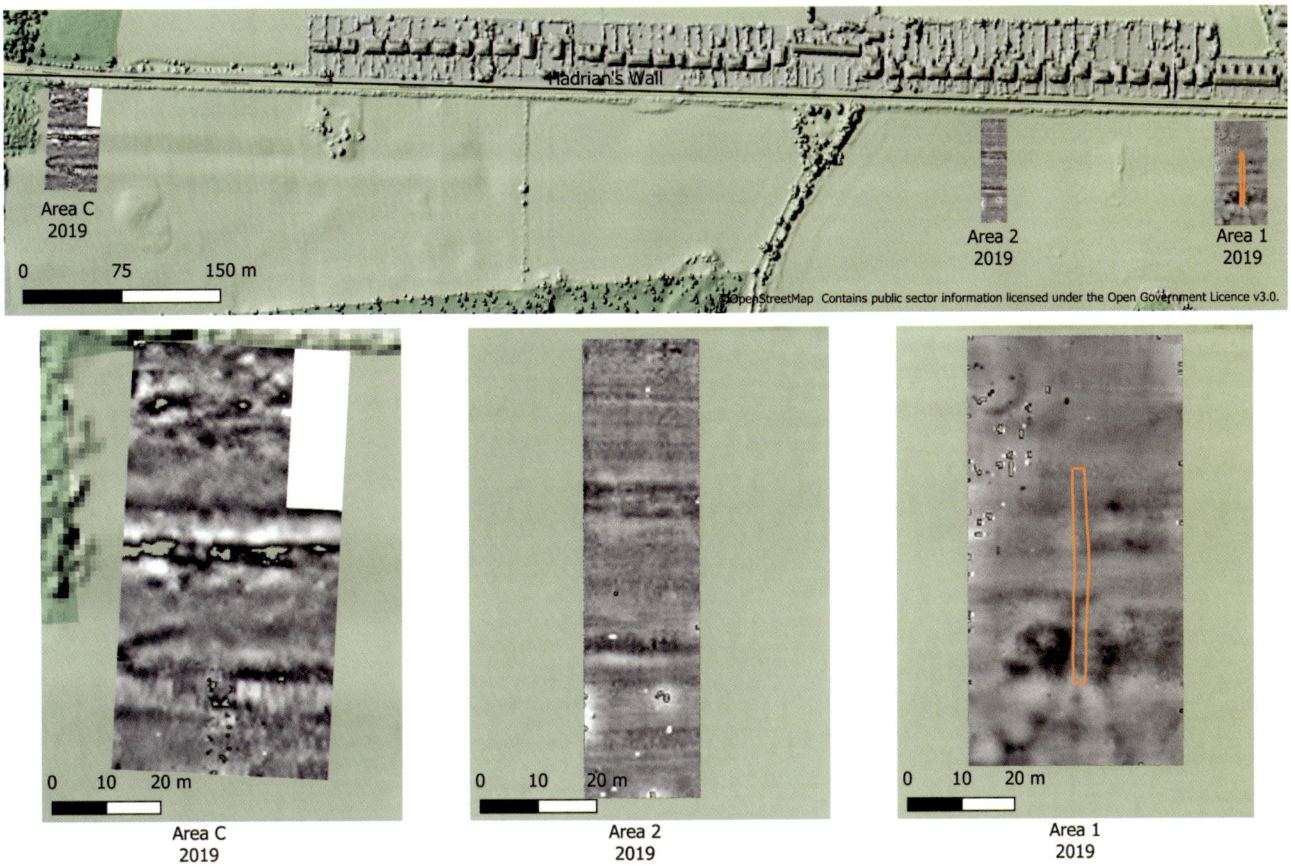

Figure 2.4: The location and results of three resisitivity surveys as transects across the Vallum. The location of the trench is indicated with the orange rectangle.

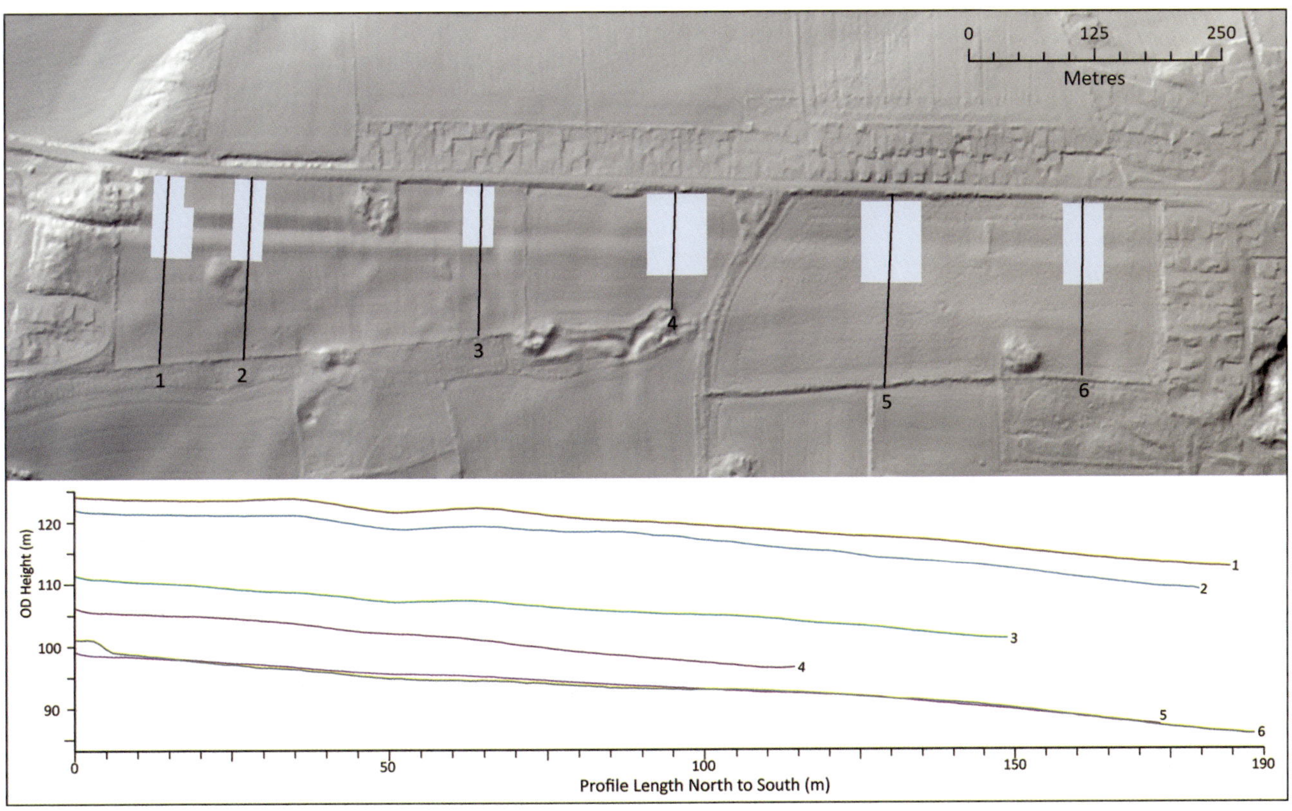

Figure 2.5: The location and comparative profiles of six topographic surface transects across the Vallum relative to the location of the gradiometry surveys.

Excavation

It was decided the most constructive approach was to focus limited excavation on the most easterly field, where damage to the Vallum was expected to have been greatest. A trench 40 m long north–south by 2 m wide was laid perpendicularly across the courses of the Vallum mounds and ditch, within the area covered by the most easterly geophysics transect in the field (Figs 2.2, 2.3, and 2.4). Initial removal of topsoil was completed with a mechanical digger, and subsequently finished by hand (Fig. 2.6). The ground surface drops by *c.* 2.3 m from the north to the south end of the trench, beyond and to the south the ground falls away more steeply. For most of the trench, the interface between disturbed soils and undisturbed geological layers were found at a depth of 0.5–0.7 m. This interface was seen throughout the trench except where the fill of the ditch was located. In that location a sondage was dug against the east-facing side of the trench to investigate the ditch. This intervention reached a depth of 1.5 m from the current ground surface. The combined length of the trench and excavation to full depth allowed the recording of the Vallum ditch profile and an environmental sample to be taken of ditch fill.

Figure 2.6: The excavation trench across the Vallum, looking south.

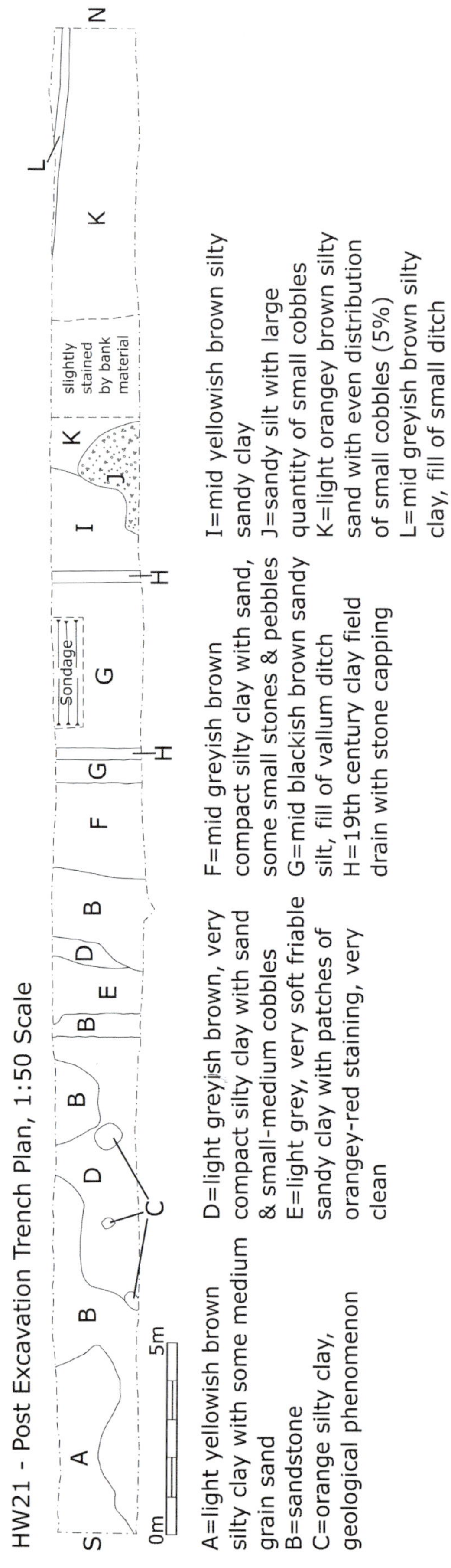

Figure 2.7: The full plan of the trench.

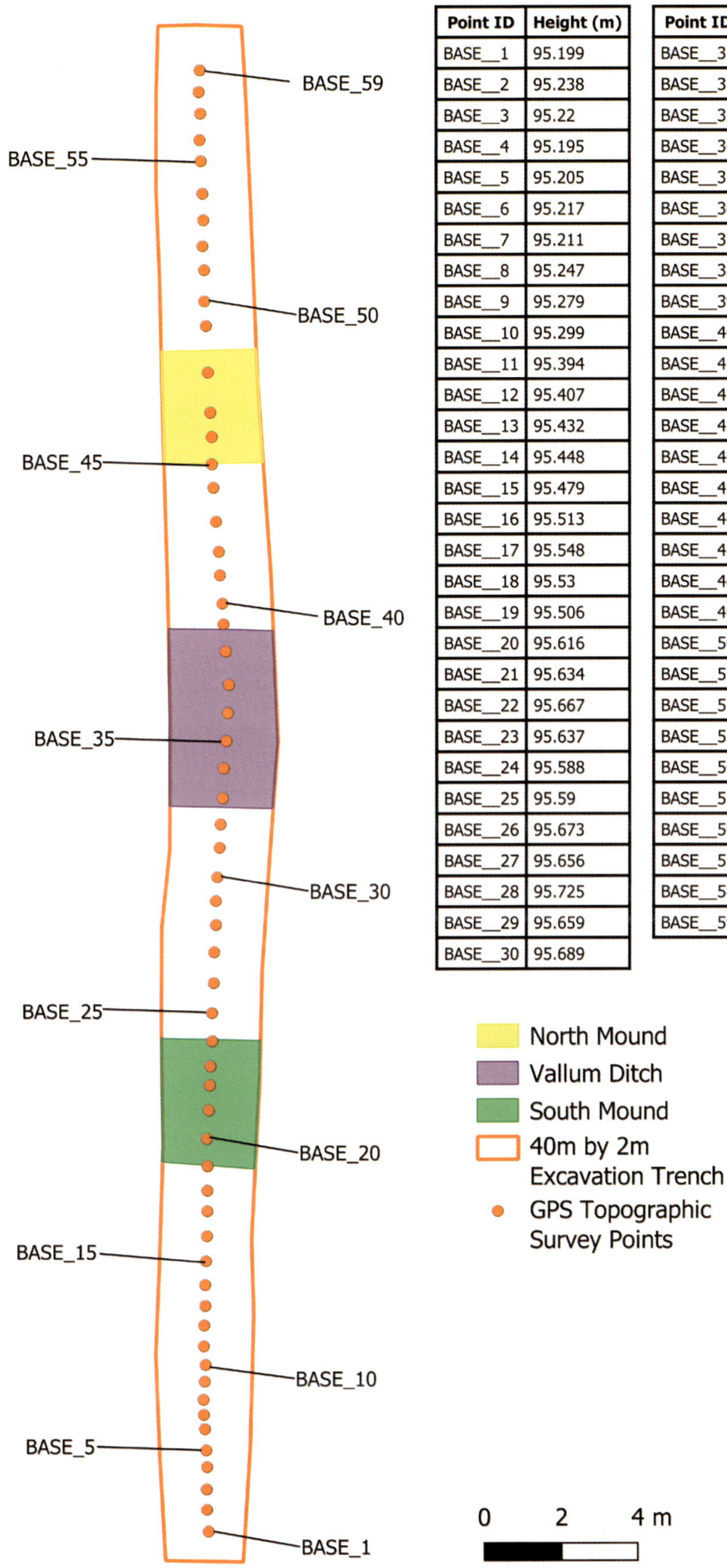

Point ID	Height (m)	Point ID	Height (m)
BASE_1	95.199	BASE_31	95.728
BASE_2	95.238	BASE_32	95.749
BASE_3	95.22	BASE_33	95.788
BASE_4	95.195	BASE_34	95.808
BASE_5	95.205	BASE_35	95.792
BASE_6	95.217	BASE_36	95.791
BASE_7	95.211	BASE_37	95.75
BASE_8	95.247	BASE_38	95.765
BASE_9	95.279	BASE_39	95.847
BASE_10	95.299	BASE_40	95.965
BASE_11	95.394	BASE_41	96.137
BASE_12	95.407	BASE_42	96.31
BASE_13	95.432	BASE_43	96.399
BASE_14	95.448	BASE_44	96.413
BASE_15	95.479	BASE_45	96.415
BASE_16	95.513	BASE_46	96.434
BASE_17	95.548	BASE_47	96.477
BASE_18	95.53	BASE_48	96.539
BASE_19	95.506	BASE_49	96.661
BASE_20	95.616	BASE_50	96.639
BASE_21	95.634	BASE_51	96.645
BASE_22	95.667	BASE_52	96.714
BASE_23	95.637	BASE_53	96.885
BASE_24	95.588	BASE_54	96.991
BASE_25	95.59	BASE_55	97.064
BASE_26	95.673	BASE_56	97.089
BASE_27	95.656	BASE_57	97.066
BASE_28	95.725	BASE_58	97.114
BASE_29	95.659	BASE_59	97.229
BASE_30	95.689		

Figure 2.8: The trench with the position of the Vallum north and south mounds and ditch coloured, accompanied by the position of survey points and their height OD.

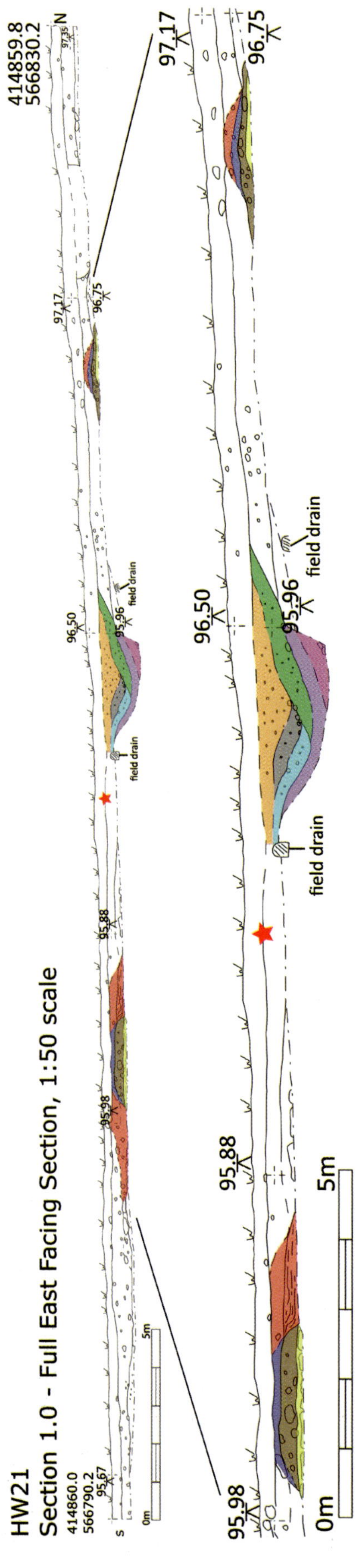

Figure 2.9: The full profile of the trench, with the Vallum features coloured. The position of the single sherd of Roman pottery is indicated by the red star.

The very slight remains of the north and south mounds, the full east-facing section of the trench and the ditch profile were drawn and recorded, along with an overall plan of the base of the trench.

The local underlying geology is composed of the mudstones, siltstones, and sandstones of the Lower Coal Measures Formation with drift geology of heterogeneous glacial till comprising clay, sand, gravel, and cobbles of a range of sizes.

The Vallum ditch was located in the excavation trench along with likely traces of the largely destroyed north and south mounds (Figs 2.7, 2.8 and 2.9). No marginal mounds or other features were detected. The ditch survived to a depth of *c.* 1.4 m below ground level, and was about 5 m wide at its spread and truncated top. The ditch was almost certainly deeper, but excavation could not continue safely below the depth reached. The south mound remains had been reduced to a maximum height of 0.4 m and *c.* 3.7 m in width, although a downslope spread of more stony material may have been mound foundations, taking the width to more like 6 m. The north mound was of a similar width, up to 3.65 m wide but survived to only *c.* 0.2 m high. The nature of the mound traces is discussed further below. The ditch was cut through the sandy clay of glacial till. The south mound was founded on an area of sandstone, the north mound on an area of gravelly sand and clay within the very varied till. Slight traces of a possible lower ground surface survived under both mounds, but the turf appeared to have been stripped from the area before the mounds were raised, possibly to be used in the construction of mound cheeks.

The Vallum ditch

The ditch was located at between 14.5–19.5 m from the north end of the trench, its darker siltier fill very clear against the yellowish colours of the varied till deposits to the north and south (Fig. 2.10). The maximum width of the ditch just below ploughsoil was at least 4.5 m, but the sides had been disturbed by the insertion of two parallel 19th-century ceramic field drains 4.5 m apart running west–east along the margins of the ditch (see H on Fig. 2.7). The ditch's profile had also been disrupted and truncated by repeated ploughing and possibly also by the traffic of heavy machines associated with coal mining as well as agriculture. Excavation had to stop at nearly 1.5 m down from ground surface, at which level the ditch was *c.* 2.5 m wide. Until *c.* 0.9 m down from ground surface both the sides were gently sloping at about 45°. The southern side was much less clear and appeared to continue on that gradient. The northern side thereafter became steeper at about 70°. This was likely to be closer to the original lower profile of the ditch.

In section the silty fills of the ditch were a maximum of 0.85 m deep below the plough soil, with a 0.15 m deep stained interface with 0.1 m of redeposited boulder clay evident below (Fig. 2.11). That lowest visible fill of the ditch – the silty, stained sandy clay – may well have been material slumped and settled from the upper sides of the ditch. The silty fills above were organic, mid to dark blackish brown sandy silts (20:80) with *c.* 5% clay and 20% poorly sorted gravel, pebbles, and occasional small cobbles. The gravel, pebble, and small cobble content and the compaction varied slightly within the fill, and there were clear tip lines. The ditch fill was gravellier than the U-shaped ploughing infill at the top of the recorded section. There was some charcoal in the fill and an environmental sample (ES1) was taken from 0.7 m depth in the ditch, from the fill interpreted as deliberate backfill. This environmental sample produced no charred plant remains but a low concentration of >2 mm wood charcoal: a fragment of roundwood charcoal gave radiocarbon date ranges of 1213–1263 cal AD (at 1σ and 68.3%) and 1172–1269 cal AD (at 2σ and 95.4%) (SUERC-105487).

The first ditch fill of stained clay may have been slump from the sides, after which the ditch seems to have begun to silt up naturally, predominantly from the north and up-slope. This silting was marked on its upper surface by a trickle of larger pebbles and small cobbles between 40–80 mm. The ditch then appeared to have been partially,

Figure 2.10: (A) The Vallum ditch in profile, mid-excavation, as seen in the west section. (B) The Vallum ditch profile (same location) on completion of the excavation.

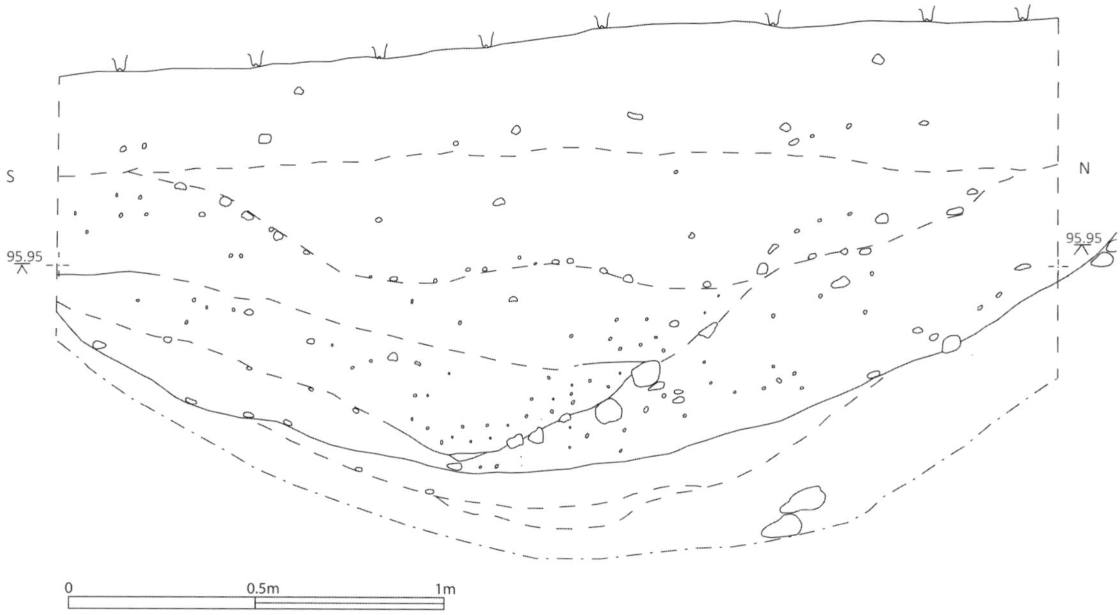

Figure 2.11: Section drawing of the Vallum ditch, west section.

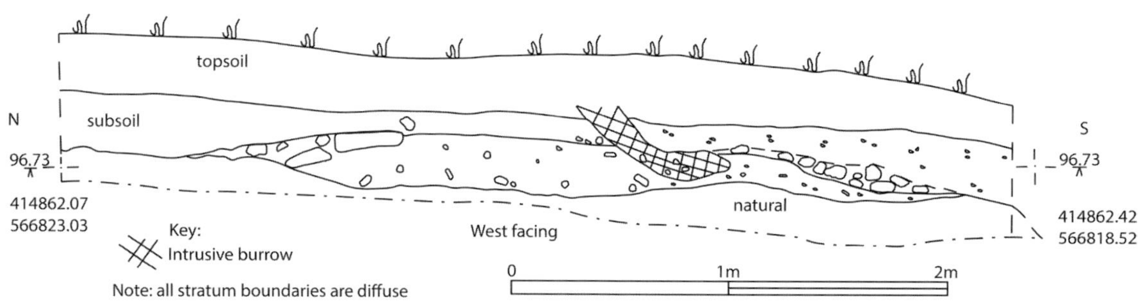

Figure 2.12: Section drawing of the Vallum north mound, east section.

and deliberately, backfilled from the south, with the tip line-marked silts being less compact and stonier. The truncation of the ditch, if – as elsewhere – the ditch was around 3 m deep (Breeze 2015, 1), meant the complete process of filling and levelling could not be traced and any interpretation must be viewed with caution because of the level of disturbance. But after the backfilling, subsequent ploughing completed the job of obscuring and infilling the ditch. There was no evidence for the ditch having been revetted in either turf or stone, or being recut. The ditch almost certainly survives to a greater depth than recorded.

No artefacts were recovered while excavating the ditch sondage and cleaning its profile but, in the subsoil just to the south of the ditch, were found a fragment of clay pipe bowl and an abraded sherd of Roman pottery, Corbridge White Ware (COR WH, see Fig. 2.9).

The north mound

The mounds survived as ghosts of their original surface construction. Excavation caught the effects of the settling and build-up of water and damper soil against the upslope foundations of the mounds (most clearly seen at the south mound: Fig. 2.16), and the altering of the soil around due to the incorporation of material used in the foundations, core, and possible turf and stone revetting. The north mound's remnants were located between 7–10 m from the north end of the trench (Fig. 2.12). The mound had been constructed above gravel and pebble-rich sandy clay, with a band of grey clay possibly representing traces of a buried land surface. The surviving tail of the mound was only around 5 m north of the spread northern edge of the Vallum ditch, suggesting that the north mound was relatively close to the ditch (see discussion below).

It is difficult to be certain of construction of the likely north mound from the traces uncovered. The mound foundations may have had a sandy boulder clay base, with a gravelly, silty sand core (Figs 2.13 and 2.14). Core material survived to a maximum of 0.2 m, possibly somewhat displaced from its original location in the mound, and may have been glacial till deposits excavated from the ditch-line. There were many larger pebbles, and the occasional larger cobble up to 0.3 m

Figure 2.13: The Vallum north mound, as revealed in the west section.

long, in the core material. The occasional flatter cobble provided slight evidence for revetting, or stone kerbs. More convincing evidence, given the hugely degraded character of the mounds, was unlikely to have survived. The clayey, northern edge of the remains was marked by iron panning, presumably caused by iron-rich water trickling down-slope and pooling against less permeable mound material. The grey silty sand laminated with the iron panning might suggest use of turf cheeks in the construction of the mound foundations.

The south mound

The south mound had been constructed above an area of sandstone bedrock and the traces were found between 25 and 32 m from the northern end of the trench. The surviving remains were therefore *c.* 5.5 m south of the southern edge of the Vallum ditch. This gap is similar to that recorded between the northern edge of the ditch as found and the identified north mound.

As to the north, the south mound archaeology is best described as representing the materials used in construction rather than providing structural detail. Again both the west- and east-facing sections (Figs 2.15 and 2.16) suggested the foundations may have included redeposited natural sandy clay, with a core of gravelly, cobble-rich silty sand. The southern mound remains were perhaps better preserved and contained a higher proportion of larger sub-angular cobbles up to 0.25 m and one angular flatter stone *c.* 0.4 m long that may have been kerbing or revetting. The mound material survived to a height of *c.* 0.4 m and 2.6 m in width, although a downslope spread of more stony material may have been mound material, taking the width to more like 6 m. A grey clay layer above the sandstone may have been a thin layer of the subsoil onto which the mound was constructed. Even more clearly than at the edge of the northern mound remains, the clayey, northern edge of the south mound was richly laminated with sandy clay, gritty silt deposits and iron panning (Fig. 2.17, right-hand side of the photograph). This may represent the remains of turf cheeks altered by post-depositional processes and in particular the effects of iron-rich water.

Artefacts

Only one artefact of note was found, a single Roman ceramic sherd identified as Corbridge white ware (COR WH). The sherd was found in the subsoil just south of the Vallum ditch, which also included a kaolin pipebowl fragment, indicating a mixed or disturbed subsoil, probably relating to historic agricultural activities.

Discussion

The excavation demonstrated that the Vallum elements survive very poorly in the furthest east of the fields under investigation. The field has been ploughed and worked in modern times from west to east, and from north to south (Fig. 2.2) and this – along with earlier agricultural use – has flattened and nearly eradicated the mounds. The area was also mined for coal. The disturbed mound remains are clearly visible as broad, lighter bands of soil via GoogleEarth, suggesting considerable spreading, shifting, and turning of the mound material (Fig. 2.18); the below-ground deposits proved to be little more than collapsed and displaced vestiges of the original earthworks. Those vestiges did provide evidence for the natural material – glacial till and clay – excavated in creating the ditch being used as foundation and core material for the mounds. The mounds seem to have been carefully constructed with probable use of turf cheeks and possibly stone kerbing or revetting. The surviving edge of the north mound was recorded only around 40 m from the likely line of the Wall curtain running under the B6528, in a stretch where the Vallum does on the whole run closer to the curtain Wall than elsewhere. Further west where the surviving stretch of the curtain stands, the north mound is closer to 20 m south of the curtain. The north mound as found was *c.* 3.2 m wide, the berm to the spread north lip of the ditch only about 4.5 m wide, and the berm from the southern edge of the ditch to the south mound around 5.2 m. The south mound remains may have been as wide as 6 m, if a southern tail of stones is included, but the more convincing survival of core elements was *c.* 3.7 m wide. It cannot be reiterated firmly enough that these measurements capture only damaged remnants of the original earthworks. The combination of destruction and slope militated against more precise measurements.

It was very difficult to estimate the original depth and width of the ditch, especially as land drains had been inserted east–west along the ditch margins, but it may have been relatively narrow as the surviving spread if also truncated top was only about 5 m wide. Below the land drains the ditch narrowed to only around 2.5 m.

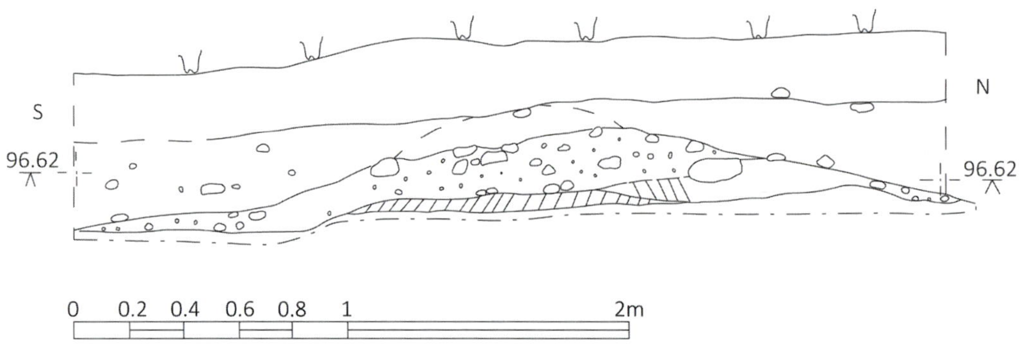

Figure 2.14: Section drawing of the Vallum north mound, west section.

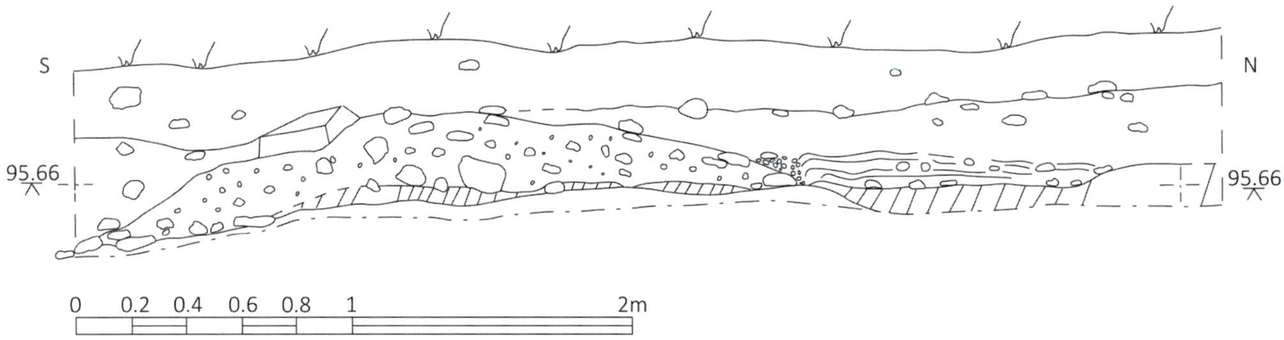

Figure 2.15: Section drawing of the Vallum south mound, west section.

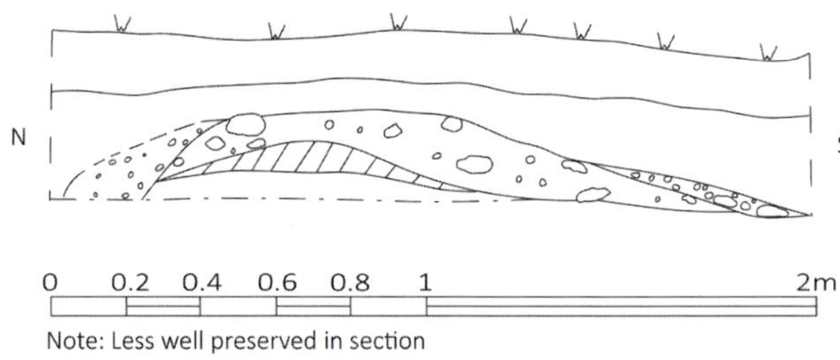

Figure 2.16: Section drawing of the Vallum south mound, east section.

Originally the ditch sides may have been angled at 70° and possibly included some clay lining. The ditch was at least partly backfilled deliberately, after initial slumping of the upper clay sides and some natural silting, before being finally infilled and all but levelled by the effects of repeated ploughing. The deliberate backfilling was radiocarbon dating to the late 12th–13th centuries, at a time when agriculture in the area was expanding. The ditch bottom was not reached in this excavation, but the ditch survived to a depth of *c.* 1.4 m below the current ground surface. The overall width of the Vallum complex at this location is difficult to determine but may have been closer to the 30 m width found at Wallhouses than the 37.5 m of the Vallum at Appletree in Cumbria (Wilmott and Bennett 2009, 134).

Figure 2.17: The northern edge of the Vallum south mound, as seen in the west section.

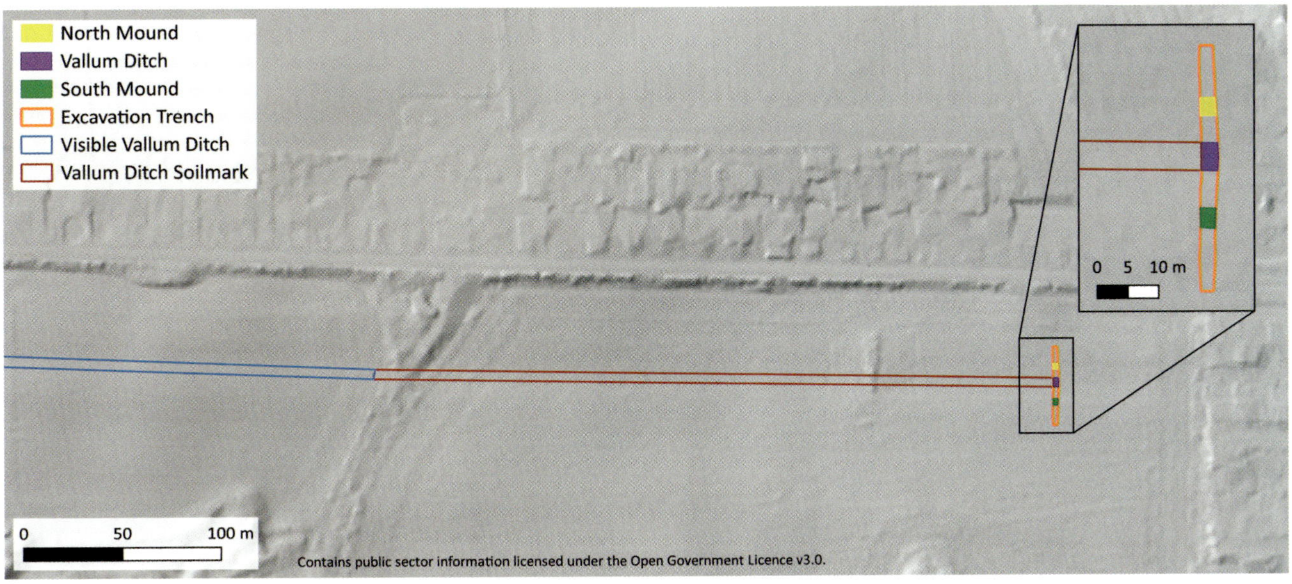

Figure 2.18: Interpretation of the excavation results, projecting the line of the Vallum west over LiDAR.

Even in their much diminished state, the components of Vallum complex recorded here can be compared to other investigations of the ditch and mounds. In a recent review of Vallum studies, David Breeze noted that research to date had revealed there was 'little in the way of uniformity in the various elements of the Vallum' (2015, 17). This excavation has added to that picture of local diversity in the details of construction and layout.

The model against which Vallum measurements have been compared (overall width 35.5 m, mounds 6 m wide, with 9 m berms either side of a 6 m wide, 6 m deep ditch (*e.g.* Breeze 2006, 54–55), while giving a general impression of scale, has been challenged by almost every investigation of the Vallum. This observation comes with the obvious caveat that dimensions have been variously and differently affected by the afterlife of the monument in several locations. Rather than sticking slavishly to a brief, the Vallum surveyors modified the design of the Vallum in response to local soils and landscape (Bennett and Turner 1983, 74). This is well-illustrated by the results gathered in seven more recent Vallum excavations (Wilmott and Bennett 2009). While many mound width measurements accord reasonably well with the model, north mound widths range from 4.4 m recorded at Wallhouses to 9.2 m at Appletree (Cumbria), the south mound from 5.5 m at West Denton to 8.5 m at Appletree, berms from less than 5–9 m and the ditch width from less than 6–10 m (Wilmott and Bennett 2009, 134).

More locally, to the west of the current site and just southwest of the exposed stretch of curtain in Heddon, the south mound was found to be only about 4.6 m wide, and founded on clay subsoil with the core constructed from sand and stone taken from the rock-cut ditch (Tait 1962, 142–143). At Throckley to the east, the Vallum berms were only about 5 m wide (Bennett 1983, 41). The Vallum mounds investigated in Wall-mile 9 – as here at Heddon – had been virtually levelled in a ploughed field but were visible as pale bands in the soil surface. The mounds survived to similar heights to those at Heddon and were also composed of sandy clay and silty sands (Wilmott and Bennett 2009, 77–79). Again, as at Heddon, further afield at Appletree (Cumbria) the mounds were constructed on ground stripped of turf and topsoil (Wilmott and Bennett 2009, 111). Evidence for stone revetting or kerbing and for the use of containing and guiding turf cheeks has been found at several sites including Heddon (Breeze 2015, 5 and 17); builders used local turf and clay, stone and other subsoils dug from the ditch for the mounds creating an inevitable diversity in mound construction materials, reflecting the local soil and geology.

The Heddon Vallum elements, although in poor condition, add to the picture of the Vallum as a construction driven by the determination to engineer a considerable ditch flanked at some distance by mounds, with the details of construction shaped by the local landscape. The relatively narrow overall Vallum at Heddon, with the monument also sitting close to the curtain Wall, may have been designed to situate the ditch and mounds on the brow of a slope that immediately south becomes a much steeper drop towards the Tyne (Figs 2.1 and 2.5). The less-steep crest location, while providing good views, would have made constructing the Vallum less challenging. The steeper hillside later contributed to the erosion of the Vallum exacerbating soil movement downslope under the impact of the ploughing.

The excavation at Heddon-on-the-Wall, although limited in scope, has provided some significant information about the condition and character of the Vallum in this stretch of Hadrian's Wall. Ploughing and possibly also mining have had a huge impact on the monument's condition and if the agricultural regime is unchanged the mounds will disappear within a few years and the ditch will continue to be eroded.

3

Geophysical survey of the curtain at Thirlwall and Drumburgh

Alex Turner

Geophysical survey was undertaken at two locations along the Wall focusing particularly on identifying traces of the curtain. These surveys were intended to be followed by excavation, but circumstances did not allow for that possibility. Namely the impact that the COVID-19 pandemic had on project timelines in combination with access to land in relation to the agricultural calendar. However, both surveys detected traces of the Wall curtain and/or ditch.

Thirlwall

Thirlwall was a site of interest for a number of reasons. In the first instance, the course of the curtain, the ditch, and the Vallum is not readily visible above the ground, though a low mound running east–west signals the location of the curtain. Secondly, stone from the Wall was used to substantially build Thirlwall Castle in the 14th century, approximately 50 m north of the curtain. Basic calculation indicates that 200–334 m of Wall was required to provide a suitable volume of material to build Thirlwall Castle (Collins *et al.* 2023b, 90), and investigation of the curtain at this location provided an opportunity to explore a confirmed historic episode of robbing and re-use of Roman fabric. Thirdly, the course of the Vallum is unconfirmed in this location, and investigation hoped to demonstrate a more certain course for that aspect of the monument. Gradiometer and electrical resistance surveys were undertaken in the field to the southwest of Thirlwall Castle. The surveys were accompanied by a programme of topographic survey using a high-definition terrestrial laser scanner.

Location, topography, and geology

The survey area was located 0.8 km north of Greenhead and 2.25 km east of Gilsland (Fig. 3.1). It lies between milecastle 46 to the east and milecastle 47 to the west and is 0.8 km northwest of the Roman fort of Carvoran (Magna).

The survey areas were laid to pasture and bounded by hedges and fences to the east and south. Large metal gateways were present but the survey areas were positioned to avoid ferrous interference with the gradiometer survey. The survey area was also sited to avoid the patch of land to the west of the survey that formed a bog with thick grass and reeds that was unsuitable for both resistivity and gradiometer survey. This area can be seen as significant depression on the digital terrain model (DTM) derived from Ordnance Survey contour data and the Environment Agency's 1 m resolution LiDAR data (Fig. 3.2).

Examination of the contour and LiDAR data shows a 1.5 m slope from north to south across the survey area. The elevation profile (Fig. 3.3) clearly shows the remnant earthwork of the wall. The slope in the west to east direction is less pronounced and is 1 m at its maximum. At its western edge, the surveys border the boggy area that can be seen as a distinctive depression on the LiDAR. The sharp edges that mark the limits of much of this area would suggest that it is either an artificial construct or a natural feature that has been managed. The lower topography either side of the line of the Wall, as it crosses this feature, might be a good indication that some of the remains of the Wall are still *in situ*. Observation of field conditions at the wettest part of the year showed that much of this area is under water for significant parts of the autumn/winter. Fortunately, adequate drainage within this field enabled the collection of some excellent results from the resistivity survey. Waterlogged areas can cause amorphous positive and negative anomalies that, when classified, are often seen as natural. This may explain some of the lack of results in the southern half of the gradiometer survey.

The underlying bedrock geology was largely sandstone in the northern half of the survey and limestone,

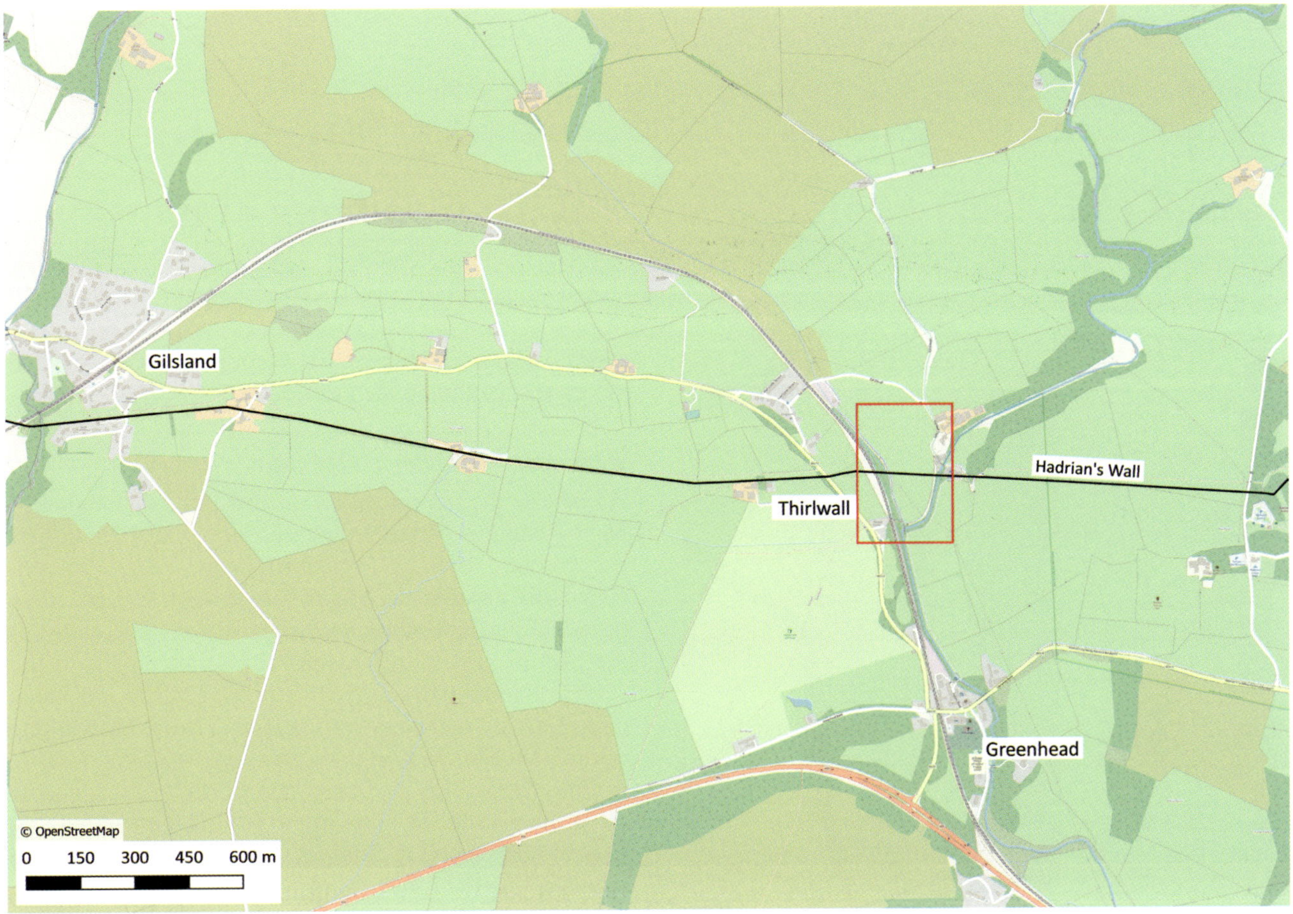

Figure 3.1: Location of the survey area.

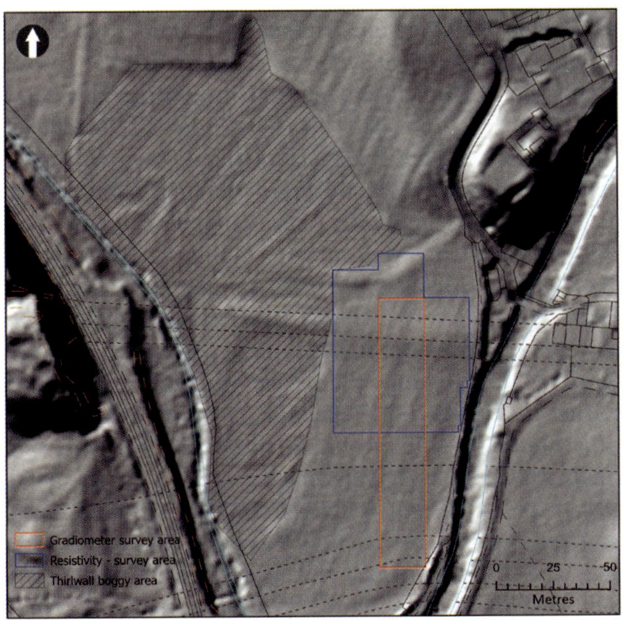

Figure 3.2: LiDAR digital terrain model (DTM) with the location of the resistivity and gradiometer survey areas. The remnant line of the Wall curtain is clearly visible in the northern half of the survey areas, and the boggy round west of the survey is visible as a semi-circular and uneven depression.

sandstone, siltstone, and mudstone in the lower lying southern half of the survey. The castle at Thirlwall is built on a sandstone outcrop and this extends westward into the field along its eastern boundary. Above this the superficial geology is largely a mixture of clay, silt sand, and gravel with an area of Till (diamicton) at the northern edge. The soil is a clay to sandy loam with an area of clayey to silty loam mimicking the same area as the Till (diamicton). None of the geological elements present on the site represent a problem for either resistivity or gradiometer survey.

Survey methodology

Fourteen 20 × 20 m full and partial survey grids grid were laid out using a Leica GNSS differential survey grade GPS connected to the Leica RTK Smartnet network. Three grids (5, 8, and 11) were common to both the resistivity and gradiometer surveys. The two survey areas were kept largely separate to enable both types of survey to be undertaken concurrently. In addition to the geophysical survey, a topographic model of the survey field was created using a Faro Focus X330 phased-based laser scanner. A total of 71 scans of the survey area and its surrounds were made and this was used to create a detailed

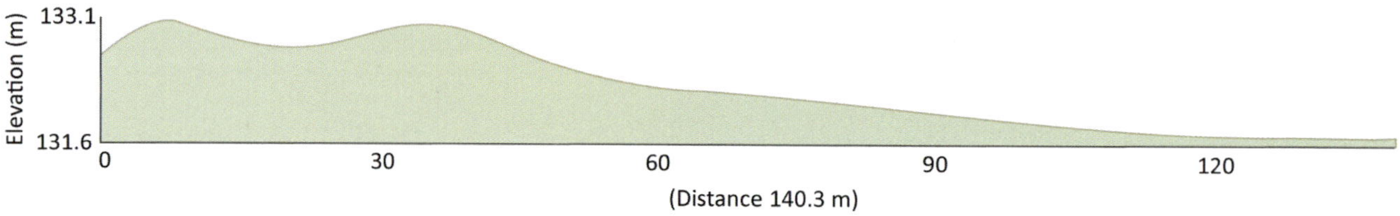

Figure 3.3: The north–south elevation profile across the survey area.

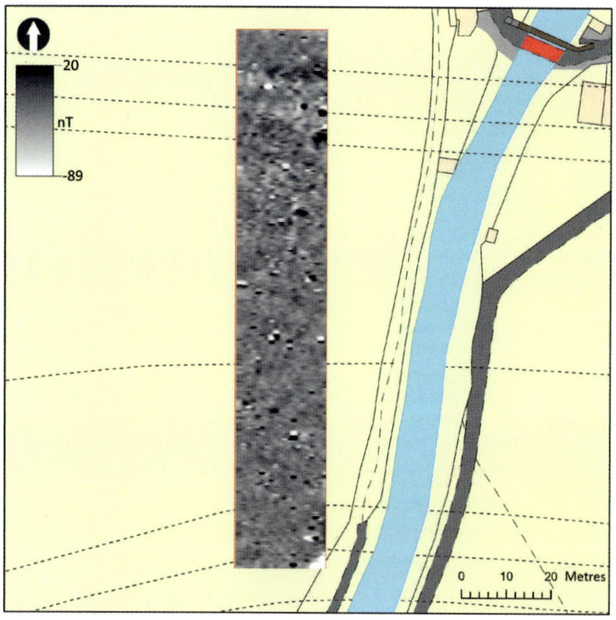

(A)

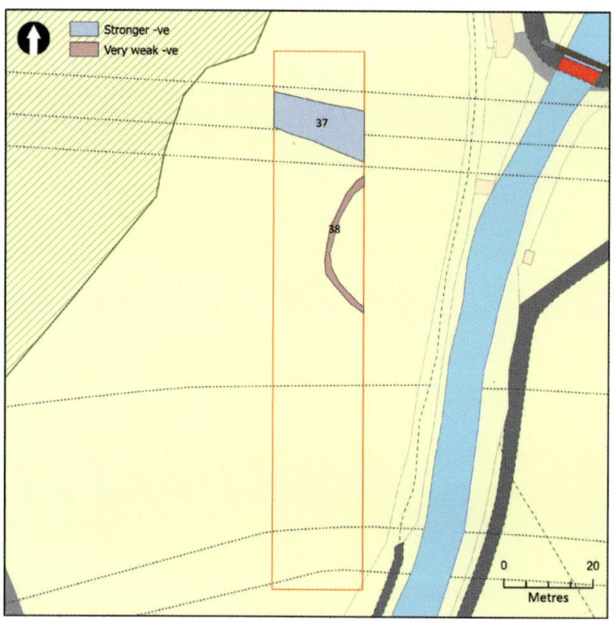

(B)

Figure 3.4: (A) Thirlwall gradiometer survey results. (B) Interpretation of the gradiometer survey results.

model of the survey areas in relation to the surrounded structures, including the castle.

Reference to historic Ordnance Survey

As part of the interpretation process, an examination of all the editions of the Ordnance Survey at 1:2500, was carried out. Historic GoogleEarth images were also consulted for the first decade of this century but provided no additional information of significance. The study of the historic maps showed that the arrangement of the survey field boundaries was much the same as it is today (Fig. 3.6A). Even the railway was in existence at the time of the First Edition County Series map as The Newcastle & Carlisle Railway had been opened as a through route on 18 June 1838. The line of the Wall is marked but it is only on the second revision of the 1:2500 County Series published in 1921 that the Military Way and the Vallum were added.

Gradiometry survey results and interpretation

The data was processed using Geoplot 4 and exported as a raster image to the ArcGIS 7.1 project for the survey (Fig. 3.4A). Only basic processing was necessary within Geoplot 4. The grids were despiked with a threshold of +/- 3SD and the Zero Mean Traverse filter was applied to reduce any striping as a result of changes in the orientation of the gradiometer during zig-zag survey. A uniform High Pass Filter, to filter any changes in the geological background, was applied with a window of 10 readings in both the X and Y direction. Interpolation was carried out between traverses so that the final data had an X and Y resolution of 0.25 m. The plots were then scaled and georeferenced to the British National Grid in ArcGIS using coordinates derived from the differential GNSS.

The scaled and georeferenced geophysics plots were used to produce an interpretive overlay within ArcGIS. Each of the drawn polygons or polylines was given a unique reference number that is used within the interpretive discussion (Fig. 3.4B). Two key features were identified. No. 37 was a stronger negative response coinciding with the line of the Wall curtain. No. 38 was a very weak negative response that mirrors the sub-circular feature on the resistivity survey. If this feature were complete, it would be *c*. 30 m in diameter. This may be an earlier, prehistoric enclosure, though no definitive stratigraphic relationship could be determined from the geophysical surveys.

Resistivity survey results and interpretation

The data was processed using the same software as the gradiometer survey. The data was despiked with a threshold of ± 3SD and then a Gaussian high pass filter was applied with a window of 10 reading in the X and Y directions to minimise the effect of background geology. A low pass filter with a window of 1 reading in the X and Y directions was used to smooth the data and enhance any large weak features. Interpolation of the data was carried out in the X and Y directions to give data plots with a final spatial resolution of 0.25 m × 0.25 m. This was an equivalent resolution to the gradiometer data. The results revealed few archaeological anomalies, consistent with the results from the gradiometer survey (Fig. 3.5A).

Six key features were identified via resistivity. No. 1 was a Linear feature consisting of a series of high resistance responses running roughly parallel to the wall. It seems to have a relationship with [2] and may possibly be the remains of a trackway associated with a route across the boggy area. No. 2 was a curvilinear, high resistance feature that follows the edge of part of the boggy area. It may be infill along the edge of this feature. No. 35 was a linear feature with a higher response that runs parallel to the Wall curtain to the north. This could be a response from the edge of the ditch. Nos. 3 and 4 were high resistance linear features indicating the line of the Wall curtain, but patchy at the west end. Nos. 5–9 and 29–34 were areas of high resistance that are part of the makeup of the Wall curtain. This patchy response may well reflect the systematic robbing of material from the curtain to build Thirlwall Castle. Nos. 17–26 were areas of high resistance that appear unconnected. They could be rubble from the dismantling of the curtain but could equally represent natural deposits within the subsoil. Nos. 11–15 and 36 are a series of high resistance responses form a semi-circular feature that may represent an early enclosure and is also seen within the gradiometer data [38].

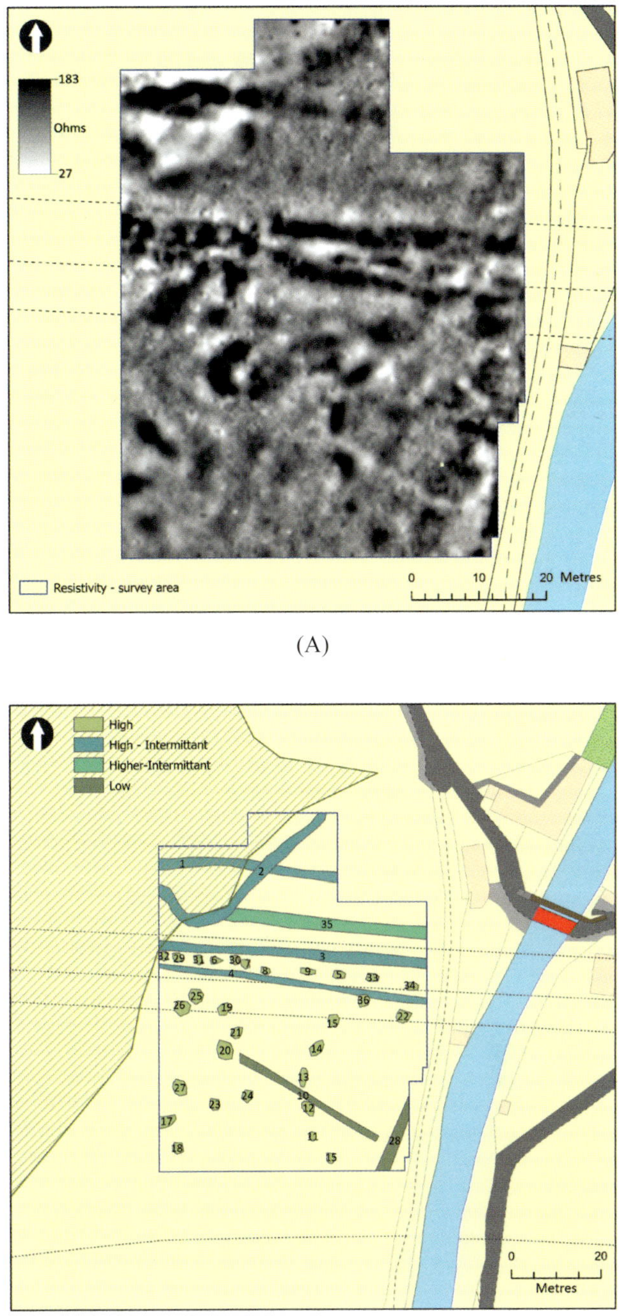

Figure 3.5: (A) Resistivity survey results. (B) Interpretation of the resistivity survey results.

Summary

There was limited success with the gradiometer survey, particularly at the southern end of the field, and this could be due to changes in the level of waterlogging of the ground. The resistivity survey was far more successful in detecting sub-surface features including the remains of the Wall curtain and possibly the ditch. Significantly, the Vallum and the Military Way do not appear in the gradiometer survey even though their line, as shown on the post-1921 Ordnance Survey, should cross the survey area. A further resistance survey to the south of the one completed was unable to take place due to waterlogging and land access issues. Given the results from the northern survey this is something that would be worth considering in the future.

Though the Wall curtain can be seen as a very low-lying mound with the naked eye in the field south of Thirlwall Castle, the geophysical survey suggests that this is not simply an artefact of the robbing of its stone. At least some rubble and possible foundations can be confidently assumed to have survived *in situ*, though not necessarily to the same degree in every location. Another interesting

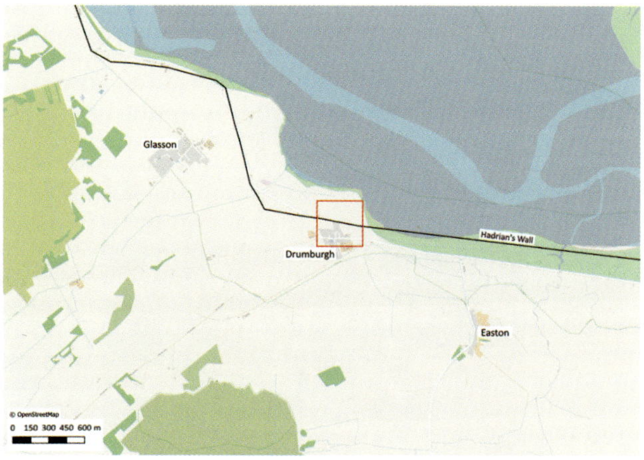

Figure 3.6: Location of the Drumburgh survey area.

result is the possible prehistoric enclosure south of the curtain; this adds to the already existing evidence of a settled and farmed landscape directly on the line of the Wall prior to its construction, though exact dating remains contentious.

Drumburgh

Drumburgh was a site of interest for a number of reasons, similar to Thirlwall. First, the course of the curtain, the ditch, and the Vallum is not readily visible above the ground, and the course of the Wall is uncertain to the east of the site as it crosses Burgh Marsh. Second, stone from the Wall or the fort at Drumburgh was used to substantially build Drumburgh Castle in the 14th century, really a fortified manor house, approximately 130 m south of the curtain, and notably south of the platform of the small Roman fort at Drumburgh. Third, the Wall was originally built in this location in turf and only subsequently rebuilt in stone; it was hoped that some traces of the Turf Wall might also be encountered.

The Roman fort at Drumburgh sits on a small drumlin or knoll that rises above the otherwise flat and low-lying land at this western end of the Wall. Historically, this land was more prone to flooding, and it is clear that there have been numerous phases of improvements to land drainage and flood defences to this area of the Solway Plain from the medieval period. The combination of historic improvements and robbing of the Wall means that there is less data for the Wall in the west than in the central and eastern sectors. The survey allowed for a modern assessment of prospective survival of the Wall in the vicinity of Drumburgh fort and at the western edge of Burgh Marsh, which could further elucidate the relationship between the Wall and the Marsh. Gradiometer and electrical resistance surveys were undertaken in the survey area across three modern fields, part of which lies within the area of the Roman fort and subsequent medieval enclosure and the rest to the east of the fort up to the western edge of Burgh Marsh. The site is centred on Ordnance Survey grid reference NY 26430 59900.

Location, topography, and geology

The site is located within the village of Drumburgh, between the villages of Glasson, 1.5 km to the west and Easton, 1.5 km to the east (Fig. 3.6). The nearest major settlement is Carlisle 17 km to the east. The survey area was laid to pasture and divided by a series of hedgerows that divided the survey area into three main sections. Metal gates, wire along the field boundaries and feeding troughs were problematic for gradiometer survey. Due to Drumburgh's position on a raised knoll the ground conditions remained dry during the survey. The only area that was not surveyed due to waterlogging was the northern edge of the medieval grange ditch (Fig. 3.7). The overhanging trees in this area also precluded any survey in this area.

Examination of the LiDAR data shows that Drumburgh lies on a distinctive knoll raising it above the surrounding low-lying landscape (Fig. 3.8). The southern part of the survey area was largely flat but dropped away significantly to the north and east. In the survey area to the east of Drumburgh House the change in slope was 8.5 m from west to east and 2 m from south to north. In the fields to the west of Drumburgh House the slope in the areas to the south of the enclosure ditch is 2 m from south to north but beyond the ditch to the northern end of the field the slope greatly increases and is in excess of 10 m. The enclosure ditch has a maximum depth of 1.5 m on the eastern side and presented a challenge for consistent survey with a gradiometer. In addition, the central field undulated considerably due to the survival of medieval ridge and furrow.

The underlying bedrock geology was part of the Mercia mudstone group consisting of mudstone with gypsum-stone and/or anhydrite-stone. These stones are diamagnetic and therefore have no effect on magnetic survey techniques. The superficial geology consisted of a mixture of Gretna Till formation – Diamicton, saltmarsh deposits – clay and silt and intertidal sandflat depots – silt and clay. The soil map showed that the majority of the survey was covered with a loam soil with only the eastern edge having a mixing of sand, clay, and loam. This geological combination, when not waterlogged, enabled good survey results to be obtained using either gradiometry or resistivity survey.

Survey methodology

The gradiometer survey grid consisted of a total of 30 squares each measuring 30 × 30 m, laid out using a Leica GNSS differential survey grade GPS connected to the Leica RTK Smartnet network. Temporary grid pegs were used to mark out the grid but the livestock in the fields meant these had to be removed overnight and relocated the following day. In practice this had very little impact on survey speed. The survey grid coordinates were derived from Mastermap

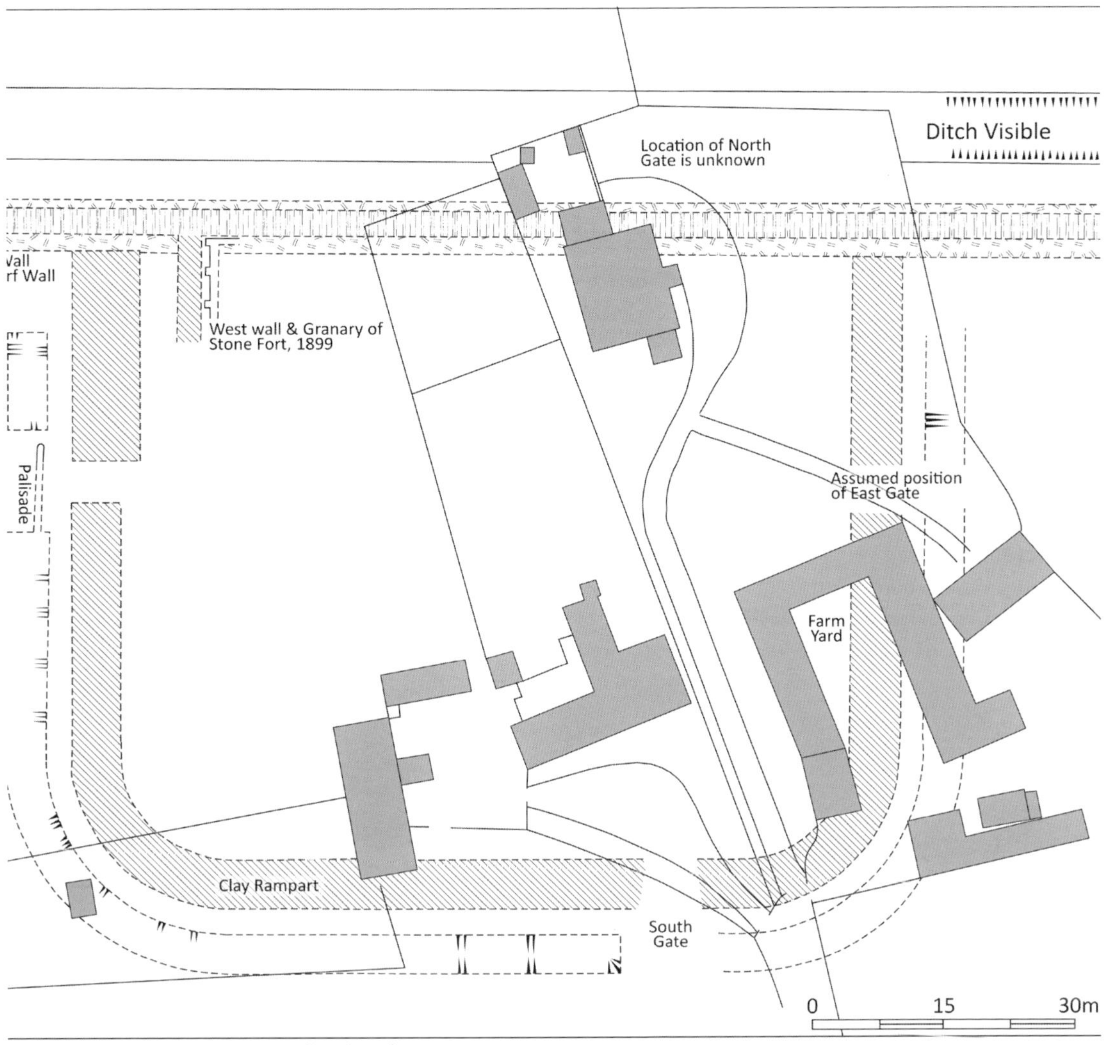

Figure 3.7: Richmond's 1947 plan of Drumburgh overlain by modern polyline data.

digital data and stored as a feature class within the survey ArcGIS geodatabase. Grids were numbered sequentially in a south–north series of west–east columns. Due to the restricted size of some of the fields in the survey area a number of the grids were partial. These were laid out as simple rectangles. The grid layout, where possible, was chosen to avoid close proximity to the ferrous intrusions within the field but in order to survey the area in close proximity to the feeding troughs and gates some ferrous disturbance was unavoidable. The area covered by a resistivity survey was unaffected by ferrous intrusions.

The resistivity survey consisted of 10 grids with 20 × 20 m squares laid out using a Leica GNSS differential survey grade GPS connected to the Leica RTK Smartnet network. Temporary grid pegs were used to mark out the corners of the grids that were aligned to the British National Grid. The survey grid coordinates were derived from Mastermap digital data and stored as a feature class within the survey ArcGIS geodatabase. Grids were

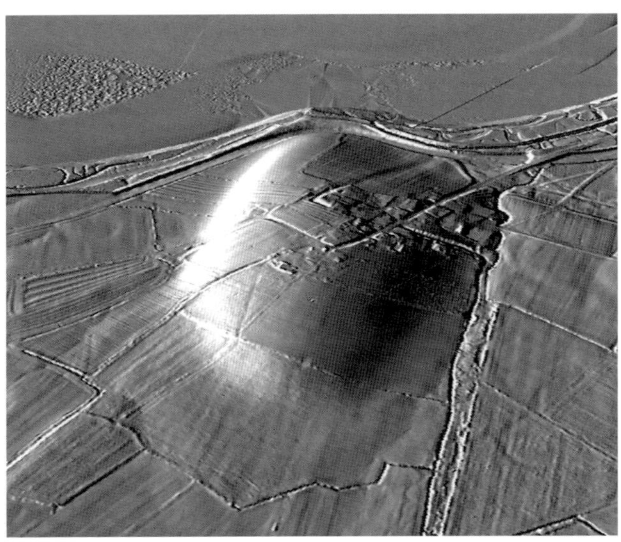

Figure 3.8: LiDAR imaging showing Drumburgh's location at the top of a knoll.

Figure 3.9: Overview of the gradiometer survey results.

numbered sequentially starting in the southwest corner of the survey. Due to obstructions in parts of the survey area, four grids were partial. Data was collected at 1 m intervals in both the X and Y direction. The survey was only conducted in the western portion of the survey area.

Reference to historic Ordnance Survey

As part of the interpretation process, an examination of all the editions of the Ordnance Survey at 1:2500 was carried out. Historic GoogleEarth images were also consulted for the first decade of this century but provided no additional information of significance. The study of the historic maps showed that the arrangement of the survey field boundaries to the east was the same as it is today, but there has been significant change in the field boundaries to the west of Drumburgh House. In the southwest corner of the area the orchard has now been replaced by a bungalow and the east–west boundary to their north no longer exists. On this map the fort is marked incorrectly as Tunnocelum (Ravenglass) rather than Congavata, probably following Bruce's 1867 publication of MacLauchlan's survey of Drumburgh. When the 1:2500 Ordnance Survey first revision was published in 1900, Tunnocelum has been replaced by the simple word fort. The Ordnance Survey National Grid edition for 1970 shows some of the current changed field boundaries and the bungalow in the southwest corner is present at this point. The other noticeable change is the expansion to the north of the garden of the Grange enclosing more of the remains of the fort.

Gradiometry survey results and interpretation

The data was processed using Geoplot 4 and exported as a raster image to the ArcGIS 7.1 project for the survey. Only basic processing was necessary within Geoplot 4. The grids were despiked with a threshold of ± 3SD and the Zero Mean Traverse filter was applied to reduce any striping as a result of changes in the orientation of the gradiometer during zig-zag survey. A uniform High Pass Filter, to filter any changes in the geological background, was applied with a window of 10 readings in both the X and Y direction. Interpolation was carried out between traverses so that the final data had an X and Y resolution of 0.25 m. The plots were then scaled and georeferenced to the British National Grid in ArcGIS using coordinates derived from the differential GNSS. The results from the gradiometer survey (Fig. 3.9) clearly show the line of the ditch in the field to the east but are also badly affected by

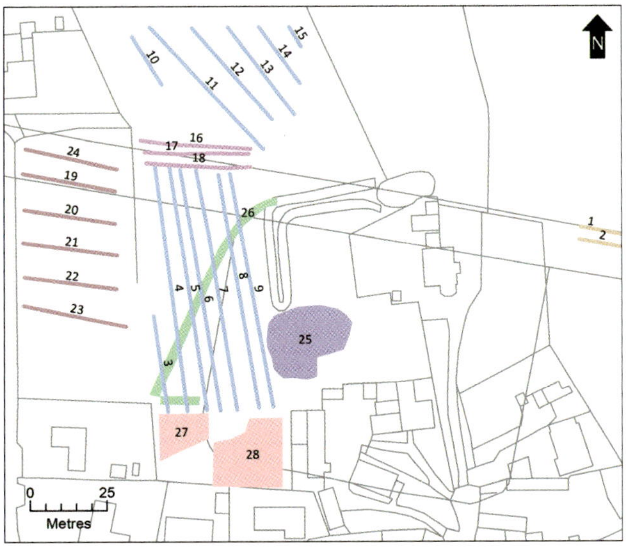

Figure 3.10: Interpretation of the gradiometer survey results, western part.

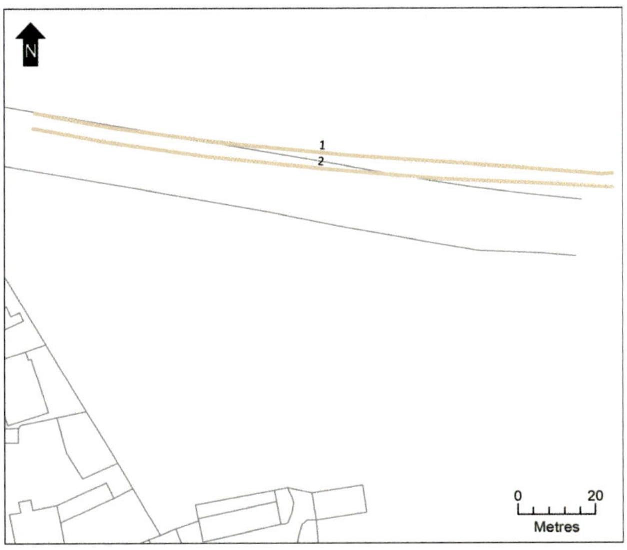

Figure 3.11: Interpretation of the gradiometer survey results, eastern part.

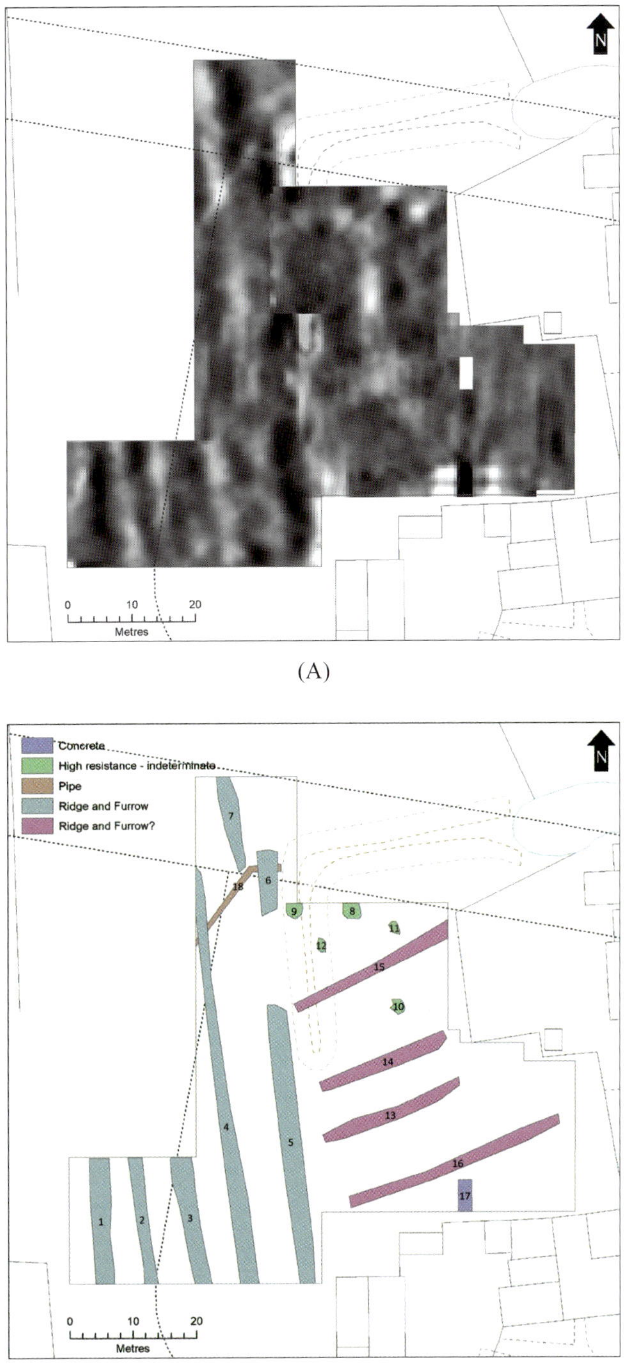

(A)

(B)

Figure 3.12: (A) Plot of the resistivity survey results – black is high and white is low. (B) Interpretation of the resistivity survey.

a drainage pipe and a large pit filled with ferrous material in the fields to the west of Drumburgh House.

The scaled and georeferenced geophysics plots were used to produce interpretive overlays within ArcGIS. Each of the drawn polygons or polylines was given a unique reference number that is used within the interpretive discussion (Figs 3.10 and 3.11). Nos. 1–2 consists of two parallel linear bands with a positive response. They represent the edges of the Wall ditch and can be traced back to the extension of Drumburgh House where the ditch was uncovered during building works. It is also clearly visible on the LiDAR plot (Fig. 3.8). Nos. 3–15 and 19–24 are the remains of medieval ridge and furrow. This is most pronounced in the central field where it runs south to north. These features are also clearly visible on the LiDAR (Fig. 3.8). Nos. 16–18 are parallel linear features that probably form part of a section of ditch visible as an earthwork at the western edge of the survey area. No. 25 indicates a large area with a massive dipolar response indicating the present of substantial quantities of ferrous metal. Anecdotal evidence suggests that this is a pit that was later filled with rubbish. No. 26 is a drainage pipe the empties into the northern section of the medieval enclosure ditch. Nos. 27–28 are two areas of highly disturbed ground that may be related to garden activity. It is shown as belonging to Grange Cottage, with what looks like an orchard, on the Ordnance Survey 1:2500 maps for 1900 and 1925.

Resistivity survey results and interpretation

The data was processed using the same software as the gradiometer survey. The data was despiked with a threshold of ± 3SD and then a Gaussian high pass filter was applied with a window of 10 reading in the X and Y directions to minimise the effect of background geology. A low pass filter with a window of 1 reading in the X and Y directions was used to smooth the data and enhance any large weak features. Interpolation of the data was carried out in the X and Y directions to give data plots with a final spatial resolution of 0.25 × 0.25 m. This was an equivalent resolution to the gradiometer data. The plots were then scaled and georeferenced to the British National Grid in ArcGIS using coordinates derived from the differential GNSS. The results from the resistivity survey (Fig. 3.12A) primarily highlight linear features pertaining to post-Roman activities.

The scaled and georeferenced geophysics plots were used to produce interpretive overlays within ArcGIS. Each of the drawn polygons or polylines was given a unique reference number that is used within the interpretive discussion (Fig. 3.12B). Nos. 1–7 are the remains of the medieval ridge and furrow that was visible within the field and ran in a northwest to southeast direction. Nos. 8–12 are patches of high resistance that could represent buried rubble or masonry. Some of them appeared to be within the line of possible ridge and furrow (nos. 13–16). Nos. 13–16 are features that produced a similar response to nos. 1–7 and could be the remains of further ridge and furrow running in a southwest to northeast direction. This is by no means certain and crucially, visible evidence was absent within the topography of this area. No. 17 is the remains of a concrete hard standing. No. 18 is a pipe that exits into the ditch at the northern edge of the survey.

Summary

The lack of real success with both gradiometry and resistivity surveys in detecting significant sub-surface features is surprising given the location of the survey area in relation to the line of the curtain and ditch. There seems to be no evidence from the geophysics of even the slightest remains of the Turf Wall, wider than the subsequent Stone Wall. Simpson *et al.*'s (1934, 132) account of the discovery of turret 56b suggests that it was a Turf Wall turret on the southern edge of a 5 m berm. If this were the case, it is possible that the resistivity survey did not extend far enough south to catch any Wall features. However, the gradiometer survey extended 25 m south of the line of the ditch and also failed to reveal anything of great significance. Although not currently visible, the supposed line of the Vallum is marked on earlier maps but this was significantly further south to that of the survey area. Unfortunately, ground-penetrating radar equipment was unavailable at the time of survey, which would have provided deeper ground penetration across the line of the curtain and ditch to determine if the destruction and/or robbing of the Wall was thorough or simply that the trace remains are too deep relative to modern ground surface to register through geophysical survey.

4

The curtain at Port Carlisle: survey and excavation

The survival of the Wall in the western sector is rather variable, with few above-ground remains of the curtain visible west of turret 52a (Banks East). There are more visible remains of the ditch and the Vallum but survival is still variable. West of Carlisle, the curtain almost disappears. Thus, the opportunity to investigate the curtain near the village of Port Carlisle on the Solway Firth provided an excellent opportunity to build on the relatively fragmentary knowledge of the western terminal miles of the Wall. A very short stretch of the curtain survives above ground 700 m west of the village of Port Carlisle and 200 m west of milecastle 79 (Fig. 4.1). Here the Wall runs through a number of fields aligned off the coastal road to the north, with the curtain acting as or providing the foundation for the southern boundaries of the run of fields. The boundaries are mostly thin drystone field walls or low embankments topped with a hedge. The Vallum is only a short distance to the south and occasionally also acts as a field boundary, but is very substantially levelled.

At the Port Carlisle site, the stretch of exposed curtain survives in association with a field gate, with exposed *in-situ* facing stones west of the gate (Figs 4.2 and 4.6); other buried remnants are encompassed in the bank and hidden in thick hedging to the west of the standing curtain and east of the gate. The Vallum is not visible on the ground in the next field immediately to the south, nor is the ditch readily apparent in the field north of the curtain, though the field boundaries to the east and west preserve a minor dip that demarcates its position.

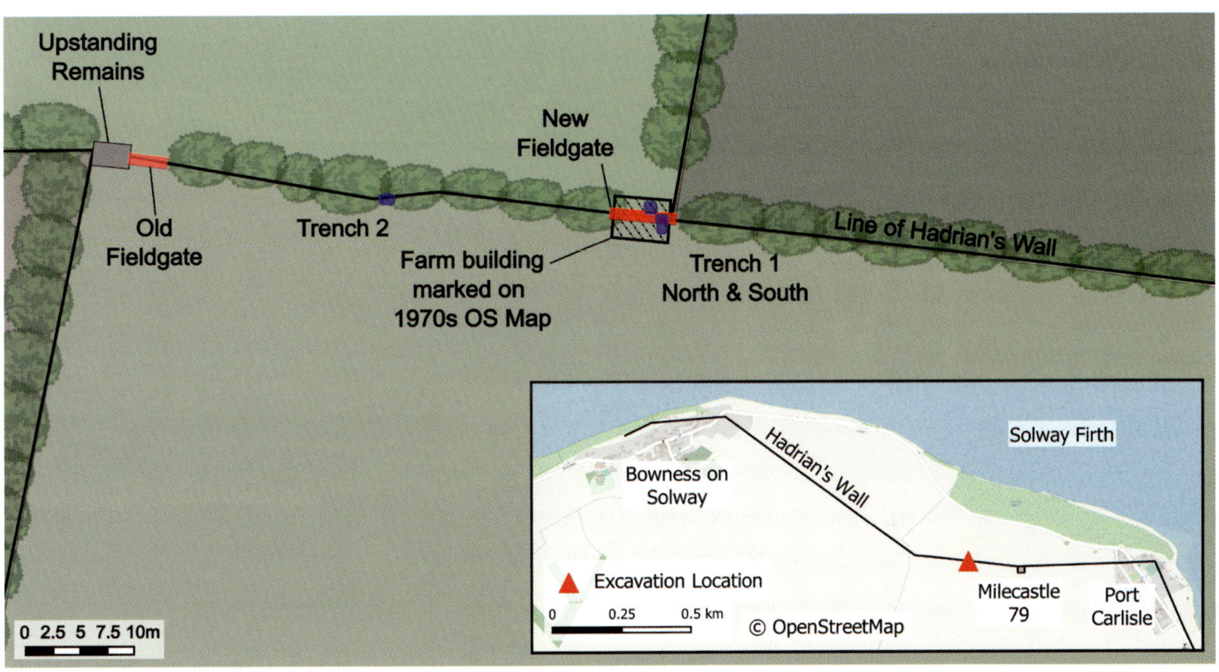

Figure 4.1: Location of the site, with the position of trenches and other key features of the fieldwork noted.

Figure 4.2: The portion of Wall curtain in situ, *west of the existing field gate.*

This length of curtain has been vulnerable for many years. The width of the long-standing farm gate through the curtain is too narrow for farm machinery of recent decades, and the exposed stonework of the curtain has been buffeted by passing tractors and other equipment. The curtain here was in urgent need of consolidation, and the farmer in need of a larger gate. In discussion with the landowner and Historic England, a plan was formed. Formerly, an outbuilding had been located further east on the line of the curtain. The 1970 OS map confirmed the site and presence of the building (see Fig. 4.1 above), and indicated that it was likely the Wall curtain had been demolished to ground level in that location. Work at Port Carlisle, therefore, was planned first to assess the survival of the curtain in that specific stretch, with the aim of inserting a new, larger farm gate at the position of the former outbuilding, and second to consolidate the surviving length of standing stone curtain, mitigating any further damage.

Geophysical survey was undertaken to the north and south of the curtain, contained within the two immediate fields between which the curtain acted as a boundary. Following this, two trenches were excavated. Trench 1 was located at the proposed position of the new gate, across the entire width of the curtain. Trench 2 was sited between Trench 1 and the existing farmgate on the south face of the curtain and hedge, where the exposure of two adjacent facing-stones indicated a good location to investigate the condition of the curtain. The excavations revealed that the survival of the curtain in this length east of the gate has almost certainly been overestimated in previous accounts, with the only confirmed undemolished curtain found around the historic farm gate.

Archaeological background

Earlier editions of the *Handbook to the Roman Wall* note that the Wall, including exposed sections, could be traced clearly from Port Carlisle to Bowness, generally positioned 100–200 m south of the road. At that time some of the exposed sections were still several feet high – apparently gunpowder was needed to demolish part of the curtain – and Bruce identified likely indications of the ditch in a few locations (Blair 1895, 239).

Milecastle 79 is just over 220 m east of the still-surviving length of the Wall. The milecastle was first excavated in 1949. Turf predecessors to the milecastle were well preserved, unlike the stone Wall levels (Richmond and Gillam 1952b). A section was recorded through what survived of the south face of the Stone Wall: only one course *c.* 0.21 m high remained of the curtain, here 2.6 m wide. That single course was founded on footing-flags *c.* 0.08 m high and *c.* 2.75 m wide. The core above the *in-situ* course was set in 'hard white mortar'; a core so hard that, echoing Collingwood Bruce's remarks, 'between Port Carlisle and Bowness it was customary to remove it in the nineteenth century by blasting' (Richmond and Gillam 1952b, 23). At the time of this excavation the section standing 245 yards to the west of the milecastle was described as 'massive', attesting to the quality of the construction work (Richmond and Gillam 1952b, 23). Presumably the short, diminished length visible today is a small survival of that section. The excavators also recorded that the turf and stone milecastles and Wall had been built on an artificial platform 'built of alternate layers of gravel and turf forming the surface upon which not only the mile-castle but the Turf Wall itself had hereabouts been erected' (Richmond and Gillam 1952b, 27). This platform was *c.* 1.4 m high over the glacial till sub-soil. The exact limits of the 'platform' could not be traced but the excavators interpreted it as running under the Wall in both directions and constructed to raise the structures above the high spring and neap tides of the estuary (Richmond and Gillam 1952b, 26). Milecastle 79 was excavated again as part of English Heritage's 'The Hadrian's Wall Milecastles Project: 1999–2000' (Wilmott 2009b, 193–197). Those small-scale, targeted investigations within milecastle 79 revealed structural evidence for both the turf and stone milecastles but found little conclusively to confirm the existence of an extensive constructed platform. Excavation across the east wall of the milecastle and into the interior found turf phase features and beneath those a layer of turf material 'which can be identified as part of the turf and gravel platform upon which the milecastle was constructed' (Wilmott 2009b, 197). The Stone Wall measured 2.83 m wide at its thin flag foundations, with the first course narrowing to 2.64 m wide (Wilmott 2009b, 195).

Geophysical survey

Gradiometry and resistivity surveys were completed in the fields immediately adjacent to the surviving Wall curtain and historic farm gate. The gradiometry results (Fig. 4.3) perhaps reflect differences in drainage and superficial deposits north and south of the Wall – the northern field margin regularly floods in winter – and picks up other geological variations. On the resistivity plot (Fig. 4.4)

Figure 4.3: Gradiometry grids and survey results relative to the position of the trenches and existing and new farm gates.

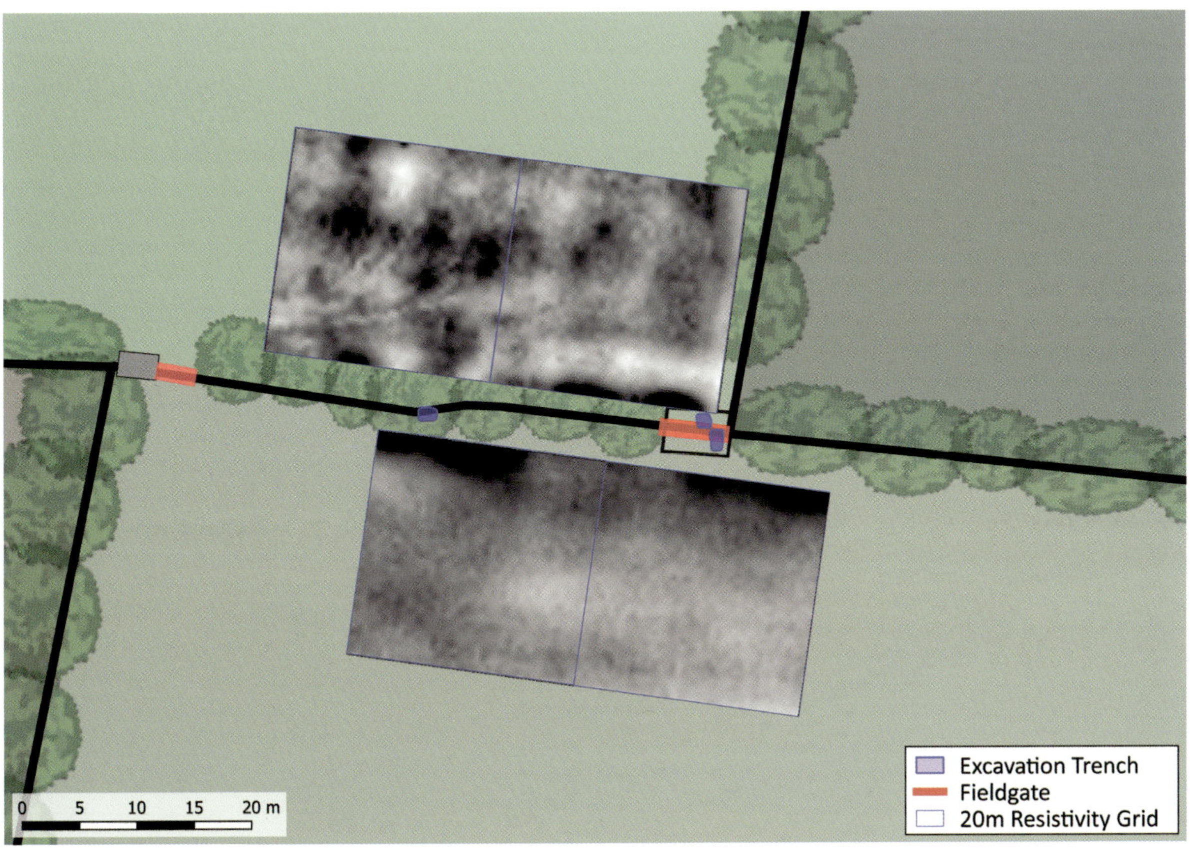

Figure 4.4: Resistivity grids and survey results relative to the position of the trenches and existing and new farm gates.

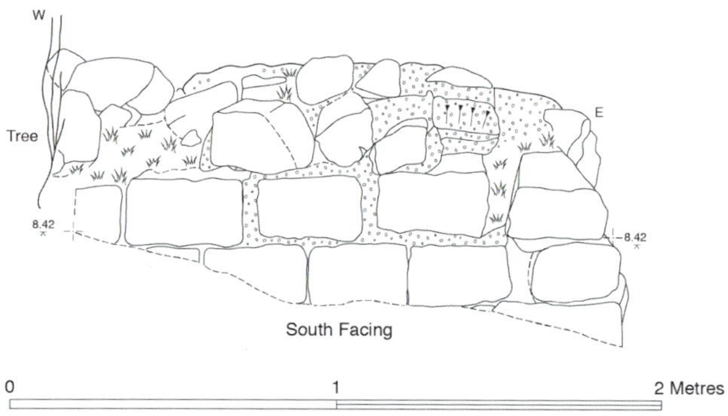

(A)

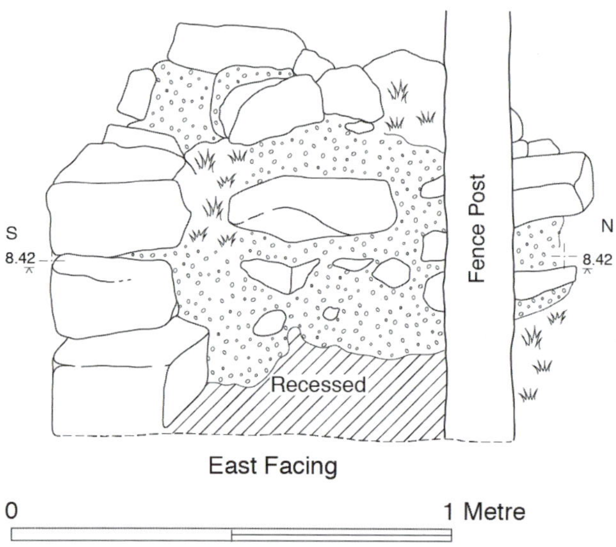

(B)

Figure 4.5: (A) Elevation drawing of the south face of the curtain, west of the existing field gate. (B) Section drawing of the curtain (east-facing) immediately west of the field gate.

the two low anomalies south of the field boundary in the vicinity of Trenches 1 and 2 are suggestive of building remains or considerable disturbance. Richmond and Gillam (1952, 28) concluded the ditch was absent around milecastle 79 and there is no conclusive evidence for the ditch in these surveys. However, the resistivity plot does indicate a band of low resistance just north of the hedge-line in the east and this may indicate the line of a ditch in an area which still holds water easily today. Slight dips in the north–south fence lines just north of the Wall line to the west and east may also hint at a Wall ditch. The many attempts to improve drainage in the fields over the years may offer another explanation for the dips.

Standing remains of the Wall curtain

The curtain remains were drawn (Fig. 4.5) and digitally modelled via photogrammetry (Fig. 4.6). A visual and measured survey of the mostly thick hedgerow was carried out between the gateway and the field corner where Trench 1 was located. In only two places was the hedge growth sparse: in the vicinity of Trench 2 (see below), and further east in the location of Trench 1, where a building was recorded on the 1970 OS map. Wall remains could not be seen through the vegetation, except in the location of Trench 2.

The upper surfaces of at least six faced curtain stones – possibly foundation stones by comparison with the standing remains or a first course indicating a footing – were visible flush with the ground in the opening of the present gateway (Fig. 4.7). A field drain running north–south cuts between those stones in the middle of the opening, and a section of surviving Stone Wall foundations and any possible Turf Wall remains might in future be obtained by careful excavation around the breach made by the drain. The standing curtain remains east of the gate, clearly visible in April 2019, were well hidden by April 2021

Figure 4.6: A photogrammetric model of the existing field gate, showing the position of the curtain west and east of the existing field gate, and the facing and core stones in situ *at ground level.*

beneath hedge regrowth of vegetation. This was cleared and supressed when the consolidation and refencing works were completed, but demonstrates the rapidity with which vegetation growth can obscure and potentially damage the curtain.

Excavation

Two trenches were excavated (Fig. 4.8). Trench 1 extended across the curtain line in the southeast corner of the northern field, where it was hoped to locate a new farm gate. This trench measured 3 m north–south, including a small 0.6 m extension to the south, by 2 m west–east and was excavated as a northwest and a southeast quadrant, split by the line of the modern hedge overlying the course of the curtain. Trench 2 was just over 2 m west–east by just under 2 m north–south and was located to investigate an apparently *in-situ* and unrecorded line of south-facing wall stones. Trench 1 was excavated down to undisturbed subsoil or bedrock and Trench 2 as far as was necessary to establish that the facing stones were re-deposited. None of the deposits or layers were suitable for environmental sampling, for use in dating or assessing conditions within the Roman period. Either the organic content had been leached out by water drainage and flooding, or layers were too heavily disturbed.

Trench 1

Trench 1 was located to investigate the line of the Wall in the location of an agricultural building shown on the 1970 Ordnance Survey map (Fig. 4.1). The trench was divided between north and south of the likely Wall-line, with the northern quadrant off-set from the southern quadrant to create a complete section through the area without removing the wooden fence on top of the bank. The line of the Wall in Trench 1 was preserved by an embankment composed of earth, stone, and mixed vegetation with a barbed wire fence across the top. The northern and southern parts of Trench 1 were significantly different, with much more disturbance apparent in the layers forming the southern slope of the bank, partly as a result of the construction and demolition of the building located on the 1970 OS map. The northern slope had been more affected by flood deposits and the effects of a rising and falling water table. However, the layers could still be correlated from north to south, and together demonstrated that all the facing stones had been removed in this area, and that Wall core had been re-purposed both to revett the hedge bank and construct a foundation surface for the building. Further disturbance had been caused by the digging of a rubble drain south of the curtain and by the digging out and redeposition of flood deposits on the northern side. The southern extension to the trench was made to confirm

Figure 4.7: Possible foundation stones of the south face of the Wall surviving at ground level.

the character of the rubble drain and the absence of any foundation stones.

There is also a notable difference in level between the southern and northern field either side of the hedge bank. This may be explained by the presence of a natural relict riverine/estuarine bank. The character of the natural glacial till material found below the archaeology in Trench 1, and in particular the discovery of bedrock at a high level south of the bank, might support this hypothesis (see below). The 1949 excavation of milecastle 79 suggested that the Turf and Stone Walls and milecastles were constructed on top of an artificial platform of alternating turf and gravel, raised to secure the milecastle and Wall against flooding from the Solway (Richmond and Gillam 1952b, 27). However, the evidence from Trench 1 supports the hypothesis that the raised roll in the ground evident in the LiDAR is at least in part a natural glacial feature (Fig. 4.8). The resistivity plot delineates sinuous possible glacial features in the field south of the Wall, with the suggestion of a ditch north of the Wall in this stretch (Fig. 4.4). The linear pooling of water in wet conditions

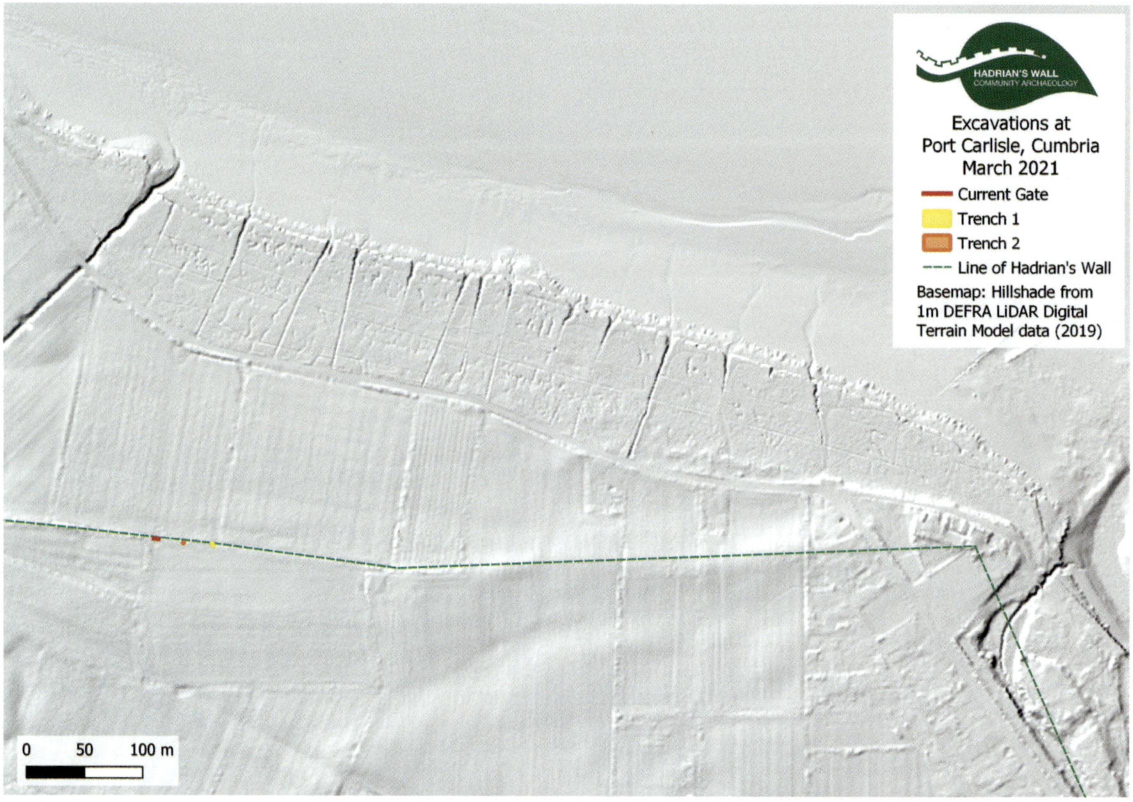

Figure 4.8: The line of the Wall curtain over a LiDAR model, showing the presence of a low ridge underlying the curtain. The gate and trenches are also located.

just north of the hedge-line in the area of Trench 1 might also reflect the presence of the back-filled Wall ditch.[1]

The two halves of Trench 1 were positioned so as to each form a quadrant to the north and south of the line of the Wall curtain. The central axis of Trench 1 ran 1.2 m up the southern bank and 1.2 m down the northern bank, offset so that the western side of the southern half became the eastern side of the northern half. Both offsets were 1 m wide. The southern side of the trench was covered with long rough grass amidst ivy and other vegetation. The northern side had very little grass and more nettles, ivy, and small saplings.

The turf, vegetation, topsoil, and upper layers were removed across both trench areas south and north of the hedge bank and along the likely Wall line (Fig. 4.9). Excavation on both sides continued until natural glacial till was reached, 0.5 m below the level where *in-situ* foundation and facing stones were recorded in the historic farm gate *c.* 50 m to the west. A small extension, 0.6 m wide was added to the southern trench to be certain there were no remaining *in-situ* facing stones. Much of the stone in the lower levels of both areas appeared to be redeposited core material, but both Trench 1 north and south were very disturbed by later construction and destruction and drainage works. The excavation thus confirmed that a new and wider gate could be inserted in this stretch of the hedge bank without disturbing any surviving *in-situ* archaeology.

The deposits, south of the hedge bank

Natural geology (1004) was reached in the southern half of the trench at *c.* 7.82 m OD. Sandstone bedrock stained with mineral deposits was encountered in the south of this part of the trench. This may have been part of a relict natural 'sea bank'. Otherwise the natural drift geology was a mixed and reworked sandy clay of glacial till and fluvial deposits, with some cobbles and stone shatter. There were more stones, shatter, and grit at the interface between the till and the layer above (1001). None of the boundaries were clear in this area, with extended interfaces between layers. Layer (1001) was found across Trench 1 and nearly 0.4 m deep in the middle of the hedge bank. There were fewer stones overall in the lowest 0.25 m of interface with (1004) below, with sub-rounded cobbles similar to those in the glacial till predominating over larger sub-angular shatter. In the upper part of layer (1001) yellow sandstone rubble made up *c.* 80% of the context. Most were sub-angular cobbles but with a considerable number of larger sub-angular stones up to 0.2–0.4 m. This latter stone was more likely to have made up the substance of curtain core material and contrasted with the large, rounded beach cobbles of red sandstone readily available on the shore of the Solway Firth just to the north. The lowest level of this compact stony layer (1001) lay just below ground level of the southern field (Fig. 4.10).

Figure 4.9: (A) Trench 1 south, looking west and north from south of the line of the Wall. (B) Trench 1 south, looking at the east section.

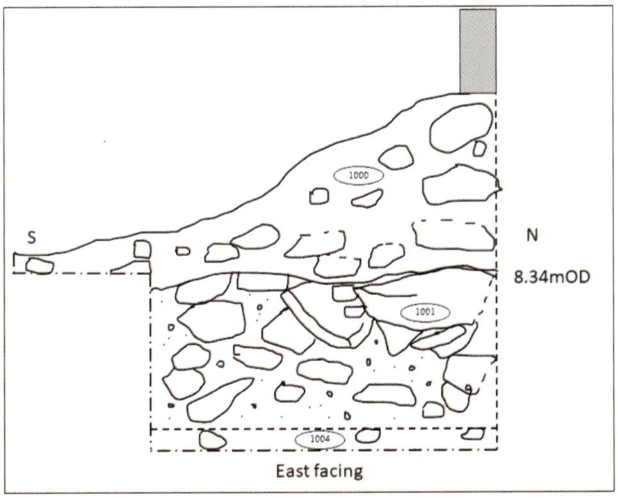

Figure 4.10: Section drawing of Trench 1, south, west section.

Overall, layer (1001) could be characterised as stone, including likely Wall core, compacted over time by water action washing out the soil matrix and by the erection of an agricultural building in the area between the 1950s and 1970s. The stone may have been used in creating the hedge bank, with some also used for the building base before being piled back up again to reform the hedge bank after the building was removed.

Above (1001) was the sandy field soil, rubble, turf, and vegetation of the field bank (1000). The gritty, sandy silt soil contained at least 50% stone: poorly sorted, sub-angular and rounded yellow and red sandstone cobbles and stone shatter, with two large round red sandstone cobbles (0.4 m in diameter). This layer was up to 0.5 m deep in the north by the wooden fence on top of the bank. (1000) with the upper part of (1001) form the hedge bank. The farmer remembers recreating the bank after the outbuilding blew down in the 1970s.

A small extension was dug 0.6 m south from Trench 1 down to just below the level at which any surviving *in-situ* curtain foundation might be found. Sandy silt layer (1006) contained 50% sub-angular and sub-rounded cobbles of yellow and red sandstone, with the more sorted and smaller cobbles comprising the backfill of the rubble drain clearly visible. The extension clarified the line of the field drain running west–east, but discovered no facing stones or foundations (Fig. 4.11).

The deposits, north of the hedge bank

Natural geology was also reached in Trench 1, north of the wooden fence and bank on the line of the curtain. Excavation stopped at 8 m OD, about 0.25 m into the interface (1005) between the field bank layer above and the mixed natural glacial till and fluvial deposits below. There had been more reworking of this layer

Figure 4.11: Trench 1, south, with the position of the post-Roman drain indicated.

than to the south, caused by the flooding of the lower northern field and a rising and falling water table. The northern field is about 0.2 m lower than the one to the south and in October 2020, the southeast corner of the field, adjacent to Trench 1 north, was under water. The boundary between this interface (1005) and the field bank (1003) above was clearer north of the fence, than to the south. Sandy silt (1003) was equivalent to (1001) to the south, and was also up to 0.5 m deep in the centre of the bank. However, (1003) contained far fewer stones than to the south, being only *c.* 10% sub-rounded cobbles and occasional larger sub-angular shatter; (1003) and (1002) above also produced several very corroded iron fragments, probably from agricultural equipment, and mostly found at the boundary between (1003) and the layer above. Layer (1003) thus comprised material piled up to recreate the field bank including silty flood deposits mixed with glacial till material, cobbles, and some possible wall core. There was far more soil and fewer larger stones in (1003) than the equivalent deposit to the south, suggesting Trench 1 south may have been closer to the line of the curtain but also indicating the silt deposition resulting from flooding (compare Fig. 4.12 with Fig. 4.9).

Layer (1002) comprised the upper makeup of northern half of the field bank with topsoil and vegetation. The gritty, sandy silt was up to 0.25 m deep. The layer was

Figure 4.12: Trench 1, north, looking south from north of the line of the Wall.

c. 15% stone: the larger sub-angular stones may have been re-purposed Wall core, but most of the stone was smaller sub-rounded and sub-angular red and yellow sandstone cobbles and pebbles. The top of this layer rose from ground level in the north at *c.* 8.25 m OD to the wooden fence line at *c.* 8.9 m OD.

Trench 2

Trench 2 examined a stretch of the southern field bank where the scrubby hedge growth was confined to the steeper northern slope and a line of at least four apparently *in-situ* Wall facing stones were visible through the patchy turf and vegetation (Fig. 4.13). The limited excavation aimed to record the location of the stones and to investigate possible explanations for the gap in vegetation. The trench demonstrated that the facing stones were not *in situ*: alterations had been made to the bank, at least one drainage ditch had been dug, and an agricultural building built and demolished in the trench area before the 1860s. This disturbance explained the condition of the hedge. Some Victorian brick, bottle-glass, and pottery were found.

The trench was sited to run SSW–NNE for nearly 1.8 m from the lower part of the cattle-eroded bank beneath the line of facing stones up to the stones themselves. The trench was 1.2 m wide. The area had been under rough turf, with patches trampled away by cattle (Fig. 4.14). The turf and topsoil were removed across the entire trench and excavation continued to the layer beneath those disturbed by an agricultural building, probably demolished in the early–mid-19th century. This limit of excavation was also well below the level (*c.* 8.3 m OD) at which *in-situ* Wall facing and foundation stones were recorded around the field gate *c.* 25 m to the west.

The deposits

The earliest layer (2006) encountered in Trench 2 was seen in the southern half of the trench, the northern half having been cut away by the west–east ditch/rubble

Figure 4.13: The location of Trench 2 before excavation, noting the putative line of in-situ *facing stones.*

Figure 4.14: Trench 2 after excavation, looking north. The facing stones were not in situ, *but repositioned following destruction of a 19th-century outbuilding.*

drain [2005] also seen in Trench 1. Layer (2006) was a gritty, dark greyish brown, sandy silt with frequent sub-rounded pebbles but also a considerable number of larger sandstone cobbles and sandstone shatter (at least 40%). This appeared to be a subsoil containing some redeposited and spread Wall core material. The layer would have been created over time as facing stones were robbed, the field bank was reshaped, and repeated ditches were cut in attempts to improve drainage. Finally, layer (2006) was levelled to construct a firm surface for raising the agricultural building (Fig. 4.15). On the basis of associated 19th-century materials and the absence of the building on OS maps, it is assumed it was constructed in the early–mid-19th century and removed before the 1860s. All the boundaries between layers in Trench 2 were very diffuse and the layers disturbed and full of redeposited material.

A west–east ditch [2005] had been cut through this layer (2006). This ditch – probably a French or rubble drain – is visible today as a very slight dip south of the field bank and running along the entire length of the field boundary. Although the ditch line was heavily truncated and probably disturbed by attempts to run another drain from it northwards, it had been at least 0.5 m wide. The ditch was completely back-filled and covered to create the foundations for a probably relatively small, earlier than mid-Victorian agricultural building. The upper fill of the ditch (2002) was subsequently mixed with demolition debris from the removal of that building: it was impossible to discern the boundary between remaining ditch fill/rubble fill and levelled demolition debris. The combined, reworked layer comprised a friable, humic, dark greyish black, sandy silt with small pebbles and in the lower layer more than 50% small-medium sorted cobbles. It was found across the trench, thinning to the south and deepening to 0.25 m in the centre of the ditch to the north (Fig. 4.16). Eight sherds of 19th-century bottle glass, a bone knife handle, and many fragments of hand-made bricks were collected from (2002). The upper

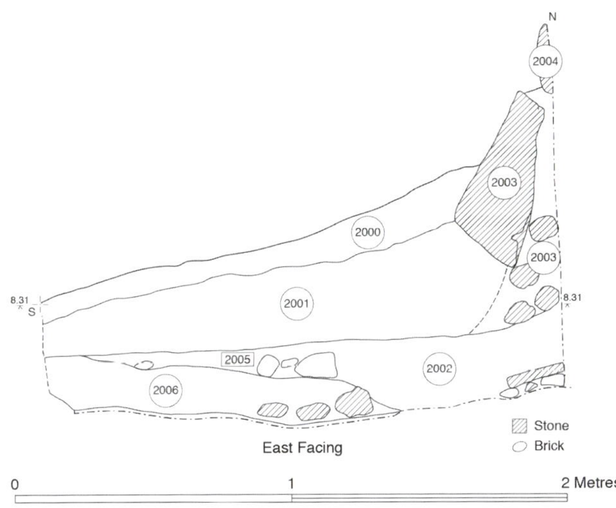

Figure 4.15: Section drawing of Trench 2, west section.

layer was composed of levelled dumps of material – in particular, brick fragments – and finds clustered in different areas of the trench.

After the removal of the structure, the field bank was rebuilt using many cobbles and some larger sandstone blocks, the majority of which latter stones could have originated as Wall core, all held together by clayey silt soil (2003). Finally, a number of curtain facing stones, which may already have been re-used in the building, were lined up along the bank to complete the restructuring (2004). Four of these were visible, three at the top of the trench and one to their immediate west. The three stones in Trench 2 were similar in size to those recorded in the *in-situ* courses to the west by the field gate, averaging at around 0.3 m long by 0.18 m high. However, the stones were either not re-set in the bank with the front faces outwards or they had twisted in settling and/or been disturbed. Only the stone to the immediate west and most eastern of the stones in the trench might be facing approximately the right way.

Figure 4.16: Photograph of Trench 2, west section.

A gritty sandy silt soil (2001) had formed over the site of the building and the re-formed bank, thinner to the south and deepening to 0.4 m deep up the bank, capped with a rough turf, well-trampled by cattle.

Discussion

The trenches demonstrated a considerable degree of cumulative disturbance and damage to the Wall. The investigations also showed the Wall in this length appeared to have been constructed on a relict glacial riverbank. There was no evidence for the curtain having been raised on an artificial platform. The targeted excavations did not reach far enough north to determine whether the north ditch had existed. Only redeposited Wall core remained in the excavation locations, with just four repositioned facing stones in Trench 2. After the stripping of the facing stones in the past, any remaining *in-situ* core material in the trench areas had been moved and redeposited during repeated attempts to improve drainage and also by the construction and demolition of two agricultural out-buildings. The surviving curtain courses around the gateway are a fortuitous survival in this hedge-line, protected by their usefulness in supporting and delineating the gate.

There was no evidence for Turf Wall survival, hardly surprising given the repeated disturbance and flooding. The flooding of the lower, northern field had clearly undermined the core material remaining after removal of the facing stones; the slump of Wall core northwards was clearly seen during the consolidation work that followed these excavations.

Note

1 We are grateful to Tony Wilmott and Humphrey Welfare for a helpful discussion of these points.

5

The curtain at Walltown Crags: survey and excavation

The Wall at Walltown Crags follows the line of the steep crags of the Whin Sill, enhancing the visual drama of the monument. The curtain here presents a contrast between well-consolidated survival and complete destruction by the 19th and 20th century quarrying west of the stretch investigated by WallCAP and then, to the east, a more prosaic buried length of Wall appearing as a scrub-covered, rubbly earth bank. However, the *c.* 30 m length of buried curtain immediately east of Walltown Quarry was investigated in the early 20th century, and left exposed to the elements after the work. Over the past 100 years or so, the exposed remains have suffered gradual deterioration through intrusive vegetation and the tumble and collapse of unconsolidated fabric, creating a Heritage At Risk site. Furthermore, there was no detailed report or publication of the 20th-century excavations. This short length of exposed stone curtain thus provided an opportunity to reassess the curtain at Walltown Crags through limited excavation, followed by conservation work to arrest further degradation of the monument (Fig. 5.1). To understand better the effects of over 100 years of exposure, two trenches were located to investigate both the area of the Edwardian excavation and also a previously unexplored portion of the still-buried curtain.

Archaeological background

As no report was made, the exact condition of the curtain at the site prior to the Edwardian excavations is not known, but it was most probably a linear, rubble-rich earth mound.

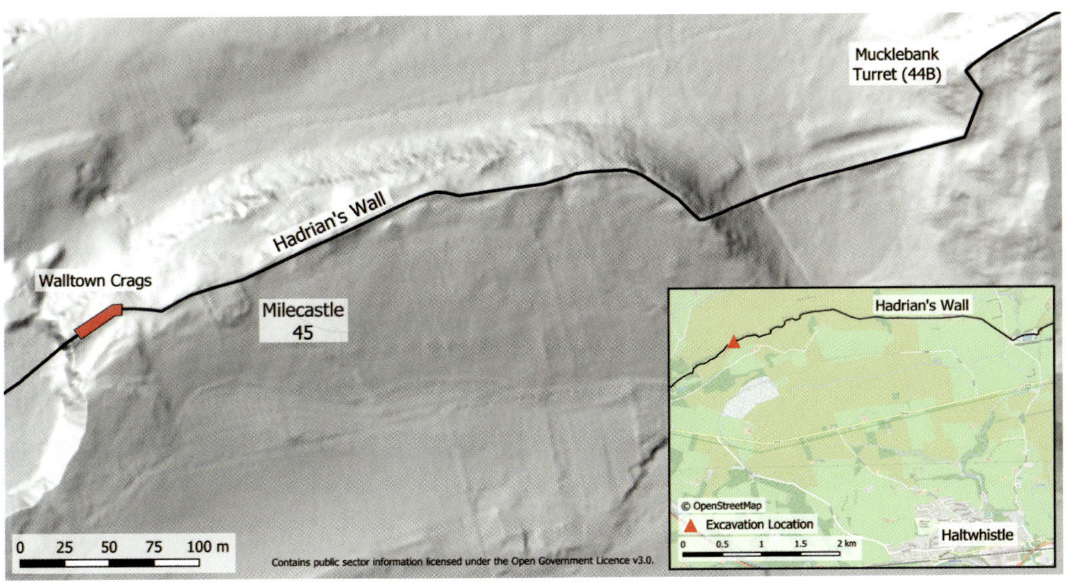

Figure 5.1: The location of the site, indicating the position of the Edwardian excavation, milecastle 45 and turret 44b (Mucklebank) over a LiDAR model. Walltown quarry east (modern) is at the west end of the Edwardian trench.

Figure 5.2: The stone curtain looking east, as revealed by the Edwardian excavators. The low mound to the right of the curtain is the spoil heap from the Edwardian diggers. Note the rising slope as the Wall runs east.

The Edwardian excavators will have removed any scrub from the mound and the immediately adjacent areas and then stripped off turf and soil to expose the Wall remains. We cannot be certain what Wall height this removal of overburden revealed. The surviving remains may indicate approximately the height of the stone curtain as uncovered in the early 20th century, but it may also have survived – perhaps in a more tumbled state – to a greater height. A shallow trench dug along the southern face of the curtain, running for over 30 m, can be seen today, delineating the extent of Edwardian work (Fig. 5.2). South of this trench is a low stone-rich embankment formed from the spoil heap of the excavation. This has created a micro-ridge between the curtain and a relatively high and craggy outcrop of bedrock a few metres to the south, with a more boggy and peaty area between the ridge and the craggy outcrop. The south face of the curtain is well defined by the shallow trench north of the spoil heap. The north face of the curtain is less clearly defined. There is no obvious remaining excavation ditch, though this may be a result of a combination of factors. The narrow berm between the north face of the curtain and the edge of the crags is uneven, and in some places drops steeply. Furthermore, this face is more dramatically exposed to the prevailing weather conditions, and between the weather and gravity, it is clear that more tumbled stone has fallen to the north of the curtain than to the south.

The closest structure to the site is milecastle 45 (Walltown Nick), located *c.* 50 m east of the site. The milecastle has not been excavated under modern conditions, but the structure survives in sufficient detail as earth embankments to identify it as a long-axis milecastle. Pits and robber trenches visible on the ground indicate exploration and stone robbing of uncertain date. The only other site that has been archaeologically investigated in the immediate vicinity is at King Arthur's Well, just under 0.5 km east of the WallCAP site (OAN 2020). Excavated in 2008, before a new flagged section of the Hadrian's Wall Path National Trail was laid, the site lies immediately south of the Wall curtain, and northeast of Walltown Farm in Wall-mile 44, at the base of one of the steep nicks cutting through the Whin Sill escarpment. Surviving as the earthwork remains of a sub-rectangular stone structure lying perpendicular to the Wall, and perhaps attached to its southern face, the feature does not conform in size or location with the regular Wall milecastles and turrets. On excavation the stone structure was interpreted as having two phases. The earlier phase encompassed part of the west wall of the building and an internal hearth. Radiocarbon determinations from the

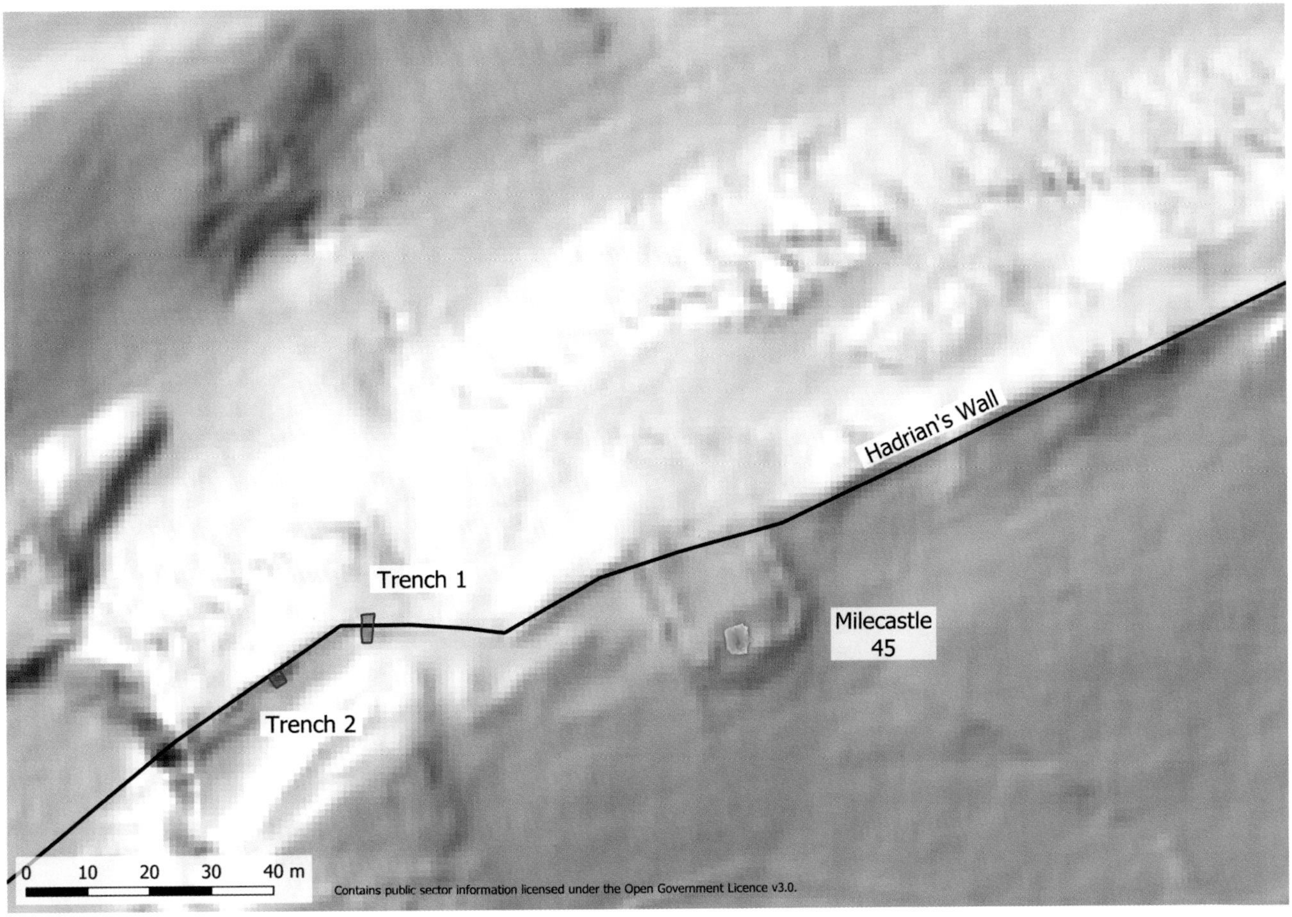

Figure 5.3: The locations of Trenches 1 and 2 and the line of the curtain, on LiDAR.

hearth produced date ranges in the early–middle Iron Age and late 1st to mid-3rd centuries AD but the presence of 'Romanised' pottery led the excavators to prefer the later dates. In its second phase, the building was 5.4 m wide east–west and more than 4.4 m north–south, and although the excavators could not be certain, the building was most likely constructed against the already standing curtain wall and used through the 2nd–mid-3rd centuries AD. The purpose of the building is difficult to determine: an additional Wall control point was unnecessary as turret 44b (Mucklebank) sits on the crags only 250 m to the northeast, with commanding views of the bottom of Walltown Nick, but if the dating is correct then the structure was presumably sanctioned by Roman military authorities. The limited nature of the investigation meant no information could be gathered about the character of the Wall curtain itself at this location.

Turret 44b (Mucklebank) was discovered in 1891 and excavated in the following year (Breeze 2006, 278). The topographical position of the turret, and its location relative to the Narrow Wall curtain, at the turn where the curtain follows a V-shaped course to the south to cross Walltown Nick, have been interpreted as indicating that this turret was probably built later than the original Hadrianic building programme (Symonds and Breeze 2016, 13–14). This tentative dating could perhaps be extended to this entire sector of curtain along Walltown Crags, and therefore point towards the potential of this area to provide dating evidence pertaining to the construction of the Wall. As part of the remedial works carried out in conjunction with the WallCAP 2020 excavation at Walltown Crags, repair and consolidation was undertaken at this turret.

Excavation

Two trenches were excavated at Walltown Crags. Trench 1 ran across the full width of the Wall curtain immediately east of the Edwardian trench, measuring 5 m north–south and 1.5 m in the south widening to 2 m on the northern side of the curtain. Trench 2 was 2 m square and lay across the Edwardian spoil-bank and ditch south of the curtain (Fig. 5.3). Both were excavated down to undisturbed subsoil or bedrock. The buried environment was very dynamic and possible cuts and boundaries between archaeological layers had been obscured by the working of water, roots and worms in sandy soils, the slippage of stones and soils down slopes, and the impact of heavy stone tumble on ground surfaces and previous collapses.

The intention was to sample any soils with the potential to produce environmental information or material

Figure 5.4: Trench 1 from the south following removal of the turf.

suitable for radiocarbon dating. Unfortunately, none of the deposits or layers were suitable for sampling. Either the organic content had been leached out by trickling water or layers had been too heavily disturbed, often by the processes of collapse. Furthermore, no artefacts or material culture were encountered in either trench. Further detailed information on each trench can also be found in Appendix 2.

Trench 1

Trench 1, just beyond the eastern end of the Edwardian excavation, ran across the curtain and revealed phases of Wall collapse to the south that had happened both before and after the Edwardian digging. This trench was located on a shallow bend southwards in the curtain, and where the curtain runs up a slope rising gently from west to east. Preservation of the curtain was different on its north and south faces, with the north face having notably fewer courses of facing stones. The foundations of the south face were laid directly onto bedrock, and up to six courses and the indication of a seventh survived, to over 1 m in height. The north face was excavated to reveal one surviving course and to give a sense of the different nature of the collapse on that side; excavating to a greater depth would have destabilised the structure. Trench 1 also encompassed the rounded end of the Edwardian spoil bank in its southwestern corner. The trench dipped slightly from the south face of the Wall, then rose across an area south of the curtain undisturbed by the earlier excavation (Fig. 5.4). Between the topography, the Edwardian trench, and the orientation of the monument, this resulted in a trench that was roughly trapezoidal. The trench's western side was 5 m long north–south and the eastern side 5.1 m north–south; the southern side was 1.5 m wide and the northern edge 2 m in length. Rough grass, moss, and small plants, interspersed with exposed core material, covered the domed top of the curtain and were left in place to prevent further erosion.

The turf, topsoil, and upper layers were removed across both trench areas south and north of the curtain; the curtain was not disturbed below the uppermost layers, and the areas of the trench to the north and south of the curtain were excavated separately. Bedrock and undisturbed subsoil were reached in a 1 m-long sondage against the southern face of curtain, which was 0.6 m wide, north–south. Core and tumble material were removed cautiously from the north face of the curtain to reveal the uppermost undisturbed, surviving course, encountered at a lower level than the undisturbed courses to the south. It is probable that this uncovered course of facing stone on the north face was the second or third course above foundation. Excavation along the north face then stopped to ensure the remaining fabric and berm was not destabilised.

The deposits south of the curtain

The earliest layers revealed in excavation related to the building of the Wall curtain in this location. Bedrock was reached in the sondage against the south-facing Wall courses (Fig. 5.5). Despite being vertically fissured in the same way as the bedrock also reached in Trench 2, the dolerite columns here were un-weathered, flat-topped and sharp-edged. The bedrock in the location of Trench 1 was, therefore, almost certainly buried when the Wall was laid out, but the curtain builders would have been aware that the bedrock was likely to be relatively level at the top of the crags as its surface was then visible in other areas, including at the site of Trench 2. In preparing the ground for curtain construction in the Trench 1 area the Roman builders clearly dug down to ensure the foundation course was laid onto the solid whinstone not far below the turf. The top of the bedrock in Trench 1 at 249.82 m OD is at a very similar height to the bedrock in Trench 2, which has an uneven top but lies between 249.88–250.25 m OD (see below).

The character of the lowest layer excavated in front of the south face (1009) suggested the foundation course, which comprised slightly larger, rougher stones than those of the courses above, was re-buried after it was built. That layer (1009) was gritty, silty clay sand packed with well-sorted subangular sandstone cobbles very similar to layer (2005) in Trench 2, there also associated with the bedrock. The upper spit of (1009) was much siltier and may be the leached and degraded remains of a ground surface. The remainder of the layer below was redeposited natural subsoil backfilling a wide, shallow foundation trench and/or disturbed natural subsoil. No cut for such a trench was found in the sondage. It may be located beyond its southern edge, but few cuts survive to be detected in such sandy, wet environments.

Above layer (1009) up to 0.8 m depth of collapse and tumble (1005) from the Wall had accumulated before a period of relative stability during which a turf layer (1006) had time to develop. The collapse mostly comprised stones – around 80% of the layer – which were predominantly unworked core stones of a range of sizes from smaller cobbles at 0.1 m square, through to the majority at 0.25–0.35 m wide, but included some facing stones

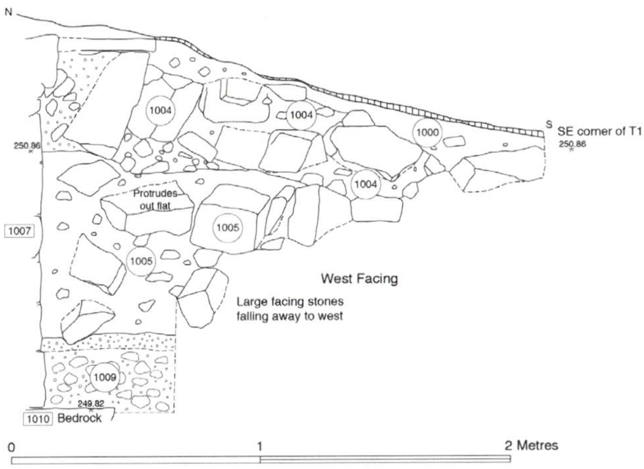

(A)

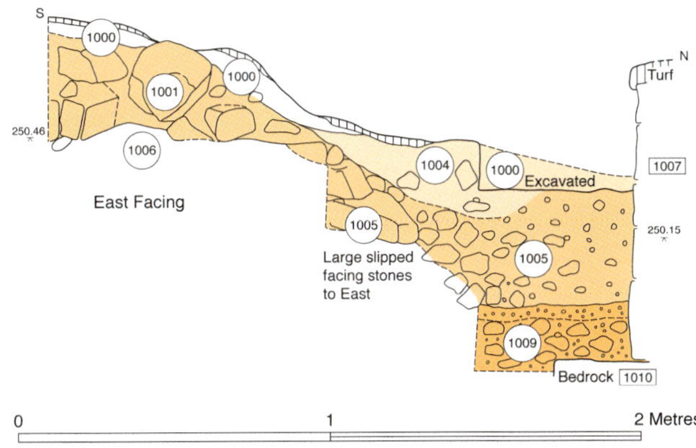

(A)

(B)

Figure 5.5: (A) Section drawing of Trench 1, south, east section. (B) Photograph of the east section of Trench 1, south.

(B)

Figure 5.6: (A) Section drawing of Trench 1, south, west section in colour. (B) Photograph of the west section of Trench 1, south.

similar in size to *in-situ* examples. Three of these had slipped together in a rotated line from the Wall behind. Overall, (1005) contained a higher proportion of the larger stones than the later collapse layer above, (1004). The soil matrix was homogenous gritty sand silt.

(1005) was clearly formed by pre-early 20th century collapses of the Wall (Fig. 5.6). It was impossible to distinguish whether the layer was predominantly the result of one or two major collapses, or of a steady succession of smaller ones, or linked to episodes of robbing. The presence of more of the larger stones and of some facing stones and especially the three displaced facing stones perhaps indicates the absence of systematic robbing as a major factor in some of the collapses. The homogeneity of the soil matrix testifies to the effects over a long period of water trickle and worm activity.

Over tumble (1005), the decayed Edwardian-period turf ground surface (1006) survived very patchily, sloping down very gently from the curtain over the tumble for just under 1 m before rising gradually under the rounded end of the spoil bank and towards the higher ground south of the Wall. The turf-line had endured better under the curved end of the Edwardian spoil bank in the southwest corner of Trench 1. Here a near continuous, thin, purple black layer remained in a small quadrant. Beyond the protective bank later falls of large stones and core material (1004) had clearly damaged the ground surface, leaving only slight traces to be discovered.

Over that turf, in the southwest corner of the trench, a half section of the rounded end of the spoil bank (1001) was investigated. Around 60% of the bank, which was up to 0.4 m high, consisted of poorly sorted stone with some larger sub-angular stones up to 0.3 m long, and was probably predominantly core material. The earlier excavators may have picked any more useful facing stones out of the tumble they were removing from behind the curtain. In Trench 1, the spoil bank may have been less eroded than in Trench 2 but tumble from the bank had clearly slipped northwest into the end of the ditch and northeast to inter-mingle with post-Edwardian collapse from the south side of the curtain.

Spread over both the earlier tumble (1005) and the tail of the spoil bank was an accumulation of post-Edwardian excavation collapse and tumble (1004) from the Wall, up to 0.4 m deep in the northeast corner against the south face of the curtain, thinning to the south over the earlier tumble and the skirt of the spoil bank, and to the southwest and west over (1005) and down into the old excavation ditch. The dynamic interaction between the layers of spoil and tumble is captured in the drawn sections through the layers (Figs 5.5 and 5.6); in this steeply sloping and mobile environment there is both kinetic mixing in the dip between the slopes to north and south, and blurring of boundaries between and within layers. This later phase of collapse or collapses resulted in a more mixed layer than (1005) below, with more lenses of grit and sand, and patches of developed soil. It contained fewer of the larger stones, but was still 60% poorly sorted sandstone, with some stones up to 0.35 m long and one or two possible facing stones. The dynamics of the fall of material from the Wall southwards was apparent in the downslope tail of larger stones, with smaller stones and shatter building up behind the curtain to hold up larger stones of subsequent collapses. Trench 1 was located on the gentle curve of the curtain southwards at this point on Walltown Crags; the impact of the Edwardian work may have destabilised the curving structure beyond the eastern end of the ditch and precipitated much of the collapse evidenced in (1004).

Subsequently, there was a long enough period without considerable collapse to allow the soil and turf (1000) to develop, although still punctured by larger stones. By this time, the top of the tumble was close to the top of the surviving core. The stones in this turf-topped layer south of the curtain seemed more likely to have been dislodged and slipped onto the ground from the standing curtain than to have fallen as part of more significant disruption. Turf (1000) was excavated south of the curtain, left *in situ* on top of the Wall, and then selectively removed only as necessary towards the base of the northern face. Poorly sorted stones still comprised around half of the layer with a less homogenised soil matrix of grit, silty sand, and organic lenses.

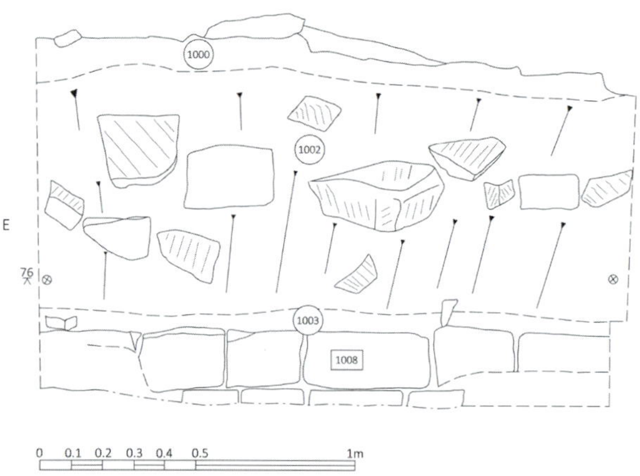

(A)

(B)

Figure 5.7: (A) Section drawing of the north face of the Wall curtain. (B) The north face of the Wall curtain, looking west.

The deposits north of the curtain

The layers across the core to the north and towards the base of the north face of the curtain were unpicked carefully. Underneath the turf, rubble, and topsoil of (1000), a layer of slipped and collapsed core material (1002) of uneven depth was removed across an area 0.6 m north–south by 0.9 m east–west over the core and in front of the north face of the curtain, to expose the top of the uppermost surviving course of facing stones (Fig. 5.7).

Some stones in (1002) were up to 0.35 m long, a few were worked, the majority were around 0.25 m in length, with the smallest ones around 0.1 m. More of the larger stones were found in the east of the trench closer to the bend. Below this, over the facing stones was a thin layer of gravelly sandy silt (1003) with a good deal of moderately sorted smaller pebbles and grit and very few larger stones. This appeared to be degraded core material under the collapse and slippage of core materials that had accumulated over the *in-situ* facing stones below. The collapse of core material from the curtain was greater to the north than to the south in Trench 1, and this can be explained by the proximity of the steep crags and the absence of more facing stones from the north face. Excavation stopped once the surviving upper course of facing stones had been revealed.

The south face of the curtain

The south face of the Wall [1007] was revealed built directly onto bedrock with a distinctive foundation course and five further courses surviving to a height of *c.* 1.15 m above bedrock (Fig. 5.8). The courses, here relatively even, comprised roughly squared blocks of sandstone. Within the trench, five complete courses survived from the bedrock up and including the footings course (0.97 m high max.); five stones of the eastern end of a sixth course remained (1.2 m in length). Only one fully *in-situ* stone survived of the seventh course, with a second to the east situated above the last visible stone of the course below. The latter stone had slipped slightly southwards and was re-bedded as part of the repair work that followed the excavation. Stones and soil of core material, consolidated with moss and grass rose a further 0.5 m above and behind the facing stones.

The distinctive footing course was laid directly on the crisp, flat un-weathered bedrock and was probably buried after construction; this course comprised slightly bigger blocks with rougher faces; all four stones recorded were 0.25 m high, only two were visible for their full length in the sondage, these were 0.23 m and 0.35 m wide. The footing stones also protruded for up to 0.05 m from the face of the course above. The stones of the five courses above, visible in the Roman period, were between 0.13–0.18 m high (majority *c.* 0.18 m) by 0.2–0.3 m wide (majority *c.* 0.25 m). The third course up from bedrock had slightly thinner stones, between 0.13–0.14 m high; the stones of the sixth course were closer to sub-square, with one stone 0.18 m high by 0.13 m wide.

The stones were roughly squared, with relatively un-weathered sharp edges and corners, contrasting to the mossy and smoothed courses visible to the west of the trench. There was no evidence at all for repairs or for bonding, although any degraded remains of mortar may have been weathered out and dispersed into the sandy environment by water and bioturbation. One facing stone of harder rock stood out on the fourth course up from bedrock. This stone was 0.18 m high and 0.27 m wide, slightly sparkling and pinkish with sharper edges and corners than the surrounding sandstones; it may be an exceptional sandstone shaped from a small discrete formation in the quarry that its neighbouring facing stones were sourced from, or it may be a completely different and more exotic stone. Certain identification could not be made without recourse to taking a physical sample, which was not feasible within the scope of the work. The curtain in Trench 1 was recorded as *c.* 2.18 m thick, measured from the outer faces of the facing stones to the north and south.

The north face of the curtain

One complete course of the northern face of the Wall was uncovered in Trench 1, and the top 0.05 m of the course below [1008]. As to the south, the courses were formed of squared rubble sandstone blocks. For the six stones of the upper course completely revealed, heights ranged between 0.17–0.19 m and widths between 0.24–0.34 m. The stones of the top course were more weathered than those of the south face. Deliberate robbing aside, this crag-edge face had collapsed to a lower level than the southern one, with much of the core and any remaining facing stones having fallen down the face of the crag (Fig. 5.7). Comparing heights above sea level of the top course on the north face with the upper complete course on the south side it is likely that the foundation course survives beneath the partially visible northern course. The top of the uncovered north face course was at *c.* 250.45 m OD, that of the upper near-complete course on the south side at *c.* 251 m OD; on the south side a level of 250.45 m OD would neatly correspond to the top of the second course above the foundation course. There was no evidence for repair or bonding of the north face, unless the thin gritty layer of (1003) was in part created by the decay of sandy bedding mortar.

In general, the character of the collapse north of the curtain had differences from that to the south. The north face is more exposed to the force of wind and rain and much of the material collapsing from the Wall would be lost down the face of the rapidly steepening crag. At least three more courses had been lost from the north face than to the south, and there may have been more slippage and gradual slumping of facing stones to the north. However, the considerable remaining height of exposed core material – around 1 m – partially consolidated by turf, moss, and small plants seemed to be holding up reasonably well, although it will undoubtedly be gently deteriorating without the protection of the facing courses.

Trench 2

Trench 2 examined the Edwardian excavation running along the south face of the Wall. Here again there was

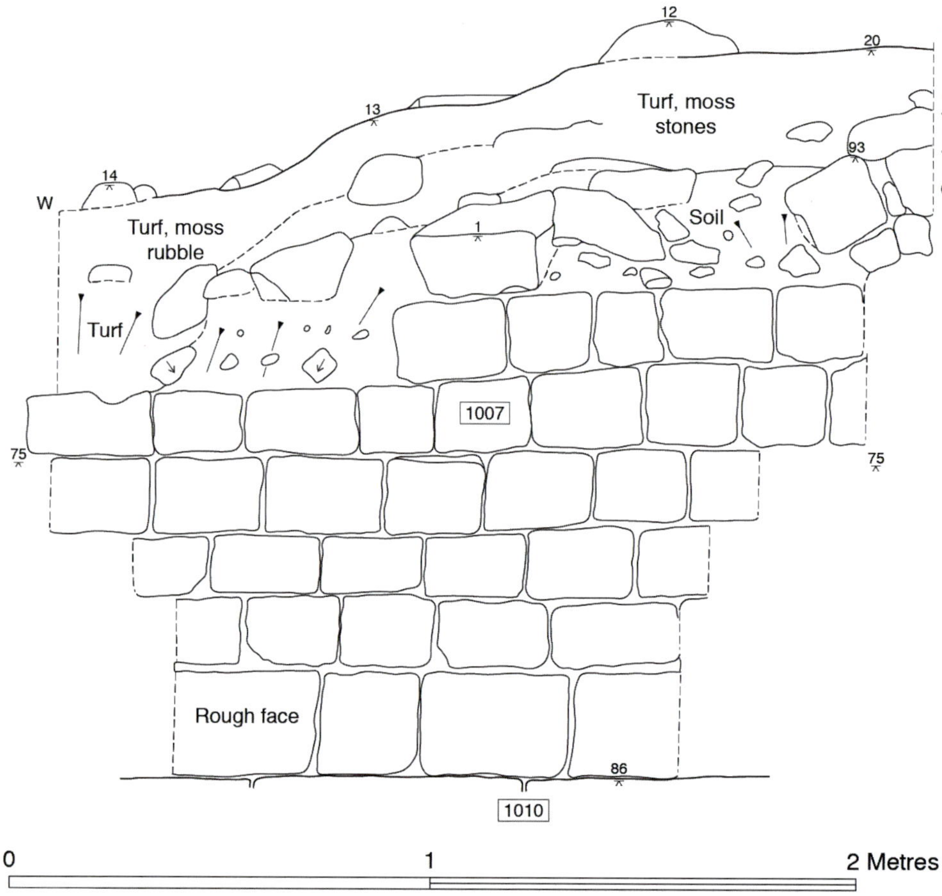

(A)

(B)

Figure 5.8: (A) Section drawing of the south face of the Wall curtain. (B) Photograph of the south face of the curtain.

evidence for phases of collapse and the Wall curtain was built directly onto bedrock. That weathered bedrock must have been exposed and visible at the time the Wall was constructed onto it. Up to three courses of the southern face survived. The excavators left no finds behind; there were none in either trench. The Edwardian work can be characterised more as a simple attempt to expose a length of the Wall face than any more rigorous investigation.

Trench 2 was sited to run NW–SE from the top of the Edwardian spoil bank running parallel to the curtain, across the Edwardian excavation ditch and up to the south face of the curtain. In this area the patchy turf and moss growing amidst the exposed core of the curtain had merged with the rough, thick grass of the ditch below to obscure the facing stones more visible to either side of the section (Fig. 5.9). The trench was 2 m square with the southern half of the trench being the spoil bank and the northern half the shallow ditch. Turf and moss were not removed from around the core so as not to further de-stabilise the top of the curtain: excavation began at the top of the surviving courses of Wall. The turf and topsoil were removed across the entire trench and excavation continued to undisturbed subsoil and bedrock in the northeastern half of trench against the Wall (Fig. 5.10).

The deposits

The oldest layer uncovered in Trench 2 related to the building of this section of the Wall. Across the width of the trench, layer (2006) comprised a mixture of sandy subsoil and sandstone cobbles, and was excavated to a maximum depth of 0.2 m for about 1 m southwards from the curtain and its bedrock foundation, before it disappeared under later wall tumble (2003). At the final level reached this layer was clearly undisturbed subsoil, and the material excavated was either the subsoil back-fill of an original shallow Roman foundation trench merging into undisturbed subsoil, or simply surface-disturbed *in-situ* subsoil. The upper spit of this layer had probably been removed and/or further disturbed by the Edwardian excavation. There was no evidence for a foundation trench cut nor of disturbance caused by repair, but any cut was likely to have been obliterated by the impact of collapsing curtain material.

Although obscured by the Edwardian excavators' ditch and bank, the natural ground surface here slopes down, away from the Wall before rising unevenly to the sheltering craggy outcrop to the south. The lowest layer reached in the southern half of the trench (2003) was pre-early 20th century Wall collapse, excavated to a depth of 0.3 m, which had fallen down the slope away from the Wall-face. This had probably accumulated over a long period, as the result of several episodes of minor and some more major collapses along with or stimulated by stone-robbing.

(A)

(B)

Figure 5.9: (A) The location of Trench 2 before excavation. (B) Trench 2 after initial removal of the turf, revealing one course of curtain built directly on bedrock.

Up to three-quarters of the sandy layer was tightly packed stones, with a higher proportion of larger sub-rectangular stones than the Edwardian spoil above, and including some facing stones. Some hints of soil development between stones supported the idea that the layer evidenced several episodes of curtain degradation whether natural or human-instigated. On the slightly higher ground to the north the depth of (2003) that originally lay above (2006) had been removed by the Edwardian excavation. The patchy turf layer (2002) developed over tumble (2003) indicated a longer period of relative stability in the Wall remains. The degraded early 20th-century turf ground surface (2002) had been cut away by the earlier excavation just south of the curtain, surviving better beneath the Edwardian spoil bank. However, the turf growth would originally also have been discontinuous, interrupted by the large stones left by pre-Edwardian collapses.

In the southern half of the trench turf (2002) was preserved beneath the spoil bank created during the

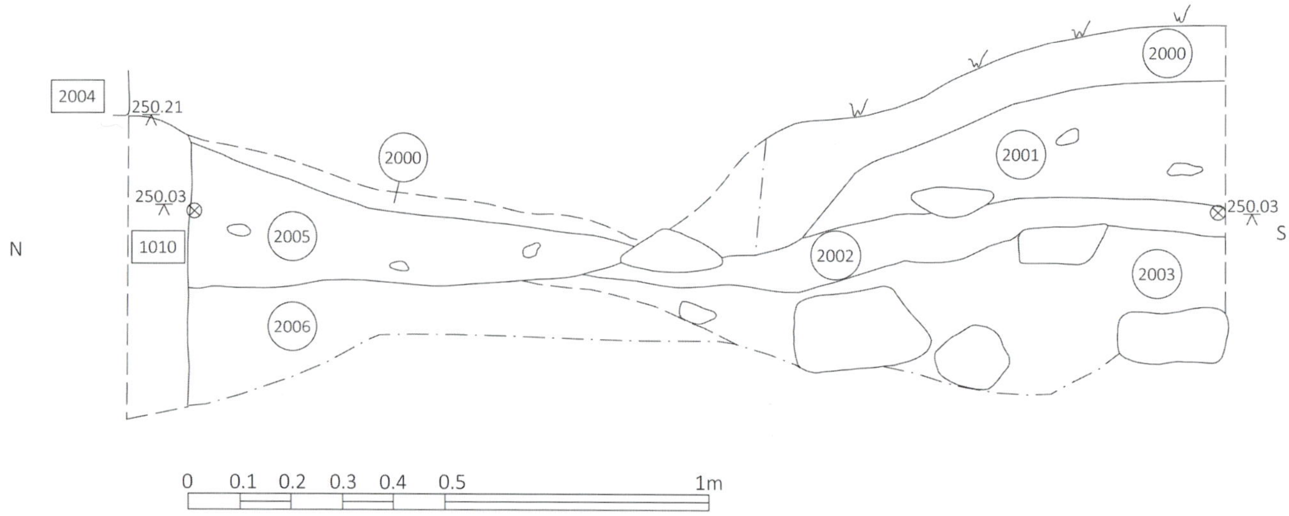

(A)

(B)

Figure 5.10: (A) Section drawing of Trench 2, east section. (B) Photograph of the east section of Trench 2.

Edwardian excavation. The 2 m wide linear bank runs parallel to the curtain for just over 30 m at about 1 m from its southern face. In the slot excavated across it in Trench 2 the bank was between 0.2–0.25 m deep, diminished by slump and walkers' and animals' trampling. Around half of the bank-material comprised poorly sorted stone, with only two larger stones amongst them. The spoil was probably mostly core material; the earlier excavators may have removed any more useful facing stones dug out from the tumble. Digging the shallow Edwardian ditch to the north of the bank had removed not only the contemporary turf (2002), but also the accumulation of pre-Edwardian collapse and disturbance (2003), and probably some of subsoil/backfill (2006) below.

In the century that followed the ditch had slowly and partially refilled with sandy silt (2005). This deposit was 0.25 m deep against the Wall and thinned to the southeast downslope, and formed mostly of smaller stone tumble and core material with patches of decayed turf amidst the soil and stones. The layer also likely contained drifts of material from the spoil bank to the south. Over the spoil bank and the tumble to the north, a rough, reed-rich and mossy grass has grown over sandy soil (2000). This topsoil layer was also very stony: mostly smaller stones but with occasional sub-rectangular stones up to 0.3 m; the area over the soil bank was stonier than to the north.

The south face of the curtain

Up to three courses of the curtain were revealed in Trench 2 (Fig. 5.11). The courses were the lowest of the Wall, with the bottom two foundation courses built directly onto whinstone bedrock. The vertically riven, jagged, uneven character of the bedrock was demonstrated clearly in the small crags rising to the south of the trenches. Four vertical sections of that bedrock were seen in Trench 2, with smoothed and rounded edges and corners (Fig. 5.11). The three columns of bedrock in the east and centre were higher and supported a footings course that began in the west as regular stones, reduced in the east to levelling chockstones between the higher bedrock and the course above. The lowest bedrock element in the west was less weathered and two stones were seen of a third Wall course which fitted between the lower bedrock and the foundation course above. To improve stability the foundation course over the higher bedrock protruded up to 0.15 m out from the regular course above (Figs 5.11 and 5.12). The stones of the highest surviving course were more regular in size (0.2–0.25 m wide by 0.1–0.15 m high) and slightly smaller on average than the stones of courses seen in Trench 1. The big stones of core material visible above the trench and along most of this stretch of the Wall were probably thrown up onto the curtain, along with some facing stones when the clearing was done for the Edwardian work.

The bedrock in Trench 2 was considerably more weathered than that in Trench 1, suggesting this area of bedrock was exposed above the surrounding rough turf when the curtain was constructed, and indeed probably remained exposed for some time thereafter. The stones of the foundation courses above bedrock were also more weathered and rounded than those in south-facing Wall in Trench 1; the full height of the Wall may have been above ground in the Trench 1 location during the Roman period. The stretch of Wall between Trench 2 and Trench 1 is broadly level with the bottom of the lowest course in the west of Trench 2 at 249.86 m OD and the bottom of foundation course in Trench 1 at 249.82 m OD.

(A)

(B)

Figure 5.11: (A) Section drawing of the south face of the Wall curtain in Trench 2, with surviving facing stones illustrated and the surviving mound of core captured only in terms of height. (B) Photograph of the south face of the curtain in Trench 2.

Discussion

The Walltown Crag trenches provided a rare opportunity to look at the construction of the Narrow Wall curtain, in particular in Trench 1 where the Wall had been buried for some time. The Narrow Wall is usually around 2.29 m wide (Breeze 2006, 53): the stretch in Trench 1 accords well with this at about 2.18 m wide. The foundations of the Narrow Wall seen elsewhere have been rough stones set in and sealed with clay, but at Walltown the footing course was laid directly onto bedrock. The sizes of the stones in the regular courses were a little larger than the average given by Breeze (2006, 54) at 15 cm by 25 cm. The Roman builders constructed the stretch of curtain at Walltown on the edge of the crags and directly onto bedrock where possible. To lay the footings they cleared the ground along the planned line of the structure and then built both directly onto exposed bedrock (Trench 2) but also dug down to buried bedrock (Trench 1); it is not clear whether the digging down was contained within a shallow foundation trench or was rougher soil-shifting. The course

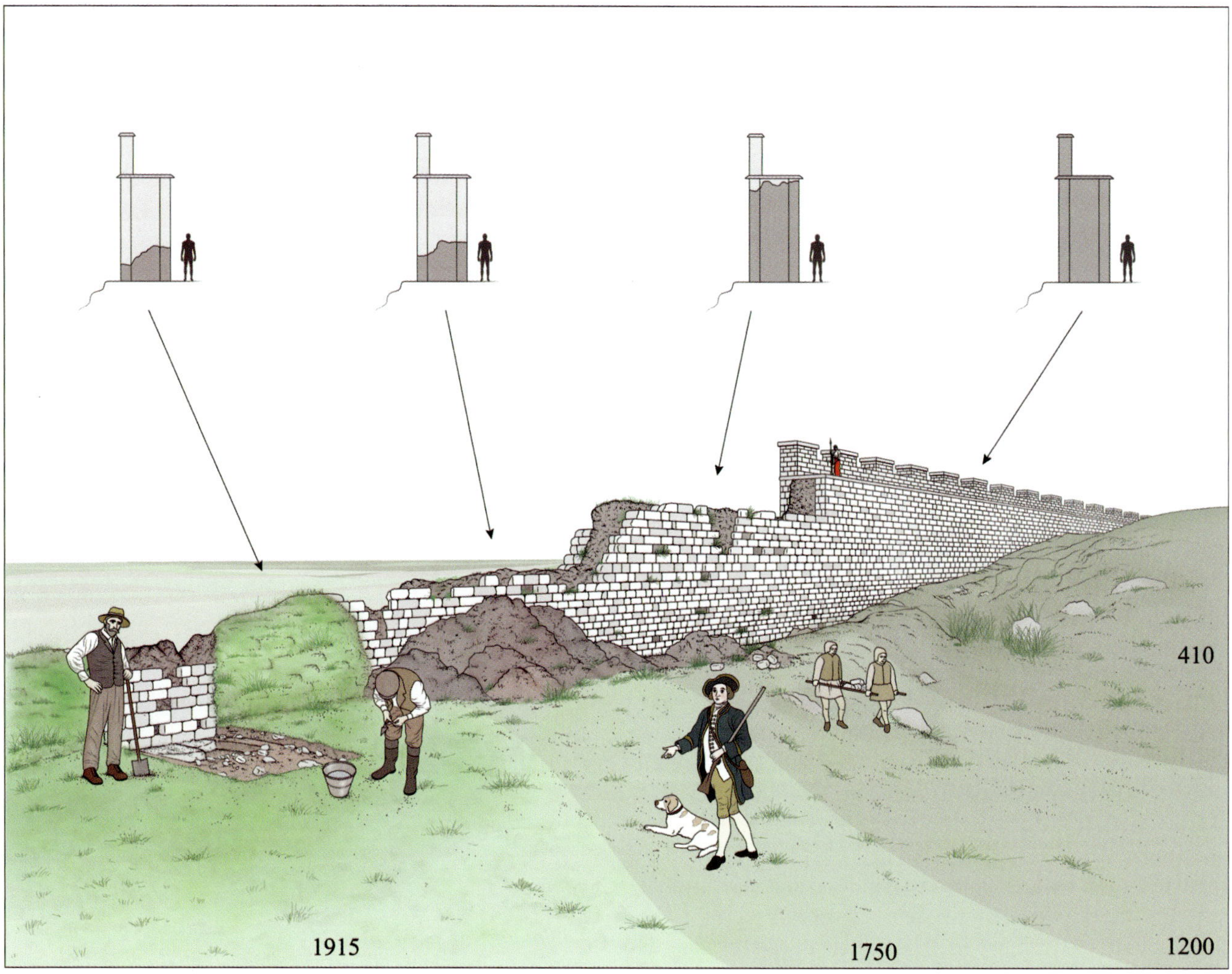

Figure 5.12: A prospective reconstruction of phases of ruin and collapse at Walltown Crags, based on evidence from the excavations. Illustration by Matilde Grimaldi.

of the Wall here is also 'unusually sinuous' as it follows the crag-top (Collins and Symonds 2019, 38–39): it seems the choice of the line of the Wall along Walltown Crags was partly driven by an intention to maximise the crag location by following the highest crest and also to lay the footings on solid and relatively level bedrock, closest to the surface towards the crag-edge.

The relationship between the foundation course laid directly onto bedrock and the course above is interesting. In Trench 1 the larger foundation stones are offset from the course above by 0.05 m; in Trench 2 the stones laid above the two westernmost columns of bedrock are also slightly offset. This parallels offset foundation courses found at other locations on the Narrow Wall. The construction of the foundations in Trench 2 is more unusual, and this may partly explain the offset, but the offsetting also appears in Trench 1 above the more level bedrock.

No repairs of the curtain were apparent in the courses uncovered in either trench, and no convincing bonding material was discovered. The phases of collapse recorded suggest that, perhaps after some early and probably major episodes of robbing, the Wall was diminished by sequences of collapse, sometimes provoked by minor robbing. No certain historic episodes of robbing can be confirmed, but the presence of a fortified tower or pele at Walltown farm less than 1 km southeast of the trenches, known to be present from at least 1279, may indicate the end-result of some stone-robbing (Whitworth 2000, 65 and 70). The Edwardian excavation may have precipitated a collapse in the Trench 1 area, in a stretch already weakened by taking a gentle curve to the south. The collapses to the north, where the Wall face was more exposed and perched above the crags, resulted in the loss of more facing courses (Fig. 5.12).

Very little more was discovered about the purpose of the Edwardian excavation, but it appeared more like a simple venture to expose the north and south faces of the curtain than any more complicated investigation.

The excavations at Walltown Crags, although limited in scope, have provided important information about the

Wall curtain in a section of the Wall that has not been investigated for many decades. Significantly, this length of curtain was not consolidated by early Wall scholars and enthusiasts: the very short length of curtain investigated in Trench 1 had not been exposed to the elements for many centuries.

The excavations confirmed that the curtain Wall was *c.* 2.18 m wide in Trench 1, and that exposed bedrock served as the foundations for its construction. The first course of squared masonry appears to have been offset *c.* 0.05–0.15 m from the face of the foundation course, and this first course of masonry consists of blocks that are larger than those in the courses above. An unusual practice observed here was the use of smaller chockstones to establish more level coursing and secure larger squared masonry blocks in place. In Trench 1, a thinner layer of facing stones may have been an attempt to create a very modest string course.

More significant is the fact that there was no proven use of mortar, or any other bonding agent, for the facing stones or core material. However, the exposure of the curtain after repeated collapses and natural processes of weathering, erosion, and bioturbation may have completely degraded any mortar or bonding agents. There was also no evidence for repair or rebuilding, although that might be found beyond the two small trenches. At least two episodes of collapse and tumble were observed in both Trenches 1 and 2: the second episode is related to the early 20th-century excavations, and provides a useful *terminus ante quem* for the first episode of collapse and tumble. Unfortunately, no evidence to enable dating was encountered in either trench.

There has been very little investigation into the history of collapse of the Wall, with the most insightful account provided by the recent excavations of the curtain at Buddle Street, Wallsend (Bidwell 2018); here, the building of the curtain compressed a sandy soil and altered the previous drainage and movement of subsurface water, resulting in multiple episodes of collapse and repair of the curtain. No such evidence was found at Walltown, though this is explained by the very different subsurface geologies: sandy drift geology at Wallsend compared to surface and just sub-surface bedrock at Walltown. Perhaps more directly comparable is the more confidently dated episode of curtain collapse at Sycamore Gap, which sealed a coin hoard dated to AD 350 or later (Crow in Daniels 1989, 51). However, this emphasises that episodes of collapse should be considered as localised events influenced by underlying ground conditions, water erosion, exposure to weather and vegetation damage.

6

The Wall-crossing at Cam Beck: survey and excavation

The Castlesteads estate sits in a rolling landscape of woods and pasture with occasional small arable fields, shaped by the course of the Cam Beck (Fig. 6.1). The line of the Wall here more often cuts across modern fields rather than surviving in and being followed by current farm boundaries; this route for the Wall was perhaps chosen as a compromise between good sight-lines and easier slopes for construction, but with sufficient height to avoid low-lying and marshy ground. The point where the Wall crosses the Cam Beck also provides more solid geology for construction purposes.

Figure 6.1: An aerial view of the Cam Beck looking northwest, indicated by the sinuous band of trees, with the line of the ditch visible east of the beck between the scrub and the trees, along with Trench 2, and the line of the curtain indicated by the lighter band of soil west of the beck heading toward the farm.

A significant feature of the landscape is the Cam Beck itself, a generally shallow watercourse rarely more than 3 m in width, gently winding in a north–south direction. Between the Wall and the area south of Castlesteads fort, the beck runs through flatter lands – at least in the vicinity of the beck. Even with modern drainage the land is frequently damp and historically would have been very marshy. East of the current course of the beck and south of the Wall is a low bluff or headland, on which the fort at Castlesteads was built. To the north of the Wall, the beck runs through a shallow valley of varying steepness; there are many good fording locations. Significantly, where the Wall crosses the beck, it has carved a relatively narrow gorge into the soft red sandstone bedrock for approximately 50 m in length. The side walls of the gorge are steep – vertical in some places – and where the Wall crosses the beck, the gorge is 30 m wide with asymmetric walls: the east bank is 8 m deep and the west 13 m. Compared to the rivers North Tyne and Irthing, the Cam Beck is a minor river crossing for the Wall (Bidwell and Holbrook 1989; Morgan and Bidwell 2015); however, the character of the gorge would have necessitated considerable investment in engineering and construction to carry the Wall across.

The scheduling for the Wall stops at the east and west banks for this gorge, as there was no evidence for the monument and how it interacted with the feature. There is a seemingly natural weir in the bedrock at the north end of the gorge, crescentic in plan and approximately 1 m in height, on which a later stone weir was built to enhance the height. Worked stones that appeared to be Roman and associated with the weir have been observed in the past and hypothesised as originating from a Roman bridge (Hill 2009), but no focused research into the linear elements of the Wall had ever been conducted in this area. The key aim of fieldwork at Cam Beck was to resolve the question of how the Wall interacted with the Cam Beck, and determine if any evidence could be found for any bridgeworks in this location.

Archaeological background

There has been very little archaeological investigation of either the Turf or Stone Walls and related structures in the vicinity of the Cam Beck crossing, or of the fort of Castlesteads, identified as Roman *Camboglanna* (Fig. 6.2). The Wall was originally built in turf in this area, subsequently rebuilt in stone, though the exact

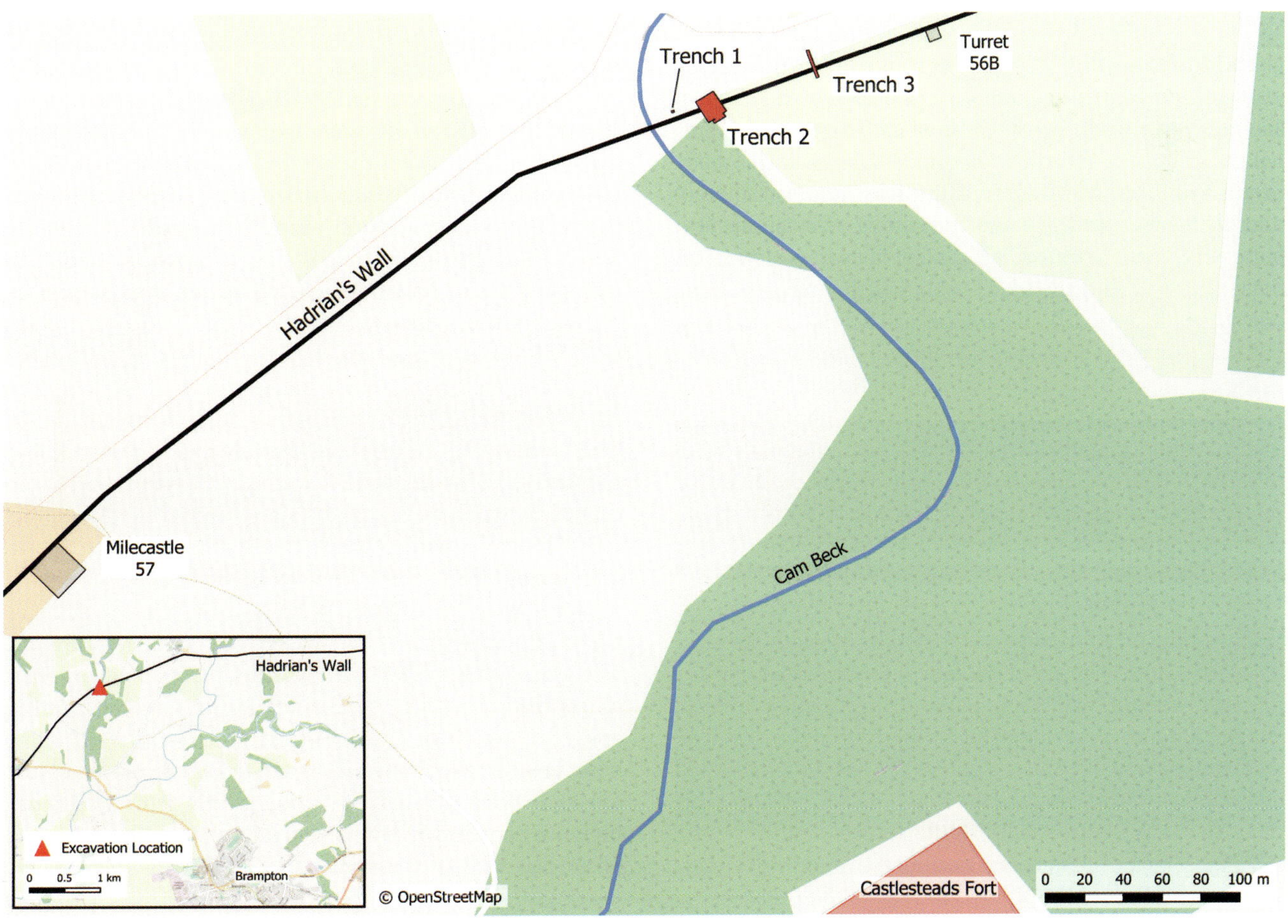

Figure 6.2: The location of the site, with the position of trenches and other key features of the Wall indicated.

date of this rebuilding is uncertain. Along the line of the Wall, milecastle 56 at the village of Walton has not been found and, although turret 56a near the farm of Sandysike has also not been located, the Wall itself was encountered in excavations in 1933, where it rested on deep masonry foundations 2.9 m wide: a 'massive substructure of large sandstone blocks, stepping boldly downhill' (Simpson *et al.* 1934, 131). In the field on the east bank of the Cam Beck, where the WallCAP excavation was located – as in the wider area – there are no visible remains of the Wall curtain above ground, but its northern ditch can be traced running west, downslope to the beck and in the sides of the gorge. An account of the destruction of the Wall in the area in 1791 for 'near half a mile' in length indicated it was 2.44 m wide with large facing stones and a core of alternating layers of rubble 0.3 m thick and mortar 0.1 m thick, identifying this stretch as Intermediate Wall that until that time survived to an estimated height of at least 0.7–1 m (Carlisle 1794, 64; Breeze 2006, 328–329). Though specific lengths cannot be identified, in the Middle Ages the manor of Walton was in possession of Lanercost Priory, located approximately 3.5 km to the east, and largely constructed from re-used Wall fabric, almost certainly including material from the later Castlesteads estate and the vicinity of Walton and Cam Beck (Collins *et al.* 2023b, 93–95).

Wall turret 56b was detected in minor excavations only 140 m upslope of the curtain's crossing-point of the Cam Beck (Simpson *et al.* 1934, 132). The turret, sitting on the brow of a break of slope down to the beck would have had an excellent view of the river crossing. The turret remains were in poor condition but projected 0.84 m north of the Stone Wall. Its south and east walls were completely removed and eroded; the remainder were reduced to clay-and-rubble foundations and the excavators commented on the softness of the degraded stone, which could be sliced with a spade 'as easily as cheese' (Simpson *et al.* 1934, 135). The heavily truncated curtain remains investigated at the turret were described as built on flag-footings over foundations of varying depths. Between T56a and T56b the excavators suggested that the Wall's foundations were relatively shallow, and the curtain was clearly again of Intermediate width. Milecastle 57 across the beck to the west is presumed to lie beneath Cambeckhill Farm which makes extensive use of Wall stones in its fabric.

There are more clues in old maps as to the fate of the Wall and the fort structures, as they pass through the Castlesteads estate. The earlier manor seen on McLaughlin's mid-19th-century map was sited south of the current house and presumably made use of Roman structural stone. The later manor house constructed in 1791 is still inhabited and sits just outside and south of the Vallum, with the fort beneath the walled garden. The late 18th-century vogue for estate beautification, as well as the building of this new house, may have accounted for a considerable amount of removal of Wall and fort stones. The farm buildings within the manor's curtilage, as well as old farms such as Sandysike and Swainsteads would also have easy access to the plunderable Roman structures.

The fort is detached from the Wall curtain, like the forts at Carvoran and Carlisle, situated on a bluff overlooking the short length of gorge where the curtain crosses the Cam Beck. Castlesteads is unique, however, in that it is still situated to the north of the Vallum, which takes a larger than normal deviation south of a parallel course to the curtain to include the fort. Excavations of the fort site in 1934 confirmed the location and dimensions of the eastern and western stone walls and gates as well as the southern wall of the fort and one external ditch (Richmond and Hodgson 1934). The little stonework of the fort walls found *in situ* was of red sandstone, with Hadrianic pottery found on a surface north of the east gate. Drastic levelling of the fort platform for construction of the walled garden in 1791, unfortunately, has left almost no stratigraphy, with exploration of the internal space encountering only 'virgin' soils and clay. The excavations also determined that *c.* 30 m of the fort had been lost due to natural erosion of the bluff. Significantly, the remains of a turf rampart pre-dating the stone fort were encountered at the southeast angle tower of the stone fort, indicating an earlier phase of military occupation. Geophysical survey south of the fort confirmed the course of the Vallum as well as several enclosures relating to extramural settlement associated with the fort (Biggins and Taylor 2007). In 1741, the external bathhouse was located and partly excavated northeast of the fort (Collingwood 1922, 201). Given the absence of surviving stratigraphy and limited excavation, the surviving inscriptions and coins are the best testimony to the fort having a broad occupational history that stretches from the Hadrianic construction of the Wall up to the early 5th century.

Geology and subsoils

The underlying bedrock of the area is the Kirklinton Sandstone Formation, characterised by a rusty-red colour, especially when wet, that is a relatively soft sandstone that weathers easily and is prone to splitting along its planes of bedding. This is the uppermost bedrock of the solid geology and that which can be observed in the sides of the gorge, laying over the Calder Sandstone Formation. The general softness of the Kirklinton sandstone is visible in the gorge, where fractures in the stone are readily apparent as a result of freeze-thaw and root actions, along with erosion from the beck or surface run-off. Where exposed in large faces, as in the gorge, there is a much higher susceptibility of this formation to collapse, slip, and other damage. However, there are variations within the formation that include harder wearing rock, for example the shelf that forms the natural weir (see below).

Although visually dominated by the red colours of the local sandstone, the drift geology around the Cam Beck site is relatively varied. The superficial deposits over the sandstone comprise mixed river terrace sands and glaciofluvial deposits of sand and gravel of geologically diverse material from earlier geological epochs. The geological diversity can be found along the course of the Cam Beck, which acts as a corridor for transport of exposed materials downstream, particularly during episodes of flooding.

These glaciofluvial deposits were found in the base of Slot 1 in Cam Beck Trench 2 (2021) at a maximum depth of 44.37 m OD, or about 1.2 m below ground surface. These were yellowish grey coarse stained sands with occasional lenses of fine gravels over a basal coarse gravel layer: context (2034) in Trench 2. Over those deposits lay lower and relatively undisturbed subsoils: context (2023) in the extension to Trench 2 and (2030) in the main trench. The subsoils were friable, non-homogenous, gritty yellowish orange variably silty sands, with some small pebbles and coarse gravel. A similar but more disturbed layer was encountered in 2019 in Trench 3, context (3003). Only further excavation will reveal to what extent these subsoils were redeposited or disturbed natural layers.

Condition survey of Cam Beck Gorge

Rob Collins and Nicky Garland

In advance of archaeological fieldwork, a condition survey and archaeological assessment of the Cam Beck gorge was completed (Fig. 6.3). The aim was to undertake a close visual inspection of the historic weir, the geological conditions of the gorge, and to confirm the extent to which any potential remains or ruins of a presumed Wall-crossing could be identified within the area. This work followed on that undertaken by Peter Hill and summarised in an unpublished report to Historic England (Hill 2009).

The Cam Beck is a sinuous stream, generally flowing north to south. The beck for most of its length is not at the bottom of a gorge, though it has carved a channel of varying depth that can be understood as a shallow or steep ravine for much of its length. Many locations, particularly south of the line of the Wall are much flatter with the channel of the beck achieving 1–2 m depth relative to the ground surface of its eastern or western banks. The beck has carved a gorge through the red sandstone of the Kirklinton Formation for approximately 50 m at the location where the Wall crosses the beck. Under normal water-flow conditions, the depth of the beck is typically less than 1 m in its centre, and frequently less than 0.5 m; there are deeper pools and channels within or following bends in the beck. The deepest areas of the beck within the area of survey were immediately above

Figure 6.3: The historic weir from the base of the gorge formed by the Cam Beck, looking west-northwest. The position of the Wall ditch can be seen in the broad V-shape behind the weir.

and below the weir. Above the weir, the floor of the beck was approximately 1–1.7 m below the surface; below the weir, a depth of at least 2 m was recorded, though it is possibly deeper closer to the weir. Due to decomposing litter and silt on the bed of the beck, an exact depth was not possible to confirm.

The Wall, and subsequently the weir are positioned to exploit the tactical and structural advantages offered by the gorge. Namely, the gorge is one of the few locations along the length of the Cam Beck where east–west crossing of the beck can be very closely monitored and prohibited. Located approximately 150 m north of the position where the Wall crosses the beck, there is a ford used for at least the last 50 years by the Cambeck Hill and Swainsteads Farms either side of the beck; this ford is likely to have been used for many centuries, based on the gently sloping holloway that frames a 3 m-wide track on its east bank. Within 50 m south of the line of the Wall, the land on the west bank of the beck is very low and provides easy access; the east bank is still steeply sloped due to the bluff where the fort was located. However, within 200 m, the east and west banks are both low and the beck is easily fordable.

Regardless of the slope of the banks, the course of the beck is generally wooded, with a belt of deciduous trees and ground-based scrub providing further strength to the banks, in bands at least 5 m wide, and considerably wider in many locations. This tree cover, beneficial to the beck and local plant and wildlife, presented challenges in both airborne and ground-based archaeological survey techniques.

The Historic Weir

A large crescentic weir was constructed at an unknown date on a similarly shaped shelf that is likely to have been carved from the bedrock at the base of the gorge.

This shelf is positioned almost entirely north of the line of the Wall where it crosses the beck, with the exception of the western terminal, which extends across the line of the ditch and sits below the berm of the Wall on the west bank, terminating where it meets another roughly squared shelf of bedrock projecting from the west bank that extends a further 12 m south (Fig. 6.3).

No evidence was visible to determine the extent to which the weir shelf was a natural feature or manmade. The original extended crescent shape of the shelf may have been natural, and subsequently enhanced through human action (Fig. 6.4). The shelf is vertical, and though unproven this may be the result of quarrying. The only certain feature that is a result of human intervention is a deep U-shaped trough that has been carved in the eastern end of the shelf, which has been filled with coursed blocks at an unknown date (Fig. 6.5). One of the blocks, on the eastern edge had distinct tooling marks present, as observed in the original Hill 2009 survey. It is also worth noting that the blocks within this U-shaped feature were of a different shape to those used to build up the weir.

The weir consists of large, dressed blocks with squared ends and beds and a sloped outer face laid in five or six courses. The sloped outer faces range from 45–60°, creating a dam that provided further height over the base of the beck by 1–2 m. The uppermost layer consists of concrete poured and smoothed over the stones, now missing in many places, also post-dating and sealing cast-iron stakes that were likely added to the weir in the later 19th–early 20th century as reinforcement. It is uncertain when the weir was first constructed, however, repairs to the weir in 1741 found and removed a Roman altar (RIB 1983). This confirms that earlier constructions of the weir incorporated Roman stonework. No definitive Roman blocks in the weir were identified at the time of the survey, though two stones of similar shape and dimensions to those in the weir were found downstream (see Table A2.4, nos. 1, 3) as well as during excavations in Trench 2 (see below). This latter example is perhaps the best indirect evidence that suggests the large blocks that make up the current weir were re-used from Roman structures.

Stonework associated with the weir

Damage to the upper courses at the east terminal of the weir has been sustained over the course of time through a mix of retreat of the beck, soil formation, and advancement of woodland and scrub vegetation. The damage is most apparent from dislodged stonework at the base of the weir's eastern terminus and extending along the base of the eastern bank. As the stones were piled, it was not possible to make an exact count though where possible, measurements were recorded (Table A2.3). It is also possible that some of these stones were removed and redundant from earlier repairs to the weir, and/or piled from their removal from collapsed Roman structure(s).

Figure 6.4: The central and eastern portions of the historic weir, with coursed stones sitting on bedrock.

Figure 6.5: A U-shaped cut in the bedrock at the east end of the weir, subsequently infilled with coursed blocks.

Above the weir, and in part due to the presence of the weir, the beck has swept west into the bank creating a slightly deeper channel and pool. At this end of the weir, a number of large, dressed blocks, stones, and slabs have been arranged in an L-shape in conjunction with squared and dressed bedrock to create a spillway or possible sluice gate at the western terminal of the weir, just north of where the weir gives way to the cut shelf of the west bank (Fig. 6.6). The stonework is positioned in parallel and perpendicular to the north–south course of the west bank, though individual stones have been dislodged through flood action. Many of the stones are covered in patches of moss and lichen above the waterline. A total of nine stones were recorded (see Table A2.2), four of which retained lewis holes and other cut spaces. It is possible that further dressed stones are below the water line. As arranged, the lewis holes and rebates do not appear to contribute to the current structure, confirming that they have been appropriated or re-used from another structure. These stones are consistent in size, shape, and dressing with stones found from the Roman bridges at Chesters and Willowford (Bidwell and Holbrook 1989), and are almost certainly re-used Roman stones. The date of construction of this spillway, however, could not be determined. This channel allows water to flow over the weir, but its position renders it vulnerable to blockage from detritus.

South of the weir on the east bank a line of 27 stones projected out of the soil of the bank, roughly level with the top of the weir for a distance of approximately 5 m (Fig. 6.7). The line of stones is not horizontal, but gently rises from south to north in a shallow curve, finishing with a more horizontal (but unlevel) surface at the north end. The stones do not project equally; rather, they are staggered as if to form a bond, and stones below this feature piled as the base of the bank suggest a larger structure that has collapsed due to erosion of the bank or flood action.

The individual stones are similar in size and shape, but irregular. Tool marks were visible on the faces of some of these. The dimensions of these stones are recorded in Table A2.1, and this area was subject to a very small excavation trench (Trench 1), that determined these stones were laid directly onto a shelf of bedrock,

Figure 6.6: Dressed stones, almost certainly re-used Roman stones, arranged in an L-shaped plan to create a spillway at the west end of the weir.

possibly mirroring that of the western bank, and that the stones themselves were probably laid in the 19th or early 20th century. Further dressed and/or quarried stones at the base of the bank and sitting above and within the beck were also recorded on the assumption that these stones were part of the same structure, but no longer *in situ* due to erosion or flood action.

It seems most likely that these stones were laid as a paved viewing surface or platform, making use of the existing shelf of bedrock on the eastern bank.

Miscellaneous worked stones

Evidence for Roman stonework was sought downstream from the position of the weir, on the basis that seasonal flooding may have dislodged stone over the course of many decades and centuries. Four stones were encountered between 100–150 m downstream of the weir (Table A2.4). All appear to have been worked or shaped, but the only stone that is most probably Roman is no. 3, which had a circular socket cut into the centre of a face that compares favourably with other stones bearing sockets from various turret and fort sites along the Wall, marking the positions of doors.

Figure 6.7: Stones projecting from the east bank of the gorge. (A) Looking south-southeast. (B) Facing directly east.

Geophysical survey

Alex Turner

Gradiometry and resistivity surveys were undertaken in advance of excavation. The survey area was laid to pasture and separated from the woodland to the north and west by a wire fence. The ditch to the north of the survey area was crossed by made ground that incorporated a draining pipe and a substantial quantity of building rubble. At the time of the gradiometer survey, the gateway was undergoing repair to correct drainage problems between it and Sandysike Farm, 400 m to the east. No further obstructions were present.

The sloping topography of the field to the north of the survey flattened out as it reached the survey area but a significant short sharp slope existed parallel to the fence at the northwest end of the survey. The earthwork and ditch of Hadrian's Wall to the northeast of the survey promoted a slight increase in the response from the resistivity due to the increased drainage in this area. The sharp slope presented a challenge for the gradiometer survey but this was overcome by significantly decreasing the data collection speed in this area.

The local geology (discussed above), particularly the soil makeup, impacted on the effectiveness of the survey. The plough soil layer is a sandy-loam with a loam soil to the northeast and south, with the dominant minerals being quartz and feldspar with some silica. The background sub-surface makeup of the survey area was deemed, in this case to be suitable for both electrical resistance and gradiometer survey. The only limiting factor was that the eastern boundary of the site was prone to flooding and that the electrical resistance survey should be conducted during drier spells of weather. This flooding is unlikely to have been caused by the underlying geology and is more likely to be due to an aged and broken field-drainage system. Examination of the survey results showed a number of varied linear responses in this area that probably represent these compromised drains.

The results of the gradiometry and resistivity surveys (Figs 6.8 and 6.9) revealed few archaeological anomalies. The lack of real success with both gradiometry and resistivity surveys in detecting significant sub-surface features is surprising given the location of the survey area in relation to the line of the Wall curtain and ditch. There seems to be no evidence from the geophysics of even the slightest remains of the Turf Wall. Simpson *et al.*'s (1934, 132) account of the discovery of turret 56b suggests that the turret was on the southern edge of a 5 m berm. If this were the case, it is possible that the resistivity survey did not extend far enough south to catch any Turf Wall features. However, the gradiometer survey extended 25 m south of the line of the ditch and also failed to reveal anything of great significance.

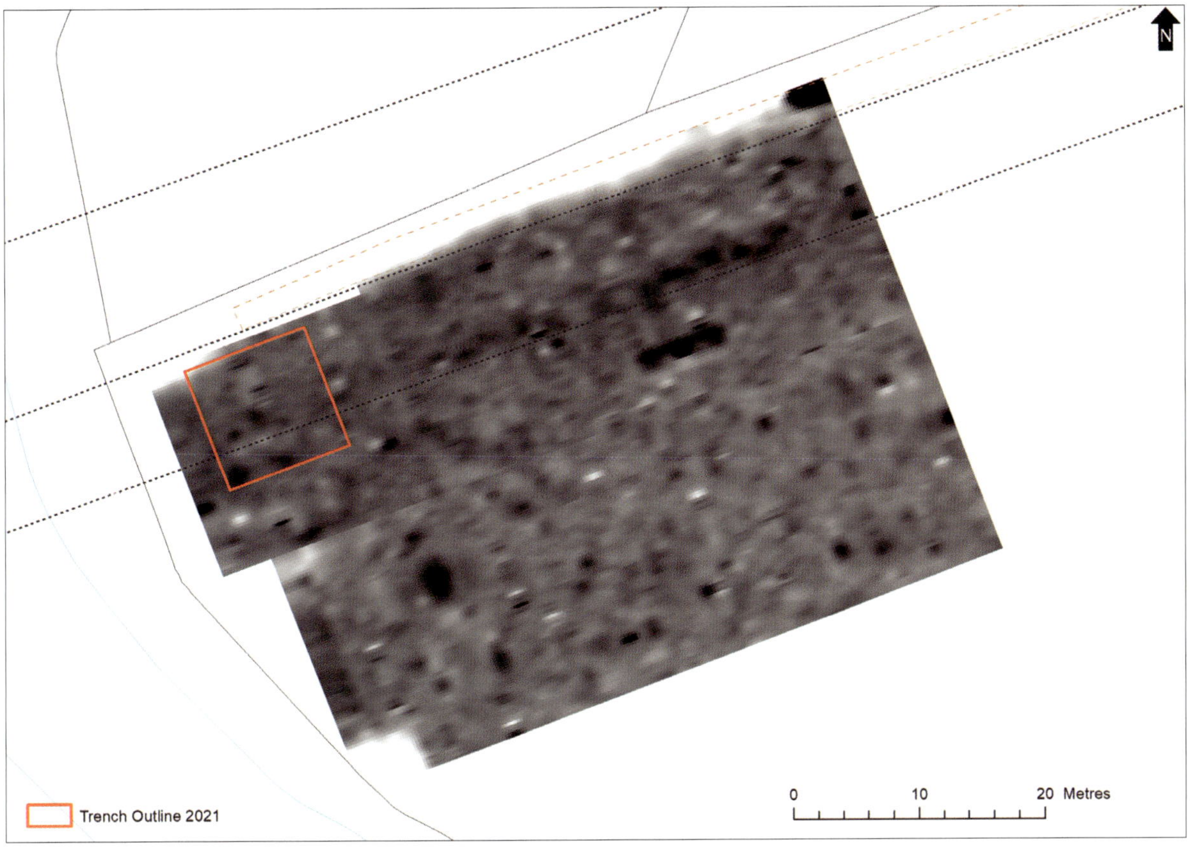

Figure 6.8: Results of the gradiometry survey east of the Cam Beck, with the position of Trench 2 indicated.

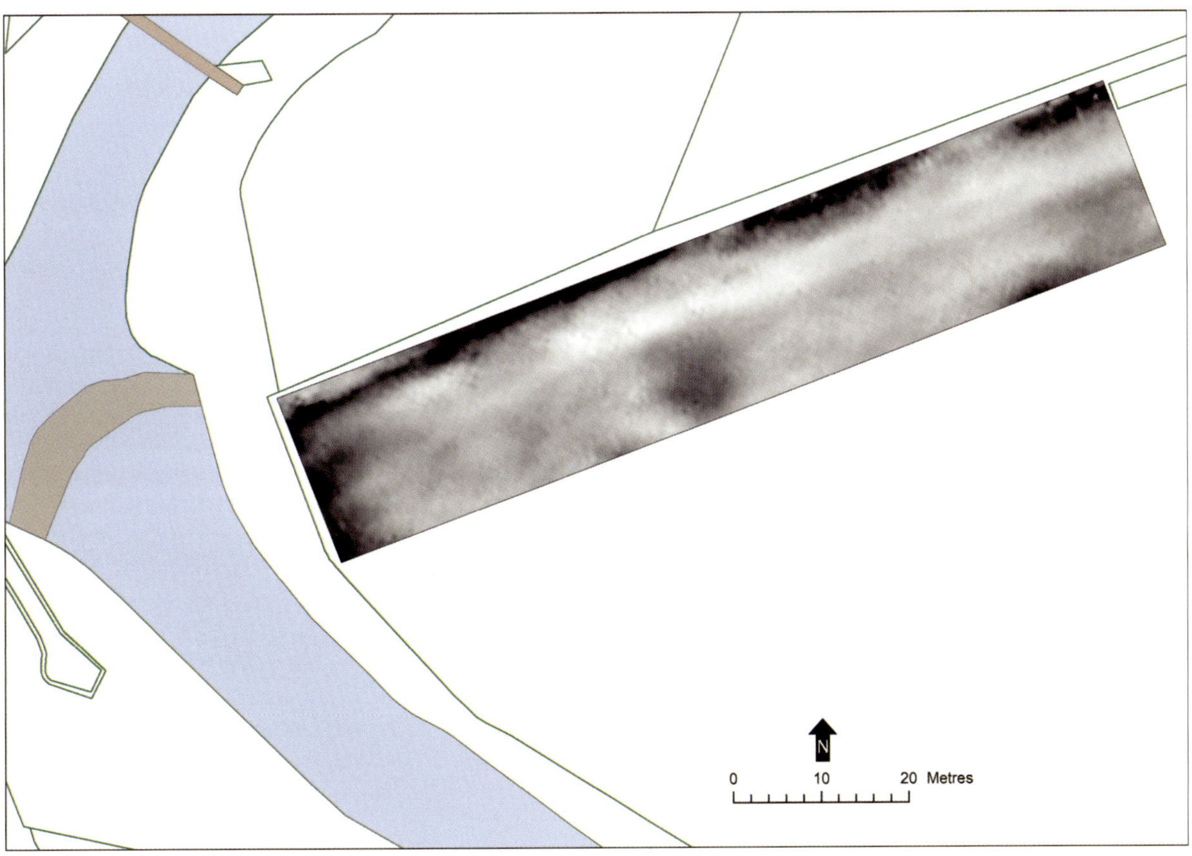

Figure 6.9: Results of the resistivity survey east of the Cam Beck.

Excavation

Two small trenches were excavated in 2019, one in the east bank of the gorge, to investigate what appeared to be worked and *in-situ* structural stones (Trench 1), and one across the likely line of the curtain in the pasture to the east of the Wall's assumed crossing point of Cam Beck (Trench 3). Trench 2, the largest trench, was excavated in 2021 at the westernmost edge of the pasture bordered by the treeline and the gorge (Fig. 6.2).

Trenches 1 and 3

Trench 1 investigated a line of sub-rectangular stones [1001] projecting from the east bank of the beck, north of the line of the curtain Wall and ditch, in an approximately 1 m square trench. This work confirmed that the stones were almost certainly part of a post-medieval feature. The only artefact helping date the structure was a single cast-iron stake (cat. no. 23; Fig. 6.25), dating to *c.* 1790–1945, found in association with the stones. The stone blocks thus appear to have been laid on a shelf of bedrock [1002] between the late 18th to early 20th century to create a viewing platform with a prospect of the gorge and beck.

Trench 3, *c.* 8.5 m long by 2 m, uncovered the lowest courses of stone rubble [3004] associated with the core of the Stone Wall (Fig. 6.10). The assumed width of the core, with additional width for robbed facing stones, indicated an overall curtain width of *c.* 2.6 m, consistent with earlier excavations that identified the curtain here as the Intermediate Wall (Breeze 2006, 54). Degraded mortar associated with this possibly *in-situ* core suggested the stone Wall in this location may have been built using mortar, or that a later and considerable rebuild of the stone curtain included the use of mortar (*pace* Carlisle 1794). A few larger lumps of mortar were recovered and identified as *opus caementicium*: a very hard mortar, made of small and medium gravels and pebbles mixed with lime and chalk and used for bonded Roman structures (see Appendix 2). No evidence was found for the Turf Wall. No artefacts were recovered from the trench.

The Trench 3 results point to long-term collapse of upper courses of the stone curtain, with one or more periods of robbing. A discrete phase of robbing is recorded for 1791 for a length estimated as 0.8 km (Carlisle 1794), but the exact location is uncertain and this certainly does not preclude the possibility of earlier robbing, and the re-use of Roman red sandstone fabric at Lanercost is likely from this sector of the Wall. Robbing concentrated on facing stones, leaving the lowest courses of core rubble more-or-less *in situ*. Following the last phase of robbing and/or destruction, possibly as late as 1790, arable ploughing extended north across the line of the stone curtain. This left most of the remaining core rubble (stone clusters 1–3) arranged in loose east–west lines aligning with ridges from pre-mechanical ploughing. Modern arable agriculture subsequently levelled this ridge-and-furrow leaving an almost flat relict ploughsoil (3003) under the turf.

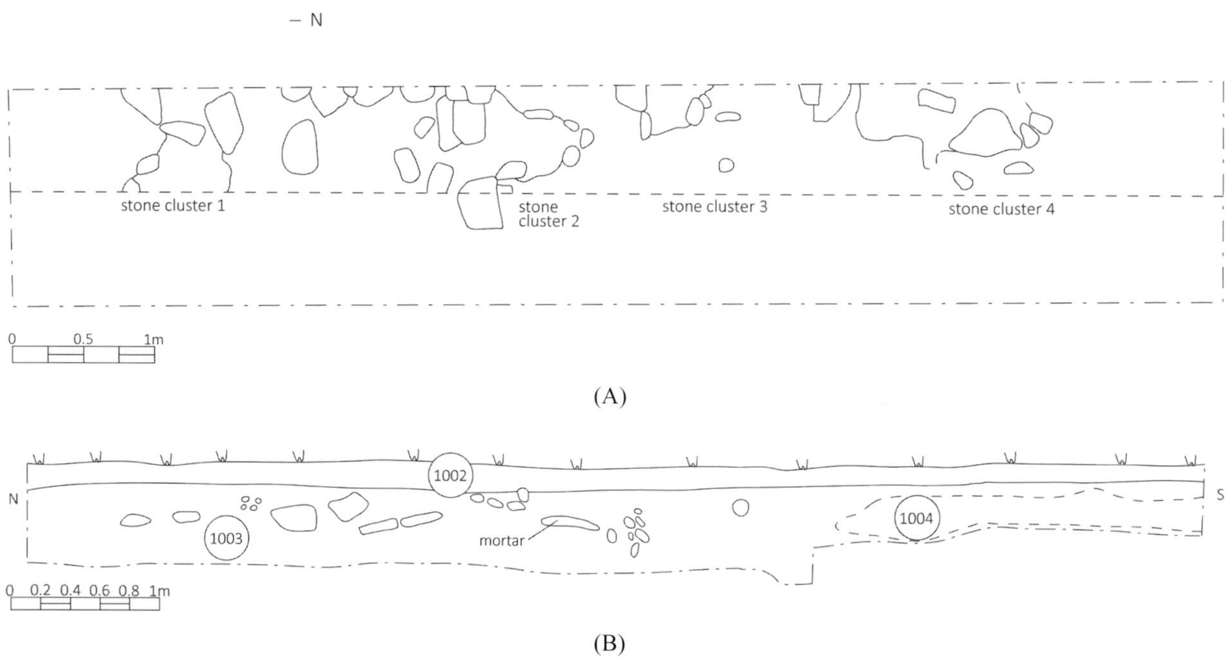

Figure 6.10: (A) Plan of Trench 3 at Cam Beck, mapping the positions of notable clusters of stones and cobbles. (B) The east section of Trench 3. (1004) corresponds with stone cluster 4, and is surviving traces of the Stone Wall core.

Trench 2

Trench 2 was located as close as possible to the point where the curtain was assumed to cross the beck gorge to the west, and also to encompass the line of the Wall as indicted by the north ditch in the field to the east; tall mature trees at the top of the gorge and the edges of the north ditch by the gorge also impacted on trench location, positioned to avoid the larger roots of those trees (Fig. 6.2). The geophysics had not revealed evidence for possible bridging structures (Figs 6.8 and 6.9). Trench 2 was 10 m near west–east by 12 m near north–south with a 6.5 m west–east by 2 m north–south extension from the southern edge of the original trench (Fig. 6.11). This extension was added during initial machining as the presence of a large stone and charcoal-rich deposits right on the southern baulk suggested significant archaeology just to the south of the original trench limit. The trench sloped down relatively steeply to the north and more gently to the northwest towards the ditch and beck ravine respectively from *c*. 47 m OD in the south to 46.1 m OD in the north and from *c*. 46.9 m OD in the southeast to 46.4 OD in the northwest.

The turf and topsoil were removed using a mechanical digger, and a deep 5.2 m long north–south slot to natural geology was excavated using a 0.75 m wide ditching bucket under a careful watching brief (Slot 1 in Fig. 6.11). All subsequent excavation was done by hand with 100% sieving. The soils were very sandy, creating a dynamic deposition environment: possible cuts and the boundaries between the sandier layers and deposits were therefore obscured by the effects of worm and water action and by both pre-modern and more recent ploughing. Clarifying stratigraphical relationships was further complicated in several areas by the presence of robber trenches around the stone Wall and all the related structures. Natural subsoils were reached in many parts of the trench but there is further work to be done to discover the full size, context, and depth of the building sequences in the south and southwest of the trench. Excavation of the trench revealed a sequence of activity in the Roman period that began with the Turf Wall and ended with a stone tower and presumed bridgework. Any late and post-Roman evidence has been lost to truncation.

The Turf Wall and associated building (Structure 1)

Some of the earliest evidence for activity was found preserved below subsequent construction in stone in Slot 3 on the western edge of the trench (Figs 6.12 and 6.13). Deposit (2014) was suggestive of Turf Wall foundation remains, and a likely outline of a turf building block was preserved on the northern edge of the context. An environmental sample taken from (2014) produced some wood charcoal but also a high concentration of the black spherical fungal sclerotia *Cenococum*, supporting the interpretation of the layer as turf (see Simmons in Appendix 2). The radiocarbon date ranges taken from two pieces of different roundwood charcoal from that sample both agreed and covered the Turf Wall construction period: 125–203 cal AD (at 1σ and 68.3%) and 107–230 cal AD (at 2σ and 88.2%), SUERC-105491; and 125–204 cal AD (at 1σ and 68.3%) and 108–230 cal AD (at 2σ and 88.7%), SUERC-105492.

Overall, the 2.4 m length of context exposed in the 0.7 m wide slot was damp, yellowish brown silty sand with a darker greyish, black and very silty, organic layer preserved below the surviving tower foundations [2011] (see below), including the possible turf outline. The later robber trenches around the subsequent tower structure had truncated the turf remains to the north and south in that location, but the turf line was also captured in the west-facing section of the deep slot to natural. That thin turf line ran for 1.5 m south from 1.75 m south of the southern edge of the later stone curtain (Fig. 6.14).

A building stratigraphically contemporary with the Turf Wall was excavated 4 m south of and detached from the Turf Wall, designated as Structure 1 (Figs 6.12 and 6.15). The remains uncovered were the southeastern end and northern wall of a west-northwest to east-southeast aligned structure, with stone-founded walls and a well-laid cobble interior with a hearth built into the floor (Structure 1: [2025] and [2026]). The structure was built onto and into a layer excavated as (2024) and (2031): a stained, mixed silty sand with frequent lenses of white clay, iron panning and scattered small cobbles and pebbles. Dominated by redeposited natural sand and consolidated with clay, this truncated layer was probably created initially by traffic and activity during construction. Just over 5 m of the northern wall-line of the building were uncovered, with the hint of a return beginning at the western end of northern wall; only 2.5 m of the return at the eastern end were seen within the trench. The foundations were between 0.7 m to 1 m wide, but did not survive beyond 1 m in length to the south-southwest and 1.5 m to the west-northwest from the visible corner. To the west the foundations were thoroughly robbed out, with a clear robber trench [2029] seen in section, and to the south both robbed and disturbed by later activity associated with the construction of Structure 2. The northeast corner of the foundations of the building survived best, with a rubble and sandy earth core faced with roughly coursed sub-square and sub-rectangular stones of red sandstone; larger stones up to 0.3 m long formed the outside northeastern corner.

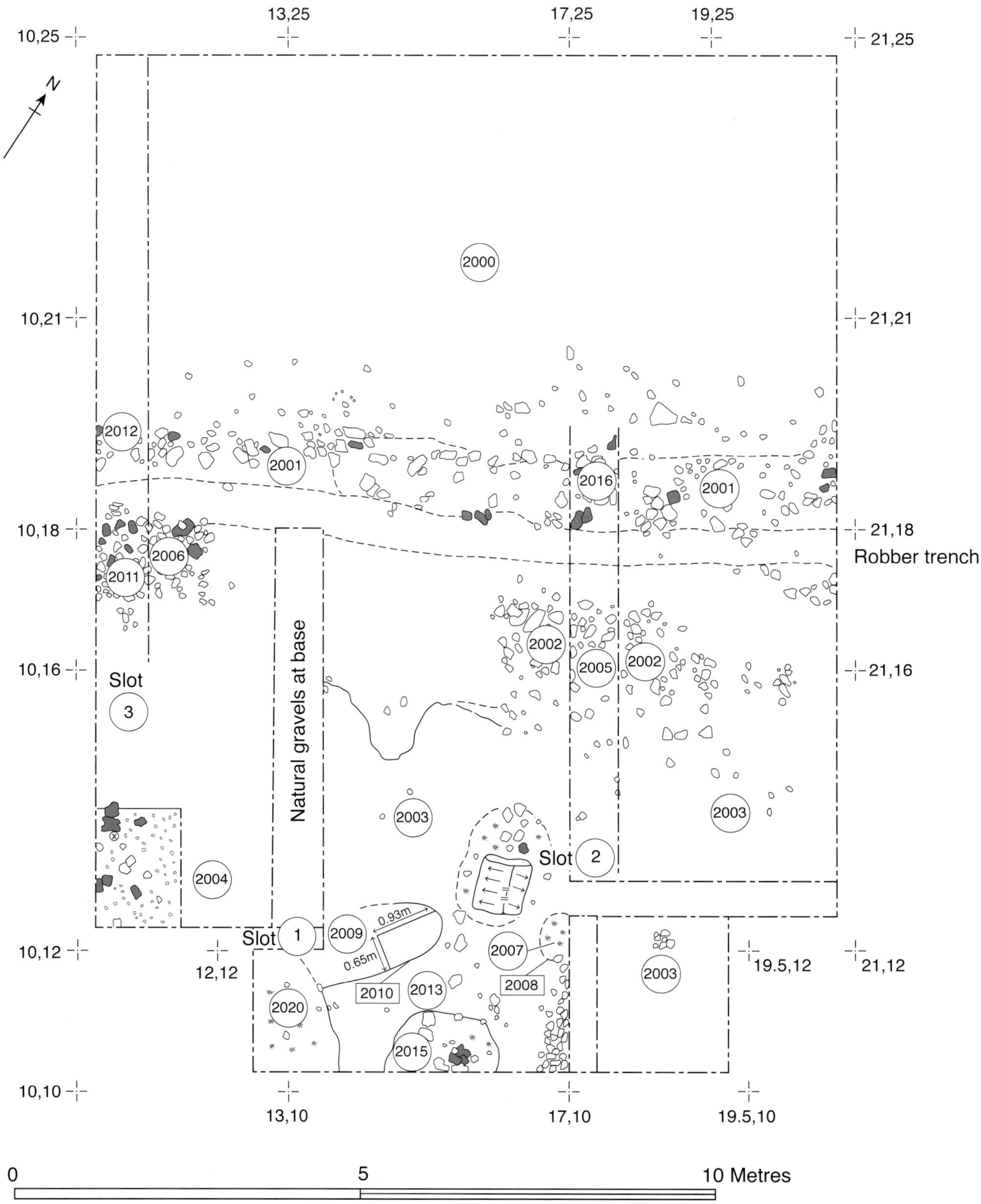

Figure 6.11: Plan of Trench 2 indicating key features and contexts.

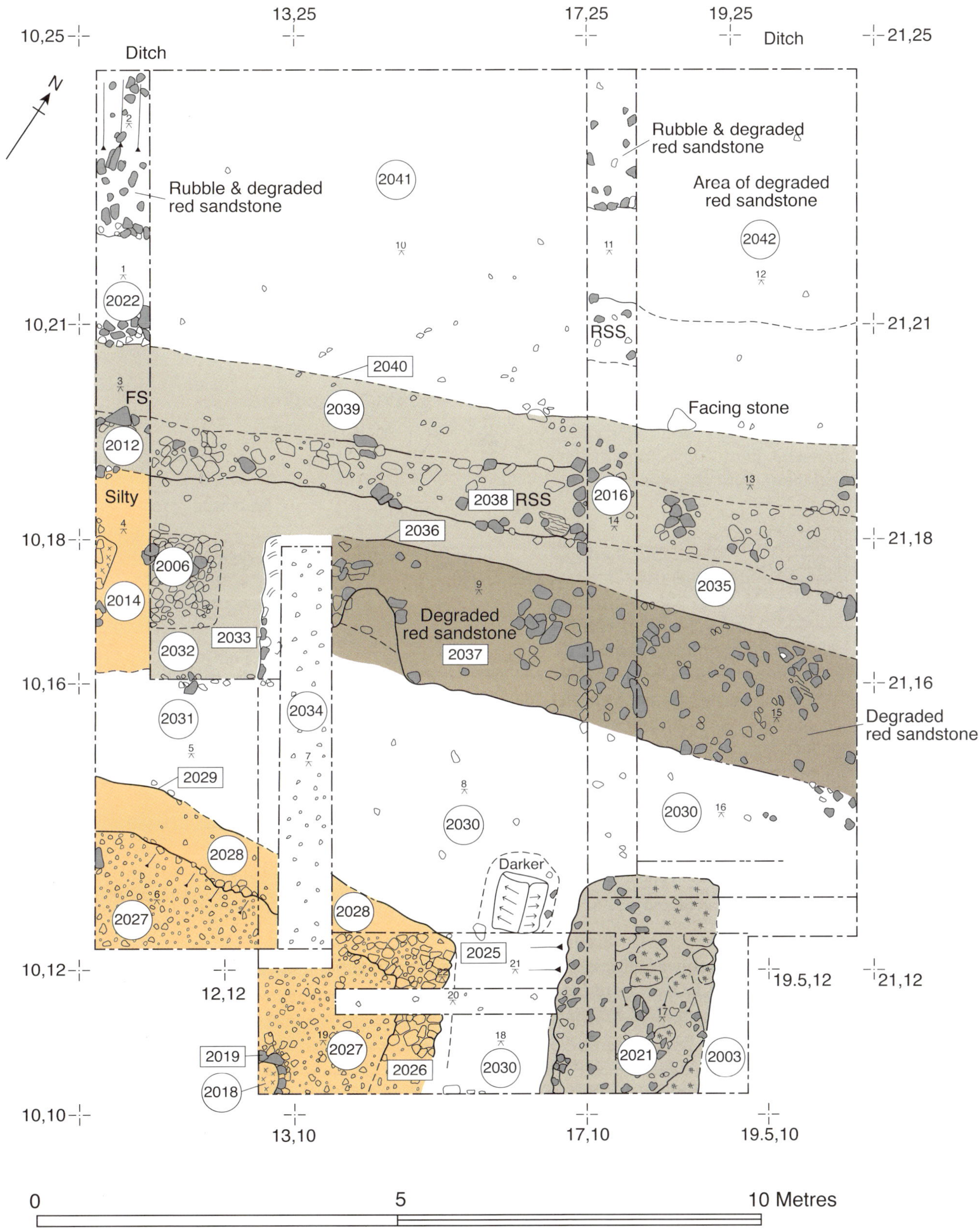

Figure 6.12: Plan of Trench 2 indicating identified structural features in discrete colours.

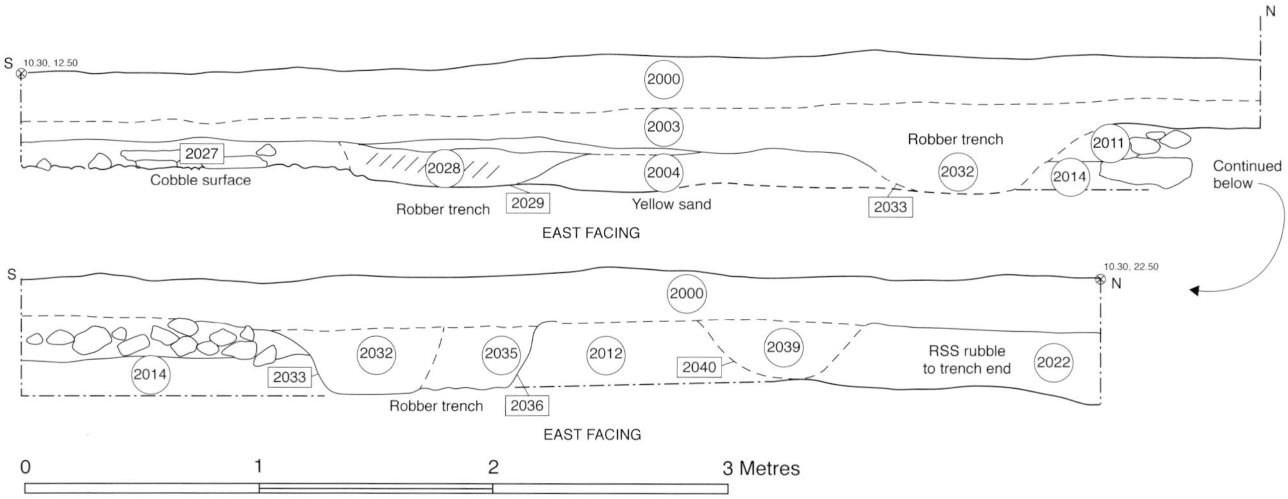

Figure 6.13: West section of slot 3 located along the northwest edge of Trench 2.

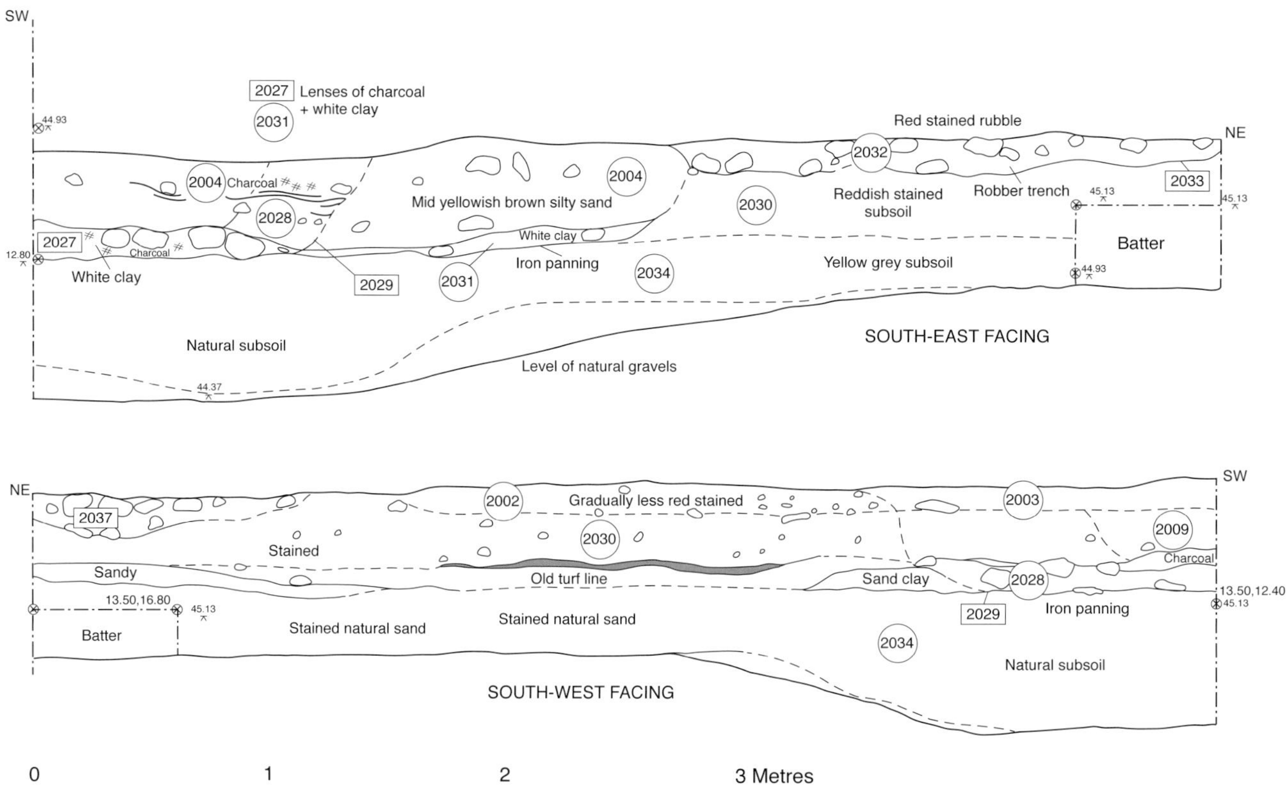

Figure 6.14: The west and east sections of the northern end of slot 3 located along the northwest edge of Trench 2.

The compact cobbled interior of Structure 1 survived well and was formed of tightly packed cobbles of near-uniform size [2027]. An area was uncovered of 5 m west-northwest to east-southeast by up to 2 m in width. The cobbles were 0.1 m in length and set in a matrix of charcoal-rich sandy silt, white clay and gravel and pebbles. A stone-lined hearth or oven base [2019], found quadranted by the southwest corner of the trench sides, sat 1.25 m from the internal side of the eastern wall and 1.7 m from the northern wall. It had been built into the floor with a lining of single depth, heavily burnt harder sandstone cobbles *c.* 0.1–0.2 m in length. The quarter of the feature excavated was 0.4 m west–east by 0.6 m north–south. The hearth appeared to have been

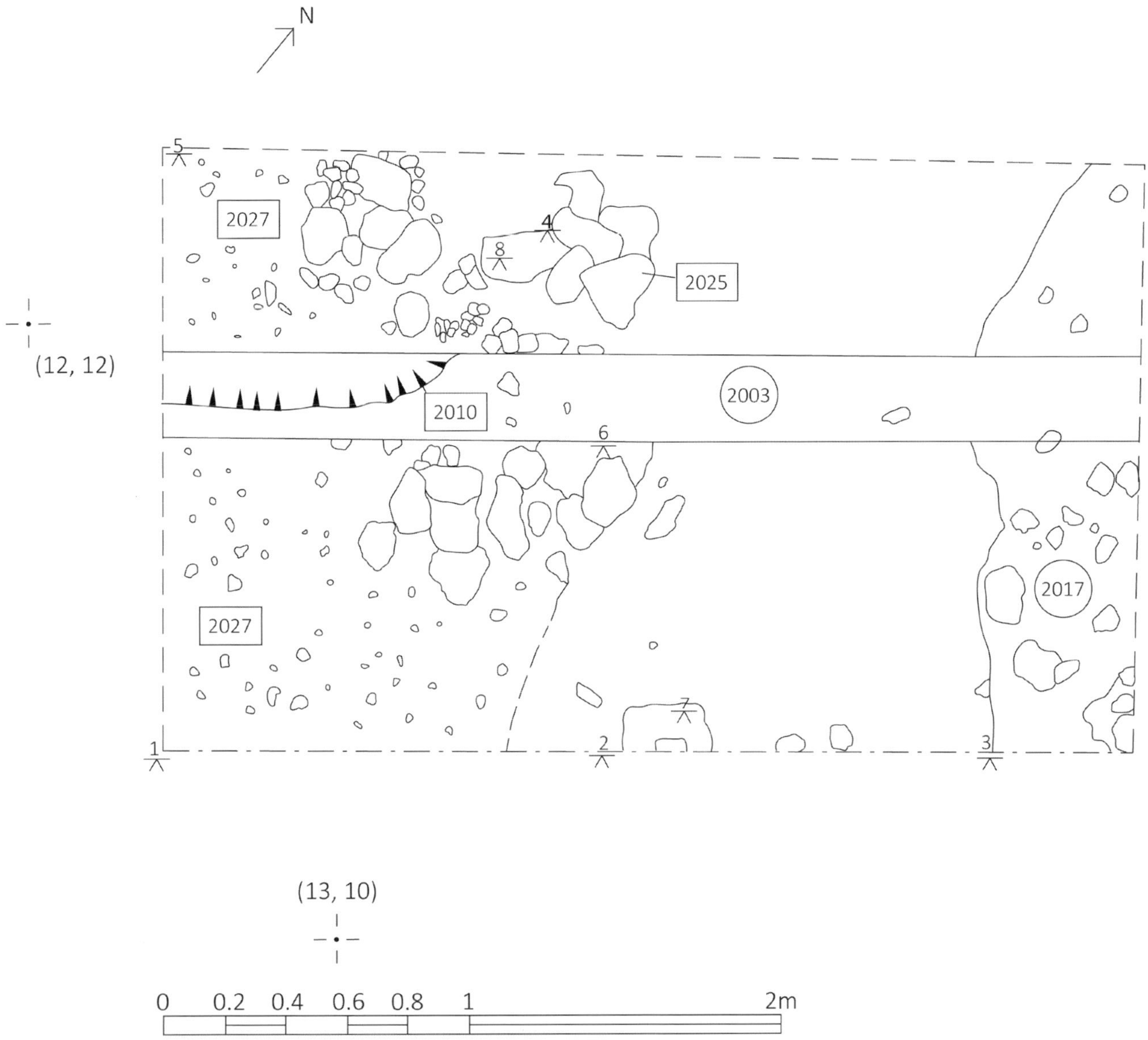

Figure 6.15: Plan of the area in Trench 2 where Structure 1 was detected.

constructed at the same time as the floor was laid, with a tight fit between oven stones and pebbles. The hearth or oven fill (2018) was 90% charcoal in brownish black silty sand and 0.4 m deep. Heavy iron panning marked the base of the feature (Figs 6.12 and 6.16). The environmental sample for this fill contained a very high concentration of wood charcoal, mostly hazel, alder and birch with some oak, ash and elm, and a little wheat cereal grain. Radiocarbon dates were secured on two samples of different roundwood charcoal from the fill and matched very well with the ranges for the building of the Turf wall: 125–204 cal AD (at 1σ and 68.3%) and 108–230 cal AD (at 2σ and 88.7%), SUERC-105496; and 60–130 cal AD (at 1σ and 58.7%) and 26–205 cal AD (at 2σ and 95.4%), SUERC-105497.

Three iron artefacts were found in the hearth fill: a hobnail (cat. no. 5), a bolt (cat. no. 18), and stone clamp (cat. no. 19) along with some very fragmentary burnt bone and a small nodule of *opus caementicum*. The structural iron artefacts and the *opus caementicum* were likely to have been introduced into the fill when the building was demolished. Structure 1 has been identified as a free-standing tower: the significance and interpretation of this is explored below.

Demolition of the Turf Wall and Structure 1

Above the wall foundations, floor and hearth of Structure 1 was a relatively deep layer (0.3 m) comprising disturbed occupation layers – including internal floor deposits – mixed with demolition spread and redeposited

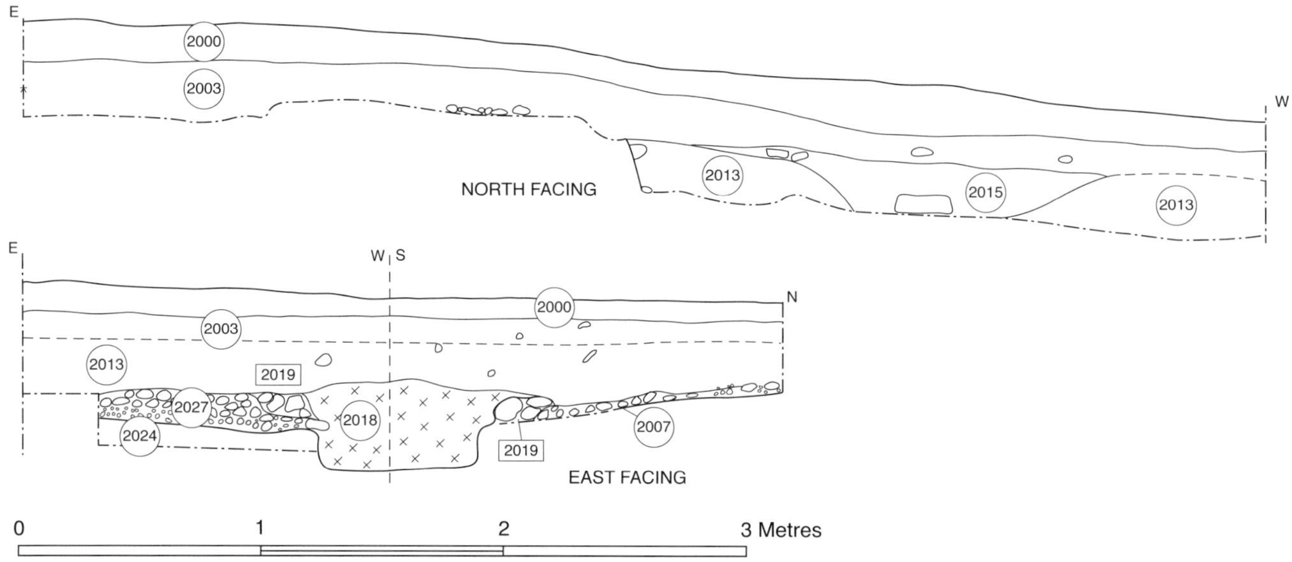

Figure 6.16: The south and west sections across Structure 1.

natural gravels and sands, merging into a poorly developed sub-soil above: contexts (2013) – with (2020) – and (2004). The latter was excavated from above the building in the southwest corner of the main trench, and the others over Structure 1 in the extension. Layer (2013) was very mixed reddish and dark, humic and gravelly silty sand, with small-medium pebbles and cobbles, and a concentration of charcoal directly over the hearth area (Fig. 6.16). The environmental sample produced considerable quantities of wood charcoal including oak, suggesting that the demolition may have included the burning of structural wood. Seven iron nails and other unidentifiable iron fragments were also found in the layer, lending weight to this theory. Roundwood charcoal from the environmental sample produced radiocarbon dates ranges of 72–133 cal AD (at 1σ and 49.5%) and 58–210 cal AD (at 2σ and 91.6%), SUERC-105490. Other finds were a composite metal object (cat. no. 3) and pottery. Just above Structure 1's floor level in (2013) nine sherds including the base of the same flat-rimmed bowl were found (OXID1); this may well have been a product of the pottery industry at Brampton just a few miles to the southeast (AD 100–150/200). The only other pottery was a sherd of Greyware (see below).

As (2013) thinned to the east of the building it merged into layer (2020) – a humic silty sand with well-sorted, small pebbles and occasional clay lenses and charcoal – which poorly developed subsoil had begun to form where the deposit was less influenced by disturbed occupation layers and demolition debris. This was the layer onto and into which Structure 2 was constructed (see below). An area of demolition (2007) spread east of and linked to (2013)/(2020) was discovered below Structure 2; this may also have been at least partly a make-up layer for the construction of the later building, re-using material from the demolition of Structure 1. (2007) was a gritty, gravelly, and charcoal-rich sandy silt with black and red patches, and much evidence for burning. The upper spit was dominated by a spread of mostly burnt small cobbles and pebbles which were probably a foundation layer for Structure 2. One iron bolt or nail was found, as well as a sherd of amphora (BAT AM1) and two sherds of Greyware. As elsewhere in this layer there were also tiny and fragile fragments of burnt bone.

In the southwest corner of the main trench the area of this extensive and varied demolition layer above and north of Structure 1 was excavated as (2004). Like (2013), above the eastern end of the building and (2020), this was a reddish, gravelly and pebbly, humic silty sand, with small lenses of white clay above the internal cobbles. The white clay suggested that there may have been at least areas of clay and small pebble floor within the building. Loose, larger cobbles, similar to those found in the building's wall core, were also found above and protecting the tightly packed and undisturbed cobble floor. Some possible fragments of mortar linked to the larger cobbles disintegrated on touch. The environmental sample produced wood charcoal and seeds of wild plants – vetch, nettle, and small-seeded grass – and heather. The radiocarbon date ranges on two samples of roundwood charcoal were again broadly second century, but with a later emphasis than those from Structure 1 and the Turf Wall: 154–214 cal AD (at 1σ and 54.9%) and 120–238 cal AD (at 2σ and 95.4%), SUERC-105488; and 112–170 cal AD (at 1σ and 42.7%) and 60–215 cal AD (at 2σ and 94.2%), SUERC-105489. Along with burnt bone fragments too small and fragile to collect, this layer, like (2013), contained four iron nails, as well as two iron fittings (cat. nos. 20 and 21), suggesting structural demolition. Other finds were a hobnail (cat. no. 4), possible stone pendant (cat. no. 10) and pottery: six sherds of amphorae (BAT AM1), one sherd of Greyware and three of unsourced sand-tempered ware. This layer was cut by the robber trench [2029] that had removed the structure's northern wall [2025] in this area. The robbing left a clear, stone-free margin of silty sand (2028) 0.6–0.7 m wide and 0.4 m deep running 5.5 m WNW–ESE, cutting into and dividing (2004) along the line of the wall.

The Stone Wall and associated bridging structures

The area covered by Trench 2 is situated on a relatively level knoll where the ground, having sloped towards the gorge from Sandysike Farmhouse in the east, rises slightly and then levels before dropping away to the beck. This knoll has in more recent times been very shaded by trees on the field margins, and the combination of very stony, root-threaded soil and shade in a tight corner has deterred farmers from ploughing the slight platform. There was no evidence for modern plough strikes or the effects of ridge and furrow. As a result, unlike in Trench 3, the basal foundations of Wall structures have survived.

However, only the lower layer of core rubble foundations of the Stone Wall survived *in situ* [2038] (Fig. 6.17). These undisturbed Wall remains ran across the trench, the first 3.5 m eastwards from the west baulk ran near west–east and the remaining 6.5 m angled slightly more south. The surviving foundations were *c.* 1 m wide and no more than 0.2 m deep with no discernible flagstone-like foundation course remaining, as found for the Wall at Turret 56b (Simpson *et al.* 1934). The full depth of the foundations was seen in both north–south slots across the curtain. Most of the core stones (*c.* 60%) were soft local red sandstone cobbles, often sub-square and *c.* 0.2 m. The remaining stones were a harder, lighter more sub-angular sandstone cobbles up to 0.35 m long with occasional more diverse greywackes and other fluvial-glacially deposited materials. The matrix for the stones (between 20–40% of the context depending on location) was reddish brown coarse, slightly silty sand. Although a few lumps of *opus caementicium* had been found in association with the more disturbed rubble core found in Trench 3 (see above), there was no evidence that mortar had been used in Wall construction in Trench 2. While it is possible that fine roots and other disturbance could have eradicated any vulnerable, porous mortar, *opus caementicium* had survived similar if not more hostile conditions in Trench 3.

The Stone Wall layers excavated above foundations [2038] comprised crushed, truncated, and disturbed rubble core (2012) and (2016). The matrix for the stones in both layers was gritty silty sand with occasional paler, yellower patches of degraded sandstone. It is just possible at least some of these paler patches were lime mortar but the highly degraded nature of the lenses meant it was impossible to be certain: they were undoubtedly predominantly sand. Layer (2012) was *c.* 0.1 m deep and excavated from above *in-situ* core in Slot 3 against the western baulk; the stone content varied from local red sandstone river cobbles up to 0.15 m to larger subangular sandstone fragments between 0.1 m–0.3 m. The latter predominated. To the north and south of (2012) almost stone-free bands indicated the robber trenches (see below). One possible damaged sub-triangular facing stone was found in the northern robber trench, measuring *c.* 0.18 m high, 0.2 m wide and 0.3 m deep. Voids amidst the rubble suggested larger stones – either facing stones or more useful large core cobbles – may have been removed.

Layer (2016) in the central north–south Slot 2 was very similar, with robber trenches [2036] and [2040] to south and north again quite distinct from the disturbed and degraded upper layer of the stone curtain core. Within the matrix for the rubble, three sherds of pottery were found, two of Black Burnished Ware (BB1), and one of Greyware (GREY) providing a *terminus post quem* for the context of AD 120 (see Hudak below). One complete possible facing stone was found on the edge of the robber trench just northeast of (2016). This was also sub-triangular and 0.18 m high, 0.35 m wide, and 0.32 m deep.

Bridging tower

The stone foundations [2011] found sealing the Turf Wall remnants (2014; see above) were for a square or rectangular structural feature south of and built against – and most probably onto the top of the stone curtain (see Fig. 6.26). This may have been a bridge tower or a simpler supporting structure, which also provided access to the bridge. The robbing of the structure's facing stone meant there was no possibility that evidence for any ground-level entrances into the building had survived, as at Chesters bridge abutment (Bidwell and Holbrook 1989, 21–24). The foundations were fully investigated in Slot 3, which ran the full length western baulk, and comprised over 80% well-sorted and well-packed rounded sandstone river cobbles between 0.16–0.2 m in diameter. Over 100 were removed in an area just 1.8 m north–south by 0.7 m west–east and 0.2 m deep (Fig. 6.13). The matrix for the cobbles was reddish brown sandy silt; no finds were made. A much more disturbed layer, about 0.1 m deep and above [2011] was interpreted as the upper more disturbed and looser cobbles of the foundations (2006). The matrix was the same but fewer of the carefully selected cobbles survived and most were displaced. No artefacts were found.

Robber trenches associated with the bridging structure

Both [2011] and (2006) were cut into by the robber trench for south-facing stone curtain facing stones [2036], as well as by robber trench [2033], running along the eastern and

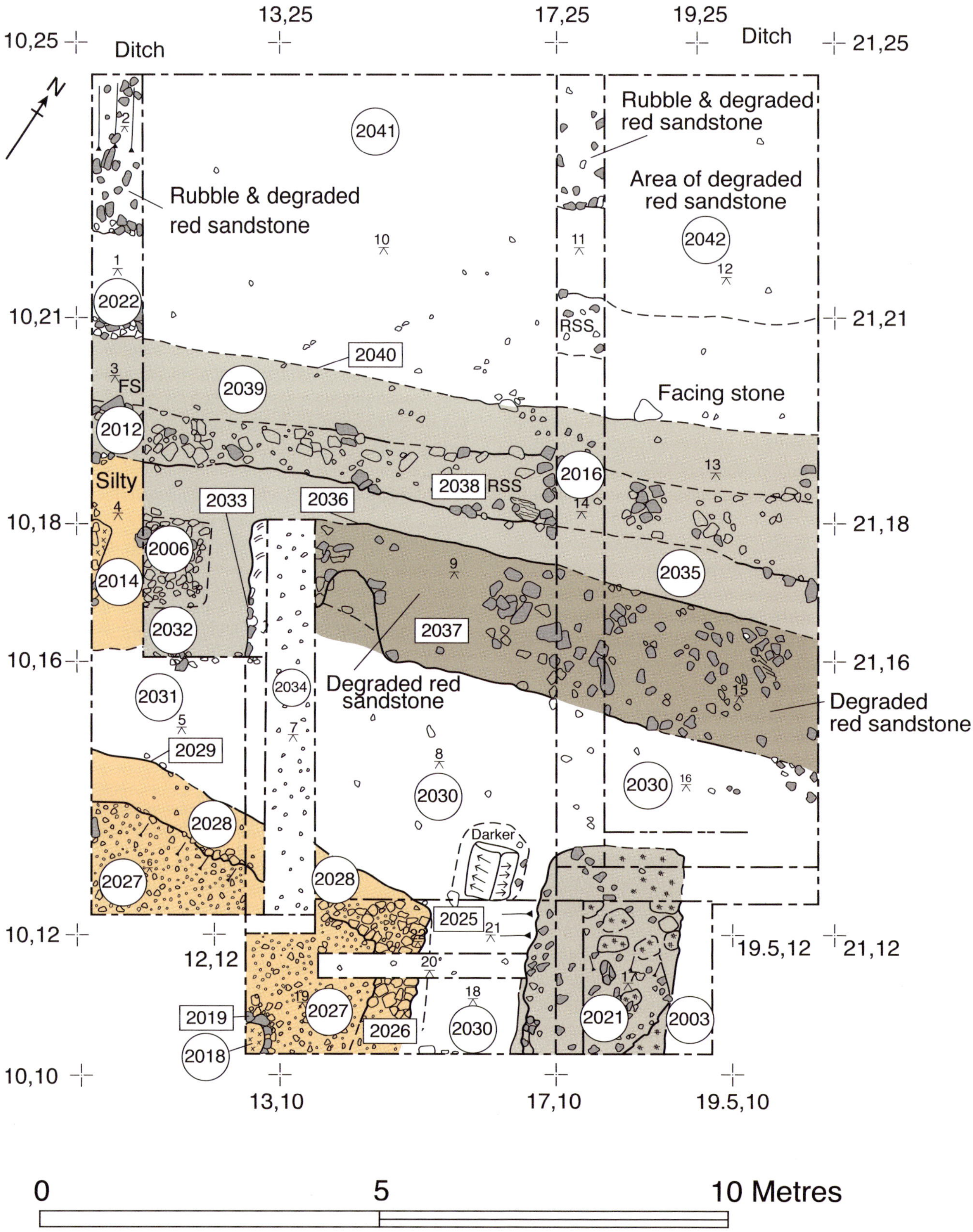

Figure 6.17: Plan of Trench 2, with colours distinguishing distinct phasing associated with particular features.

southern sides of the tower, presumably again targeting facing stones, this time of the tower's walls. This implies the tower was added to the completed stone curtain, possibly immediately, and then later dismantled to access curtain facing stones. The trench for [2033] around the tower was *c.* 0.6 m wide at its spread top and up to 0.4 m deep, U-shaped and with near vertical sides, 2.5 m long north–south on the eastern side, with *c.* 2.3 m west–east revealed on southern side. The tower walls were thus about 0.5 m wide originally. The tower robber trench was filled with (2032): reddish brown coarse, gritty silty sand with very occasional pebbles and small red sandstone cobbles. No artefacts were recovered. The relationship with the robber trench for the southern facing stones of the curtain [2036] was uncertain (see below).

Including the width of the robber trench to the south, the structure ran just over 2 m south from the putative south face of the curtain and was up to 2.3 m wide west–east, including the tower robber trench to the east. However, the foundations clearly continued west into the baulk. As the tower was constructed against the Stone Wall curtain it may have been without facing stones on the northern side but the clarity of the southern robber trench for the retrieval of facing stones in this area suggests the curtain was raised and faced before the tower.

Ramp or steps base

A second bridge-related structure was found immediately south and abutting the curtain. These were the rectangular rubble foundations [2037] for either a ramp or stairs, again, like the tower, built against the stone curtain. The ascent would have been made from east to west (Fig. 6.26). The foundations were fully excavated in Slot 2 and exposed in area; they comprised very crushed and degraded red sandstone sub-square and sub-rectangular cobbles, and occasional paler and harder, rounded sandstone cobbles in a sandy silt matrix. The un-crushed cobbles were up to 0.5 m long. The foundations were *c.* 8m long near east–west as revealed and 2 m wide, and were butting against – and likely constructed after – the curtain had been completed. The remaining foundations were up to 0.15 m deep. Without clear horizontal stratigraphy it was not possible to be completely certain about the chronological relationship between the ramp and the curtain, and the tower-like structure and the ramp. However, the vertical stratigraphy suggested that the ramp may have been a slightly later addition to the Wall and tower arrangement, with spread ramp material stratigraphically above the upper disturbed elements of the tower (2006).

In Slot 2, running north–south through the near centre of the trench, more of the foundations were seen as (2005), where the smaller pebbles and cobbles of the lower foundations as well as the larger sandstone rounded and sub-angular cobbles were excavated. The cut of the southern robber trench [2036] was seen especially clearly in section in this slot, dug into the remains of the ramp or stairs.

Structure 2

Set back from and south of the Wall, and from the same broad phase as the ramp and curtain-joined tower, was a second free-standing building, designated Structure 2 (Figs 6.17 and 6.18). This structure was built into demolition and levelling layer (2007) – see above – which had accumulated over the remains of the earlier building. Structure 2 was situated only about 1.5 m to the east of Structure 1, but the buildings followed different alignments, with Structure 2 running north-northwest to south-southeast at right-angles to the course of the curtain Wall and ramp. The short northern end of sub-rectangular Structure 2 faced the Wall leaving a gap of only about 1.5 m between the building and the southern side of the ramp or stairs. Also unlike Structure 1 this was a timber building. The clearly defined clay and cobble floor was bounded to the east by a north-northeast to south-southwest trending band of clean sandy silt, suggesting a possible wall trench. A similar band may have existed to the west and north but merged with underlying subsoils (2013)–(2003). The clay and rubble foundations for the interior of Structure 2 [2021] delineated an area 2.15 m wide internally by 3 m long near north–south as excavated – the building continued into the southern trench-edge. Adding the width of the wall trenches would indicate a building over 2.5 m wide. The lower floor layer was a slightly silty sand matrix with large white clay lenses and copious charcoal, combined with red sandstone cobbles selected to be between 0.1–0.15 m in length. The upper floor layer was similar with white clay lenses and abundant charcoal; the cobbles however were more disturbed, less well-sorted and less evenly distributed. There were hints of truncated internal post-holes or post-pads, *c.* 0.2 m in diameter and

Figure 6.18: The area of Structure 2, looking west.

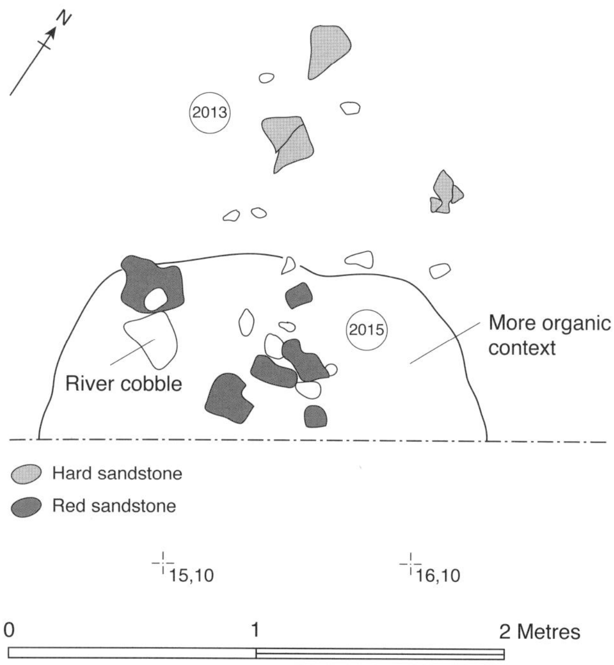

Figure 6.19: Plan of the destruction deposits associated with Structure 2.

packed with red sandstone, in the north centre and middle west of the building, perhaps supporting the roof. No artefacts were found in either of the floor layers.

Above the remains of Structure 2 was a relatively deep layer comprising a demolition layer and levelling layer becoming a poorly developed subsoil (2003). This layer was excavated as (2001) and (2002) over the remnants of the stone curtain, tower and ramp. Layer (2003) in the trench extension over the detached buildings was a fairly humic sandy silt with siltier and gravelly patches and clay lenses, especially over Structure 2. A sherd of Greyware pottery was found and two sherds of unsourced Severn Valley Oxidised ware (SVW OX2), along with a hobnail (cat. no. 6), a structural nail (cat. no.17) and a fragment of worked flint (cat. no. 9). There were obviously fragments of burnt bone in the layer but these disintegrated on excavation.

In the southern extension of the trench two distinct spreads of demolition-related material were also excavated from the truncated surface of levelling layer (2003) (Fig. 6.19). These were probably linked to the dismantling of Structure 2. Running into the centre of the extension's southern baulk, deposit (2015) was excavated in a semi-circle *c.* 1.8 m west–east by *c.* 0.7 m north–south, and at most 0.2 m deep. The deposit was a humic sandy silt with patches of concentrated charcoal and burnt clay, and a heap of cobbles in the centre. These were similar in size and types of stone to the floor of Structure 2, including red sandstone cobbles, occasional burnt river cobbles and angular, harder sandstone cobbles, with some pebbles. The finds included some fragments of burnt bone, possible slag, and a number of iron artefacts: a single hobnail and three hobnails clearly discarded together – perhaps attached to a scrap of boot-sole – (cat. nos. 7 and 8), and four structural nails (cat. nos. 11–14). The pottery comprised four sherds of Greyware, a sherd of unsourced Severn Valley Oxidised ware (SVW OX2) and three sherds of Black Burnished Ware (BB1). An environmental sample taken from one of the charcoal-rich lenses contained a high concentration of wood charcoal and was the only sample to contain evidence for metal-working and slag. This raises the possibility that some metal-working may have been carried out in Structure 2. The charcoal, burnt clay, and structural nails within the deposit also suggest the building may have been burnt down. The radiocarbon date ranges from (2015) were later in emphasis – reaching more into the 3rd century – than from those related to Structure 1 and its demolition at: 157–193 cal AD (1σ and 30.7%), 198–230 cal AD (1σ and 28.0%) and 122–240 cal AD (2σ and 95.4%), SUERC-105576.

The second distinct spread (2009) within the generalised demolition and levelling layer was found 1 m to the northeast of (2015) (Fig. 6.20). This appeared like a ditch-end on the surface but resolved into a sub-oval pit [2010], *c.* 0.4 m deep and *c.* 1.2 m west-southwest to east-northeast by *c.* 1 m wide. Like (2015) the dump of material was humic sandy silt with abundant charcoal but with only occasional clay lenses. There were fewer cobbles but most of these, and the smaller pebbles, were burnt. The lower level of the deposit may have been dug into and merged with the upper disturbed remains of earlier Structure 1. The sides of the pit were rough and collapsed but in the south steep and to the east gently sloping. The finds included the usual fragments of burnt bone that disintegrated on excavation, two sherds of Greyware and one of Severn Valley Oxidised ware (SVW OX2), along with some very fragmentary iron. The environmental sample contained grass seed and wood charcoal. The radiocarbon date ranges were reasonably similar to those from (2015) but with a more decided 3rd-century emphasis: 206–251 cal AD (at 1σ and 56.2%) and 153–255 cal AD (at 2σ and 73.0%), SUERC-105572.

In the main trench the levelling layer and poorly developed subsoil was excavated as (2001) and (2002). (2001) was located over the line of the stone curtain and is described below. (2002) was excavated south of the curtain in the main trench, over the remains of the tower built against the curtain and the ramp. Here the development of a subsoil was clearer in the sections. The reddish brown silty sand contained poorly sorted sub-angular pebbles up to 0.03 m long, but with about a third of the stones being red sandstone cobbles up to 0.4 m. This reflected the range

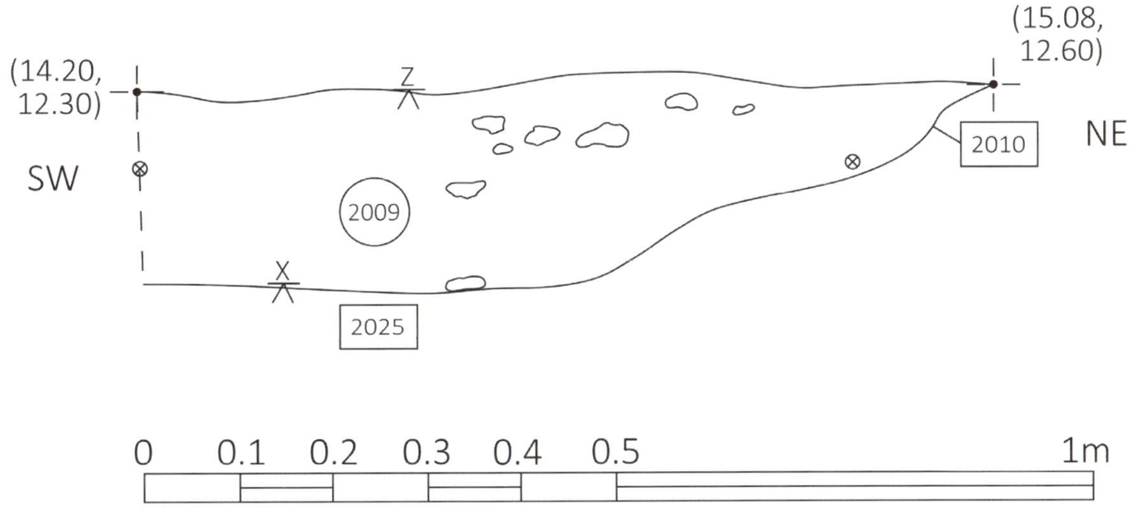

Figure 6.20: Section drawing of sub-oval pit [2010] associated with the demolition of Structure 2.

of stones found in the surviving foundations of the ramp or stairs. No other artefacts were recovered.

The final discovery in the levelling layer was an isolated large stone (Figs 6.17 and 6.21). When this was lifted by the mechanical digger at the end of the excavation it proved to be very similar to the stones used to construct the weir (see above), although less worn having not been subjected to years of weathering by the beck. The stone was 0.79 m deep, 0.66 m wide and 0.27 m high, with deep tooling on its upper surface and a sloped front edge (Fig. 6.21). It had presumably been dropped or discarded during a phase of concerted robbing of bridge structure stone, with some of the stones at least being used to build up the weir. Unfortunately, as discussed above, there is no certain date for that phase of construction of the weir, but it was important to have discovered evidence linking the weir stone with the Roman stonework bridging the beck.

Wall tumble and robbing detritus

Extensive stone tumble was seen north of the curtain and down-slope towards the ditch in both Slot 2 and Slot 3, suggesting some progressive collapse of the Wall as well as concerted dismantling, as in Trench 3 (see above). In Slot 3, against the western baulk and north of robber trench [2040] (Figs 6.13 and 6.17), two bands of red sandstone cobbles were excavated in a matrix of red slightly silty sand (2022). Just north of the robber trench in a band *c.* 0.5 m wide the stones were on average larger, comprising sorted red sandstone cobbles, sub-square ones up to 0.2 m and sub-oval up to 0.3 m. These were a combination of tumble from the Wall to the immediate north and the detritus left from the robbing and dismantling.

Figure 6.21: A large stone associated with a levelling layer, similar in size and shape to those used in the construction of the weir, looking north.

One metre northwards and downslope was a 3 m long spread of rolled tumble and collapse towards the ditch, with a range of less well sorted stones and fewer of the largest sizes. A broadly similar pattern was seen in central north–south Slot 2, although this was not excavated to the depth of Slot 3, and west and east of that slot to the north of the curtain: layers (2041) and (2042). Only smaller rubble core stones and shatter were found beside the northern robber trench [2040], with mostly larger red sandstone core material excavated downslope. No artefacts were found in any of these robbing and rolled collapse tumbles except for a sherd of post-medieval pottery in (2022).

Robber trenches for the Stone Wall curtain

Ascertaining with confidence the level from which the robber trenches alongside the curtain and around the bridging structure/tower had been cut was not possible. The upper layers in Trench 2 had clearly been truncated by agricultural and farm animal activity over the centuries, if not by intensive ploughing, as well as by a degree of soil creep downslope to the north, northwest and southeast. As the robber trenches by the Wall were apparent as soon as top and subsoil had been machined away it seems most likely that they had been cut from a now lost ground surface above layer (2001), which had accumulated over the more disturbed curtain core layers and rubble tumble described above. Disturbed layer (2001) was only 0.1 m deep, and concentrated over the line of the remaining rubble core of the Wall and was yellowish-reddish brown sandy silt with siltier areas around clusters of core material. Some of the sub-angular stones were larger – up to 0.3 m – and sat among sorted cobbles up to 0.15 m long and some river cobbles. Only two sherds of pottery were recovered, one of Greyware and one of post-medieval pottery, along with one iron nail. The robber trenches were also cut from a surface above layer (2002), which covered the remains of the ramp (see below).

The robber trenches themselves, [2036] for the south-facing stones and [2040] for the north-facing, were filled with (2035) and (2039) respectively. Both fills were reddish brown gritty silty sands containing occasional pebbles and very occasional smaller red sandstone Wall core stones. Neither fills produced any finds. The edges of southern robber trench [2036] were often diffuse but were on the whole much clearer than robber trench [2040] to the north. The course of both trenches was indicated most clearly by the contrast in stone content with surrounding layers. The cut north of the Wall was clearest in centre of the trench, but the edges were mostly quite difficult to discern in plan. For both trenches, however, cuts were quite obvious in section (Fig. 6.13). Where the cuts were clearest the trenches were *c.* 0.7 m wide, and up to 1 m wide where they were more diffuse. The Stone Wall therefore *c.* 2.3–2.4 m wide with foundations apparently up to *c.* 0.4 m deep. However, the foundations were probably shallower before the disturbance caused by the dismantling. This confirms the Wall here was of Intermediate Wall construction.

Subsoil and clean-up layer

The uppermost layer over the remains of the Cam Beck bridging point was the subsoil and clean-up layer (2000), removed across the main trench after the machine stripping of 0.2 m in depth of the rough turf and field topsoil. This gritty, sandy silt was between 0.2–0.3 m deep and contained scattered poorly sorted pebbles, and rounded and subangular cobbles up to 0.2 m in length, with a few larger red sandstone cobbles concentrated over the Wall-line. Five modern pottery sherds were found under the turf and Roman pottery at the interface with the contexts below. These latter were found mainly with the discarded bridging structure stone and in the southwest corner of the main trench, above the remains of Structure 1, and comprised one sherd of Black Burnished Ware, 27 of Greyware and one of an unsourced fine reduced ware. Other finds were a very corroded iron nail (cat. no. 16), a whetstone (cat. no. 1), and a copper alloy mount (cat. no. 2), all of which were most probably Roman.

Field-walking west of the beck

Immediately west of the Cam Beck, the northern side of a sub-triangular modern field corresponded to the line of the Wall (Fig. 6.22). The northern boundary was historically determined by the Wall ditch, and subsequently delineated by drystone fieldwall containing re-used Roman fabric, though positioned on the berm between the curtain and the ditch; the Wall ditch has broadened over centuries through use as a farm track. The southern boundary of the field is defined topographically, as a short steep slope to the south, with the ground south of the field acting as marshy pasture. Following annual ploughing and seeding for grass, a day was spent field-walking and metal-detecting the field in a grid pattern. No certain Roman building material or artefacts were found, and the vast majority of objects recovered were ceramics of mid-19th century or more recent date. Some large lumps of mortar were recovered, but these were inconclusive in terms of dating and most likely of modern date.

The most significant evidence was structural in nature, but offers only tentative evidence. The northeast corner of the field, on the line of the Wall, had a number of large sandstone slabs and stones visible in the ploughsoil. There was not enough of the stone visible to support a detailed

Figure 6.22: An aerial photograph of the ploughed field that the Wall runs through to the west of the beck.

plan, but their size tentatively suggests surviving Roman fabric near the west bank of the beck. Furthermore, looking eastward from this point, a clear colour distinction in soils was visible. The soils overlying the line of the Wall and to its north up to the fieldwall were greyer in appearance, with the line of the Wall further marked by a very dispersed linear arrangement of stones 0.10–0.30 m in length. South of the line of the Wall, the soil was more consistently red.

Another surface feature was also observed. Two discrete areas of irregular shape, each *c.* 5–10 m in diameter, were identified by a high incidence and concentration of lighter, buff-coloured sandstones and river cobbles. The stones did not present any clear structural arrangement; however, the concentration relative to the surrounding soil was distinct. Furthermore, the two concentrations were positioned relative to the southern boundary of the field. This may offer tentative evidence of a paved road leading west-southwest from the putative west end of the bridge over the Cam Beck.

Roman and post-Roman pottery

Eniko Hudak

The Roman pottery was hand examined and where deemed necessary fresh breaks were created to be studied under hand lens (10× magnification). The pottery was recorded by context and by fabric, and fully quantified and catalogued using the standard measures of sherd count, weight, and Estimated Vessel Equivalents (EVEs), in accordance with the latest guidelines for archaeological ceramics (PCRG, SGRP, MPRG 2016). A 'context considered date' was determined for each context (except the topsoil layers) containing Roman pottery. This date represents a cross-section of the fabric and form dates present in the given context providing a *terminus post quem* (TPQ) for deposition but is not dependant on its stratigraphic relationships.

The data was recorded into a relational database with the help of fabric and form codes of the National Roman Fabric Reference Collection (Tomber and Dore 1998), the

Table 6.1: Quantification of the Roman ceramic assemblage per fabric by sherd count, weight (g), and EVEs.

Fabric code	*Fabric expansion*	*Sherd count*	*Weight (g)*	*EVEs*
BAT AM 1	Baetican (early) amphorae	7	423	
BB1	Dorset Black-burnished Ware 1	6	19	
FINE	Unsourced Fine Sand-tempered ware	1	4	
GREY	Unsourced Reduced (grey) Sand-tempered ware	40	208	0.64
OXID	Unsourced Oxidised Sand-tempered ware	3	8	
OXID1	Unsourced Oxidised Sand-tempered ware, micaceous	9	214	0.50
SVW OX 2	Severn Valley Oxidised ware 2 (unsourced)	4	143	
Total		70	1019	1.14

Hadrian's Wall Ceramic database of TWM Archaeology (Tyne & Wear Museums 2008–2009), and a set of custom four-letter codes describing the main characteristics of the fabrics. Forms were recorded with the help of a range of relevant local typologies and corpora including the Hadrian's Wall Ceramic Database, Gillam's Types of Roman Coarse Pottery Vessels in Northern Britain etc. Post-Roman ceramics were recorded by sherd count and weight to establish a basic quantitative and context distribution assessment.

Roman pottery: overall assemblage condition, composition, and dating

A small assemblage of 70 sherds weighing 1.019 kg and representing 1.15 EVEs was recovered from the excavations. The condition of the pottery is moderate. Most fragments are abraded and only a few appear to be freshly broken. Sherd size ranges from 1–152 g, and while no complete vessels are present, two fragmented near-complete vessels were identified. Mean sherd weight is 14.6 g indicating a degree of redeposition had taken place.

Signs of use-wear or post-firing modifications are limited with only one vessel showing external sooting/ burning, although there is a complete base with internal organic residue, which would benefit from further analysis. No graffiti, post-firing holes, or reshaping of sherds were noted.

A limited range of Romano-British and imported Continental fabrics are present in the assemblage spanning the entire Roman period in date (Table 6.1). Unfortunately, the assemblage is too small for detailed compositional and functional analysis, thus a list of fabrics and forms present is provided.

Romano-British fabrics in the assemblage include unsourced sand-tempered wares (GREY, OXID, OXID1, FINE), most likely of fairly local origin, Dorset Black-Burnished Ware 1 (BB1), and Severn Valley Ware and similar fabrics (SVW OX 2). Continental imports are restricted to Baetican Dressel 20 olive oil amphora fragments (BAT AM 1). There are no Samian wares or mortaria in the assemblage.

Unsourced sand-tempered reduced wares (GREY) are the most frequently recorded fabric by sherd count, whereas Baetican amphora sherds account for most of the site assemblage by weight. Diagnostic sherds in GREY represent a minimum of three different vessels: rims of two necked figure-7 rim jars and rim, body, and base sherds of a necked carinated jar. The carinated jar is of interest as it is an early form, dated to between AD 50–150 to its broadest extent, and most likely to be of early 2nd century date here.

The only other fabric present in considerable quantities is Severn Valley Ware (SVW OX 2) and fragments of a single vessel in an oxidised, micaceous, sand-tempered fabric, which may be a product of the Brampton potteries (OXID1, Paul Bidwell, pers. comm.). SVW OX 2 is represented by body and base sherds, including the complete base with the organic residue. Fragments in the OXID1 fabric all belong to the same vessel, a flat-rimmed bowl very similar to Gillam 217 although the carination does not survive (Gillam 1970, fig. 23), which is dated to the early 2nd century AD. Similar bowls in oxidised sand-tempered wares were found in Period 1 contexts at Birdoswald (pre-Stone Fort, Hird 1997, 239 and fig. 155/22), and from the Period 1/2 *praetentura* contexts at Wallsend fort (Rushworth and Croom 2016, fig. 22.12/22). Vaguely similar reeded-rim carinated bowls in Fabric 16 at Old Penrith, with a possible source at Scalesceugh, are dated to around AD 90–130 (Austen 1991, 137). All other fabrics, OXID, FINE, and BB1, are represented by small numbers of body sherds only, and only the latter could be more precisely dated, to after AD 120.

Pottery distribution

Roman pottery was recovered from nine individually numbered contexts including the topsoil, several layers, demolition deposits, and the remains of the curtain Wall. Individual context assemblages are all small comprising less than 30 fragments each, in fact apart

Table 6.2: Distribution of Roman ceramics per context by sherd count, weight, and EVEs.

Context	Sherd count	Weight (g)	EVEs	Context Considered Date
2000	29	129	31	–
2001	1	6		Intrusive PMED?
2003	3	129		AD 40–400+
2004	10	295		AD 50–200
2007	3	171	11	AD 50–200
2009	3	10		AD 40–400+
2013	10	215	50	AD 100–150/200
2015	8	51	13	AD 120–400+
2016	3	13	9	AD 120–400+
Total	70	1019	114	

from the topsoil, only two contexts contained more than 10 fragments (Table 6.2), which shows the dispersed and redeposited nature of the assemblage. The largest and the most well-dated context assemblages are described in detail below.

Layer (2004) in the southwest corner of the main trench produced 10 sherds of Roman pottery weighing 295 g. It consists of Dressel 20 amphora fragments in the earlier Baetican fabric (BAT AM 1, mid-1st–late 2nd centuries AD), and base sherds in unsourced reduced and oxidised sand tempered wares.

Layer (2013) yielded a total of 10 sherds weighing 215 g. All fragments but one (GREY body sherd) belong to the same OXID1 flat-rimmed bowl with 50% of its rim circumference present, which may be from the Severn Valley (see above). This bowl type is dated to the early 2nd century AD (Gillam 1970, fig. 23/217 and see above).

Although both layer (2015) and remains of the curtain Wall (2016) produced meagre amounts of pottery (Table 6.2), they both included fragments of BB1. These suggest a TPQ of AD 120 for these features.

The post-Roman pottery

Only seven fragments of post-medieval/modern pottery weighing 43 g were recovered from the excavations (Table 6.3). Most sherds were recovered from the topsoil, but one fragment each was found in layers (2001) and (2022), which are either intrusive or related to the robbing or demolition activities associated with these features.

Conclusions

Overall, a small Roman pottery assemblage was recovered during the excavations including a limited range of material, most likely representing a subset of a regular occupation range. Although most of the fragments could only be broadly dated to the Roman period, diagnostic sherds and fabrics could be dated to the early–mid-2nd century AD. Whilst the small size and dispersed and disturbed nature of the assemblage limit the discussion beyond providing dating and allows restricted comparison with other assemblages in the area (see above), the presence of early 2nd-century AD forms is of intrinsic interest.

Table 6.3: Distribution and quantification of the post-Roman pottery.

Context	Fabric	Sherd count	Weight
2000	PMED	5	41
2001	PMED	1	1
2022	PMED	1	1
Total		7	43

Artefacts

Rob Collins

Across the two seasons of fieldwork at Cam Beck a small amount of material culture was recovered. This is almost certainly reflective of the structures identified through excavation and linked to their usage as a Roman watch post and/or bridge crossing of the Cam Beck. A total of 25 individual objects were recorded and catalogued (below), with a further 11 entries consisting of a range of nails and other related structural objects, quantified by number of fragments and weight. These objects were recovered through excavation, metal detecting of the spoil heap, and a small number during environmental sample processing. Some nails were recorded individually, on the basis of their state of preservation. Objects of certain modern date, *i.e.* post-Second World War, were not recorded.

Overall, the assemblage is very strongly dominated by nails and structural ironwork. Given the shallow stratigraphy, this points to demolition of a substantial structure or structures, which may also have included burning. Excavation of the Wall curtain does not typically produce any Roman assemblage (see the Walltown excavations in Chapter 5), and this again reinforces the interpretation that more is happening at Cam Beck than a typical curtain construction.

There is no closely datable artefact. It should also be noted that the ironwork is presumed to be Roman, largely on the basis of contextual analysis, though strictly speaking there is very little ironwork that is diagnostically Roman. Therefore, some ironwork in the highest contexts and layers could be of more recent date (*c.* 1800–1950), or a mix of Roman and modern materials. Cast iron was identified and removed from the assemblage for analysis as best as could be identified through varying levels of corrosion and preservation.

Table 6.4: Artefacts recovered during the Cam Beck excavations, summarised by context.

Context	*No. of nails*	*No. of artefacts*	*Objects of interest [cat. No.]*
2000		3	Whetstone [1], cu alloy mount [2]
2003	1	4	Flint flake [9], hobnails [6]
2004	4	4	Possible stone pendant [10], hobnail [4]
2013	7	1	Unidentified composite object [3]
2015	5	6	2 hobnails [7, 8], otherwise all nails
2018		2	Hobnail [5], clamp [19]

In the following analysis, context of discovery is placed in parentheses ( ), and the number provided is the catalogue number in brackets [ ] found here.

Analysis by trench and context

All artefacts recorded, with one exception, were from Trench 2.

Trench 1 had a large cast iron stake of 19th- or 20th-century date, found above a positioned layer of stones, disturbed from its original position by root action. Similar stakes are visible within the river weir, and are part of a later 19th- or early 20th-century refurbishment of the weir.

Contextual analysis is summarised in Table 6.4, noting any contexts with more than three recorded artefacts, and any key artefacts. The presence of artefacts in relevant contexts is also noted in the stratigraphic narrative above. Significantly, all the contexts listed in the table below are of Roman date, independently confirmed via radiocarbon dating, with the exception of (2003).

Discussion by category of material

The vast majority of recorded finds are nails and other structural fittings. This largely points to substantial building in timber, which could be related to the various structures on site. Another possibility is that at least some of these nails are from disturbed contexts relating to the construction and subsequent destruction of the Turf Wall. Also, the presence of a few larger pieces of corroded ironwork, one of which could be a clamp [19] to tie stones together also suggests some of these structures were larger. This supports the hypothesis of some sort of bridging system linked to this location.

In addition to the comments above, it is worth noting there are three objects of further interest.

Recorded as a single object due to the effects of corrosion, a series of three complete hobnails [8] were lost *in situ* presumably with the fragment of boot/sandal sole that they were attached to. The arrangement highlights how the objects were arranged on the sole, and the corrosion also preserves the void of the leather lost with the hobnails, now decayed and absent. From the same context (2015) is a probable hobnail head [7] which is flatter and approximately twice the diameter of the other three, perhaps a more decorative hobnail. Regardless, this points to the deposition (whether primary, secondary, or tertiary) of a substantial portion or complete item of footwear.

A small stone [10], shaped very much like a ground-stone axehead of Neolithic date, but in miniature, was found in (2004). It is possible that this was a miniature axehead pendant, suspended with organic material. However, there is no trace of the stone being worked or for any suspension, or of having any relationship with human activity. The object was selected in the excavation on the basis of its striking shape, which was distinct from the local stones and pebbles that naturally occur in the soils at the site. It is perhaps interesting that these objects are mostly from the layers relating to building destruction.

Three fragments of an unidentified object [3] from (2013) are intriguing. All three fragments relate to the same object, though they do not all fit neatly together. The section of the largest fragment reveals the outline of something in iron, surrounded by a mixed matrix of iron corrosion, lead, and copper-alloy. Based on the very fragmentary nature, it has not been possible to identify the object.

Catalogue

Individual objects are recorded here in this catalogue, with the catalogue numbers referred to in the primary text/reporting of the site. Measurements are given in millimetres (mm) and grams (g). The category 'Date' refers to the dating associated with the object form or typology, where present, and not to the date of the context. An asterisk * after the object indicates illustration in Figure 6.23.

1. Whetstone*
   Context: CB21.2000
   Date: 43–410 (Roman)
   Length: 71
   Width: 20
   Thickness: 19
   Weight: 64
   Object category: tool
   Material(s): stone
   Description: A water-worn sub-rectangular cobble, with multiple smoothed faces from sharpening metal objects, with one particularly smoothed face.

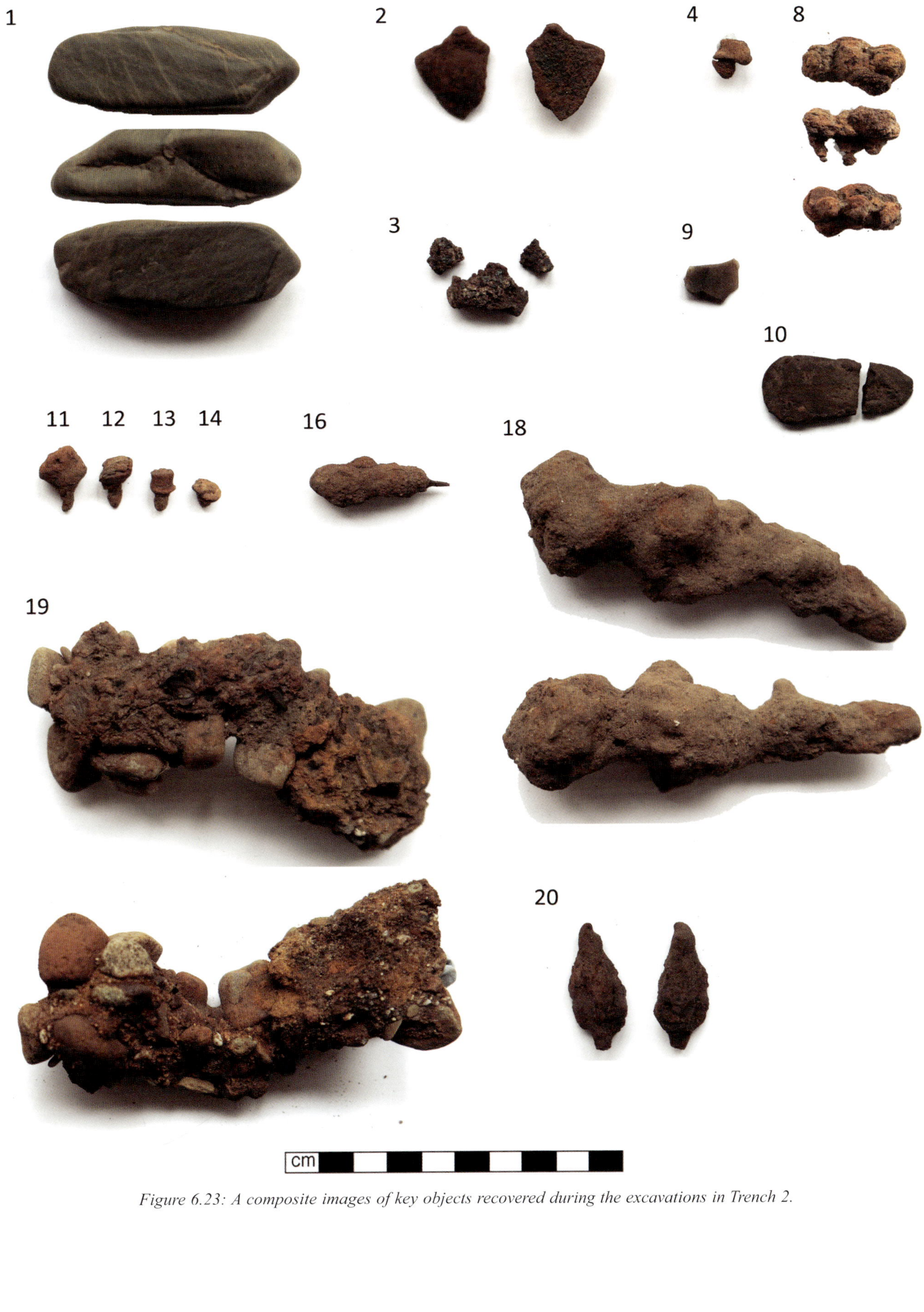

Figure 6.23: A composite images of key objects recovered during the excavations in Trench 2.

2. Mount*
Context: CB21.2000
Date: 43–410 (Roman)
Length: 30
Width: 23
Thickness: 10
Weight: 7
Object category: fitting
Material(s): cu alloy
Description: A corroded fragment of a mount, sub-triangular in plan with irregular, abraded edges. A raised oval with an incised central line is visible in typical Roman 'coffee bean' shape. The upper face bears the appearance of iron corrosion, but the flat underside has a scaly green patina.
Note: This object was found via metal detecting in the spoil from the indicated context.

3. Unidentified object*
Context: CB21.2013
Date: 43–410 (Roman)
Length: n/a
Width: n/a
Thickness: n/a
Weight: 6
Object category: uncertain
Material(s): cu alloy, lead, iron
Description: Three fragments of an unidentified compound object, the core of which is iron and possibly an open box or cylinder shape, surrounded by corroded lead and copper alloy.

4. Hobnail*
Context: CB21.2004
Date: 43–410 (Roman)
Length: 13
Width: n/a
Thickness: 7
Weight: 0.5
Object category: militaria
Material(s): iron
Description: A wrought iron hobnail.

5. Hobnail
Context: CB21.2018
Date: 43–410 (Roman)
Length: 12
Width: 7
Thickness: 3
Weight: 2
Object category: militaria
Material(s): iron
Description: A corroded wrought-iron hobnail adhering to a larger globule of corrosion, also containing charcoal.

6. Hobnail
Context: CB21.2003
Date: 43–410
Length: n/a
Width: n/a
Thickness: n/a
Weight: 1
Object category: miltaria
Material(s): iron
Description: The corroded head of a wrought-iron hobnail, in three fragments.

7. Hobnail
Context: CB21.2015
Date: 43–410 (Roman)
Length: 16
Width: 13
Thickness: 7
Weight: 2
Object category: militaria
Material(s): iron
Description: The corroded head of a large, wrought-iron hobnail retaining the base of the shaft.

8. Hobnail*
Context: CB21.2015
Date: 43–410 (Roman)
Length: 30
Width: 13
Thickness: 19
Weight: 4
Object category: militaria
Material(s): iron
Description: A line of three corroded hobnails, complete, retaining their original position relative to each other through fusion of corrosion, indicating that these were part of a linear arrangement on the sole of the sandal or boot.

9. Flake*
Context: CB21.2003
Date: uncertain
Length: 12
Width: 14
Thickness: 4
Weight: 1
Object category: uncertain
Material(s): flint
Description: A flake of flint that appears to be the result of shatter rather than directly knapped, in that there is no bulb of percussion. This does not preclude it as waste from human activity.

10. Pendant (possible)*
Context: CB21.2004

Date: 43–410 (Roman)
Length: 45
Width: 20
Thickness: 4
Weight: 3
Object category: dress accessory
Material(s): stone
Description: An unworked, water-worn stone that bears the shape of a miniature groundstone axehead. There is no visible evidence of working on the stone, though the stone bears evidence of flaking along its natural bedding. Its use as a pendant is possible and unproven. The stone has fragmented into two halves.

11. Nail*
Context: CB21.2015
Date: 43–410 (Roman)
Length: 20
Width: 15
Thickness: n/a
Weight: 2
Object category: structural
Material(s): iron
Description: The corroded head and upper shaft of a wrought-iron nail.
Note: Found in a flot sample.

12. Nail*
Context: CB21.2015
Date: 43–410 (Roman)
Length: 15
Width: 13
Thickness: n/a
Weight: 1
Object category: structural
Material(s): iron
Description: The corroded head and upper shaft of a wrought-iron nail.
Note: Found in a flot sample.

13. Nail*
Context: CB21.2015
Date: 43–410 (Roman)
Length: 12
Width: 7
Thickness: n/a
Weight: 1
Object category: structural
Material(s): iron
Description: The corroded shaft of a wrought-iron nail, bearing a small collar.
Note: Found in a flot sample.

14. Nail*
Context: CB21.2015
Date: 43–410 (Roman)
Length: 8
Width: 9
Thickness: n/a
Weight: 0.5
Object category: structural
Material(s): iron
Description: The corroded head and upper shaft of a wrought-iron nail.
Note: Found in a flot sample.

15. Nail
Context: CB21.2006
Date: 43–410 (Roman)
Length: 9
Width: 13
Thickness: 7
Weight: 1
Object category: structural
Material(s): iron
Description: The corroded head of a wrought-iron nail found adhering to an irregular burnt cobble.

16. Nail*
Context: CB21.2000
Date: 43–410 (Roman)
Length: 43
Width: 15
Thickness: n/a
Weight: 6
Object category: structural
Material(s): iron
Description: The corroded shaft of a wrought-iron nail, with the pointed end visible and not surrounded by a matrix of corrosion.
Note: Found in the spoil heap with a metal detector.

17. Nail
Context: CB21.2003
Date: 43–410 (Roman)
Length: 57
Width: 18
Thickness: 10
Weight: 12
Object category: structural
Material(s): iron
Description: A large, corroded wrought-iron nail, with the lower shaft slightly bent.

18. Bolt or spike*
Context: CB21.2018
Date: 43–410 (Roman)
Length: 117
Width: 35
Thickness: 24
Weight: 118
Object category: structural

Material(s): iron
Description: A large, corroded bolt or spike, the general shape of which can be seen through corrosion, including a substantial head.

19. Clamp or bracket*
Context: CB21.2018
Date: 43–410 (Roman)
Length: 122
Width: 42
Thickness: 25
Weight: 160
Object category: structural
Material(s): iron
Description: A corroded mass agglomeration, including numerous pebbles arranged in a rough L-shape around an iron object, suspected to be a clamp or bracket used for structural purposes.
Comparanda & reference: Bidwell and Holbrook 1989, 128, fig. 90.

20. Fitting*
Context: CB21.2004
Date: 43–410 (Roman)
Length: 38
Width: 18
Thickness: 14
Weight: 7
Object category: structural (possibly)
Material(s): iron
Description: A corroded length of nail or rod, with other unidentifiable iron fittings corroded against it.

21. Fitting
Context: CB21.2004
Date: 43–410 (Roman)
Length: 44
Width: n/a
Thickness: n/a
Weight: 609
Object category: structural (possibly)
Material(s): iron
Description: A corroded globule of iron, in which a small tubular length of iron is visible in section on one face of the globule, which is firmly attached to a small, irregular stone slab, roughly pentagonal in shape.

22. Unidentified
Context: CB21.2003
Date: 20th century (Modern, probably)
Length: 56
Width: 42
Thickness: 7
Weight: 20
Object category: agricultural
Material(s): iron
Description: A corroded fragment of iron 'plate'-style fitting, sub-trapezoidal in plan. The underside is less corroded and bears evidence of fitting to another object, with corroded rivets in place. The fragment is most probably machine made and therefore modern.

23. Stake (Fig. 6.24)
Context: CB19.1000
Date: 19th–20th century (Modern)
Length: 482
Width: 40
Thickness: 28
Weight: 1675
Object category: structural
Material(s): iron
Description: A large cast-iron stake of square section, with some surface corrosion along all faces and bearing a sub-square head.

24. Nails (highly fragmentary)
Context: CB21.2003 (×1 fragment)
Weight: 3
Context: CB21.2004 (×3 fragments)
Weight: 12
Context: CB21.2004 (×1 fragment)
Weight: 10
Context: CB21.2007 (×1 fragment)
Weight: 28 (possible bolt)
Date: 43–410 (Roman)
Object category: structural
Material(s): iron

Figure 6.24: A cast-iron stake found associated with the stones projecting out of the east bank of the gorge, in Trench 1.

25. Quartz pebbles
    Context: CB21.2009 (×4)
    Weight: 17
    Context: CB21.2009 (×2)
    Weight: 5
    Context: CB21.2013 (×1)
    Weight: 3
    Context: CB21.2013 (×2)
    Weight: 12
    Context: CB21.2013 (×4)
    Weight: 27
    Context: CB21.2015 (×2)
    Weight: 23
    Context: CB21.2015 (×3)
    Weight: 33
    Material(s): quartz

26. Chestnut shells
    Context: CB21.2022 (×1)
    Weight: 0.1 (fragment)
    Context: CB21.2023 (×2)
    Weight: 17
    Material(s): plant (shell)

The Wall at Cam Beck

As far as can be determined from the fieldwork conducted in 2019 and 2021, there is no evidence for direct pre-Roman activity on the line of the Wall at Cam Beck. Excavations, however, have revealed a sequence confirming the presence of the Turf Wall and an associated structure on the east bank of the Cam Beck, and its subsequent replacement by the Stone Wall. Furthermore, the Stone Wall seems to have incorporated a bridge over the beck, as well as another structure immediately south of the curtain. The presence of Structures 1 and 2 were unexpected, and are new to the complex of Hadrian's Wall, while also shedding light on its construction and use.

Evidence for the Turf Wall survived in one location in Trench 2, preserved below a later Roman structure. This consisted of the shape of an individual turf block visually distinguished by a dark band of highly organic silty material. Sampling of this block confirmed the feature as a degraded turf block and also produced sufficient material for radiocarbon date ranges covering the 2nd century at 95.4% but focused on 125–203/4 cal AD at 68.3% (see above). Though these ranges do not provide an exact date of construction of the Turf Wall at Cam Beck, they are clearly within the timeframe of construction, *c.* 120–122. The full width of the Turf Wall could not be identified, but a minimum width of 2.4 m was determined in section.

The presence of a freestanding stone-walled structure to the south of the Turf Wall was unexpected. (Structure 1). Only two walls of the structure were located within the trench, so the full dimensions could not be confirmed. Those lengths that were preserved of the northeast corner measured 0.7–1 m in thickness, and the surviving stone foundations and robber trench indicate a minimum width of *c.* 5.5–6 m. Given the size of the walls of the structure and its position and orientation on the ground and relative to the Turf Wall, it is reasonable to project the structure as square in plan and infer that this was a tower. At present, we can only be certain that the foundations of the tower were built in stone, with the presence of robber trenches indicating that at least a few courses of stonework were present, and possibly more. Environmental samples of burnt debris found remains of charred oak, suggesting that elements of the tower were also built in timber. Free-standing towers south of the curtain are not a feature of the Wall, but the arrangement of a tower positioned closely behind a turf or earth embankment or timber palisade is known from the Upper-German and Raetian *limes*, also constructed under Trajan and Hadrian (Baatz 2000, 42–49). Known as watchtowers (Wachtürme), approximately 900 examples are known from that particular frontier; they are located between 100–1,100 m apart and were built in timber or stone. Stone towers are square with sides 4.8–6 m in length, and 0.7–1 m thick (Kreiger 2015, 38). The Trajanic/Hadrianic towers tend to be built in timber, sometimes on stone foundations, with stone towers a feature of the mid–later 2nd century and after. At Cam Beck, the extent of stone use for Structure 1 is uncertain; stone may only have been used to create a stable foundation, the lowest courses, or even one or more storeys. The limitations of the evidence from Cam Beck make further comparisons difficult, but on the existing evidence a tower remains the most likely interpretation for the structure. The date of the tower was determined by the associated pottery and radiocarbon date ranges almost identical to those from the Turf Wall construction, focused on the early–mid to late 2nd century (see above).

Cam Beck is the first site along the Wall that offers not only an insight into a minor river crossing, but also how this was approached by the Turf Wall. There is absolutely no evidence to indicate whether or not the Turf Wall – say in the form of a timber palisade – was carried across the Cam Beck gorge. The presence of the freestanding tower, however, suggests that the Turf Wall may have stopped on each bank of the Cam Beck. The tower is positioned behind the Turf Wall, but as close as possible to the east bank of the gorge, and it is sited such that the northwestern face is oriented toward the beck and gorge. Furthermore, the presumed height of a tower would elevate any watcher and provide better observation of the gorge floor. This arrangement would not stop or hinder traffic using the beck or gorge to cross the line of the Wall, but it would ensure that it was under observation. This interpretation has been favoured for illustration purposes (Fig. 6.25).

With the demolition of the Turf Wall and its replacement by the Stone Wall this arrangement changed. Part of the demolition process for the tower and perhaps the

Turf Wall included burning, on the basis of spreads of charcoal and burnt materials in the demolition deposits stratigraphically between the tower's construction and the Stone Wall's construction. This may have provided a reasonably rapid way in which to clear away any rotted timber and loosen compressed turf and soil in preparation for rebuilding the Wall in stone. The demolition of Structure 1 and thus by association likely also of the Turf Wall was probably during the mid–later 2nd century (see radiocarbon dates for the destruction layers above Structure 1 above). The exact date of replacement with the stone-built curtain cannot be determined but as the date ranges for the destruction of Structure 2 are broadly later 2nd into earlier 3rd century the dates for construction of the stone curtain are likely to fall in the later 2nd century.

Regardless of dating resolution, there is a clear sequence of activity. First, the curtain was rebuilt in stone to the intermediate gauge. The exact width of the curtain's foundations cannot be determined, due to post-Roman stone robbing, but a reasonable projection of the total width being 2.3–2.4 m based on the width of the rubble core and the robber trenches fits best with the intermediate gauge, rather than the broad or narrow gauges of curtain. The curtain was built to some height, perhaps even full height, before a new feature was added.

A square tower or platform, composed of three faces abutting against the south face of the curtain, was constructed. Probably at least 5 m square, this structure provided an extension to the south face of the curtain at the top of the east bank of the gorge. After this tower or platform was added, the traces of a rectangular structure were added immediately to the east and again abutting the south face of the curtain. Though these structures were heavily robbed like the curtain itself, they are most readily interpreted as inter-related structures. The tower or platform would have provided greater structural stability to the curtain as it approached the Cam Beck gorge, as well as a stronger foundation for building across the gorge. The rectangular structure to its immediate east is best understood as the surviving foundations of a ramp or stairway that provided access at ground level up to the height of the tower/platform, and presumably also the curtain. Combined, these provide strong evidence for some sort of bridging across the Cam Beck gorge. This interpretation is reinforced when the immediate topography is further considered. The west bank of the gorge is *c.* 5 m higher than the east bank; the addition of a tower on the east bank provides a means of elevating the height of a bridge or rampart to the level of the western bank. Furthermore, the arrangement of a tower serving as an

Figure 6.25: A reconstruction of the Turf Wall phase at Cam Beck, with Structure 1 presented as a tower to observe the gorge. Illustration by Matilde Grimaldi.

entry and possibly also a structural reinforcement to bridgeworks is paralleled at both Chesters and Willowford (Bidwell and Holbrook 1989). Similarly, the survival of the bases of piers at Chesters and Willowford bridges suggest spanning arches of *c.* 10 m; at Cam Beck with the width of the gorge *c.* 30 m, a bridge would have required three spanning arches, requiring two piers and a further column/pier integrated with the Wall curtain on the east bank and west bank, perhaps built from the narrow bedrock shelves still visible in the gorge. This interpretation has been illustrated in Figure 6.26, with the possibility of the bridge being anchored at each end by a tower or a bastion/platform.

The primary difference between Cam Beck and Chesters and Willowford is one of scale and phasing. There is no surviving evidence for the subsequent expansion of the bridge at Cam Beck; the proposed bridge at Cam Beck is suitable only for pedestrian traffic, assuming that any bridge was no wider/deeper than the tower built against the south face of the curtain, assuming the full scale and depth of the tower incorporated the curtain as well. In this regard, it seems more likely that access to the east tower from the ground utilised steps, rather than a ramp. It is feasible that subsequent expansion of bridgeworks has been destroyed by post-Roman robbing and other forms of truncation, but it seems unlikely that all archaeological evidence for subsequent Roman phases of bridge expansion would be completely destroyed. Therefore, it seems most likely that the bridge across the Cam Beck remained of a scale suitable for pedestrian traffic, and this makes sense when considered in the wider landscape setting and Roman infrastructure.

The course of the Wall at Cam Beck makes good use of a rare phenomenon in this stretch of the Cam Beck – solid geology on the east and west bank. South of the line of the Wall, the land flattens to either side of the beck and is both marshy and very easily forded. North of the line of the Wall the terrain is more rolling but without adding any significant advantage to position. In contrast, the chosen position has several advantages. For the building of the Wall, in both its turf and stone phases, the land is higher and would keep the Wall construction off structurally unsuitable marshy ground more prone to compression. The Wall-crossing at the gorge also provides more solid geology for a heavy structure like a bridge. For tactical purposes, the gorge creates a funnel or channel for any traffic seeking to cross the line of the Wall – an effective pinch-point that facilitates observation and control of the terrain. Fording the beck is considerably easier only a short distance to the north and south of the line of the Wall.

Figure 6.26: A reconstruction of the Stone Wall phase at Cam Beck, showing stone towers added to the curtain at each end of a bridgework that carries the curtain across the gorge, accessed by stairs behind Structure 2. Illustration by Matilde Grimaldi.

Furthermore, the position of the fort at Castlesteads, detached from the curtain and *c*. 500 m to the south, has implications for expected levels of use of any bridge across the Cam Beck. Wheeled traffic and bulk goods would be expected to be sent to or leave from the fort, and will have made use of the Military Way and a presumed ford further south that met the fort's logistical needs in terms of greater accessibility. In this regard, the fordability of the beck and water-table of the immediately adjacent lands may have been primary factors in the planning of the Roman military landscape in this locale.

Little can be said about Structure 2 with any certainty, except that it is an exception as a Wall structure. No other locations are known to have detached timber buildings associated with the stone curtain that are not otherwise part of a fort and adjacent settlement. This most likely demonstrates the rather narrow and curtain-bound focus of previous mural excavations rather than any exceptionalism of Cam Beck. The stratigraphy and dating, however, is undeniable, and Structure 2 appears to be linked with the building of the Stone Wall and/or the bridge works. It is uncertain how long it stood, but broadly from the later 2nd–early–mid-3rd century (see radiocarbon dates above), and it may also have been destroyed by fire.

The post-Roman history of the site is archaeologically defined by episodes of collapse and robbing. Though the exact locations are uncertain, the Wall was robbed of material for the construction of Lanercost priory in the later 12th and early 13th century, as the manor of Walton was part of the priory's holdings. It is uncertain when the first weir was constructed, though one had already been built by 1741, when repairs to the weir recovered a Roman altar (RIB 1983). The only other specific date for an episode of robbing or destruction is the demolition of the curtain in 1790 (Carlisle 1794). Subsequent changes in the manor grounds and surrounding farms and fields added further episodes of robbing and/or destruction, though these are not dated.

Though the dating is often imprecise, the motivation for robbing is clear. The Wall provided readily accessible and re-usable stone for building, in a location with rather variable outcrops of rock. Re-used Roman stone is readily visible in Walton church, as well as any number of local farms and cottages, especially those pre-dating the mid-19th century. This, however, also highlights an interesting quality of the local red sandstone. The re-used Roman fabric appears as solid today as it must have seemed when freshly quarried and shaped, but it is also a stone that is prone to weakening when thoroughly exposed to wet conditions, and high levels of pressure or compression. As described in 1934 and encountered during recent excavations, the sandstone is easily degraded and takes on a claylike quality under wet conditions or breaks down into sandy lenses or lumps of very hard compressed soil, both of which become challenging to detect in the natural red topsoils of the locality. Careful excavation and recording surmounted these challenges, but they are factors that should be considered in future excavations.

7

Corbridge: survey and excavation

The Roman town of Corbridge lies on the north bank of the River Tyne, just west of the modern village of Corbridge and 4 km south of Hadrian's Wall (Fig. 7.1). Even before the Wall was built, Corbridge was a strategically important military location, and later in the Roman period developed into a significant town and military base. Roman activity began at Corbridge in the early AD 80s, with the building of the first in a sequence of four forts. By the later 2nd century, with the construction of Hadrian's Wall and its recommission after the Antonine occupation of lower Scotland, Corbridge's military focus had shifted to a small legionary base and supply depot, surrounded and surpassed by a rapidly expanded and extensive town.

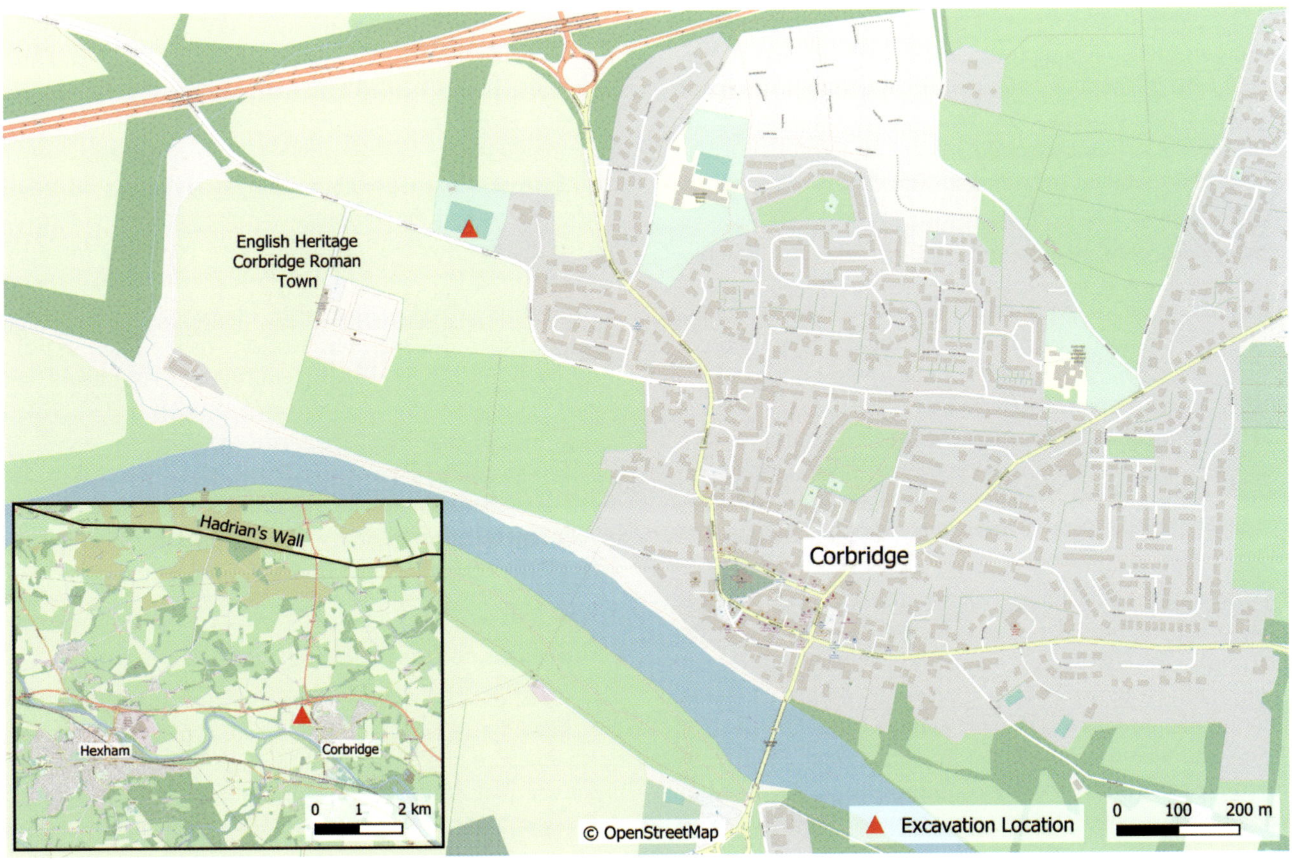

Figure 7.1: Location of the excavation site relative to English Heritage site of Corbridge Roman Town and the modern village.

Corbridge's location underpinned its growth: sitting on the north bank of the river at a bridgeable point and straddling the junction of two major Roman roads. North–south Dere Street linked the legionary fortress and later provincial capital at York to the Antonine Wall; running east–west, the Stanegate connected its eastern terminus at Corbridge to the western terminus at Carlisle. Like Corbridge, Carlisle's origins were as an army fort, and the Stanegate linked a series of forts and fortlets from the later Flavian to Hadrianic periods, *c.* AD 80–120. This key strategic position sustained the early forts, and then the town behind the Wall, through the fluctuating fortunes that followed changes in imperial policy, troop withdrawals to deal with continental wars, and local uprisings and attacks. On current evidence, the town reached its greatest extent and probably also its largest population in the 3rd century. By the mid-3rd century, the town of Carlisle had been granted *civitas* status for the Carvetii. There is no evidence that Corbridge was made a *civitas* but it remains a possibility. By the 4th century the Roman town had shrunk from its 3rd-century peak, probably to within defensive walls. The bridge across the Tyne collapsed at an uncertain date, but occupation on some scale continued in the town until the 5th or 6th centuries. After that the main focus of the settlement shifted east to the historic core of the modern village of Corbridge, with St Andrew's church known from at least the 8th century and probably the later 7th century.

The excavated remains of the Roman town displayed at the English Heritage site of Corbridge feature the urban core of the late 2nd to early 3rd century town and legionary compounds. The Stanegate runs through the town, dividing the consolidated archaeology. The urban centre is dominated by a massive courtyard building and huge granaries north of the Stanegate, and two military compounds south of the road, later merged into a single compound. A water supply links the two sites, running in a channel from the north into a fountain, and then routed under the Stanegate to tanks supplying the compounds.

However, the full extent of the town and its cemeteries remain concealed below surrounding fields. Early 20th-century excavations uncovered roads and strip buildings north of the town centre and up to Corchester Lane, roughly along whose route the later town defences were discovered (Birley 1959; Bishop 1994; Bishop and Dore 1988). Extensive geophysical survey undertaken by the Corbridge Roman Station and Environs Project (CRSEP) directed by Ian Haynes and Alex Turner (2017–2019) had already demonstrated that, before any later encircling defences, Corbridge extended north beyond the modern Corchester Lane, west across the Cor Burn, and also east under the modern village (Fig. 7.2). Fields further to the west and northeast also appeared to contain cremation cemeteries, as well as the mausoleum at Shorden Brae, west of the Cor Burn and north of the Stanegate.

As the largest town in northeastern *Britannia* and indeed the northernmost town in the entire Roman Empire, Corbridge is a significant site in understanding processes and practices of Roman urbanism at both the regional and international scale. Indeed, it was almost certainly fundamental to the operation and occupation of Hadrian's Wall, along with the town at Carlisle. However, there is much that is poorly understood about Roman Corbridge and WallCAP had the opportunity to address some of these research questions in a discrete package of fieldwork focused on the playing field west of Corchester Towers and separated from the English Heritage site by the modern road. Most of the excavations at Corbridge were undertaken in the early 20th century, and the contemporary archives do not record at the level of detail considered best practice by today's standards, complicated by the stratigraphic complexity of the site. This has left questions around dating and inter-relationships between structures and strata. Site phasing, therefore, is not as confidently understood in detail as it is for some other sites in the Wall corridor. Related to this, and the post-Roman history of the site, the final phases of occupation are poorly dated, and have been subject to progressive truncation over much of the town's area due to arable agriculture. Also, the outer zones have received far less archaeological attention than the centre of the Roman town.

WallCAP repeated geophysical survey over the playing field and followed with two seasons of excavation (Fig. 7.3). This revealed that the northward continuation of Dere Street, after re-routing through Corbridge, ran into the field. A west-northwest to east-southeast spur road, apparently lined with buildings, cut across the field. Earlier maps and the geophysics indicated that archaeology in the field would inevitably have been disturbed by medieval and later ploughing, probable field drains, and landscaping linked to the large house – later school – located just to the east. Excavations in the playing field in 2019 and 2021, joined by hundreds of volunteers, set out to determine how well the archaeology had survived and to investigate the character of the northern sector of the Roman town. Two discrete structures located to the north and south of the branch road, respectively, were investigated, supported by a programme of scientific dating and analysis of the material culture.

Landscape context: geology and topography

The river terrace west of modern Corbridge on which the Roman town is located slopes gently towards the north bank of the Tyne, with a slightly steeper drop to the river just south of the town. The Cor Burn flows north–south into the Tyne only 250 m from the centre

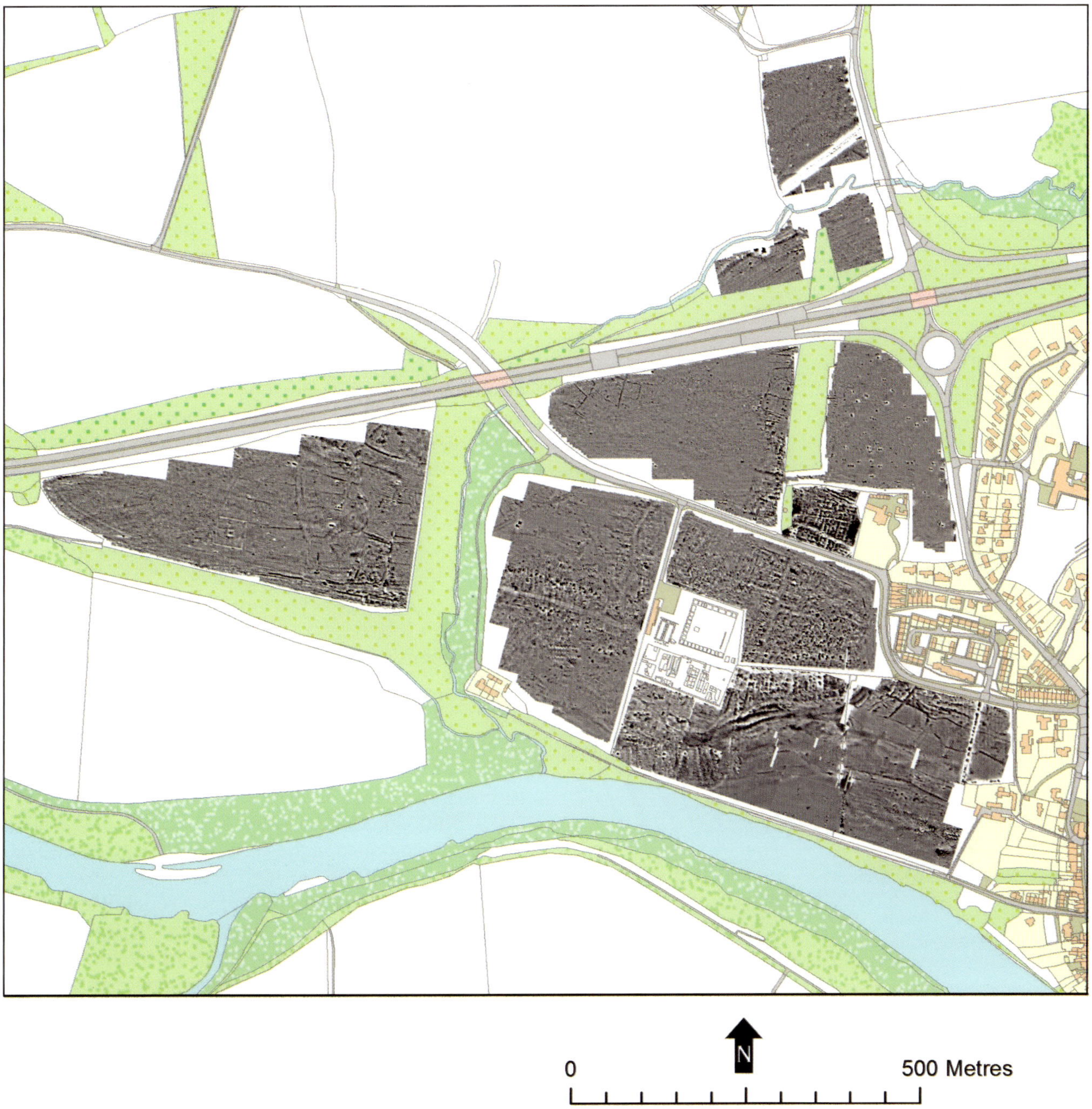

Figure 7.2: The extent of Roman Corbridge as revealed by gradiometry courtesy of the Corbridge Roman Station and Environs Project. Access to the Beaufront Estate for the project was kindly given by permission of A. Cuthbert. © I. Haynes and A. Turner.

of the English Heritage site, having described a gentle loop around the wider site from the northeast to the west. Although the exact course of the burn will have altered over time the river terrace also tilts slightly towards the stream's valley (Fig. 7.1).

The underlying geology of the area is the Stainmore formation of mixed mudstones, sandstones, and limestones. The bedrock is overlain by Devensian Till superficial deposits, dominated by clay. Observations during the Corbridge excavations by the WallCAP geologist recorded the sandstones and glacial cobbles used in Roman constructions onsite. The sandstones could not be sourced, but were probably brought from more than one location. The cobbles were greywackes (sandstone) and lava; they were either river cobbles or had been transported to the area by ice-sheets from the Southern Upland terrains and reworked into

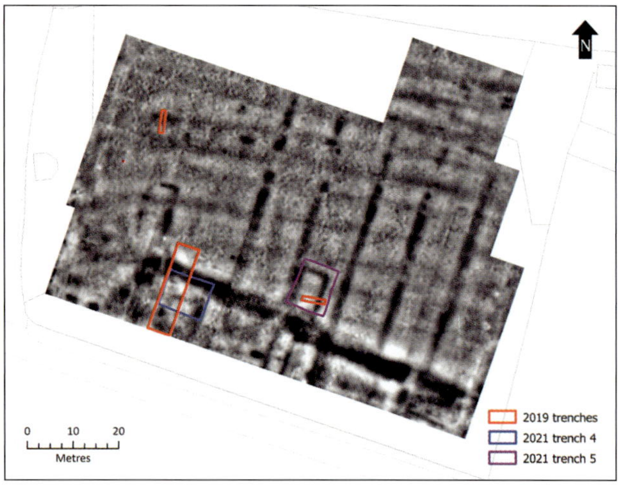

(A)

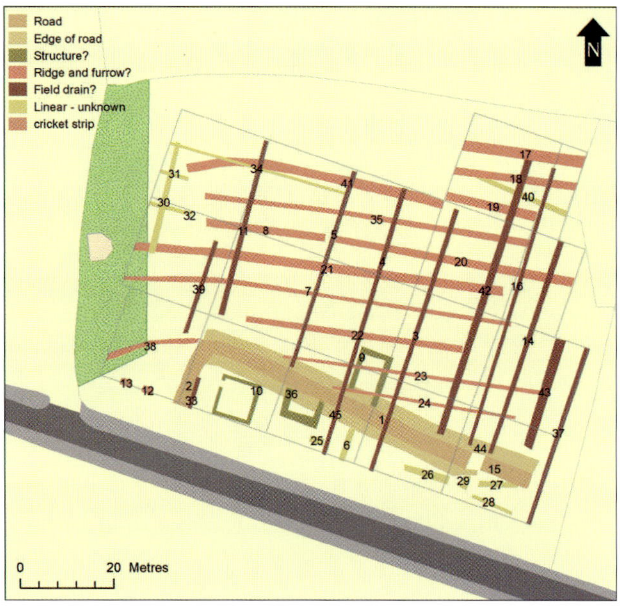

(B)

Figure 7.3: (A) Resistivity survey results with trench locations. (B) Interpretation of the resistivity survey results.

local fluvio-glacial deposits. Significantly, this indicates a relatively diverse sourcing of geological materials for the construction of buildings, roads, and other monuments in Roman Corbridge.

Archaeological background

Corbridge has benefited from a high volume of archaeological investigation via survey (aerial, geophysical, and topographic) and excavation. The site is further advantaged, in contrast with other Roman towns of Britain, by the shifting east of the settlement in the early medieval period; this means the Roman period settlement is largely unencumbered with contemporary buildings and settlement. In this regard, Corbridge is archaeologically more accessible than Carlisle, the other Roman town in the immediate hinterland of Hadrian's Wall.

At present, there is limited evidence for pre-Roman settlement at Corbridge, though it is certain that the landscape was settled in the late pre-Roman Iron Age. The large multivallate hillfort crowning Warden Hill, 7 km northwest and overlooking the confluence of the North and South Tyne, is a suitable candidate for a high status Iron Age settlement. No archaeological fieldwork has been undertaken at the site, but aerial photography and fieldwalking have revealed internal circular buildings and what appears to be a Romano-British settlement overlying the northwest ramparts (Historic England 1994). Three enclosures were identified by aerial photography at Bishop Rigg, on the northwest fringe of the subsequent Roman town and east of Shorden Brae, but excavation failed to obtain a certain date for the enclosures. Similarly, a palisaded enclosure with a circular building was found beneath the fort and subsequent town (Richmond and Gillam 1955, 221–224). Morphologically, the settlements at both sites fit within the Iron Age, but they may have been abandoned prior to Roman settlement. The internal area of one of the enclosures appears to have been quarried by the Romans (Jobey 1979). Though settlement structures are more limited, there are a number of occurrences of prehistoric artefacts and other features (Bishop and Dore 1988, 7).

The Roman name for Corbridge has been given in a small number of sources: as Corstopitum in the *Antonine Itinerary* (originally compiled in the early 3rd century) and Corielopocarium in the *Ravenna Cosmography* (originally compiled in the early 8th century). However, given the transmission history of these two sources, the given names for Corbridge are almost certainly corrupted (Breeze 2006, 416). The Vindolanda writing tablets identify a place named Coris, which in nominative form becomes Coria. As used in contemporary documents dating *c.* AD 92–105 and recurring in multiple tablets (*e.g.* TV 154, 176, 292), Coria is the most probable Roman name for Corbridge. Some agreement in the name of the locals may be found in an altar inscription (RIB 1142), recording the slaughter of a band of Corionototae. This altar, found during the late 19th-century rediscovery of the 7th-century crypt at Hexham Abbey, was thought to originate from Corbridge, but Bidwell (2010) has argued that it probably originated from Chesters. Regardless of which site the altar was obtained from, the Corionototae can reasonably be argued to be a name of the local 'tribe'.

The earliest known Roman site is at Red House farm, west of the Roman town, where evidence for a fort was revealed by a single ditch 254 m in length and internal timber buildings (Hansen *et al.* 1979). The full size of the installation is unknown, but east of this enclosure, a large stone bathhouse was excavated in 1955–1957 (Daniels 1959). Though the stone-built baths indicate an intention for longer-term occupation, the site seems to have survived for only 10–20 years, centred on the AD 80s. It is presumed that the fort was founded in the AD 70s. The site was abandoned in the AD 80s, and replaced with a new fort site to the east in the location of the eventual Roman town.

The main site consisted of six discrete phases attributed to one or more forts preceding the Roman town, dating *c.* AD 86–163, identified through a series of excavations across the 20th century (see Forster and Knowles 1910; 1911; 1912; 1913; 1914; 1915; Birley and Richmond 1938; Richmond and Birley 1940; Richmond 1943; Richmond and Gillam 1950; 1952a; 1953; 1955; Bishop and Dore 1988; Hodgson 2008). The early forts consisted of turf-and-timber constructions, with stone buildings not appearing until *c.* 140 with most buildings constructed in stone by 160. The date of abandonment or conversion of the final fort is uncertain, but more recently has been suggested as *c.* 163. The levelling of the fort defences was followed by new buildings engaged in industrial activities, and the large and well-constructed courtyard building known as Site XI. The building was never fully finished, but its form and high-quality construction suggest it was to house large scale activity, variously argued as being storage, production, a forum, and as a market. The failure to complete the complex may have been because of a widespread fire, evidenced in excavation locations throughout the town and known as the 'Corbridge destruction deposit', dating anywhere between *c.* 165 and 185. It was after this fire that the layout of Corbridge as displayed today began to emerge, with the construction of a series of new buildings. Though never completed, parts of the large Site XI building were used in later phases of the town, and seemed to have provided a centre for the new town, with the aqueduct and fountain laid to its west, and the construction of stone-built replacements for the granaries. The deposition of a smith's chest containing different sets of *lorica segmentata* and other items known as the Corbridge hoard seems to date to this period of transition from fort to town (Allason-Jones and Bishop 1988).

The town was built around the two major roads that cemented its strategic position. The Stanegate ran east–west through the centre of the town, and a stone bridge carried Dere Street across the Tyne, meeting the Stanegate west of the town centre and the continuing north in two branches from the town, one west of the granaries and one east of Site XI. South of the Stanegate, across from Site XI and the granaries, two legionary compounds allowed the Roman army to retain a presence in the town. Eventually, these merged into one larger compound with traces of a more monumental gate into the complex visible on site. The town seems to have expanded rapidly, and various artefacts, inscriptions, and architectural stonework point to a thriving settlement with temples, shops, and workshops, alongside domestic occupation. There is a predominance of strip buildings, aligned with the gable end to the street, and built with stone and timber. The artefactual record is quite rich, with products from a range of long-distance sources, and good evidence for manufacturing. An urban defensive circuit has also been suggested from antiquarian observations, but there is no conclusive modern evidence for any town walls. Cemeteries are known to the west and north of the town, with geophysics highlighting likely cremations (see Fig. 7.2).

Two examples suffice to demonstrate the wealth and prestige of the settlement. A large stone-built tower-tomb in a 10 m square-walled enclosure was constructed in the 2nd century as a mortuary monument at Shorden Brae (Gillam and Daniels 1961), indicating an individual or family of some wealth and significance. A large silver platter bearing a mythological scene, known as the Corbridge lanx, is the only surviving vessel of a larger hoard of silver vessels dating to the later 4th century (Haverfield 1914; Brendel 1941). Coins attest to occupation of the town continuing at least into the early 5th century, and a small number of other objects, for example cruciform brooches, indicate some activity dating to the later 5th and 6th centuries (Hedley 1937). However, the stratigraphy of the later Roman phases of the town seems to have suffered from agricultural damage over the centuries.

Precise dating of specific structures and phases is often complicated by the early 20th-century date of the excavations that have provided the most detailed and extensive investigations of the early forts and town. Intensive research of that archive supported by further fieldwork resulted in a stronger understanding of Corbridge in the 2nd and 3rd centuries (Bishop and Dore 1988), and the site continues to benefit from scholarly attention to material from on the site and in Hexham (*e.g.* Bidwell 2010; Hodgson 2010).

Corchester Playing Field

The WallCAP excavations took place on the playing field north of Corchester Lane, 0.8 km northwest of the centre of the village of Corbridge and 0.2 km northeast of the English Heritage site exhibiting the central area of Corbridge Roman Town (Fig. 7.1). The field is owned by the local Parish Council, managed by English Heritage, and well-used by locals and visitors. The WallCAP work was the first modern excavation of Roman Corbridge and the only one to date that has resulted in scientific dating.

The playing field is a small part of the extensive area of Scheduled Monument number 1006611, and is included on Historic England's *Heritage at Risk Register* due to the damage being caused to archaeology by arable ploughing of the surrounding fields. The field itself has been ploughed in the past and heavily landscaped in more recent times, before finally being levelled in the 1930s for use as a playing field. The 1777 Corbridge West Field enclosure map, shows a series of post-medieval (and possible earlier) strip fields. Although no sign of medieval ridge-and-furrow survives in the field today, it was clearly evident in the geophysics (see below).

In the 1930s, Corchester Playing Field was used by the boys' school based in Corchester Towers, the large house next to the field to the east. The school magazines for 1936–1939 describe excavations by staff and pupils in the playing field that uncovered substantial Roman structures and recovered numerous finds including pottery and metalwork. Unfortunately, the reports provide only limited descriptions of what was discovered, with no plans detailing the position of, or features within, the trenches. Some references suggest the trenches may have been in the far southwest of the field, just beyond the 2019 and 2021 excavations. The WallCAP excavations were an opportunity to determine the condition of archaeological remains that had survived the earlier ploughing and later landscaping of the playing field but the information is also relevant to the archaeology under the immediately surrounding – and still ploughed – fields.

Geophysical survey

Alex Turner

The site, having been levelled for use as a playing field, is now largely flat but with a noticeable northeast to southwest gradient towards the Cor Burn and the Tyne. The current playing field boundaries were established by the 1860s, when the area was within a sub-rectangular field 182 m west–east by 107 m south–north, with its long southern side running along Corchester Lane. A substantial house, Corchester Towers, was built within the easternmost third of the field during the 1880s. The house first appears on the 1890s Ordnance Survey maps; a pavilion is also marked on the field's western boundary on those editions, suggesting the construction of the house was accompanied by landscaping of the rest of the field to its west. Corchester Towers became a school in 1891 (Waugh 2020, 9) and the conversion of the field to the school rugby pitch probably accounts for the large number of north–south field drains detected in the geophysical surveys; many of these field drains may now be broken.

The playing field has been surveyed several times. The first survey was undertaken in 1976, using both resistivity and magnetic survey, and revealed building plots north and south of a near east–west road (Bartlett 1976). More recently, the playing field was surveyed with a gradiometer by Wardell Armstrong Ltd. These results showed the potential complexity of the building plots themselves and the likely line of Dere Street running north–south beyond the field.

WallCAP surveys were completed in 2019 (Fig. 7.3). The gradiometer output was less clear than previous results; the resistivity survey was more successful, revealing that the northward continuation of Dere Street, after re-routing through Corbridge centre ran into the field (anomaly 2). A near west–east spur road apparently lined with buildings ran east across the field from Dere (anomalies 1 and 15). When the 2019 results are compared to the transcription of cropmarks and excavation results compiled by Bishop and Dore (1988, 335; Fig. 7.3), anomaly 2 aligns well with Eastern Dere Street to the south of Corchester Lane. North of the spur road it seems likely that a later field drain obscures the continuation of Dere Street further north. The lower resistance anomalies 44–45 running alongside the spur road proved on excavation in Trench 4 to result from the roadside ditches and water conduit.

Anomalies 3–5, 11, 14, 16, 33, 37, 39 and 43 were interpreted as a series of north-northeast to south-southwest field drains, none of which intruded into areas excavated in 2019 and 2021. Anomalies 7–8, 17–24, 35, 38, and 41 were interpreted in 2019 as the remains of ridge and furrow and proved to be such where furrows were excavated crossing both Trench 4 and 5 in 2021. High resistance anomalies 9, 10, and 36, perpendicular to the road, were suggested as indicating buried structural remains. Anomaly 9 did indeed accurately reflect the layout of the building excavated in Trench 5 in 2021. Anomaly 10 within Trench 4 was discovered to be a smoothing out of the interaction of many superimposed stone structural remains and filled-in ditches in a complex archaeological sequence. To the east of Trench 4, anomaly 36 is likely to reflect part of a large and possibly high-status building, indications of which were found in Trench 4. In the southeast of the field, high resistance, linear anomalies 6 and 25–29 also seem most likely to be recording partially surviving stone structures. To the northwest and north, anomalies 30–32 (perhaps especially 32) and 40–41 could reflect more structural elements, but their longer and straighter character might suggest they are related to more recent landscaping and drainage. Areas of high resistance 12 and 13 were correlated with the cricket practice strip.

The geophysical surveys were difficult to interpret as the anomalies were responses to truncated archaeology, disturbed in its upper levels and with complex stratigraphy. The features within those layers interacted to create anomalies hard to understand as individual features: anomaly 9 was the exception to this rule.

Excavation

Two seasons of excavation were undertaken, in 2019 and 2021, with a break caused by the COVID-19 pandemic. Trenches 1, 2, and 3 were completed in 2019, and Trenches 4 and 5 in 2021 (Fig. 7.3). Trench 2 had no archaeological features, so was not reopened or further explored, while the initial results from Trenches 1 and 3 in 2019 helped with the positioning of Trenches 4 and 5 in 2021.

Work in 2019 was hindered and then halted by extremely wet weather, which water-logged and flooded the trenches. Also, de-turfing and all digging was done by hand so progress was slow. However, the hand-excavation meant that the depth of the topsoil and disturbed subsoils were well-sampled and in 2021 excavation could begin with a mechanical digger stripping out those layers down to just above undisturbed archaeology. The playing field area had been ploughed in medieval and modern times, and then substantially landscaped both when Corchester Towers was built in the east of the original field in the 1880s and subsequently. The old ploughsoils and field soils were fairly deep at 0.3–0.35 m and a considerable amount of archaeology had clearly been destroyed by the past work on the field. Dating from the WallCAP excavations suggests that archaeology post-dating the later-3rd century has been lost. Below that layer, however, the truncated Roman archaeology survived relatively well and, when compared with the Edwardian excavations to the south of Corchester Lane, appeared to survive at a higher level (Foster and Knowles 1914). This may be because the playing field has not been subjected to 20th and 21st-century ploughing, and this raises concerns for the survival of the archaeology in the surrounding fields still in cultivation.

Both of the 2021 trenches were opened using a mechanical digger. Guided by the results from 2019, between 0.30–0.35 m of turf, topsoil and subsoil were removed under close observation. The spoil heaps were scanned thoroughly with metal detectors and around a 3% sample of spoil hand-sorted and sieved. All the remaining excavation was done by hand, with 100% sieving of all significant contexts and at least 33% sieving of all contexts, with the proportion sieved increased if sieving produced any artefacts. The spoil heaps continued to be checked by metal detectorists throughout the excavation. Summaries of Trenches 1 and 3 are provided, but the evidence from both of these trenches is fully integrated into the interpretation of Trenches 4 and 5, respectively.

Trench 1

Trench 1 was located to investigate the WNW–ENE spur road and a possible rectangular structure (Fig. 7.3). The trench was 20 m long, encompassing the full width of the road, 5 m wide and excavated to a maximum depth of 0.35 m. As hand-dug topsoil and subsoils (1001), (1002), (1004) and (1006) together were 0.3–0.35 m deep, the work in 2019 exposed archaeological features but did very little further exploration. Much of the pottery and almost all of the small finds recovered came from the relict ploughsoils and disturbed subsoils: only 62 sherds came from undisturbed the Roman features and layers below (see below and Appendix 1).

The removal of the disturbed subsoils in Trench 1 revealed the spur road's surface, roadside ditches and flagging, and a rough yard surface with pits and possible gullies south of the road. The 2021 Trench 4 encompassed the full width of Trench 1 and 8 m of the north–south length (Fig. 7.4).

Description

The 2019 excavation exposed the full 3.85 m width of the near west–east road (1008). This road surface, along with layer (1016) below, was equivalent to layers (4001) and (4015) as excavated in 2021 (see pp. 104 and 105), and comprised medium and large sub-rounded stone cobbles tightly packed within a silty matrix. One sherd of abraded Samian was found in the matrix, along with a scattering of brick from demolished Roman buildings amidst the cobbles. In 2021 the last surviving road surface, when excavated just east of the location of Trench 1, also incorporated demolition debris, used in areas of patching. Limited areas of the road surface (1008) and of layer (1016) below were explored in a small sondage. Layer (1016) was interpreted as an earlier metalling formed of smaller cobbles; this may rather have been foundations for (1008). A flagged area south of the road, investigated further in 2021, was exposed in 2019 as (1007), when it was observed that ploughing had broken the large slabs *in situ*.

To the north of the road, and beyond the northern edge of 2021 Trench 4, the 2019 trench uncovered the roadside ditch [1022], approximately 0.8 m wide; this was not excavated, but was of similar width and with a similar fill to the ditches along the south side of the road excavated in 2021.

The extensive layer (1009) south of the road and the flags, 4 m north–south by 5 m wide, was recorded in 2019 as a clay- and pebble-rich silt, and interpreted as a rough yard surface, although large areas of this layer clearly included remaining subsoil (Fig. 7.4). Very little of (1009) was excavated in 2019, with no finds recorded; much of it was dug as subsoil (4000) over late, rough cobble surface (4011) in 2021. That cobble surface of small-medium sub-rounded stones was also observed in 2019 in a small sondage as (1015), but not excavated. The top stony fill of the cremation pit [4045] excavated in 2021 was not recorded in 2019, remaining obscured by the pebble-inclusions of the subsoil.

Cut features that lay beyond the southern edge of Trench 4 in 2021 were investigated in 2019. These features were cut into an occupation surface (1013) which seemed very similar in composition, inclusions, and depth to the extensive yard surface excavated in 2021 (see below). Layer (1013) contained 22 sherds of Roman pottery, the fabrics suggesting a mid-2nd-century date for the layer; this date range was consistent with radiocarbon dating obtained in 2021. In a small sondage an underlying levelling/demolition spread (1010), more fully investigated in 2021, also produced a number of sherds of Roman pottery. Interestingly this lower layer also contained a smithing hearth cake (circular or oval and plano-convex accumulations of slag, which formed inside a blacksmith's hearth),

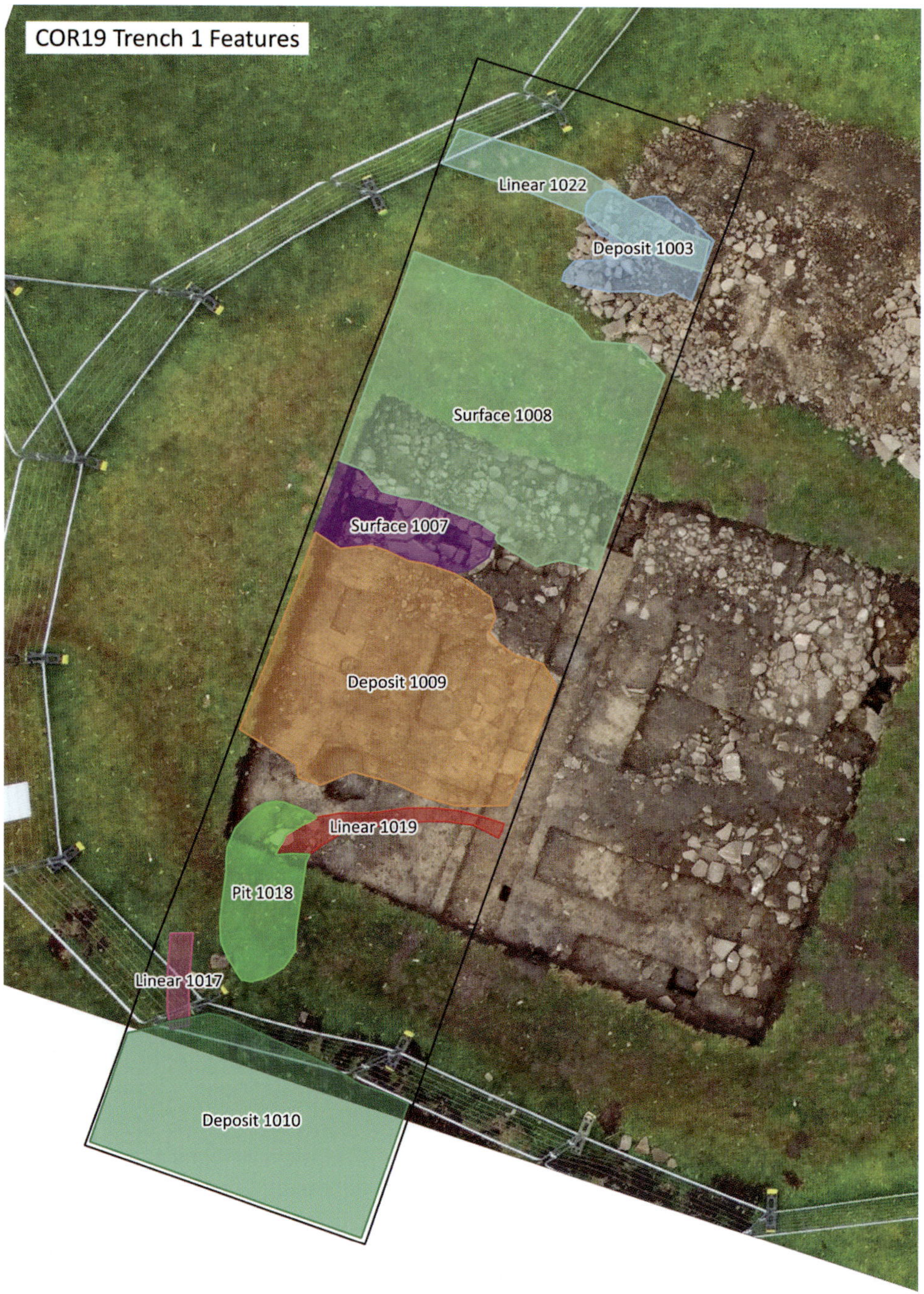

Figure 7.4: Features identified during the 2019 excavation superimposed on an aerial photograph of Trench 4 in 2021.

thus reinforcing the idea that the yard was used for some time for metal-working and specifically smithing (report in Appendix 2).

The Roman-period cut features investigated in 2019 were a shallow pit [1018] (Fig. 7.5) and a possibly associated curvilinear, narrow and shallow gully [1019]. A small part of the pit reached into the southern end of Trench 4 but was not re-excavated in 2021. The pit was 1.6 m long, 0.8 m wide and only 0.35 m deep, packed with medium to large cobbles in a sandy silt matrix (1012), within which were four sherds of Roman pottery. It was difficult to interpret the purpose of these features: the original suggestion was these may have been for drainage. The number and arrangement of late pits and ditches in the yard area discovered in 2021 challenges the simplicity of this interpretation but the sequence and character of later activity remains hard to understand.

The 2019 excavations revealed the full width of the road and confirmed that there had been considerable activity to the south of its line. Further excavation of features

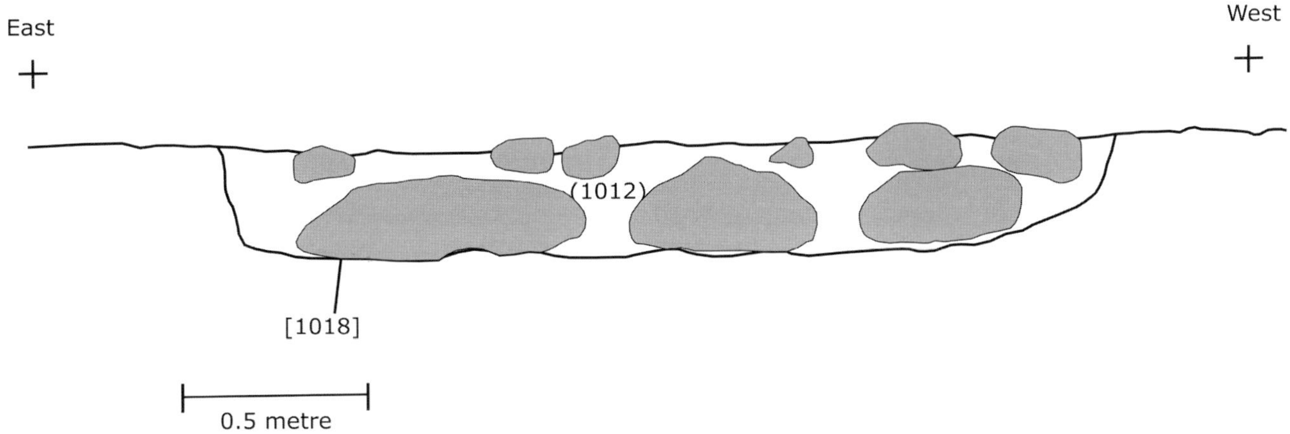

Figure 7.5: The south section of pit [1018].

in 2021 enabled the full complexity of the archaeology to be characterised.

Finds and dating

The pottery assemblage from Trench 1 overall was very mixed in date, from a Gillam 237 mortarium (AD 60–90) to a Gillam 163 jar (AD 360–400) and many fabrics between. Over 70% of that material, however, was from the ploughsoils and subsoils. Pottery from the undisturbed Roman contexts was more limited in date range, from around the mid-2nd to the mid-3rd centuries with perhaps an emphasis on the mid–late 2nd century (see below).

Only two Roman recorded finds were from secure contexts: an iron horse harness buckle (cat. no. 68) from occupation surface (1013); and a fragment of a small crucible (cat. no. 75) from another surface (1021). The remaining Roman objects were from the disturbed layers and included: three coins, an enamelled disc brooch, a finger ring, a ceramic counter, and an iron vessel rim fragment. Other artefacts in glass – bowl, jug, and bottle sherds – and a few unidentified but probably structural iron objects were all from the same layers.

Trench 3

Trench 3, 5 m long and 1 m wide, was located in the centre south of the playing field, targeting a possible rectangular structure observed in the geophysical survey (Fig. 7.3). The entirety of this small trench was encompassed by Trench 5 in 2021 (Fig. 7.6). The hand-dug old ploughsoils and disturbed subsoils were represented by layers (3001), (3002), (3003), and (3004). Both Roman and post-Roman pottery was retrieved from these layers. In total only 60 sherds of Roman pottery were found: 38 of these were from undisturbed features and layers with Roman-only material. A fragment of a Roman copper-alloy brooch was found in (3002), along with an iron hinge and unidentifiable iron artefacts.

Description

At the eastern end of Trench 3, north–south wall foundations [3005] were uncovered, running across the width of the trench. The wall was 1.1 m wide; a small slot was excavated across it showing the foundations were 0.25–0.3 m deep and constructed from large, un-mortared, sub-oval stones. This was found to be part of the eastern wall [5037] of the rectangular building uncovered in full plan in 2021.

In 2019 two different deposits were excavated west and east of wall foundations [3005]. A small amount of deposit (3006) to the east was excavated before rising groundwater halted work. This clay-rich, pebbly silt was excavated as (5034) in 2021, when it was interpreted as a levelling layer within a domestic annex to the main workshop building, mixed with some subsoil. (3006) contained three sherds of Roman pottery and three unidentifiable iron structural artefacts. To the west of the wall in 2019, deposit (3007) a yellow silty clay, produced 24 sherds of Roman pottery, including a number of everted-rim jars and beaker fragments, six unidentifiable iron artefacts, and an iron bracket. This was interpreted in 2019 as a possible floor deposit and was linked in 2021 with yellow clay layer (5003), which was a secondary floor, perhaps patching the earlier flooring surfaces within the building (see below).

The western end of Trench 3 was dominated by a stony deposit [3008], interpreted as a second wall foundation but not excavated in 2019. In fact, this was a stone layer sealing feature [5038] within the building, uncovered in 2021. Immediately east of [3008] was a sub-circular area of burnt material (3009), composed of bright red silty clay, and measuring 0.87 m long and 0.49 m wide. Again, (3009) was not excavated but was interpreted as remains of a hearth or a kiln. In 2021 this was excavated as (5021) and shown to be the redeposition and spread raked-out debris from an oven to the west. Underlying (3009), and (3007) to the east, was a brown silty clay (3010),

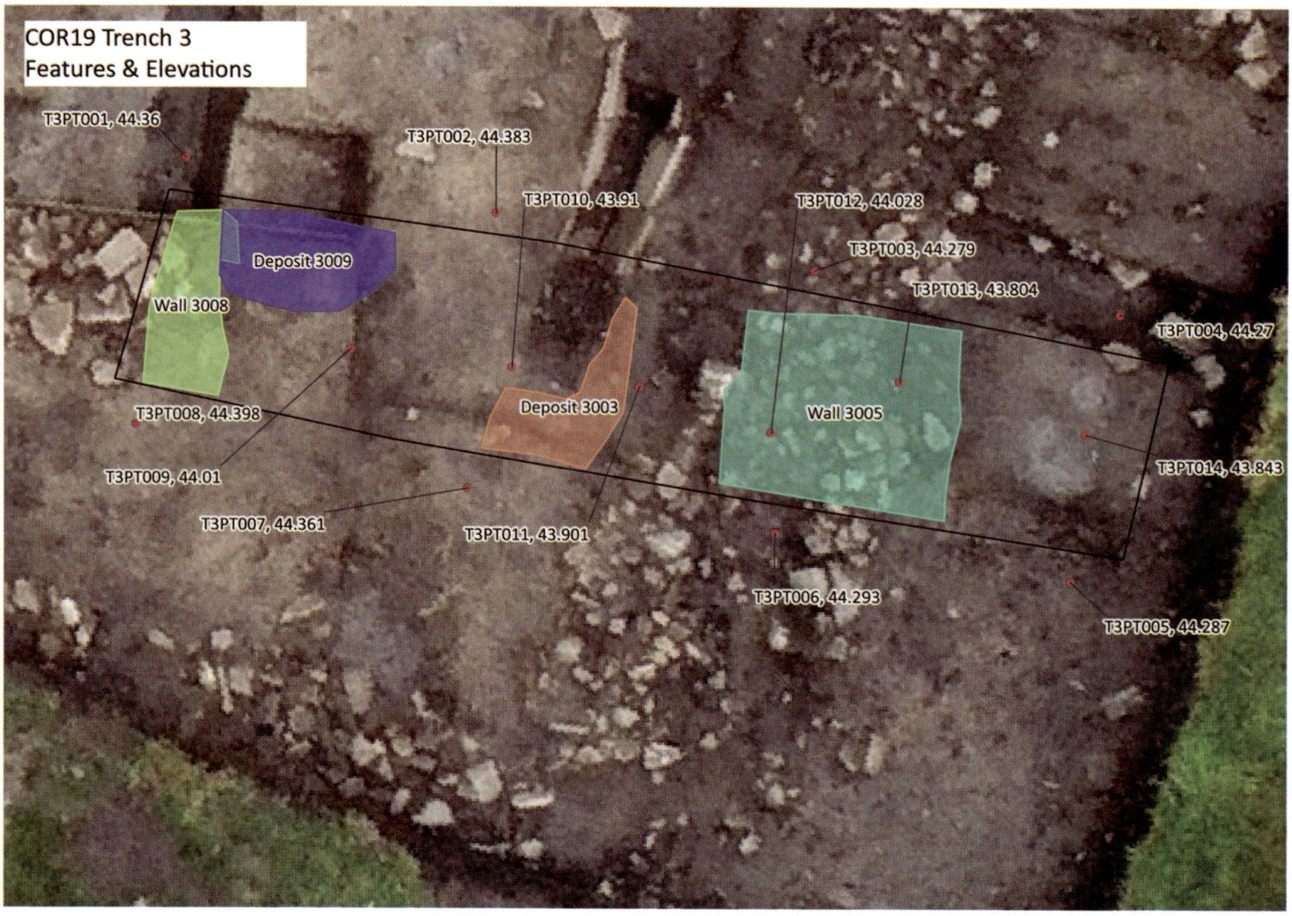

Figure 7.6: Features identified during the 2019 excavation superimposed on an aerial photograph of Trench 5 in 2021.

with pebble inclusions and clay lenses. This layer was explored in a small sondage and seen to be at least 0.1 m deep before rising water halted excavation. Eleven sherds of Roman pottery were found, including Samian and amphorae, and an iron mount. This internal floor deposit was excavated as (5020) in 2021. The 2019 excavation produced sufficient evidence to indicate that a Roman building was present, more fully characterised in the 2021 excavations.

Finds and dating

Overall, the pottery covered almost the entire Roman period but pottery from secure Roman-only contexts, including everted-rim Greyware jars and a Gillam 226 bowl both with intersecting ARCS decoration, suggested a similar date range to that for Trench 1, roughly mid-2nd to mid-3rd centuries, but with perhaps a slightly later lean towards the early–mid 3rd century.

Trench 4

Positioned to explore more of the length of the spur road and of the building detected in geophysics, as well as features observed in 2019, Trench 4 was 10 m west–east by 8 m north–south. The most western 5 m of Trench 4 encompassed the full width of Trench 1 and 8 m of its length (Fig. 7.4). The work in 2019 had confirmed the considerable truncation of the archaeology, including by ENE–WSW plough-strikes, and recorded *in-situ* archaeology at *c.* 3.4 m deep. A total of three phases were identified across the trench, dating broadly from the mid-2nd century up to the early 4th century.

The turf and upper topsoil, to a maximum depth of *c.* 0.35 m, were removed by machine, with the spoil being sampled for finds and the remaining spreads of relict ploughsoil, 2019 backfill and upper subsoil excavated by hand. Those sandy silt layers (4000) contained considerable amounts of sandstone cobble and shatter, ploughed up and disturbed from underlying Roman buildings and surfaces. The soil also produced plenty of pottery, the overwhelming majority of which was Roman (244 sherds; 80.1% of the total), including large sherds of finewares, Samian, mortaria, and amphorae. Only 58 sherds of post-Roman pottery were found during the excavation of Trench 4, and all of those were in (4000). As well as stone, the building material in (4000) included Roman tile, brick, *imbrices*, and mortar (see Appendix 2). There were many animal bone fragments; the leg bone of a crane was

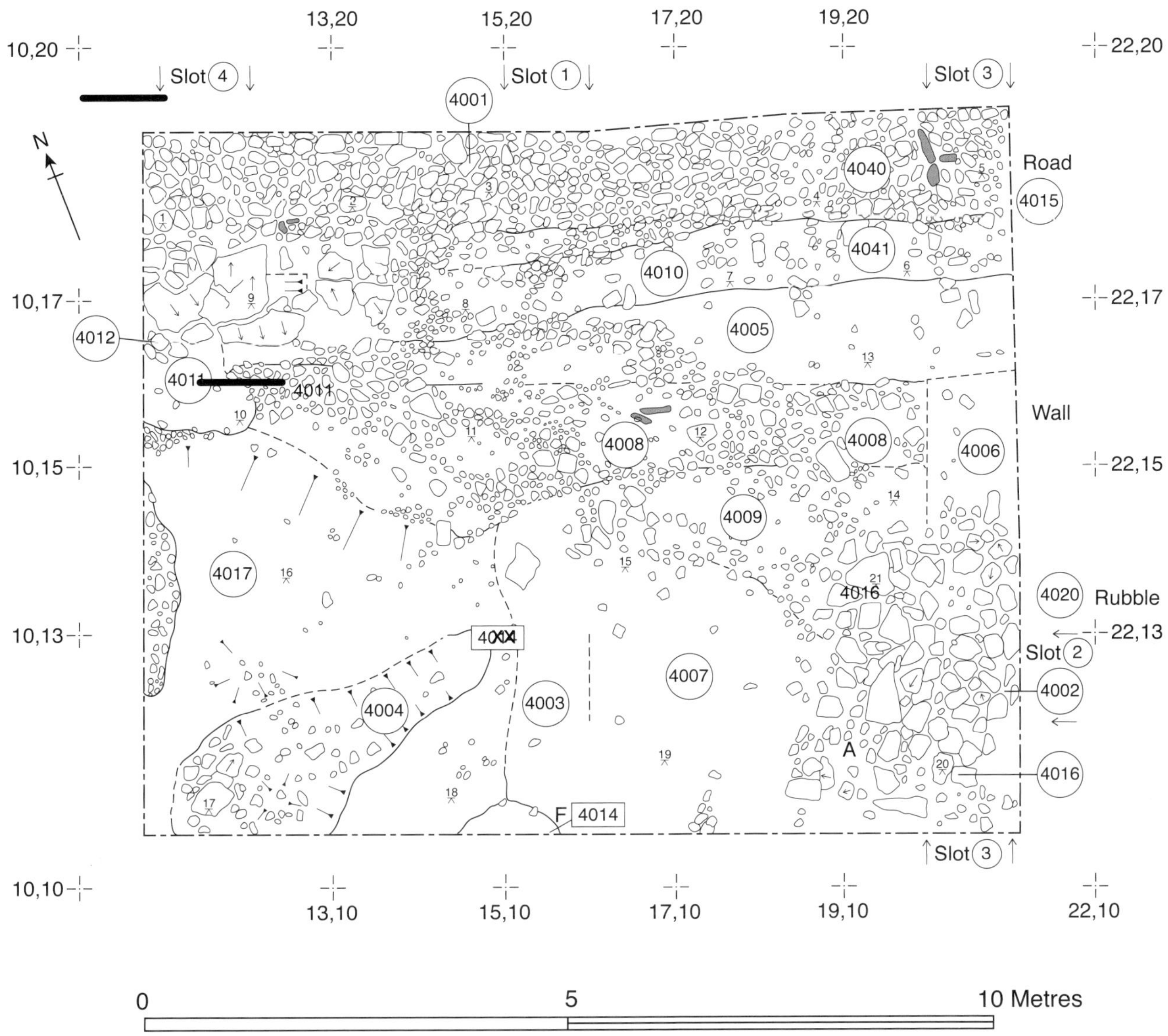

Figure 7.7: Plan of Trench 4 after removal of the top soil and initial subsoil.

found at the interface with the fill of pit [4045], discussed below (p. 212; report in Appendix 2). Roman lead artefacts were retrieved, included a weight and fitting, and many iron items mainly hobnails and structural nails. The slag, copper alloy tweezers, stone smoother, and stone pestle testified to metalworking and domestic activity. There was one coin, a denarius of Marcus Aurelius issued AD 155–157 (cat. no. 2).

All the finds indicated complex Roman archaeology below the relict ploughsoil, with distinct areas of archaeology immediately visible beneath (4000) (Fig. 7.7). These included: the west–east spur road running across the top of the trench, with an area of large flags immediately south of the road surface in the west; a likely roadside ditch alongside the road in the centre-east; areas of cobbling to the south of the road in the west and centre; more substantial structural remains south of the road in the east of the trench; and cut features in the southwest of the trench. The features in the west of Trench 4 tied up with the archaeology revealed in 2019, when the road, western flagging – and cut features to the south of that – were recorded with very little further excavation.

Phase 1: the west–east road

About half the width of the west–east road was uncovered in 2021, running across the full length of the northern edge of the trench: 1.5 m wide in the west and 1.2m wide in the east (Figs 7.7 and 7.3). The road was investigated

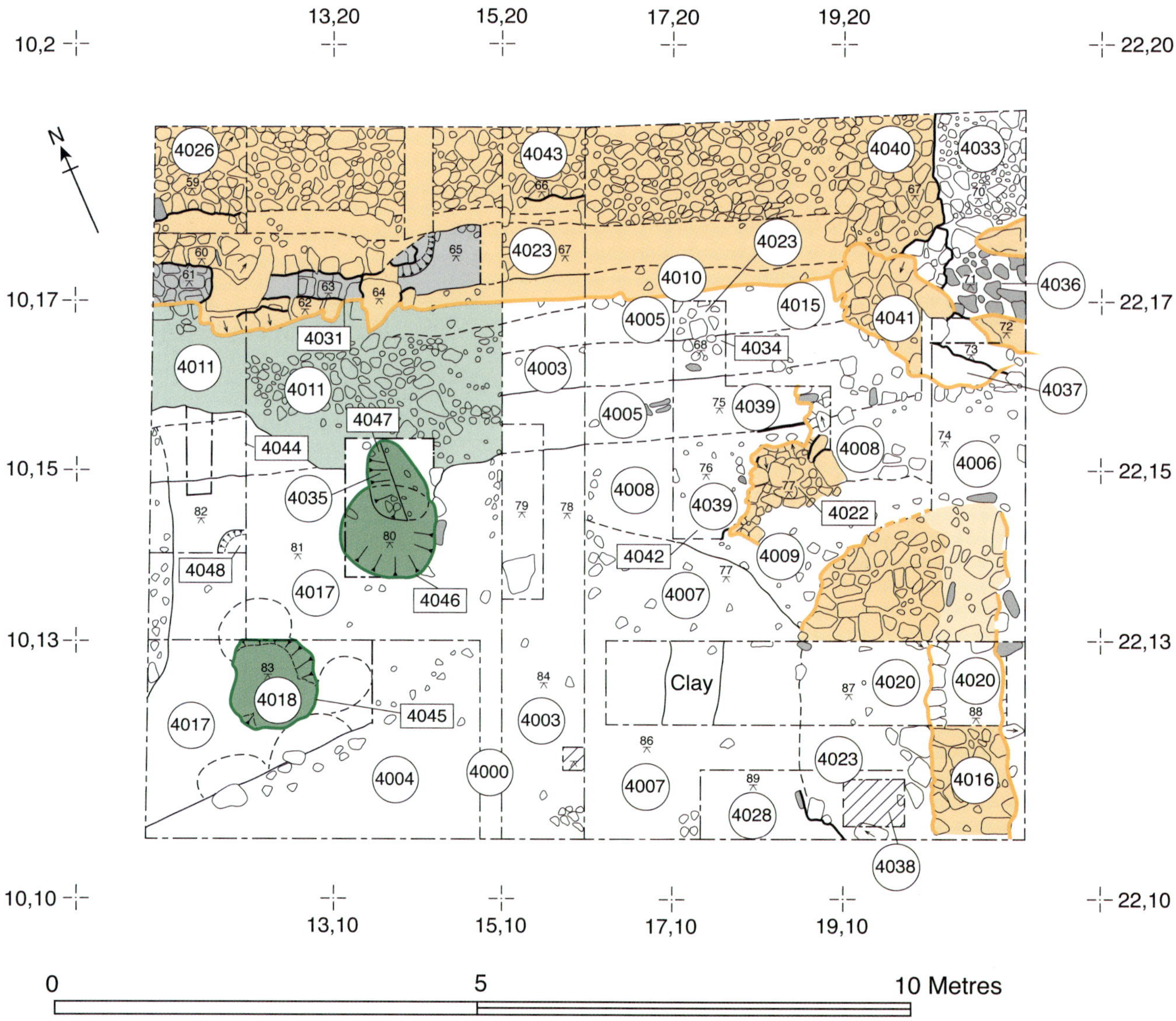

Figure 7.8: Plan of Trench 4, phases 1 and 2.

in detail in three north–south slots, in the west, centre, and east of the trench. The central slot gave a complete section through the road and its re-laying, although as the entire site was truncated it is possible if not likely that other repairs and later re-surfacing(s) were lost to ploughing. The western slot investigated the relationship between the paved-over water conduit and the road, and the eastern slot explored the structural impact on the road of the high-status building south of the road and on the eastern edge of the trench.

Central slot across road

In the centre slot a 1.5 m north–south width of the road was investigated, reaching undisturbed clay under the foundations (4043) of the earliest version of the road (Figs 7.8 and 7.9, section 4.03). This first road was either narrower than the subsequent metalling or ran a little further north. There was evidence for the foundation stones being anchored in yellow clay, and those cobbles were definitely sealed with a clay layer 0.2 m deep, into which the road surface was set (4023). The majority of the stones of foundations (4043) were sub-square or sub-rectangular, and 0.1–0.3 m long by 0.15 m wide, creating a layer *c.* 0.15 m deep, with 85% cobbles set in a matrix of pebbly, gritty clayey silt. Only three abraded sherds of Roman pottery were found among the foundations, along with gnawed cattle rib fragments.

The road surface (4023) above had slumped south of the foundations into the truncated roadside ditch, shifted by later work on the road. The surface stones were bedded

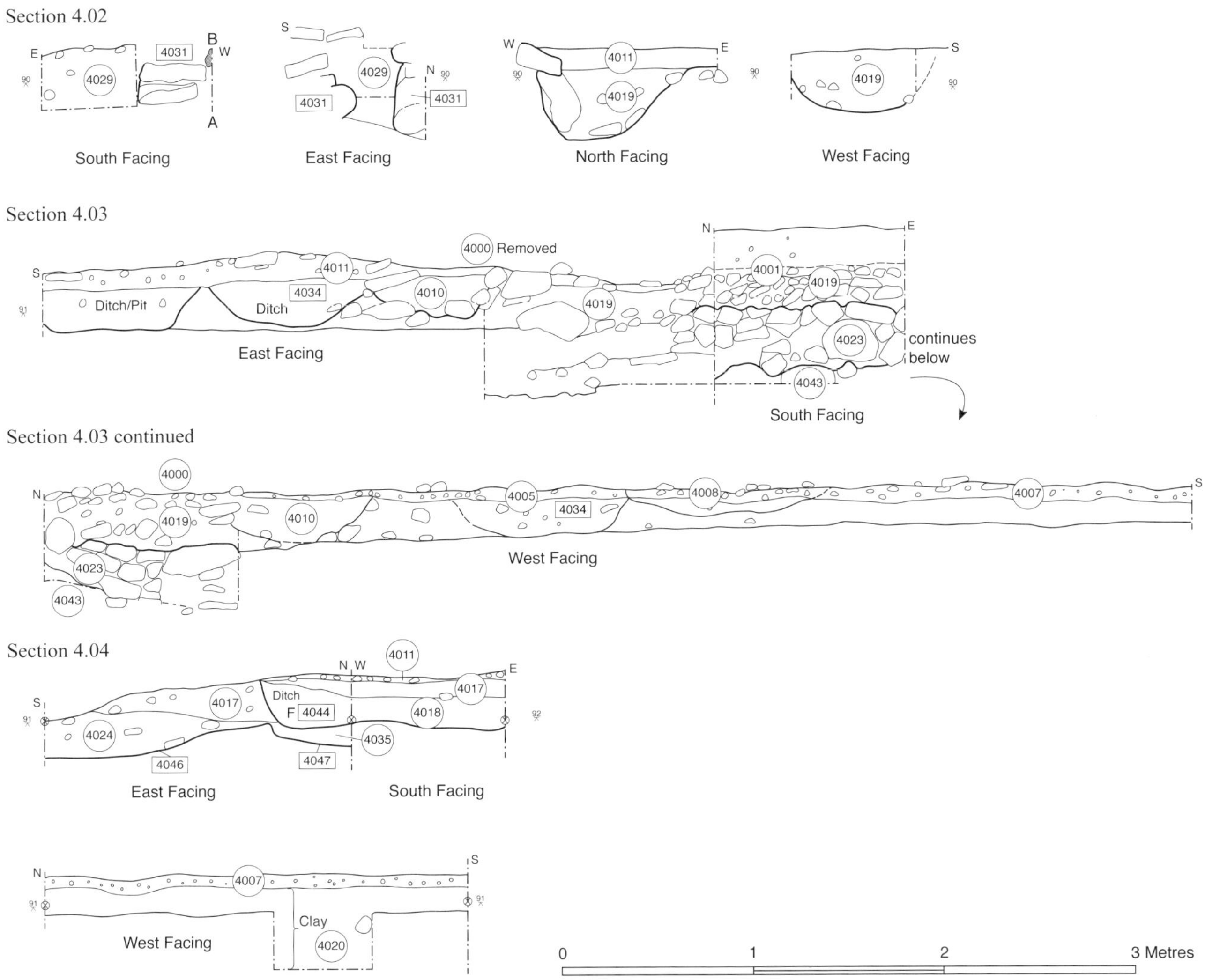

Figure 7.9: Section drawing of various features from Trench 4, phase 1.

in yellow clay and dominated by flatter sub-angular cobbles up to 0.4 m long, with the majority being well-sorted and *c.* 0.2 m by 0.1 m, with a few smaller packing stones, in a slightly silty clay matrix. The tightly packed road cobbles ran up to 1 m south from the northern edge of the trench, with the siltier and spread road-side ditch fill and slipped stones extending a further metre from the road-edge. The truncated ditch survived as an open U-shape only 0.2 m deep. Stones from surface (4023) had slumped down the ditch's northern side. Finds came predominantly from the ditch sides and included Roman brick and half-a-dozen abraded sherds of Roman pottery, dated like those from the foundations broadly to the mid-2nd to mid-3rd centuries. One sherd was of a very fine fabric with a possible but unidentifiable graffito.

Eastern slot across the road

The foundations of the first road were also reached in this slot [(4036) equivalent to (4043): see above] and comprised angular stones and rounded cobbles less than 0.2 m long in a matrix of evenly sized pebbles and sandy yellow clay (Figs 7.10 and 7.11, sections 4.10 and 4.11). Again the foundations were bedded in yellow clay and produced only fragmentary cattle bone and a few abraded sherds of Roman pottery. Immediately above this layer was packed yellow clay (4033), about 100 mm thick; together these two layers provided a firm foundation for surface stones (4032) [equivalent to (4023): see above]. Most of the stones were well-sorted between 0.2–0.3 m long and both rounded and angular, creating a layer up to 0.3 m thick with a pebbly, sandy silt matrix. To the south the contemporary roadside ditch survived as a truncated, spread and slumped 0.8 m-wide band of silty material with very few stones, but where most finds were made. After some initial silting the ditch had been rapidly backfilled with silty material that included debris from building alteration and/or demolition, including window glass, structural nails, mortar, and *imbrex* fragments. The backfilling prepared for the relaying of the road and refashioning of the ditch. The notably different

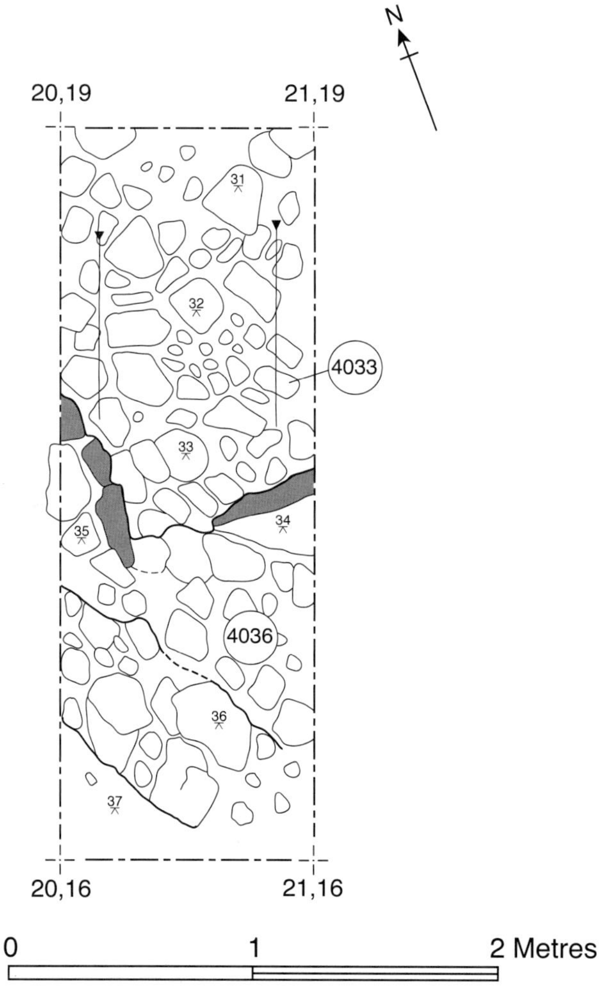

Figure 7.10: Plan of the early road surface in Trench 4.

stones just above and either side of this degraded ditch belonged to the reworking of the roadside ditch in the following phase.

Phase 1: the yard area

No buildings or features could be linked with the first road, other than one small, shallow pit [4048] caught only in section in the west. But the road was in use during a period when the area to the south was possibly cleared of any existing buildings (probably stone-founded but predominantly wooden) and then certainly levelled in preparation for new construction by the spreading of a debris and charcoal-laminated clay layer.

Levelling layer

This extensive layer below later yard surfaces was sampled in several locations south of the road-line. In the centre east area of the trench, where the foundations of the Phase 2 smithy building were set into it, the clay- and charcoal-rich layer (4039) was at least 0.2 m deep and contained considerable amounts of fragmentary, abraded animal bone, the identifiable bone predominantly cattle with some pig; over 40 sherds of pottery dominated by amphorae and greyware; slag and coal; and structural nails, as well as *opus caementicium*, fired clay, Roman brick and fire-cracked stone (Fig. 7.11, sections 4.05, 4.06, 4.07, and 4.08).

The levelling layer was investigated as (4028) in another slot, 0.8 m wide west–east and 5 m long excavated east–west along the southern baulk from the southeast corner. Here layer (4028) was cut by a later north–south wall and acted as bedding for later paving. The layer was very similar to (4039), silty and clay- and charcoal-rich with iron panning. Finds in (4028) under the flagging comprised fired clay and abraded sherds of pottery; to the west beyond the flagging only pottery was found, and almost exclusively sherds of Samian. The fired clay, as elsewhere, was likely from demolished ovens or hearths, so (4028) could indicate the demolition of Phase 1 workshops or at least ovens and hearths, like layer (4039) discussed above. A 0.5 m square sondage was dug into (4028) to test its depth, in the area just under the flags. Layer (4038) was up to 0.3 m deep and contained a considerable amount of burnt bone from cattle and caprids, three sherds of pottery, fragments of iron objects, and *imbrex*.

The clayey redeposited spread was also found across the west of the trench, here as (4018). The western end produced relatively less structural debris but was especially clay-rich and investigated across a wider area, 5 m north–south by 4 m, as there were no later buildings to constrain excavation. The finds included chalk, fired clay and *imbrex*, burnt bone fragments, jug and bottle glass, and 18 sherds of pottery, dominated by greyware. Several later pits and ditches were cut down into (4018) – discussed below.

The character of the levelling layer indicates that either there had already been considerable activity in the immediate vicinity to generate the debris and detritus spread to level the area, or it was brought in from close by. The brick and structural finds suggest earlier buildings and/or ovens had been demolished. As layer (4039) is not significantly different in artefact finds or composition from any of the other fills and layers from the subsequent yard Phase 2, it seems reasonable to propose that there was similar, if perhaps less intense, domestic, and industrial activity in the immediate and/or surrounding area in the first phase. The finding of a hearth bottom in this layer in 2019 only reinforces this reinterpretation.

Phase 1: finds and dating

The pottery from the first road and the levelling layer was broadly from the mid-2nd to mid-3rd centuries, with perhaps an emphasis on the 2nd century; most of the sherds were relatively small and abraded. Other finds were few, predominantly structural nails in the east and glass in the west.

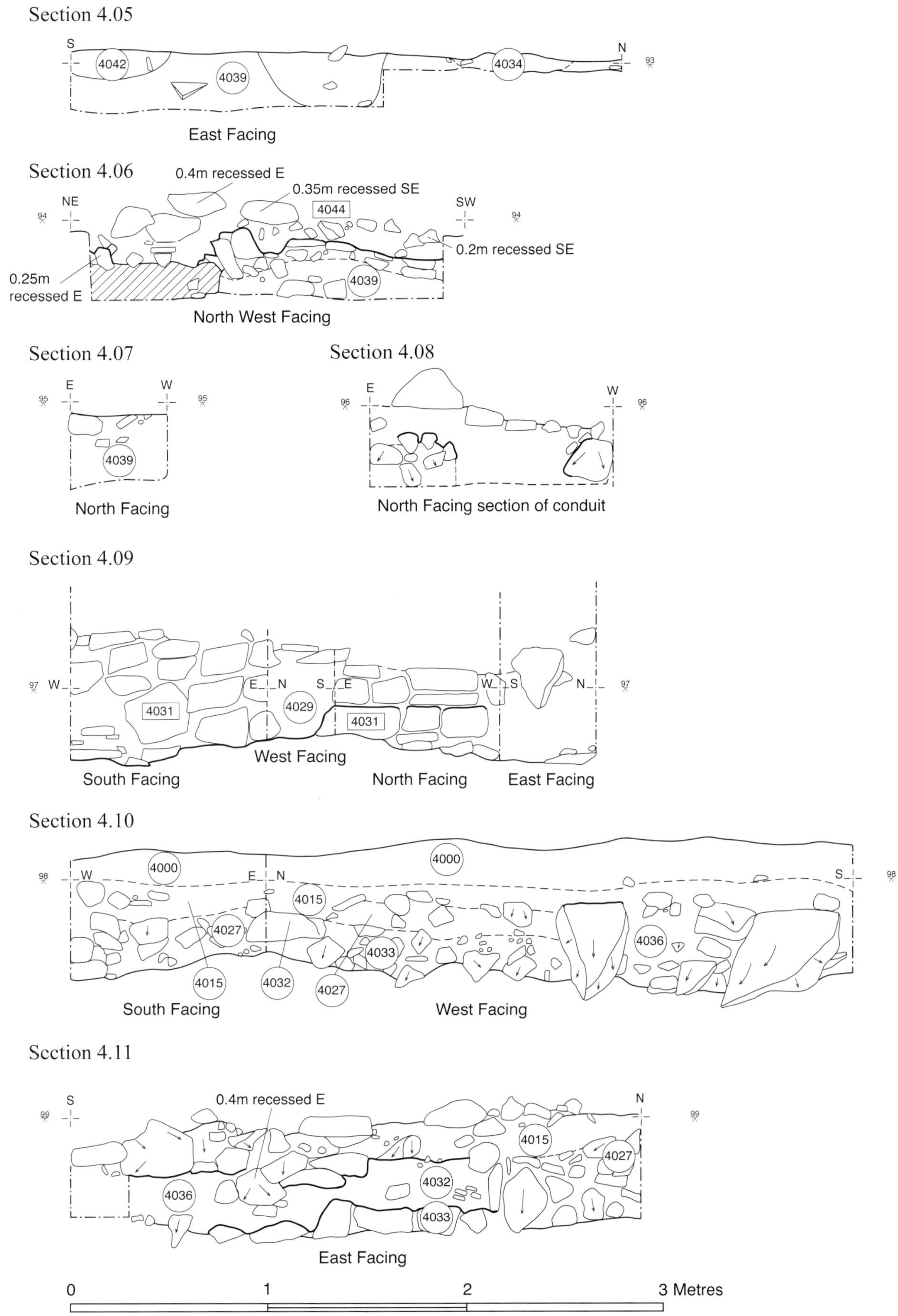

Figure 7.11: Section drawings of foundations and roads from Trench 4, phases 1 and 2.

Phase 2: the west–east road and yard

The second road with its water conduit in the west was contemporary with a phase of activity in the yard better represented in the archaeology, with a probable smithy and evidence for metal-working, possibly butchery and certainly the disposal of rubbish. Small timber buildings, if they existed in the yard, were impossible to detect amidst the disturbed and truncated layers of this phase, although structural nails might hint at their presence. Small pits and other cut features may have supported storage barrels or troughs, or aided drainage. In the east, the slight remains of a north–south, wide and well-built stone wall, and the range of associated finds, suggested the yard belonged to a high-status building located to the east of Trench 4.

Central slot across the road

The first road was overlain by a second layer of foundation stones (4019) and its ditch cut by a new ditch [4010] for the re-laid road. Around half the foundation stones of (4019) were well-sorted cobbles up to 0.2 m long, and half more variable larger and sub-square stones up to 0.4 m long, packed in clayey silt. (4019) was 0.2 m deep and, at 1.5 m wide as excavated, reached further south than the surface below. The finds were very similar to those from the first road, with just half-a-dozen abraded sherds of Roman pottery. The latest surviving road surface (4001), although disturbed and truncated by post-Roman activity, was nonetheless tightly constructed of evenly sized sub-oval and sub-rectangular cobbles, mostly around 0.2 m long, and bedded in yellow clay laid over the foundation stones (4019). Only a few abraded sherds of Roman pottery were found in the silty matrix, along with fragmentary bone and a Neolithic flint drill (cat. no. 88). Some stones that appeared to be patchy repairs of the road surface had plaster or mortar adhering, suggesting re-used structural material. These repairs may have been carried out in Phase 3, as the yard and associated building fell out of use.

The road-side ditch [4010], around 0.8 m wide in its spread condition, ran near west–east alongside the new road. It was truncated, with only up to 0.2 m in depth surviving and, like the ditch below, an open U-shape. The fill was silty clay that became siltier and pebblier with depth, with clay lenses suggesting the ditch was originally lined with yellow clay. The finds from the lower siltier fill were strikingly different from those found in the ditch below, suggesting a period of increased domestic and industrial activity in the yard to the south. There were considerable amounts of fragmentary animal bone including cattle and pig; nearly 70 sherds of pottery, including a large amphora sherd with a handle stub; iron artefacts including hobnails and structural nails; slag, clunch, and plaster. The overwhelming majority of artefacts were in the lower silty southern side of the ditch suggesting material thrown or slipped in from a busy yard; the structural debris including the clunch and plaster was overwhelmingly from the more disturbed upper layer of the fill. The heavy fraction of the environmental sample from the silt contained much hammerscale and also vitreous material supporting the idea that iron-working – almost certainly blacksmithing – was being carried out in the yard. The building identified as a likely smithy lay just to the southeast on the other side of the ditch.

The fill of this ditch [4010] was also investigated – as [4021] – in a small slot just to the east (Fig 7.9) where it had been cut by later ditch [4034], associated with the late phase of pits discussed below. This stretch of the southern side of the roadside ditch had been very badly disturbed and included stones that had slumped in from both the smithy structure to the south and the road surface to the north. The stones in the ditch comprised large cobbles similar to the road stones, and smaller cobbles and large, long sub-triangular stone with a smooth scalloped edge which may have come from the building in the centre of the trench. The ditch fill contained half-a-dozen fragmentary pottery sherds, some bone and three structural iron nails. All the finds were down the southern side of the ditch; the few sherds of pottery were of a similar range of fabrics to the considerable assemblage from [4010] including Samian, amphorae sherds, and Black Burnished Ware. The heavy fraction of the environmental sample from this section of the ditch contained some bone, metal, slag, hammerscale, and charred vitreous material. The radiocarbon dates from the sample were 201–238 cal AD (at 1σ and 39.8%) and 123–246 cal AD (at 2σ and 95.4%), SUERC-105500, suggesting that the most productive phase of activity in the yard could have been early 3rd century, possibly beginning in the 2nd century.

Eastern slot across the road

The laying of the new road foundations (4027) [equivalent to (4019) – see above] included the construction of a more elaborate roadside ditch in this area. Although badly damaged by later collapse and truncation, the ditch was flanked and channelled by two huge triangular stones, which emerged from the eastern edge of the trench (Figs 7.8, 7.11 section 4.10, and 7.12). These were presumably linked to some structural ditch-feature continuing to the east and connected with the likely high-status building south of the road and almost entirely outside the trench to the east. Each of the stones was laid near west–east and at least 0.5 m of each stone lengthways was uncovered. Further lengths of the stones were well-anchored in the trench-side. The sub-triangular stones sloped gently west and towards their pointed ends, creating a channel about 0.65 m wide; the northern stone was 0.4 m wide, the southern slightly wider, and both were maximum 0.2 m thick. The *in-situ* foundation stones of the new road (4027) lay north of the channel and comprised cobbles and sub-rectangular stones up to 0.37 m long, packed with well-sorted, smaller cobbles and pebbles in a clayey silt matrix. The camber of the road survived here and the foundations sloped gently towards the south and the channel. The ditch fill between the large triangular stones was humic and contained both charcoal and some finds. There was no pottery, but clunch and fragmentary bone. Above (4027), [equivalent to (4001) in the centre slot], was a disturbed layer of road surface stones (4015) bedded patchily in clay, with evidence for later repair. Most of the layer comprised cobbles and sub-angular stones between 0.1–0.15 m long in a sandy silt matrix, with one larger and some smaller areas of clay and pebble patching. As in other areas of this upper road, larger stones were packed around with evenly sized smaller stones to create a more level surface.

The eastern end of the road was explored further just to the west of the slot discussed above, as there were indications of structural collapse onto the road from the yard (Fig 7.8). The disturbed and truncated archaeology was very difficult to untangle but a structure [4041]–[4022] had stood south of the roadside ditch and is discussed further below. The near west–east wall foundations [4041] survived very poorly, running alongside and south of the ditch for about 3 m. Stones [4040] from that wall appeared to have collapsed onto the road surface to the north and across the partially in-filled roadside ditch, as the yard buildings were demolished and/or fell out of use. Some of the stones of [4040] were quite large: sub-oval cobbles and sub-rectangular stones up to 0.35 m long were partially covered by silty soil and smaller cobbles, suggesting collapsed wall stones and core. Only a few sherds of Roman pottery were found in that core material.

The road in the west of the trench and the stone water course

The surviving second road surface in the west, equivalent to (4001) centre and (4015) east had been investigated in a 2019 sondage as (1008). The remaining undisturbed road surface was excavated in a north–south slot as (4026) to explore the relationship of the road with the stone water course SG[4031]. This did not go beyond exposing the foundations of the second road. The flags south of the road, (1007) in 2019, were partially lifted to reveal the stone water conduit below.

The road stones (4026) north of the flags were set in yellow clay as elsewhere and retained a slight southwards camber. The vast majority of the stones were well-sorted cobbles and sub-angular stones up to 0.2 m long, with a few larger stones towards the southern edge. Six large, rounded stones up to 0.34 m long were set in a 0.4 m wide band of white clay on the road edge. Fragments of cattle, sheep, and pig bone, coal, an iron artefact, and 13 abraded pottery sherds dominated by Greyware and

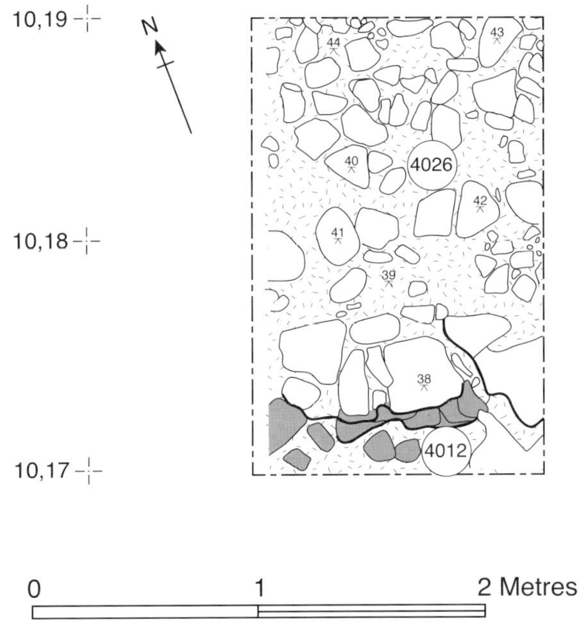

Figure 7.12: Plan of the phase 2 road surface in Trench 4.

amphorae were found amidst the stones. The ends of the coursed side stones of the water conduit SG[4031] were also set into the white clay, suggesting the second road and the conduit had been constructed together.

The large flags (1007) capping the conduit, probably to allow road traffic in and out of the yard. comprised at least 10 roughly shaped flags. Three much larger ones were up to 0.85 m long and fitted together in sub-square, L-shaped and crescent-shaped pieces. These were surrounded by smaller sub-triangular and sub-square flags between 0.3–0.4 m long, knitted into the larger stones of the road edging to the north (Fig. 7.7). The conduit SG[4031] below was *c.* 0.5–0.6 m wide with a flagged base and rough coursed stone sides between three to five courses deep. Three metres of the conduit survived in the trench, disappearing into the trench-side in the west; in the east the channel feeding it ran from the north under the road to join the eastern end of the conduit (Figs 7.7, 7.8, 7.11 section 4.09, 7.12 and 7.13 section 4.01). The eastern end was *c.* 0.35 m deep; the conduit deepened gradually to nearer 0.8 m in the west.

The fill of the conduit was investigated in three slots across its course, from west to east: (4012), (4029), and (4030) (Figs 7.13 and 7.11 section 4.09). Investigating fill (4012) in a 0.75 m wide slot, it appeared that the watercourse had first been partially blocked with washed-in organic-rich material and then slowly silted up. Here the sides of the conduit were rough coursed and four–five courses high, with the 0.6 m wide base stone-lined with rough, small sub-oval and sub-square flags. The fill was very humic and gritty, with heavy iron panning and some smaller cobbles and fragments

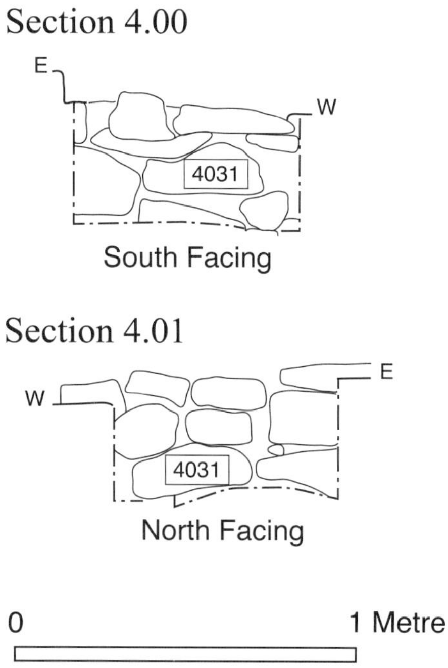

Figure 7.13: Sections of the conduit associated with the phase 2 road in Trench 4.

of sandstone in the lower fill; most of the pottery, other artefacts and bone (pig and sheep, some of which was burnt) were found in the upper siltier deposits. These finds included over 20 sherds of Roman pottery (mostly Lower Nene Valley ware, Greyware, and Black Burnished ware), some undiagnostic ceramic building material, and iron objects such as hobnails and studs. The environmental samples from (4012) contained charred plant remains, and wood charcoal, with fragments of bone, and considerable slag and hammerscale in the heavy fraction. The radiocarbon dates from the upper siltier fill were: 351–408 cal AD (at 1σ and 61.9%) and 329–418 cal AD (at 2σ and 78.7%), SUERC-105498; and from the lower in-fill: 281–330 cal AD (at 1σ and 52.2%) and 225–362 cal AD (at 2σ and 95.4%), SUERC-105499. This suggests that the conduit was less well-maintained during the late 3rd to earlier 4th century and perhaps gradually silted up thereafter.

The second investigation of the conduit fill (4029) was in a slot 1 m to the east of the first. Here the conduit was narrower, *c.* 0.5 m wide; the fill was also gritty and very humic but with only a small amount of gravel and occasional small cobbles in the lower spit. Like the stretch of conduit investigated to the west, the channel was slightly higher in the east (0.36 m E–0.41 m W), creating a gentle fall in the watercourse towards Dere Street. The fired clay and ceramic building material found in (4029) were mostly in the lower fill with the other finds, including three abraded pottery sherds and fragments of bone, in the upper siltier layer. The bone included a cat pelvis. The environmental sample results were very similar to the first slot but with even more copious hammerscale.

The final intervention across the conduit (4030) explored where the end of the stone-built conduit met roadside ditch [4010]. This junction had been badly disturbed but it was clear in section that the feeder for the conduit had come from the north under the road before turning west under the flags. The relationship with the roadside ditch(es), both in terms of construction and stratigraphy could not entirely be unravelled but the conduit was deeper than and cut through the earlier roadside ditch. Conduit fill (4030) was very similar but less humic than the conduit fills to the west, with only a few abraded pottery sherds in the siltier upper layer. A Bronze Age barbed and tanged flint arrowhead was found at the base of conduit (cat. no. 87). The arrowhead is of particular interest when considered alongside the dating for the cremation discussed below. By contrast over 50 sherds of Roman pottery were found in the fill of the open roadside ditch just east of the junction, including many amphorae and Greyware sherds, along with burnt bone fragments, hobnails, and a range of ceramic building materials including clunch, tile and *imbrex*, and fired clay.

Phase 2: the yard and its structures and features

After the ground south of the road was levelled using the deposits described above, it became a busy yard. The more extensive and laminated clay-dominated yard surfaces across the trench while similar in composition, contained finds and inclusions that reflected activities predominating in different areas. Thus, although the various layers merged into one another they gave some impression of a variety of uses. The subsequent destruction in the Roman period of the buildings in the yard and the pit and ditch-digging that followed complicated the interpretation of the archaeology. Later ploughing and landscaping further truncated and disturbed the archaeology. However, the yard was clearly used for metal-working and contained at least one stone-founded building. The more substantial stone wall remains in the east belonged to a building standing mostly beyond the trench, but probably of some status.

The yard surfaces

The surfaces encountered across the yard were inevitably very heterogenous, built up of thin layers and spreads of earth, clay, charcoal, and debris with some paving and areas of cobbling (Figs 7.7 and 7.8). In the west over levelling layer (4018), and south of the flagging over the conduit, the external floors were excavated as (4017) and were composed of charcoal-rich silty clay with evidence for disturbed but bedded-in patches of rough cobbling using rounded stones up to 0.15 m long. Presumably the cobbling reinforced areas of heavy traffic or focused working. As well as fragmentary bone, some identifiable as pig and sheep, and Roman brick, the finds included iron nails, a lead plug, Roman bottle glass and 47 sherds of pottery – from Samian fragments, including a base with two repair rivet holes, and Lower Nene Valley Colour-coated ware sherds, to amphorae and Greyware.

To the east the depth of the floors were sampled in a central north–south slot as (4003). A small depth of the layers had been removed in 2019 as (1015) but no finds were made. [The small square cut feature in south of the slot in (4003) was the remains of a sump dug in 2019 in an attempt to drain Trench 1.] Layer (4003) was *c.* 0.15 m deep, very similar in composition to (4017), but with more lenses of yellow clay. The clay, as with all these external surfaces could have been remnants of clay working floors and the greater proportion in (4003) may have been linked to working areas around the smithy. The patches of pebbles and smaller cobbles frequent in all the related yard layers were pressed into the clay to improve the surface in at least some areas of the yard, and particularly around the small building and south of the flagged crossing of the water conduit. A stone post-pad (0.38 m by 0.35 m) in the centre west of the slot, may have supported part of the wooden superstructure of building [4022] to the east, discussed below. The building may have been open to the west. The sections created by excavating this slot showed some of the inter-relationships between the roadside ditches discussed above and picked up the courses of the later ditches dug through the yard surfaces (Fig. 7.9 sections 4.03 and 4.04). Within (4003) were fragments of degraded animal bone, iron nails, 21 sherds of Roman pottery, including some Samian, fired clay (CAM3) and a possible smoothing stone.

Layers (4005) and 4007) in the eastern part of the trench, although related to the small building and to more deliberate paving, were also a continuation of the yard floors and are discussed with layers (4008) and (4009) below. These latter two layers merged with the surrounding floors (4005) and (4007) but contained direct evidence for the character of the building.

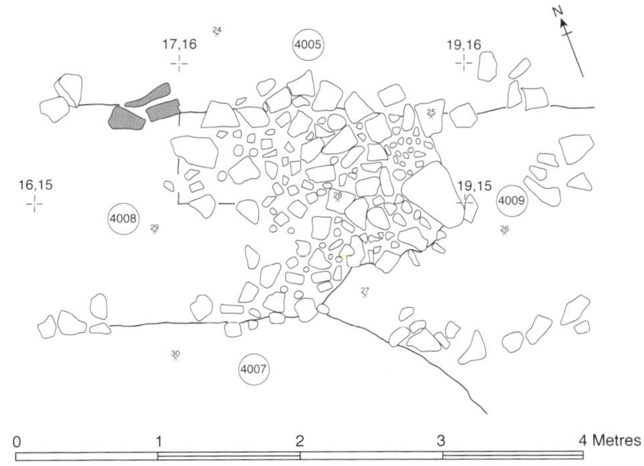

Figure 7.14: A plan of surviving flagging associated with the west wall of a substantial building in the east of Trench 4.

Figure 7.15: The remains of the phase 2 smithy and associated flagging in Trench 4, looking west.

The smithy and related surfaces

The small building stood in the east centre of the yard (Figs 7.7, 7.8, and 7.10), but its exact layout was extremely difficult to determine. The surviving, slumped foundations and lower courses [4022] were found as a near north–south, open arc facing west, which may originally have been a corner, or a twisted stretch of a wall linked in a corner with the remnants of near west–east wall [4041] to the north. An intervention around 2 m^2 explored the depth of the building's remains. The foundations were built into the underlying spread of midden-type Phase 1 deposits (4039) (Fig. 7.11 sections 4.05, 4.06, 4.07, and 4.08).

The structural remains [4022] and [4041] can best be explained as the low stone foundations and lowest wall course(s) for a wood and plaster walled workshop, possibly open to the west and perhaps also partially open-sided. The post-pad found to the west beyond the concentration of walls may have supported the frame of the open west side. The building, likely about 3 m near west–east by up to 4 m, may have been used, at least part of the time, for metalworking as there was a significant amount of slag and hammerscale in related contexts, including in the roadside ditch silting to the north. Two to three courses of the north–south wall foundations [4022] remained, in a length of *c.* 1.3 m curved by slumping and facing near northwest (Fig. 7.11 section 4.06; Fig. 7.15). The stones were sub-rectangular *c.* 0.15–0.3 m long and *c.* 0.1 m high, and the wall was about 0.25 m wide. The matrix for the slumped and displaced stones contained considerable amounts of fragmentary animal bone and 10 sherds of abraded Roman pottery; structural nails, white lime mortar, and fired clay; window glass and sherds from a blown glass vessel, and a lead candlestick (cat. no. 50). There were traces in layers (4008) and (4009), to the east and southeast of these foundations, of further stone structural traces and a cobbled area leading to patchily surviving flagging [4016]. This flagging was laid next to the substantial north–south western wall [4020] of the building to the east (Figs 7.7, 7.8, and 7.14).

The clustering of stone in layer (4008) in the centre east of the trench above the building perhaps indicated it had been near square (or perhaps sub-circular), with one wall [4041] running just south of the roadside ditch, and the southwards return and southeast corner in the east surviving as [4022]. Some of the stones of [4041] had collapsed across the road, but the remaining foundation stones were evenly sized, mostly rounded cobbles up to 0.3 m long, with smaller packing cobbles in the core and a clayey silt backfill of the likely foundation trench. Eight sherds of Roman pottery, including Mancetter-Hartshill Whiteware and amphorae sherds, and animal bone fragments were found in the backfill, along with a fragment of a copper alloy brooch (cat. no. 8). Although there was certainly a building in this location, it must be emphasised that the disturbed nature of the archaeology makes the details of shape, size, and construction far from certain.

About 1 m to the east of the smithy (Fig 7.11 section 4.05) a small, probably contemporary pit [4042] was caught in section. Shallow at *c*. 0.15 m deep and *c*. 0.5 m in diameter, the pit was back-filled with clay- and charcoal-rich material very similar to the clay floors and contained only one sherd of Greyware.

Layer (4008) was an area of about 4 m west–east by *c*. 1.5 m north–south encompassing the remains of the building's walls. This gritty layer contained many small clay lenses and a considerable amount of cobbles and sandstone shatter, with three long (up to 0.4 m), thin orthostatic stones marking the putative west–east wall-line, and a few larger stones similar to those in the courses surviving below. The matrix included 34 sherds of Roman pottery, dominated by Greyware and Black Burnished ware, but with some Samian; as well as a large number of bone fragments and structural nails, with fired clay, *imbrex* and Roman brick, lead casting waste and ironworking slag.

Layer (4006) between (4008) and the trench edge to the east, was effectively a continuation of (4008) but seemed to comprise both displaced traces of the west–east wall of [4041] and the wider north–south wall [4020] of the building to the east (discussed below). The sandy silt was 25% cobbles and larger pebbles – possible wall core – and contained fragmentary bone, an iron nail and 13 sherds of pottery, mostly Greyware. Layer (4009) to the south of, and also related to, (4008) may have been linked more to the interior of the building and its near north–south eastern wall. The stones and matrix were very similar, although there were fewer cobbles and larger stones in the centre (interior) of the layer. The clustering of stones in the west of the context suggested a partial north–south return parallel to that represented by [4022]. Like [4022] the arrangement of those stones had a curved trend. Thus it is possible the structure was actually more sub-oval or sub-circular than sub-rectangular. The finds were also similar to (4008): eight sherds of pottery, mostly Samian, and bone and iron fragments.

North (4005) and south (4007) of those three connected and building-related layers, were contexts which seemed much more in the character of disturbed exterior surfaces: part of the yard surrounding the building. It is important to reiterate here that because of the degree of later disturbance – ploughing and landscaping – all these later layers are somewhat mixed, with yard floor and building-related deposits truncated and in the upper laminations mixed with the finds-rich and demolition-influenced subsoils. Both (4005) and (4007) contained much less stone and no hints of structure. Surface (4005) lay south of the road and north of (4008), spreading over the first roadside ditch. It was a firm, clayey layer with only occasional sandstone cobbles. Found in it were 31 sherds of Roman pottery, dominated by Greyware and Samian, some fine ceramic building material (CAM2), the largest amount of animal bone on the site at over 100 fragments, with all the identifiable bone being cattle, a considerable amount of ironworking slag and a possible smithing hearth cake. These finds suggest debris accumulating outside the building, including during a time when it was in use as a smithy.

South of the building was a more extensive surface (4007), some 4 m long west from the remains of the north–south wall discussed below, and 4 m wide from (4008) to the southern edge of trench. (4007) was explored to its full 0.2 m depth in a 1 m wide slot, running west–east from the north–south wall (Figs 7.7 and 7.8). (4007) was very similar in composition to (4005) – and the other yard floors – but had more abundant charcoal and iron panning, especially to the west. The finds decreased in quantity to the west but included ceramic building material (CAM 3), iron artefacts including nails, some animal bone (all the identifiable bone was from cattle), and 17 sherds of pottery, over half of which was Greyware with no Samian but a sherd of amphora. The environmental sample from the base of the layer contained charred plant remains, some wood charcoal and abundant bone in the heavy fraction. This sample produced radiocarbon dates of 111–171 cal AD (at 1σ and 42.3%) and 60–215 cal AD (at 2σ and 94.1%), SUERC-105501. This date has a broader range at 2σ but suggests a later 2nd century bias for the earlier period of use of the yard.

The north–south house wall

The most eastern north–south investigation also uncovered the best surviving remains of north–south wall [4002] and [4020], running 4 m north from the southeast corner of the trench up to the roadside ditch (Figs 7.7 and 7.8). This wall had been thoroughly dismantled to its foundations but would have been double-faced and about 1 m wide. The upper, spread layer of wall remains [4002] was 85% stone, dominated by large cobbles up to 0.3 m long and smaller in-fill cobbles from the core, with one or two displaced facing stones; a couple of *in-situ* facing stones were found below. The core matrix was clayey silt, 0.2 m deep and contained four sherds of Roman pottery, including an amphora handle, and a hobnail. One of the larger stones appeared to have been worked with a chamfer and possible joint. Only the lowest foundation stones survived substantially *in-situ* as two parallel lines of rough-faced stones [4020] with some patches of clay-bonded cobble core. A few sherds of pottery were found in the core, along with bone fragments and some fired clay (CAM3). Many of the facing stones were around 0.3 m long, suggesting a relatively substantial wall, continuing south beyond the trench. Some of the wall seemed to have collapsed onto, or been dismantled with debris left on, the area of flagstones [4016] outside and to the west of the wall, with most of the useful wall material subsequently removed.

Flagged area

The area of sandstone flag paving [4016] that lay between wall [4020] and the smithy to the east was *c.* 1.5 m wide and 4 m long. There was evidence for damage occurring during the dismantling of wall [4020] and probable rough patching of the area in the subsequent Phase 3. The paving survived best in the north and the southeast corner and here was well-laid, running up to the wall and formed of flat but varied sub-square (up to 0.2 m by 0.3 m by 0.08 m) and sub-triangular flags (up to 0.4 m by 0.3 m by 0.1 m), and flatter smaller cobbles carefully fitted together. The flags were laid in pebbly, silty soil. The finds included a few sherds of pottery, including Samian, and an amphora handle with a stamp (possibly of Callistus); burnt bone, with identifiable fragments being pig and sheep; iron artefacts, including seven structural nails; and several glass sherds from the body of a cup and a jug handle. These finds were suggestive of domestic activity linked to the house to the east.

Pits in the west of the trench and west–east ditches

Two intercutting pits dug through the truncated yard surface (4017) and into the levelling layer (4018) below were covered by a late rough pebble surface (4011), discussed below, and may have belonged to a slightly later phase of the yard's use. The first pit [4047] was sub-oval in plan (0.9 m by 0.5 m), oriented near north–south, with almost vertical sides and a shallow U-shaped base but only 0.3 m of its depth remained. Its fill (4035) was very silty and clay-rich: lenses of clay suggested the pit may have been clay-lined or capped with clay. Much of the surviving fill had been removed by subsequent pit but what remained contained 18 sherds of pottery of a range of fabrics suggesting a first half of the 3rd century date for the filling of the pit along with iron structural nails and fragmentary bone. The second, circular and later pit [4046], cut into the southern end of backfilled [4047], was more substantial, just over 1 m in diameter, and surviving to 0.4 m deep with steep sides and a near flat base. The fill (4024) was similar to the earlier pit: very silty and humic, with lenses of clay from a possible lining and capping. The finds were dominated by a considerable amount of animal bone – all the identifiable bone was cattle – but included burnt clay and stone, iron artefacts, a cast lead shank, and 26 sherds of pottery, including Samian. The burnt clay, stone, and nails came from the upper spit of the fill, the pottery from the lower fill. The original purpose of these pits is impossible to know, but they were finally levelled with demolition debris.

Two west–east ditches running just south of the roadside may also have been dug later in the yard's use. F[4034] was a U-shaped ditch up to *c.* 0.8 m wide seen most clearly in two interventions in the centre and around the small building (Figs 7.8 and 7.11 section 4.05). The stratigraphical relationship between roadside ditch [4010] and ditch [3034] could not be confirmed because of truncation and disturbance. Ditch [3034] had partly silted up and then possibly been capped with yellow clay, like pit [4046], before finally being levelled with cobbles and debris. The late rough cobbled surface (4011) also ran over the central stretch of the ditch. Structural nails and fired clay Type 3 were recovered from the upper disturbed layer, while the slag, animal bone (dominated by cattle bone, including some burnt rib fragments), bottle glass sherds, and pottery were mostly found in the siltier, lower fill. The 29 sherds of pottery were dominated by Greyware; a roughly shaped yellow sandstone, sub-circular gaming counter was discovered with the pottery (cat. no. 42).

A second west–east ditch [4044] ran just south of [4034], and was even harder to characterise. This ditch was captured most clearly in the western sections, but also in the central slot and east central excavation of building remains. Only *c.* 0.2 m of its depth survived. The backfill excavated in the west produced only a couple of sherds of Roman pottery but fragments of imbrex, brick, tile, fired clay Types 1 and 3, and some non-diagnostic ironworking slag. There was no stratigraphical relationship with ditch [4034] but ditch [4044] was also covered by rough cobble surface [4011]. Ditch [4044] did, however, cut backfilled pit [4046], possibly hinting at a sequence of ditch digging.

These ditches may have been inserted to improve drainage. The flooding experienced in Trench 1 in the same area as Trench 4 in 2019 demonstrated the poor draining capacity of the soil. The ground in the Roman period probably sloped more to the west and the south-running tributary of the Tyne. Ditches F[4034] and F[4044] might have helped keep the yard dry, channelling water with the slope of the ground towards a north–south roadside ditch. The roadside ditches may have been less well-maintained in the later yard period. There is also the possibility that over time the presence of the conduit had interfered with the operation of the roadside ditches and necessitated the construction of new drainage channels.

Phase 2: finds and dating

The radiocarbon dates for the earlier spit of yard (4007) and backfilling of the roadside ditch for the Phase 1 road (4021) both possibly suggest a later 2nd into earlier 3rd century range for the first period of intensive use of the yard. This might push Phase 1 into the mid-2nd century. The artefacts are consonant with the dating of Phase 2. Glass ranged from 1st century to 3rd century in date, with an emphasis on 1st- to 2nd-century forms. The pottery was similar in span to Phase 1, with the same predominance of mid–late 2nd- to early–mid-3rd-century fabrics and forms. However, the yard floors such as (4008), (4017), and (4028) were spot-dated by the pottery to the first half of the 3rd century as was the initial silting of the second roadside ditch (4021) and the lower flagging layer (4016). Other Phase 2 artefacts were of a broad date range, fitting comfortably into the ranges indicated by the pottery and scientific dates.

There are suggestions of a secondary phase of yard activity, involving the digging of pits and ditches, the former perhaps linked to more transitory activities and the latter to help with drainage as roadside ditches choked up and became less effective.

Phases 3: overview

It was impossible to be entirely confident about the phasing of the later features, including a number of pits and ditches. Some may have been contemporary with the smithy, for example pit [4042] near the smithy, and pits [4046] and [4047] in the west, discussed above. These pits may also have been part of a later and less structured use of the yard area. Others were later again and heavily truncated and most probably belonged to the last phase of archaeology surviving in the trench. That final phase only partially survived and was badly affected by later ploughing and landscaping but seemed to represent a period of contraction after the smithy and probably the main building had been demolished. During this period, some ditches and pits may have been dug, the road was patchily repaired, areas of rough cobbling and paving laid and an unusual cremation burial made. This cremation pit was the one most clearly cut from a level above the surviving archaeology and may belong to a later Phase 3b or even a putative Phase 4. However, how long after any of the pits it was dug remains impossible to say.

Phase 3: later flagging and cobbled surfaces

Flagged areas

There were suggestions of repair or re-surfacing of flagging [4016] with areas of double layers of flagstones; the upper layer was rougher. As has been noted above in discussing the roads the upper surface of the second road had been patched with material dominated by demolition debris, including tile, brick, and stone with mortar and plaster attached. Wall stones from the smithy may also have been re-purposed to patch or flag the eastern end of the road [4040], or even to create a later crossing over the partially infilled roadside ditch.

In the east of the trench, paved area [4016] had been repaired with double layers of flags creating a rough secondary surface.

Cobble surfaces

The disturbed, rough cobble surface (4011) found south of the road in the west of the trench covered over earlier yard surfaces and backfilled pits (seen in 2019 as 1009). The rough surface was formed of pebbles and a range of cobbles up to maximum of 0.15 m pressed into an uneven and patchy layer of yellow clay. It stretched for about 4 m west–east from the western trench edge, merging into structural demolition layers in the east and thinned to the south, merging with the pebbly spread top fill (4004) of pit [4045]. The surface was often hard to distinguish from 2019 backfill and the lower subsoil (4000). Few finds were recorded, with just a few fragmentary bones and a few pottery sherds.

Pits and ditches

The pit [1018] and linear cut feature [1019] discussed above may be part of this phase.

A fragment of late ditch [4037], dug after the buildings within the yard had been demolished and through the remains of the wall [4041] was discovered in the east of the trench. This open U-shaped ditch was about 0.8 m wide and very shallow, disturbed, and truncated, with a couple of sherds of Greyware in its fill. This may have been a re-cut of ditch [4034].

Phase 3b: Pit [4045]

In the southwest corner of Trench 4 a large pit [4045] was discovered, dug from a surface lost to ploughing and other disturbance (Fig. 7.8). This may have been a surface contemporary with the late cobbling but was probably later. Historic truncation was more severe and disturbance deeper in this area of the trench, with the trough of a medieval furrow cutting across it, and the upper fill (4004) of the pit was spread and merged with the 2019 backfill of cut features pit [1018] and gulley [2019]. The cut for the pit was very difficult to discern as it had been backfilled with material of the same composition as it was cut into. There were also hints in the clay-rich yard layer (4017) surrounding the pit of the ephemeral traces of the very bases of other pits cut from a higher level. Whether these were covered by or dug through late cobbled surface (4011) was impossible to say.

Pit [4045] was probably first dug as one large pit to receive the extremely large Greyware storage jar buried in it, with the pit being immediately enlarged to enable a number of complete pots to be stacked around the top and upper sides of the jar. This was achieved by making smaller, shallower cuts into the sides of the main pit (Fig. 7.16), creating a sub-oval, lobed pit up to 1 m in diameter, with near-vertical, stepped sides surviving up to 0.5 m deep and a flat base. A large flat sub-oval stone (0.3 m by 0.35 m and 0.08 m thick) sat in the bottom onto which the large storage jar had been placed. The top of the GREY2 jar had been badly crushed, although many sherds of the upper body sherds were retrieved from the surrounding pit fill, (4025), (4013) and (4004), but the base and half of the lower body survived intact. Two and possibly three post-firing holes had been deliberately drilled into the lower wall of the vessel, equally spaced around the base, suggesting a deliberate modification for a specific purpose.

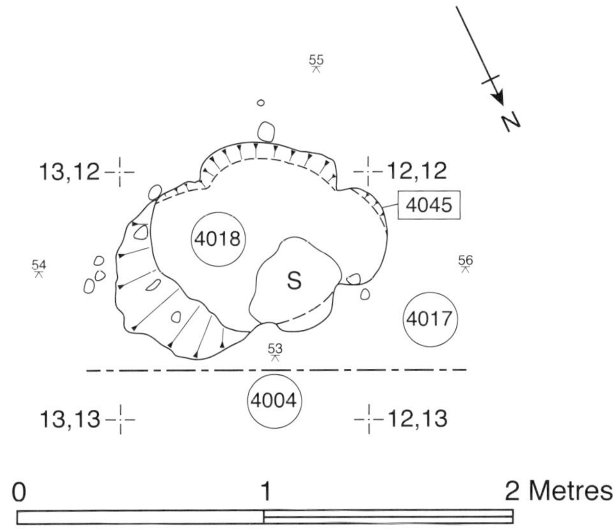

Figure 7.16: A plan of the pit [4045].

The bone in the pit

The undisturbed and unbroken lower half of the jar was packed with burnt bone and this undisturbed deposit was removed in its entirety as Environmental Sample 6. This produced copious burnt and tiny fragments of bone in all the fractions, as well as very little charcoal and charred plant remains (see report in Appendix 2). An iron Roman chain ring with flat faces was also found in the sample (cat. no. 12). The majority of the unidentifiable bone from all the sieve sizes was white and calcined, indicating burning at temperatures in excess of 600ºC. Less than a third of the bone could be identified (and some of the cremated bone must have been lost to truncation) but the identifiable bone was all caprid sheep/goat including fragments of skull, vertebra, tibia, and heel bone (see Appendix 2). This perhaps suggests the burning of a complete animal. None of the bone in the pot fill could be identified as human. Only one fragment of the bone was suitable for radiocarbon dating and produced a Bronze Age date: 2489–2449 cal BC (at 1σ and 34.1%); 2497–2341 cal BC (at 2σ and 81.3%), SUERC-105783, discussed further below.

The back fill (4025) surrounding the lower complete part of the pot contained a few sherds of animal bone, one identifiable as cattle, another as sheep and more like the bone found in other ditch fills, surfaces, and pits in the trench. The upper and more disturbed pit backfill comprised some calcined bone from the jar mixed with other bone, the former mostly found amidst the pots packed over the jar. One uncalcined fragment was identified as sheep while two burnt but not calcined fragments from amongst the pots around the upper half of the jar were from roe deer. These were interpreted as having come from roasted joints of meat and suggest hunting and feasting (see Appendix 2). A crane bone was recorded from just above the jar in (4000); finds of crane bone are rare on Roman sites and have been linked to high-status or military sites (Allen 2009).

The fills

That humic lower back fill (4025) also contained lenses of yellow clay that may have been the remains of a lining. The 54 sherds of pottery in (4025), as well as fine wares and Samian, included several sherds from the large storage jar and others from a South Essex/North Kent wares wide-mouthed bowl, which joined with rim and body sherds from pit fill (4013) above and (4000) above the pit. This pottery was used in northern *Britannia* from the later 2nd century onwards, and become the major coarse ware source during the 3rd century (Croom 2016). Other finds were bottle and cup glass, fired clay Type 1, and iron artefacts including a wrought iron fitting (cat. no. 63).

Pit fill (4013) above was much more disturbed, and comprised a mix of some of the contents of the large jar with the surrounding backfill, along with several fragmented but complete and near-complete vessels, which must originally have been stacked as whole pots above and around the shoulders storage jar. Five of these vessels were Samian ware, all of late 2nd century date and included: 17 sherds amounting to a complete bowl of Central Gaulish Samian with the decorator's stamp of Lastuca of Lezoux (dated to AD 160–185); the complete profile and over half of a very large East Gaulish Samian rouletted dish, stamped by Paternus viii of Rheinzabern, dated after AD 160; many joining rim and body sherds of a late 2nd-century Central Gaulish Samian Dr36 type dish with barbotine leaf decoration on its rim; and joining fragments of the upper half of a Samian Dr38 flanged bowl, the lower interior of which showed a very heavy wear pattern, probably caused by repeated stirring or grinding. The flange of another Dr38 form had been removed and carefully rubbed flat (Fig. 7.22).

Other near-complete vessels included: the complete profile of a decorated BBW bowl dated after AD 160, matched with joining sherds from (4000) above the pit (Fig. 7.25, RP1). Also found were two more complete profiles of plain-rim decorated 'dog' dishes in DOR BB (Fig. 7.25, RP2); joining rim fragments of a decorated wide-mouth Greyware bowl in both (4013) and (4000) (Fig. 7.25, RP3), and sherds of a decorated and black-slipped beaker probably imported from Trier (Symonds 1992 Group 35; dated to AD 200–275 (Fig. 7.25, RP5); and sherds making up the complete rim of the vessel and parts of the body of a decorated SENK type 10 jar were recovered from (4000) and (4025) – dated to AD 120–230/250 (Monaghan 1987) but appearing in mid–late 3rd-century contexts at Wallsend (HWCD; Fig. 7.25, RP10).

Other pottery from (4013) comprised: Dressel 20 amphora fragments, including a handle; BB2, CNG BS, GREY everted-rim jar sherds; LNV CC beaker fragments; a MAH WH M78 mortarium rim sherd; a sherd of SVW OX 2; and a fragment of a WW cupped-rim flagon.

The mixed backfill also contained several glass sherds including from a flagon, an early and rare cast polychrome bowl and a heat-distorted jug; a copper-alloy headstud brooch (cat. no: 7); a ring from the contents of the jar, and a copper alloy and iron mount (cat. no. 67). The spread fill (4004) above (4013) clearly contained pit fill but was extremely disturbed, including by the excavation in 2019 of the later features stone-filled pit [1018] and gully [1019]. The high clay content might suggest the pit had been capped with clay. The 26 sherds of pottery were much more abraded but included some larger sherds of BBW, Greyware and amphorae; alongside the burnt bone were fragments of imbrex, Roman brick and tile; iron nails and hobnails and a cast copper-alloy mount (cat. no. 16).

The cremation burial

The pit and its contents were obviously a cremation burial, with the large jar packed with cremated bone and stacked round with complete and impressive ceramics representing a deliberate and rich structured deposition. However, this 'burial' raises many questions. The Bronze Age, mid-3rd-millennium BC radiocarbon date range is difficult to explain as the burial is otherwise so decidedly Roman from the container to the complete pots buried with the cremation jar. Was the cremation conducted in an area where Bronze Age cremations had been made – the fire pit dug down into a mound perhaps – and earlier cremated bone swept up with the Roman material? There are traces of Bronze Age occupation in the vicinity (Bishop and Dore 1988) and Trench 4 did produce a Bronze Age barbed and tanged arrowhead, often found with burials (4030; cat. no. 87). No radiocarbon date could be secured for the Roman deposition of the bone, but the stratigraphy and finds could indicate a mid to later 3rd century event. If the cremation included a person, then according to Roman custom, the burial should be located outside the town. Does this belong to a period of urban contraction post-dating the raising of town walls by the 4th century?

All the identifiable bone in the surviving undisturbed fill of the jar was caprid and, although this cannot rule out the possibility that a person was cremated, the identity of the bone might suggest an extravagant offering to domestic deities, involving animal sacrifice and feasting with the burial of the remains of the feast – including crane and roe deer – with the cremated, sacrificed goat/sheep and the striking dinner service. Animal sacrifice was widely practised in Roman Britian (Robinson 2002), but this is an unusually elaborate one. Buried burnt offerings have also been discovered as foundation deposits for buildings (Woodward and Woodward 2004), but this commemorative feast and offering seems more likely to have been marking a different but clearly notably important occasion.

Phase 3: finds and dating

Relatively little pottery came from Phase 3 features, except for the cremation pit. Sherds from the late ditches [3034] and [4037] could have a mid–later 3rd-century emphasis. The dating of the cremation pit remains challenging. One of the near complete vessels, a SENK type 10 jar, appeared in mid–late 3rd-century contexts at Wallsend. Other finds and ceramics have the same wide range as previous phases. The dates for the silting of the conduit provide the only other dating brackets for the site, with the lower silting focused on a mid–later 3rd, possibly into early 4th-century date and the final silting in the 4th century. This later range perhaps fitting with the contraction of the town, or at least urban activities and settlement on this site, and the abandonment of the conduit system.

Trench 4, Phases 1–3: Discussion

Though it is possible that earlier activity took place in the area of Trench 4, the earliest evidence encountered during these excavations was for possible metal-working and other industrial/domestic activities in Phase 1 dating to around the mid-2nd century. There may have been related, and less permanent, wood-dominated buildings, but there was no certain evidence for this. These activities could have been linked to the military base, to the south or provide evidence for the earliest 'urban' activities as Corbridge began to develop as a town. Another possibility is that this was a discrete farm or small settlement north of the army base during the 160s–170s. Phase 1 ended with a levelling deposit. This could be conceivably linked to the unrest or disruption that stalled building on Site XI, with the levelling layer related to the 'Corbridge Destruction Deposit' (see Hodgson 2008; McCluskey 2022). Or the levelling may have been undertaken in advance of the expansion or further planning and development of the town.

Phase 2 is the most archaeologically rich phase, during the time of the rapid expansion of the town, with a probable later 2nd- into earlier 3rd-century range for the first period of intensive use of the yard which dominates Trench 4. This period also saw the building and occupation of the house to the east, to which the yard belonged. Ceramics and artefacts suggest a high-status house, possibly with military connections. The quality of the structural remains, the findings of, for example window glass, *imbrices* and fine ceramics, all testify to the standing of the building and to occupants of some wealth and status. This phase saw the rebuilding of the spur road, the laying of a road-side water conduit, and the construction of a small building, used as a smithy for at least some of its life. The building had low stones walls, perhaps open to the west with a wooden superstructure that may plausibly have been partly open-sided.

Phase 3 begins in the mid-3rd century and corresponds to some changes with the digging of ditches, perhaps to combat drainage problems, and of pits that may have held barrels or founded other small structures. Subsequently, and perhaps only a little later, the stone buildings seem to have been demolished, and patchy rough external paving and cobble surfaces laid. The road surface was also inexpertly patched and possibly other pits and ditches dug. The latest activity in the trench associated with the Roman period is the unusual and lavish cremation burial or burnt animal offering in a pit. A date for this deposit in the later 3rd century is most likely on the basis of the ceramics found in the pit. It is feasible that further activity on site occurred in the later 3rd and 4th centuries, but post-Roman agriculture and landscaping has truncated the latest Roman archaeology. It is, however, notable that very few 4th-century ceramics were recovered, even in disturbed subsoils, and this points to a probable changed use of the site, away from domestic and craft activities.

Trench 5

Trench 5 was located *c.* 16 m the east of Trench 4 and on the northern side of the spur road to investigate what appeared in the geophysics to be a stone-founded strip building facing the street (Fig. 7.3). Trench 4 was 10 m north–south by 8 m west–east and entirely encompassed Trench 3 from 2019 (Fig. 7.6). Excavation in 2019 had confirmed the considerable truncation of the archaeology, with *in-situ* archaeology at *c.* 0.3 m deep; the furrows of the ENE–WSW pre-modern plough-strikes were more apparent in Trench 5.

Turf, topsoil, and upper subsoil (5000) were removed by machine to a depth of *c.* 0.3 m, after which – as with Trench 4 – excavation of the remaining disturbed layer continued by hand, with the same sieving and sampling protocols. Those clayey, sandy silt layers contained some cobbles and stone shatter, clearly concentrated over the emerging wall-lines. A total of 375 sherds of Roman pottery were recovered from (5000), 27% of the total trench assemblage. The condition of the pottery in the trench was generally poorer than Trench 4, with smaller, more abraded sherds. More post-medieval pottery was also recovered from layers below (5000) indicating a greater degree of mixing and disturbance. Most of the pottery in (5000), however, was Roman with a range of wares and forms, but with notably more Greyware sherds compared to Trench 4. Building material included clunch, *opus signinum*; and fragments of *tegulae*, *imbrices*, Roman brick and tile, and fired clay. As well as hobnails, iron structural nails, and an iron latch, Roman period finds comprised a brooch pin, two gaming counters – one stone, one ceramic – sherds of glass vessels, non-diagnostic slag, and a fragment of lava quern stone. The animal bone fragments were in poor condition; all identifiable bone was cattle.

The building outline was visible immediately below (5000) (Fig. 7.17), with wall foundations up to 1 m wide delineating an interior *c.* 4.75 m wide by *c.* 8.25 m long, short side facing the road. There were no gaps for doorways indicating that surviving layers were foundations only. The stony layer [3008] and burnt deposits (3009) recorded in 2019 were also revealed; it was obvious immediately that they belonged to a separate circular feature within the southwest corner of the building.

Phase 1: early ground surface and wall

Below part of the foundation cut for a wall of the Trench 5 building there were hints of an earlier structure and a related surface. The earlier structural feature [5033] was found below the western wall in a slot across the width of the foundations [5035]; the surface was found below the north wall [5036] and above natural clay, and may have been internal or external.

The structural element [5033] was only seen in 1 m-wide slot but appeared to be a wall constructed on a slightly different alignment – more NNW–SSE. Only the upper surface was seen, built of rounded and some sub-angular cobbles *c.* 0.15 m long. The matrix and a thin soil layer over the stones was a clayey silt containing some corroded iron fragments. The western wall of the later strip building may have used this structure as a base for its foundations. The surface (5032) into which the northern wall's foundation trench [5036] was cut, was a highly organic sandy silt with some small pebbles, up to 0.15 m deep and sitting on natural clay. A collapse of the sides of the foundation trench had deposited some intrusive post-medieval brick and tile into (5032) from the subsoil to the north but the remainder of the finds were Roman and included hobnails and 15 sherds of pottery dated to early–mid-2nd into early 3rd century. An environmental sample (ES8) produced copious wood charcoal, charred vitreous material and fragments of bone.

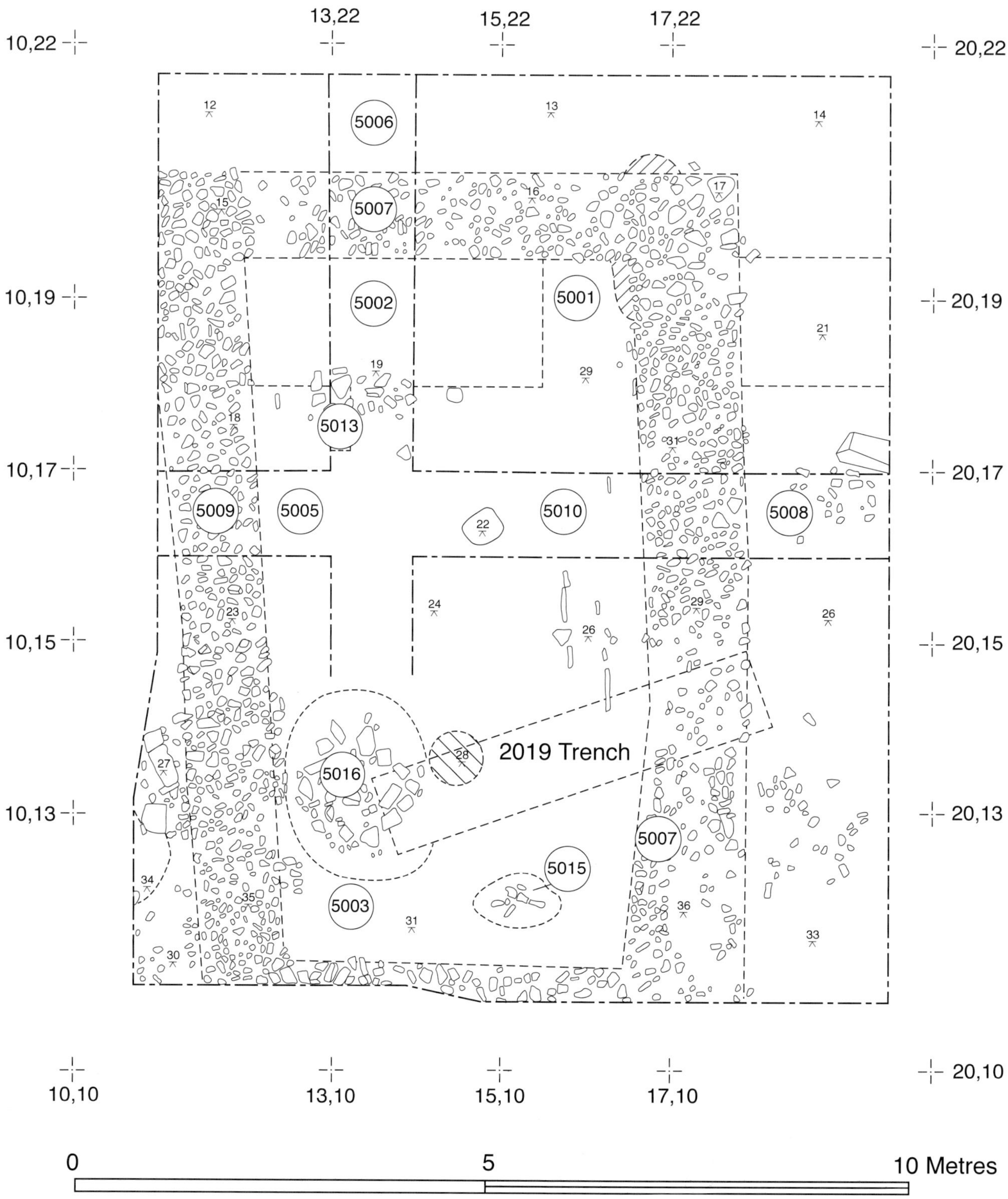

Figure 7.17: The plan of Trench 5.

Phase 1: finds and dating

A radiocarbon date range was secured for the lowest level of the early surface (5032): 68–132 cal AD (at 1σ and 51.9%) and 57–209 cal AD (at 2σ and 90.8%), SUERC-105508. These relatively broad ranges might suggest a later 1st to early 2nd century date but could equally focus on the 2nd century. Combining this with the abraded pottery, dating might lean towards an early–middle 2nd century range.

Phase 2: overview

The strip building had two distinct layers of stone foundations. It was impossible to determine whether these represented a rebuilding or simply the original construction approach. The building had an eastern annex, which could only be partially explored but seemed more domestic in character.

Later disturbance and truncation and the consequent loss of horizontal stratigraphy also made it difficult to be certain about the chronological relationships of features within the building. A hearth [5028] in the near centre of the building may have been earlier than the oven [5022] in the southwest or the trough [5018] in the east centre, or may rather have gone out of use earlier. The stone-filled pit [5016] that covered the remains of the oven was part of Phase 3 discussed below, that also included a small pit [5015] next to the southern wall.

Phase 2: the foundations of the strip building

The east, west, and north walls were examined in slots across their widths (Figs 7.17 and 7.18). The western wall foundations [5035] were built on the Phase 1 foundations; the first Phase 2 foundation layer (5011) was 1.06 m wide and up to 0.4 m deep – and thus up to 0.2 m deeper than the northern and eastern equivalents, perhaps built deeper to utilise or compensate for the earlier structural feature. Sub-angular and sub-rounded cobbles, ranging in size between 0.08 m and 0.2 m, were used to construct the layer with more of the larger stones on the exterior face of the foundations. The sandy silt matrix contained two unidentified iron artefacts, a very corroded wrought iron escutcheon (cat. no. 38), bone fragments and over 20 sherds of Roman pottery of a range of fabrics. An intrusive post-medieval sherd testified to the considerable disturbance just to the west of the foundations, partially caused by a medieval furrow but also by later activity. The foundation layer above (5009) was *c.* 0.2 m deep and 1.07 m wide but built of better sorted and mostly sub-rounded cobbles between 0.1–0.15 m with smaller infill of more angular stones. The matrix was very similar, if more charcoal-rich: four sherds of Roman pottery were found of a likely mid-2nd to mid-3rd-century date range and few fragments of bone. The overall depth of the surviving foundations was *c.* 0.6 m.

The northern wall and eastern wall foundations were very similar. The slot through east foundations [5037] was the only location where the foundation cut could be discerned (Fig. 7.18C); the slot also gave a glimpse of the very disturbed remains of west–east foundations that may have supported the northern wall of the annex.

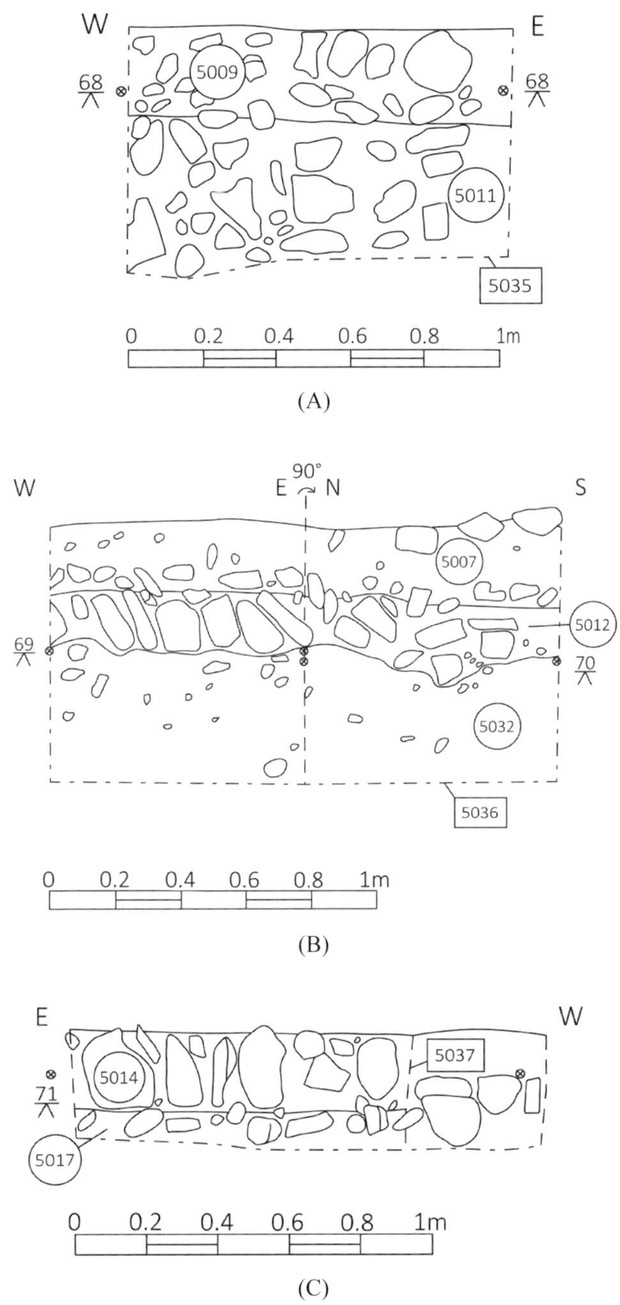

Figure 7.18: (A) The section through the west wall of the building. (B) The section through the north wall of the building. (C) The section through the east wall of the building.

This appeared likely to have been a butt join and the annex added to the main building rather than built with it. The lower east foundations (5017) were 1 m wide and 0.15 m depth was excavated. Sub-rounded and sub-angular cobbles between 0.1 m to 0.2 m long were laid in a rough herring bone pattern. A thin *c*. 0.07 m bedding layer of pebbly silty clay had been spread to take the second layer of foundations. The finds included non-diagnostic ironworking slag, some cattle bone and teeth fragments, three unidentified iron artefacts and bottle glass fragments. The foundation layer above (5014) was *c*. 0.25 m deep and utilised bigger sub-rounded and sub-angular stones mostly around 0.2 m and up to 0.27 m long, in a similar silty clay matrix. No artefacts were found.

The northern wall foundation [5036] trench cut into surface (5032) discussed above and was then raised in a very similar fashion to the eastern foundations (Fig. 7.18B). The full depth of the 1 m-wide lower foundations (5012) was reached at *c*. 0.2m, and showed the trench was first packed with a layer of small cobbles onto which larger and more angular cobbles were laid in a herringbone pattern, finally a thin layer of silty bedding clay laid over the top of the first layer of foundations. Twenty sherds of Roman pottery were found in the matrix, with a date range from the mid-2nd century onwards, along with bottle glass, animal bone, and an unidentifiable copper-alloy artefact (cat. no. 85). The upper foundations (5007) were up to 1.1 m wide and 0.2 m deep with the same silty clay matrix. The sub-rounded and sub-angular cobbles were well-sorted and mostly around 0.2 m long. There were more obvious attempts to interlock stones, using smaller cobbles and pebbles to level rough courses. Only three sherds of Roman pottery were found, along with some Roman brick fragments, mortar and fired clay, and an iron nail. Building material found in the foundation layers probably came from the demolition of earlier structures.

The southern wall foundations were just caught by the positioning of Trench 5, but seemed to be less substantial than those of the other three sides, perhaps indicating a structure open-fronted to the road. When pit [5015] was investigated, the stones of the foundations in that area seemed to be little more than a disturbed and perhaps spread single layer. However, the bulk of the foundation's width remains south of the trench.

Phase 2: structures within the building

The hearth and related surface

The disturbed remains of a fairly crude hearth [5028] (Fig. 7.19) were found just north of the centre of the building, some of the partly displaced stones had been used to cap the hearth, other *in-situ* flags formed a rough, semi-circular structure formed of five larger sub-rectangular but irregular flat stones, between 0.3–0.5 m long with smaller stones infilling. These delineated an area 1.55 m east–west by 0.6 m north–south by *c*. 0.18 m deep and probably open to the northeast. The fill was very charcoal-rich, ashy, clayey silt but much of the centre of the feature was taken up by a large and unidentifiable iron object (cat. no. 84), that was relatively flat and very corroded with an integral hooked shank. Four other unidentifiable iron objects were found with it, as well as a crudely cast lead disc surrounding a wrought iron loop (cat. no. 56). This was perhaps an object used on the hearth in cooking or an industrial process. Clay-rich, ashy material laminated with iron panning had accumulated above the iron object. A small amount of fragmentary bone, some burnt, came from the matrix surrounding the object, along with a hobnail and 14 sherds of Roman pottery dominated by Greyware, with dating likely to be from the earlier–mid-2nd century up to the end of the century. The environmental sample produced considerable amounts of wood charcoal but little else. A radiocarbon date on roundwood charcoal from the sample produced date ranges of 154–210 cal AD (at 1σ and 54.0%) and 118–236 cal AD (at 2σ and 94.1%), SUERC-105509, thus with a focus on the mid to later 2nd century.

The hearth was associated with a lower floor area (5030) part of the layer dug as (5019-5020-5023-5024-5027-5031), and discussed below, but possibly as a lower spit of that floor. The oven [5022] nearly 3 m to the south of the hearth seems to have been constructed into this floor. The (5030) layer was explored in a north–south slot running from the hearth to the oven and excavated to a depth of 0.15 m. It comprised silty clay-clayey silt and was charcoal-rich with fragments of fired clay and burnt stone. A fragment of tubular blue glass bead (cat. no. 20) was found, along with a small amount of burnt and unburnt animal bone, three structural nails and 25 sherds of Roman pottery, again dominated by Greyware.

The lower floor layer

The less-disturbed, lower floor layer within the main building was sampled in slots and in areas as (5019-5020-5023-5024-5027-5031). Generally a slightly sandy, silty clay with variable but often considerable amounts of charcoal, the floor had been roughly paved in limited areas, presumably where there was heavy foot traffic or a focus of activity. These areas were above and around the hearth [5028] and just to the northwest in (5019). Overall this layer also contained more ceramics and other finds than the quite disturbed yellow clay floor sealing it.

The distribution of bone within the lower floor was uneven. The areas around the hearth [(5020), (5023) to the east and (5031) to the south] contained more fragments, some burnt, with all the identifiable bone from cattle,

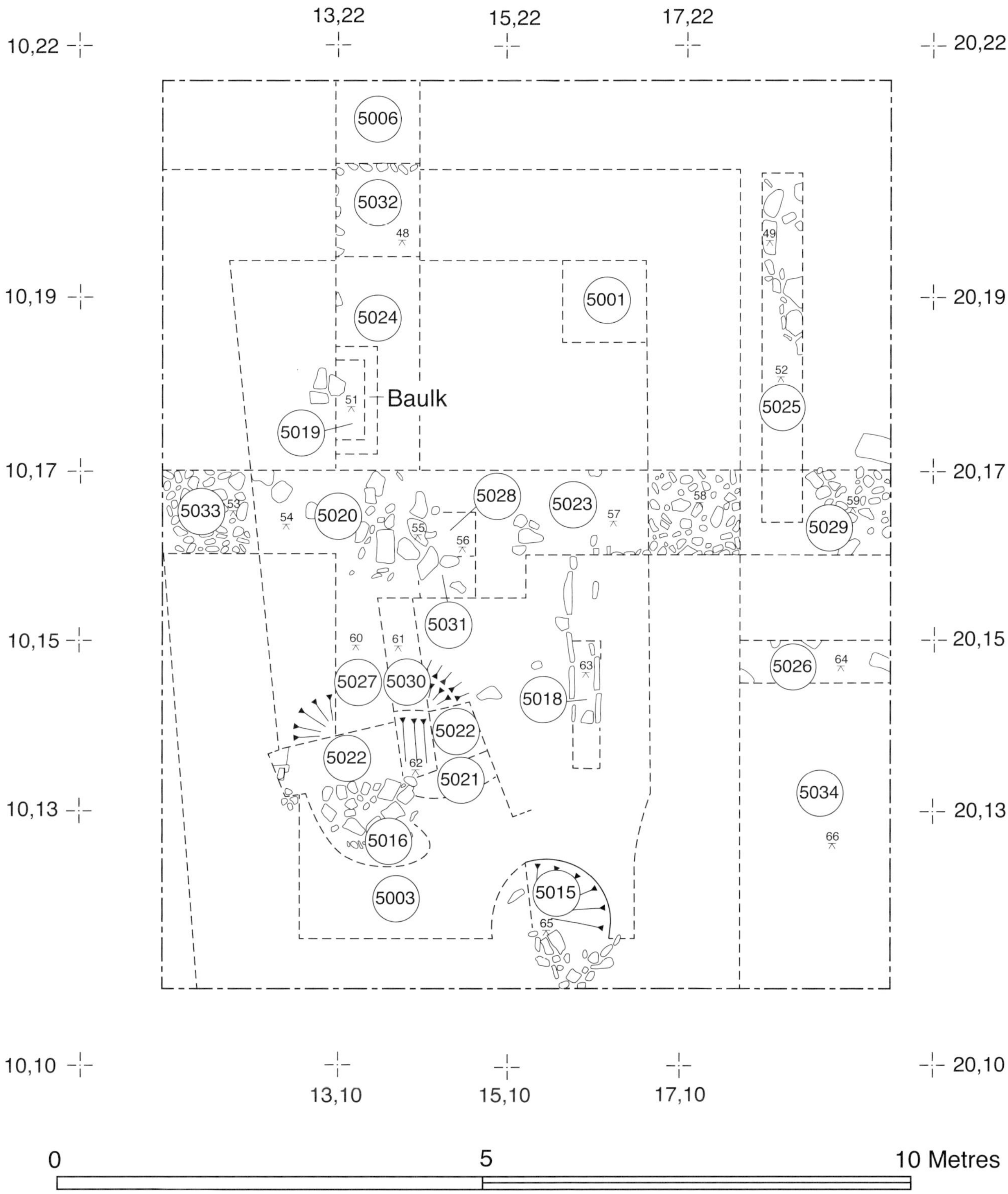

Figure 7.19: A plan of the building in Trench 5, focusing on internal features.

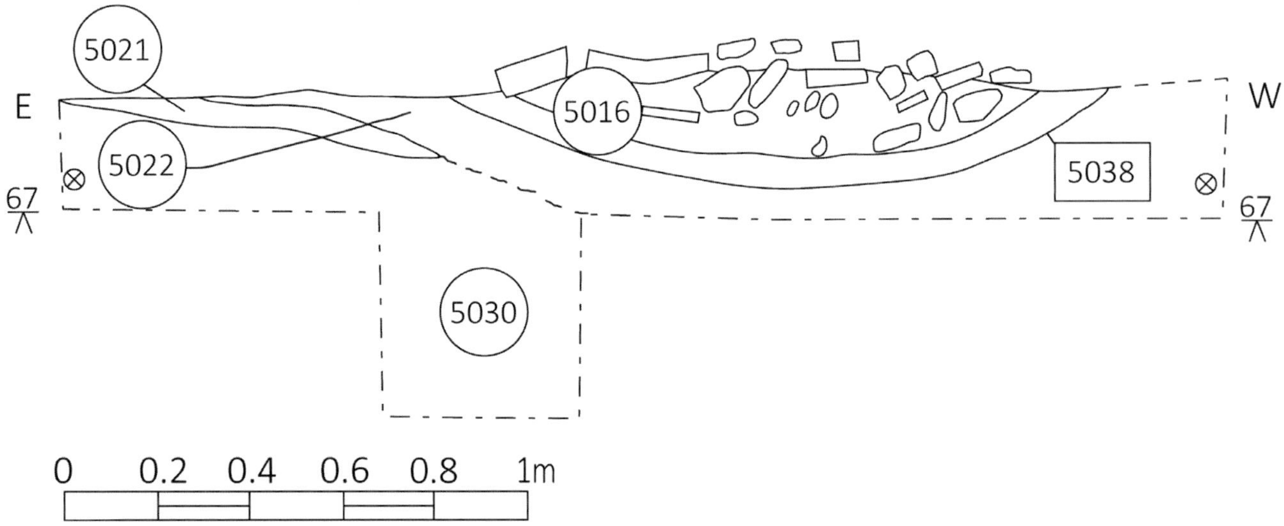

Figure 7.20: A section of the oven or hearth [5022], located in the southwest corner of the building in Trench 5.

except for one pig bone, while areas to the north and northwest in the building (5019) and (5024) contained very little bone.

The area around the hearth also produced abundant unidentifiable structural iron artefacts and some slag, while the northern end of the building produced only structural nails. The former were perhaps from a hearth-related structure and evidence for occasional smithing, while the latter may have come from the wooden superstructure or furniture at the back of the building. The pottery also showed some possible patterning. Around the hearth, although Greyware dominated and there was a certain amount of Samian, the fabrics were more varied and considerable numbers of sherds were found. Area (5020) around the hearth was especially productive, with around 80 sherds including from amphorae, fine wares and a beautifully burnished Black Burnished ware fabric. (5027) between the hearth and the oven was another pottery sherd-rich area with lots of Greyware but also nearly 20 sherds of a fine oxidised fabric. Fewer sherds were found in the northern end of the building, with very little in (5019) in the northwest and a small assemblage from the north (5024) dominated by Greyware. There were very few other finds but a fragment of a copper-alloy dress accessory (cat. no. 18) came from (5024) in the north of the building, along with part of a scabbard slide (cat. no. 24), and a blue glass bead (cat. no. 27) from (5027) near the oven.

The oven and the trough

The oven/hearth [5022] located in the southwest corner of the building was cut into floor layer (5030) (Figs 7.19 and 7.20) and was in use at the same time as the lower floor. Before the floor was sealed by a yellow clay layer, the oven had been thoroughly dismantled with any stone elements removed; its use as the base for a clay-lined pit [5038] in the following phase further disturbed the remains of the feature. The silt clay remains, 0.35 m deep, covered an area 1.6 m near east–west and 1.2 m near north–south and were full of burnt stone shatter, fired clay, vitrified material, and charcoal. A few calcined cattle bone fragments and 16 structural nails were found in the remains, along with over 70 sherds of pottery and a copper alloy pin head (cat. no. 14). The environmental sample (ES5) produced high concentrations of wood charcoal, low concentrations of cereal grain and hazel nutshell, but a moderately high concentration of heathland wild or weed plant seeds. These results were very similar to those obtained from the trough [5018] to the east, and distinct from the assemblages in the trench's other environmental samples, perhaps indicating that the two features may have worked together.

To the east of the sub-oval remains of the oven a spread of orangey red burnt clay 0.1 m thick and 0.9 m long by *c.* 0.8 m wide represented the remaining rake out from the oven. No finds were made and the environmental sample (ES4) produced only burnt clay in the heavy fraction.

The stone-lined trough [5018] was located around 1 m east of the oven and aligned north–south. The depth of the trough was constructed of long thin stones, four of these survived on the eastern side and six on the western side, creating a feature around 1.6 m long, 0.36 m wide and up to 0.42 m deep, including the cobble base. The stones were *c.* 0.5 m high, *c.* 0.25–0.3 m wide and between 0.2 m and 0.4 m long. Above a thin layer of packed pebbles and small cobbles the trough base may have been clay-lined. The silting of the trough was a clay- and charcoal-rich silt; the environmental sample (ES3), like that of the oven produced a high concentration of wild or weed plant seeds from grassland or heath and considerable amounts of wood charcoal. A number of iron nails and unidentified iron artefacts came from the silting, as well as hobnails and a lump of lead casting slag. The fill also contained bone fragments, some identified as pig as well as cattle, both unburnt and calcined. Over 40 sherds of pottery were found, dominated by Greyware but as elsewhere, covering a range of fabrics including finewares, with a spot date from the mid-2nd century to the end of the 2nd century. Two radiocarbon dates were obtained, one from the fill of the trough giving date ranges of 121–204 cal AD (at 1σ and 68.3%) and 69–218 cal AD (at 2σ and 95.4%), SUERC-105502, indicating the trough may have filled up during the 2nd century. How much of this happened during the active use of the trough is another matter. The occupation deposit into which trough was constructed gave ranges with a slightly earlier emphasis of 77–166 cal AD (at 1σ and 59.7%) and 60–211 cal AD (at 2σ and 93.3%), SUERC-105506.

The domestic annex

The domestic annex to the east was explored in two east–west slots (5026) and (5029) and the area just to the north in a north–south slot (5025). Deciding the north–south length of the annex was challenging: there were hints of a west–east wall from the east wall of the strip building at around 6 m north from where geophysics suggested the road-edge would run (discussed above). Both (5026) and (5029) lay within this area. However, extremely disturbed structural remnants further to the north (seen in (5025) could possibly suggest the annex was longer with a west–east partition wall. Beyond the first 2 m, most of the annex's width lay east of Trench 5.

Both floor layers (5026) and (5029) were silty clay with a little charcoal, very similar to the occupation layers within the strip building. Small amounts of burnt and unburnt animal bone were found as elsewhere in the floors, but more iron nails and unidentified iron structural artefacts. And although dominated by Greyware, the small areas excavated produced relatively high pottery sherd counts. Other finds were somewhat different, of a higher quality and perhaps objects more associated with women. A silver decorative mount (cat. no. 51) and a lead spindle whorl came from (5026) (cat. no. 74); a corroded radiate coin (cat. no. 3) and half of a faience melon bead from (5029) (cat. no. 22).

The floor/external surface area (5025) to the north was very similar in composition and inclusions to (5026) and (5029), also relatively rich in pottery sherds and structural iron artefacts. The most notable find in (5025) was a fragment of a blue glass bangle with a trailed yellow glass pattern (cat no. 19).

The disturbed and restricted area available for exploration of this eastern occupation area makes it very hard to be confident about its character, but it may have been more domestic. Most of the small finds might be linked to a female presence and the structural ironwork might suggest furniture and fittings.

Phase 2: finds and dating

The Phase 1 dating of the wall foundations suggested an emphasis on the early–middle 2nd century for the construction of the strip building. The Phase 2 dates for the fill of the trough ranged across the 2nd century and into the early 3rd century, while dates for the hearth deposits were more focused on the second half of the 2nd century. The pottery dates on the whole ranged from the mid-2nd century across the 3rd century including some ceramics with rim forms dated to the mid- to later 3rd century and more Greyware forms dated to after AD 250 than Trench 4. Several of the DOR BB 1 bowls and jars had decoration indicting a date after AD 250. Although the condition of the pottery – mostly small and abraded – testifies to the disturbance within the trench, it is possible that Phase 2 activity in the strip building continued well into the 3rd century.

Phase 3: overview

Very little survived of this final, truncated and very disturbed phase of activity in the strip building. The pottery suggests (see below) that the building may have still been in use into the early 4th century but evidence for the character of that activity is slight. The mixing evident in the upper archaeological layers also means that some of the assemblage in this phase is undoubtedly intrusive. However, the earlier floor and partially dismantled hearth were sealed with a yellow clay layer (5001)-(5002)-(5003)-(5004)-(5005)-(5010)-(5013), a small pit was dug next to the southern wall foundations [5015] and a larger stone-filled pit [5038] covered the remains of the oven.

The clay floor

This strip building floor layer, like the preceding one, was investigated in slots and small areas (Fig. 7.19) and although a similar silty clay, was notable for lenses and patches of yellow clay. Across the clay floor a scattering of structural nails and iron objects were recovered along with fragments of mostly calcined animal bone, all of the identifiable bone was cattle. There were more fragments of demolition debris, such as tile, brick, and mortar in this layer (Appendix 2). In the north of the building there were fewer other finds although (5001) and (5002) together contained around 70 sherds of mostly very abraded pottery, dominated by Greyware, suggesting a date range from mid-3rd into mid-4th centuries (as well as a few intrusive post-medieval sherds). Both window and bottle glass fragments came from (5002). A little further towards the middle of the building (5013) and (5019) contained very little pottery and a few structural iron objects; (5013) included a small area of rough flagging.

The centre of the building (5004)-(5005)-(5010) produced more pottery, including amphorae sherds and a range of finewares, but less structural debris and fewer iron objects. A stone counter (cat. no. 45) and an iron hinge (cat. no. 59) came from (5004), bottle and jug glass from (5005). The area further south (5003) around the pit [5038] dug into the remains of the oven was the most finds-rich and included a lead counter (cat. no. 46), considerable amounts of pottery – over 60 sherds, with a later 3rd-century date range – and unidentifiable iron objects. However, the many sherds of a large Horningsea Reduced ware storage jar with internal combing marks found in (5003) next to pit [5015] belonged to a single vessel that had been standing upright in the shallow pit. These pots have been identified at Wallsend, South Shields, Newcastle, and Benwell and are thought to be of mainly 3rd-century date (see below; Croom 2016, 58).

Pits [5015] and [5016]

Pit [5015] was sited right up against the foundations of the southern line of the building, which may have supported a more open frontage. The southern side of the pit had been disturbed either by foundation stones being dragged into the feature by ploughing or by a late reworking of the building frontage. The truncated pit, 1.75 m east–west by 0.95 m north–south was cut into the clay floor (5003) with 0.15 m of depth surviving. An open bowl-shaped and lined with pebbly yellow clay the upper fill comprised a silty clay and half-a-dozen medium to large cobbles that appeared to have supported the large, 3rd-century Horningsea Reduced ware storage jar mentioned above. There may have been other pots in the pit, perhaps a Greyware vessel, but the other sherds of pottery were small and not joining and were more likely to be residual in the back fill or intrusive from disturbance. The corroded fragment of a polyhedral terminal

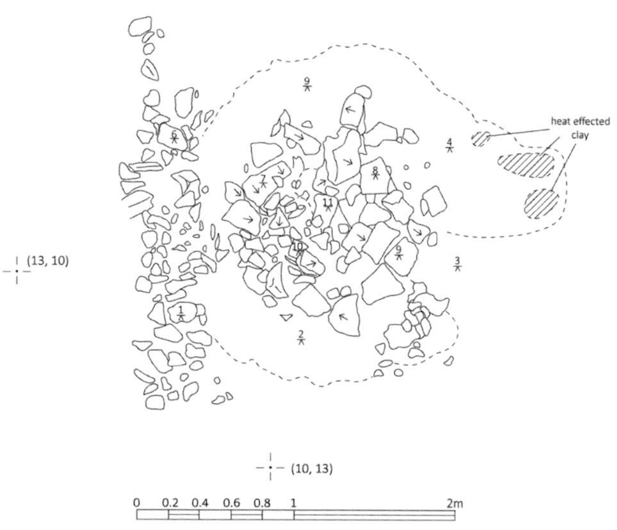

Figure 7.21: Plan of a sub-circular pit cut into the remains of the over or hearth [5022].

of a copper-alloy pin or penannular brooch (cat. no. 9) was found, along with unidentifiable slag, an iron nail and other iron objects. The environmental sample (ES1) taken from the lower fill contained very little other than charred vitreous material.

The much larger sub-circular pit [5038] (Figs 7.20 and 7.21) less than 1 m to the northwest of [5015], was cut into the remains of oven [5022]. Oriented near north–south the pit was 1.45 m east–west by 2 m north–south and up to 0.3 m deep with gently sloping, yellow clay-lined sides and an open concave base. The silty clay fill of the pit (5016) was packed with poorly sorted angular and sub-angular cobbles between 0.1 m and 0.35 m long; although slightly spread by ploughing, it appeared that the stone fill had been used to create a level surface. Only three sherds of pottery and three iron structural objects were found amongst the stones. The environmental sample (ES2) from the base of the pit under the stones produced a low concentration of charred plant remains and a few fragments of roundwood charcoal. A radiocarbon date range of 204–250 cal AD (at 1σ and 58.8%) and 130–254 cal AD (at 2σ and 80.4%), SUERC-105507, suggests activity well into the 3rd century (see pp. 97–98 for the link to Trench 3).

Just to the east of [5038] and cut into (5021) was a large trapezoidal stone 0.4 m wide by 0.55 m long and 0.07 m deep, which also sealed the oven remains. The base was burnt. This may, like pits [5015] and [5038], have been the base or support for something standing within the building.

Domestic annex

Two layers (5034) and (5008) excavated in the domestic annex probably belonged to this phase, although (5034), the upper layer, was very disturbed and will have contained intrusive material. (5008) was from a west–east slot, with hints of a northern wall in the north of the slot; again like the internal deposits in the strip building, (5008) seemed to be the remnants of a clay floor. The finds included some animal bone and iron artefacts, as in the main building, the base of a small glass bottle and just under 50 sherds of pottery, dominated by Greyware but including 10 sherds of Samian, one of which may have been reworked to form a counter; the assemblage suggested a later 3rd-century date. The layer above (5034) across the whole of the eastern annex in the trench was very disturbed but contained window and bottle class, some Roman pottery – again with a likely later 3rd-century date range – and iron objects.

A layer of the same broad phase to the north of and outside the strip building (5006), included a couple of sherds of pottery and likely building demolition debris, such as fragments of mortar, clunch, fired clay, and a considerable number of structural iron nails and iron fragments.

Phase 3: finds and dating

It is difficult to date Phase 3 but it seems likely to represent activity from the early to mid-3rd century through the 3rd century, with the surviving features focused on the first half of the 3rd century. The pottery from the more mixed and disturbed layer and topsoil also indicates activity into the 4th century, thus later than in Trench 4.

Trench 5, Phases 1–3: discussion

The building in Trench 5 was a strip building similar to those excavated beside Dere Street to the south of Corchester Lane (Forster and Knowles 1914, 300). With stone foundations and possibly a few courses of stone wall supporting a timber superstructure, the building may have had an open or partly open frontage onto the road. The wall foundations had a characteristic lower layer of herringbone design, except the western wall, which may have been built re-using the foundations of an earlier building.

The pottery was distinctly different from that in Trench 5, with a fair amount of later pottery dating to the 4th century. The distribution of finds in the main surviving Phase 2, focused on the second half of the 2nd century, suggests zoned or designated use of space, with the oven and trough in the south and the hearth in centre seeing more activity, while the northern part of the building was perhaps used more for storage and furnishings. The annex to the east appeared more domestic in character. It is difficult to interpret what was happening in Phase 3 but perhaps the building was being used more for storage.

Roman and post-Roman pottery

Terra Sigillata and Samian Wares

Felicity C. Wild

The 2021 excavations produced about 312 sherds of Samian ware. With the exception of a large pit (4013), which produced the greater part of five vessels (discussed below), the sherds were mostly very small, including scraps of as little as 0.5 g in weight. With many pieces too small or featureless to be ascribed to a form, it is impossible to estimate with any degree of accuracy the proportions of different forms and origins. A rough estimate based purely on a sherd count suggests that about 88% were Central Gaulish and 10% from East Gaul: the Central Gaulish ware was from Lezoux or its outliers, with one sherd possibly from Les Martres-de-Veyre, while the East Gaulish ware was probably mainly from Rheinzabern, with one decorated bowl from the Argonne. Six small sherds, weighing a total of 19 g, including one of decorated ware, were South Gaulish and Flavian-Trajanic in date. These were clearly residual in context.

The rest of the material formed a uniform group of late 2nd-century date or, in the case of the East Gaulish ware, late 2nd to 3rd century, all of which is likely to have remained in use into the 3rd century. The commonest plain forms were dishes of form 31 and 31R (Lud. forms Sa and Sb), form 36 and other late forms. Earlier 2nd-century forms such as 27, 18/31, and 18/31R were conspicuous by their absence. By the later years of the 2nd century, decorated ware from Central Gaul clearly became more difficult to obtain, which would account for its relative scarcity here.

Identifiable forms, excluding scraps, are listed below, though it must be borne in mind that decorated scraps, however small, can be attributed to form 37 (no sherds attributable with certainty to form 30 were found), whereas plain sherds are of uncertain form, and do not appear in the figures. Although there were 26 pieces of Central Gaulish ware showing decoration, most were too small or insignificant for identification and the number of publishable pieces was small for a site such as Corbridge.

South Gaulish: 37 (1), 27 (1), 18, or 18/31 (3?)
Central Gaulish: 37 (26), 33 (8), 18/31 or 31 (3), 31 (9), 18/31R or 31R (2), 31R (16), 36 (8), 38 (4), 45 (5), 72 (3?), 68? (1), Lud Tf (1)
East Gaulish: 37 (4), 27? (1), 33? (1), 31 or 31R (Lud Sa or Sb) (6), 36 (1), Lud TbR (1), Lud Tg (1).

Comparatively few cases of repair or reworking were noted. Three sherds showed rivet holes or possible traces of riveting; a form 38 in the large pit group (4013) discussed below had had its flange systematically removed and rubbed smooth, a sherd of gritted mortarium had been trimmed into a disk and similar trimming may have been attempted on one other small piece.

The Samian ware from the large pit (4013) is of particular interest. Apart from a few scraps and small sherds, including one of South Gaulish form 37 datable to *c.* AD 80–110 and another, from Central Gaul, dating to AD 125–150 (no. D2 below), all doubtless residual in context, it contained the greater part of five different vessels, all of late 2nd-century date:

1. Seventeen sherds of Central Gaulish form 37, amounting to a complete bowl, with the stamp of Lastuca of Lezoux (D5 below).
2. Five sherds amounting to about 65% of a large East Gaulish dish, diameter 300 mm, stamped by Paternus viii of Rheinzabern. The form is a rouletted version of Lud. Tb (S2 below). The potter's output seems to have been almost entirely restricted to dishes, mainly of forms 31 and 32 and their rouletted versions.
3. Five sherds of a large Central Gaulish form 36, with 39% of the rim present.

4. Seven sherds of a Central Gaulish form 38 with 54% of the rim present. The interior is heavily worn, removing any traces of a potter's stamp.
5. A single sherd amounting to 35% of the rim, probably from another Central Gaulish flanged form 38 rather than the less common cordoned form 44. The flange (or cordon) has been carefully removed and rubbed flat. The rubbing implement was wide enough to scar the wall above the flange. The interior appears unworn.

Decorated ware

In the following report, figure types are quoted from Oswald 1936–37 (O.), Central Gaulish motifs from Rogers 1974 (Rogers), East Gaulish types and motifs from Ricken and Fischer 1963 (R&F), parallels from Stanfield and Simpson 1958 (S&S). Potter and die numbers and dates are from Hartley and Dickinson 2008–12 (NoTS). Each entry below is illustrated in Figure 7.22.

D1. Form 37, Central Gaulish. A panelled bowl with wavy-line borders, probably in the style of Drusus ii of Lezoux, with his ovolo (Rogers B15). Panels show a festoon (Rogers F60) containing a bird to left (O.2298?). A bowl with his signature shows the festoon with a similar bird to right (S&S, pl. 88, 5). He also used vertical rows of large circles (Rogers 1999, pl. 42,1). The type in the right-hand panel is uncertain. *c*. AD 125–145. (4010)

D2. Form 37, Central Gaulish, showing a festoon with the leaf (Rogers H73) used by the potter X6 (Catullus) (S&S, pl. 74, 2–4). *c*. AD 125–150. (4013)

D3. Form 37, Central Gaulish, with a stag (O1704) used by Attianus ii, Cinnamus ii, and later by Doeccus i. In this case, the sherd is likely to be by one of the earlier potters, probably Cinnamus. *c*. AD 135–180. (4013)

D4. Form 37, Central Gaulish, with a panel containing a medallion with the urn (Rogers T15), used on bowls in Cinnamus ii style. *c*. AD 140–180. (4003)

D5. Form 37, Central Gaulish, with the mould stamp of Lastuca of Lezoux (die 1a). Decoration shows the ovolo (Rogers B114) and a scroll with the leaf (Rogers H37) in the upper concavities and medallions with flying birds (O.2316, O.2324) in the lower. Lastuca appears to have been a mould-maker for Paternus v, though occasionally, as here, he put his own stamp in the mould. He does not appear to have made plain ware. The ovolo and types were all used on bowls stamped by Paternus, though only the leaf has been recorded on bowls with Lastuca's stamp. It is interesting to note that Stanfield and Simpson record a stamp of his from Corbridge (S&S, p. 189), though there is no illustration of it. Under Paternus (S&S, pl.104, 10) they illustrate a bowl, also from Corbridge, with identical decoration to this one apart from a different space-filler next to the leaves. It does not appear to show a potter's stamp. *c*. AD 160–185. (4013)

D6. Form 37, Central Gaulish, slightly burnt, in the style of Banvus of Lezoux. Decoration shows the ovolo (Rogers B24), a vertical border of corded beads (Rogers A34) and festoons (cf. Rogers 1999, pl. 14, 17, and 18). A bowl from South Shields (S&S, pl. 139, 7) shows similar panel decoration with a bird (O. 2296) of which the head may possibly be in the right-hand panel here. *c*. AD 175–200. (4000)

D7. Form 37, East Gaulish, in an orange fabric typical of the Argonne potteries. The sherd is badly abraded, with only traces of a dull, orange slip surviving. Decoration shows a large, tongueless ovolo with three borders surrounding a narrow core (possibly Chenet and Gaudron 1955, fig. 54bis, O6, though their drawing, from a mould, is not completely clear) and the leaf (probably *ibid*., fig. 58k). The ovolo and leaf occur together on a bowl illustrated by Deru and Feller (2005, fig. 7, 47).[1] *c*. AD 150–200. (5031)

D8. Form 37, East Gaulish. Two sherds, one of base, the other showing the bestiarius (O.1125A, R&F. M199) used by Helenius ii of Rheinzabern. The light orange fabric with matt, orange slip is not typical of Rheinzabern, though Joanna Bird notes that at New Fresh Wharf, London, there were Rheinzabern bowls in a 'pale yellowish fabric with coarse orange slip' (Bird 1986, 144), of which this may be another example. The type on the left is too fragmentary to identify, though there is a tendril on the right, ending in a leaf. *c*. AD 170–200. (5027, 5031)

D9. Form 37, East Gaulish, showing the ovolo (RF E41) used by Primitius i of Rheinzabern. Too little survives of the decoration for further identification. *c*. AD 200–260? (NoTS) (5026)

Potters' stamps

Apart from the decorated bowl of Lastuca (no. 5 above), the excavation produced only four potters' stamps, of which only one was complete. The letters on one were too uncertain for identification.

S1. [MERC]ATo[Scrap, probably of form 31, Central Gaulish, with part of die 5a or a' of Mercator iv of Lezoux. A form 31 with this die has already been recorded from Corbridge. *c*. AD 160–200. (5000)

S2. [PATIIRN]VSFII Form Lud. TbR, East Gaulish, with die 3a of Paternus viii of Rheinzabern. The die occurs in a group of unused vessels from New Fresh Wharf with a suggested date of *c*. AD 235–245. The date given by NoTS for his work as a whole is *c*. AD 160–260. (4013)

S3. SECVNDINI Form 33, Central Gaulish, with die 4a of Secundinus vi of Lezoux. *c*. AD 160–190. COR 19 (1006)

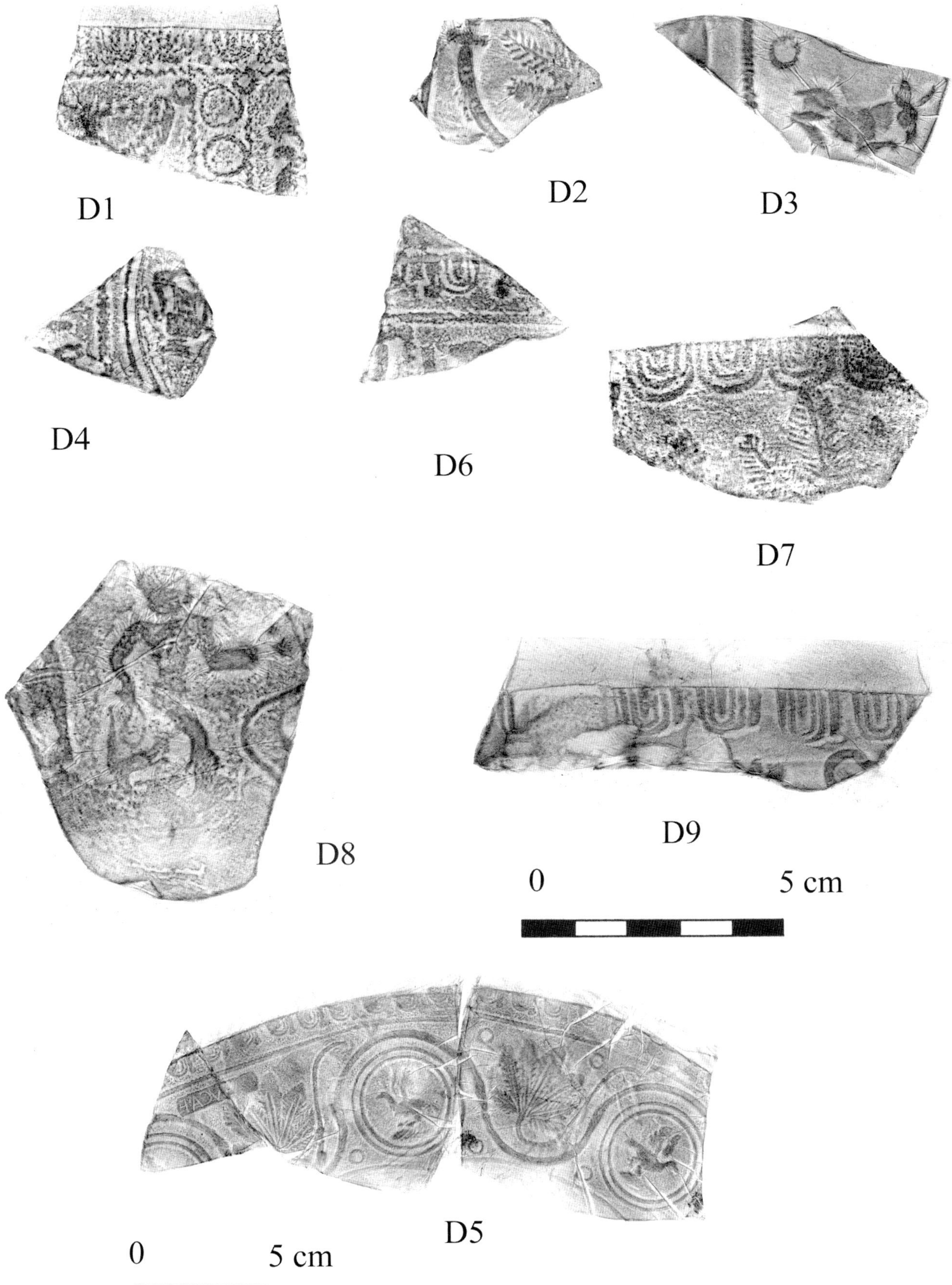

Figure 7.22: Decorated sherds of Samian.

Coarse and fine wares

Eniko Hudak

Pre-Construct Archaeology Ltd. (PCA) was commissioned by Newcastle University to undertake the post-excavation assessment of the ceramics recovered during the 2021 excavations of the Hadrian's Wall Community Archaeology Project (WallCAP) on land within the playing field to the north of the Corbridge Roman Town site (COR21). The following report represents a detailed assessment of the Roman pottery, and a short assessment and statement on the post-Roman pottery retrieved from the fieldwork.

Methodology

The Roman pottery was hand examined and where deemed necessary fresh breaks were created for more detailed study under hand lens (10x magnification). The pottery was recorded by context and by fabric, and fully quantified and catalogued using the standard measures of sherd count, weight, and Estimated Vessel Equivalents (EVEs), in accordance with the latest guidelines established by the Study Group for Roman Pottery (PCRG, SGRP, MPRG 2016). A 'context considered date' was determined for each context (except the topsoil layers) containing Roman pottery. This date represents a cross-section of the fabric and form dates present in the given context establishing a *terminus post quem* for deposition but is not dependant on its stratigraphic relationships.

The data was recorded into a relational database used by PCA specialists, which is ultimately based on the standards established by the Museum of London Specialist Services, with the help of fabric and form codes of the National Roman Fabric Reference Collection (Tomber and Dore 1998), the Hadrian's Wall Ceramic database of TWM Archaeology (HWCD, Tyne & Wear Museums 2008–2009), and a set of custom four-letter codes describing the main characteristics of the fabrics. Forms were recorded with the help of a range of relevant local typologies and corpora including the Hadrian's Wall Ceramic Database, the type series established for Catterick (Bell and Evans 2002), Gillam's (1970) *Types of Roman Coarse Pottery Vessels in Northern Britain,* etc. For a full list of fabric codes and expansions, and relevant typologies see Table 7.1.

Post-Roman ceramics were recorded by sherd count and weight to establish a basic quantitative and context distribution assessment.

Table 7.1: Fabric codes and expansions with a list of relevant typologies.

Fabric category	*Fabric*	*Fabric expansion*	*Reference*	*Typologies used*
Amphorae	BAT AM 1	Baetican (Early) amphora 1	NRFRC	Martin-Kilcher 1987; University of Southampton 2014
	BAT AM 2	Baetican (Late) amphora 2	NRFRC	Martin-Kilcher 1987; University of Southampton 2014
	GAL AM 1	Gaulish amphorae 1	NRFRC	N/A
	GAL AM 2	Gaulish amphorae 2	NRFRC	N/A
	NAF AM 1	North African (Lime-rich) amphorae 1	NRFRC	N/A
Imported Coarse Wares	NOG WH 5	North Gaulish White ware 5	NRFRC	N/A
Romano-British Coarse Wares	DOR BB 1	Dorset Black-burnished ware 1	NRFRC	Hadrian's Wall Ceramic Database
	BB2	Black-burnished ware 2 (wheelmade)	N/A	Hadrian's Wall Ceramic Database
	BBS	Black-burnished style ware	N/A	Hadrian's Wall Ceramic Database
	BUFF	Unsourced buff sand-tempered ware	N/A	N/A
	CALC	Unsourced calcite-tempered ware	N/A	N/A
	CRA RE	Crambeck Reduced Ware	NRFRC	Corder 1937; Bidwell and Croom 2010
	GREY	Unsourced reduced coarse sand-tempered ware	N/A	Hadrian's Wall Ceramic Database
	GREY1	Unsourced reduced coarse sand-tempered ware (hard fabric)	N/A	Hadrian's Wall Ceramic Database

(Continued)

Table 7.1: (Continued)

Fabric category	Fabric	Fabric expansion	Reference	Typologies used
	GREY2	Unsourced reduced coarse sand-tempered ware (black surface)	N/A	N/A
	GRIT	Unsourced gritty ware	N/A	N/A
	GROG	Unsourced grog-tempered ware	N/A	N/A
	HOR RE	Horningsea Reduced ware	NRFRC	N/A
	HUN CG	East Yorkshire ('Huntcliff') Calcite-gritted ware	NRFRC	Gillam 1970; Bidwell and Croom 2010
	LTW	Local Tradition Ware	Bidwell and Croom 2002	N/A
	MISC	Miscellaneous fragments	N/A	N/A
	OXID	Unsourced oxidised coarse sand-tempered ware	N/A	Hadrian's Wall Ceramic Database
	OXIDF	Unsourced oxidised fine sand-tempered ware	N/A	Hadrian's Wall Ceramic Database
	SENK	South Essex/North Kent reduced coarse wares	Hadrian's Wall Ceramic Database	Hadrian's Wall Ceramic Database
	SHEL	Unsourced shell-tempered ware	N/A	N/A
	SVW OX 2	(Unsourced) Severn Valley Oxidised ware 2	NRFRC	N/A
	VER WH	Verulamium Region White ware	NRFRC	N/A
	WS	Unsourced white-slipped ware	N/A	N/A
	WW	Unsourced white ware	N/A	N/A
Imported Fine Wares	CNG BS	Central Gaulish Black-slipped ware	NRFRC	Symonds 1992
	CNG CC 1	Central Gaulish (White) Colour-coated ware 1	NRFRC	Symonds 1992
	MOS BS	Moselkeramik Black-slipped ware	NRFRC	Symonds 1992
Samian	LEZ SA 2	Lezoux Samian 2	NRFRC	NoTS
	SAM	Samian (unsourced)	N/A	Webster 1996
Romano-British Fine Wares	CC	Unsourced colour-coated ware	N/A	N/A
	COL CC 2	Colchester (Late) Colour-coated ware 2	NRFRC	N/A
	CRA PA	Crambeck Parchment Ware	NRFRC	Bidwell and Croom 2010
	FINE	Unsourced fine sand-tempered ware	N/A	N/A
	LNV CC	Lower Nene Valley Colour-coated ware	NRFRC	Perrin 1999
	LON FR	London style fine reduced ware	NRFRC	N/A
	MICA	Unsourced mica-dusted fine ware	N/A	N/A
Imported Mortaria	NOG WH 4	North Gaulish White ware 4	NRFRC	N/A
	SOL WH	Soller White ware	NRFRC	N/A
Romano-British Mortaria	COR WH	Corbridge White ware	NRFRC	N/A
	CTR WS	Catterick White-slipped ware	NRFRC	Bell and Evans 2002
	LNV WH	Lower Nene Valley White ware	NRFRC	Perrin 1999
	MAH WH	Mancetter-Hartshill White ware	NRFRC	Bell and Evans 2002
	MORT	Unsourced mortarium	N/A	N/A
	OXF WH	Oxfordshire White Ware	NRFRC	Young 1977

Table 7.2: Quantification of the Roman pottery assemblage per fabric by sherd count, weight (g), and EVEs.

Fabric	*SC*	*%SC*	*Wt(g)*	*%Wt*	*EVEs*	*%EVEs*
BAT AM 1	46	1.86%	2092	5.62%	0.07	0.20%
BAT AM 2	46	1.86%	4946	13.28%	0.82	2.35%
BB1	241	9.76%	3382	9.08%	4.23	12.11%
BB2	119	4.82%	1440	3.87%	1.57	4.49%
BBS	1	0.04%	9	0.02%	0.04	0.11%
BUFF	55	2.23%	285	0.77%	0.61	1.75%
CALC	3	0.12%	60	0.16%	0.05	0.14%
CC	5	0.20%	70	0.19%	0.14	0.40%
CNG BS	22	0.89%	44	0.12%	0.13	0.37%
CNG CC 1	1	0.04%	2	0.01%	0	0.00%
COL CC 2	1	0.04%	13	0.03%	0	0.00%
COR WH	3	0.12%	47	0.13%	0	0.00%
CRA PA	1	0.04%	93	0.25%	0.38	1.09%
CRA RE	7	0.28%	49	0.13%	0.05	0.14%
CTR WS	2	0.08%	50	0.13%	0.05	0.14%
FINE	10	0.41%	38	0.10%	0.21	0.60%
GAL AM 1	2	0.08%	26	0.07%	0	0.00%
GAL AM 2	5	0.20%	37	0.10%	0	0.00%
GREY	718	29.08%	7054	18.94%	9.99	28.60%
GREY1	50	2.03%	663	1.78%	1	2.86%
GREY2	23	0.93%	2860	7.68%	0	0.00%
GRIT	11	0.45%	76	0.20%	0.17	0.49%
GROG	13	0.53%	309	0.83%	0	0.00%
HOR RE	109	4.41%	2405	6.46%	0	0.00%
HUN CG	4	0.16%	60	0.16%	0.16	0.46%
LEZ SA 2	12	0.49%	793	2.13%	1	2.86%
LNV CC	128	5.18%	564	1.51%	1.73	4.95%
LNV WH	2	0.08%	33	0.09%	0	0.00%
LON FR	3	0.12%	11	0.03%	0	0.00%
LTW	9	0.36%	242	0.65%	0.24	0.69%
MAH WH	41	1.66%	1574	4.23%	1.37	3.92%
MICA	8	0.32%	50	0.13%	0.07	0.20%
MISC	6	0.24%	13	0.03%	0	0.00%
MORT	2	0.08%	52	0.14%	0	0.00%
MOS BS	28	1.13%	89	0.24%	0.06	0.17%
NAF AM 1	2	0.08%	1	0.00%	0	0.00%
NOG WH 4	1	0.04%	71	0.19%	0	0.00%
NOG WH 5	5	0.20%	19	0.05%	0	0.00%
OXF WH	3	0.12%	81	0.22%	0.05	0.14%
OXID	177	7.17%	868	2.33%	1.08	3.09%
OXIDF	54	2.19%	394	1.06%	0	0.00%
SAM	310	12.56%	3596	9.65%	6.83	19.55%
SENK	92	3.73%	2235	6.00%	2.14	6.13%

(Continued)

Table 7.2: (Continued)

Fabric	SC	%SC	Wt(g)	%Wt	EVEs	%EVEs
SHEL	3	0.12%	15	0.04%	0	0.00%
SOL WH	1	0.04%	16	0.04%	0	0.00%
SVW OX 2	16	0.65%	114	0.31%	0.03	0.09%
VER WH	14	0.57%	51	0.14%	0	0.00%
WS	9	0.36%	55	0.15%	0.41	1.17%
WW	45	1.82%	203	0.54%	0.25	0.72%
Total	2469	100.00%	37250	100.00%	34.93	100.00%

The Roman pottery

Overall assemblage condition, composition, and dating

A total of 2,469 sherds of Roman pottery weighing 37.25 kg and representing 34.93 EVEs were recovered from the 2021 excavations at Corbridge. The pottery is in relatively good condition with numerous large sherds, fresh breaks, and moderate levels of sherd abrasion. Sherd size ranges from 1 g fragments to large sherds weighing in excess of 1.3 kg, and several fragmented near-complete, and complete vessels are also present. Mean sherd weight is at 15.1 g, which together with the amount of pottery recovered from the topsoil (see Pottery Distribution below) and the levels of abrasion observed, imply a significant degree of redeposition and residuality.

Several examples of use-wear and post-firing modifications were observed in the assemblage.

Nine vessels bear one or more post-firing holes, some of which are most likely evidence for repair while others show a change of function of the vessel. A further four sherds appear to have been trimmed or re-worked into counters, and there is only one potential graffito. Evidence for use-wear is more limited with two examples of internal limescale and another six with external soot all indicating cooking, and one vessel (apart from mortaria) with significant internal wear patterns implying vigorous or extensive stirring and/or grinding.

There is a great variety of fabrics represented in the assemblage (Tables 7.1 and 7.2), all of which are well attested in the area. These include a wide variety of Romano-British material of local origin, as well as regional imports from Yorkshire, Dorset, the South East, Cambridgeshire, the West Midlands, and a quantity of pottery that could not be assigned to a known production centre with confidence. Continental imports are also well represented in this assemblage incorporating Baetican, Gaulish, and North African amphorae, fine and coarse wares from Germania and Gaul, and of course a significant quantity of Samian ware. Whilst these fabrics and forms encompass the entire Roman period in date with several broadly dated examples, there appears to be an emphasis on fabrics and forms dated to the mid–late 2nd to early–mid 3rd century AD.

Coarse wares

Coarse wares dominate the site assemblage accounting for 74.5% of total sherd count, 66.5% of weight, and 67.25% of all EVEs (Table 7.2, Fig 7.23A). Unsourced sand-tempered grey (reduced) wares, (GREY, GREY1, and GREY2), are most frequent with 32% of total sherd count, 28.4% of weight, and 31.4% of EVEs. A quantity of GREY sherds is likely to be of fairly local origin, the northeast or more specifically Corbridge itself, as attested by the small number of rim fragments of high-shouldered and everted/angular rim jars that were produced in Fabric 2 here during the late 1st century (Dore 1998: types JA3–8). There are, however, a number of fragments recorded as GREY, which may originate from the Lower Nene Valley (rare, but appears in the area, Bidwell and Croom 2002, 153–154), the Horningsea potteries, East Yorkshire, or the South East, but they could not be assigned to these production centres with confidence. Two distinctive fabric variants of reduced sandy grey wares were recorded under their own fabric codes. GREY1 signifies sherds in a very hard pale grey fabric, while all GREY2 sherds belong to the same vessel, the complete lower part of a very large storage vessel with abundant sand temper and a black surface with three post-firing holes near its base. Forms in the GREY fabric range represent a variety of functional categories including flagons, jars, beakers, bowls, dishes, and lids, but only jars are quantitatively significant. The most frequently recorded jar type is the Black-burnished style everted-rim cooking jar (SENK type 5.1, HWCD), which is generally dated to after AD 120.

Dorset Black-burnished ware 1 (DOR BB 1) is the second most commonly occurring fabric type in the assemblage with 9.8% of count, 9.1% of weight, and 12.1% of EVEs. The BB1 industry was a major supplier of coarse wares to the north during the 2nd century AD and later again from the late 3rd century AD (Croom 2016, 58). The BB1 forms occurring in the assemblage provide evidence for both periods of supply including several plain-rim dishes and triangular-rim bowls broadly dated to after AD 120, a near complete example of a Gillam 226 bowl dated to after AD 160, and rim and body sherds of the late type everted-rim cooking jar with burnished obtuse lattice decoration dated to after AD 250.

Black-burnished ware 2 from the South East (BB2) and 'allied' fabrics of similar date and origin (SENK, South East/North Kent, also known as South-Eastern reduced ware SERW – Croom 2016, 58; Bidwell and Croom 2018, 199ff.) also form a significant component of the site assemblage. BB2 accounts for 4.8% of total sherd count, 3.9% of weight, and 4.5% EVEs, while SENK for 3.7%, 6% and 3.9% respectively. These fabrics reach the North from the late 2nd century AD onwards and become the major coarse ware suppliers during the 3rd century AD (Croom 2016). Forms in these fabrics in the COR21 assemblage include a number of triangular-rim bowls (SENK types 14, 15, 17, 18), everted-rim jars (type 5), a variety of necked jars (type 6), wide-mouth bowls (type 10), plain-rim dishes (types 12 and 13) and lids.

The only other pottery type present in considerable quantities is Horningsea reduced ware (HOR RE) with 4.4% of sherd count and 6.5% of weight. Only body sherds are present, most of which likely belong to the same large storage jar with internal combing/wiping marks. HOR RE storage jars have been recognised at Wallsend, South Shields, Newcastle, and Benwell (Croom 2016, 58) and appear to have been imported at the same time as BB2 and SENK and thus probably of mainly 3rd-century AD date.

All other coarse wares in the assemblage are under 3% of weight each, only a few of which were assigned to a known production centre (*e.g.* Severn Valley ware, Verulamium Region White ware, East Yorkshire Calcite-gritted ware). Of interest are the small number of rouletted pentice beaker fragments in North Gaulish coarse ware (NOG WH 5, Richardson 1986, 107, late 2nd to 3rd centuries AD) and sherds in 'Local Traditional Ware' (LTW, also known as Local Handmade Ware – Gerrard 2012) from a jar similar to Gillam 156. LTW are vessels made in the Iron Age tradition throughout the Roman period (Bidwell and Croom 2002, 169–170). Examples of potential LTW cooking pots with simple everted rims have been found at Corbridge in 3rd-century AD deposits (Bidwell and Croom 2002, 169–170, citing Birley and Richmond 1938).

Mortaria

The coarse ware assemblage includes a total of 56 sherds of mortaria weighing 1.932 kg and representing 1.47 EVEs (Table 7.2, Fig 7.23A). The bulk of the mortarium assemblage consists of Mancetter-Hartshill products (MAH WH, 1.7% of total sherd count, 4.2% of weight, and 3.9% of EVEs), which became the main suppliers of mortaria to the north by the 3rd century AD (Hudak 2013). There are no examples of the early MAH WH products with the mixed quartz and sandstone trituration grits (pre-AD 140), and the range of rim profiles present are dated to the mid–late 2nd to mid–late 3rd centuries AD (types M78, 82, 89, 93, 96, 97; Bell and Evans 2002). All other mortarium fabrics are present with 1–3 fragments each including Corbridge White ware, Catterick White-slipped ware, Lower Nene Valley White ware, Oxfordshire White ware, one sherd of the mid-1st- to 2nd-century Verulamium White Ware, one of a mid–late 1st-century AD import North Gaulish White ware, and another import, Soller White ware. Most of the mortaria are worn and appear to have been discarded at the end of their use-life. There are no stamps present.

Fine wares

Fine wares including Samian account for 21.4% of the assemblage by sherd count, 14.4% by weight, and 30.2% of all EVEs (Table 7.2, Fig 7.23A). Of the non-Samian fine wares Lower Nene Valley Colour-coated ware (LNV CC) is the most prominent comprising 5.2% of the assemblage sherd count, 1.5% of weight, and 5% of EVEs. Diagnostic sherds in LNV CC are almost exclusively of beakers including cornice rim beakers and a range of funnel neck beakers with a variety of decorative techniques (rouletting, underslip-barbotine swirls, dots, animals, barbotine scale decorations, indentations, white paint). There is only one example of a post-AD 250 flanged bowl in LNV CC (Perrin 1999, fig. 64/255–262), and two small rim fragments of Castor Box lids (Perrin 1999, fig. 62/208–213). There is a considerable amount of imported non-Samian fine wares: Central Gaulish black slipped ware (CNG BS, AD 150–250) and Moselkeramik (MOS BS, AD 200–275) indented and rouletted beakers, including several refitting fragments of one from Trier (Group 35, Symonds 1992). There is only one example of a Crambeck Parchment ware bowl (CRA PA, AD 300–400+) with red-painted decoration on its flange.

Samian

There is a total of 322 fragments of Samian ware weighing 4.389 kg and representing 7.83 EVEs, accounting for 13% of total sherd count, 11.8% of weight, and 22.4% of EVEs (Table 7.2, Fig 7.23A). The Samian is assessed in full above, and only a brief summary is provided here for inclusion in the wider ceramic analysis.

One complete and several near-complete Samian vessels were identified in the assemblage, all from the same context (see Pottery Distribution below). The complete but fragmented example is a decorated Dr37 type bowl, complete with a decorator's stamp in the decoration: [LASTVCA.F] retrograde, the stamp of Lastuca of Lezoux dated to AD 160–185 (NoTS online). There are joining fragments of a Dr38 type flanged bowl (AD 150+) with 54% of its rim present and with very heavy internal wear-patterns. The complete profile of a very large dish with a partial stamp (Ludowici TbR type, 65% of rim) and rim and body sherds of a Dr36 type dish with barbotine leaves (43% of rim) were also recovered from this feature. Other than the complete/near-complete vessels there is a high number of diagnostic Samian fragments including a variety of Dr37 bowls, Dr18/31 and Dr31, and Dr36 dishes, a small number of cups and even fewer mortaria – one fragment of which was reworked into a counter. Other than the decorator's stamp and the stamp on the LudTB dish.

Amphorae

Amphora sherds total 101 fragments, 7.102 kg, and 0.89 EVEs (4.1% of total sherd count, 19.1% of weight, and 2.6% of EVEs) (Table 7.2, Fig. 7.23A). As usual from any Roman site in Britain, Southern Spanish (Baetican) Dressel 20 olive oil amphora fragments are the most common in both the 'early' and 'late' fabric variants (BAT AM 1, BAT AM 2). Four rim fragments of Dressel 20 amphorae were recorded, two of which are the Martin-Kilcher rim type 91, dated to between AD 150–210 at Kaiseraugst (Martin-Kilcher 1987, Beilagen 1–2). There is one Dressel 20 handle with a stamp, which is unfortunately too abraded to be read precisely. Legible letters comprise [C.L.S...], and it may be a stamp of Callistus dated to the second half of the 2nd century AD, which had been found at Corbridge previously (Callender 1949, fig. 2/16, CEIPAC 15836). This, however, remains a speculation. Other than Dressel 20 sherds, in the BAT AM 1 and 2 fabrics there are two fragments, which may derive from Dressel 23 vessels, the smaller version of the late Dressel 20 type, and a single example of a 1st–2nd-century AD Haltern 70 type (a container of defrutum or olives). Other amphora fabrics include a few fragments of Gauloise wine amphorae and two miniscule flakes that may be of a late Roman North African amphora. There are no obvious signs of any secondary use for the amphora fragments.

Functional composition

Functional analysis of the site assemblage shows a clear prevalence of jars with 13.03 EVEs, or 48% of all EVEs (excluding Samian forms, Fig. 7.23B). Black-burnished style everted rim cooking jars are the most common jar type and overall form type in the assemblage with five EVEs. These are generally dated to after AD 120–125, but many BB1 examples are of the late rim type with obtuse lattice decoration dated to after AD 250. Other jars include a range of necked jars, mostly in SENK, some narrow-necked examples, and even fewer of the late Roman hooked-rim type. The next most important functional category in the assemblage are bowls and dishes with 4.94 EVEs and 2.28 EVEs respectively (26% of total excluding Samian), with the BB-style triangular rim bowls and the Gillam 226 type bowls and plain-rim 'dog' dishes. Beakers and mortaria are the last two categories with more than 5% of EVEs each (9% and 6% respectively). While the high percentage of jars suggests a predominance of food storage and preparation, serving vessels (flagons, beakers, dishes, and some bowls) for the consumption of food are also well-represented in the assemblage.

Pottery distribution

Roman pottery was recovered from 71 individually numbered contexts (including the topsoil and the subsoil) from Trenches 4 and 5 (Table 7.3, Fig. 7.24).

Table 7.3: Distribution and dating of the ceramics per context.

Context	*SC*	*Wt(g)*	*EVEs*	*Context Considered Date*
4000	302	4107	3.76	–
4001	6	249	0.07	AD 190–240
4002	4	577	0.21	AD 150–160/300
4003	21	101	0.23	AD 150–200/260
4004	26	193	0.16	AD 120–150?
4005	33	375	0.74	AD 150–250
4006	13	93	0.06	AD 120–250
4007	17	154	0.27	AD 160–250
4008	34	460	0.38	AD 200–250
4009	8	49	0.13	AD 90/120–150
4010	69	1471	0.97	AD 190–200/240
4011	7	37	0	AD 150–200
4012	22	150	0.4	AD 150–200
4013	197	7900	4.92	AD 200–250
4016	11	603	0.08	AD 150–200
4017	47	414	0.85	AD 250–260/300
4018	18	90	0.18	AD 150–200
4019	8	92	0.14	AD 150–260
4020	7	73	0.05	AD 150–300
4021	7	43	0.13	AD 150–250
4022	10	102	0.22	AD 200–220/250
4023	7	46	0.07	AD 150–250
4024	28	246	0.19	AD 150–200
4025	54	895	1.13	AD 200–250
4026	13	165	0.11	AD 150–200
4028	22	351	0.41	AD 200–250
4029	2	14	0.07	AD 120–250
4030	53	1355	1.26	AD 200–250
4033	1	22	0	AD 50–200
4034	29	362	0.62	AD 180–200/250
4035	18	152	0.06	AD 200–250
4036	3	124	0.18	AD 150–210
4037	3	49	0.07	AD 140–300
4038	3	15	0	AD 40/120–260
4039	38	1241	0.32	AD 150–250
4040	3	23	0.01	AD 150–260
4041	8	119	0	AD 140/160–200
4042	1	38	0.15	AD 120–400+
4043	3	27	0	AD 150–300
4044	2	4	0	AD 40–400+
5000	510	4645	5.05	-
5001	28	309	0.19	AD 150–250*
5002	48	377	0.16	AD 150–250*
5003	150	2563	1.08	AD 250–275*
5004	9	78	0	AD 140–250

(Continued)

Table 7.3: Distribution and dating of the ceramics per context. (Continued)

Context	*SC*	*Wt(g)*	*EVEs*	*Context Considered Date*
5005	27	247	0.23	AD 250–260/300
5006	2	2	0	AD 40–260
5007	3	39	0.15	AD 150–400+
5008	49	248	0.36	AD 250–275
5009	4	36	0	AD 150–260
5010	20	530	0.41	AD 250–400+
5011	25	223	0.43	AD 250–400+*
5012	22	159	0.19	AD 150/270–400+
5013	8	34	0	AD 120–400+
5015	50	688	0.33	AD 150–200*
5016	3	12	0	AD 150–400+
5018	42	271	0.36	AD 250–275
5019	16	142	0.09	AD 150–200
5020	84	1338	1.24	AD 250–260/300
5022	72	522	0.36	AD 200–250
5023	35	411	0.93	AD 300–400+
5024	44	234	0.6	AD 270–300/400+
5025	39	247	0.55	AD 270–300
5026	52	560	0.55	AD 270–400+
5027	73	532	0.79	AD 200–250
5028	14	38	0.07	AD 120–150/200
5029	5	299	0.16	AD 150–250
5030	25	324	1.07	AD 150/200–250
5031	28	265	0.46	AD 200–260
5032	15	99	0.17	AD 120–150/250
5034	19	244	0.35	AD 250–260/300
Total	2679	38297	34.93	

Individual context assemblages are mostly small, with 49 contexts containing less than 30 fragments, 18 contexts with medium-sized assemblages (31–100 sherds), and two large context assemblages (over 100 sherds) excluding machine stripped topsoil contexts (4000) and (5000). The trench assemblages with details on the largest feature assemblages are described in more detail below.

Trench 4

A total of 1100 sherds of Roman pottery weighing 22.229 kg and representing 18.6 EVEs were recovered from Trench 4 contexts (Fig 7.24A). A significant amount was retrieved from the topsoil layer (4000) totalling 244 sherds weighing 3.755 kg, 3.76 EVEs. The pottery from this trench is in good condition with little abrasion, several large sherds showing complete profiles of vessel forms, and a relatively high mean sherd weight of 20.2g.

Even though a great variety of Roman fabrics were identified in the assemblage (43), nearly 88% of the trench assemblage by weight is made up of only 10 different fabrics. Over a quarter of the trench assemblage weight comprises Baetican amphora fragments (BAT AM 1, BAT AM 2, 5.767 kg combined). There are three Dressel 20 rims, two of the Martin-Kilcher 91 type dated to AD 150–210, and the stamped handle of potentially very similar date.

Samian (SAM and LEZ SA 2) is the second most significant fabric group in this trench assemblage with 13.7% of sherd count, 13.5% of weight, and 28.3% of all EVEs, including all the complete/near-complete vessels described above, most of which post-date AD 150. Reduced grey wares follow: GREY2 with only 1.9% of sherd count but 12.7% of weight, all from the lower half of the same very large storage jar with two or three post-firing holes near the base. GREY is more fragmented with 22.6% of sherd count and 11.5% of weight including a high number of diagnostic sherds of everted-rim cooking pot jars (post-AD 120), and other jars, bowls, and dishes (24.4% of EVEs).

The only other fabrics present in significant quantities are BB2 and SENK, DOR BB 1, and lastly, MAH WH mortaria, which all provide significant dating evidence (Fig. 7.24A). Diagnostic sherds in SENK include type 6.1 necked jars (AD 180+, HWCD) the fragmented complete rim and profile of a type 10 wide-mouthed bowl, which type is dated to AD 120–230/250 (Monaghan 1987, type 4A2) but appears in mid–late 3rd and 4th century deposits at Wallsend (HWCD). BB2 forms are mostly type 5 cooking jars and type 15 triangular rim bowls, and the complete profile of a type 18 rounded-rim bowl/dish dated to after AD 190 (HWCD). There is a high number of rim sherds and complete profiles of vessels in DOR BB 1, mostly plain-rim dishes with burnished intersecting arc decoration and one example of a Gillam 226 type bowl generally dated to after AD 160. MAH WH mortarium forms, beaded-and-flanged, reeded collared, and reeded hammerhead, are also of late 2nd to 3rd century in date (M78, M89, M93, and M97 Bell and Evans 2002), and further 3rd-century vessels include imported North Gaulish coarse ware pentice beaker fragments and black-slipped wares such as the rouletted indented beaker from Trier (Symonds 1992, AD 200–275).

The functional composition of the trench assemblage is similar to that of the overall site assemblage with a prevalence of jars and high percentage of serving vessels.

The main fabric and form types in this trench give an overall date of late 2nd to mid, possibly late 3rd century AD. This is further reiterated by the virtual absence of typical 4th-century AD fabrics and forms, such as East Yorkshire Calcite Gritted ware Huntcliff jars or Crambeck Parchment ware mortaria. The only fragment of HUN CG in this trench was recovered from the topsoil.

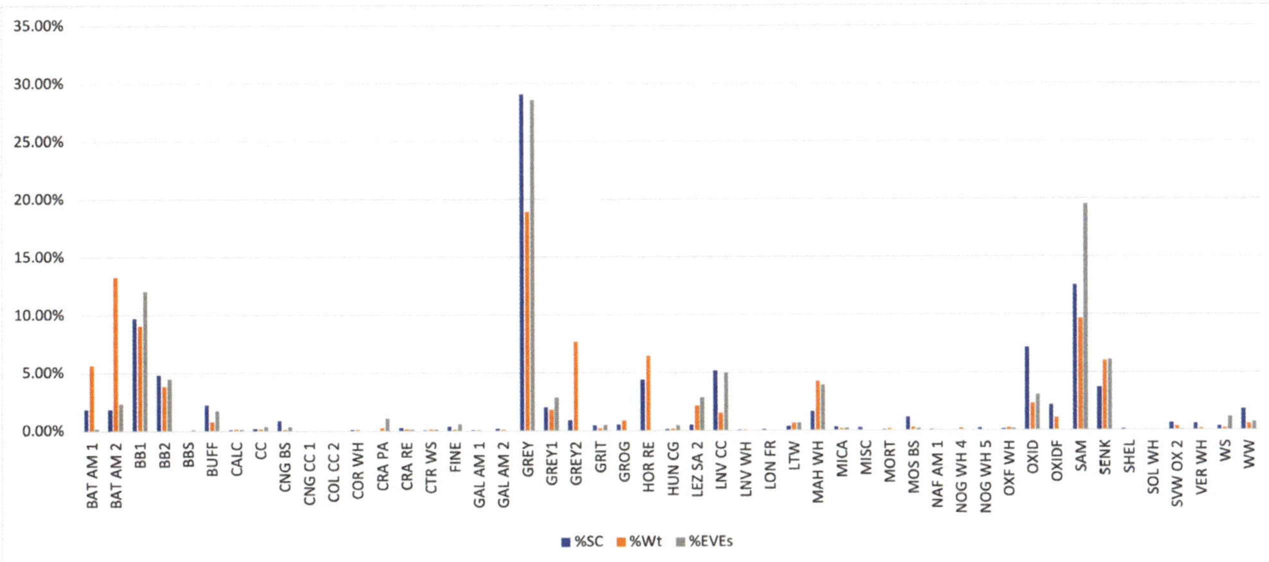

(A)

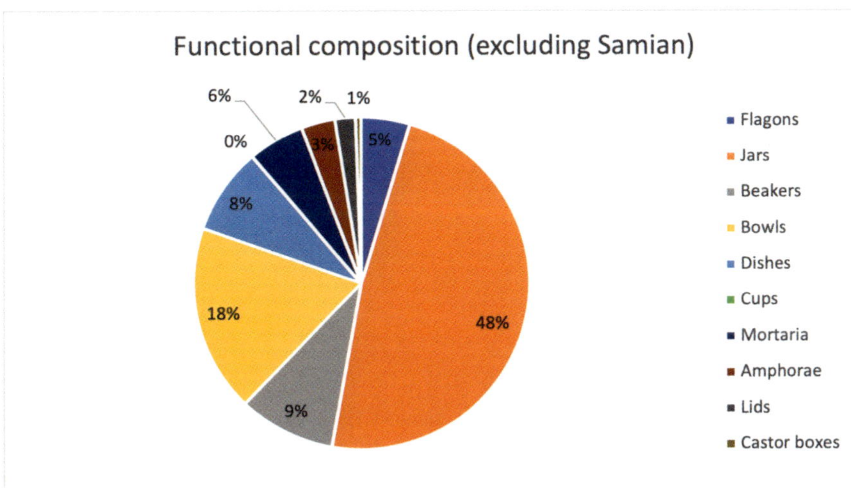

(B)

Figure 7.23: (A) Graphical breakdown of ceramics by fabric. (B) Graphical breakdown of vessel form / function.

Fills (4013) and (4025) of possibly intercutting pits

Of intrinsic interest are the assemblages recovered from fills (4013) and (4025) of intercutting pits in the southwest corner. Fill (4013) contained a substantial assemblage of Roman pottery totalling 197 sherds weighing 7.9 kg and representing 4.92 EVEs. It includes several fragmented complete and near-complete vessels (Fig. 7.25):

- Fragmented complete profile with 32% of the rim present of a DOR BB 1 Gillam 226 bowl with burnished intersecting arcs decoration. Additional joining sherds (22% of rim) were recovered from (4000). Dated to after AD 160. Fig. 7.25, RP1.
- Complete profiles of two plain-rim 'dog' dishes in DOR BB 1 with burnished intersecting arcs decoration and burnished swirls on the outside of the base of one. Dated to after AD 120/5. Fig. 7.25, RP2.
- A GREY1 wide-mouth bowl with fine combed wavy line decoration on its shoulder and 23% of its rim present. Joining rim fragments (13% of rim) were recovered from (4000) and additional sherds with the same combed wavy line decoration may also belong to this vessel. Potentially a 3rd-century AD type. Fig. 7.25, RP3.
- The complete lower half and additional body sherds of GREY2 large storage jar (2.407 kg). There are two, potentially three post-firing holes in the lower vessel wall, equally spaced around the base, suggesting the function of the vessel was intentionally modified. Additional sherds in the same fabric were also retrieved

from (4025) and also from (5001) in Trench 5. Broadly dated to the Roman period. Fig. 7.25, RP4.

- Fragments of one imported, black-slipped beaker with rouletted decoration and elongated indentations. Most likely from Trier (Symonds 1992, Group 35). Dated to AD 200–275. Fig. 7.25, RP5.
- Fragmented but complete LEZ SA 2 Dr37 decorated bowl with decorator's name in the decoration (Lastuca, Lezoux). Dated to AD 160–185. See entry D5 in the Samian report and Fig. 7.25, RP6.
- Joining fragments of the upper half of a Samian Dr38 flanged bowl with 54% of its rim present. The lower interior shows a very heavy wear pattern, potentially a sign of prolonged use for stirring or grinding. The form type is generally dated to after AD 150. Fig. 7.25, RP7. There is one fragment of another Dr38 form with the flange removed (see entries 4 and 5 in the Samian report).
- Numerous joining rim and body sherds of a Samian Dr36 type dish with barbotine leaf decoration on its rim, 39% of the rim extant. From Central Gaul, dated to the late 2nd century AD. See Samian report entry 3 and Fig. 7.25, RP8.
- The complete profile of a very large Samian dish, Ludowici type TbR, 65% of the rim present. Part of the maker's stamp survives reading]VSFII]. From East Gaul, potter Paternus viii dated to after AD 160. See Samian report entry S2 and Fig. 7.25, RP9.
- Near-complete profile with fragmented complete base of a SENK type 10 jar with wavy line decoration in a cordon. Rim sherds making up the complete rim of the vessel were recovered from (4000) and (4025). The type is dated to AD 120–230/250 (Monaghan 1987) but it appears in mid–late 3rd century AD contexts at Wallsend (HWCD). Fig. 7.25, RP10.

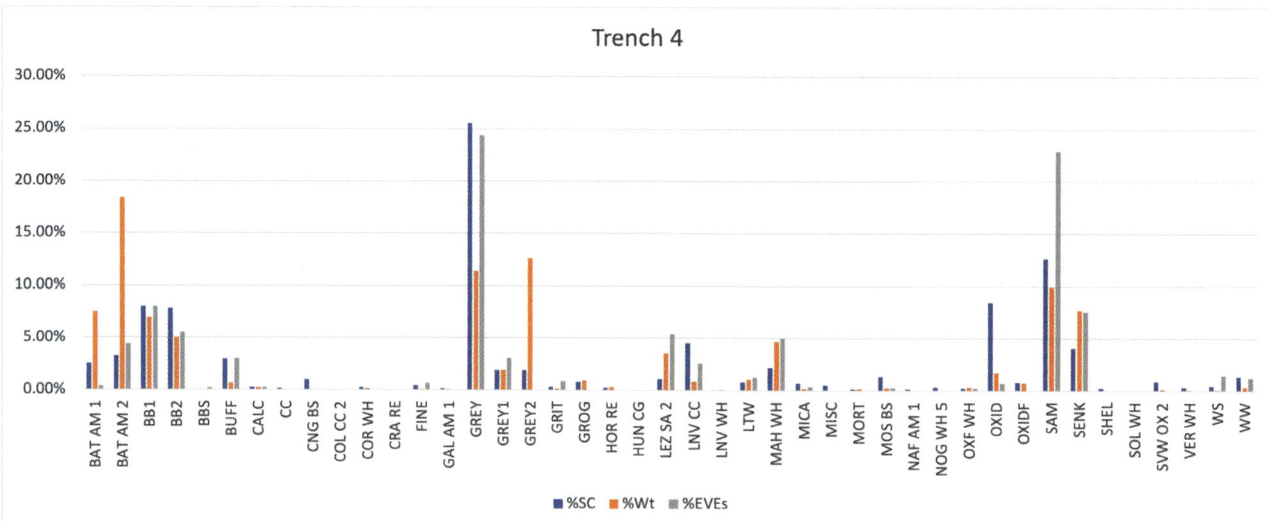

(A)

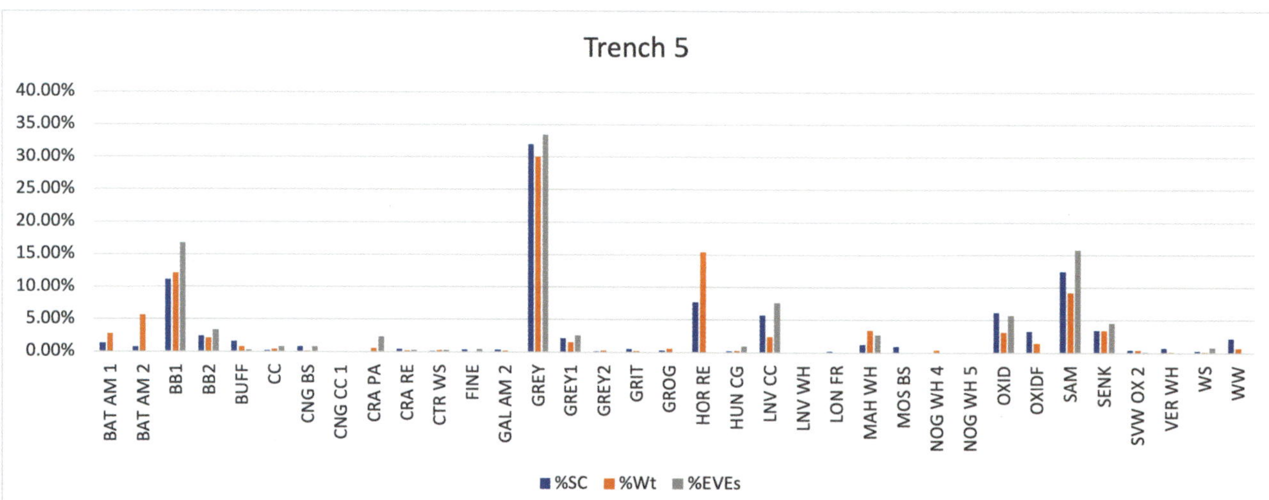

(B)

Figure 7.24: (A) Breakdown of fabric from Trench 4. (B) Breakdown of fabric from Trench 5.

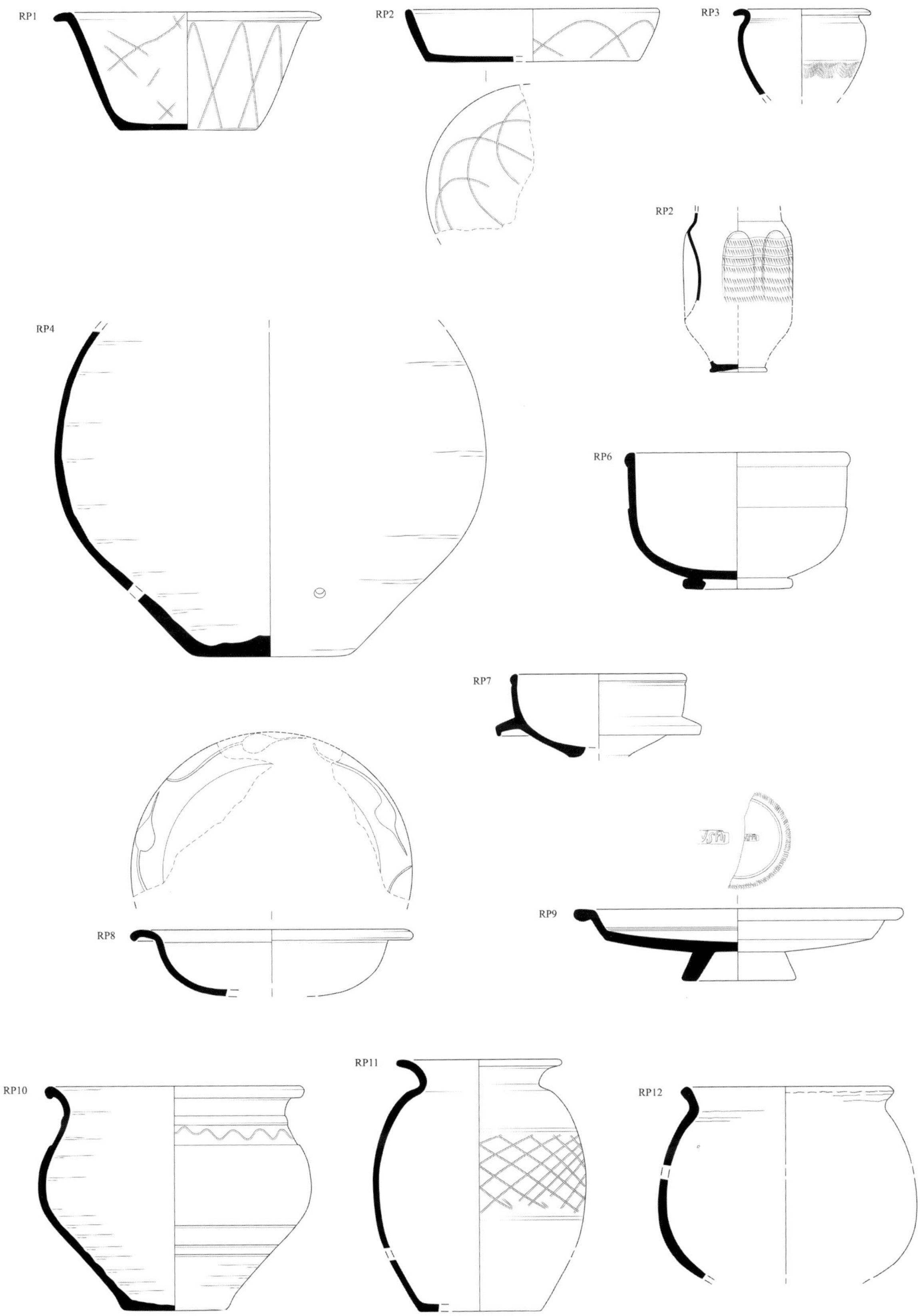

Figure 7.25: Illustration of vessels from fills in Trench 4. Illustration by Cate Davies.

Other pottery from the fill consists of (amongst others) Dressel 20 amphora fragments, including a handle, BB2, CNG BS, GREY everted-rim jar sherds, LNV CC beaker fragments, a MAH WH M78 mortarium rim sherd, a sherd of SVW OX 2, and a fragment of a WW cupped-rim flagon. The date of the forms suggests a deposition date within the first half of the 3rd century AD including some potentially retained material. Although it may be an example of refuse disposal, the high number of complete/near-complete vessels and the placement of the large storage jar in the centre of the pit indicates structured deposition.

Fill (4025) yielded a significantly smaller assemblage of 54 sherds (0.895 kg, 1.13 EVEs), but it incorporates several fragments of vessels from (4013). There are nine additional sherds of the large GREY2 storage jar and joining rim and body sherds of the SENK type 10 wide-mouth bowl. Additional sherds from the latter were also recovered from the topsoil (4000).

Other features with larger assemblages

A total of 69 sherds weighing 1.471 kg (0.97 EVES) were recovered from fill (4010) of the ditch to the south of the road. Over half of this by weight is made up of BAT AM 2 Dressel 20 body sherds, and only GREY and BB2 is present in considerable quantities. The latter includes the complete profile of a type 18 round-rimmed bowl, which is dated to after AD 190 (HWCD). The small amount of Samian from the fill includes two vessels with post-firing repair holes, and there is also a GREY sherd with a post-firing hole.

Fill (4030) of drain/conduit and associated fills (4029) and (4012) produced a total of 77 sherds of Roman pottery weighing 1.519 kg and representing 1.73 EVEs. Again, Dressel 20 amphora sherds comprise over half of the feature assemblage by weight, including one of the rims dated to AD 150–210. The only other fabric present in quantity is LTW with rims of a jar very similar to Gillam 156, a type which had been found at Corbridge in 3rd-century deposits (see above). The presence of a lid-seated jar in a gritty fabric very similar in form to Gillam 153 may support a later 3rd-century infilling for the feature (Bidwell and Croom 2010).

Trench 5

A total of 1369 sherds of Roman pottery weighing 15.021 kg and representing 16.33 EVEs were recovered from Trench 5 contexts (Fig. 7.24B). A substantial amount was recovered from (5000) topsoil: 375 sherds, 4.024 kg, 5.05 EVEs. The condition of the pottery from this trench is poorer than of Trench 4 with higher levels of abrasion and a low mean sherd weight of 10.97g. This, the amount of post-Roman pottery recovered from layers other than the topsoil (5000), and the number of cross-context joins indicate a greater level of redeposition (through later activity) had taken place.

The composition of this trench assemblage is markedly different to that of Trench 4 (compare 7.24A and B). While a wide range of Romano-British and imported fabrics were also identified in this assemblage (35), five fabrics account for 72.7% of the assemblage by weight. The most frequently recorded fabric is GREY with 31.9% of total sherd count, 30.1% of weight, and 33.4% of EVEs. Diagnostic sherds in GREY represent a minimum of 55 different vessels, mostly Black-burnished style everted-rim cooking jars (AD 120+), but forms dated to after AD 250, such as flanged bowls and hooked-rim jars are also present. HOR RE follows with 7.7% of total sherd count and 15.5% of weight and 0 EVEs. All sherds in HOR RE most likely belong to the same large storage jar with internal wiping/combing, but no diagnostic sherds survive. As noted above, this vessel is also likely of 3rd-century AD date. DOR BB 1 is also prominent with 11.2% of sherd count, 12.2% of weight and 16.8% of EVEs of approximately 29 different vessels. There are rim sherds and complete profiles of Gillam 226 and 227 bowls (AD 160+), plain-rim dishes with intersecting arcs decoration, and everted-rim cooking jars. Several of the everted-rim jars are the later type and are also decorated with burnished obtuse lattice (also one of the plain-rim dishes), which indicates a date after AD 250.

The last two significant fabric categories in this Trench assemblage are Samian with 12.5% of sherd count, 9.2% of weight, and 15.7% of EVEs, and Baetican amphorae with 2.1%, 8.5%, and 0% respectively. SENK, BB2, and MAH WH are all below 4% of weight each, the latter including some later rim profiles such as M96 and M105 (mid–late 3rd century AD, Bell and Evans 2002). Some of these fabrics, along with NOG WH 4, VER WH or the jar forms potentially made at Corbridge, are bound to be residual even within Roman contexts, but the extent of this is difficult to judge.

The functional composition of the Trench 5 assemblage is again like that of the site assemblage overall, with a strong presence of jars and perhaps even higher proportion of bowls/dishes and beakers.

Although the fabric and form composition of the Trench 5 assemblage shows a stronger presence of post-AD 250 material than within Trench 4, 4th-century AD forms and fabrics are still scarce. There is a small amount of Crambeck reduced ware, one example of a Crambeck Parchment ware bowl with red-painted decoration (Bidwell and Croom 2010, fig. 4.8/54, AD 300–400), and three fragments of HUN CG from the topsoil, which may hint that activity extended into the earliest years of the 4th century AD, but it does not appear to be significant. Contexts incorporating the latest dated pottery from this trench are: layers (5003), (5005), (5008), (5010) sealing the main occupation deposits, deposits (5011) and (5012), which appear to be part of the foundation of the stone wall, fill (5018) of a stone-lined trough, occupation deposits (5020), (5023), and (5024) within the building, and (5025) and (5034) to the east of the building.

Conclusions for the Roman ceramic assemblage

Overall, the Roman pottery assemblage recovered during the excavations includes a great variety and range of material spanning the entire Roman period in date. Activity in Trench 4 appears to be of mainly early–mid-3rd century AD in date with very restricted evidence post-dating AD 250. The assemblage from Trench 5, however, incorporates significantly greater amounts of pottery dated post-AD 250, a significant proportion of which was derived from well-stratified occupation layers and features. Thus, activity in the excavation area post-dates the establishment of the civil town at Corbridge (McCarthy 2005; Hodgson 2008). Given the scarcity of forms and fabrics typical of 4th-century AD date in the area, it is unlikely that the activity extended into the latest Roman period. The functional composition of the assemblages indicates activities relating to food storage, preparation, and consumption (the full occupation range), while the presence of several pottery gaming counters implies other leisure activities. It is tempting to interpret the high percentage of vessels related to the consumption of food and drink and the counters as potential commercial activities in buildings fronting the roads leading to/from the town, this is purely speculation and it must be tested against other artefactual and structural evidence from the site. Nonetheless, flagons (for serving drinks) are rather rare in the assemblage, which may argue against this hypothesis.

The post-Roman pottery

A total of 210 fragments of post-Roman ceramics weighing 1.047 kg was recovered from the 2021 WallCAP excavations (Table 7.4). The material comprises largely post-medieval and modern material with very few possible medieval fragments.

The post-Roman material was retrieved from eight individually numbered contexts including the topsoil/subsoil from both excavation trenches. In Trench 4 all post-Roman sherds were recovered from (4000). In Trench 5 most of the post-Roman fragments were also recovered from the topsoil/subsoil (5000), however, a small number of sherds were found in layers directly below (5000) and from features beneath where they might be intrusive.

Table 7.4: Quantification and distribution of the post-Roman ceramics.

Context	*SC*	*Wt(g)*	*Fabric*
4000	58	352	PMED
5000	135	621	PMED
5001	1	1	PMED
5002	4	8	PMED
5003	1	1	PMED
5008	1	2	PMED
5011	1	9	PMED
5015	9	53	PMED
Total	210	1047	

Glass

Sally Cottam

A total of 137 fragments of glass were examined, from 31 individual contexts. Of these 73 were identified as Roman and eight as very probably Roman (including melted lumps), and these 81 fragments were catalogued. Nearly all were vessel fragments, six came from windows and there was one glass bead. The other 56 fragments ranged in date from the late 18th to the 20th/21st centuries. Most of these modern fragments, where identified, came from window panes, wine bottles and small medicine/ointment bottles. Part of a late 18th-century ribbed ale glass was also identified (context 5000). One small fragment of a colourless plastic container (context 1002) was also in the assemblage.

Nearly all the Roman glass was in a stable condition, though fragments from two of the vessels were very shattered (nos. 1 and 3/4). Fragments were generally small and there were no large sections of any vessel, and no full profiles. The deposition was typical of normal domestic activity, whilst the small size of the fragments and the near absence of joining pieces may indicate that broken glass was being collected, perhaps for recycling.

The vessel glass

The polychrome fragment no. 1 is a very small, but the thickness of the body and the combination of opaque white glass in a translucent purple ground indicate that it came from a non-blown (cast) polychrome vessel. Several forms of cast bowl use this colour combination, and although no ribs are evident on this small piece, perhaps the most likely source for this fragment is a convex ribbed bowl (pillar moulded bowl). These bowls have a straight rim, a convex body with vertical ribs, and a flat or slightly concave base (Isings 1957, form 3a/b; Price and Cottam 1998, 44–46). Polychrome pillar moulded bowls are generally rare after the early Flavian period, although an example with opaque yellow rods in a green ground has been found previously at Corbridge (Bulmer 1955, 119; Charlesworth 1959, 36). This bowl may therefore have been used during the earliest years of Roman activity at Corbridge, and as a polychrome glass vessel was likely to have been a valued item. Purple bowls with opaque white and/or opaque yellow elements have been found in northern Britain at military sites such as York (Yorkshire Museum no. YORYM: 1995.432), Strageath (Price 1989, 197 no. 1 fig. 100) and Camelon (unpublished) and also at early sites not connected to a Roman military base, such as Scotch Corner (Cool 2020, 467, no. 597, fig. 5.67) and Stanwick, North Yorkshire (Price 2016, 262, nos. 1–2, fig. 13.1). No. 1 was found in a deposit with a pottery assemblage suggesting deposition during the first half of the 3rd century, and the possibility that it may come from a later form of purple and white cast polychrome vessel cannot be ruled out. These later polychrome vessels are unusual, but a purple and opaque white plate on a foot ring is known from Piercebridge, County Durham, and dated to the 2nd or 3rd centuries AD (Price 2002; Cool and Price 2008, D.10.8, fig. D.10.1 no. 1).

The form of no. 2, the yellow/green tubular base fragment, cannot be determined as this type of base is common to a number of 1st–2nd-century vessels. The diameter suggests a relatively small vessel, perhaps a small bowl, such as the yellow/green bowl with a horizontal fold around the body, from Felixstowe, Suffolk and now in the British Museum (BM online catalogue 1853,0815.24).

No. 3 is the rim and body of a colourless cylindrical cup of a type found commonly throughout the Roman world on sites dating from the mid-2nd to early 3rd centuries (Isings 1957, form 85b). The complete vessel would have had a vertical rounded rim, a straight side curving to a horizontal base and a tubular pushed in base ring, probably with an additional trailed base ring near the centre of the base (Price and Cottam 1998, 99–101). No. 4 has the same rim, but it is slightly thicker and may therefore come from a second cup. Many similar cups are known from sites in the Hadrian's Wall region, including Corbridge (Bulmer 1955, 128, 14; Allen 1988, 293, nos. 43–44, fig. 132). Three cups of this type were amongst the glass grave goods in the cemetery at Brougham, Cumbria, where they occurred in 3rd-century burials (Cool 2004, 119, 124, 166–167, 367, nos. 102.17, 107.9, and 186.8, figs 4.92 and 4.154) and others are known from Vindolanda (Price 1985, 207 nos. 8–11, fig. 77), Housesteads (Charlesworth 1971, 34–35, nos. 4 and 5) and Carlisle where at least 30 were identified at Blackfriars Street (Price 1990, 170–172, MF 69–72, nos. 22–30, fig. 161).

No. 5 has a similar vertical rounded rim, but comes from a blue/green vessel, probably a large cup or bowl. The colour and form of the rim suggest a 2nd–3rd-century date, but no further information on the form is visible. No. 8, a blue/green tubular base ring, cannot be closely identified, and could come from a 1st–3rd-century bowl or jug.

At least two blue/green jugs are represented by nos. 6, 6a, and 7. The curvature of the rim of no. 6 suggests that it may come from a jug with a pouring spout. Several jug types of the 2nd–3rd centuries have spouts that were formed by either pushing in the sides of the rim or pulling out part of the rim into a point whilst the glass was still hot. Whilst no. 6 cannot be firmly identified as either pushed-in or pulled-out, the contour of the rim edge is more suggestive of a pulled-out spout. Jugs with spouts usually have a globular or a squat, discoid body (Price and Cottam 1998, 157–161). No. 6 had a narrow ribbon handle and was probably quite a small vessel. At the point where the handle is attached to the rim, the glass has been pinched whilst still hot to form two projections. This decorative feature is occasionally used on late 1st- and 2nd-century jugs, and can be seen on a complete blue/green discoid jug with a pulled-out spout from a burial dated to the second half of the 2nd century AD at Colchester (Thorpe 1935, 21, pl. 8a; Colchester Museum Online catalogue no. COLEM:JOS.229.dup).

In northern Britain spouted jugs occur quite frequently. A colourless jug with a similar pulled-out spout came from a deposit dated to the 2nd–3rd centuries at Catterick (Cool and Price 2002, 223, no. 38, fig. 334), and jugs with pouring spouts are also known from Binchester (Price and Worrell 2010, 312, nos. 246–247) and Carlisle (Price and Cottam 2010, 247–248, no. I37 fig. 129). No. 7 might possibly be a handle fragment from the same jug, but is more likely to come from a different vessel. No. 6a has a rim that has been folded out and in and flattened, and comes from a further vessel, probably a jug or flask.

Blue/green glass bottles, used for storing and serving liquids and semi liquids, are usually the most common vessels on sites occupied in the 1st and 2nd centuries, and this is the case here, where around 60% of the vessel glass was identified as coming from bottles. These vessels were usually quite sturdy, with folded rims, short cylindrical necks, and short angular handles. Various shapes of bottle were produced. In the 1st century, cylindrical bottles were common, whilst square bottles were used both in the 1st century and throughout the 2nd century (Price and Cottam 1998, 191–198). At least two cylindrical bottles, represented by body fragments from trenches 4 and 5, are in this group of glass.

Square bottles were formed by being blown into a multi-piece mould and have distinctive straight sides and flat bases, which often have a raised design. Although there are no 45-degree corners amongst the body fragments here, it is likely that most of the flat bottle fragments listed were from square bottles, as these were very common. Three joining body fragments, from trench 5, appear to be from a bottle with a hexagonal body, a type used in the late 1st and 2nd centuries. These too were blown into a mould and also have a flat base, again usually with a raised design (Price and Cottam 1998, 198–200). Three bases with raised designs have been identified (nos. 8–9 plus a listed fragment). Two show part of a circle, probably from a design of concentric circles, which is the most common pattern on mould-blown bottle bases. The third also has part of a curved raised design, but the full pattern cannot be reconstructed.

Window glass and objects

Six fragments from trenches 4 and 5 came from at least three window panes. Window glass is a common find on Roman sites in Britain. As well as for residential buildings, glass panes were extensively used in bath houses. A considerable number of fragments were found during excavations at the Red House bathhouse about 1 km west of this site (Daniels 1959, 140). Two main types of window glass were produced during the Roman period. The fragments here come from panes with one matt surface and one smoother surface, usually termed 'matt/glossy' window glass. These features indicate that one side of the pane had contact with a flat surface during manufacture, a theory supported by recent experimental research (Taylor 2003). 'Matt/glossy' panes are found in association with buildings dated from the 1st–3rd centuries though no doubt some windows of this type continued *in situ* into the 4th century.

A near complete flattened hexagonal glass bead was found in trench 5 (cat. no. 21 below in Artefacts). Green hexagonal beads are quite frequently found on Roman sites and appear to have been most popular in the 3rd and 4th centuries (Guido 1978, 96–97). Most glass beads are found as single items, presumably losses from a necklace or bracelet, although complete necklaces are known from burials (Guido 1979, 297–300, pl. 1a). Two green hexagonal beads are already known from Corbridge (Guido 1978, 216), six came from Coventina's Well, Carrawburgh (Allason-Jones and McKay 1985, 39 no. 1290) and others occur at Vindolanda (Birley 2006, 27, fig. 1.12), Birdoswald (Price and Cottam 1997, 274 no. 26 fig. 185) and elsewhere in the Hadrian's Wall region. A small fragment of an opaque blue glass bead was also found in trench 5 (cat. no. 20) and an incomplete blue faience melon bead (cat. no. 22). Melon beads are extremely common at the sites along Hadrian's Wall.

Three blue/green melted lumps came from trench 1 (COR19 1002). These are of a colour that could identify them as Roman but they could also be modern. One has a very small piece of unidentified bone attached.

Summary

During the Roman period, glass was being used at this site for a variety of functions; as tablewares, storage vessels, for windows and for personal adornment (necklace). The Roman glass assemblage represents a minimum of 11 vessels, at least four windows and three beads. The true number of vessels may be greater, as it is difficult to identify individual vessels amongst the many body fragments, particularly the bottles. The glass ranges in date from the 1st to at least the 3rd century. The cylindrical bottles are the only two vessels that can be firmly placed in the 1st century, although the polychrome bowl (no. 1) is also likely to be early. The colourless cups (nos. 3–4) and the blue/green jug (no. 6) belong to the later 2nd and early 3rd centuries. Many of the vessel fragments (*c.* 60%) came from 1st–2nd century blue/green bottles, a proportion fairly typical of 1st–2nd-century sites with a military connection. The polychrome bowl was probably a valued item, and is not particularly common in northern Britain, but the other recognised vessel forms are types commonly found on other sites in the region.

Catalogue

Following the category of glass, significant pieces are given a catalogue number and associated context, followed by a brief description and where feasible, a date of associated production. Measurements follow in mm, using the following abbreviations: Dims = dimensions; T = thickness; PH = present height; BD = base diamter; RD = rim diameter.

Non-blown, polychrome

1. COR21 4013
   Three joining purple and opaque white body fragments, ?bowl. Thick-walled convex body. Translucent purple ground, opaque white roundels/spirals. Surfaces lightly weathered.
   Dims: 18 × 11 T:4

Blown, yellow/green

2. COR19 1002
   Base fragment, bowl/beaker. Edge of wide lower body tapering into diagonal tubular pushed-in base ring and slightly concave base. Dark streaks in base. Edge of base ring worn.
   PH: 13 BD. 60 T: 2 3
   COR21 4017 – body fragment

Colourless

3. COR21 5023
   6 rim and body fragments, four joining, cup. Vertical rim, edge rounded. Straight side.
   PH: 12 RD: *c.* 70 T: 1–3

4. COR21 5022
   Rim and body fragment, cup. Vertical rim, edge rounded. Straight side.
   PH: 10 T: 2–3.5

Body fragments

COR21 5024 – convex
COR21 5025 – three fragments, two joining, slightly heat distorted
COR21 4025 – straight sided
COR21 4016 – five fragments, ?lower body. Trace of edge of base.
COR21 5000 – straight sided

Blue/green

5. COR21 5027
Rim and body fragment, cup/bowl. Vertical rim, edge rounded. Straight side.
PH: 10 RD: *c*. 110 T: 1.5–3

6. COR19 RF13 1006
Rim and handle fragment, jug. Vertical rim (?part of spout), edge rolled in. Upper part of narrow ribbon handle, attached at horizontal angle to rim edge. Two vertical rounded projections on upper attachment.
PH: 16 Handle width: *c*. 18
6a. COR21 5000 – Small fragment, part of folded rim, ?jug

7. COR21 4016
Handle fragment, jug. Part of ribbon handle, expanding out slightly. One edge folded over to form uneven central ridge. Part of broken edge worn.
Handle width: 20–21 T: 3–6

8. COR21 4022
Base fragment. Trace of edge of body. Narrow tubular base ring, slightly concave base.
PH: 12 BD: 75

Body fragments

COR21 5027 – thin walled, possibly indented side

Undecorated

COR19 1002
COR21 4013 – slightly heat distorted
COR21 4018
COR21 5000
COR21 5005
COR21 5006
COR21 5022

Blue/green bottles

Small fragment, ?edge of handle
COR21 5022

Shoulder/body fragments

COR21 4018
COR21 5000 West wall
COR21 5017
COR21 5020
COR21 5027

Cylindrical bottles, body fragments

COR21 4023 – Bubbly, uneven glass
COR21 5020 – three fragments
COR21 5022 – ?cylindrical bottle

Flat, straight sided body fragments, bottles

COR19 1002 – three fragments, different bottles
COR19 1012
COR21 4013
COR21 4017
COR21 4025
COR21 4032
COR21 4034
COR21 5000 – two fragments
COR21 5005
COR21 5012 – three joining fragments, ?hexagonal bottle
COR21 5015
COR21 5017
COR21 5018
COR21 5024
COR21 5034 – two fragments, different bottles

9. COR21 5008
Base fragment, small bottle. Trace of edge of body, slightly concave base. Raised circle on underside of base, Pontil scar at centre of base. Worn.
Diameter of raised circle: *c*. 40 T: 4–6.5

10. COR21 5000
Body and base fragment, bottle. Straight sided body. Flat base. Raised curved design on underside of base.
PH: 12 T: 6–7
COR21 5000 – base fragment, part of raised circle on underside
COR21 5002 – small chip, ?base

Window glass (matt/glossy)

COR21 5000 – pale blue/green, rounded edge
COR21 4022 – blue/green
COR21 5002 – blue/green
COR21 4032 – blue/green
COR21 5034 – blue/green
COR21 5031 – pale green

Beads

See Artefacts below.

Melted lumps, ?Roman

COR19 1002 – three blue/green irregular lumps, one with small area of bone attached

Artefacts (incl. coins)

Rob Collins

Across two seasons of fieldwork in the playing field at Corbridge, a considerable amount of material culture was recovered, reflecting the urban nature of the site. A total of 98 individual objects were recorded and catalogued (below), with a further 157 entries consisting of a range of nails and other unidentified structural and production objects, quantified by number of fragments and weight. These objects were recovered through excavation, metal detecting of the spoil heap, and a small number were found during environmental sample processing.

The small finds were examined directly, identified, and recorded to a database to facilitate analysis and cataloguing. Objects were assigned a database number as they were recorded, and new catalogue numbers were assigned during analysis to best cluster objects of related function/category. Weights were taken following washing of objects, but before any conservation and are therefore subject to change. Objects were photographed and composite images have been produced in an illustration programme. Objects of modern date, *i.e.* post-the Second World War, were not recorded, of which there were approximately 20.

Analysis is based on context, and identification of an object (where possible) to a specific type or function and to a broader category of activity. Some objects and categories, such as 'fittings', remain ambiguous, as the given fitting could be part of an item of costume, furniture, transport, or even structural/domestic objects.

Overall, there is an interesting mix of objects that is generally reflective of the urban character of Roman Corbridge. Significantly, there is a majority of material that points to production and other economic activities, rather than domestic occupation. Unsurprisingly, given the importance of Corbridge's location in the Hadrian's Wall corridor, and the fact that it originated as a Roman fort, there is some evidence of military presence/activity. For an urban site, very few coins were discovered, totalling five of Roman date.

Closely datable material is sparse. Of the coins, only one was found in a secure context and there are too few to provide a reasonable analysis of coin loss. Most of the other objects have quite long production periods, often for the entire Roman period. When a shorter period of production can be identified, this is highlighted. It should also be noted that the ironwork is presumed to be Roman, largely on the basis of contextual analysis, though strictly speaking there is very little ironwork that is diagnostically Roman. Therefore, some ironwork in the highest contexts and layers could be of more recent date (*c.* 1800–1950), or a mix of Roman and modern materials. Cast iron was identified and removed from the assemblage for analysis as best as could be identified through varying levels of corrosion and preservation.

In the following analysis, context of discovery is placed in parentheses ( ), and the number provided is the catalogue number in brackets [] found here.

Analysis by trench and context

Using context numbers, objects can be assessed relative to the trench they were found in, ideally providing some notion of the overall character of the trench.

Trench 1 had 17 recorded artefacts and a handful of unidentified ironwork thought to be structural in function. The trench provided three of the five Roman coins from the site [1, 4, 5] (1002) and many of the unambiguous late 19th–early 20th-century objects [91–94] (1002). An enamelled disc brooch [6] (1002) and fragmentary finger ring [15] (1004) were found, as well as a number of objects from (1006) that included an iron vessel rim fragment [38], a ceramic counter [45], and a flint flake [90]. An iron buckle [69], consistent with heavy buckle forms used for horse harness was also found (1013).

Trench 2 provided a window latch [96] of late 19th/early 20th-century date.

Trench 3, with seven recorded artefacts and 18 fragments of unidentified structural ironwork, is dominated by iron and objects pertaining to structural features and fittings. Notable exceptions include a corroded fragment of copper alloy likely to be a brooch fragment [17] (3002), and the iron hoop from a stave-built tankard [40] (3009).

Trench 4 has 32 recorded artefacts and 163 fragments/remains of ironwork and slag. The overwhelming majority of this latter material is structural and points to both stratified and unstratified/disturbed remains of one or many Roman structures making use of nails. Recorded artefacts are mixed, with no dominant category, and includes hobnails, a few dress accessories, the base ring of a glass ewer and other traces of ceramic vessels, a stone counter, and a possible lead candlestick. In summary, a mixed assemblage pointing toward mixed domestic activities and some limited artefactual evidence for production activities.

Trench 5 has 41 recorded artefacts and 207 nails and other structural ironwork and slag, again pointing to one or more Roman structures built with nails. This trench boasted the most artefacts recorded, and in terms of functional categories, was very mixed. A number of objects of militaria were found, primarily hobnails, but also a sword scabbard slide [24] (5024). Dress accessories included glass beads and a fragment of a glass bangle [19] (5025). The majority of game counters were found in this trench, and metal fittings pointing to eating and drinking, such as a corroded escutcheon/vessel mount [39] (5011). A few bits of metal slag and stone smoothing stones also point to production work.

Contextual analysis is summarised in Table 7.5, noting any contexts with more than three recorded artefacts, and any key artefacts, with the exception of 1000/2000/3000/4000/5000.

Table 7.5: Summary of artefacts and material culture by context.

Context	*No. of iron/slag*	*No. of artefacts*	*Objects of interest [cat no]*
1002		6	Disc brooch [6]
1003	10	1	Cut stone counter [45]
1006		6	Iron vessel frag [38], looped mount [61], lead weight [71]
3004	7	1	Hinge socket fitting [59]
3007	6	1	Iron bracket [63]
4005	8		
4007	7		
4008	8	1	Lead cast waste [78]
4010	9	1	Hobnail [25]
4013		3	Headstud brooch [7], jewellery chain ring [12]
4016	8		
4039	8		coal
5002	10		
5004		3	Stone counter [46], hinge plate [60], smoothing stone [80]
5005	3	1	Iron fitting [66]
5027		3	Glass bead [21]
5008	18		
5015	8	2	Prob penannular brooch [9], lead plug/seal [36]
5018	10	2	Hobnail [34], lead slag [79]
5020	22+	5	Lead disc around incompl iron loop + 4 fe fragments [85]
5022	16	2	Pin [14], hobnail [32]
5025	19	2	Glass bangle [19], brooch pin [11]
5026	20		
5031	9		

Discussion by category of material

Objects have been assessed relative to functional categories of use to provide a brief overview of the evidence for particular activities. In addition to the comments below, it is worth noting two objects of uncertain attribution, but which are particularly interesting.

A cast silver mount, in a circular pelta shape [52] was a find decorative element for some dress accessories or piece of furniture, though its exact attribution cannot be certain.

A fragment of a roughly cast lead 'vessel' or item [51] can probably be identified as a candlestick.

Finds relating to transport can be difficult to identify, but a highly corroded iron buckle [69] is substantial enough that it best parallels examples associated with horse or ox harness. An iron with a rectangular base [70] can also be reasonably identified as a terret, and therefore from a wagon, cart, or chariot.

Dress accessories

A total of 18 (poss. 19) objects have been identified as definitely or probably belonging to a functional category of dress accessory. This includes six brooches and one possible brooch fragment: disc brooch [6]; headstud brooch [7]; P-shaped brooch [8]; penannular brooch terminal [9]; a spring-pin from a brooch [10]; and a hinged brooch pin [11]. Of these, the disc brooch and headstud brooch were probably made between *c.* AD 75–200, while the P-shaped brooch was produced *c.* AD 175–250. The penannular brooch polyhedral terminal is from a smaller from, that could date *c.* AD 50–250.

A small cast ring, probably part of a chain or link for jewellery [12] is among a small selection of other jewellery items, including a fragmented earring [13], a pin [14], and the bezel of a finger ring [15]. An incomplete pair of tweezers [23], pressed flat can be understood as an accessory for appearance or a medical implement.

Three small beads were recovered, one incomplete cylindrical, one an elongated box-shape with a flattened hexagonal section, and a faience melon bead [20, 21, 22], probably of later 1st–3rd-century date. A fragment of a glass bangle, Kilbridge-Jones type 3J, is of a similar date. The green glass bead could be later in date, as its form is typically dated to the 3rd–4th centuries, though on the basis of associated material from other contexts in the trench, a 3rd-century date seems most likely.

Militaria

Finds of military objects were generally confined to hob-nails, totalling 10. The exception is a sword scabbard slide [24] that fits within 2nd–3rd-century production dates.

Leisure

A total of eight discoidal or small domed counters were found, cut or ground in stone or cut in ceramic. One counter was cast in lead with a more decorative appearance [47]. All could arguably be used for playing a game. Of the total, six were found in Trench 5.

Eating and drinking

A number of objects attest to eating and drinking, notably the remains of an iron hoop nailed or riveted to a stave-built tankard [40] (3009), though it is possible that this is a fragment of a larger hoop from a barrel; given that no further certain Roman material is known from Trench 3, it is possibly not Roman in date (though see [98]).

A rim fragment from an iron vessel [38] and what appears to be a corroded drop-shaped escutcheon from another vessel [39] point to cooking in the Trench 1 and 5 areas. Two lead plugs/seals may also attest to ceramic repair [36, 37]. Though not quantified here, substantial numbers of ceramic vessel sherds were also collected, as well as evidence for vessel glass.

Production

A range of artefacts point to production activities. Two lead spindle whorls [74, 75] are indicative of spinning wool, from (4000) and (5026) respectively. A small and fine ceramic crucible [76] (2021) points to working of soft metals, and lead production waste [77–79] was found in three contexts (5000, 4008, and 5018). As many as five smoothing stones [80–84] were found, three from Trench 4 and two from Trench 5.

Structural evidence

Various fittings, primarily in iron, but also in lead, suggest considerable amounts of building fabric in timber or other soft materials. For example, a corner bracket [81] that would be found on a chest or item of furniture, and two different components of large iron hinges [59, 60] were found in (3004, 5004); the first of these has a loop fitting to form a socket, while the second is more of a broad plate.

A hooked fitting [98] (3005) was found within the stone wall.

Prehistoric evidence

Three items of flint were recovered during the excavations. A secondary flake [90], very abraded, was found in (1006), while (4001) produced a reworked drill of Neolithic form [89], and a Bronze Age barbed-and-tanged arrowhead [88] was found in (4030).

Modern evidence

Seven items point to the early history of the site as a playing field, and its previous use as the gardens of Corchester House. Of the former, a 10 centimisi coin minted in 1893 in Italy, an enamelled school badge, a clothing pin/fastener, and button are all machine made and possibly lost during recreational activities. Two iron latches and 19th-century vessel glass almost certainly relate to the garden phase of the land.

Catalogue

Individual objects are recorded here in this catalogue, with the catalogue numbers referred to in the primary text/reporting of the site. Measurements are given in millimetres (mm) and grams (g). The category 'Date' refers to the dating associated with the object form or typology, where present, and not to the date of the context.

Coins (Fig. 7.26A)

1. Denarius of Antoninus Pius
   Context: Cor19.1002
   Date: 143–144 (Roman)
   Length: 12
   Width: 12
   Thickness: 1.8
   Weight: 3
   Material(s): silver
   Condition: W/W
   Reference: RIC III Antoninus Pius 109A
   Description: Obverse: Laureate bust right, inscribed ANTONINUS AUG PIVS PI-VS PP TRP COS III. Reverse: Caduceus with crossed cornucopiae, inscribed IMPERATOR II.

2. Denarius of Marcus Aurelius
   Context: Cor21.4000
   Date: 155–157 (Roman)
   Length: 17
   Width: 17
   Thickness: 1.9
   Weight: 2
   Material(s): silver
   Condition: SW/SW
   Reference: RIC III Marcus Aurelius 437
   Description: Obverse: Uncrowned bust right, inscribed [AVRELIV]S CAES [ANT]ON AVG PIIF. Reverse: Virtus standing left holding parazonium and spear, inscribed TR POT XI COS II.

Figure 7.26: Artefacts from the Corbridge excavations. (A) Coins.

3. Radiate, unidentified ruler
Context: Cor21.5029
Date: 260–285 (Roman)
Length: 12
Width: –
Thickness: 2.5
Weight: 2
Material(s): cu alloy
Condition: VW/VW
Reference: –
Description: Incomplete and very worn, corroded and illegible on both faces, but with the lines of a radiate crown visible.

4. Radiate (barbarous)
Context: Cor19.1002
Date: 275–285 (Roman)
Length: 19
Width: 20
Thickness: 1.5
Weight: 1
Material(s): cu alloy
Condition: VW/VW
Reference: –
Description: Chipped edges and very worn. Obverse: radiate bust right. Reverse: unidentifiable central figure. Contemporary copy.

5. Nummus, House of Valentinian or Theodosius
Context: Cor19.1002
Date: 379–387 (Roman)
Length: 13
Width: 15
Thickness: 0.8
Weight: 2
Material(s): cu alloy
Condition: VW/VW
Reference: –
Description: Clipped edges and very worn, with no surviving inscription. Reverse: emperor facing left, raising a kneeling woman, facing right. REPARATIO REI PVB reverse type.

Dress Accessories (Fig. 7.26B)

6. Disc brooch
Context: Cor19.1002
Date: 75–200 (Roman)
Length: 21
Width: 21
Thickness: 1
Weight: 3
Material(s): cu alloy
Description: A cast but incomplete example, missing the hinged pin and hooked rest of the catchplate. The surface has a central circle with a hollow cell missing enamel (traces of white) surrounded by a sunblaze or star motif in red enamel and outer triangles in blue enamel. Each cell/field is framed by cast integral relief.

7. Headstud brooch
Context: Cor21.4013
Date: 75–200 (Roman)
Length: 32
Width: 22
Thickness: 15
Weight: 8
Material(s): cu alloy
Description: A cast, incomplete corroded headstud brooch retaining the hinge pin. A central ridge on the head is found above an oval-shaped headstud.

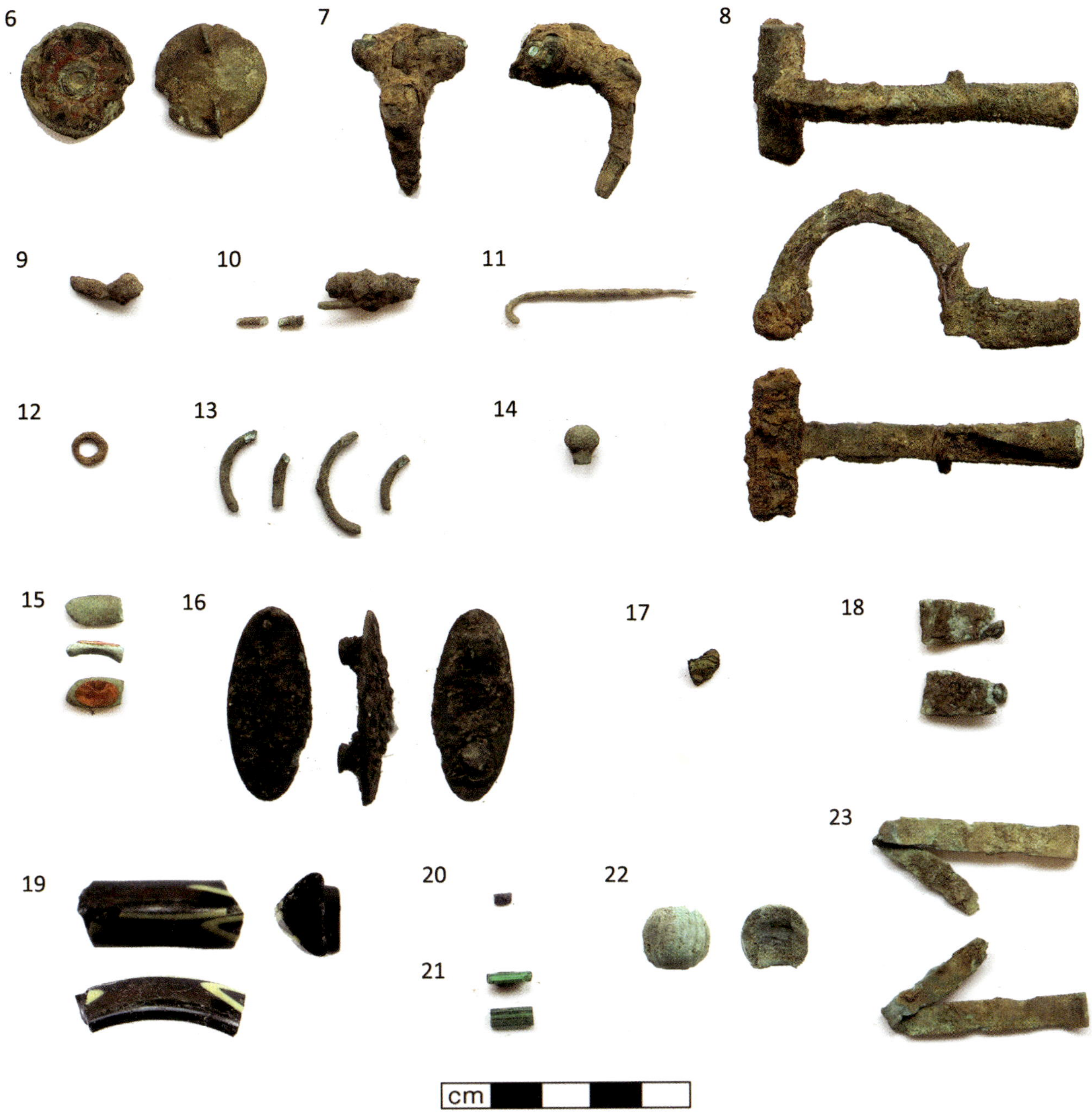

Figure 7.26: Artefacts from the Corbridge excavations. (B) Dress accessories.

8. P-shaped brooch
Context: Cor21.4041
Date: 175–275 (Roman)
Length: 56
Width: 27
Thickness: 9
Weight: 13
Material(s): cu alloy
Description: A near-complete cast P-shaped brooch bearing a cylindrical head, a bow with a triangular section and a projecting disc near the base, and a shallow step separating the bow from the foot. A portion of the catchplate has fragmented off in antiquity. The pin is missing, but spring remains corroded *in situ*.

9. Penannular brooch / dress pin
Context: Cor21.5015
Date: 43–410 (Roman)
Length: 10
Width: 6
Thickness: 2.5
Weight: 1
Material(s): cu alloy
Description: A corroded fragment of a penannular brooch or dress pin, with *c.* 6 mm remaining of the frame of the brooch or shaft of the pin, and a polyhedral head at an angle relative to the frame/shaft.
Note: Found in a flot sample.

10. Brooch pin
Context: Cor21.5000
Date: 50–200 (Roman)
Length: 7
Width: 18
Thickness: 3
Weight: 2
Material(s): cu alloy
Description: The coiled spring and base of a pin made from a wrought wire, probably from a bow brooch. The pin shaft survives for a length of *c*. 8 mm, with two further short lengths of pin shaft *c*. 4 and 6 mm in length, respectively.

11. Brooch pin
Context: Cor21.5025
Date: 50–410 (Roman)
Length: 39
Width: 2
Thickness: 2
Weight: 2
Material(s): cu alloy
Description: A near complete hinged pin from a brooch, probably a bow brooch on the basis of its length.

12. Jewellery chain link / ring
Context: Cor21.4013
Date: 43–410 (Roman)
Length: 7
Width: 7
Thickness: 1
Weight: 0.6
Material(s): cu alloy
Description: A small corroded ring typical for use jewellery.
Note: Found in a flot sample.

13. Earring
Context: Cor21.4013
Date: 50–410 (Roman)
Length: 23
Width: n/a
Thickness: 1.2
Weight: 0.8
Material(s): cu alloy
Description: Four fragmentary lengths of copper-alloy wire, probably forming an earring of Allason-Jones type 3 or 12.

14. Pin
Context: Cor21.5022
Date: 50–410 (Roman)
Length: 9
Width: 8
Thickness: n/a
Weight: 0.5
Material(s): cu alloy
Description: A sub-spherical head of a pin with the top of the shaft, which is circular in section.

15. Finger ring
Context: Cor21.1004
Date: 100–250 (Roman)
Length: 12
Width: 6
Thickness: 3
Weight: 2
Material(s): cu alloy
Description: A fragment of a finger ring, consisting of an oval-shaped bezel with an oval inset retaining degraded enamel or glass paste 'gem' imitating carnelian. No trace of a carving remains on the 'gem'. The rest of the hoop of the ring is missing, but in profile the hoop has a flat bezel, short angled shoulders and a circular frame. The bezel is lentoidal in section.

16. Mount
Context: Cor21.4004
Date: 43–410 (Roman)
Length: 37
Width: 16
Thickness: 2
Weight: 7
Material(s): cu alloy
Description: A very corroded copper-alloy mount, consisting of an oval plate with cast integral cylindrical shanks on the underside near each end of the plate. The shanks also have flat bases. The corrosion on the face of the mount, its underside and the shanks suggest contact/deposition with corroding iron.

17. Brooch or other dress accessory fragment
Context: Cor19.3002
Date: 43–250 (Roman)
Length: 7
Width: 5
Thickness: 1.5
Weight: 0.4
Material(s): cu alloy
Description: A small fragment of cast copper alloy bearing decoration in relief, part of a larger curved dress accessory. Possibly the fragment from a brooch, such as a trumpet brooch, a finger ring, or some other dress accessory. Though obscured by corrosion, the relief is typical of the native Romano-British 'Celtic' style dating to the 1st–3rd centuries.

18. Dress accessory
Context: Cor21.5024
Date: 43–410 (Roman)
Length: 18
Width: 8
Thickness: 3
Weight: 3
Material(s): cu alloy
Description: A corroded and folded fragment of cast copper alloy from a bracelet or finger ring or some other dress accessory such as a strap end or pendant. The folded portion consists of a flat oval, one end of which has been torn. The opposite end widens from the tapered end of the oval and has evidence of an abraded break.

19. Bangle
Context: Cor21.5025
Date: 60–200 (Roman)
Length: 33
Width: 15
Thickness: 7
Weight: 6
Material(s): glass
Description: A glass bangle fragment of blue glass, triangular in section, with trailed yellow glass mixed on the upper surface. Kilbride-Jones type 3J.

20. Bead
Context: Cor21.5030
Date: 43–410 (Roman)
Length: 4
Width: 4
Thickness: 1
Weight: 0.1
Material(s): glass
Description: A fragment of a tubular opaque blue glass bead.

21. Bead
Context: Cor21.5027
Date: 200–410 (Roman)
Length: 9
Width: 4
Thickness: 1.3
Weight: 0.9
Material(s): glass
Description: A green glass bead, rectangular in plan and a very flattened hexagonal section with a circular bore through its length.

22. Bead
Context: Cor21.5027
Date: 43–410 (Roman)
Length: 12
Width: 14
Thickness: 3
Weight: 0.3
Material(s): faience
Description: An incomplete melon bead in faience. Though included in this section with other dress accessories, melon beads have also been associated with horse harness.

Medical/Toiletry (Fig 7.26B)

23. Tweezers
Context: Cor21.4000
Date: 43–410 (Roman)
Length: 41
Width: 8
Thickness: 1.1
Weight: 2
Material(s): cu alloy
Description: A flat rectangular strip of copper-alloy sheet that has been folded to create two arms for the tweezers. One end is missing, but the surviving end curves inward slightly. The fold in the tweezers has been crushed and creased, so that the arms are flush against each other.

Militaria (Fig. 7.26C)

24. Scabbard slide
Context: Cor21.5024
Date: 100–275 (Roman)
Length: 78
Width: 15
Thickness: 3.5
Weight: 17
Material(s): cu alloy
Description: An incomplete cast scabbard slide missing its lower terminal. The upper terminal is triangular and flat, while the main bar of the slide is tapered in plan and D-shaped in section. An incised central line is visible down its length with hatched angled lines from the outer edge to the centre creating a chevron pattern.

Figure 7.26: Artefacts from the Corbridge excavations. (C) Militaria.

25–34. Hobnails

No.	*Context*	*Length*	*Width*	*Thickness*	*Weight*	*Material*	*Note*
25	Cor21.4010	15	10	3	2	Iron	Hemispherical head with off-centre shaft, curved into a J-shape. Corroded.
26	Cor21.5028	15	9	3.5	1	Iron	Hemispherical head with off-centre shaft, curved into a J-shape. Corroded.
27	Cor21.4000	19	14	4	1	Iron	Large, hemispherical head with off-centre shaft. Corroded.
28	Cor21.4000	16	8	5	1	Iron	Mostly corrosion, but hemispherical head visible through corrosion.
29	Cor21.5000	15	10	3	1	Iron	Hemispherical head with off-centre shaft. Corroded.
30	Cor21.5000	25	10	4	3	Iron	Hemispherical head with off-centre shaft, curved into a J-shape. Corroded.
31	Cor21.5000	–	–	–	1	Iron	Corroded head only. From flot sample.
32	Cor21.5022	–	–	–	4	Iron	3 corroded hobnails. From flot sample.
33	Cor21.4012	–	–	–	5	Iron	6 corroded heads of hobnails. From flot sample.
34	Cor21.5018	–	–	–	6	Iron	5+ corroded head and other fragments. From flot sample.

Eating and Drinking (Fig. 7.26D)

35. Plug / seal
Context: Cor21.5015
Date: 43–410 (Roman)
Length: 38
Width: 27
Thickness: 1.5
Weight: 14
Material(s): lead
Description: An irregular and incomplete cast sheet of lead with a rectangular lug. The face of the sheet with the lug bears ridges in low relief, suggesting it was a plug or seal for a ceramic vessel.

Figure 7.26: Artefacts from the Corbridge excavations. (D) Eating and drinking.

36. Plug / seal
Context: Cor21.4017
Date: 43–410 (Roman)
Length: 28
Width: 22
Thickness: 1
Weight: 13
Material(s): lead
Description: An irregular sub-circular disc bearing a raised rectangular shank on one face and the disc of the base bent 'upward'. An oval hole is found as the base of the fold, in line with the shank.

37. Vessel
Context: Cor19.1006
Date: 43–410 (Roman)
Length: 75
Width: 50
Thickness: 3
Weight: 32
Material(s): iron
Description: A corroded rim fragment of a wrought iron vessel, probably a cauldron or similar form. The rim is everted with corrosion on the outer face below the rim that may belong to a separate iron hoop used for suspension. The likely diameter of the vessel when complete is 250–300 mm.

38. Escutcheon (vessel)
Context: Cor21.5011
Date: 43–410 (Roman)
Length: 35
Width: 24
Thickness: 15
Weight: 4
Material(s): iron
Description: A highly corroded petal or drop-shaped mount. Corrosion obscures evidence for breaks or missing components. The shape is similar to button-and-loop fastener heads, though the latter are typically made in copper alloy.

39. Hoop from tankard
Context: Cor19.3009
Date: 43–410 (Roman)
Length: 97
Width: 25
Thickness: 8
Weight: 69
Material(s): iron
Description: A fragment of a small iron hoop used in stave-built vessels, in this case a wooden tankard. Approximately 40% remains, in a somewhat flattended C-shape with breaks at each end. The entire surface is corroded in varying degrees, but nail/tac heads can be seen on the upper face, and the shafts of these on the inner face. Some of these may have been larger and decorative on the basis of a large circular corrosion scar. The tankard would be approximately 20 mm in diameter.

40. Pestle
Context: Cor21.4000
Date: 43–410 (Roman)
Length: 65
Width: 48
Thickness: 30
Weight: 143
Material(s): stone
Description: An oblong ground stone with an abraded end, suggesting breakage of a larger/longer stone.

Leisure (Fig. 7.26E)

41. Counter
Context: Cor21.5000
Date: 43–410 (Roman)
Length: 25
Width: 22
Thickness: 7
Weight: 8

Figure 7.26: Artefacts from the Corbridge excavations. (E) Leisure.

Material(s): stone
Description: A discoidal water-worn pebble, with possible further polishing or grinding.

42. Counter
Context: Cor21.4034
Date: 43–410 (Roman)
Length: 38
Width: 36
Thickness: 9
Weight: 19
Material(s): stone
Description: A roughly shaped yellow sandstone disc of sub-circular shape.

43. Counter
Context: Cor21.5000
Date: 43–410 (Roman)
Length: 27
Width: 27
Thickness: 8
Weight: 6
Material(s): stone
Description: A sub-circular coal-like geological material of mostly black colour, cut in a sub-circular shape.

44. Counter
Context: Cor19.1003
Date: 43–410 (Roman)
Length: 55
Width: 51
Thickness: 12
Weight: 55
Material(s): stone
Description: A large sub-circular cut stone counter, or possibly small 'pot lid'.

45. Counter
Context: Cor21.5004
Date: 43–410 (Roman)
Length: 27
Width: 25
Thickness: 7
Weight: 10
Material(s): stone
Description: A ground stone discoidal counter.

46. Counter / game piece
Context: Cor21.5003
Date: 43–410 (Roman)
Length: 17
Width: 8
Thickness: 6
Weight: 6
Material(s): lead
Description: A rectangular block cast with moulding to include a swollen base and top, with a central horizontal ridge. One face is less exaggerated than the other. The upper and lower faces both have a shallow groove across the central width. In appearance, it is reminiscent of a knuckle bone, and it is perhaps this emulation that suggests its function as a counter or game piece.

47. Counter
Context: Cor21.5000
Date: 43–410 (Roman)
Length: 17
Width: 17
Thickness: 8
Weight: 4
Material(s): ceramic
Description: A sub-circular disc cut from a sherd of Samian ware.

48. Counter
Context: Cor19.1006
Date: 43–410 (Roman)
Length: 15
Width: 10
Thickness: 5
Weight: 1
Material(s): ceramic
Description: A wall sherd of a Samian vessel cut into a sub-circular discoidal shape.

49. Counter
Context: Cor21.5000
Date: 43–410 (Roman)
Length: 21
Width: 21
Thickness: 6
Weight: 6
Material(s): ceramic
Description: A greyware vessel sherd cut in a sub-circular disc shape.

Lighting (Fig. 7.26F)

50. Candlestick (possibly)
Context: Cor21.4022
Date: 43–410 (Roman)
Length: 23
Width: 35
Thickness: 20
Weight: 63
Material(s): lead
Description: A fragment of a solid, simple cast lead 'vessel' in crude cuplike form, less than 50% complete, consisting of a sub-circular base with walls flaring up and outward. The internal surface of the walls is rough and unfinished, and a casting sprue can be seen on one edge of the base.

50

Figure 7.26: Artefacts from the Corbridge excavations. (F) Lighting.

Fittings (Fig. 7.26G and H)

51. Mount
    Context: Cor21.5026
    Date: 43–410 (Roman)
    Length: 17
    Width: 19
    Thickness: 0.75
    Weight: 1
    Material(s): silver
    Description: An incomplete silver mount, cast as a shell with C-shaped scrolls to either side of the base. The outer edge of the shell is scored with small triangular notches, and a central incised line runs from the base to the outer edge, flanked by two curvilinear lines forming a simple hourglass shape. The reverse is undecorated, and there is an abraded spur along the base edge indicating a break.

52. Shank
    Context: Cor21.4024
    Date: 43–410 (Roman)
    Length: 43
    Width: 7
    Thickness: 6
    Weight: 15
    Material(s): lead
    Description: A cast shank or leg of rectangular plan, with slight bending at the thicker end with and abraded irregular section suggesting breakage. The narrower end is abraded and may have been the terminal.

Figure 7.26: Artefacts from the Corbridge excavations. (G) Fittings (in white metal).

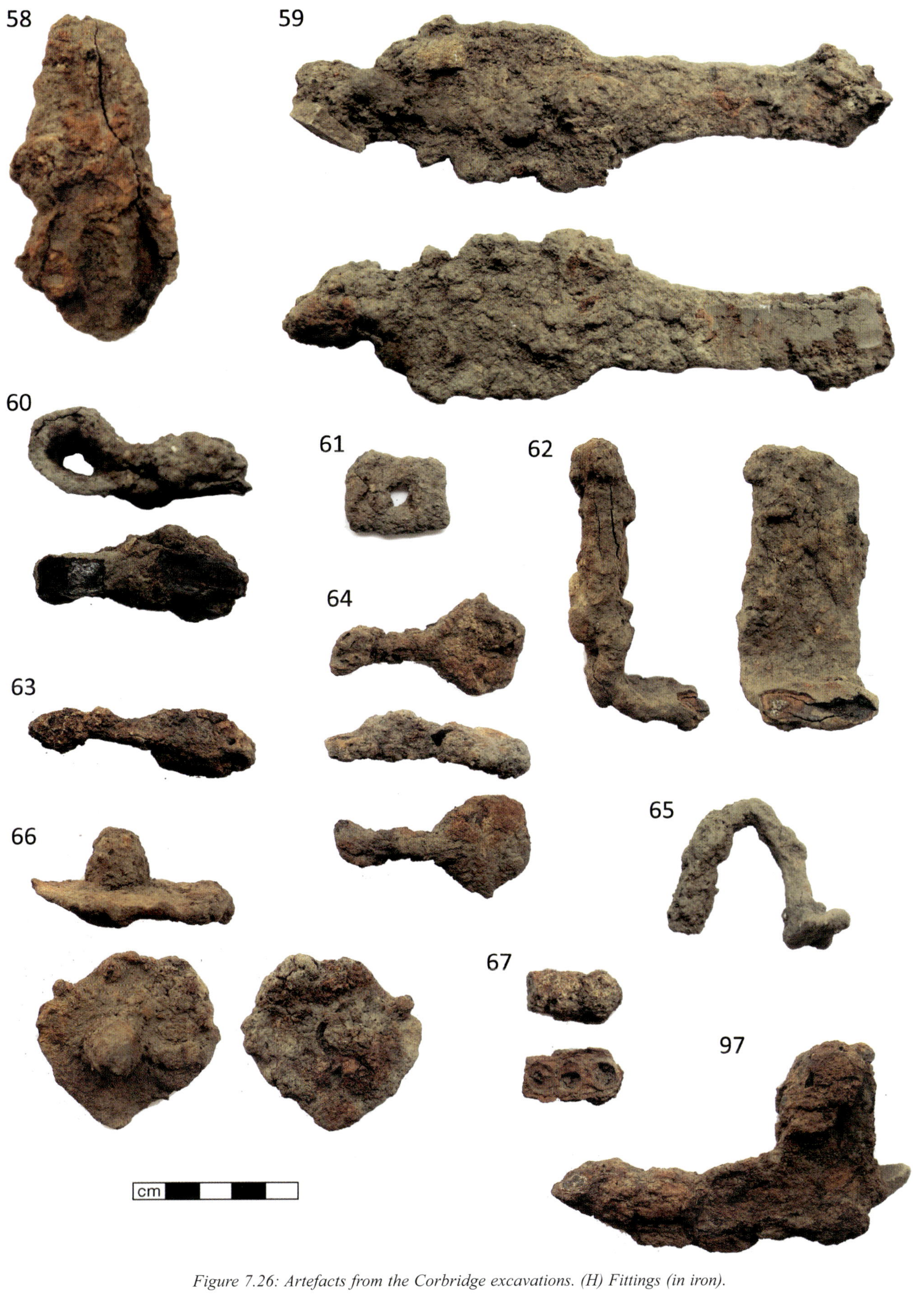

Figure 7.26: Artefacts from the Corbridge excavations. (H) Fittings (in iron).

53. Plug / seal
Context: Cor21.4000
Date: 43–410 (Roman)
Length: 46
Width: 37
Thickness: 6
Weight: 41
Material(s): lead
Description: An incomplete discoidal (oval) plug or seal, missing approximately 25% at one end. The upper face is irregularly convex, while the lower face has an irregular, damaged centre, suggesting the breakage or removal from a surface in antiquity.

54. Mount
Context: Cor21.5034
Date: 43–410 (Roman)
Length: 26
Width: 30
Thickness: 1
Weight: 8
Material(s): lead
Description: An incomplete sub-circular discoidal mount with a rectangular strip curved to form a hook for attachment.

55. Frame
Context: Cor21.4000
Date: 43–410 (Roman)
Length: 52
Width: 21
Thickness: 12
Weight: 55
Material(s): lead
Description: A gently curved rectangular length of lead framing, D-shaped in section.

56. Fitting
Context: Cor21.4000
Date: 43–410 (Roman)
Length: 36
Width: 26
Thickness: 14
Weight: 20
Material(s): lead and iron
Description: An irregular lead disc cast around a bent iron shank, presumably to fix the iron in place. The shank is sub-circular in section and *c.* 8 mm in diameter.

57. Washer
Context: Cor21.5028
Date: 43–410 (Roman)
Length: 27
Width: 21
Thickness: 3
Weight: 5
Material(s): lead
Description: An incomplete sub-circular washer with a central, circular perforation.

58. Hinge socket
Context: Cor19.3004
Date: 43–410 (Roman)
Length: 95
Width: 43
Thickness: 20
Weight: 128
Material(s): iron
Description: A flat strap of iron folded on itself to form a loop and allow the arms or tails of the strap to be riveted or nailed together.

59. Hinge plate
Context: Cor21.5004
Date: 155–410 (Roman)
Length: 180
Width: 51
Thickness: 10
Weight: 155
Material(s): iron
Description: A flat piece of iron forming the strap / plate of a large hinge. The entire surface is covered in corrosion making the exact plan of the pate difficult to determine, but possibly with a wider, curved portion at the inner end, such that it has a slight oval shape with the rectangular extension of the hinge protruding from one end. A small ceramic sherd (Nene Valley ware) adheres to the corrosion matrix.

60. Looped mount
Context: Cor19.1006
Date: 43–410 (Roman)
Length: 63
Width: 12
Thickness: 5
Weight: 41
Material(s): iron
Description: A flat strap of iron folded on itself to leave a sub-circular loop, with the tails overlapping to take rivets or nails for attachment to a surface.

61. Fitting
Context: Cor21.5027
Date: 43–410 (Roman)
Length: 33
Width: 27
Thickness: 6
Weight: 6
Material(s): iron
Description: A corroded fragment of iron strap with a circular perforation to take a missing rivet or nail, slightly convex in section.

62. Bracket
Context: Cor19.3007
Date: 43–410 (Roman)
Length: 78
Width: 37
Thickness: 15
Weight: 83
Material(s): iron
Description: A corroded fragment of iron strap in an L-shape, serving as a reinforcement bracket.

63. Fitting
Context: Cor21.4025
Date: 43–410 (Roman)
Length: 70
Width: 20
Thickness: 20
Weight: 17
Material(s): iron
Description: A highly corroded fitting consisting of a slightly curved length of iron with one half a larger conical shape, and the opposite half a slighter conical shape. The larger half appears to have a cylindrical shank as if to fit in a socket.

64. Fitting
Context: Cor21.5034
Date: 43–410 (Roman)
Length: 57
Width: 28
Thickness: 13
Weight: 17
Material(s): iron
Description: An incomplete corroded fitting, symmetrical when complete, consisting of discoidal terminals connected with a short arm perpendicular to the plane of the terminals.

65. Fitting
Context: Cor21.5005
Date: 43–410 (Roman)
Length: 45
Width: 58
Thickness: 7
Weight: 28
Material(s): iron
Description: An incomplete corroded U-shaped fitting, retaining one discoidal terminal perpendicular to the square-sectioned loop.

66. Mount
Context: Cor19.3010
Date: 43–410 (Roman)
Length: 56
Width: 52
Thickness: 20
Weight: 33
Material(s): iron
Description: An incomplete corroded sub-circular discoidal mount with a central sub-conical shank, riveted through to the underside of the disc.

67. Mount
Context: Cor21.4013
Date: 43–410 (Roman)
Length: 30
Width: 16
Thickness: 13
Weight: 4
Material(s): copper alloy and iron
Description: A highly corroded fragmentary length of a metal mount, probably from furniture consisting of three surviving hollow domed heads, partially obscured by corrosion, with an iron shank through a flat strip of copper alloy. The underside preserves the outline of the domed heads.

97. Fitting
Context: Cor19.3005
Date: 43–410 (Roman)
Length: 91
Width: 60
Thickness: 12
Weight: 103
Material(s): iron
Description: A corroded hooked fitting, broadly L-shaped in plan and rectangular in section, notably found within the stone wall deposits, presumably as a result of deposition during the collapse of the wall, from its original position of being hammered/placed in the wall face.

Transport (Fig. 7.26I)

68. Buckle
Context: Cor19.1013
Date: 43–410 (Roman)
Length: 45

Figure 7.26: Artefacts from the Corbridge excavations. (I) Transport.

Figure 7.26: Artefacts from the Corbridge excavations. (J) Trade and exchange.

Width: 45
Thickness: 8
Weight: 27
Material(s): iron
Description: A highly corroded C-shaped buckle and separate pin. The buckle frame has been distorted in shape prior to corrosion, with one arm bent inward. The pin (30mm length) is incomplete, with more recent break through the corrosion at the hinged end and more ancient loss of the full length. Its size suggests a buckle from horse harness.

69. Terret
Context: Cor19.3010
Date: 43–410 (Roman)
Length: 67
Width: 60
Thickness: 10
Weight: 61
Material(s): iron
Description: A corroded iron circular fitting with a stem or shank, consistent with fittings for waggons, carts, and chariots.

Trade and exchange (Fig. 7.26J)

70. Weight
Context: Cor19.1006
Date: 43–410 (Roman)
Length: 25
Width: –
Thickness: 18
Weight: 86
Material(s): lead
Description: A roughly cast cylinder.

71. Weight
Context: Cor21.4000
Date: 43–410 (Roman)
Length: 34
Width: –
Thickness: 12
Weight: 71
Material(s): lead
Description: A roughly cast off-centre and shallow cone.

Production (Fig. 7.26K and L)

72. Weight
Context: Cor21.4034
Date: 43–410 (Roman)
Length: 24
Width: 22
Thickness: 22
Weight: 6
Material(s): ceramic
Description: An unfinished or damaged clay weight, intended to be conical and identified by the suspension loop and upper portion of the object. It is presumed that on drying the clay cracked and broke.

73. Spindle whorl
Context: Cor21.4000
Date: 43–410 (Roman)
Length: 27
Width: 27
Thickness: 10
Weight: 36
Material(s): lead
Description: An irregular disc, D-shaped in section with a central perforation.

74. Spindle whorl
Context: Cor21.5026
Date: 43–410 (Roman)
Length: 22
Width: 22
Thickness: 10
Weight: 26
Material(s): lead
Description: A disc with a central perforation, bearing some corrosion on the outer surface.

75. Crucible
Context: Cor19.1021
Date: 43–410 (Roman)
Length: 26
Width: 24
Thickness: 1.5
Weight: 4
Material(s): ceramic
Description: A large fragment of a small crucible, from a bowl-shaped base to a flaring rim, with likely metallic slag or residue adhering to the inner face.

Figure 7.26: Artefacts from the Corbridge excavations. (K and L) Production.

76. Waste
Context: Cor21.5000
Date: 43–410 (Roman)
Length: 33
Width: 12
Thickness: 15
Weight: 7
Material(s): lead
Description: An irregular cone of lead casting waste.

77. Waster
Context: Cor21.4008
Date: 43–410 (Roman)
Length: 34
Width: 8
Thickness: 3
Weight: 4
Material(s): lead
Description: An irregular casting waste in L-shape, almost certainly resulting from a rectangular object in a mould.

78. Slag
Context: Cor21.5018
Date: 43–410 (Roman)
Length: 35
Width: 25
Thickness: 20
Weight: 21
Material(s): lead
Description: A globular and aerated lump of lead casting slag, roughly conical in shape.

79. Smoother
Context: Cor21.5004
Date: 43–410 (Roman)
Length: 87
Width: 33
Thickness: 11
Weight: 57
Material(s): stone
Description: An oblong ground stone with a D-shaped section, probably used for grinding and/or smoothing.

80. Smoother
Context: Cor21.5000
Date: 43–410 (Roman)
Length: 81
Width: 47
Thickness: 10
Weight: 63
Material(s): stone
Description: An incomplete oblong stone ground on all faces, with a slightly abraded brake at one end, with an estimated 25% missing.

81. Smoother
Context: Cor21.4000
Date: 43–410 (Roman)
Length: 57
Width: 46
Thickness: 9
Weight: 42
Material(s): stone
Description: A sub-circular discoidal stone with all faces and edges ground smooth.

82. Smoother
Context: Cor21.5000
Date: 43–410 (Roman)
Length: 90
Width: 83
Thickness: 57
Weight: 628
Material(s): stone
Description: An irregular cobble, smoothed on every face and edge with the exception of one sub-rectangular portion of a broad face, which retains the likely original pitted surface, suggesting a loss of 2–3 mm surface through smoothing.

83. Smoother
Context: Cor21.4003
Date: 43–410 (Roman)
Length: 77
Width: 59
Thickness: 55
Weight: 424
Material(s): stone
Description: A sub-oval cobble with flattened upper and lower faces. All faces have been smoothed, and the broken end is well abraded.

Unidentified

84. unknown
Context: Cor21.5028 and 5020
Date: 43–410 (Roman)
Length: –
Width: –
Thickness: –
Weight: 333
Material(s): iron and lead
Description: A large corroded flat iron object with an integral hooked shank (incomplete) found in Cor21.5028. Five further objects from Cor21.5020 were found with it, including a crudely cast lead disc surrounding an incomplete iron loop.

85. unknown
Context: Cor21.5012
Date: 43–410 (Roman)
Length: 21
Width: 16

Thickness: 3.5
Weight: 2
Material(s): cu alloy
Description: A fragment of a sub-rectangular, uncertain flat object.

86. unknown
Context: Cor21.5027
Date: 43–410 (Roman)
Length: –
Width: –
Thickness: –
Weight: 6
Material(s): cu alloy
Description: Three irregular fragments, highly friable and corroded of an uncertain copper-alloy object.

Prehistoric / flint (Fig. 7.26M)

87. Arrowhead
Context: Cor21.4030
Date: Bronze Age
Length: 22
Width: 15
Thickness: 3.5
Weight: 0.8
Material(s): flint
Description: A knapped barbed-and-tanged arrowhead of Bronze Age form.

88. Drill
Context: Cor21.4001
Date: Neolithic
Length: 33
Width: 20
Thickness: 10
Weight: 3
Material(s): flint
Description: A knapped drill of T-shaped plan, with likely secondary knapping on the tip of the broken drill bit.

89. Flake
Context: Cor19.1006
Date: uncertain
Length: 36
Width: 22
Thickness: 7
Weight: 7
Material(s): flint
Description: A secondary flake from flint knapping.

Modern (19th–early 20th century) (Fig. 7.26N)

90. Coin, 10 centemisi (Italy)
Context: Cor19.1002
Date: 1893
Length: 32
Width: 30

Figure 7.26: Artefacts from the Corbridge excavations. (M) Prehistoric.

Thickness: 0.9
Weight: 10
Material(s): cu alloy
Condition: VW/VW
Description: All details in very low relief. Obverse: bust right, inscribed UMBERTO III / RE D'ITALIA. Reverse: wreath with a star at the top, inscribed 10 / CENTEMISI / 1893 in centre.

91. School Badge
Context: Cor19.1002
Date: 20th century
Length: 23
Width: 23
Thickness: 1.2
Weight: 7
Material(s): cu alloy with enamel
Description: A pointed, shield-shaped badge with a blue enamel surface, with Vice Captain in cast relief diagonally upward left-right. The pin is missing from the reverse, though the base of the hooked catch, loop, and pin hinge all survive.

92. Pin
Context: Cor19.1006
Date: 1875–1950 (Modern)
Length: 83
Width: –
Thickness: –
Weight: 6
Material(s): cu alloy
Description: A composite pin, with a cast spheroid head (now flattened) fixed to a cast shaft. The opposite end has threading surviving on the shaft, suggesting another head or fixture, making it a dress pin rather than a hair pin.

93. Button
Context: Cor19.1002
Date: 1875–1950 (Modern)
Length: 15
Width: 15
Thickness: 0.5
Weight: 1
Material(s): cu alloy
Description: A circular discoidal back of a composite button, with a shank for the loop, though the loop itself is missing.

Figure 7.26: Artefacts from the Corbridge excavations. (N) Modern.

94. Vessel
    Context: Cor21.4001
    Date: Modern
    Length: –
    Width: –
    Thickness: 1
    Weight: 1.5
    Material(s): glass
    Description: Two fragments of very translucent vessel glass, from the upper body of the vessel, bearing thin, white opaque bands as decoration.

95. Latch for window / cupboard
    Context: Cor19.2002
    Date: 19th–20th century
    Length: 228
    Width: 54
    Thickness: 10
    Weight: 203
    Material(s): iron
    Description: A semi-corroded hooked fitting, broadly J-shaped, with the end of the shaft flattened and bearing rivets on one face, demonstrating attachment to another fitting. A simple hooked latch common to windows, cupboards and similar.

96. Latch
    Context: Cor21.5000
    Date: 19th–20th century
    Length: 90
    Width: 25
    Thickness: 8
    Weight: 34
    Material(s): iron
    Description: A modern, machine cast corroded iron hooked-latch fitting, the swivel end obscured by corrosion. The latch is broadly L-shaped in plan, but the terminal of the L curves back under itself to form a hook/partial loop to slot over a peg or nail. Similar fittings can still be seen in historic houses.

Nails and other unidentified iron objects (Roman)

A number of nails and other iron objects / remains in varied states of preservation were found across numerous contexts. These are summarised in Appendix 2.

The northern fringe of Corbridge Roman town

The WallCAP trenches, in the playing field west of Corchester Towers and north of the English Heritage site, explored the northern fringe of the Roman town as determined through extensive geophysical survey and aerial photographs (Fig. 7.2). The trenches were also located north of the known extent of the later 1st to early 2nd-century forts at Corbridge. The absence of any unambiguously military structures in the trenches, therefore, is not surprising.

Very little material was found that pre-dated the mid-2nd century, and this fits with the accepted chronology of the development of the Roman town, which also emerged from the later 160s and 170s. In general, the evidence for activities across all the Roman phases and features can be best understood as reflecting the urban period of Roman Corbridge. The majority of activity can be confidently dated in the mid–late 2nd century up to the mid–late 3rd century. There are hints of 4th-century activity, particularly in Trench 5 in terms of material culture, but the *in-situ* archaeology does not survive for the later Roman centuries. This is probably the result of post-Roman truncation and destruction, over centuries of agricultural use, and the subsequent development of the field as grounds for Corchester Towers, and then further levelling to create the playing field. The later 4th-century material, minimal as it is, may also relate more to later use of the spur road than to roadside settlement activity.

There are a few aspects of previous excavation that help further contextualise the new WallCAP work. The first is the path of Dere Street north from the Stanegate. The line of Dere Street has been confidently identified 400 m north of the early forts (and also north of the playing field), and western and eastern branches have been identified within the town centre. These branch roads have not been fully traced to determine where they converge, assuming they are contemporary, nor is there sufficient evidence to decide their relative chronology and usage. Both the east and west branches of Dere Street can be identified in Figure 7.2, although their courses cannot be seen north of Corchester Lane. The east branch road of Dere Street, however, can be projected north from the town centre across Corchester Lane to just west of Trenches 1 and 4. This establishes a direct path from the yard and house in Trench 4 to the centre of the town. The trunk road running east–west and linking Trenches 4 and 5 could thus be interpreted as a route providing a corridor around the town's eastern perimeter.

This linkage to the town supports the interpretation of the buildings found during the excavations. The yard and small structure in Trench 4 housed small-scale manufacturing, including blacksmithing on the basis of quantities of iron and slag. Metalworking was not restricted to the outer edges of Roman Corbridge, as revealed in previous excavations; metalworking has been evidenced in several locations, not least in the legionary compounds south of Dere Street. The Trench 4 yard in which the smithing was conducted was bounded to its north and west by roads; its southern extent was beyond the limits of the trench. But it was a large yard, suggesting a good working space that could support work at a reasonable scale. Furthermore, the house to which the yard was attached appeared to be a relatively substantial structure, on the basis of the well-built and wide stone foundations of its western wall. Window glass was also found in the trench. The facts combined suggest a property owner of some wealth. Located at the northern fringe of the town, the smithy was also well placed to serve travellers as they entered or left Coria.

The building found in Trench 5 provided some evidence for domestic occupation, but it was clearly a strip building with its southern gable end as the street frontage. The building produced a hearth in its southern half, along with numbers of sherds for vessels used in the eating and drink. Though it is not possible to be certain, the building could be interpreted as a tavern, eatery, or some other roadside service venue. This is not to deny any purely domestic use. The owners probably lived in the eastern half of the structure in the annex. It is perhaps reasonable to suggest an upper story based on the finds of iron and lead fittings.

During the 3rd century this particular street on the northern fringe of Roman Corbridge was an active part of the town, engaged in trade and production, and not designated for solely domestic occupation (Fig. 7.27). The later 3rd and 4th centuries, however, are poorly understood. The structured pit deposit in Trench 4, although reasonably interpreted as a cremation burial, cannot be fully understood. No human bone could be determined in the vessel's contents – only animal bone – although very little bone could be identified. The vessels found in the pit, the stratigraphy and their state of preservation, support deposition in the mid-3rd century. But the top of the pit has been truncated, removing the possibility of stratigraphically linking it with other features in the yard, so the pit could post-date the latest use of the yard. Another possibility can be considered: rather than a human cremation burial, perhaps this was a ritual deposit in which a cremated animal offering was made in association with a range of vessels. This could have been a foundation deposit for an overlying and now lost building or a closing deposit marking the end of the activities in the yard.

The lack of any evidence for 4th-century activity is intriguing. Is this the result of destruction and truncation in more recent centuries, or it is a genuine absence of activity in this part of the Roman town? The putative urban defences observed by antiquarians have yet to be identified by any archaeological excavation, but it would be reasonable to infer that a Roman town so close to Hadrian's Wall could have had a defensive circuit. This problem is not unique to Corbridge; it is also found at

Figure 7.27: A reconstruction of the east–west trunk road and the buildings facing it based on the excavated evidence. The distance between the areas of Trenches 4 and 5 have been compressed for artistic reasons. Illustration by Matilde Grimaldi.

Carlisle. If the antiquarian-observed urban defences were genuine, however, they were located south of the playing field, prompting speculation about whether the town walls of Roman Corbridge ever existed, but also about the timing of their construction. If they were raised early in the town's development, perhaps in the boom under the Severans (early 3rd century) seen elsewhere in the town, then this portion of the town was extra-mural. If constructed in the later 3rd or 4th century, this may provide a context for the putative abandonment of the site, with the town contracted inside of the walls. Until the question of the walls can be resolved, this has to remain as speculation.

Another absence was evidence for the 'Corbridge destruction deposit', a widespread and violent fire event seen across much of the centre of the town. This can be dated to *c.* 163–195, and its absence may provide a *terminus post quem* for construction on the site. More likely is that the fire did not extend as far north as the playing field trenches. Though a direct link cannot be made, the mid–later 2nd-century levelling layer of Phase 1 in Trench 4 is consistent with activity seen in central Corbridge relative to the 'Corbridge destruction deposit'. Phase 1 could be interpreted as initial urban activities related to the early post-fort activities at Corbridge; it could also reasonably be interpreted as part of the replanning of Corbridge in the wake of the destruction event. It is this latter that is favoured here, and this indicates that this northern fringe was likely to have been part of the original planning for the civil town of Corbridge.

The general character of the stratigraphy in the WallCAP trenches fits that observed elsewhere in the town (*e.g.* Bishop and Dore 1988), although there are notable differences. The archaeological deposits were less deep. This is to some extent a result of the truncation noted above, but this particular location also had a briefer period of occupation. However, given that the modern ground level of the playing field is lower than that of the surrounding fields, later Roman archaeological stratigraphy may survive. In the future it would be interesting to compare the WallCAP trenches to archaeological remains in other fields outside of the English Heritage site.

Note

1 We are grateful to Joanna Bird for providing the parallel and its reference.

8

Conclusion

During the course of the Hadrian's Wall Community Archaeology Project, a total of seven sites on the Wall or within the larger corridor were investigated through archaeological survey and excavation. A further three locations benefited from consolidation of collapsed or partly ruinous fabric, accompanied by a watching brief. The work at these 10 sites, reported in detail in previous chapters and in the following appendices, has provided significant new information for each site, but more importantly has expanded our understanding of the entire monument. At sites under direct threat WallCAP interventions arrested deterioration and allowed the sites to be removed from Historic England's national Heritage At Risk register (*e.g.* Steel Rigg, Port Carlisle); at other sites work contributed fundamental new information that will directly enhance future management of that site (*e.g.* Cam Beck, Corbridge) or of sites with similar features and threats (*e.g.* Heddon-on-the-Wall, Walltown, Steel Rigg). Previous chapters are intended to stand on their own. In this chapter, we reflect upon the cumulative insights and benefits gained through the entire programme of WallCAP's Heritage-At-Risk work.

Insights from each site

A number of insights and new discoveries were made through archaeological fieldwork at each site. These need not be considered in detail, as full discussions can be found in each chapter, but looking at the sites together highlights the cumulative benefits of the geographically wide-ranging approach deployed by WallCAP.

Heddon-on-the-Wall

The Vallum was investigated as it ran across three fields between Throckley and Heddon-on-the-Wall, prompted by visibly differential survival across each field moving from mechanised modern arable use in the eastern field to long-term designated pasture in the westernmost field. This differential survival is visible to the naked eye: the mounds and ditch present clear earthworks in the pasture field, but in the central and eastern fields can only be detected in slight dips that indicate the position of the ditch under drystone wall field boundaries. Historic maps and aerial photos also track the decreasing preservation of the Vallum in the central and eastern fields, which WallCAP confirmed via geophysical survey. The most significant element of the fieldwork, however, was the trench excavated across the full width of the Vallum in the easternmost field where the monument was expected to be poorly preserved. Such long trenches are exceedingly rare in more modern archaeological investigations of the Wall, and this allowed WallCAP to collect environmental samples for analysis. The stratigraphically lowest sediments of the ditch fill produced sufficient wood charcoal to provide radiocarbon date ranges of 1213–1263 cal AD (at 1σ and 68.3%) and 1172–1269 cal AD (at 2σ and 95.4%), (SUERC-105487). This suggests that at this location, the Vallum was largely undisturbed until the 13th century.

The measurements and features of the Vallum at Heddon vary in detail from other sites, but also fit within the spectrum of Vallum measurements and features observed elsewhere. The mounds produced slight evidence for stone revetting or kerbs, were constructed after the ground was stripped of turf and using local clay, stone and other subsoils dug from the ditch. The Vallum was also located closer to the Wall than in many locations to exploit the views and less sloped ground at a break of slope. As noted previously, whatever the principle and theory behind the Vallum for the Roman planners and architects, in practice the details of Vallum construction were executed in response to local soils, geological conditions, and topography (Bennet and Turner 1983, 74).

Thirlwall

Thirlwall provided an optimal site to investigate the relationship between historic destruction of the Wall, its visibility in the archaeological record, and the current condition of the monument in close proximity to a 14th-century castle built some 50 m north of the line of the Wall curtain and substantially of Wall stone. Geophysical survey at Thirlwall confirmed some level of survival of the stone curtain and ditch, and identified a potential prehistoric enclosure to the south of the curtain. Due to circumstances beyond the project's control, WallCAP was not able to follow up this survey with the intended trench across the line of the curtain and ditch, and another to assess the enclosure. However, this work has provided a suitable foundation for excavation going forward.

Drumburgh

Drumburgh was another location at which historic destruction, in this case of both the curtain and the fort, has left many questions about the current state of preservation and potential. However, the local conditions constrained how much could be discovered through survey. The drumlin upon which the Roman fort was built has also been the core location of subsequent medieval to modern settlement. Geophysical survey in available areas detected sub-surface traces of ridge-and-furrow, but these either masked or had significantly destroyed Roman deposits. At this site, excavation would be necessary to address questions and concerns about the survival of any Roman layers.

Port Carlisle

Work at Port Carlisle was driven by the need to reduce damage to a surviving exposed portion of stone curtain to either side of an agricultural field gate. Excavation revealed complete destruction of the stone curtain in two different trenches, which was previously believed to be partially preserved in the hedge beyond the visible surviving stretch. The trenches found evidence for demolished agricultural outbuildings at both locations, and this highlighted the historic exploitation of the curtain as a field boundary in the Solway area, even while its stone fabric was thoroughly robbed for re-use elsewhere. The work also discovered that the curtain had been built to follow a relict natural sea bank, so raising it above the danger of flooding from the Solway Firth to the north. The curtain had survived around the field gate only because it was useful as a support for the gate. The confirmed destruction of the curtain further into the hedge, however, enabled the relocation of the gate to the east and the insertion of a larger gate suitable for modern mechanical agriculture. The formerly endangered section of surviving curtain could then be cleared of vegetation, consolidated, and fenced off to protect it from the cattle using the pasture. This work saw the removal of the site from Historic England's Heritage At Risk register.

Walltown Crags

Excavation at Walltown was undertaken to reassess an Edwardian investigation, which had uncovered a length of surviving curtain courses immediately east of Walltown quarry, and to consolidate fabric in danger of collapse. The visible Wall courses were compared with those that remained buried within rubble and rough grass just beyond the end of the earlier excavation. The WallCAP excavations made significant findings about Roman builders' approach to preparing the ground in advance of laying the curtain foundations. The ancient ground surface, presumably a thin layer of soil and/or turf, was stripped away to expose the bedrock and the curtain was constructed directly onto the solid geology. Chock stones and blocks and facing stones of irregular sizes were used in the lower course of the curtain to establish level courses on the uneven bedrock surfaces (as observed on the exposed south faces in Trenches 1 and 2). This is not a practice typically observed elsewhere, and indicates a commitment to sturdy construction. However, this sector of curtain may have been raised later in the Hadrianic building programme (Symonds and Breeze 2016), and so it is possible challenges faced in building at other locations provided guidance on how best to build the curtain at Walltown. The excavations also revealed a long term and phased process of collapse and dismantling of the curtain, seen in the layers of collapsed fabric to the south of the curtain and the presence or absence of facing stones among the rubble.

Cam Beck

The line of the Wall at Cam Beck necessitated crossing a relatively modest gorge carved by the beck, with no evidence of how this had been achieved by the Romans. Stonework associated with the historic weir in the beck suggested that the Romans had bridged the gorge, but this was no more than a hypothesis (Hill 2009). Excavations at the eastern crossing point found a highly disturbed and thoroughly robbed sequence, which nonetheless provided evidence for the initial Turf Wall, its subsequent replacement with the Stone Wall, and the approach the Romans took towards crossing the gorge in each phase.

During the Turf Wall phase, the corner of a stone-founded, detached building (Structure 1) was discovered immediately south of the line of the curtain. The exact width of the base of the Turf Wall could not be determined from the slight remains uncovered, so the distance between Structure 1 and the eastern base of the Turf Wall remains uncertain. The building was not aligned quite parallel to the Turf Wall, was structurally independent of it but stood only a couple of metres to the south of the Wall. Structure 1 is perhaps best interpreted as a free-standing tower. This is the first occurrence of such a structure along the entire Wall, but a good parallel for this arrangement of a ditch fronting a turf-and-timber barrier with a tower behind can be seen in the Upper German and Raetian *limes*. For Hadrian's Wall, the free-standing tower seems to have been adopted specifically to monitor the gorge, which then suggests the Turf Wall did not bridge the gorge.

The Stone Wall replaced the Turf Wall, and after construction of the stone curtain – at least at the surviving lowest courses – a stone tower was added to and abutted the curtain on the eastern bank of the gorge. A sub-rectangular stone platform was then laid immediately south of the curtain and east of the tower, which was probably the foundations for stairs or a ramp. Thus, the Stone Wall was supplemented with a tower that most likely served as an access point for a bridge across the gorge. The combination of a tower and ramp has been observed at major river crossings along the Wall at Chesters and Willowford (Bidwell and Holbrook 1989); Cam Beck presents a scaled-down version. In contrast with Chesters and Willowford, however, there was no evidence at Cam Beck for subsequent expansion of the bridge. The Cam Beck bridge seems to have remained as a pedestrian crossing. The west bank was not excavated, but it is inferred that a matching tower was located at the opposite end of the bridge. A second detached building was also found associated with the Stone Wall phase, roughly contemporary to its construction or built only a short time later. The function of Structure 2 is uncertain, but was built in timber with a clay floor and was aligned at right angles to the line of the Wall.

Corbridge

Excavations at Corbridge were carried out at the northern fringe of the Roman town, and focused on two trenches. These confirmed an absence of evidence of military structures, with the earliest Roman structures appearing in the mid–late 2nd century. The westernmost trench revealed evidence for a yard for industrial activity (smithing), and the western wall of a large structure just inside the eastern edge of the trench. The yard and smithy were located at the junction of a north–south road, almost certainly the eastern branch of Dere Street leaving the centre of Roman Corbridge, and an east–west trunk road. A substantial drain separated the yard from the paved roads, and environmental samples and ceramics indicate that the drain silted up in the later 3rd into 4th centuries. The peak of activities in the yard, which also featured a number of pits seems to date to the 3rd century. A conspicuous pit appeared to be a cremation burial, containing a large storage jar with burnt animal bone material and a number of mid-3rd century ceramics. Bizarrely, radiocarbon dating of a fragment of animal bone returned a Bronze Age date. Interpretation of this feature remains unclear, but it was undoubtedly Roman and possibly a foundation or closing deposit.

The easternmost trench was located over a strip building lying to the north of the east–west trunk road. A series of features and material culture were found to suggest that this was a tavern, eatery, or some other roadside venue. The building seems to have been in use from the 2nd century into the 4th century, though very little could be interpreted post-dating the 3rd century.

Evidence from both trenches indicates very active structures and life in the later 2nd and 3rd centuries, supported by good dating via ceramics and radiocarbon. Truncation of the site can be associated with post-Roman agriculture, landscaping to create a garden in the 19th century, and subsequent transformation of the garden into a playing field. This has obscured and demolished any 4th-century and later layers, but it is notable that very little evidence dated to the 4th century, and what was present was predominantly found in the eastern trench. This may suggest contraction of the town towards its core in the 4th century, though this remains a tentative interpretation. However, comparison of current ground levels in the Playing Field with fields surrounding the English Heritage site indicate that there may be greater survival of the later Roman levels in some of those.

The significance of local landscape

Across each of the sites investigated above, the character of the local landscape was clearly a significant element shaping the detail of the construction of the Wall, its subsequent use and post-Roman afterlife. Landscape, or more specifically, topography has long played an importance of assessing the tactical attributes of the Wall (*e.g.* Hodgson 1840), though a wider and more holistic contextualisation of the Wall within the landscape is far more limited in the literature (*e.g.* Woodside and Crow 1999; Symonds 2020). The Wall was clearly conceived as a unified monument, but the execution of this vision was modified several times during the building programme, in response to actual conditions on the ground, but also to socio-cultural and environmental factors (see Chapter 1). In this regard, there is always a balance to be found between the characteristic elements and features of the Wall at a given location, and the locally specific conditions that demanded changes to 'the vision'.

Prolonged time at any given site during the course of fieldwork provides the opportunity to assess the local landscape – topography, hydrology, meteorology, etc. – in conjunction with the emerging archaeological evidence. The different environmental conditions of upland and lowland locations were immediately apparent. For example, near surface bedrock provided a solid foundation for the construction of the stone curtain at Walltown; whereas the course of the Wall at Cam Beck appeared to have been dictated by the best path relative to the beck, bridging and fording points, and adjacent marshy land; at Port Carlisle, in a littoral rather than riverine location, a relict sea bank and the impact of possible flooding also influenced the route of the Wall. At each location, the weather will have been a different challenge once the Wall was built.

Port Carlisle would have been prone to coastal flooding, as well as seasonal and diurnal changes to water levels due to the tides. Cam Beck had to be able to withstand seasonal river flooding. On the crags at Walltown, the curtain was very exposed to prevailing weather, which had more prolonged and sustained impact than flooding on the Wall's condition. Indeed, the final day of backfilling the trenches at Walltown saw a progression of rain, hail, and a brief snowy blizzard!

The local geology also influenced the building materials available. Good hard sandstones were locally available at Heddon, Corbridge, and Walltown Crags. Cam Beck was situated just west of a major faultline that resulted in softer red sandstones being the most immediately available building material. At Port Carlisle, sandstones of the St Bees formation had to be imported from some miles distant for construction. The accessibility of stone as a building material as well as its attributes influenced how each building stone was shaped (in terms of size) and subsequently how these stones were arranged in the building of the curtain. During the course of WallCAP, considerable data was gathered that demonstrates a wide range of building styles in the curtain, even from the earliest Hadrianic phases (Collins *et al.* 2023b). Compare, for instance, the use of chock stones in association with facing stones built directly on bedrock at Walltown to the laying of a cobbly foundation at Cam Beck, and more level coursing at Port Carlisle.

These local landscape conditions also very strongly related to socio-cultural conditions on the ground, and this proved particularly significant in the post-Roman centuries, what we can call the Wall's Roman afterlife.

The Wall's Roman afterlife

Following centuries of Roman occupation, the use of the Wall and its installations, and its remains become much more highly localised. The extent to which sites along the Wall continued to be occupied or exploited depended quite largely on the larger settlement pattern of any given time. For example, there appear to be a number of Wall forts that were occupied into the 5th or 6th centuries and in some instances even later, and the towns of Corbridge and Carlisle were probably always occupied at some scale (Collins 2012). But the prevailing political conditions will have introduced changes to the broader settlement pattern. For example, the foundation of a Norman castle and royal court over the remains of the Roman fort at Newcastle and subsequent early medieval monastic foundation, shifted the political centre of the region away from Corbridge and downriver to Newcastle. In contrast, Walltown Crags was not local to any large population centres, and any farms will have not been located on the top of the crags. Yet Walltown may offer a reasonably good example of a 'natural' sequence of ruin of the Wall, with minimal human impacts.

Collapse along the south face of the curtain at Walltown could be detected in discrete phases, though each phase may represent a prolonged period of time. Significantly, it is the earlier phase of collapse, broadly dating *c.* 450–1900 that had more facing stones amidst the rubble, and notably at lower positions within the rubble though still mixed. Upper portions of this collapse had fewer facing stones that suggest some selection and removal of these by locals for re-use. Episodes that may be related to robbing are the building of a medieval tower and subsequent modification and expansion of the farm into the later 19th century. The second distinct phase of collapse was stratigraphically later and overlain the spoil of the Edwardian diggers. Changing ground conditions instigated by those excavations resulted in a shift downhill of rubble.

At Heddon, though the curtain was not accessible for excavation, the Vallum ditch fill dates to the 13th century, broadly speaking. This would coincide with a general trend of population expansion in medieval England, in which new land was claimed or repurposed for agriculture and settlement. The Vallum is positioned near the southern edge of a shelf overlooking the north slope of the Tyne valley, but the lands it runs through were deemed worthy of taking in for some use; more specifically, this could also be linked to the growing importance of Newcastle, only some 11 km to the east and still linked by a direct east–west road that paralleled the Wall. Medieval robbing of the Wall also took place in the stretch east of the Cam Beck in the late 12th and early 13th centuries to build Lanercost Priory, as the vill was part of the priory's estate. Specific locations, however, are uncertain, but there was further confirmed dismantling in 1791 under the new owners of the Castlesteads estate.

Agricultural needs will have always played a large part in the Wall's afterlife, and from the medieval period to the present day, there is a steady trend of consolidating small field systems into larger single field conglomerations that facilitate improvements in arable technologies, like mechanised tractors. Dismantling the Wall curtain, infilling the ditch, levelling the Vallum mounds and infilling its ditch will all have made more land accessible to the plough in lowland areas. This activity can be seen at Heddon, Cam Beck, and Port Carlisle in one form or another. In upland areas surviving linear features had benefits to livestock management, as at Walltown. Where the ruins of Roman installations and buildings were not repurposed for farms or some other occupation, dismantling of Roman ruins provided ready building stone, all the more valuable in locations where good building stone was not available in local outcrops, like Port Carlisle. Thankfully, large-scale industrial destruction of the Wall is limited, most visibly to 19th- and 20th-century industrial quarrying at Cawfields and Walltown. Over the long term, however, many of the less impactful activities (ploughing, the taking of stone here-and-there) have accumulated. Bearing in mind the sequence at Walltown, where there was minimal human interaction in post-Roman centuries, the lesson is very clear. Human interactions with the Wall tend to accelerate processes of destruction. This conclusion is very clearly seen in all the site-focused chapters of this book.

However, the past 200 years has also seen the increased value and understanding of our surviving heritage, and this is very true for the Wall. Various antiquarian observations and artistic renderings of the monument and its associated material culture survive from the 16th century and after, and from the 19th century there are explicit attempts to preserve the monument from further destruction. This was an active motivation in the formation of John Clayton's portfolio of Wall properties (McIntosh 2019). Indeed, repair and consolidation at Steel Rigg and the Cat's Stairs (see Appendix 2) was largely undertaken on fabric that had already had at least one phase of repair. At Port Carlisle, though the curtain was not preserved, progressive reworking of field boundaries still fossilised some elements of the monument.

Future research

WallCAP adopted an interdisciplinary approach, with two discrete strands of activity – Heritage At Risk (HAR) and Stone Sourcing and Dispersal (SSD) – bringing archaeology and geology together to investigate Hadrian's Wall. As highlighted above, excavation of sites under the HAR strand also had bearing on the SSD strand (detailed in Collins *et al.* 2023b). However, the significance of the post-Roman history of Wall sites is often overlooked, and as the fieldwork reported in this volume shows, there are still significant discoveries to be made.

Cam Beck provides an excellent example. A fundamental reason for the fieldwork was to understand how the Wall builders might have dealt with 'minor' river crossings. Not only were the remains of bridging structures found, but new detached structures were discovered, only a few metres south of the curtain. This highlights just how structure-focused the excavation of Hadrian's Wall has been: ground to the north of the ditch or south of the curtain is rarely excavated. There is clear potential for new insights to be gained by positioning trenches to encompass surrounding ground, and so considering the landscape context as well as the structural sequence and history of the monument.

Across the time of WallCAP, the combination of geological and archaeological methods and data generated new information on Hadrian's Wall and its surrounding landscape. In addition to new archaeological information and interpretation, WallCAP has also been able to understand and in a few instances arrest historic and contemporary degradation of the monument. WallCAP's research has been ground-breaking in many ways, but it is also just the beginning. By taking an interdisciplinary approach and a more landscape-informed perspective, new avenues for future research have been identified and existing understandings of the Wall challenged. From foundations laid by this research, it is hoped that further investigation will continue to enhance our appreciation and understanding of Hadrian's monumental erection.

Appendix 1

Contexts

Contexts registers for each site where excavations were undertaken can be found in this appendix. These are presented by each site, arranged alphabetically by site name and captured in a table for each trench. The context numbers correspond with the narrative text in the relevant chapter.

Cam Beck

CB19: Trench 1			
Context no. *Type*	*Physical relationships* ***Levels mOD***	*Description* ***Interpretation***	*Drawings*
1000 layer	Above all	Loose organic-rich sandy loam, containing mix of leaf-litter and twigs/branch fragments in various states of decomposition. The loam is a brown to dark brown colour. The topsoil also contained substantial tree roots, most of which were retained/left undisturbed. A reasonably large root (*c.* 0.12 m in diameter) ran in a roughly north–south direction at the base of the layer. Found trench wide: 1 m × 1 m Depth of the deposit varied due to steep ground slope of the bank, with a minimum depth of 0.2 m and a maximum of 0.44 m. ***Naturally formed topsoil, primarily a result of decomposition of woodland litter in combination with some erosion of soils from the erosion of the riverbank. Removed by hand, sieved.***	
1001 structure	Below (1000) Above (1002)	A single layer/surface of large, elongated prepared stones laid on bedrock (1002). Within the trench, three long rectangular blocks projected out of the cut sides of the trench immediately below the topsoil (1000). Only one block could be measured in its entire length, as 0.55 m × 0.23 m; the remaining two blocks extended back into the east section of the trench, and were further obscured by substantial tree roots. These two blocks measured 0.75+ m × 0.18 m and 0.54+ m × 0.16 m. At least three smaller boulders were also present in the east wall of the trench. These may represent tumble from higher up the slope of the bank that could belong to the topsoil (1000) or packing/revetment positioned at the same time as the long rectangular blocks, but subsequently disturbed from tree roots and landslip. Of these boulders, only one could be measured (0.18 m × 0.16 m) **Finds**: An iron spike/stake *c.* 0.3 m in length was found laying across the two adjacent stone blocks in a manner suggesting it had been disturbed/moved from its original position by bioturbation. It is directly comparable to examples visibly incorporated into the weir. ***Laid course of blocks to establish a path or platform cut into the east bank of the beck, associated with landscaping of the estate (19th–20th century).***	

(Continued)

CB19: Trench 1			
Context no. *Type*	*Physical relationships* ***Levels mOD***	*Description* ***Interpretation***	*Drawings*
1002	Below (1001)	Bedrock consisting of soft red sandstone that is visible in both the east and west banks of the beck. It was uncertain if the bedrock was cut/altered to take the stone blocks (1001), or if a naturally formed ledge or shelf was exploited. The topsoil (1000) directly overlay the bedrock in spaced between blocks of 1002. ***Natural bedrock***	

CB21: Trench 2			
Context no. *Type*	*Physical relationships* ***Levels mOD***	*Description* ***Interpretation***	*Drawings*
2000 layer	Above all ***Top: 46.1–47***	Friable, dry, dark orangey brown, gritty sandy silt, 30:70 (topsoil) to 40:60; stones: poorly sorted pebbles and rounded and subangular cobbles max. 0.2 m, mostly red sandstone, *c.* 10%. Some larger cobbles above putative Wall line running near W–E across trench and in sub-rectangular area south of Wall. Trench wide: 10 m W–E × 12 m N–S and 6.5 m × 2 m southern extension. 0.2–0.3 m deep. Trench slopes down to NW and W towards ditch and beck ravine. Considerable root disturbance and bioturbation. **Finds**: 5 sherds modern pottery under turf; RB pottery at interface with contexts, especially near large stone in S of trench and in SW corner of extension: 1 sherd BB1; 27 sherds GREY; 1 sherd fine; very corroded Fe: nail × 1, Cat no. 16; smudges of degraded bone and CBM; whetstone, Cat no. 1; Cu alloy mount, Cat no. 2: <1% ***Rough pasture, field soil and clean-up layer across trench. Top 0.2 m removed with digger; clean-up by hand.***	100
2001 layer	Below (2000), Cut by [2036] and [2040] above/related to (2012) and (2016); same as (2002) and (2003) ***Top: c. 45.9–46.7***	Friable, dry, mid yellowish-reddish brown sandy silt (40:60), with siltier areas around clusters of core material; some larger sub-angular stones up to 0.3 m and sorted cobbles max. 0.15 m, some river cobbles *c.* 50%. 10 m W–E by *c.* 1.2 m wide N–S, with robber trench visible to S of core material, esp. in W. 0.05–0.1 m depth of matrix and small pebbles removed to clarify Wall line. Considerable root disturbance and bioturbation. **Finds**: Fe fragment; 1 sherd of GREY and 1 sherd modern pottery at interface with (2000); 1 flint: >1% ***Robbed remains of curtain Wall: matrix and stones. Facing stones removed, line of wall core remaining and possibly distorted by ploughing. Remaining core stones cluster along the line; these clusters notable for lack of red sandstone cobbles and dominance of paler, finer more angular sandstone.***	100
2002 layer	Below (2000) south of Wall-line; above (2005), (2032); cf. (2022), (2041) (2042) 18,16 ***Top: c. 46***	Friable, soft, mid reddish brown silty sand (45:55–50:50); poorly sorted subangular pebbles up to 0.03 m *c.* 10%, majority of stones *c.* 0.1 × 0.15 m, larger red sandstone cobbles up to 0.4 m *c.* 30%. Dominated by degraded red sandstone, with occasional rounded river cobble. *c.* 7m W–E by *c.* 4m N–S; 0.05 m removed. Fine roots and worm activity. **No finds**. ***Matrix and stones: layer below (2000) south of the Wall-line including disturbed upper layers of remains of robber trench for south facing stones of Wall and of sub-rectangular structure south of Wall line and robber trench.***	100, 1.00

(Continued)

CB21: Trench 2			
Context no. *Type*	*Physical relationships* ***Levels mOD***	*Description* ***Interpretation***	*Drawings*
2003 layer: S extn	Below (2000), (2009) and (2015); above (2017) 18.25, 11.25	Friable, yellowish brown (dry) to reddish brown (damp) sandy silt 45:65 with siltier patches; charcoal in cut features and siltier patches; small pebbles and sub-angular shatter *c.* 2–5% with patch of gravel 1.15 m W–E by 0.9 m N–S revealed on S side of extension. Lenses of white clay in eastern 2 m. Across extension 6.5 m W–E by 2 m N–S; *c.* 0.1–0.2 m removed. Fine roots and worms. **Finds**: burnt bone fragments; worked flint scraper; RB pottery incl. base: 1 sherd Greyware; 2 sherds SVW OX2 unsourced Severn Valley Oxidised ware (AD 40–400). ***Layer below clean-up in southern extension with darker, more humic and charcoal-rich cut features revealed as well as more clay area in east.***	100, 101, 104, 105, 1.00, 1.03
2004 layer	Below (2000), (2028); above [2019], [2027]; same as (2013)/ (2020 11, 13	Friable reddish-orangey brown (when damp), sandy silt (40:60); small, rounded pebbles *c.* 5%; small lenses of white and pink clay above cobbles; occasional quartzite pebble; large red sandstone cobbles in SW corner; charcoal flecks, concentrated over cobble surface below. Possible mortar fragments, disintegrated on touch. 3.5 m W–E × 1.5 m N–S; 0.1 m removed. Fine roots and worms **Finds**: burnt bone fragments, RB pottery: 6 sherds BAT AM1, 1 sherd GREY, 3 sherds OXID; corroded Fe incl. poss. nails × 4: 2 × Fe fittings, Cat nos 20 and 21; hobnail × 1, Cat no. 4; poss. stone pendant, Cat no. 10: >2% **Spot date**: AD 50–200 **ES (environmental sample) 1**: wild seeds – vetch, nettle and small-seeded grass – and heather. Some wood charcoal. ***In SW corner of main trench: siltier area with large sandstone cobbles in furthest SW: reveals tightly packed cobble surface below. Cobbled surface has clear border marked by larger cobbles with stone-free deposit running WNW–ESE beyond: likely robber trench. Possible fragmentary remains of white clay and pebble floor above cobbles?*** ***RC14: 1. AD 154–214 (54.9%, 1σ); AD 120–238 (95.4%, 2σ); 2. AD 112–170 (42.7%, 1σ; AD 60–215 (94.2%, 2σ).***	100, 1.00
2005 layer	Below (2002) in Slot 2; above [2037] 17.25, 16	Friable in N (likely in robber trench for Wall facing stones), slightly more compact in S, mid-reddish brown in N and lighter orangey brown in S; silty sand in N nearer Wall siltier to the S; 40–50% poorly sorted small pebbles, red sandstone rounded and sub-angular cobbles, occasional paler and harder sandstone. Red sandstone degrading and soft. In Slot 2 (0.7 m W–E × *c.* 2 m N–S); 0.03–0.06 m removed. Fine roots and worms. **No finds**. ***Remains of foundations of bridging structure S of Wall and southern robber trench. Nearer Wall more large red sandstone cobbles; to S more rounded cobbles.***	100
2006 structure	Below (2002), (2032); above [2011], [2037] 10.5, 19	Friable, mid reddish brown when damp, sandy silt (40:60); 60% well-sorted river cobbles and occasional RSS sub-angular fragments *c.* 0.06 m, occasional larger stone; occasional charcoal flecks. *c.* 1.2 m N–S by 1.5 m W–E; 0.05–0.1 m removed. Fine roots and worms. **No finds**. ***Matrix and upper, looser cobbles of foundations of sub-square or sub-rectangular structural feature south of and butting Wall line in west of trench. Better preserved in west. Probable support for bridging point, with Wall robber trench to N and robber trench for structure walls to E and N.***	100

(Continued)

CB21: Trench 2

Context no. *Type*	*Physical relationships* ***Levels mOD***	*Description* ***Interpretation***	*Drawings*
2007 spread	Below (2003), (2017), (2021); related (2013) 16.25, 12	Friable yellowish brown with black and red patches, gritty and gravelly sandy silt (30:70); upper layer 60% red sandstone small cobbles and pebbles, most burnt. Removed as (2013) to east. 2.15 m N–S by 0.3 m W–E as revealed, by 0.3 m deep. Fine roots. **Finds**: RB pottery: 1 sherd BAT AM1, 2 sherds GREY; burnt bone fragments; Fe nail/bolt × 1: > 1%. **Spot date**: AD 50–200 ***Appeared to be sub-oval pit feature on surface. Excavated in box-section due to diffuse boundaries. Proved to be spread of burnt stone and charcoal with less stony, charcoal-rich silty layer with finds below. Structure 2 lies above it and (2007) may be make-up for Structure 2 and/or disturbed material on edge of Structure 2 resulting from its demolition, both possibilities likely including elements of destruction material from Structure 1 and surrounding surfaces.***	100
2008 cut	Not used	(2007) spread and possible surface related to Structure 2 not fill	
2009 deposit	Below (2003); above (2013) (2020); related to (2015) 14, 12	Friable, dark blackish brown, humic sandy silt (30:70) with occasional clay lenses; 5% small pebbles with occasional larger rounded cobble and quartz pebble, many burnt; abundant charcoal. Increasingly silty and clay with depth. 0.93 m W–E by 0.65 m N–S as excavated; 0.2 m in depth removed. **Finds**: RB pottery: 2 sherds Greyware, 1 sherd SVW OX 2, unsourced Severn Valley Oxidised ware (AD 40-400); Fe fragment; burnt bone fragments: >1% **ES 2**: 2 × 10l buckets: small grass seed, some wood charcoal. ***In centre N of S extn (after second extension to W): possible ditch-end or pit? Resolved into probable demolition-related deposit into a pit over robbed-out wall face of Structure 1. Excavated initially as half section of 'end'. RC14: AD 206–251 (56.2%, 1σ); AD 153–255 (73.0%, 2σ).***	100, 103, 1.00, 1.04
2010 cut		Not used	
2011 structure	Below (2006); above (2014) 10.5,19	Friable, mid reddish brown sandy silt (40:60); 1% small pebbles, 80% well-sorted river cobbles 0.16–0.2 m (100 removed), occasional larger sub-angular fragment red sandstone; occasional charcoal flecks in S and towards base of (2011). 1.8 m N–S by 0.7 m wide in slot; 0.1–0.15 m depth removed. Large and fine roots and worms. **No finds**. ***Excavation in N–S Slot 3 against W baulk of foundations of poss. tower bridging structure south of Wall. Foundations comprise mostly rounded cobbles. Slot 3.***	100, 1.03
2012 structure	Below (2001), (2035), (2039), cf. [2016] 10.5, 19.5	Friable, mid reddish brown gritty silty sand (30:70) with paler yellower patches of degraded sandstone/mortar; flecks of degraded sandstone/mortar, occasional pebbles, and river cobbles 0.1–0.15 m, 10–15%: larger subangular sandstone fragments 0.1 m–0.3 m <5%; v occasional flecks of charcoal. 0.7 m W–E in slot by *c.* 2 m N–S; *c.* 0.1 m removed. One damaged facing stone: 0.18 m high, 0.2 m wide and 0.3m. **No finds**. ***Remains of Wall core material as excavated in Slot 3 against W baulk. To south some voids appeared suggesting larger stones left in robber trench.***	106

(Continued)

CB21: Trench 2			
Context no. *Type*	*Physical relationships* **Levels mOD**	*Description* ***Interpretation***	*Drawings*
2013 layer	Below (2003), (2007), (2015), 2021; above (2018), [2027], same as (2020) 15, 11	Friable, non-homogenous yellowish red, mid reddish brown and greyish black gravelly silty sand (40:60); 15% small-medium pebbles and cobbles with sandy, coarse gravel (redeposited natural); SW corner has 30–40% charcoal directly over hearth. 3.75–4 m W–E by 2 m N–S from west baulk of S extension; 0.25 m deep. **Finds**: pottery rim at 45.54 mOD, pottery base = 9 sherds OXID1 (Brampton) flat-rimmed bowl; 1 sherd GREY RB; unID composite metal object, Cat no. 3; Fe fragments, Fe nails × 7; burnt bone fragments: *c.* 3%. **Spot date**: AD 100–150/200 **ES 3**: 1 × 10 l bucket from area of concentrated charcoal: high concentration of wood charcoal incl. oak. ***Mix of redeposited natural gravelly sand and charcoal-rich silty material, covering hearth and cobbled surface: likely mix of internal floor deposits and demolition/destruction layer of Structure 1 merging into poorly developed sub-soil.*** ***RC14: AD 72–133 (49.5%, 1σ); AD 58–210 (91.6%, 2σ).***	1.02
2014 layer	Below (2011); over (2030) LOE 10.5, 19	Friable, mid–dark yellowish brown damp silty sand (45:55) with darker greyish, siltier and more organic layer just below structure [2011], with possible turf outline on northern edge; darker and siltier than matrix of [2011] above; some v. small pebbles, v. occasional small cobbles some burnt, v. occasional quartz pebble; flecks of charcoal or organic material. 0.7 m W–E in slot by 2.4 m; 0.15 m removed. Roots. **No finds.** **ES 4**: 1 × 10l bucket from area of possible turf: high concentration of black spherical fungal sclerotia *Cenococum* confirms interpretation of turf; some wood charcoal. ***Possible area of turf Wall foundations preserved beneath tower bridging structure. Excavation reached into robber trenches to N and S, which had removed the line of possible turf. Slot 3.*** ***RC14: 1. AD 125–203 (68.3%, 1σ); AD 107–230 (88.2%, 2σ); 2. AD 125–204 (68.3%, 1σ); AD 109–230 (88.7%, 2σ).***	106, 1.03, 1.03
2015 deposit	Below (2003); above (2013) 15.5, 10.5	Friable, dark yellowish, orangey brown humic sandy silt (30:70); patches of concentrated charcoal *c.* 10% of matrix; heap of red sandstone in centre as excavated up to 0.2 m, occasional burnt river cobble and harder sandstone angular cobble, and pebbles, *c.* 10%; *c.* 1.8 m max W–E by *c.* 0.7 m N–S, *c.* 0.2 m deep and semi-circular against the baulk. **Finds**: Fe slag; Fe artefacts: 2 × hobnails, Cat nos 7 and 8 (latter 3 × hobnails lost together); 4 × nails, Cat nos 11–14; RB pottery: 3 sherds BB1, 4 sherds GREY, 1 sherd SVW OX2; fragments of burnt bone: *c.* 2% TPQ: AD 120 **ES 5**: from charcoal-rich area: moderately high concentration of wood charcoal. ***Spread/dump of demolition/burnt material with lenses of burnt clay; over developing subsoil (2013); possibly linked to demolition of Structure 2?*** ***RC14: AD 198–230 (28.0%, 1σ); AD 122–240 (95.4%, 2σ).***	101, 104

(Continued)

CB21: Trench 2			
Context no. *Type*	*Physical relationships* ***Levels mOD***	*Description* ***Interpretation***	*Drawings*
2016 structure	Below (2001), (2035), (2039) c.f. [2012] 17.5, 18	Friable, mid-reddish brown gritty silty sand (30:70) with occasional paler yellower patches of degraded sandstone; flecks of degraded sandstone or possible mortar, occasional pebbles, river cobbles 0.1–0.15 m, *c.* 10%: larger subangular sandstone fragments 0.1 m–0.3 m 40% within Wall-line; v. occasional flecks of charcoal. 0.7 m W–E in slot by 4 m N–S, extending into robber trenches either side of foundations where far fewer and smaller stones, mostly red sandstone (*c.* 2% pebbles). Extensive Wall core tumble (*c.* 30%) was seen to the north of the Wall-line, down-slope towards ditch. Roots. **Finds**: RB pottery in matrix: 2 sherds BB1, 1 sherd GREY: >1% TPQ: AD 120 ***Remains of and matrix for curtain Wall in N–S Slot 2.***	106
2017 layer	Below (2003); upper layer of (2021); over (2007) and (2013) 18.25, 11.25	Friable, light reddish brown silty sand (40:60) with greyish white clay lenses (*c.* 30%: more clayey in N up to 60%); at least 50% poorly sorted and various angular pebbles and small cobbles av. 0.04 m, some harder sandstone, some larger soft red sandstone and occasional river cobble fragments; abundant charcoal, *c.* 0.2 m deep: depth variable. Area 2.25 m long near N–S as revealed and 2 m wide without likely wall trenches. 2 flat RSS possible post-pads on surface in N centre and middle W, *c.* 0.2 m in diameter and packed with red sandstone cobbles. Fine roots. **No finds**. ***Cobbly, clay floor: likely remains of internal surface for Structure 2. Possible truncated and disturbed post-holes with packing in N centre and W middle of floor. The floor was bounded to the SE corner of the extension by an NNE–SSW trending band of clean sandy silt, suggesting a possible wall trench. A similar band may have existed to the north but merged with (2013)–(2003) subsoils.***	104, 105, 107
2018 fill	Below (2013), (2020); fill of [2019]; part of [2027] 12.5,11	Friable, mid–dark brownish black silty sand with 90% charcoal; very few small pebbles. 0.4 m W–E × *c.* 0.6 m N–S quadrant in SW corner of extension, by 0.4 m deep. Heavy iron panning at base of hearth. Fine roots. **Finds**: Fe artefacts: 1 × hob nail, Cat no. 5; 1 × bolt, Cat no. 18 and stone clamp, Cat no. 19; fragmentary burnt bone; CBM: *opus caementicum*: *c.* 2 % **ES 6**: cereal grain, wheat and very high concentration of wood charcoal, mostly hazel, alder, birch etc. with some oak, ash and elm. ***Charcoal-rich fill of remains of hearth/oven in Structure 1. RC14: 1. AD 125–204 (68.3%, 1σ); AD 108–230 (88.7%, 2σ); 2. AD 60–130 (58.7%, 1σ); AD 26–205 (95.4%, 2σ).***	102, 106, 107, 1.02
2019 structure	Below (2013); filled by (2018); part of [2027] 12.5,11	Built into compact pebble surface forming interior floor/courtyard of Structure 1. Lining comprised single depth of harder sandstone cobbles 0.1–0.2 m sub-square, sub-triangular and sub-rectangular, all of which were burnt. A quarter curve of the feature was revealed 0.4 m W–E × 0.6 m N–S. ***Stone-lined hearth or base of oven in Structure 1. The feature appeared to have been constructed at the same time as the pebble floor had been laid with a close fit between oven stones and pebbles.***	102, 106, 107, 1.02

(Continued)

CB21: Trench 2			
Context no. *Type*	*Physical relationships* **Levels mOD**	*Description* ***Interpretation***	*Drawings*
2020	Below (2007) and (2009); above [2025]; same as (2013) 15, 11	Friable, mid-reddish brown, occasionally humic silty sand (25:75) with occasional clay lenses; well-sorted small pebbles 5%; occasional charcoal. 2 m N–S × 3 m W–E in extension, W of structure 2, over Structure 1 in the W; 0.1 m deep. **Finds**: Fe object; burnt bone fragments: > 1% ***Layer of disturbed, poorly formed subsoil over Structure 1 wall foundations; eastern version of (2013), which accumulated over Structure 1, less influenced by occupation deposits and into which Structure 2 built. Influences by destruction of Structure 1.***	ctxt sheet
2021	Below (2017); above (2007) 18.5, 11	Light yellowish slightly silty sand and white clay lenses with copious charcoal in patches and flecks and 40% RSS cobbles and pebbles, max. 0.2 m most 0.1–0.15 m; *c*. 0.2 m deep. Area 3 m long near N–S as revealed and 2.15 m wide without likely wall trenches. ***Clay and rubble foundations for interior of Structure 2. There were hints of internal post-holes or post-pads and the lack of rubble around floor suggested the walls may have been wooden.***	104, 105, 107
2022	Below (2001); cut by [2040]; same as a (2041) in Slot 3; LOE 11, 23	Friable mid reddish brown silty sand; 20% sorted red sandstone cobbles: sub-square up to 0.2 m near robber trench; and up to 0.3 m sub-oval cobbles, poorly sorted and on av. larger in the north near the ditch. In slot 1 m W–E × 4 m N–S. **Finds**: one sherd intrusive post-medieval pottery; fragment animal bone: > 1% ***North of Wall and robber trench in Slot 3: detritus left from robbing, tumble from Wall to immediate north and larger, rolled tumble and collapse downslope in ditch.***	106
2023	Under (2024), (2031), B1; same as (2030). Lower spit of (2013)? 16, 11	Friable, non-homogenous mid yellowish orange gritty, gravelly silty sand (40:60); 10% small-medium pebbles and cobbles with sandy, coarse gravel (redeposited natural). 0.1 m thick across extension. **No finds**. ***Poorly developed, stained and disturbed sub-soil in extension, into which Building 1 constructed.***	106 1.03
2024 layer	Below (2013) [2027]; above (2023); same as (2031) 13, 10.5	Firm-friable mid orangey brown and light orangey yellow gritty, coarse silty sand with clay lenses and iron panning. Under [2027] *c*. 30% sub-angular and rounded cobbles and occasional pebbles. 0.1 m thick seen in 0.2 m long intervention. **No finds**. ***0.2 m slot dug against southern baulk through [2027] just west of hearth [2019]. Stained layer below yard/floor; similar to (2031).***	1.02
2025 structure	Below (2004)/ (2013), (2020); above (2030) (2031) 14, 12	1 m wide by max. 1.5 m length revealed. Corner survives best and the foundations do not survive beyond a metre in length to the south and 1.5 m to the west. To the west they have been robbed out, to the south possibly robbed and also disturbed by later activity, perhaps associated with Building 2. Rubble coursing facing clearer in stretch north of baulk. With larger stones up to 0.3 m long on the outside corner. ***Foundations for WNW–ESE Building 1 wall around interior [2027]: courtyard or building wall, north of baulk in southern extension.***	106, 107

(Continued)

CB21: Trench 2			
Context no. *Type*	*Physical relationships* ***Levels mOD***	*Description* ***Interpretation***	*Drawings*
2026 structure	Below (2004)/ (2013); above (2030) (2031) 14.5, 11	0.7 m wide by 1 m long revealed south of 0.4 m wide W–E baulk. Foundations with rough rubble coursed facing of sub-square and sub-rectangular RSS stones *c.* 0.2 m max. with core of sub-oval and sub-triangular small RSS cobbles and pebbles in gritty sandy silt matrix. ***Foundations for near N–S Building 1 wall around interior [2027]: courtyard or building wall, south of baulk in southern extension.***	106, 107
2027 structure	Buts [2026], [2025]; below (2004), (2009), (2013); above (2023) 11.5, 11.5	Matrix: friable to firm mid reddish brown sandy silt (40:60) with lenses and flecks of charcoal and iron panning and considerable patches of white clay *c.* 30%. 85% well-sorted and tightly packed circular and sub-oval cobbles .*c* 0.1 m in diameter with gravel and pebbles around the stones. 5 m long WNW–ESE by max. 2 m wide as revealed. ***Cobble/pebble surface of interior floor or courtyard of Building 1***.	102, 106, 107, 1.00, 1.02
2028 fill	Fill of [2029]; below (2003) 11, 14	Friable dark reddish brown silty sand (30:70) with 3% small pebbles, charcoal and siltier lenses. **No finds.** ***Fill of robber trench for north wall of Structure 1, seen in Slot 1.***	106, 1.00
2029 cut	Filled by (2028); cuts (2004), [2027], (2030), (2031) 11, 14	0.6 m wide × 5.5 m long by *c.* 0.4 m deep along northern edge of Structure 1 west of surviving stone foundations. ***Robber trench around Structure 1, seen in Slot 1, west of area where foundations survive [2026].***	106, 1.00
2030 layer	Below all contexts; same as (2023); above (2034)	Friable, patchy, yellowish brown (dry) to reddish brown sandy silt 45:55 with sandier and gravelly lenses; small pebbles and sub-angular shatter *c.* 2–3%. **No finds.** ***Lower subsoil, across main trench. Poorly developed soil? Lower, less disturbed spit of (2003)***.	106, 107, 1.00
2031 layer	Below (2004), [2025], [2027]; cut by [2029] above (2030), (2034); same as (2024) 11.5, 15	Friable mid orangey yellow silty sand (30:70) with occasional gravel, small RSS cobbles, frequent lenses of white clay and iron panning. To north of the building and cut by the robber trench. Area 2 m² max. and 0.1 m deep. **No finds.** ***Yellow sand and clay layer under (2004) and Building 1 seen in deep slot and extension. Redeposited natural sand (2034) associated with Building 1, perhaps layer created by traffic and activity during building***?	106, 1.00
2032 fill	Fill of [2033]; below (2002) 12, 17.5	Friable, light reddish brown coarse silty sand (20:80); gritty with very occasional pebbles and small RSS cobbles. **No finds.** ***Fill of robber trench around likely tower/support structure for bridging point south of Wall-line. Seen to N, E and S***.	106, 1.00
2033 cut	Below (2002), filled by (2032), cuts (2006) (2011) (2030); (2035) uncertain 12, 17.5	0.6–0.7 m wide on two sides of tower E and S; max. 0.4 m deep, U-shaped, near-vertical sides, spread and truncated top. 2.5 m long N–S on east side, 2.2 m W–E revealed on south side. Walls likely *c.* 0.5 m wide originally. ***Cut for robber trench around two sides of likely tower/support structure for bridging point south of Wall-line. The robber trench was detected E and S of structure [2011] that would have abutted the Wall.***	106, 1.00
2034 natural	Below all contexts 13, 16	Seen in Slot 1. Yellowish grey coarse stained sands with occasional lenses of fine gravels excavated to coarse gravel layer. Generally *c.* 25 m deep under (2030) and (2023), dipping to 0.5 m deep in south of slot at 44.37 mOD. ***Natural glaciofluvial sands and gravels***.	106, 1.00

(Continued)

CB21: Trench 2			
Context no. *Type*	*Physical relationships* ***Levels mOD***	*Description* ***Interpretation***	*Drawings*
2035 fill	Fill of [2036]; below (2000) 16, 18	Friable, light reddish brown coarse, gritty silty sand (20:80) with very occasional pebbles and very occasional smaller RSS Wall core stones. **No finds.** ***Fill of robber trench for S-facing facing stones of Wall.***	106
2036 cut	Filled by (2035); cuts (2001), (2022) [2038], (2041) (2042); relnship [2033] uncertain 16, 18	Edges often diffuse but much clearer than robber trench [2040] to north: lack of stones indicates the trench, which is 0.7 m wide where the cuts are clearest and up to 1 m wide where they are more diffuse. Wall therefore *c.* 2.3–2.4m wide with foundations up to *c.* 0.4 m deep. Foundations were probably originally shallower before robbing disturbance. ***Robber trench for S-facing facing stones of Wall.***	106
2037 structure	Below (2005) (2006); cut by [2036]; above (3030) LOE 17, 16	Excavated in Slot 2 and in area. Red sandstone rounded sub-square and sub-rectangular cobbles up to 0.5 m long, very crushed, degraded and disturbed: *c* 33%. Structure 8 m near W–E as revealed and 2 m wide; abutting and poss. later than the Wall-line. Remaining foundations up to 0.15 m deep. **No finds.** ***Sub-rectangular foundations for ramp/stairs to bridging point abutting Wall.***	106
2038 structure	Below (2001), (2012) and (2016) LOE 16,19	Friable, light reddish brown coarse silty sand (20:80); harder sandstone, more sub-angular cobbles up to 0.35 m long, and softer red sandstone cobbles often more sub-square and *c.* 0.2 m, 40–70%; *c.* 1 m wide × 10 m near W–E. First 3.5 m from west baulk v. near W–E and remaining 6.5 m angle slightly south. Foundations shallow, no more than 0.2 m, with diffuse lower boundary; no discernible flagstone-like foundation course. No sign of mortar. **No finds.** ***Remains of core/foundations of curtain Wall, running near W–E across trench: crushed, truncated and disturbed.***	106, 1.03
2039 fill	Below (2000) fill of [2040] 16,19	Friable, light reddish brown coarse, gritty silty sand (20:80) with occasional pebbles and smaller RSS Wall core stones. **No finds.** ***Fill of robber trench for N-facing facing stones of Wall.***	106
2040 cut	Filled by (2039); cuts (2001), (2022) [2038], (2041) (2042) 16,19	Cut clearest in centre of area revealed, with a facing stone discovered on edge at 18, 19.5. Edges mostly diffuse but lack of stones indicates the trench, which is 0.7 m wide where the cuts are clearest and up to 1 m wide where they are more diffuse. Up to *c.* 0.4 m deep. Wall therefore *c.* 2.3 m wide. ***Robber trench for N-facing facing stones of Wall.***	106
2041 layer	Below (2001); cut by [2040]; same as (2042)/(2022) LOE 15, 22	Unexcavated, except in Slot 3 where N of Wall-line excavated to greater depth than in Slot 2 to the east. N of robber trench [2040] Wall core rubble – RSS cobbles and pebbles – then larger RSS core material downslope for 2 m to N edge of trench. All in reddish brown silty sand matrix, cf. (2039) and see (2022). Area 6 m W–E × 4.5 m N–S. **No finds.** ***N of Wall in NW of trench: detritus left from robbing, tumble from Wall to immediate north and rolled tumble downslope in ditch.***	106
2042 layer	Below (2001); cut by [2040]; same as (2041)/ (2022) LOE 19, 22	Smaller rubble just north of [2040] robber trench, likely result of collapse/robbing; large red sandstone stones found 4–5.5 m north of Wall-line, likely tumble from Wall-core; both in reddish brown silty sand matrix. Area 3 m W–E × 5 m N–S, east of Slot 2. **No finds.** ***Red sandstone destruction and collapse rubble and Wall-core tumble north of Wall-line, seen in N–S Slot 2 and in NE corner of trench N of Wall-line under (2001).***	106

CB19: Trench 3			
Context No. *Type*	*Physical relationships* ***Levels mOD***	*Description* ***Interpretation***	*Drawings*
3001 layer	Above all	Friable, dark orange-brown gritty, sandy-silt loam containing occasional small rounded and sub-angular pebbles (max 0.02 m diameter). The layer was uneven in thickness across the trench, varying between 0.01–0.04 m. ***Bottom interface of turf with topsoil, distributed across entire trench; removed by hand.***	
3002 layer	Below (3001); above (3003)	Compacted red-brown loam found across entire trench. Contained some areas of higher compaction of silty loam. Relatively consistent layer in colour and compaction, however, varying in thickness from 0.1–0.2 m. The layer was consistently at its thinnest in the southern portion of the trench, overlying the putative rubble of the Wall curtain (3004). Very sterile/clean soil. ***Compacted subsoil below turf/topsoil, suspected as relict ploughsoil prior to conversion of field to pasture in the 1970s (date of conversion provided by farmer). Excavated by hand.***	
3003 layer	Below (3002); above (?)	Red-brown sandy loam, slightly compacted at higher levels and more loosely compacted at lower levels. Found across entire trench. Maximum thickness 0.66 m. No lower boundary identified, the lower levels were sufficiently loose and sandy as to possibly constitute a different layer, for which the boundary was not recognised. Four distinct clusters of large stone and associated patches of degraded sandy mortar were found within the deposit, each aligned roughly E–W. The three northernmost clusters clearly sat within the deposit, and probably represent rubble material from the Wall curtain. The stones were ranging in size from 0.06–0.4 m length, some of which had been worked to a rough standard. The fourth, southernmost cluster (3004) may lay atop a different layer. Finds: A base fragment of a post-medieval, 19th-century ceramic vessel, found within the layer between the second and third stone clusters, at a depth below that of the clusters. A roughly dressed block that is a probable facing stone for the Wall curtain was removed from the northernmost cluster of stones. ***Relict post-Roman ploughsoil, with the only datable evidence the 19th-century pot base. The cluster of stones suggests prospective ploughing in an E–W orientation, such that stone rubble was moved into ridges between plough furrows.***	
3004 structure	Below (3003); above (?)	A dense concentration of irregular stone boulders/rubble approximately 1 m in diameter N–S, with a notable additional cluster of boulders/rubble approximately 0.75 m in diameter N–S to the north of the concentration. The largest stones were 0.3–0.4 m in length, and up to 0.25 m thick, mostly irregular in their shape, though some could be described as roughly dressed. The stones are a sandstone, densely stacked or piled without evidence of much disturbance. No facing stones were identified within the cluster, though degraded, sandy mortar could be found in denser pockets of sand mixed with the surrounding soil matrix (3003) as well as between some of the rubble. No objects were found. ***The putative remains of the stone Wall curtain, likely the core, with tentative evidence of mortar bonding or patching. Facing stones removed, but no clear stratigraphic remains of a robber trench identified. Southern extent not confirmed. Base of deposit not revealed/investigated. As the entire concentration has a length N–S of 2 m, it is likely that the northern portion is displaced rubble core, while the rest is*** **in situ.**	

Corbridge

Trenches 1–3 from Corbridge were incorporated into the full excavation interpretation, but were originally recorded in a slightly different manner. The original recording was retained.

Context number	*Context type*	*Fill of*	*Context description*	*Spot date*
			COR19: Trench 1	
1001	Layer		Topsoil, covering trench	
1002	Layer		Ploughsoil, underlying topsoil 1001	
1003	Layer		Stony spread underlying deposit 1006 at northern end of trench	
1004	Layer		Dark brown clayey silty layer underlying 1002 at southern end of trench	
1005	Layer		Intermittent clay deposit underlying 1004 at southern end of trench – possible surface?	
1006	Layer		Interface layer between 1002 and 1003	
1007	Layer		Large paving stones (fragmented) against street surface 1008	
1008	Layer		Road surface comprising of medium and large sub-rounded cobbles to north of 1007	AD 120–250
1009	Layer		Possible yard surface comprising of medium sub-angular and sub-rounded cobbles to south of 1007	
1010	Layer		Layer of brown clay and pebbles at southern end of trench (unexcavated)	AD 125/150–160
1011	Fill	1017	Mid-grey silty clay fill of linear feature	med or post-med?
1012	Fill	1018	Mid-greyish brown silt/clay stony fill of pit 1018	AD 120–250
1013	Layer		Mixed yellow clay deposit – possible occupation surface?	AD 120–130/160
1014	Fill		Fill of plough mark 1024	
1015	Layer		Metalled surface beneath layer 1009 (unexcavated)	
1016	Layer		Metalled surface beneath layer 1008 (unexcavated)	AD 120–250
1017	Cut		Cut of linear feature orientated broadly N–S	
1018	Cut		Cut of sub-circular pit 1018 – filled by stony deposit 1012	
1019	Cut		Curvilinear feature 1019 lead into pit 1017, probably contemporary	
1020	Fill	1019	Fill of curvilinear feature 1019	
1021	Layer		Deposit at north-western corner of trench, overlying linear 1022	possibly medieval?
1022	Cut		E–W orientated linear (not excavated), possible roadside ditch?	
1023	Fill	1022	Fill of linear feature 1022	
1024	Cut		Cut of plough mark	
			COR19: Trench 2	
2001	Layer		Topsoil, covering trench	
2002	Layer		Ploughsoil, covering trench	
2003	Layer		Dark brownish grey silty clay deposit	

(Continued)

COR19: Trench 3				
3001	Layer		Topsoil, covering trench	
3002	Layer		Ploughsoil, underlying topsoil 3001	
3003	Layer		Stony spread deposit underlying plough soil 3002	
3004	Layer		Interface between underlying stone deposit 3003 and ploughsoil 3002	
3005	Masonry	3011	Foundation of wall, orientated broadly N–S	
3006	Layer		Deposit abutting eastern face of wall foundation 3005 – possible backfill?	AD 120–250
3007	Layer		Clay deposit abutting western face of wall foundation 3005 – thin intermittent layer	AD 250–300
3008	Masonry	3012	Foundation of wall, orientated broadly N–S at western end of trench	
3009	Layer		Burnt clay deposit. Possible edge of furnace/hearth	
3010	Layer		Layer clay deposit overlaid by burnt deposit 3009, possible occupation deposit	AD 160–250
3011	Cut		Cut for foundation wall 3005. Not visible during excavation	
3012	Cut		Cut for foundation wall 3008. Not visible during excavation	

COR21: Trench 4			
Context no. *Type*	*Physical relationships* ***Levels mOD***	*Description; finds* ***Interpretation***	*Drawings*
4000 layer	Over all contexts	Friable, greyish black gritty and humic sandy (slightly clay) silt (15:85); less silty and inc. clayey/sandy with depth; limestone shatter, degraded limestone; limestone cobbles sub-angular, sorted up to 200 mm, some burnt; charcoal flecks: all inclusions *c.* 10–15%. Trench-wide 10 × 8 m × max. 0.4 m depth. Boundaries clear to rubble in E, road surface to N and yellowish-brown clay below. Roots and bioturbation. **Finds**: considerable amount of pottery (majority RB, some big crisp sherds – incl. mortaria, amphorae, Samian; occasional medieval and 18th/19th century); CBM, incl. RB imbrex, tile and brick and white lime mortar; daub, plaster; bone fragments, incl. crane over [4045]; Pb artefacts incl. Pb weight and fitting; Fe artefacts incl. hobnails, 16 nails and slag; RB Cu alloy tweezers; RB stone smoother and stone pestle: *c.* 2% of context. **Coin**: Marcus Aurelius denarius AD 155–157. ***Turf and relict plough/topsoil soil and subsoil removed by digger to 0.35m depth. Western c. 4 m N–S encompasses Trench 1 (2019).***	Sections
4001 layer	Below (4000); over (4019); related [4010] 15.5, 18.5 ***Top: 44.48***	Friable-firm (dry), yellowish grey sandy silt (20:80) with yellower, clayey lenses; more stone and clay-rich with depth; upper layer: rounded and sub-angular cobbles, from 70 × 60 mm to majority 80% *c.* 180 × 230 mm; lower layer: rounded and sub-angular cobbles, some flatter stones, sizes from majority 90 × 110 mm to few 130 × 230 mm and one 250 × 240 mm: 70%; some stones appeared to have plaster adhering, poss. re-used structural material; area 1m wide in slot by 2 m N–S with 1.20m N–S of road surface and 0.8 m poss. ditch to south; bioturbation. **Finds**: bone fragments; worked flint: Neolithic drill; clay pipe; Fe artefact; 6 × RB sherds, esp. in lower layer of cobbles: *c.* 1% of context. ***W–E road surface in Slot 1: upper layer of surviving cobble road. The cobbles were bedded in clay. To south a more clay band with fewer cobbles: upper, very disturbed and truncated surface of ditch [4010].***	Plan 400

(Continued)

COR21: Trench 4			
Context no. *Type*	*Physical relationships* ***Levels mOD***	*Description; finds* ***Interpretation***	*Drawings*
4002 layer structure	Below (4000); related (4007); over [4020] 20,12.5	Friable, (damp) dark brown, clayey silt (30:70); tiny amount charcoal; 1% small pebbles; 85% stone: 40 small core stones 60–70 mm, flag stones 30–40 mm thick, 12 large cobbles 300 mm × 180 mm; 1 m by *c.* 2 m W–E × 0.2 m deep; bioturbation. **Finds**: worked stone – possible joint and chamfered; plaster; 4 × RB sherds incl. BBW Greyware and amphora handle; hobnail. ***Disturbed E face of double-faced N–S wall; stones removed possible wall core, facing. East end slot 2.***	Plan 400
4003 layer	Below (4000); F(4014); same as (4007); over (4020) 15.5, 12.5	Compact (very dry), mid brownish grey, clayey silt (50:50) with more brownish yellow clay lenses and lenses brown clayey silt; W side esp. clayey; occasional charcoal, flecks of CBM, limestone shatter, occasional pebbles: *c.* 3%; 1 m W–E × 5 m N–S × 0.15 m deep. **Finds:** degraded animal bone; Fe nails; 21 × RB sherds incl. Samian; smoothing stone: 5%. ***Slot 1, working from southern baulk. Stony feature in SW corner of Slot, sump from 2019 trench (4014). 5 m N, possible post pad 0.38 × 0.35 m. Possible interior clay surface. Transition between (4007) interior and area of (4003), more industrial?***	Plan 400
4004 fill	Below (4000); poss. below (1009), same as (4011); above (4013); fill of [4045] 13,12	Compact (dry), blackish brown silty clay from 20:80 to 50:50 with occasional more friable lenses of yellowish brown; limestone shatter, small river cobbles and pebbles *c.* 5% and *c.* 5% charcoal; *c.* 2 m SW–NE × 1 m × 0.1 m removed; roots and worms. **Finds:** burnt bone; CBM incl. imbrex, RB brick and tile; fired clay Types 1 and 3; 5 × Fe artefacts incl. nails, hobnail and slag; 26 × RB sherds incl. BBW, Greyware, amphorae, some large; Cu alloy mount: *c.* 10% ***Spread upper fill of sub-oval feature of pit/intercutting pits in SW corner of trench. Cut into dark silty humic material and filled with similar matrix so cuts very difficult to discern. The spread also merged into the backfill of stone-filled pit [1018] and gully [1019], excavated in 2019 and trending SW to NE. Excavation in 2021 concentrated on the pit(s) to the NW of those 2019 cut features.***	Plan 400 404 405
4005 surface	Below (4000); related to (4015) [4034] 19, 16.5	Firm yellowish grey, gritty and dry slightly sandy, silty clay 30:70, 40:60; occasional cobbles, limestone grit and shatter *c.* 5%; *c.* 2 m N–S × 4 m W–E; roots, burrows and worms. **Finds:** 31 × RB sherds incl. Samian; CBM; considerable amounts of animal bone; iron metalworking slag: *c.* 3%. ***Area south of road and ditch in the east with fewer stones and cobbles; over earlier ditch.***	
4006 layer	Below (4000); same as (4008); cut by [4037] 21.5, 15	Friable, dry greyish brown sandy silt (20:80); angular cobbles, small sub-rounded cobbles and pebbles: 25%; occasional charcoal; 1 m W–E against E baulk by 1.5 m N–S × 0.35m deep; roots and worms. **Finds**: fragments of bone; 13 × RB sherds; 1 × Fe nail. ***N–S Slot 3: stony area in east of trench south of (4005) and north of (4002), likely remains of W–E wall foundation. Also related to (4008) further west?***	
4007 layer	Below (4000); (4002); below/ same as (4003) 17.5, 12.5	Compact and dry, light pinkish brown (greyer when dry) clayey silt; in E occasional charcoal, pebbles, small limestone shatter some burnt, one flagstone and suggestion of robbed out facing; abundant iron panning, finds decrease to west but charcoal and iron panning increases; *c.* 4 m W–E × 1 m × 0.2 m (slightly deeper in area of w wall-face); roots and worms. **Finds**: possible plaster; CBM; 7 × Fe artefacts, incl. nails; animal bone; 17 × RB sherds. **RC14:** 111–171 cal AD (1σ: 68:3%) with 13.1% possibility of 183–203 cal AD; 60–216 cal AD (2σ: 94.1%) **ES 4:** charred plant remains; some wood charcoal; HF: abundant bone. ***West of structural area (4002), possible. Excavated in Slot 2 W–E. Rubble spread and disturbed flags in west over clay-rich surface. To immediate west, possible remains of western face of wall in east of area, with rubble free extent to west.***	Plan 401

(Continued)

COR21: Trench 4			
Context no. *Type*	*Physical relationships* ***Levels mOD***	*Description; finds* ***Interpretation***	*Drawings*
4008 layer	Below (4000); above (4022) 16.5, 15.5	Friable (damp) firm (dry), light greyish black gritty, sandy/clayey silt (20:80 to 15:75); pebbles, cobbles and limestone shatter *c.* 10%; *c.* 7 m W–E × 1 m N–S in E to 1.5 m N–S in W × 0.1 m deep; roots and worms. **Finds**: 34 × RB sherds; considerable bone incl. teeth; Fe fragments incl. nails; CBM incl. fired clay Type 3; imbrex and roman brick; ironworking slag. ***Line of possible path/wall foundations W–E across trench or tumble from wall and remains of cobbled surface: related to (4009)? South of possible wall?***	Plan 401
4009 layer	Below (4000); above (4022) 17, 14	Friable, dark greyish brownish black gritty, clayey/sandy silt (30:70) matrix; occasional pebbles, rounded and larger cobbles and larger limestone shatter: 10%; occasional charcoal; *c.* 3.5 m W–E × *c.* 1 m N–S × 0.1 m deep; roots and worms. **Finds**: 8 × abraded RB sherds; bone and Fe fragments, incl. 1 × nail: <1% ***Area of damaged cobble path/surface or disturbed and truncated wall foundations W–E across trench: related to (4008). Runs up to post pad in west; stones of cobble surface in west have curved shape, convex to west. South of possible wall?***	Plan 401
4010 feature	Below [4034]; same as (4021); above (4019); cuts [4023] 16, 17.5 (centre) 20.5, 15.5 (E)	Compact dry yellowish grey silty clay (35:65), changing to darker clayey silt (50:50) fill below surface; cobbles and pebbles *c.* 5%; 1m W–E × *c.* 1 m wide ditch (spread at top) × 0.15 m depth excavated; roots and worms. More pebbles *c.* 0.1 m down in fill. Open U-shaped ditch, truncated. 0.2 m deep max. by 0.8–1 m wide. **Finds**: considerable animal bone incl. cattle and pig; 69 × RB sherds incl. large amphora sherd with handle; 10 × Fe artefacts, incl. hobnail and nails; slag; CBM and clunch; plaster. Most finds from southern edge of ditch. **Environmental sample (ES) 1**: vitreous material; Heavy Fraction, HF: bone and hammerscale. ***W–E ditch to south of later road, excavated in two N–S slots. Possibly cutting ditch and surface below connected to earlier version of road.***	
4011 layer	Below (4000); above F[4044] (4017), (4018) 20.5, 15.5	Firm (very dry), greyish yellow gritty slightly silty clay; cobbles and pebbles: *c.* 50%; some charcoal flecks and iron panning flecks: 1–2%; 1 m W–E by 1.2 m N–S as investigated in N–S slot on W baulk; roots and worms. **Finds**: fragmentary bone, abraded pottery sherds RB x7: < 1% ***Area of level yellow clay and cobble surface south of flagged area south of road in west. Seen in 2019 as 1009.***	
4012 fill	Below (4000); same as (4029), (4030) 11, 17	Friable (damp), gritty and humic brownish black clayey sandy silt (20:80), occasional grey clay lenses further down; homogenous for first 0.15m then clay lenses, silty lenses and heavy iron panning; pottery associated with siltier deposits; 0.2 m down occasional cobbles and limestone fragments; 0.4 m deep in E and 0.4 m deep in W. **Finds**: animal bone some burnt; 22 × RB sherds incl. poss. Nene Valley; CBM; 1 small sherd glass; Fe fragments, incl. hobnail and studs. **ES 2 and 3**: charred plant remains, wood charcoal; HF: bone, slag and hammerscale. **RC14**: 351–408 cal AD (1σ: 61.9%); 329–418 cal AD (2σ: 78.7%); 281–330 cal AD (1σ: 52.2%); 225–362 cal AD (2σ: 95.4%) ***Silty matrix just below flags and large cobbles south of road and fill of coursed drain. Filled with dumps of material initially then silted u***p.	

(Continued)

COR21: Trench 4			
Context no. *Type*	*Physical relationships* ***Levels mOD***	*Description; finds* ***Interpretation***	*Drawings*
4013 fill	Below (4004); above (4025); fill of [4045] 13, 12 ***Top: 44.13–44.03***	Friable (siltier) to firm (more clay) mid blackish brown, slightly clayey slightly sandy silt 20:80, with yellower clay lenses; abundant charcoal, occasional gravel and grit; abundant iron panning around clay; 0.85 m N–S by 1.25 m W–E and up to 0.43 m deep. **ES 6,** fill of Greyware jar: some charred plant remains, some wood charcoal; >4mm HF: considerable bone and a metal ring. **Finds:** CBM: fired clay Types 1 and 3, RB tile, chalk; pottery: 197 × RB sherds, many joining sherds and near complete vessels incl. near complete large Greyware jar, Samian incl. highly decorated, BBW, Greyware, domestic fineware sherds, amphora handle; much fragmentary unburnt, very burnt bone incl. roe deer; **glass**: flagon sherds; early and rare polychrome bowl; 3 joining sherds; heat-distorted glass jug sherd. **SFs**: Cu alloy RB brooch; Cu alloy RB ring (in flot); Cu alloy and Fe mount; Fe nail. ***Lower less disturbed fill of pit in SW corner cut through later cobbling, demolition spread, redeposited yellow clay and earlier yard; tear-drop shape resolving into SW-NE trending pit with collapsed sides. Probably one large central pit with smaller pits dug into circumference, all containing pottery stacked around large central Greyware jar. Clay lenses possibly collapsed lining***?	Plan 405
4014 feature	Below (4000); above (4003) 15.25,10.75	***Remains of small square sump cut during COR 2019.***	
4015 layer	Below (4000); over [4021] and (2027); related to (4040) 20.5, 18.5 ***44.42***	Friable, greyish black (dry) gritty slightly sandy v slightly clay silt (20:80); limestone shatter and pebbles *c.* 3%; cobbles and sub-angular limestone blocks, 20 cobbles 0.1 × 0.1 × 0.15 m, 40 small cobbles 0.05 m diameter, 40 between the sizes: 70%; v. occasional charcoal and iron flecks; 1 m W–E × 1.25 m N–S in Slot 3 × *c.* 0.2 m; roots. Smaller stones on top, large stones underneath with curved area of clay with almost no stones ringed by larger stones. **Finds:** v. occasional bone; undiagnostic CBM fragments. ***Upper, disturbed, truncated and repaired road surface as excavated in Slot 3.***	
4016 layer/ structure	Below (4000) (4007); butts [4020]; above (4028) 20,11.5 ***44.33***	Firm (dry) light greyish brown sandy silt (30:70) matrix; pebbles and limestone shatter 3%; larger rubble, both large cobbles and sub-rectangular sandstone *c.* 60%; occasional charcoal; 1.5 m N–S × 4 m W–E. Large sub-triangular cobbles up to 0.4 × 0.3 × 0.1 m (2), flatter sub-square stones 0.2 × 0.3 × 0.08 m (10), smaller sub-triangular and sub-square stones (20), flatter flagstones 0.05 m thick (4). Investigation extended west in N–S slot 0.5 m wide, beyond rubble/ flags; two layers of stones. Flagged area up to 1.5 m W–E by 4 m N–S by 0.2 m deep. **Finds:** 8 × RB sherds incl. amphora handle with stamp; burnt bone incl. pig and sheep; Fe fragments, incl. nails × 7; glass: jug and cup fragments, incl. handle. ***Rubble and remains of flagging W of N–S wall in SE corner. Flags, rubble and soil matrix.***	
4017 layer	Below (4000), (4011); same as (4003) above (4018) (4024) 15.5, 22.5 ***44.34***	Friable-firm, yellowish grey gritty silty clay (20:80) with darker siltier lenses; charcoal flecks: damaged cobble surface: large pebbles, occasional cobbles 0.15 m and some limestone shatter 30%; 1 m × 5 m NE × 0.1 m deep, in slot and elsewhere. **Finds**: fragmentary bone; 47 × RB sherds incl. repaired Samian base; RB brick; 5 × Fe fragments incl. nails; Pb seal; bottle glass. ***Yard layer: non-homogeneous, below damaged cobble surface and over redeposited clay surface and cobble surface in centre slot (poss. thin destruction levelling layer beneath those surfaces). In slot S of ditch/ water conduit.***	

(Continued)

COR21: Trench 4

Context no. *Type*	*Physical relationships* ***Levels mOD***	*Description; finds* ***Interpretation***	*Drawings*
4018 layer	Below (4011) (4017); cut by [4045] [4046] [4047] same as (4028), (4038) (4039) 13, 13.5 ***44.19***	Firm (very dry) blackish, greyish, brownish yellow, gritty slightly sandy silty clay (20:80) with siltier lenses; occasional limestone shatter and cobbles *c.* 0.1 m, smaller pebbles; iron flecks and panning and charcoal *c.* 3%; 5 m N–S from S baulk and 4 m from W baulk merging with (4003) and (4007) to east. **Finds:** chalk, fired clay type 1, imbrex; bunt bone fragments; jug and bottle glass; 2 × Fe artefacts; 18 × RB sherds. ***Redeposited clayey surface in centre west, north of (4004), in Slot 4 and across whole yard area; influenced by pits and levelling demolition layers above.***	Plan
4019 layer/ structure	Below (4001); above (4023); linked to [4010] 15.5, 19.5 ***44.32***	Friable, orangey, yellow brown clayey silt (20:80) with darker siltier burning influenced lenses with iron panning and iron flecks; 75% 0.15–0.2 m cobbles and pebbles to larger sub-square limestone fragments up to 0.4m larger stones 50% by volume and 50% poorly sorted but larger cobbles; occasional charcoal; 1 m in slot by 1.5 m N–S × 0.2 m deep. **Finds**: fragmentary bone; CBM; 6 × RB sherds. ***Lower layer of road cobbling in central Slot 1. Possible patching and repair and slump into earlier ditch? Possibly an earlier road edge to N of later road edge with backfilled ditch just to south.***	
4020 layer/ structure	Below (4000); (4007); butted by [4016]; above (4028) (4038) 20, 13.5	Firm greyish brown, clayey silt matrix; 70% stones with some smaller shatter and pebbles; charcoal; possible plaster; *c.* 2 m², *c.* 0.1 m removed. **Finds:** 7 × RB sherds; bone fragments; chalk, fired clay Type 3. ***Remains of N–S wall linked to flagstones to west. The wall had been thoroughly dismantled but* c. *1 m wide, running 4 m north from south-east corner of the trench. Only the lowest foundation stones survived as two parallel lines of facing stones with some patches of cobble core. Many of the remaining facing stones were around 0.3 m long, suggesting a relatively substantial wall above; some facing stones could also be seen running south and north of Slot 2.***	
4021 feature	Below (4015), above (4027); same as [4010] 19.5, 17.75	Firm-friable, greyish brown, slightly silty clay (20:80) with sizeable clay lenses; some charcoal; 60% large cobbles and large limestone stones, with some smaller cobbles and large, long sub-triangular stone with smooth scalloped edge in north; 1 m in slot × ?1.5 m. Under relatively stone-free surface many more stones in this area south of wall-line. Fill and southern side of degraded ditch; side was likely part of open U-shape but so disturbed it was difficult to discern. **ES 5**: heavy fraction: some bone, metal, slag, hammerscale, charred vitreous material. **RC14**: 201–238 cal AD (1σ: 39.8%); 123–246 cal AD (2σ: 95.4%) **Finds**: 6 × RB sherds; fragmentary bone; 3 × Fe nails. ***Slot 3. Area south of road and north of possible wall. Ditch, probably same as [4010], with slumped material from wall to south and road surface to north. Good drawing on context sheet.***	
4022 feature	Linked (4008), (4009); above (4039) 16, 15.5	Friable when damp, clayey silt (30:70); occasional fine gravel; charcoal, degraded limestone, rounded pebbles, iron panning *c.* 1%; L-shaped slot 1 m N–S × 2 m W–E and extra 1 m in W by 0.6 m wide × 0.15 m deep. **Finds**: considerable amounts of badly abraded animal bone; 10 × RB sherds; Fe artefacts, incl. 3 × structural nails; Pb. candlestick; window glass and blown glass vessel; white lime mortar; fired clay Type 1. ***Central structure in trench. Remains of later cobbled surface with stone structural elements and patchy flagging to south. Likely low stone foundations and wall for open-sided workshop in yard.***	

(Continued)

COR21: Trench 4			
Context no. *Type*	*Physical relationships* ***Levels mOD***	*Description; finds* ***Interpretation***	*Drawings*
4023 feature	Below (4019); above (4043); cut by [4010] 15.5, 19.5	Friable, gritty, greyish yellow, slightly silty clay (20:80) ditch fill, over lower darker spit, then clay-rich again; stones of road: large cobbles and flatter sub-angular limestone up to 0.3m bedded in yellow clay, 4 large stones 0.25–0.3 m by 0.12–0.17 m, majority 0.07–0.1 m by 0.08–0.1 m and some smaller *c.* 0.06 m; iron panning; *c.* 2 m N–S × 1 m. Ditch: open U-shaped, truncated *c.* 0.15 m deep and 0.8–1 m wide. Lowest road stones associated with yellow clay and some very large 0.35–0.4 m by 0.25 m, sub-angular and flattish. Only *c.* 20% smaller cobbles, with most stones *c.* 0.2 m. **Finds**: only from ditch edges: 6 × RB sherds; RB brick; bone fragments, degrading on excavation. ***Lower cobble road layer in central slot – c. 0.9 m N–S – merging into fill of disturbed road ditch to south, up to 1 m wide. Included earlier, wider ditch, with slump of stones from south down the side. 0.2 m down another layer of road cobbles encountered (4043), wider and reaching under ditch.***	
4024 fill	Below (4011); fill of [4046]; above (4035) 14, 13.5	Friable dark brown, gritty sandy clayey silt (30:70) with yellower clay lenses, especially in centre of pit; burnt limestone fragments, up to 0.15 m. *c.* 3%; charcoal; 0.9 m N–S by c. 0.7 m W–E (quadrant); 0.3–0.4 m deep. **Finds:** considerable animal bone much very degraded, cattle; Fe nails and fitting; Pb artefact; 26 × RB sherds; CBM and fired clay. ***Pit south of road in west centre of trench. Cuts pit [4047].***	
4025 fill	Below or lower spit (4013); fill of [4045]; cuts (4017) 12,12.5 ***Top: 44.10–44.26*** ***Bottom: c. 43.5***	Friable, brownish black gritty, slightly sandy slightly clayey silt (30:70) with yellowy orange lenses of clay; occasional small pebbles and small limestone shatter, few bigger pebbles and charcoal: 5%; edges collapsed and cuts very difficult to distinguish as filled with same material cut into; spread fill of pits cover 3 m SW–NE and 1.5 m NW–SE, max. depth 0.35–04 m. Large flat sub-oval stone (0.3 × 0.35 × 0.08 m) sat under the large greyware pot (with hole), with iron panning and CBM fragments surrounding. **Finds**: 53 × RB sherds, incl. fine wares and Samian; 3 × poss. Fe artefacts, incl. Fe fitting; burnt bone; bottle and cup glass; fired clay Type 1 with iron attached, CBM and RB brick; ironworking slag ***Fill of intercutting pits, excavated in west after removal of large Greyware pot and large sherds Samian; fill from around jar. Pit(s) punch through to levelling layer very similar to pit fill; so of what was excavated as fill could be underlying occupation layer similar in phase to (4028).***	
4026 layer	Below (4000); 11.5, 18 ***44.29***	Matrix: friable, gritty dry greyish brown slightly sandy silt with lenses of yellow clay and W–E band of very firm white clay, *c.* 0.4 m wide × 0.02 m deep; gravel, small pebbles, limestone shatter and charcoal: 5%; **road stones**: 6 large sub-angular stones 0.25 × 0.25 m; *c.* 80 sub-angular and cobbles 0.15 × 0.2 m and a few smaller cobbles; 6 large, rounded stones set in band white clay av. 0.23 m with biggest 0.34 m; stones below more disturbed layer set in yellow clay and seem to have slight N–S gradient. **Finds**: bone fragments: cattle, sheep and pig; CBM, 13 × RB pottery sherds mostly Greyware and amphorae; Fe artefact; coal. ***Upper layer of N–S road in western N–S slot, disturbed by 2019 excavation. With large stones edging conduit to south.***	

(Continued)

COR21: Trench 4			
Context no. *Type*	*Physical relationships* ***Levels mOD***	*Description; finds* ***Interpretation***	*Drawings*
4027 layer	Below (4015); above (4032); related [4010] [4021] 18.5, 20.5 ***Top: 44.26N–44.06S*** ***Bottom: c. 44***	Matrix: mid orangey brown to blackish brown, slightly sandy clayey silt (20:80) with both more humic and more clay lenses; occasional charcoal, degraded limestone occasional CBM flecks, gravel and grit; small up to 0.1 m shatter and pebbles used as packing: 5%; **road stones**: 0.37 × 0.2 m cobble × 1; sub-rect. 0.35 × 0.15 m stone × 1; 2 × sub-rounded 0.25 × 0.2 × 0.1 m; 612 × smaller sub-rounded cobbles 0.15 × 0.10 × 0.1 m; 6 × sub-square and sub-rect. 0.1 × 0.15 × 0.1 m; sub-square 0.25 × 0.26 × 0.19 m; lump of possible plaster/mortar; area of pebbles set in clay 0.4 × 0.3 m at 0.6 m below ground surface. **Finds**: clunch and fragments CBM; fragmentary bone: < 1%. ***Lower layer of W–E road in NE corner comprising very large stones with camber. Line of roadside ditch unclear.*** *V. good drawing on context sheet*	
4028 layer	Below (4016) (4020); above (4038) in SE corner 20.5, 11	Friable-firm, dark orangey brown, slightly sandy, clayey slit (30:70), inc. clayey to west, as move beyond area under flagging; gravel, pebbles ocas. smaller cobble; iron panning; iron flecks and panning abundant in east; 0.8 m N–S by 5 m × 0.08 m. **Finds**: around wall area: chalk and fired clay Type 1; ironworking slag; bone fragments; Fe nail; 11 × RB sherds; in more clay area to W: RB pottery incl. 11 × sherds Samian. ***Siltier context under rough flagging around possible W–E wall and to west, in slot against S baulk. Likely occupation/yard surface onto which later rough flagging laid and wall has collapsed.***	
4029 fill	Same as upper (4012), (4030) 12.75, 17.25 **c. *44.46***	Friable and damp (even in heat), dark blackish brown slightly sandy clayey gritty and humic silt (20:80); small amount gravel, occas. small pebbles, charcoal flecks and degraded bone fragments, some burnt; *c.* 5%; 0.8 m wide W–E by 0.5 m × 0.41 m deep W and 0.36 m E. **Finds**: plaster, mortar; abraded sherds 3 × RB sherds; Fe artefact; CBM fragments and fired clay Type 2; chalk; fragments of bone, incl. cat pelvis: < 1% **ES 7**: Charred plant remains and wood charcoal; HF: bone, slag, copious hammerscale. ***Below flags in second slot across conduit: E of large flag and the first N–S slot across conduit. Fill of likely conduit/drain, beneath flags.***	
4030 fill	Same as (4012) (4029) 14.25, 17	Friable, mid blackish brown slightly sandy clayey gritty and humic silt (30:70), less humic than (4029); small amount gravel, occas. small pebbles and cobbles charcoal flecks, iron panning and degraded bone fragments, some burnt; *c.* 3%; 0.8 m wide W–E, intervention just to east of final flag; more pottery in upper layer. **Finds**: 52 × RB sherds; bone, some burnt; CBM: clunch, imbrex, RB tile, fired clay Type 1; Fe artefacts incl. hobnail. **SF11**: BA barbed and tanged flint arrowhead at base of conduit. ***Fill of drain/conduit excavated in third slot across feature, E of (4029). Continues east as uncoursed and possibly earlier ditch, with feeder for conduit running from under road N–S and turning west into conduit running west, south of road.***	
4031 structure	SG for conduit	**W–E conduit/drain with coursed stone sides and flagged base.**	
4032 structure	Below (4027); above (4033) Related to (4015)/ (4010) 20.5, 18.25 ***44.4***	Friable, dark blackish brown matrix, sandy silt (30:70); 20% pebbles (0.06 × 0.05 × 0.03 m); 60% large stones: large angular stones 0.25 × 0.2. × 0.3 m; sub-rounded, 0.2 × 0.15 × 0.1 m; medium angular, 0.15 × 0.15 × 0.1 m; rounded flags, 0.2 × 0.2 × 0.1 m; charcoal 1%; 1.5 m × 0.85 m × 0.25–0.3 m deep. **Finds**: bone fragments; plaster/mortar; imbrex; Fe structural nail; bottle and window glass ***Structural stones embedded in yellow clay with pebbly matrix, collapsed into roadside ditch. An area of notably different stones on southern edge of road. In eastern N–S slot.***	

(Continued)

COR21: Trench 4			
Context no. *Type*	*Physical relationships* ***Levels mOD***	*Description; finds* ***Interpretation***	*Drawings*
4033 layer	Below (4032); above (4036) 20.5, 18.25 ***44.1***	Compact, yellowish/orangey brown slightly silty clay (20:80); occasional charcoal flecks; occasional pebble and limestone shatter; 0.7 m × 0.3 m between stones to depth 0.1 m. **Finds**: RB pottery × 1. ***Clay layer below structural stones south of the road in east.***	
4034 feature	Below (4011); cuts (4039); relationship [4010] unclear 16, 16.5	Compact, yellow clay surface – capping – over blackish brown clayey slightly sandy silt (40:60); cobbles and sub-angular limestone max. 0.2 m *c.* 40%; stones slipped into fill down sides. Ditch open U-shaped, truncated, 0.22 m deep and 0.78 m wide. **Finds**: 5 × Fe structural nails; fired clay Type 3; slag; bottle glass; ceramic weight; cattle bone fragments incl. burnt ribs; 29 × RB sherds, mostly Greyware: 3% ***Fill of U-shaped ditch running W–E, seen in L-shaped intervention in centre east trench and in centre slot. Runs just south of road ditches although truncation obscured relationship with ditch [4010] and appears to run length of trench west from small building under later cobbled surface.***	Plan 405 Sec. 4.05
4035 fill	Below (4024); fill of [4047]; cut by [4046]; above (4018) 14.5, 13	Friable dark, brownish black clayey silt (30:70), with some blackish yellow clay lenses; charcoal, gravel and small pebbles *c.* 2%. **Finds**: 2 × Fe structural nails; 18 × RB sherds incl. Samian; imbrex; cattle bone fragments: 3%. ***Fill of sub-oval pit cut by [4046] to SW. Cut into clay with thin silty fill; sealed with clay.***	Plan 405 Sec. 4.04
4036 feature	Below (4033); LOE 20.5, 17 ***43.72***	Compact, dark yellowish brown gritty, sandy silty clay (50:50); well-sorted pebbles *c.* 25 mm, charcoal: *c.* 5%; 40% larger stones angular up to 0.15 m and cobbles up to 0.2 m; 0.7 m N–S × 0.4 m W–E × 0.28 m depth. Stone content decreases with depth. **Finds**: fragmentary bone; 3 × RB sherds: <1% ***Cobble layer below yellow clay (4033) in NE corner of trench. Possible foundation layer for (4033).***	Plan 405 Sec. 4.10
4037 fill	Below (4040); same as [4034] ditch fill LOE 20.5, 16	Compact (dry), dark yellowish brown, silty clay (50:50), with paler more clay lenses; occasional pebbles and charcoal < 1%; 0.8 m W–E × 0.64 m N–S × 0.08 m depth. **Finds:** 3 × RB sherds; fragment of bone; Fe artefact: < 1% ***South of structural stones (4032) and (4033)–(4036): possible ditch fill.***	Plan 405
4038 layer	Below (4028); LOE 19.25, 11.25	Compact, mid greyish brown (dry), silty clay (50:50); grit and pebbles max. 70 mm: 5%; N–S 0.55 m × W–E 55 m × 0.35 m; sandier and fewer finds with depth. **Finds:** teeth, many bone fragments some burnt, incl. cattle and caprid; 3 × RB sherds: Fe fragments; CBM fragments: c. 5% ***Sondage in south of W–E slot: indicates occupation surface c. 0.3 m deep in this area.***	Plan 405
4039 layer	Below (4022); S of (4034); related (4042) 17.5, 15.0	Firm, baked, dark greyish brown, silty clay (50:50), interspersed with orangey brown silt layers frequent charcoal and sub-rounded river pebbles 80–150 mm; infrequent angular stones 200–300 mm; 2.9 m N–S × 1.9 m max. T-shape; 0.2 m removed. **Finds:** considerable amounts fragmentary bone incl. cattle and pig; over 40 RB sherds inc. amphorae and Greyware; slag and coal; structural Fe artefacts × 6; CBM: *opus caementicium*, fired clay Type 3, RB brick; fire-cracked stone: 162g banded sandstone, sooty and reddened: *c.* 7%. ***Levelling layer of midden-type deposits cut by structural element in east (2–3 courses of semi-circular wall remain). Pit (4042) in SW of intervention and seen in section cut by curved wall, also seemed to be cut by near W–E ditch. The layer is laminated with charcoal-rich deposits inter-leaved with siltier, less charcoal-rich layers.***	Plan 405 Secs 4.05 4.06

(Continued)

COR21: Trench 4			
Context no. *Type*	*Physical relationships* ***Levels mOD***	*Description; finds* ***Interpretation***	*Drawings*
4040 structure	Below (4000); part of [4041]; 19.5, 18.5	Matrix 15%; friable mid brown clayey silt; stones 75%: some v. large cobbles 0.35 × 0.25 × 0.2 m; sub-rectangular cobbles up to 0.2–0.35 m; smaller sub-oval cobbles 0.1–0.2 m; smaller cobble and pebble fill between stones; larger flatter stones under top layer up to 0.35 m. Finds: 3 × RB sherds; coal; animal bone fragments: < 1%. ***Collapsed stones from structure [4041] which spreads over possible roadside ditch and reveals large stones [4041] in line with conduit to west.***	Plan 405
4041 structure	Below (4000); and [4037] = [4034]; part of [4040] 19.75, 17.0	Matrix 20%: friable mid brown clayey silt; stones 80%: sub-oval and sub-rectangular, reasonably well-sorted and more rounded large cobbles, most *c.* 0.1 m × 0.3 m occasional smaller packing cobble; *c.* 1.5 m in length by 1 m wide by c. 0.2 m deep. **Finds:** 8 × RB sherds; 1 × Fe nail; animal bone fragment; fragment of Cu alloy brooch: <1%. ***Larger stones to south of road line, running along south side of ditch. Structural remains of wall related to main phase mostly lost to truncation and later disturbance.***	Plan 405
4042 feature	Below (4022) cut into (4039) related (4034) 17.5, 15.0	Firm dark greyish brown silty clay; frequent charcoal and iron staining; 0.5 m diameter, 0.15 m deep; truncated top, gently sloping sides and concave base. **Finds:** 1 × RB sherd; slag: <5%. ***Cut and fill of pit seen only in east facing section in east central intervention relating to building: fill very hard to distinguish from midden-type layers.***	Plan 405 Sec. 4.05
4043 layer	Below (4023) LOE 15.5, 18.5 ***Top: 43.90***	Matrix, 15%: mid brown gritty clayey silt; gravel, pebbles, occasional charcoal: 2% of matrix; 85% stones: occasional cobble 0.1–0.2 m, majority of stones angular, sub-square and sub-rectangular 0.1–0.3 m × 0.15 m; no small cobbles or pebbles; 1.5 m N–S × 1.5 m max. W–E, by 0.15 m deep as excavated. **Finds:** 3 × RB sherds; fragmentary bone which decayed on retrieval: < 2%. ***Large stones of narrower W–E road foundation under 0.2 m clay and set in clay in NW corner of trench north of conduit. See drawing on context sheet.***	Plan 405
4044 feature	Below (4011), cuts (4017) 11.5, 15.5	Friable, dark yellowish brown clayey, slightly sandy silt (30:70); small pebbles, occasional larger pebble, some gravel and iron panning, occasional charcoal: 3%; 0.3 m wide excavated to 0.1 m depth; seen in three interventions. **Finds**: slag; 2s × sherd RB pottery; fragments of bone; fragments imbrex, RB brick and tile, fired clay Type 1 and 3; badly abraded. ***Seen most clearly in section in western slot against baulk, in central slot and east central excavation of building remains: W–E ditch. No inter-cutting stratigraphy with other ditches by road but under later cobbles (4011).***	Plan 405 Sec. 4.03
4045 cut	Filled by (4013) (4025); cuts (4017) (4018) 12.25, 12,50	Sub-circular, truncated, near vertical sides, open near flat base; up to 0.5m deep, 1m in diameter. ***Cut for large irregular pit in SW corner. Sub-circular in plan, irregular to near vertical sides, near flat base cut into levelling deposits.***	Plan 405 Plan 404
4046 cut	Filled by (4024); cuts (4017), (4018) [4047] 13.75, 14,0	Circular in plan, truncated, sides steeply sloping base near flat. ***Circular pit in west centre of trench,*** **c.** ***1.1 m in diameter and up to 0.4 m deep, cutting pit [4047] to the north.***	Plan 405 Sec. 4.04
4047 cut	Filled by (4035); cut by [4046]; cuts (4018) 13.75, 14.9	Sub-oval/tear-drop in plan, oriented NNW–SSE, truncated, sides near vertical, base open U-shape. ***Sub-oval pit in west centre of trench, 0.9 m by 0.5 m by up to 0.3 m deep, cut by [4046].***	Plan 405 Sec. 4.04

(Continued)

COR21: Trench 4			
Context no. *Type*	*Physical relationships* ***Levels mOD***	*Description; finds* ***Interpretation***	*Drawings*
4048 feature	Under (4017) cuts (4018) 11.75, 14	Quadrant of small pit: 0.25 m width N–S by 0.3 m W–E revealed *c.* 0.1 m deep. Cut into levelling layer in west of trench, south of road. ***Small pit under yard: seen only in section.***	Plan 405
4049 structure		N–S wall in the east of the trench.	Plan 405

COR21: Trench 5			
Context no. *Type*	*Physical relationships* ***Levels mOD***	*Description; finds* ***Interpretation***	*Drawings*
5000 layer	Above all	Topsoil was friable, dry mid brownish black sandy, clayey silt. Subsoil was firm to compact mid brownish grey sandy clay; small to medium pebbles (5–10%), occasional flecks of charcoal. Trench wide: 8 m E–W × 10 m N–S, trench sloped down to the north. Considerable root disturbance and bioturbation. Evidence of plough lines across the trench running E–W. **Finds**: Ceramics (Roman through to Victorian/modern), glass sherds, metal objects (iron nails and pieces, lead, copper alloy), clay pipes. ***Playing field, subsoil and clean-up layer across trench. Top 0.3m removed with digger, clean up by hand.***	Plan 500
5001 layer	Below (5000)	Firm, dry, mid brownish grey, fine to medium grain sandy clay (20:80), with some patches of yellow clay, mid blackish grey sandy clay, and orangey red burnt clay (5–10%). Even distribution of small cobbles (5%) and a small amount of charcoal flecking. 0.92 m × 0.90 m, maximum depth 0.12 m. Some bioturbation and rooting. **Finds**: Ceramics, fired clay, Fe nails/objects. ***NE internal corner of Roman building, partially excavated area of the floor surface, with a high concentration of burnt clay, particularly large patch up against internal edge of eastern wall. Slight over digging while clearing back remaining subsoil.***	
5002 layer	Below (5000) Above (5024)	Firm to compact, dry, mid greyish brown sandy clay with 5–10% small to medium pebbles and flecks of charcoal and CBM. 3.4 m × 1.2 m, maximum depth 0.08 m. Some bioturbation and rooting. **Finds:** Sherds of black burnished ware or greyware, other ceramics, burnt animal bone, CBM, iron nail, glass. ***Partial excavation of Roman yellow clay floor surface in NW internal corner of building. Slight over digging while clearing back remaining subsoil.***	
5003 layer	Below (5000); above (5015), (5016) (5004); same as (5005) (5010) (5013)	Firm to compact, very dry, mid yellowish brown, silty clay. Contained small to medium rounded, sub angular and angular stones (5%) with an average diameter of 0.04 m, and flecks/small pieces of charcoal (2%). 3.4 m N–S × 4.45 m E–W × 0.1 m depth. Very little bioturbation or rooting. **Finds**: Ceramics including greyware and a sherd of finer decorated ware, iron nail and slag, animal tooth. ***Yellow clay layer that has been deposited and spread to seal the earlier floor surface and occupation deposits within the building.***	
5004 layer	Below (5000), (5003) (5005); same as, (5010), (5013)	Compact, dry, mid yellowish brown silty clay containing less than 1% small pebbles. Approximately 2 m by 2 m and 0.05–0.1 m depth. **Finds**: long, unidentified iron object (approximately 0.2 m long), ceramics, and possible gaming piece or counter. ***Removal of the yellow clay layer, north of the 2019 trench and west of the stone lined trough, deposited and spread to seal the earlier floor surface and occupation deposits within the building.***	

(Continued)

COR21: Trench 5			
Context no. *Type*	*Physical relationships* ***Levels mOD***	*Description; finds* ***Interpretation***	*Drawings*
5005 layer	Below (5000); above (5020) (5004); same as (5003) (5010), (5013)	Firm, dry, mid yellowish brown silty clay, with 5% small pebbles and small cobbles. 1 m N–S × 3 m E–W × 0.1 m depth. Bioturbation. **Finds**: Iron nails and pieces, ceramics including BBW. ***Yellow clay layer that has been deposited and spread to seal earlier floor surface and occupation deposits within the building. This area was located immediately to the east (interior) of the western wall of the building, and was removed from within the 1 m wide E–W slot that ran across the entire trench.***	
5006 layer	Below (5000)	Compact, dry, mid yellowish brown sandy, silty clay, with charcoal pieces up to 2cm in size (2%), small to medium cobbles (2%) and fragments of mortar/plaster (3%). 1 m × 1 m × 0.05 m. Some bioturbation. **Finds**: ceramics, fragments of mortar or plaster, iron nails ***Build-up of material to the north of the building, including some occupation and possible building demolition debris. Context is within the 1m wide N–S slot that runs the entire length of the trench.***	
5007 fill/ structure	Below (5000); above (5012); fill of [5036]; same phase as (5009), (5014)	Compact, dry, dark blackish grey silty clay with medium to large sub rounded and sub angular cobbles (80%) and some small to medium pebbles (2%). Cobbles are various sizes, with some average measurements of 0.28 m × 0.18 m × 0.15 m, 0.21 m × 0.18 m × 0.06 m, 0.25 m × 0.12 m × 0.14 m and 0.25 m × 0.17 m × 0.1 m. Area: 1 m E–W × 1.1 m N–S × 0.2 m depth. No noticeable contamination. **Finds**: ceramics, CBM, mortar/plaster, iron nail, animal bone. ***Later, 2nd phase of the stone foundations of the north wall of the building. Some of the cobbles were very roughly trapezoid shaped and placed to be interlocking within the foundations, with the sandy clay soil infilling any gaps between the cobbles. The base of this deposit was a thicker layer of the sandy clay soil with small to medium pebbles which appeared to create a more level surface for the larger cobbles to sit on. Context is within the 1m wide N–S slot that ran the entire length of the trench.***	Section 5.4
5008 layer	Below (5000); above (5029)	Firm to compact, dry, mid brownish yellow sandy clay with small (20%) to medium (40%) sub angular and angular cobbles and a 5cm piece of semi-carbonised wood. 1 m N–S × 1.63 m E–W × 0.1 m depth. Small amount of rooting and bioturbation. **Finds**: glass, ceramics including decorated vessel rim and vessel handle; animal bone and iron nail. ***Yellow clay layer that has been deposited and spread to seal the earlier occupation deposits to the east of eastern wall of the main building. The eastern end of this area may have a section of a rough rubble wall of a small annexe off the side of the main building. This area is the eastern end of the 1 m wide E–W slot that runs across the entire trench.***	
5009 fill/ structure	Below (5000) Above (5011) Same phase as (5007), (5014)	Friable, dry, mid yellowish brown, sandy silt with small to medium sub angular and angular (30:70) cobbles (80%) and large pieces of charcoal (5–7 cm). 1.07 m E–W × 1 m N–S. **Finds**: ceramics, coal, animal bone. ***Later, 2nd phase of the stone foundations of the west wall of the building, built using small to medium sized cobbles with sandy silt soil infilling the gaps between the cobbles. Context is within the 1 m wide E–W slot that ran across the entire trench.***	Section 5.3

(Continued)

COR21: Trench 5			
Context no. *Type*	*Physical relationships* **Levels mOD**	*Description; finds* ***Interpretation***	*Drawings*
5010 layer	Below (5000); above (5023); same as (5003) (5004), (5005) (5013)-(5019)	Compact, dry, mid greyish yellow sandy clay with small, rounded pebbles (2–5%). 1 m N–S × 0.1 m depth. No contamination. **Finds**: ceramics including Black Burnished Ware and Samian with decorated rim, and iron nail. ***Yellow clay layer that has been deposited and spread to seal earlier floor surface and occupation deposits within the building. This area was located immediately to the west (interior) of the eastern wall of the building, and was removed from within the 1 m wide E–W slot that ran across the entire trench.***	
5011 fill/ structure	Below (5009); within [5035] Same phase as (5012), (5017)	Friable, dry, dark greyish brown, sandy silt with medium to large sub rounded, rounded and sub angular cobbles (80%), with ranging in size from 0.08 m–0.09 m by 0.1 m–0.2 m. 1.06 m E–W × 1 m N–S. No contamination. **Finds**: ceramics, iron artefacts and bone. ***Earlier, 1st phase of the stone foundations of the west wall of the building, built using medium to large sub rounded, rounded and sub angular stones. The cobbles appear to have been placed with the larger stones towards the exterior of the foundations (west) and the smaller stones towards the interior of the building (east). Context is within the 1 m wide E–W slot that ran across the entire trench.***	Section 5.3
5012 fill/ structure	Below (5007); above (5032); fill of [5036] Same phase as (5011), (5017)	Soft, dry, dark brownish black, silty clay with medium to large sub rounded and sub angular cobbles (80%), small rounded and sub rounded 0.1 m × 0.1 m cobbles (5%), CBM or burnt clay, charcoal (especially towards the base of the wall trench), and small pebbles. 1 m E–W × 1.1 m N–S. Small amount of bioturbation. **Finds:** ceramic, glass, Cu alloy piece, iron nail, daub/plaster, animal bone. ***Earlier, 1st phase of the stone foundations of the north wall of the building. The base of the foundation trench was packed with a layer of small rounded and sub rounded cobbles onto which the medium to large cobbles were laid. These were laid in a herringbone pattern to create a stable foundation for the likely timber superstructure of the building. Between this deposit (5012) and the later, 2nd phase of the foundations (5009) was a levelling layer of soil and smaller stones, used to create a good base for the 2nd phase.***	Section 5.4
5013 layer	Below (5000); above (5019) Same as (5003), (5004), (5005), (5010)	Firm to compact, dry, mid greyish brown, silty clay with flecks of charcoal, CBM or burnt clay, small amounts of redeposited yellow clay (5%) in the soil. About 10–15 large sub angular and angular cobbles were sitting on the surface where the box section was placed. 0.87 m N–S × 0.33 m E–W × 0.16 m depth. Small amount of bioturbation and rooting. **Finds**: pottery, iron nails, animal bone. ***Box section to explore the layers of the floor surfaces in the interior of the building. Initially removed a number of stone thought to possibly be an internal dividing wall, but they were only sitting on the surface (not embedded in the soil).***	
5014 fill/ structure	Below (5000); above (5017) Same phase as (5007), (5009)	Compact, dry, dark blackish grey silty, clay (25:75) with a mix of small to medium rounded, sub rounded and sub angular cobbles (80%) (larger stones measure 0.2 m × 0.17 m, 0.27 m × 0.16 m, 0.24 m × 0.19 m). Area: 1 m × 1 m × 0.25 m. Small amount of bioturbation and rooting. ***Later, 2nd phase of the stone foundations of the east wall of the building, built using small to medium sized cobbles with silty clay soil infilling the gaps between the cobbles. A layer of soil approximately 0.07 m deep was below this context and was removed to reveal the (5017). Context is within the 1 m wide E–W slot that ran across the entire trench.***	Section 5.5

(Continued)

COR21: Trench 5			
Context no. *Type*	*Physical relationships* **Levels mOD**	*Description; finds* ***Interpretation***	*Drawings*
5015 feature	Cut into (5003)	Upper fill: friable, dry, mid yellowish brown, silty clay with 5–6 medium to large sub angular cobbles. Clay lining: compact, light greyish yellow, clay with small pebbles (2–3%). 1.75 m E–W × 0.95 m N–S × 0.15 m depth. Some bioturbation. **Finds**: glass, iron nails/objects, large amount of pottery, mostly of the same vessel found in (5003) around the pit. **SF 4**: copper alloy object. **ES 1**: charred vitreous material, a very little bone and metal. ***Small sub-oval pit, lined with yellow-grey clay and filled with friable, silty clay with several sub angular medium-large cobbles embedded in the surface. The south side of the pit was disturbed by reworking of the southern wall foundations or later ploughing.***	
5016 fill	Below (5000); fill of [5038]; cut into (5021) and [5022]	Fill: soft, dry, dark blackish brown silty clay (50:50) with small to medium angular and sub angular cobbles (60%), measuring 0.1 m × 0.1 m up to 0.35 m × 0.25 m, flecks of charcoal, occasional small pebbles. Clay lining: light greyish yellow clay. 1.45 m E–W × 2 m N–S × 0.15 m depth. No contamination. **Finds**: iron nails/objects, pottery. **ES 2**: a little charred plant remains and fragments of roundwood charcoal. ***Large pit lined with light yellow clay with dark blackish brown silty fill. The surface of the pit had a layer of packed, small to medium angular and sub angular cobbles, which created a fairly level surface. The pit is very similar to [5015] and the two pits may have been dug at the same time. Pit [5038] was cut into the remains of a possible oven or hearth [5022] and there was an area of burnt clay (5021), first seen during the 2019 excavations, to the east. Between [5038] and (50210 was a large trapezoidal stone measuring 0.4 m × 0.55 m × 0.07 m, which had been placed on top of [5022]. It had been burnt on the bottom side and was cracked into 3 pieces. This feature may be the base for something that sat within the building.***	Plan 500, 501, 502 Section 5.2
5017 fill/ structure	Below (5014); fill of [5037] Same phase as (5011), (5012)	Firm, dry, mid blackish grey, silty clay with medium sub rounded and sub angular cobbles (80%), measuring 0.1 m × 0.15 m to 0.15 m × 0.2 m. 1 m × 1 m. Some bioturbation and rooting. **Finds**: iron nail, glass, animal bone. ***Earlier, first phase of the stone foundations of the east wall of the building. The medium cobbles were laid in a rough herringbone pattern, visible in the section, to create a stable foundation for the likely timber superstructure of the building. Between this deposit (5017) and the later, second phase of the foundations (5014) was a levelling layer of soil and a few smaller stones, used to create a good base for the second phase. Not all stones were removed, so the full depth of the foundations was not reached.***	Section 5.5
5018 feature	Below (5000); cut into	Compact, dry, mid brownish grey, silty clay with charcoal (5%), small-medium rounded and angular cobbles, and some pebbles. 1.6 m N–S × 0.36 m E–W × 0.42 m max. depth. Some bioturbation and minor rooting. **Finds**: slag, iron nails, iron hobnails, pottery, animal bones and teeth. **ES 3:** Fill from trough: 1 × 10 l bucket. **ES 6**: Occupation deposit below trough: 1 × 10 l bucket. ***Fill of stone lined trough, running N–S on the east side of the interior of the building. The sides of the trough were marked by long, thin stones that were the height of the trough (approximately 0.25 m) and the bottom of the trough was packed with medium cobbles and probably clay-lined. The fill contained a higher concentration of hobnails than found elsewhere in the trench. The trough may be associated with the possible hearth or oven (5022) to the west. The trough was over-dug during excavation to sample occupation deposits below, and environmental samples of the fill and this lower deposit were collected.***	Plan 502 Section 5.1

(Continued)

COR21: Trench 5			
Context no. *Type*	*Physical relationships* ***Levels mOD***	*Description; finds* ***Interpretation***	*Drawings*
5019 layer	Below (5013)	Friable, dry, dark blackish brown, silty clay with small rounded and sub rounded cobbles (5%), CBM or burnt clay, and charcoal. 0.87 m N–S × 0.33 m E–W × 0.12 m depth. Some bioturbation and rooting. **Finds**: pottery, CBM, animal teeth, burnt bone, iron nail. ***Lower deposits in the box section, excavated to understand the development of the floor deposits within the building. Coming down onto dark, charcoal rich occupation level below with higher concentration of ceramics, charcoal, CBM and iron content, as seen in the E–W and N–S slots running the width and length of the trench.***	
5020 layer	Below (5005); above (5028); same as (5023), (5024) (5027), (5031)	Friable to firm, dry, mid greyish brown, silty clay with flecks of charcoal (3%), CBM or burn clay (3%), and large possible flagstones. 1 m N–S × 2.5 m E–W × 0.2 m depth. Bioturbation. **Finds**: ceramics, iron nails, animal bone, glass, CBM. ***Upper layer of occupation deposits within the building, containing a higher concentration of charcoal and CBM. Removal of this context uncovered a number of possible patchy flagstones, which may have been laid in an area of higher activity to try to keep the area dry or to keep the occupants out of the mud. Larger number of finds, including pottery, iron nails/ objects and animal bone. This context was in the interior of the building, to the east of the west wall of the building, in the 1 m wide E–W slot that ran across the entire trench.***	
5021 deposit	Below [5038]; above (5022)	Loose – friable, dry, medium reddish orange burnt silty clay (100%). 0.8 m × 0.8 m × 0.1 m. No contamination. **Finds**: none **ES**: 4 ***Deposit of burnt/baked clay on the eastern end of the possible hearth or oven [5022], where hot material from the hearth/oven has been raked out and baked the clay.***	Section 5.2
5022 structure	Below [5038] Above (5030)	Firm to compact, dry, mid greyish brown silty clay with charcoal, burnt material, small to medium pebbles, iron nails/objects, and burnt/baked clay. 1.6 m × 0.6 m × 0.35 m. Bioturbation and rooting. **Finds**: pottery, nails, animal bone, CBM. **SF 9**: Cu pin head. **ES 5**: 1 × 10 l bucket. ***Fill and/or remains of a possible hearth or oven. Area was later cut into by pit (5016). In order to see the feature in section, a box section was used after (5016) was half sectioned.***	Section 5.2
5023 layer	Below (5010) Same as (5020), (5024), (5027), (5031)	Compact, dry, mid blackish brown, silty clay with charcoal (5–10%), and flecks of CBM and plaster, and 2–3 angular stones (0.1 m × 0.15 m). 1 m. Small amount of bioturbation and rooting. **Finds:** pottery, animal bone, iron nails. ***Occupation deposits within the building, containing charcoal and CBM. Sherds of pottery, animal bone and iron objects also indicate generally activity in the building. Context is located directly west of the eastern wall, on the interior of the building. It is within the 1 m wide E–W slot that ran across the trench.***	

(Continued)

COR21: Trench 5			
Context no. Type	*Physical relationships* **Levels mOD**	*Description; finds* ***Interpretation***	*Drawings*
5024 layer	Below (5002); same as (5020), (5023) (5027), (5031)	Compact, dry, mid greyish brown, sandy and silty clay with occasional medium to large pebbles (0.01 m–0.02 m), 1 large sub angular cobble, and moderate amount of charcoal (some in larger chunks). 1 m E–W × 1.5 m N–S. Small amount of bioturbation **Finds**: Iron nails, pottery, glass, Cu alloy. **SF6**: Cu alloy scabbard slide. ***Occupation deposits within the building, containing an even distribution of charcoal, sherds of pottery, and iron objects. The scabbard slide indicated probably military activity in or around the building. Context is in the 1m wide N–S slot that ran the length of the trench, from the area directly south of the northern wall of the building.***	
5025 layer	Below (5029); same as (5026)	Firm to compact, dry, mid to dark greyish brown, silty clay with small, angular cobbles (2%), reveals an area of possible flagstones. Excavated in slot 3.4 m N–S × 0.5 m E–W × 0.18 m depth. Small amount of bioturbation and rooting. **Finds**: 36 × sherds RB pottery; CBM; some burnt bone; 19 × Fe nails. **SF12:** piece of a blue glass bangle with yellow patterned decoration. ***Build-up of occupation material to the east of the building. May include an area of flagstones. Finds from this area are of a more domestic nature and indicate a female presence. There may have been a living area adjacent to the main workshop building.***	Plan 503
5026 layer	Below (5034); same as (5025), (5029)	Firm, dry, mid greyish brown, silty clay with a small amount of fine sand. Contains small to medium pebbles and sub angular and angular cobbles (2–5%), charcoal and flecks of CBM. Excavated in slot 1.55 m E–W × 0.5 m N–S. Small amount of bioturbation. **Finds:** *c.* 18 × Fe nails, 52 sherds RB pottery; CBM; cattle 2 × molars, burnt and unburnt bone. **SF7**: silver decorative mount; **SF14**: lead spindle whorl? ***Small exploratory slot across the interior of the possible annexe to the east the main workshop building. Context has similar appearance and inclusions as the occupation deposits seen across the trench. Within the silty soil were patches of redeposited grey clay. Finds are of higher quality, and indicate a female presence. There may have been a living area adjacent to the main workshop building.***	Plan 503
5027 layer	Below (5000); above (5030), same as (5020) (5023) (5024) (5031)	Firm to compact, dry, light greyish brown, sandy clay with charcoal (5%) and small to medium pebbles (10%). Patches of purple staining may indicate peat deposit. Excavated in slot 2.2 m N–S × 1 m E–W × 0.25 m depth. Minimal bioturbation. **Finds**: 71 × RB pottery sherds; 4 × Fe nails and Fe fitting; cup and bottle glass, green glass bead (found while sorting finds tray, otherwise would have been a small find); CBM; small animal bone incl. teeth; fragment of Cu alloy. ***Occupation deposits within the building, containing charcoal, CBM, animal bone. This context was located in the 1m wide N–S slot that ran the length of the trench, and was between the E–W slot and the hearth/oven feature (5022).***	Plan 503

(Continued)

COR21: Trench 5

Context no. *Type*	*Physical relationships* ***Levels mOD***	*Description; finds* ***Interpretation***	*Drawings*
5028 structure	Below (5020)	Friable to firm, mid blackish grey, clayey silt with small pebbles (5–10%), charcoal (5–10%), flecks of CBM. Excavated in slot 1.55 m E–W × 0.6 m N–S × 0.18 m depth. No contamination. **Finds**: small amount animal bone, some burnt; Fe hobnail and washer; 14 × sherds RB pottery. **SF10:** large, curved, sub-circular unidentified iron object (block lifted); hearth-related? **ES7:** 1 × 10 l bucket; good amount wood charcoal. ***Fill of semi-circular structure in the centre of the building, possible an early hearth. The edge of the feature is marked with large, flat stones. Soil is very humic/organic and contains charcoal. In the centre of the structure was a large iron object, unidentified, which was block lifted to prevent any damage to the object.***	Plan 503
5029 layer	Below (5008), same as (50250, (5026)	Friable to firm, mid blackish brown with patches of more yellowish brown, silty clay, containing small to large pebbles and small rounded cobbles (20%) and charcoal (5%). Excavated in slot 1 m N–S × 1.63 m E–W × 0.08 m depth. Minimal bioturbation and rooting. **Finds**: 4 × sherds RB pottery, small amount animal bone, 2 × Fe nails, coal. **SF8**: Cu alloy coin, very corroded radiate; **SF16:** half a milky green melon bead ***Occupation deposits that have built up to the east of the main workshop building, possibly part of an annexe or domestic building associated with the workshop. Finds are generally of a higher quality than those in the workshop and indicate a female presence. Context is directly east of the east wall of the building and is within the 1 m wide E–W slot that ran across the entire trench.***	Plan 503
5030 layer	Below (5022), (5027)	Firm, damp, mid blackish grey, clayey silt in the northern end of the slot, with more yellowish grey silty clay in the southern end of the slot under (5022). Contains small pebbles (5%), charcoal flecks and larger chunks (5%), flecks of CBM, burnt sandstone (possibly associated with the oven/hearth (5022)). Excavated in slot 0.4 m E–W × 2.1 m N–S × 0.15 m. Small amount of bioturbation. **Finds**: small amount animal bone, some burnt; 3 × iron nails, 25 × sherds RB pottery. **SF15**: half of a small, bright blue moulded glass bead. ***Lower occupation deposits within the building and the edge of the hearth/oven (5022). Slot through the burnt clay and stained, possibly peat deposits seen at the bottom of (5027).***	Plan 503 Section 5.2
5031 layer	Below (5000); above (5028); same as (5020), (5023) (5024), (5027)	Firm to compact, very dry, mid greyish brown, silty clay with charcoal, CBM and a small amount of stone (2%). Excavated in slot: 1.3 m E–W × 0.55 m N–S × 0.2 m depth. No contamination. **Finds**: 28 × sherds RB pottery, window glass, iron nail, burnt and unburnt animal bone, incl. cattle. ***Occupation deposits within the centre of the workshop building, containing CBM, charcoal and animal bone. Cleared back this area to expose the possible stone lined hearth (5028). Contained a higher concentration of burnt and unburnt bone than seen elsewhere across the trench.***	Plan 503

(Continued)

COR21: Trench 5			
Context no. *Type*	*Physical relationships* ***Levels mOD***	*Description; finds* ***Interpretation***	*Drawings*
5032 deposit	Below (5012); cut by [5036]	Loose, dry, dark greyish brown, sandy silt with small stones (15%), charcoal and flecks of CBM. 1 m E–W × 1.05 m N–S × 0.25 m depth, as excavated. Bioturbation. **Finds**: CBM, 15 × sherds RB pottery, slag, iron object. **ES 8**: copious wood charcoal, charred vitreous material, bone. ***Deposit of material with a high organic content at the bottom of the foundation wall trench. Below this was the undulating surface of the yellowish brown natural clay (the only point where we reached natural across both trenches. Poss. ground surface into which building constructed.***	Plan 503 Section 5.4
5033 feature	Below [5035]; above natural; LOE	Firm, damp, mid blackish grey, clayey silt with medium rounded and angular (80:20) cobbles (85%), charcoal. Bioturbation. **Finds:** iron fragments. ***Below a layer of soil at the base of the western foundation wall for the main workshop building (5011) was a wall on a slightly different alignment to the west wall (more NW–SE). This wall was built primarily with rounded stones, with some more angular. It was uncovered on the last day of excavation and therefore only the upper surface of the wall was excavated. The western wall of the building (5011) may have used this earlier wall as a base during construction.***	Plan 503
5034 layer	Below (5000)	Soft, damp, mid blackish brown, clayey silt with small to medium pebbles (5%), charcoal, flecks of CBM; *c.* 4 m N–S by 2 m W–E as excavated. Minor bioturbation. **Finds**: decorated floor tile, iron incl. Fe fitting, 19 × RB pottery sherds, lead fitting, RB window and bottle glass. ***Clearing back over possible annex/domestic area to the east of the main workshop building, in the SE corner of the trench.***	Plan 503
5035 cut	Filled by (5009), 5011); cuts [5033]; same as [5036], [5037]	N–S aligned linear cut, roughly square in profile, with fairly straight sides and near flat base. Seen in excavation 1 m × 1.06 m. ***Cut of foundation trench for the western wall of the building. Cut was not completely clear while excavating. Cut created a roughly square trench for the foundations of the west wall of the building. Below base of cut, another N–S stone wall was uncovered (see [5033]) on a slightly different alignment.***	Section 5.3
5036 cut	Filled by (5007), (5012); cuts (5032) and natural; same as [5035], [5037]	E–W aligned linear cut, roughly square in profile, with fairly straight sides and an undulating base that followed the natural clay. Seen in excavation 1 m × 1.05 m. ***Cut of trench for the foundations of the northern wall of the building. Sides of cut were not completely clear while excavating. The foundation trench was cut down to natural clay in this location (the only point to reach natural in either trench). The base was undulating, following the shape of the clay. A small sondage, approximately 0.2 m × 0.2 m × 0.2 m, was excavated in the SE corner of this slot, through the base of the foundation trench. This was done to check to see if the base was in fact natural, or if any other features lay below the clay. Nothing was encountered and this was interpreted as natural clay.***	Section 5.4
5037 cut	Filled by (5014) (5017); cuts natural; same as [5035] [5036]	N–S aligned linear cut with fairly straight sides. The profile and base are unknown. Seen in excavation 1 m × 1 m. ***Cut of trench for the foundations of the east wall of the building. Cut was not completely clear while excavating. The slot was not fully excavated, and the base was not reached.***	Section 5.5
5038 cut	Filled by (5016); cuts [5022]	Circular, roughly N–S oriented pit with gently sloped sides and gently rounded/concave base.1.45 m E–W × 2 m N–S × 0.25–0.3 m. ***Circular pit with gently sloping sides and a flat to slightly rounded/concave base, located in the SW corner of the building. Pit was lined with yellow clay and then filled with stone and silty clay. burnt/fired clay deposit found on the east side of the feature from [5022] A large trapezoid shaped stone was found placed on the base of the pit (see (5016)). Pit was cut into (5022).***	Plans 500, 501, 503 Section 5.2

Heddon-on-the-Wall

As only one trench was excavated at Heddon, and the resulting number of contexts were limited, there is no long complex context register for this site. All contexts can be observed on the plans, sections and discussed in the text in the main report.

Port Carlisle

PC21: Trench 1			
Context no. *Type*	*Physical relationships* ***Levels mOD***	*Description* ***Interpretation***	*Drawings*
1000 layer: trench south	Above (1001) ***Top:*** ***8.93–8.85 to 8.46–8.40*** ***Bottom:*** **c. *8.40–8.30***	Friable, dry and humic, mid greyish black, gritty sandy silt (30:70); at least 50% stone: two large round red sandstone cobbles (*c.* 0.4 m); poorly sorted, sub-angular and rounded yellow sandstone cobbles and stone shatter, most *c.* 0.1–0.2 m. Layer trench-wide 1.2 m N–S, by 1 m in W–E, up to 0.5 m deep in north by wooden fence on top of bank; sloping to 0.1 m at level ground in the south. The larger sub-angular yellow sandstone may originally have been wall core material. Much root disturbance. ***Turf/vegetation, field soil and rubble forming southern field bank, rebuilt after 1970s building removed. The farmer remembers recreating the bank after the outbuilding blew down.***	
1001 layer: trench south	Below (1000); above (1004) ***Top:* c. *8.30*** ***Bottom:*** **c. *7.90***	Friable, dry, mid-yellowish/orangey brown silty sand (40:60); at least 80% yellow sandstone rubble, majority sub-angular cobbles 0.1–0.15 m; some larger sub-angular shatter 0.2–0.4 m; occasional small, rounded pebbles and grit. In lower 0.25 m far fewer stones, fewer larger and more sub-rounded stones: intersection with natural. Across trench and up to 0.4 m deep. Some bioturbation and affected by flooding and falling and rising water table. ***This compact stony layer lay at and just below ground level of the southern field. It appeared to be a spread of stone including possible wall core compacted over time by water action washing out soil and the construction of an agricultural building in the area between the 1950s and 1970s. From*** **c. *0.25 m down the layer seemed to have an extended interface with diffuse boundaries to natural.***	
1002 layer: trench north	Above (1003) ***Top:*** **c. *8.91–8.25*** ***Bottom:*** **c. *8.65–8***	Friable, root-matted mid-greyish black sandy silty sand (20:80); 10–15% medium-large cobbles; up to 0.2 m, sub-rounded and sub-angular red and yellow sandstone. Across the trench 1.2 m N–S by 1 m E–W by 0.15–0.25 m deep. Boundaries unclear. Bioturbation and water disturbance. A few very corroded Fe fragments, probably from agricultural equipment, found in this layer. ***Vegetation and makeup of northern hedge bank with wooden fence on top. Some of the stone may have been re-purposed wall core. Note the field north of the field bank is noticeably lower than that to the south by*** **c. *0.3 m.***	
1003 layer: trench north	Below (1002); above (1005) ***Top:* c. *8.65–c 8.4*** ***Bottom:*** **c. *8.29***	Loose-friable mid greyish brown, sandy silt (50:50); fine-medium sand. 10% small-medium sub-rounded cobbles. Max. depth *c.* 0.5 m in the south, thinning to *c.* 0.2 m in the north. Trench wide. Diffuse and irregular boundary with (1002); clearer boundary to (1005) as lower layer much more compact. Bioturbation, including heavy rooting, and water action. Several very corroded Fe fragments, probably from agricultural equipment found at the boundary between (1002) and (1003). ***Silty flood deposits mixed with glacial till material and some possible wall core piled up to (re)create field bank.***	
1004 layer: trench south	Below (1001); LOE ***Top:* c. *7.90*** ***Bottom:*** **c. *7.82***	Friable, damp gritty, mid blueish grey silty sandy clay (15:40:45) with purplish black siltier degraded organic lenses; some cobbles and stone shatter, mostly at interfaces, with solid bedrock encountered in the south of the trench; across the trench excavated for 0.1 m depth. Diffuse boundary to (1001). ***Natural: mixed glacial till with fluvial/beach deposits. Possible relict natural 'sea bank'.***	

(Continued)

PC21: Trench 1			
Context no. *Type*	*Physical relationships* ***Levels mOD***	*Description* ***Interpretation***	*Drawings*
1005 layer: trench north	Below (1003); over (1004) ***Top: c. 8.29*** ***Bottom: c. 8***	Friable-compact mid greyish brown silty sand (40:60); small-medium sub-rounded cobbles, pebbles and grit *c.* 20%; Layer 0.2–0.25 m across trench above natural; boundaries clear. Some bioturbation. ***Interface between field bank and natural glacial till/fluvial deposits.***	
1006 layer: trench south	Below (1001) LOE ***Top: c. 8.40*** ***Bottom: c. 8.34***	Friable, gritty mid orangey brown humic sandy silt (30:70); sub-angular, angular cobbles of yellow and red sandstone, 50%, majority 0.1 × 0.1 m, occasional larger stone 0.2 × 0.2 × 0.4 m; small pebbles and grit 10%; across 0.6 m × 1 m extension south, dug for *c.* 0.1 m until ditch line and lack of facing stones discovered. ***Small extension of Trench 1 southwards on south side. 1 m W–E by 0.6 m N–S to confirm no Wall foundations and to trace line of rubble drain. Rubble drain northern edge located and no facing stones or likely* in-situ *core material found.***	

PC21: Trench 2			
Context no. *Type*	*Physical relationships* ***Levels mOD***	*Description* ***Interpretation***	*Drawings*
2000 layer	Above (2001) ***Top: from c. 8.78–87 (N) to c. 8.29–33 (S)***	Layer of rough turf, matted with roots, some poorly sorted degraded stone shatter and pebbles (0.01–0.1 m). Across trench 2 m N–S × 1.2 m, W–E *c.* 0.1 m deep. ***Turf layer, matted roots and vegetation.***	Sec: 2.0
2001 layer	Below (2000); above (2002), (2003, (2004) ***Top: c. 8.2–8.7*** ***Bottom: c. 8.15***	Friable, dry, gritty and humic mid greyish brown sandy silt (20:80), lighter with depth (up to 40:60), with fibrous and sandier lenses; occasional small pebbles. Across trench. 0.15–0.4 m deep, thinning to S. Heavily rooted. ***Disturbed topsoil of bank and field edge.***	Sec: 2.0
2002 fill	Below (2001), (2005); above (2003), (2006); Fill of [2005] ***Top: c. 8.10 in S*** ***Bottom in ditch c. 7.85***	Friable, humic dark greyish black to blackish brown sandy silt (30:70) with some more clay lenses; grit, small pebbles and occasional cobble *c.* 10%. Across trench, thinning to nothing in S sloping gently for 1 m to N then dipping to 0.25 m deep in ditch. Rooting and bioturbation. 10% inclusions: hand-made thin brick and degraded mortar (with some evidence of paint) and some coke. Finds: 8 sherds of 19th century bottle glass; 1 bone knife handle; 2 × sherds 19th century pottery; Fe fragments. ***At least pre-/early Victorian rubble field drain (using wall core) levelled off to create foundation for likely Victorian building. This was then mixed with demolition debris from the removal of the building spread to level the area. The curtain in this area has been heavily damaged by attempts to improve field drainage: the original ditch runs W–E but may also have had N–S element, and/or a re-cut. The disturbed nature of the layers made it difficult to be certain.***	Sec: 2.0
2003 layer	Below (2001) (2004); above (2002; LOE S ***Top: c. 9.1*** ***Bottom: c. 8.3***	Friable-compact, light brownish grey, slightly clayey sandy silt (10:15:75) with some more clay lenses; *c.* 70% stones of various sizes, from cobbles to larger sandstone blacks, including facing stones of (2004) Across N of trench on bank, up to 0.6 m high but only max 0.2 m width excavated into face of bank. ***Disturbed wall core, reconstituted and piled up after demolition of building and 'refaced' with [2004].***	Sec: 2.0

(Continued)

PC21: Trench 2			
Context no. *Type*	*Physical relationships* ***Levels mOD***	*Description* ***Interpretation***	*Drawings*
2004 layer	Above (2003); below (2001) ***Top: c. 9*** ***Bottom: c. 8.4***	Three repositioned curtain facing stones: sandstone roughly faced *c.* 0.35 m wide by 0.2 m high. A fourth stone continues the line to the west beyond the trench. ***Three repositioned curtain facing stones (of four visible), with cobble revetting (2003). Presumably used in the 19th century agricultural building and then re-used to recreate the field bank after the building was demolished, before the 1860s.***	Sec: 2.0
2005 cut	Cuts (2006); filled by (2002) ***Top: c. 8.1 in S*** ***Bottom in ditch c. 7.85***	Truncated ditch with spread gently sloping west side visible in east-facing section, with 45° slope after break of slope to lowest level of ditch excavated. Bottom not quite reached (max. 0.25 m deep) and only short portion of northern return slope caught in section. 1.7 m wide as revealed across the trench, but possibly disturbed by re-cuts or ditches running to the north. ***Disturbed length of ditch/drain visible elsewhere as a slight dip running W–E to south of bank. Also seen in Trench 1. The ditch preceded the building.***	Sec: 2.0
2006 layer	Below (2002), cut by [2005] (2005); LOE ***Top: c. 8–8.1*** ***Bottom: 8, LOE***	Friable to compact dark greyish brown, gritty, sandy silt (30:70); grit; frequent sub-rounded pebbles and large sandstone cobbles *c.* 30% of context. ***Subsoil with some likely deposited and spread wall core created over time as facing stones robbed and work done to shape field bank and improve drainage.***	Sec: 2.1

Walltown Crags

WTC: Trench 1			
Context no. *Type*	*Physical relationships* ***Levels mOD***	*Description* ***Interpretation***	*Drawings*
1000 layer: whole trench	Above (1001); (1002), (1004)	Friable but heavily matted with roots, mid brown – yellower in SW corner – sandy silt (30–40: 60–70) with sandier lenses; at least 50% stone, large sandstone cobbles, sub-angular and rounded stone shatter, poorly sorted and degraded sandstone; % of stones greater nearer to the curtain to the south; sandier lenses around large stones and shatter. Layer trench-wide 5 m N–S in west, by 2 m in W–E in north, by 5.1 m near N–S in east by 1.5 m in south; depth to south of wall between 0.1 m–0.35 m close to curtain wall. Thinner to north of wall. Over wall, turf removed only as necessary. Bioturbation. ***Turf, soil and rubble south of, over and north of Wall. Turf-consolidated tumble from Wall and core material of Wall that runs N–S through middle of the trench. Trench located just east of end of Edwardian trench running south of curtain and over very slight curve south in the structure.***	Secs: 1.0, 1.1, 1.2 and 1.3
1001 layer: trench south	Below (1000) (1004); above (1005), (1006) ***Top: c. 250.83*** ***Bottom: c. 250.46***	Friable-loose with root matting, mid orangey brown silty sand (30:70/40:60); at least 60% sandstone rubble, sub-rounded, sub-angular cobbles up to 0.2 m long; sub-angular shatter up to 0.1 m; occasional small, rounded pebbles and grit. Located in SW corner of trench, quadrant 0.6 m × 0.6 m along trench edge. Max depth in SW corner 0.4 m, drops away to NE. Boundary clear to turf below. ***End of upcast bank from Edwardian trench: rounded end of long, low bank of material running parallel to Wall c. 1 m to south. Tumble from upcast has slipped north into earlier excavation ditch and NE across contemporary turf. This movement has met (1004) lower layer of post-Edwardian collapse from south side of curtain.***	Sec.: 1.3

(Continued)

WTC: Trench 1			
Context no. *Type*	*Physical relationships* ***Levels mOD***	*Description* ***Interpretation***	*Drawings*
1002 layer: trench north	Below (1000); above (1003) ***Top:* c. *251.3*** ***Bottom: 250.49–45***	Friable, root-matted orangey brown silty sand (40:60); 50–50% small-medium stones; up to 0.35 m, majority *c.* 0.27 m smaller *c.* 0.1 m; rounded and sub-angular, some worked stone; 0.6 m N–S by 0.9 m E–W by max. 0.25 m deep. Boundaries unclear. Bioturbation. ***Collapse and slip of N side of curtain. Most collapse to E, closer to bend.***	Sec.: 1.0
1003 layer: trench north	Below (1002); above [1008] ***Top: 250.49–45*** ***Bottom:* c. *250.39***	Loose-friable mid orangey brown and mid greyish brown, sandy silt (50:50); fine-medium sand. Gravellier layer with more small pebbles and stones than (1002); moderately sorted, very few larger stones. Across whole trench, max. 0.1 m deep. Bioturbation. ***Surviving and slipped core material under curtain collapse; associated with* in-situ *facing stones below.***	Sec.: 1.0
1004 layer: trench south	Below (1000); above (1001), (1005), (1006) ***Top: 250.95–250.62*** ***Bottom:* c. *250.86–250.4***	Friable to loose, some loose gritty sand and root matting, mid orangey brown sandy silt (40:60)/sandy silt (50:50); more sandy lenses than (1000); 60% poorly sorted wall collapse including a few facing stones: largest stones sub-rounded to sub-angular cobbles max width 0.35 m, medium *c.* 0.25 m, smaller 0.1 m with stone shatter, gravel, grit and coarse sand; across trench S of curtain excluding corner of (1001), 1.4 m by 1.5 m by 2 m; depth 0.1–0.4 m; boundaries clearer close to curtain, diffuse where tumble (1001) meets (1004). Bioturbation. ***Lower layer of post-Edwardian collapse, with more stones. Dynamic of fall south from gently curving Wall very apparent. Tail of larger stones with smaller stones and shatter behind, and some larger stones held back by first fall of stones.***	Secs: 1.2 and 1.3
1005 layer: trench south	Below (1004) and (1006); above (1009) ***Top:* c. *250.86*** ***Bottom:* c. *250.11*** ***Against S face of wall***	Friable-loose matrix, 75–80% stones; matrix mid orangey brown, more homogenous then (1004), sandy silt (30:70–10:90); stones, sandstone, one or two possibly igneous; mostly undressed core material with mix similar to (1004), but higher % stone overall and more larger stones; some likely facing stones, including three facing stones slipped together in a rotated line from wall behind; more grit and gravel close to the wall; across width of trench but removed in a slot, *c.* 1 m W–E by 0.6 m N–S; depth max. 0.8 m against the wall; boundaries clear with (1004) and (1009) but some blurring. Bioturbation. ***Pre-Edwardian collapse of the faced wall: impossible to discern whether predominantly the result of one collapse or of a number, or linked to robbing, but the homogeneity of the matrix might support the former idea as might the line of slipped facing stones. Possibly a collapse following episode(s) of robbing? The decayed Edwardian period turf (1006) survived in patches over (1005), dipping down from the SW corner and then gently upwards towards the wall. The turf had clearly been damaged by the fall of stones (1004). Layer (1005) was excavated to its full depth in a slot 1.2 m W–E against the wall in the north, by 0.4 m N–S.***	Secs: 1.2, 1.3
1006 layer: trench south	Below (1001), (1004); above (1005) ***Top:* c. *250.58 S, 250.72 N*** ***Bottom:* c. *250.53 S, 250.62 N***	Friable mid-purple black slightly sandy silt; no inclusions; 0.6 m × 0.6 m quadrant preserved under Edwardian spoil bank in SW corner to a depth of *c.* 0.1 m; very patchy between stones of (1004) and (1005). ***Turf-line preserved under bank of Antiquarian upcast, surviving patchily elsewhere. The Edwardian ground surface dropped slightly to north towards wall from southern trench edge, rising again very gently towards wall after* c. *0.5 m.***	

(Continued)

WTC: Trench 1			
Context no. *Type*	*Physical relationships* ***Levels mOD***	*Description* ***Interpretation***	*Drawings*
1007 structure: trench south	Below (1009); above [1010] ***Top:*** ***251.24W–251.55E*** ***Top (courses):*** ***250.97*** ***Bottom: 249.82***	Sandstone wall, southern face, uneven courses; within trench five complete courses revealed from foundation course on bedrock up (0.97 m high max.); a sixth upper course surviving in the east for five stones (1.2 m length, 1.16 m high max.), facing stones lost to west for 0.8 m length; one *in-situ* stone surviving of seventh course, slightly slipped southwards and situated above last surviving stone to west of course below; behind and rising above the courses, the stones, soil of core material, consolidated with moss and grass. Stones of upper five courses between 0.13–0.18 m high, (majority *c.* 0.18 m) by 0.2–0.3 m wide, (majority *c.* 0.25 m). The third course up from bedrock had more thinner stones 0.13–0.14 m high, the top course closer to sub-square, with one stone 0.18 m high by 0.13 m wide. The course built onto bedrock comprised bigger blocks with rougher faces, all 0.25 m high, only two visible in full length in sondage: 0.23 m and 0.35 m wide. Stones were roughly squared, with relatively un-weathered sharp edges and corners, contrasting to visible courses to west and east of the trench. No evidence at all for repairs or for bonding; the latter may have been dispersed and homogenised in the sandy environment by water and bioturbation. One non-sandstone block stood out on the fourth course up from bedrock: 0.18 m high, 0.27 m wide, a pinkish orange hard igneous stone with sharper edges and corners than the surrounding sandstone. ***South face of Wall built onto bedrock with distinctive foundation course, six courses surviving to height of* c. *1.15 m from bedrock; width of wall: 2.18 m.***	Secs: 1.1, 1.2 and 1.3
1008 structure: trench north	Below (1003); LOE ***Top (courses):*** ***250.39*** ***Bottom:* c. *250.23***	Sandstone wall, northern face; only one complete course seen and tops of course below. Comparing with south face, likely that one foundation course survives beneath partially visible course. Of six stones of course completely revealed: heights 0.19–0.17 m and widths 0.34–0.24 m. Western stones more weathered; newly revealed stones sharper as in south face. No evidence for repair or bonding. ***North face of the Wall: one complete course revealed and upper 0.05 m of one below. At least one further course below the two uncovered likely to survive but further excavation would have destabilised the face. Deliberate robbing aside, this crag-edge face had collapsed to a lower level than the southern one with most of the core and any facing stones having fallen down the face of the crag.***	Sec.: 1.0
1009 layer: trench south	Below (1005); above bedrock/ LOE ***Top:* c. *250.11*** ***Bottom: 249.78***	Friable, wet, mid-light brownish orange, gritty slightly silty sand (10:90), with clay lenses; well-sorted subangular-angular sandstone cobbles max. 0.1 m diam.; no core or wall stones, some rounded pebbles and grit, 65–70% of deposit; in slot *c.* 0.3 m deep to bedrock. Upper spit of layer *c.* 0.08 m deep much siltier with fewer stones. ***Layer corresponding to foundation course of curtain wall. Upper spit could be remains of ground surface; rest possible backfill of wall construction trench/disturbed natural subsoil.***	Secs: 1.2 and 1.3
1010 bedrock	Below [1007]/ [1008], all contexts *Top:* ***249.82 (E)*** ***259.75 (W)***	Whin Sill: dense, hard, black quartz-dolerite, here flat-topped, crisp, sharp and un-weathered suggesting it was below ground when the curtain wall was constructed, and subsequently re-buried, remaining below ground until the excavation. Three vertically divided sections of bedrock were uncovered, all three protruded horizontally out from beneath the wall for 0.25–0.28 m. A 0.2 m width of one section was uncovered in the W, a complete 0.53 m width in the middle, 0.3 m in the E. ***Top of bedrock, un-weathered, on which foundation course of the curtain wall (south face) had been constructed.***	Secs: 1.1, 1.2 and 1.3

WTC: Trench 2

Context no. *Type*	*Physical relationships* ***Levels mOD***	*Description* ***Interpretation***	*Drawings*
2000 layer	Above (2001), (2005) ***Top: from*** **c.** ***250.32–37 (top of spoil bank) to*** **c.** ***250.12–7 (in ditch)***	Friable, matted with roots, mid yellowish-orangey brown sandy silt (30:70), fine sand, with sandier lenses over spoil heap; 50% stone: poorly sorted degraded sandstone, stone shatter and pebbles (0.01–0.1 m), cobbles (0.1–0.2 m), and occasional sandstone sub-rectangular stones up to 0.3m; sandier with greater proportion of stone over Edwardian soil heap. Across trench 2 m × 2 m, *c.* 0.1 m deep, up to 0.15 m in ditch. ***Turf and topsoil layer, matted roots and moss.***	Sec: 2.1
2001 layer	Below (2000), (2005); above (2002) ***Top: 250.28 Level 83 Bottom: 249.97–250.03***	Friable to loose mid yellowish-orangey brown sandy silt, darker with depth (up to 50:50), with fibrous and sandy lenses; 50–60% stone, mostly poorly sorted as above, with 2 larger stones one *c.* 0.2 m, one up to 0.45 m long. 1 m × 1 m from S edge trench in slot running near N–S across spoil heap and ditch in E half of trench. 0.2–0.25 m deep, thinning to N. Heavily rooted. ***Part of linear*** **c.** ***2 m wide Edwardian spoil bank running parallel to Wall,*** **c.** ***1 m from southern face of curtain.***	Sec: 2.1
2002 layer	Below (2001), (2005); above (2003), (2006) ***Top: 249.9–249.98 Levels 30–32 Bottom: 249.88***	Loose-friable, with darker more compact humic patches up to 0.1 m in diameter, mid-greyish black to blackish brown sandy silt (30:70) with paler, sandier lenses around stones; grit and small pebbles *c.* 10%. 2 m N–S × 1 m W–E in slot; very variable depth up to 0.1 m. Rooting and bioturbation. ***Degraded early 20th century turf ground surface, removed by earlier excavation in N of trench, surviving better underneath early 20th century spoil bank in S. Turf however originally also discontinuous in S as formed over large stones in pre-Edwardian collapse.***	Sec: 2.1
2003 layer	Below (2002) (2005); above (2006); LOE S ***Top: 249.87–250 Levels 81–82 Bottom, LOE: 249.65***	Very loose-friable, light orangey brown slightly clayey silty sand (5:10:85) with sandier lenses around stones; up to 75% tightly packed stones, higher proportion of larger sub-rectangular/ angular stones (60% see: DSC_1200) *c.* 0.2 × 0.2 × 0.4 m including some facing stones, remaining angular cobbles up to 0.1 m; 0.1 m × 0.1 m in S end of slot; max depth excavated *c.* 0.3 m. ***Stones and core of pre-early 20th century collapse(s) of curtain wall, with some development of soil between stones. To N of the spoil bank this collapse removed by the Edwardian excavation.***	Sec: 2.1
2004 structure	Above [1010]; abutted by (2000), (2005) (2006) ***Top:*** **c.** ***250.4 Bottom: 249.86 in E, 249.95–250.05 in centre, 250.25 in W***	Up to three roughly faced, uneven courses of carboniferous sandstone curtain wall; stones in bottom two foundation courses built onto bedrock and more varied in size, from 0.35 m wide by 0.2 m high to 0.1 m^2 levelling chock-style stones. Only two stones of lowest foundation course visible in west of trench where bedrock drops by at least 0.15 m. Surviving Wall course above foundation courses missing two facing stones; remaining eight from 0.2–0.25 m wide by 0.1–0.15 m high. The complete foundation course above protrudes out from beneath the course above by up to 0.15 m. No evidence for bonding, alteration or repair. ***Curtain wall: three courses surviving built directly onto uneven whinstone bedrock, with small chock stones used to level the lower course above domed weathered bedrock outcross in the east. Two stones seen of third and lower course west of the higher bedrock, built onto bedrock below. The weathering of the rock suggests this patch of bedrock was visible when the curtain wall was constructed. Wall stones also weathered and rounded. Bottom of lowest visible course in west at 249.86 mOD (compare bottom of foundation course in Trench 1 at 249.82 mOD).***	Secs: 2.0, 2.1

(Continued)

WTC: Trench 2			
Context no. *Type*	*Physical relationships* ***Levels mOD***	*Description* ***Interpretation***	*Drawings*
2005 layer	Below (2000); above (2001), (2002), (2006) ***Top: 249.98–250.18*** ***Bottom: 249.88***	Friable mid-dark yellowish brown sandy silt (40:60), with sandy and humic lenses; 40% stone, poorly sorted from grit to 0.15 m long, both angular and rounded. In N half of slot, up to 0.25 m deep against [2004], thinning to the S. Heavily rooted. ***Post-Edwardian tumble likely formed over a longer period, with patches of decayed turf amidst the soil and stones. In this area the early 20th century excavation has removed (2002) the contemporary turf and (2003) the pre-Edwardian collapse. The layer also probably contains drifts of material from the spoil bank to the S.***	Sec: 2.1
2006 fill/layer	Below (2003), (2005); LOE N ***Top: 249.79–249.81*** ***Levels 79–80*** ***Bottom: 249.63***	Friable, mid-light orangey brown gritty, slightly silty sand (20:80) with some clayey lenses; grit; some rounded pebbles and stone shatter but predominantly well-sorted sub-angular/angular stone cobbles max. 0.1 m, *c.* 70% of context. In N half of slot against bedrock [1010]; max depth 0.2 m in N. LOE. ***Redeposited subsoil and cobbles, probably the original back-fill of the Roman foundation trench and or*** **in situ** ***subsoil when curtain constructed: no signs in surviving courses of repair. No evidence of a cut, likely to have been obliterated by later collapse. Upper spit of layer probably removed by Edwardian excavation.***	Sec: 2.1
1010 bedrock	Below [2004], all contexts ***Top: 249.88 (W) 250.25 (E)***	Whin Sill: dense, hard, black quartz-dolerite, here weathered suggesting it has been above ground for a considerable time; perhaps visible when the curtain wall was constructed, and subsequently either buried or exposed until the Edwardian excavation. ***Bedrock: weathered, four vertical columns visible with convex/ concave tops, lowest and furthest west column less weathered; furthest west 0.3 m seen, to east 0.75 m wide and protruding 0.3m from out from wall, next column 0.85 m wide and protruding 0.1 m, furthest east 0.25 m width seen, protruding 0.1 m.***	Secs: 2.0, 2.1

Appendix 2

Specialist report data

Across the many site investigations conducted by WallCAP, a series of different investigative techniques were employed generating discrete sets of specialist data. For those sites reported in this volume where detailed data of the presentation is unnecessary to locate alongside the interpretation, the data is collated in this appendix. The data is sorted into two parts. The first part consists of further information from Cam Beck and Corbridge that is supplementary to the main chapter on each site. The second part is a brief summary of fabric consolidation at Cat's Stairs, Port Carlisle, Steel Rigg, and turret 44b (Mucklebank).

Cam Beck: Gorge survey

Rob Collins and Nicky Garland

The following tables provide supplemental data on the stones in the gorge survey at Cam Beck, as discussed in Chapter 6.

Table A2.1: Dislodged stonework along eastern base of the weir. Dimensions are in metres and N/A means it was not possible to undertake measurement.

Stone number	*Length*	*Width*	*Thickness*	*Notes*
N	0.48	0.3	0.19	Partially submerged
O	> 0.3	0.24	0.12	
P	0.9	0.3	0.12	
Q	0.6	0.25	0.1	
R	0.5	0.27	0.12	
S	1.16	0.28	0.14	
T	0.66	N/A	N/A	Not accessible for measuring other dimensions
U	0.52	N/A	N/A	Not accessible for measuring other dimensions
V	0.46	N/A	N/A	Not accessible for measuring other dimensions
W				Tooling marks present on wall within U shaped cut – not accessible for measurements

Table A2.2: Dressed stones found at the western terminal of the weir, labelled A–I. Dimensions in metres, N/A indicates it was not possible to undertake measurement, due to being submerged in the water or within the soil of the bank, or some combination thereof.

Stone number	*Length*	*Width*	*Thickness*	*Notes*
A	>0.83	N/A	N/A	Lewis hole 0.16 from top of stone and 0.19 from base. Lewis hole measures 0.1 m long and 0.1 m deep (water erosion likely).
B	>0.95	N/A	N/A	
C	N/A	N/A	0.16	Mortar base separating stonework from D and B
D	0.44	0.18	0.17	

(Continued)

Table A2.2: Dressed stones found at the western terminal of the weir, labelled A–I. Dimensions in metres, N/A indicates it was not possible to undertake measurement, due to being submerged in the water or within the soil of the bank, or some combination thereof. (Continued)

Stone number	*Length*	*Width*	*Thickness*	*Notes*
E	0.95	0.8	N/A	Lewis hole 0.49 m from N edge and 0.38 m from E edge. Lewis hole measures 0.03 m wide and 0.08 m long
F	0.48	0.32	0.2	Dislodged stone 1.1 m from main blockwork. Approx. 18 tool marks on unexposed face (chisel grooves)
G	1.1	0.96	0.33	Tooling along top edge under moss – all along same orientation. Groove/cut on eastern edge, measures 0.15 × 0.13 m. A shallow groove extends from edge of the stone to the cut out. Square socket measures 0.08 × 0.045 and 0.04 m deep. Lewis hole in line with cut out (0.46 m away). Measures 0.08 × 0.045 m, depth >0.09 m
H	1.05	N/A	0.17	
I	0.97	0.53	N/A	Lewis hole centred on stone. Measures 0.08 m long and 0.03 m wide

Table A2.3: Stones projecting out of the east bank of the gorge (1–27), as well as stonework laying at the base of the eastern bank below the projecting stones and extending north toward the weir (I–XXIV). Dimensions are provided in metres, N/A means it was not possible to undertake measurement.

Stone number	*Length*	*Width*	*Thickness*	*Notes*
I	0.6	0.3	0.13	
II	0.72	0.26	>0.1	
III	0.69	0.29	0.2	
IV	0.87	0.3	0.15	
V	0.9	0.35	0.22	Tooling on north face above water line
VI	0.84	0.33	0.16	Slight groove on top, unsure if human made or natural weathering due to water action
VII	>0.76	0.33	0.13	Partially shattered
VIII	0.82	0.37	0.17	Weathered tooling on upper face
IX	0.52	0.3	0.25	
X	0.54	0.33	0.23	
XI	0.9	0.3	0.15	
XII	0.71	0.27	0.19	
XIII	>0.56	0.33	0.15	Covered in vegetation so difficult to measure exact dimensions
XIV	0.5	0.3	0.18	
XV	1.08	0.31	0.15	
XVI	0.5	0.3	0.14	
XVII	0.6	0.34	0.16	
XVIII	>0.4	>0.32	0.18	Partially obscured by stone XVII
XIX	0.54	0.387	0.22	
XX	0.7	0.29	0.13	
XXI	0.63	0.31	0.17	Possibly trapezoidal in shape
XXII	0.64	0.32	0.21	
XXIII	0.69	0.3	>0.13	
XXIV	0.88	0.24	0.16	
Below measurements from blockwork eroding out of the bank – only selected stones measured				
1		0.28	0.15	
6		0.3	0.18	
8				Possible tooling on northern face

(Continued)

Table A2.3: (Continued)

Stone number	Length	Width	Thickness	Notes
10				Wedged shape, although this may be due to weathering. Tooling at end of stone
13	>0.8	0.32	0.21	Tooling on northern face
15				Tooling on western face
16	>0.52	0.3	0.13	
18				Weathered tooling on north and western faces
19	>0.48	0.28	0.18	Tooling on western faces (worn chisel?)
20				Tooling
24				Tooling at end
27				Laminated – split into 4–5 pieces

Table A2.4: Dislodged stonework found approx. 100–150 m downstream of the weir. Dimensions given in metres, N/A means it was not possible to undertake measurement.

Stone number	Length	Width	Thickness	Notes
1	0.99	0.68	0.52	Sharpe edges indicate possible cut stone
2	0.33	0.28	0.15	Socket cut into stone, measures 0.065 m diameter and 0.035 m deep
3	0.8	0.5 (as visible)	>0.18	Partly submerged in silt and gravel
4	0.32	0.15	0.1	Loose piece of possible moulding, found 0.7 m from socketed stone (no 2)

Charred plant remains and wood charcoal assessment: Cam Beck, Corbridge, and Heddon-on-the-Wall

Ellen Simmons

Introduction

A series of bulk samples were taken during archaeological excavations at three sites investigated by WallCAP. Six samples, representing 74 L of sediment, were taken from foundation structures and buildings at Cam Beck. A total of 15 samples, representing 130 L of sediment, were taken from features associated with buildings and a road located at the northern edge of the Roman town of Corbridge. One 10 L sample was taken from the bottom of the Vallum ditch at Heddon-on-the-Wall.

Aims and objectives

- To determine the concentration, diversity, state of preservation and suitability for use in scientific dating, of any paleoenvironmental material present in the samples.
- To evaluate the potential of any paleoenvironmental material present in the samples to provide evidence for crop plants and/or wild plant foods.
- To evaluate the potential of any paleoenvironmental material present in the samples to provide evidence for the local environment or land use.

Methodology

The bulk samples were processed by the author using a water separation machine. Floating material was collected in a 300 μm mesh, and the remaining heavy residue retained in a 1 mm mesh. Flots and heavy residues were air dried. The >4 mm fractions of the heavy residues were sorted for artefacts and ecofacts. The 2–4 mm fractions were scanned by eye and the abundance of wood charcoal was recorded. The abundance of small artefacts or identifiable ecofacts such as molluscs or fish bone in the 2–4 mm fractions was also recorded. Magnetic material (such as hammerscale) was extracted from the 2–4 mm and 1–2 mm fractions using a large magnet.

The samples were assessed in accordance with Historic England guidelines for environmental archaeology assessments (Campbell *et al.* 2011) and the CIfA toolkit for specialist reporting (CIfA 2021). A preliminary assessment of the samples was made by scanning using a stereo-binocular microscope (x10–x65) and recording the abundance of the main classes of material present. All material present in the samples was quantified using a scale of abundance (- = < 10 items, + = 10–29 items, ++ = 30–49 items, +++ = 50–99 items, ++++ = 100–499 items, +++++ = > 500 items).

Preliminary identification of plant material was carried out by comparison with material in the reference collections at the Department of Archaeology, University of Sheffield, and various reference works (*e.g.* Cappers *et al.* 2006). Cereal identifications and nomenclature follow Zohary *et al.* (2012). Other plant nomenclature follows Stace (2019). The composition of the samples is recorded in Table A2.5. The seed, in the broadest sense, of the plant is always referred to in Table A2.5, unless stated otherwise. The abbreviation *cf.* means 'compares with' and denotes that a specimen most closely resembles that taxon more than any other.

State of preservation

Preservation of plant macrofossils and wood is by charring. Preservation of charred plant material is relatively poor. Most of the cereal grains are puffed and distorted, with only fragments of epidermis remaining. Preservation of wood charcoal is good, although some fragments have been affected by vitrification, whereby charcoal takes on a glassy appearance that potentially hampers identification or the recording of dendrological features.

The presence of modern roots, uncharred seeds and fly puparia in many of the bulk samples indicates the presence of some intrusive material and therefore some degree of bioturbation.

Results

Charred plant remains

Cam Beck (site code: CB21)

Low concentrations of charred plant remains, consisting of cereal grain, onion couch grass tuber (*Arrhenatherum elatius* ssp. *bulbosm*), heather family (Ericaceae) stem fragments and/or wild/weed plant seeds, were found in hearth fill (2018), layer (2004) and pit fill (2009).

Only sample 6 from hearth fill (2018) produced cereal grain, which was only identifiable as indeterminate wheat (*Triticum* sp.). The wild/weed plant seed assemblage includes brome grass (*Bromus* sp.) and orache (*Atriplex* sp.), which are typical crop weeds or plants of fertile disturbed soils. Seeds of sedge (*Carex* sp.) are also present, most of the species of which are associated with damp soils, as well as small-seeded grasses (<2 mm Poaceae). A fragment of onion couch grass tuber and a grass stem node (<2 mm culm node) were also found.

Sample 1 from layer (2004) produced a small assemblage of wild/weed plant seeds consisting of vetch/vetchling (*Vicia/Lathyrus* sp.), nettle (*Urtica dioica*) and a small seeded grass. A tuber/rhizome and a small quantity of heather family (Ericaceae) stem fragments were also present. Sample 2 from pit fill (209) produced a small grass seed.

The remaining samples were largely devoid of charred plant remains except for occasional heather family stem fragments. Sample 4 from possible turf layer (2014) produced a high concentration of black spherical fungal sclerotia, likely to be from the soil dwelling fungus *Cenococcum*, which is consistent with the interpretation of this layer as possible turf.

Corbridge (site code: COR21)

Low to moderate concentrations of charred plant remains, consisting of cereal grain, hazel nutshell (*Corylus avellana*), heather family stem fragments, tuber/rhizome and wild/weed plant seeds, were found in several samples. Cereal grains were found in a series of samples from water conduit fills (4012) and (4029) and a layer (4007) within a structure in Trench 4, as well as in possible oven fill (5016), oven fill (5022) and drain/trough fill (5018) in Trench 5.

Samples 2 and 3 from water conduit fill (4012), sample 7 from water conduit fill (4029) and sample 2 from possible oven deposit (5016) produced low concentrations of cereal grain, hazel nutshell and wild/weed plant seeds. The cereal grain assemblage includes spelt wheat (*Triticum spelta*) and indeterminate wheat. The wild/weed plant seeds associated with the cereal grain include a range of typical crop weeds or plants of fertile disturbed soils such as redshank/pale persicaria (*Persicaria maculosa/lapathifolia*), chickweed (*Stellaria media*), fat hen (*Chenopodium album*), cleavers (*Galium aparine*), scentless mayweed (*Tripleurospermum inodorum*) and brome grass (*Bromus* sp.).

Sample 3 from drain/trough fill (5018) and sample 5 from oven fill (5022) produced low concentrations of cereal grain and hazel nutshell but moderately high concentration of wild/weed plant seeds. The cereal grain assemblage includes spelt wheat and indeterminate wheat. The wild/weed plant seed assemblage includes taxa more commonly associated with grassland or heath than with cultivation such as lesser spearwort (*Ranunculus flammula*), stitchwort (*Stellaria graminea*), hemlock (*Conium maculatum*), heath grass (*Danthonia decumbens*), ribwort plantain (*Plantago lanceolata*), sedges (*Carex* spp.) and small seeded grasses (<2 mm Poaceae).

Sample 6 from the fill (4013) of a near complete pottery base produced a single seed of fat hen. A high concentration of burnt bone was also found in the heavy fraction of this sample, along with a small (approx. 8 mm diameter) flattened metal ring.

Heddon-on-the-Wall (site code: HW21)

Sample 1 from the deliberate backfill of the Vallum ditch produced no charred plant remains.

Wood charcoal

Cam Beck (site code: CB21)

Wood charcoal fragments greater than 2 mm in size were found in all the samples, although only hearth fill (2018), layer (2013) and layer (2015) produced charcoal assemblages with more than 50 >2 mm fragments.

Sample 6 from hearth fill (2018) produced a high concentration of >2 mm wood charcoal, which includes over 100 fragments of >4 mm and over 100 fragments of 2–4 mm. Preliminary examination using low power microscopy indicates that the assemblage is composed primarily of diffuse porous taxa (such as hazel/birch/alder, hawthorn/apple/pear/whitebeam, willow/poplar, cherry/blackthorn and field maple), along with some ring porous taxa (such as oak, ash or elm). Several fragments of small diameter round wood are also present.

Sample 3 from layer (2013) also produced a high concentration of >2 mm wood charcoal fragments, which includes between 10 and 30 >4 mm fragments and over

100 fragments of 2–4 mm. Most of the charcoal fragments in this sample were, however, found in the heavy fraction rather than the flot. This may be due to silt particles penetrating the vessel cavities of the wood charcoal fragments thereby reducing buoyancy. Preliminary examination indicates the presence of both diffuse porous and ring porous taxa, including some probable oak (cf. *Quercus*) with closely spaced annual growth rings.

Sample 5 from layer (2015) produced a moderately high concentration of >2 mm wood charcoal which includes between 30 and 50 >4 mm fragments and between 50 and 100 2–4 mm fragments. Preliminary examination indicates the presence of both ring porous and diffuse porous taxa, including several fragments of small diameter round wood.

Corbridge (site code: COR21)

Wood charcoal fragments greater than 2 mm in size were found in most of the samples. Foundation trench fill (5032), oven fill (5022), sub-circular stone feature fill (5028), water conduit fills (4012) and (4029), layer (4007) and drain/trough fill (5018) produced charcoal assemblages with more than 50 >2 mm fragments.

Sample 8 from foundation trench fill (5032) produced a high concentration of >2 mm wood charcoal, which includes between 50 and 100 >4 mm fragments and over 100 2–4 mm fragments. Preliminary examination indicates the presence of both ring porous and diffuse porous taxa, including occasional fragments of possible small diameter round wood.

Sample 5 from oven fill (5022) and sample 7 from sub-circular stone feature fill (5028) produced high concentrations of >2 mm wood charcoal, which include between 20 and 50 >4 mm fragments and over 100 2–4 mm fragments. Preliminary examination indicates the presence of both ring porous and diffuse porous taxa, including occasional fragments of small diameter round wood.

Samples 2 and 3 from water conduit fill (4012), sample 7 from water conduit fill (4029) and sample 4 from layer (4007) produced moderate concentrations of >2 mm wood charcoal, which include between 10 and 30 >4 mm fragments and between 50 and 100 2–4 mm fragments. Preliminary examination indicates the presence of only diffuse porous taxa, including several fragments of small diameter round wood.

Sample 3 from drain/trough fill (5018) produced a moderate concentration of >2 mm wood charcoal, which includes less than 10 >4 mm fragments and between 50 and 100 2–4 mm fragments. Preliminary examination indicates the presence of mostly diffuse porous taxa along with some ring porous taxa. Occasional fragments of small diameter round wood are also present.

Heddon-on-the-Wall (site code: HW21)

Sample 1 from the deliberate backfill of the Vallum ditch produced a low concentration of >2 mm wood charcoal, which includes less than 10 fragments of diffuse porous taxa. One fragment of >4 mm roundwood charcoal is present.

Hammerscale

Low to moderate concentrations of hammerscale were found in the heavy fractions of a small number of samples from Trench 4 at Corbridge (COR21). Samples 2 and 3 from water conduit fill (4012) produced low concentrations of between 30 and 50 pieces of hammerscale and sample 7 from water conduit fill (4029) produced a moderate concentration of over 100 pieces of hammerscale. Low concentrations of hammerscale were also found in samples 1 and 5 from roadside ditch fills (4010) and (4021).

Discussion of potential

The low to moderate concentrations of charred plant remains found in the samples from Cam Beck and Corbridge have some very limited potential to provide evidence for cereal crops. The sample from the Vallum ditch at Heddon-on-the-Wall has no potential to provide evidence for crop plants or wild plant foods.

The only positively identified crop type is spelt wheat, which is a typical crop of the Roman period and has been found at several Roman period sites in northeast England such as the Romano-British settlement at Thornborough, Northumberland, located 2 km to the south east of Corbridge (van der Veen 1992), at the Roman fort of Birdoswald (Huntley 1991; 1997), located 9 km to the east of Cam Beck and at the Roman fort of Vindolanda, located 25 km to the west of Corbridge and 28 km to the east of Cam Beck (Huntley 2003; 2007). The presence of a small quantity of hazel nutshell in the samples from Corbridge may also indicate the gathering of wild plant foods.

The cereal grain is likely to have been charred accidentally during parching, drying, or cooking and therefore suggests the presence of domestic hearth or oven waste. The low density and poor preservation of the charred cereal grain suggests that this material has been reworked and redeposited into the fills of features across the sites over time. The burnt bone and pottery fragments found in many of the samples from Corbridge that produced charred cereal grain, also suggests the presence of domestic waste.

Many of the wild/weed plant seeds from typical crop weeds or plants of fertile disturbed soils, which are associated with cereal grain in samples from Cam Beck and Corbridge, are likely to be from weeds that were brought to site along with the crops, therefore indicating the presence of by-products from crop processing, which was charred as waste or used as fuel. The wild/weed plant seed assemblages may therefore have some limited potential to provide evidence for crop husbandry practices. The presence of nitrophilous taxa such as redshank/pale persicaria, chickweed, cleavers, fat hen and brome grass, in association with cereal grain in water conduit fills (4012) and (4029), as well as in possible oven deposit (5016) at Corbridge, suggest the cultivation of nutrient rich soils.

Table A2.5: Archaeobotanical sample assessment.

Context/ Feature No.	*Sample No.*	*Context description*	*Date*	*Sample volume (l)*	*Roots (ml)/ flot volume excluding roots (ml)*	*Grain/ chaff*	*Wild or weed plant material*	*>4/ >2 mm charcoal from flot*	*>4/ >2 mm charcoal from residue*	*Notes*
Cam Beck (CB21): Trench 2										
2004	1	Organic silty layer over cobbled yard	Roman (2nd C?)	10	10/1	0/0	–	0/-	-/++	**CPR:** *Vicia/Lathyrus* spp., *Urtica dioica*, <2 mm Poaceae Tuber/rhizome (-). Ericaceae stem fragments (-) **WC:** DP (two fragments of >4mm round wood) **>4 mm HF:** Ceramic (-)
2009	2	Organic silty fill of pit [2010]	Roman (2nd C?)	20	0.1/3	0/0	–	0/-	+/0	**CPR:** <2 mm Poaceae **WC:** DP **>4 mm HF:** Ceramic (-), bone (-) Modern fallen tree seeds. *Chenopodium* (uc). *Rubus* (uc). Fly puparia. Invertebrate remains
2013	3	Charcoal rich deposit within layer over cobbled yard/ interior with hearth	Roman (2nd C?)	10	0.1/3	0/0	0	-/-	+/++++	**CPR:** Ericaceae stem fragments (-) **WC:** DP and RP (cf. *Quercus* sp. with narrow rings) **>4 mm HF:** Bone (-) Modern fallen tree seeds. *Chenopodium* (uc).
2014	4	Possible turf layer under structural foundations	Roman (2nd C?)	10	2/0.1	0/0	0	0/-	-/++	**WC:** DP, bark (2 fragments of >4 mm roundwood) *Cenococcum* sclerotia (++++) Modern fallen tree seeds.
2015	5	Charcoal rich layer within stony deposit	Roman (2nd C?)	10	2/1.5	0/0	0	-/-	++/+++	**CPR:** Ericaceae stem fragments (-) **WC:** RP and DP (six fragments of >4 mm roundwood) **>4 mm HF:** Bone (-), metal (-), slag (-) Modern fallen tree seeds.
2018	6	Charcoal rich fill from base of hearth	Roman (2nd C?)	14	20/10	-/	–	+/+++	++++/ ++++	**CPR:** *Triticum* sp. grain. >2 mm Poaceae. *Carex* sp., *Atriplex* sp. <2mm Pocaeae cf. *Arrhenatherum elatius* ssp. *bulbosum* tuber. <2 mm culm node **WC:** DP (seven fragments of >4 mm round wood) some RP Thorns (+) **>4 mm HF:** Bone (-) Modern fallen tree seeds. Fly puparia

(Continued)

Table A2.5: (Continued)

Context/ Feature No.	*Sample No.*	*Context description*	*Date*	*Sample volume (l)*	*Roots (ml)/ flot volume excluding roots (ml)*	*Grain/ chaff*	*Wild or weed plant material*	*>4/ >2 mm charcoal from flot*	*>4/ >2 mm charcoal from residue*	*Notes*
Corbridge (COR21): Trench 4										
4010	1	Fill of roadside ditch S of Roman road		10	5/0.1	0/0	0	0/0	0/0	Indet. charred vitreous material (+) **>4 mm HF:** Bone (+++), CBM (+), metal (-), hammerscale (++)
4012	2	Fill of water conduit. E half section		10	0.5/10	-/0	–	+/+++	-/++	**CPR:** *Triticum spelta* grain. *Persicaria maculosa/ lapathifolia, Stellaria media, Bromus* sp. **WC:** DP (six fragments of >4 mm round wood) some RP **>4 mm HF:** Bone (+++), ceramic (-), CBM (-), slag (-), hammerscale (++)
4012	3	Fill of water conduit. W half section		10	0.2/5	-/0	–	-/++	+/++	**CPR:** *Triticum spelta, Triticum* sp. grain. *Plantago lanceolata, Tripleurospermum inodorum*, <2 mm Poaceae. *Corylus avellana* nutshell Ericaceae stem fragments (-) **WC:** DP (five fragments of >4 mm roundwood) **>4 mm HF:** Bone (+++), ceramic (-), metal (-), slag (-), hammerscale (++)
4007	4	Silty layer internal to structure		10	0.5/10	-/0	0	+/+++	-/-	**CPR:** *Triticum spelta, Triticum* sp. grain. *Carex* sp., **WC:** DP (four fragments of >4 mm roundwood) **>4 mm HF:** Bone (+++), ceramic (+), metal (-), slag (-)
4021	5	Fill of possible earlier roadside ditch S of Roman road		6	2/0.5	0/0	0	0/-	0/0	**WC:** DP **>4 mm HF:** Bone (+), metal (-), slag (-), hammerscale (+) Indet. charred vitreous material (+)
4013	6	Fill of near complete pottery base within pit		3	0.2/<0.1	0/0	–	0/0	-/-	**CPR:** *Chenopodium album* **WC:** RP **>4 mm HF:** Bone (+++), CBM (+), ceramic (-), metal ring (-)
4029	7	Fill of water conduit E of samples 2 and 3		10	0.2/4	-/-	–	-/++	+/++	**CPR:** *Triticum spelta, Triticum* sp. grain. >2 mm culm node. *Carex* sp. <2mm Poaceae **WC:** DP (three fragments of >4 mm roundwood) **>4 mm HF:** Bone (+++), ceramic (-), CBM (-), slag (-), hammerscale (++++)

(Continued)

Table A2.5: Archaeobotanical sample assessment. (Continued)

Context/ Feature No.	*Sample No.*	*Context description*	*Date*	*Sample volume (l)*	*Roots (ml)/ flot volume excluding roots (ml)*	*Grain/ chaff*	*Wild or weed plant material*	*>4/ >2 mm charcoal from flot*	*>4/ >2 mm charcoal from residue*	*Notes*
Corbridge (COR21): Trench 5										
5015	1	Silty fill of small pit		4	<0.1/<0.1	0/0	0	0/0	0/0	Indet. charred vitreous material (+) **>4 mm HF:** Bone (-), metal (-)
5016	2	Deposit above circular stone feature: possible oven		10	2/0.5	-/0	0	-/-	0/-	**CPR:** *Triticum spelta, Triticum* sp. grain. *Galium aparine, Chenopodium album, Stellaria media* **WC:** DP (two fragments of >4 mm roundwood) **>4 mm HF:** Bone (-), ceramic (-)
5018	3	Fill of drain/ trough		10	4/10	-/0	++	-/+++	-/+	**CPR:** *Triticum* sp. grain. Asteraceae. Fabaceae. *Carex* sp. <2 mm Poaceae, *Danthonia decumbens, Ranunculus flammula, Plantago lanceolata, Chenopodium* sp. **WC:** DP (two fragments of >4 mm roundwood) some RP **>4mm HF:** Bone (+++), ceramic (-), CBM (-), metal (-), slag (-)
5021	4	Burnt clay related to oven, below (5016)		7	0/0	0/	0	0/0	0/0	**>4mm HF:** Burnt clay (++++)
5022	5	Charcoal rich silty clay: oven remains		10	0/7	-/0	++	-/+++	++/++++	**CPR:** *Triticum spelta, Triticum* sp. grain. *Conium maculatum, Stellaria graminea, Stellaria media, Asteraceae, Trifolium/Medicago, Plantago lanceolata, Danthonia decumbens*, *Carex* spp. <2mm Poaceae, *Urtica urens*, Unidentified seed (four types) *Corylus avellana* nutshell (-), Ericaceae stem fragments (-) **WC:** DP and RP (one DP and two RP fragments of >4 mm round wood charcoal) **>4 mm HF:** Ceramic (+), CBM (+++), metal (-), bone (-)
5018	6	Lower primary fill of drain/ trough below (5018)		10	0/1	0/0	–	0/-	+/+++	**CPR:** <2 mm Poaceae. Tuber/rhizome (-) **WC:** RP and DP (three fragments of >4 mm round wood) Indet. charred vitreous material (+) **>4mm HF:** Bone (+), CBM (-), ceramic (-)

(Continued)

Table A2.5: (Continued)

Context/ Feature No.	*Sample No.*	*Context description*	*Date*	*Sample volume (l)*	*Roots (ml)/ flot volume excluding roots (ml)*	*Grain/ chaff*	*Wild or weed plant material*	*>4/ >2 mm charcoal from flot*	*>4/ >2 mm charcoal from residue*	*Notes*
5028	7	Organic fill of sub-circular stone feature		10	0/10	0/0	–	+/+++	+/+++	**CPR:** *Urtica urens*, *Carex* spp. **WC:** DP and RP (one RP and five DP fragments of >4 mm roundwood) **>4 mm HF:** Bone (+), ceramic (-), CBM (-), slag (-)
5032	8	Organic deposit at bottom of wall foundation trench		10	0/<0.1	0/0	–	0/0	+++/ ++++	**CPR:** *Carex* sp. **WC:** DP and RP (two fragments of >4 mm possible roundwood) Indet. charred vitreous material (-) **>4 mm HF:** Bone (-), ceramic (-), CBM (-), slag (-)
Heddon-on-the-Wall (HW21)										
Ditch fill	1	Deliberate backfill of Vallum ditch		10	0/0.2	0/0	0	0/-	-/-	**WC:** DP (one fragment of >2 mm round wood) Indet. charred vitreous material (+)

key – = < 10 items, + = 10–29 items, ++ = 30–49 items, +++ = 50–99 items, ++++ = 100–499 items, +++++ = > 500 items. CPR = charred plant remains, WC = wood charcoal. DP = diffuse porous charcoal, RP = ring porous charcoal. HR = heavy residue. uc = uncharred

Some of the wild/weed plant seeds may, however, be from sources other than crop weeds. The wild/weed seed assemblages found in drain/trough fill (5018) and oven fill (5022) at Corbridge include a range of taxa such as lesser spearwort, stitchwort, hemlock, ribwort plantain and heath grass, which are more commonly associated with grassland or heath. Heath grass is common in Roman archaeobotanical assemblages from northern England and is one of a suite of crop weeds that have been associated with larger scale arable production and arable expansion in the Iron Age and Roman periods in northeast England (van der Veen 1992). It has also been suggested, however, that heath grass is one of a suite of taxa that may be indicators of the presence of turf, particularly when these taxa are found in association with heather family stem fragments and tuber/rhizomes (Hall and Huntley 2007, 213). Heather family stem fragments have been found at many Iron Age and Roman sites in northern England, including at Birdoswald and Vindolanda Roman forts (Huntley 1991), indicating the widespread exploitation of heathland for plant resources in the region (Hall and Huntley 2007, 213). Full sorting and identification of the wild/weed plant seed assemblage in drain/trough fill (5018) and oven fill (5022) from Corbridge may provide further evidence for the likely origin of these remains, as several of the wild/weed plant taxa found in the samples could not be identified during assessment.

The wood charcoal assemblage from Cam Beck and Corbridge has good potential to provide evidence for the availability and exploitation of local woodland. Where at least 50 charcoal fragments of a suitable size for identification are present, this is more likely to result in a representative sample of wood use, including rare taxa (Stuijts 2006). The charcoal assemblage from Heddon-on-the-Wall has no potential to provide evidence for the availability and exploitation of woodland.

The charcoal assemblages from Cam Beck and Corbridge are likely to be from mixed hearth waste and include large and small diameter wood from diffuse and ring porous taxa. These assemblages therefore have good potential to provide evidence for the use of a range of different woody taxa as domestic fuel. Comparable wood charcoal assemblages from the Roman forts at Vindolanda and Birdoswald include oak and diffuse porous taxa identified as either hazel/alder/birch, along with evidence for the use of heather as oven fuel (Huntley 1991; 2003; 2007).

Significance of the plant macrofossil and wood charcoal assemblage

Although only low to moderate concentrations of charred plant remains were found in the samples from Cam Beck and Corbridge, these assemblages are still of regional research significance as evidence for farming practices at sites associated with Hadrian's Wall. Only a small number of sites associated with Hadrian's Wall, and Roman sites in northeast England in general, have produced charred plant remains (Petts and Gerrard 2006, 155; Hall and Huntley 2007, 65). It is unlikely, however, that full sorting and identification of the charred plant remains assemblage from most of the samples would produce any significant additional evidence to that found during preliminary assessment.

The evidence for grassland and/or heathland plants found in samples from drain/trough fill (5018) and oven fill (5022) at Corbridge are of regional research significance as evidence for the exploitation of plant resources from grassland or heaths for use as fodder, roofing, bedding, fuel, or construction material. Due to the presence of more than 30 wild/weed plant seeds in these samples, including several taxa that could not be identified during preliminary assessment, full sorting and identification of this material would be expected to provide additional evidence to that found during preliminary assessment.

The charcoal assemblages from Cam Beck and Corbridge are of regional research significance as evidence for the availability and exploitation of woodland during the Roman period in northeast England (Petts and Gerrard 2006, 155). Evidence from wood charcoal assemblages can complement evidence from pollen sequences or provide evidence for woodland availability where pollen evidence is lacking. The identification and analysis of wood charcoal from sites associated with Hadrian's Wall, and Roman sites in northeast England in general, is rare (Huntley 2010, 30). The analysis of charcoal from hearths or oven deposits is a research priority to provide comparable material for wood used in industrial activity in the Roman period (Huntley 2010, 63). Analysis of the wood charcoal assemblage would also provide complimentary evidence to that potentially present for the use of plant material as fuel in the charred plant remains assemblage.

Corbridge: assessment of animal bone (COR21)

Don O'Meara

During the course of the COR21 excavations, bone was hand collected. This material totalled *c.* 6.4 kg of bone. The assemblage is represented by material from 76 contexts. The material was given a rapid assessment by the author to characterise the remains, set out here. Notes on the assessment are presented below as Table A2.6, where the context number, weight, approximate number of unidentified fragments, and general notes are presented.

Cattle: The assemblage as a whole is dominated by bones of cattle, and typically from the denser elements such as the bones of the foot, molars, and the denser parts of the vertebra. Relative to their proportions in the skeleton, there are few remains from the ribs and the midshaft of long bones. The proximal-intermediate-distal phalanges ('toe bones') made up the most common intact element, with 23 examples from the assemblage as a whole. Twenty-six cattle vertebra fragments (mainly from the centrum) were also recovered.

It is interpreted that the assemblage has been impacted by both the nature of the burial environment (relatively shallow, and in a region with typically acid soils),

Table A2.6: Animal bone from COR21 excavations summarised by context.

Context	Weight	Unid. frags	Notes on ID'd bone
1003	90	11	Cattle – 2 vertebra, carpal, fragments molars; bird femur fragment
1006	230	16	Cattle – talus, mandible frag, molar, rib, caudal vert. oyster, +fragmented teeth
1008	40	10	Cattle – vert. 2 mandible frags. Premolar frag,
1012	17	4	Cattle – distal phalange
1016	50	6	Cattle – molar, intermediate phalange, vertebra fragment
1016	145	16	Cattle – distal humerus, distal metapodial fragment, rib fragments. Very abraded
1021	39	15	Pig – 3 molars, possible mandible fragment; cattle – molar fragment
2003	4	4	Fragments of burnt bone
2004	57		Concentration of burnt bone
2018	1	1	Burnt bone fragment
3002	79	12	Sheep – 7 skull fragments, left talus,
3004	8	3	Cattle – molar, vertebra fragment, burnt bone
4000	472		See written report for further details
4001	136	22	Cattle – carpal, 2 vertebra fragments, 2 rib fragments; Sheep – molar, proximal phalange fragments
4003	43	9	Cattle – proximal phalange fragments
4004	23	19	Cattle – 2 rib fragments, calcinated and unburnt fragments
4005	660	100+	Cattle – proximal scapula, femoral head, 2 distal phalange, proximal radius, 6 vertebra fragments, distal humerus, 6 molars, 2 rib fragments, mandible fragments
4006	35	11	Cattle – 2 molar fragments, 2 intermediate phalange
4007	79	13	Cattle – 2 vertebra fragments, 2 pre-molars, 1 tibia fragment, 1 ulna fragment
4008	212	30+	Cattle 2 distal humerus, distal phalange; Pig – talus
4009	1	1	Tooth enamel fragments
4010	754	70+	See written report for further details
4010	136	15	Cattle – distal humerus, proximal scapula; Pig – pelvis fragment
4011	33	7	Cattle – distal femur; Sheep – mandible fragment
4012	118	20+	Pig – incisor; Sheep – proximal metatarsal, proximal scapula, intermediate and distal phalange, 2 rib fragments
4013	41	20+	Sheep – distal metapodial; Roe deer – proximal scapula, poss. Roe deer distal metapodial. Both R. deer fragments burnt. Half of all fragments were calcinated
4015	29	4	Cattle-orbital fragment
4016	18	1	Cattle – 3 molar fragments
4017	87	10	Pig – talus, distal femur; Sheep – proximal scapula
4018	63	14	Cattle – distal phalange
4019	20	3	Cattle – metacarpal fragment, vertebra fragment
4020	9	2	
4021	114	7	Cattle – pelvis fragment, distal metapodial, vertebra fragment
4022	422	50+	See written report for further details
4024	118	20+	Cattle – distal humerus, mandible fragment, proximal phalange, rib
4025	78	12	Cattle – proximal tibia, intermediate phalange; Sheep – distal femur
4026	227	15	Cattle – distal ulna, 2 proximal phalange, vertebra fragment; Sheep – proximal phalange; Pig – incisor
4027	6	1	Cattle – vertebra fragment
4029	48	9	Cattle – distal femur with gnawing; Cat – possible pelvis
4030	40	15	
4032	90	16	Cattle – 2 molars
4034	70	25	Cattle – talus, burnt rib fragments

(Continued)

Table A2.6: Animal bone from COR21 excavations summarised by context. (Continued)

Context	*Weight*	*Unid. frags*	*Notes on ID'd bone*
4035	31	2	Cattle – ulna head, distal tibia
4036	20	2	Cattle – vertebra fragment
4037	12	1	
4038	115	30+	Cattle – 2 molars; Sheep – mandible fragment
4039	1	1	
4039		50+	Cattle – 3 distal, 1 intermediate, 1 proximal phalange, 3 distal metapodial fragments, 2 vertebra fragments, 2 molars, 2 distal humerus fragments; Pig – molar/maxilla fragment
4041	16	2	
4042	1	1	Enamel fragments
4043	67	4	Cattle – 2 rib fragments, talus (gnawed and cut)
4044	2	1	
5000	205		Cattle – molar fragments, distal humerus fragments, proximal phalange fragments, distal metapodial, femur fragment, burnt, charred, and unburnt fragments, distal femur, horncore fragment
5001	14		Charred and calcinated fragments
5002	10	4	Calcinated fragments
5003	9	1	Cattle molar fragments
5005	5	3	Cattle – rib fragment, 3 other calcinated fragments
5008	3	5	Cattle – molar; 4 calcinated fragments
5009	3	2	
5010	29		Cattle – 2 distal phalange, 1 calcinated rib fragment
5011	84	21	Cattle – distal phalange, 2 molars, charred, calcinated, and unburnt fragments
5012	45	13	Cattle – vertebra fragment; calcinated, and unburnt fragments
5017	8	6	Cattle – molar fragment
5018	58	50	Cattle – molar, vertebra fragments; Pig – molars, distal humerus; calcinated, and unburnt fragments
5019	12	3	Cattle – molar fragments
5020	133	40+	Cattle – distal femur fragment; calcinated, and unburnt fragments
5022	32	16	Cattle – molar, rib fragment, mainly calcinated fragments
5023	126	30	Cattle – distal metapodial, molar fragments; Pig – possible burnt distal humerus
5024	7	4	Calcinated and burnt fragments
5025	17	16	calcinated and burnt fragments
5026	67	8	Cattle – 2 molars, burnt and unburnt bone
5027	40	15	Cattle – molar
5028	17	6	Burnt and unburnt fragments
5029	7	3	Calcinated fragments
5030	33	8	Calcinated bone fragments, and molar fragments
5031	84	30+	Cattle – vertebra, rib; calcinated, burnt, and unburnt fragments

and by the nature of the site type (a Roman urban/military settlement, where assemblages are typically dominated by cattle bones in the first instance).

Other remains recovered were:

Sheep: Like cattle, the denser elements from the sheep skeleton were more commonly represented. Sheep were recovered from nine contexts.

Pig: Individual numbers of pig remains were rare, with molars/incisors being the most common finds. Though less commonly recovered than sheep in terms of actual numbers, their bones were also found in nine contexts. A burnt distal humerus from (5023) likely represents the remains from a cooked joint of meat.

Cat: A possible cat pelvis fragment was recovered from (4029).

Crane (*Grus grus*): The proximal ulna of a crane was identified from context (4000). This item was sent to the Historic England laboratories in Fort Cumberland, where

Table A2.7: Summary of weights from the deposit.

Deposit	*Sample*	*>4 mm (sorted)*	*4–2 mm (unsorted)*	*2–1 mm (unsorted)*	*Total weight*	*Identified fragments?*
4013	6	24.8 g	30.3 g	26.7 g	81.8 g	Sheep/goat: skull (0.3 g), vertebral body (1.1 g), tibia (2.3 g), calcaneus (4.1 g)

it was compared against a range of possible alternatives (including swan, heron, pelican, and eagle). The confirmation identification was undertaken by Polydora Barker, who confirmed it was from a crane.

Roe Deer: two bones from a roe deer were identified from (4013). One was the proximal/articulating surface of a scapula, and the other was a distal metapodial. In both cases the bones were heavily burnt, and in places calcinated. This is suggested as deriving from roasted joints of meat.

Taphonomy

The assemblage contains a mix of bones which are unburnt, burnt, and fully calcinated. Burnt bones were identified from 17 contexts, but notable concentrations were found in (2018) and (4013) [associated with the roe deer remains]. This is likely to represent cooking meat on the joint, and gives an insight into cooking practice, such as the burnt cattle ribs from (4034), the burnt roe deer bones, and the burnt pig distal humerus from (5023).

A single fragment of bone from (4025), had the appearance of having been disturbed from a cesspit; being darker in colour, apparently better preserved, and with sand/grit strongly adhering to the surface of the bone. This bone might suggest some mixing of contexts within the life of the site, but its discovery as a single item suggests this mixing was limited.

The bones overall had average-good surface preservation, excepting those from 1016 and 4022, which were notable more abraded than others from the assemblage. Gnawing, presumably by scavenging dogs, was noted on a number of bones fragments, though was not commonly noted. It was concentrated on long-bone ends.

Significance

The remains can broadly be described as typical for a Roman settlement of the size and nature of Corbridge; *i.e.* dominated by cattle bones, with small numbers of other species, including evidence for hunting. Considering the relatively paucity of Roman skeletal remains from the broader Wall corridor (excepting Vindolanda and Carlisle), the remains can be classed as being of regional importance.

There is a strong suggestion from the remains that high-status or military type activity is represented by the remains. Finds of crane are rare from Roman Britain, but their recovery has been suggested as linked to high-status sites (Allen 2009). Additionally, the apparently roasted roe deer bones suggest hunting and feasting activity, more typically associated with the Roman military and/or high-status individuals or communities.

The remains of the crane are of broad interest for the zooarchaeology of Roman Britain. These birds can be hunted for both their meat and feathers (the latter possibility should be considered as the bones recovered was the ulna). Cranes typically live on flat areas near wetland. Along the Wall corridor there are a number of adjacent areas where this sort of environment might occur in the Roman period, such as the Brightwater Valley in Co. Durham, the coastal areas of the Northumberland coastal plain (particularly around the Bradford Kaims), as well as the wetlands between Carlisle and Burgh-by-Sands. It should also be considered that crane populations may have been present closer to Corbridge, but subsequent landscape modification and change has pushed them from their ecological niches in this area.

Corbridge: burnt bone from structured deposit

Lauren McIntyre

This report details the osteological analysis of one deposit of burnt bone (4013), interpreted as a cremation burial, found during excavations at Corbridge. The deposit was found in a truncated Greyware storage jar, deposited in an earth cut pit [4045]. This feature was dated to the Roman period, from the mid-3rd century or later. Fill (4013) also contained charcoal, charred plant remains and a metal ring. Two fragments of white bone weighing a total of 2.6 g were selected for radiocarbon dating. These fragments came from the >4 mm sieve fraction. The bone fragments dated to the Bronze Age (see Chapter 7).

The material was assessed to confirm species identification. Initial observations suggested that the bone was non-human. This was verified by a zooarchaeologist. The few identifiable fragments were sheep/goat.

Bone weights per sieve fraction are summarised in Table A2.7. Only the >4 mm sieve fraction was sorted. The 4–2 mm and 2–1 mm fractions contained a combination of burnt bone and extraneous material, such as stones. Most of the unidentifiable bone from the 4–2 mm sieve fraction was white, indicating that it had been burnt at high temperatures in excess of 600°C. Only a small proportion of the bone from this sieve fraction was charred black, so not fully oxidised, consistent with less heat exposure. The bone fragments in the other sieve fractions also appeared to be predominantly white, but more detailed inspection of these would be needed to confirm this.

Discussion and conclusions

This deposit was interpreted as a cremation burial. However, the absence of identifiable human bone might suggest something other, although less than a third of the bone could be identified. The bone was recovered from the complete base of a truncated pot, so it will never be known what the complete original deposit comprised. The fact that the identified bone is all faunal, might suggest that none of it is human, including the unidentified fragments. Perhaps a better interpretation would be as a domestic burnt offering. Here, burnt or charred animal remains found in conjunction with certain charred plant remains, have previously been interpreted as ritual offerings to domestic deities (Robinson 2002). Animal sacrifice was widely practised in Roman period Britain, and though the preferred animal varied according to the deity being appeased, sheep and goats were commonly used for this purpose (King 2005). Similar features have also been interpreted as possible foundation deposits, for example, for a new town (Woodward and Woodward 2004).

The Bronze Age date of a fragment of the burnt bone complicates interpretation. No comparative examples of burnt bone of Bronze Age date housed in a Roman ceramic vessel were found in the literature. As such it is unclear whether the burnt bone was placed in the pot intentionally, or as the result of another process. For example, the truncation of the feature should be considered in regard to the degree of post-depositional disturbance.

Corbridge: bulk finds

Rob Collins

A number of bulk objects, primarily consisting of nails and other iron objects and debris were catalogued from the excavations at Corbridge. These do not inform interpretation in any significant fashion as individual objects, the quantity is indicative of the structural and craft activity at the site. Further iron objects were found during metalwork analysis (see Table A2.10).

Contents	*Category*	*Material*	*No. of items*	*Wt (g)*	*Season*	*Context*	*Notes*
CBM	structural	plaster	3	26	Cor21	5000	
Coal	production	coal	1	17	Cor21	4039	
Coal	production	coal	1	4	Cor21	4040	
Nail	structural	Fe	1	2	Cor19	1021	
Nail	structural	Fe	2	39	Cor21	4000	
Nail	structural	Fe	3	93	Cor21	4000	
Nail	structural	Fe	3	73	Cor21	4000	
Nail	structural	Fe	1	12	Cor21	4000	
Nail	structural	Fe	3	34	Cor21	4000	
Nail	structural	Fe	2	20	Cor21	4000	
Nail	structural	Fe	3	23	Cor21	4000	
Nail	structural	Fe	1	12	Cor21	4000	
Nail	structural	Fe	1	3	Cor21	4000	corroded fragment of an iron nail, J-shaped in plan, plaster mixed with corrosion
Nail	structural	Fe	1	23	Cor21	4003	
Nail	structural	Fe	2	26	Cor21	4003	
Nail	structural	Fe	1	10	Cor21	4007	
Nail	structural	Fe	4	11	Cor21	4010	from flot sample
Nail	structural	Fe	1	6	Cor21	4024	
Nail	structural	Fe	1	24	Cor21	4028	
Nail	structural	Fe	4	74	Cor21	4034	
Nail	structural	Fe	1	10	Cor21	5000	
Nail	structural	Fe	1	7	Cor21	5000	
Nail	structural	Fe	2	40	Cor21	5000	machine cleaning
Nail	structural	Fe	1	7	Cor21	5003	
Nail	structural	Fe	1	5	Cor21	5005	

(Continued)

Contents	*Category*	*Material*	*No. of items*	*Wt (g)*	*Season*	*Context*	*Notes*
Nail	structural	Fe	1	2	Cor21	5005	
Nail	structural	Fe	1	12	Cor21	5007	
Nail	structural	Fe	1	12	Cor21	5008	
Nail	structural	Fe	1	7	Cor21	5015	
Nail	structural	Fe	1	14	Cor21	5019	
Nail	structural	Fe	2	2	Cor21	5020	
Nail	structural	Fe	2	11	Cor21	5022	
Nail	structural	Fe	6	46	Cor21	5024	
Nail	structural	Fe	2	8	Cor21	5027	
Nail	structural	Fe	1	6	Cor21	5029	
Nail	structural	Fe	2	10	Cor21	5029	
Shell			1	2	Cor21	5000	extremely weathered
Slag	production	Fe	3	109	Cor21	4000	
Slag	production	Fe	4	9	Cor21	4000	
Slag	production	Fe	1	4	Cor21	4000	
Slag	production	Fe	1	2	Cor21	4004	
Slag	production	Fe	1	8	Cor21	4007	
Slag	production	Fe	1	133	Cor21	4039	
Slag	production	Fe	4	19	Cor21	4042	
Slag	production	Fe	3	9	Cor21	5008	
Slag	production	Fe	1	4	Cor21	5030	
Slag	production	Fe	1	13	Cor21	5027	
Slag, nail	mixed	Fe	2	85	Cor21	5000	
Slag, UnID	mixed	Fe	8	183	Cor21	4000	prob incl Modern
Slag, UnID	mixed	Fe	10+	566	Cor21	5000	incl Modern
Slag, UnID	mixed	Fe	3	229	Cor21	5000	incl Modern
Slag, UnID	mixed	Fe	10+	597	Cor21	5000	
Slag, UnID	mixed	Fe	5	42	Cor21	5015	
Slag, UnID	mixed	Fe	10+	243	Cor21	5020	
Slag, UnID	mixed	Fe	5	288	Cor21	5025	
UnID	mixed	Fe	10+	238	Cor21	5000	prob incl Modern
UnID	structural	Fe	10	93	Cor19	1003	
UnID	structural	Fe	1	9	Cor19	1006	
UnID	structural	Fe	1	6	Cor19	1012	
UnID	structural	Fe	2	15	Cor19	3002	
UnID	structural	Fe	7	60	Cor19	3004	
UnID	structural	Fe	3	20	Cor19	3006	
UnID	structural	Fe	6	26	Cor19	3007	
UnID	structural	Fe	7	186	Cor21	4000	
UnID	structural	Fe	4	22	Cor21	4000	incl Modern
UnID	structural	Fe	8	117	Cor21	4000	
UnID	structural	Fe	4	65	Cor21	4000	
UnID	structural	Fe	7	141	Cor21	4000	
UnID	structural	Fe	2	38	Cor21	4000	

(Continued)

Contents	Category	Material	No. of items	Wt (g)	Season	Context	Notes
UnID	structural	Fe	2	20	Cor21	4000	
UnID	structural	Fe	1	14	Cor21	4000	
UnID	structural	Fe	1	6	Cor21	4000	
UnID	structural	Fe	2	7	Cor21	4001	
UnID	structural	Fe	3	59	Cor21	4004	
UnID	structural	Fe	1	37	Cor21	4005	
UnID	structural	Fe	2	45	Cor21	4005	
UnID	structural	Fe	3	12	Cor21	4005	
UnID	structural	Fe	2	33	Cor21	4005	
UnID	structural	Fe	1	7	Cor21	4007	
UnID	structural	Fe	4	16	Cor21	4007	from flot sample
UnID	structural	Fe	4	21	Cor21	4008	
UnID	structural	Fe	4	18	Cor21	4008	
UnID	structural	Fe	3	31	Cor21	4009	
UnID	structural	Fe	1	16	Cor21	4010	
UnID	structural	Fe	2	18	Cor21	4010	
UnID	structural	Fe	3	6	Cor21	4012	poss spherical stud heads
UnID	structural	Fe	2	25	Cor21	4013	
UnID	structural	Fe	6	71	Cor21	4016	between and under flags
UnID	structural	Fe	2	27	Cor21	4017	
UnID	structural	Fe	2	71	Cor21	4017	
UnID	structural	Fe	4	28	Cor21	4021	
UnID	structural	Fe	2	82	Cor21	4022	
UnID	structural	Fe	1	3	Cor21	4024	
UnID	structural	Fe	1	5	Cor21	4029	
UnID	structural	Fe	1	8	Cor21	4032	
UnID	structural	Fe	1	10	Cor21	4035	
UnID	structural	Fe	1	12	Cor21	4037	
UnID	structural	Fe	3	11	Cor21	4039	
UnID	structural	Fe	3	38	Cor21	4039	
UnID	structural	Fe	1	19	Cor21	4041	
UnID	structural	Fe	1	7	Cor21	5000	
UnID	structural	Fe	1	10	Cor21	5000	
UnID	structural	Fe	3	12	Cor21	5000	
UnID	structural	Fe	3	66	Cor21	5000	
UnID	structural	Fe	1	12	Cor21	5000	
UnID	structural	Fe	7	87	Cor21	5000	
UnID	structural	Fe	4	37	Cor21	5000	
UnID	structural	Fe	7	19	Cor21	5000	prob Modern
UnID	structural	Fe	4	65	Cor21	5000	
UnID	structural	Fe	9	26	Cor21	5000	
UnID	structural	Fe	7	98	Cor21	5000	
UnID	structural	Fe	2	8	Cor21	5000	
UnID	structural	Fe	3	31	Cor21	5001	

(Continued)

Contents	*Category*	*Material*	*No. of items*	*Wt (g)*	*Season*	*Context*	*Notes*
UnID	structural	Fe	3	37	Cor21	5002	
UnID	structural	Fe	5	115	Cor21	5002	
UnID	structural	Fe	2	20	Cor21	5002	
UnID	structural	Fe	4	34	Cor21	5003	
UnID	structural	Fe	1	34	Cor21	5005	
UnID	structural	Fe	5	19	Cor21	5008	
UnID	structural	Fe	5	35	Cor21	5008	
UnID	structural	Fe	3	4	Cor21	5008	
UnID	structural	Fe	1	5	Cor21	5008	
UnID	structural	Fe	1	34	Cor21	5012	
UnID	structural	Fe	2	23	Cor21	5013	
UnID	structural	Fe	1	41	Cor21	5015	
UnID	structural	Fe	1	45	Cor21	5015	
UnID	structural	Fe	2	23	Cor21	5016	
UnID	structural	Fe	1	36	Cor21	5016	
UnID	structural	Fe	10	47	Cor21	5018	
UnID	structural	Fe	10+	106	Cor21	5020	
UnID	structural	Fe	8	140	Cor21	5022	
UnID	structural	Fe	1	34	Cor21	5022	
UnID	structural	Fe	1	13	Cor21	5022	
UnID	structural	Fe	4	56	Cor21	5022	
UnID	structural	Fe	10+	73	Cor21	5023	
UnID	structural	Fe	9	33	Cor21	5023	
UnID	structural	Fe	10+	83	Cor21	5023	
UnID	structural	Fe	5	71	Cor21	5024	
UnID	structural	Fe	2	27	Cor21	5025	
UnID	structural	Fe	3	14	Cor21	5025	
UnID	structural	Fe	3	16	Cor21	5025	
UnID	structural	Fe	6	40	Cor21	5025	
UnID	structural	Fe	9	73	Cor21	5026	
UnID	structural	Fe	4	109	Cor21	5026	
UnID	structural	Fe	5	117	Cor21	5026	
UnID	structural	Fe	1	10	Cor21	5027	
UnID	structural	Fe	3	64	Cor21	5028	
UnID	structural	Fe	2	38	Cor21	5028	one corroded onto stone
UnID	structural	Fe	2	117	Cor21	5030	
UnID	structural	Fe	2	20	Cor21	5031	
UnID	structural	Fe	7	109	Cor21	5031	
UnID	tool?	Fe	2	34	Cor21	4016	between/under flags
UnID	unid	Fe	2	26	Cor21	4010	
UnID	unid	Fe	3	5	Cor21	5017	
UnID	unid	Fe	4	1	Cor21	5021	from flot sample
UnID	unid	Fe	3	7	Cor21	5023	3 polygonal and corroded fragments of an unidentified iron object
UnID	unid	Fe	2	10	Cor21	5026	

Table A2.8: Categories of slag and related materials identified from excavation.

Smithing hearth cake (SHC)	Circular or oval, and plano-convex (or concave convex), accumulations of fayalitic (Fe_2SiO_4) slag which formed inside a blacksmith's hearth (McDonnell 1991; Serneels and Perret 2003).
Non-diagnostic ironworking slag (NDFe)	Most ironworking slag assemblages include a significant proportion of fayalitic slag which lacks a diagnostic surface morphology that would allow the identification of the process(es) which produced them. In many cases, this is simply because the lumps of slag are small fragments of a larger whole; however, in some cases the lumps of slag are essentially complete but amorphous (cf. Historic England 2015, fig. 18).
Vitrified ceramic lining (VCL)	Vitrified ceramic usually showing a black vitreous (inner) face, an intermediate reduced fired ceramic layer, and an oxidised-fired (outer) layer (Historic England 2015, fig. 11).
Iron (Fe) Objects	These are usually highly corroded/concreted but usually respond to a magnet.
Coal and partially burnt coal (PBC)	Black, vitreous, light-weight, combustible material used as a fuel from Roman times onwards. Partially burn coal is usually less lustrous, sometimes porous and more friable.
Geology	Stones, rocks, etc.
Soil and Iron (Fe) concretions	Fragments of soil with iron corrosion products (sometimes almost entirely iron corrosion products (not usually magnetic).

Table A2.9: Summary of slag and related materials (weight in g, for abbreviations see Table A2.8).

Code	*Context*	*Type*	*Comment*	*Weight*
COR19	1006	VCL		71
COR19	1010	NDFe		282
COR19	1010	SHC		359
COR19	2003	NDFe	(SHC frag?)	115
COR21	4005	NDFe		5
COR21	4005	NDFe		89
COR21	4008	NDFe		19
COR21	4025	NDFe		30
COR21	4044	NDFe		129
COR21	5000	NDFe		300
COR21	5017	NDFe		4
All				1403

Corbridge: assessment of slag and related material

David Dungworth

All of the material submitted for assessment was examined visually and recorded following standard guidance (Historic England 2015). The material was divided into several categories based on surface morphology, density, porosity, colour, etc. (Table A2.8). The material was weighed by material type/form and by context.

The assessed material includes just over 1.4 kg of metalworking debris (Table A2.9), as well as smaller amounts of other materials (Tables A2.10 and A2.11). The only diagnostic ironworking material is the smithing hearth cake from (1010). The other materials provide no certainty as to the processes that might have produced them. Nevertheless, given the absence of evidence for any *other* metalworking activity (and the presence of a smithing hearth cake), it is likely that all of the non-diagnostic ironworking slag was also generated by smithing. The iron objects (Table A2.10) are not necessarily related to smithing activity and were found in many more contexts (25) than ironworking slags (9). Most of the iron objects appear to be fragments of nails or hobnails. The other materials (Table A2.11) include a small amount of coal, which was occasionally used as a fuel in the Roman period (Dearne and Branigan 1995). The remaining materials include some natural materials (stones, etc.) as well as iron-rich concretions that may represent completely corroded iron objects.

The metalworking debris recovered from the excavations at Corchester Playing Fields provides evidence for the smithing of iron. The quantity of slag is relatively modest and could have been generated in less than a week of full-time smithing.

Corbridge: building materials and fired clay

Amparo Valcarcel

The building materials were examined using the London system of classification (Betts 1995). Examples of the fabrics can be found in the reference collection of the Museum of London Archaeology Service. A fabric number was allocated to each object which specifies its composition, form, and approximate date range. As there were no ceramic building material fabric references in any of the publications accessed, the consultation of the relevant 1:50,000 geological maps for this area provided the local geological background. New tile and brick fabric were prefixed by CAM followed by 1; thus CAM1, CAM2. Some fabrics such as the fired clay and stone compared well with the London fabric codes (see description of fabrics below).

The application of a 1 kg mason's hammer and sharp chisel to each example ensured that a small fresh fabric surface was exposed. The fabric was examined at x20 magnification using a long arm stereomicroscope or hand lens (Gowland ×10).

The material collected from this site amounts to 824 fragments weighting 17.07 kg. The assemblage recovered from excavations dates mainly to the Roman period, with a few fragments of post-medieval material. Fired clay dominates the assemblage from this site, followed by ceramic building material (249 fragments, 5799 g) and stones (218 fragments, 8497 g). Most of the stones are too small to identify a form, but probably they are natural erratic material. In general, the material is in a mixed condition, although it is generally well preserved. Some structures were exposed in Trench 4, but in general the material was found in layers and fills. The loose assemblage is quite fragmented and demonstrated signs of abrasion.

Ceramic building material (249 examples, 5799 g)

The ceramic building material assemblage is dominated by fragmentary examples of Roman and post-medieval items. No contexts produced large accumulations of material, except in layers (4000) and (5000). Six different fabrics were recorded in all of the archaeological sequence. Due to the absence of previous studies on ceramic building material at this site, new fabric codes were created (CAM1, CAM2, CAM3, CAM4, and CAM5). The Roman material dates were paralleled with the Roman pottery (see Hudak, this volume) and fabrics which could be equated (Betts 1995). Examples of the fabrics can be found in the reference collection of the Museum of London Archaeology Service with the matching with London fabric type series are indicated below:

- 2279 (AD 1630–1850): Fine well fired texture, sandy fabric with moderate quartz <1 mm, occasional black/red iron oxide & calcium carbonate inclusions <1 mm, 1 fragment, 128 g.
- CAM1 (AD 120–250): sandy fabric, frequent rounded clay pellets <0.3 mm; occasional silty inclusions, & bands <6 mm in mottled clay matrix; 23 fragments, 353 g.
- CAM2 (AD 90–200): fine fabric, varying amounts of quartz, occasional limestone, siltstone, mica, and yellow silty bands, 108 fragments, 2256 g.
- CAM3 (AD 120–250): very fine texture, occasional coarse quartz, calcium carbonate and muscovite, mica 44 fragments, 535 g.
- CAM4 (AD 1450–1900): sandy fabric, very course, frequent quartz, some yellow speckles, 6 fragments, 18 g.
- CAM5 (AD 1450–1900): very course sandy fabric, frequent quartz and red iron oxide inclusions, 1 fragment, 13 g.

Table A2.10: Summary of metallic objects (weight in g).

Code	*Context*	*Type*	*Comment*	*Weight*
COR21	4004	Fe Obj	hobnail	2
COR21	4004	Fe Obj	nail	12
COR21	4005	Fe Obj		9
COR21	4006	Fe Obj		30
COR21	4007	Fe Obj		48
COR21	4008	Fe Obj	nail	32
COR21	4010	Fe Obj		19
COR21	4013	Fe Obj	nail	23
COR21	4016	Fe Obj		23
COR21	4017	Fe Obj		16
COR21	4018	Fe Obj		5
COR21	4018	Fe Obj		13
COR21	4022	Fe Obj	nail	6
COR21	4024	Fe Obj	nail	9
COR21	4025	Fe Obj		2
COR21	4025	Fe Obj	inc hobnails	142
COR21	4030	Fe Obj		42
COR21	4030	Fe Obj	hobnail	64
COR21	4034	Fe Obj	nail	1
COR21	4035	Fe Obj		314
COR21	5000	Fe Obj	nail	31
COR21	5000	Fe Obj	nail	7
COR21	5000	Fe Obj		83
COR21	5000	Pb		3
COR21	5006	Fe Obj		14
COR21	5010	Fe Obj		35
COR21	5011	Fe Obj		5
COR21	5011	Fe Obj		2
COR21	5018	Fe Obj	nail	9
COR21	5025	Fe Obj		50
COR21	5026	Fe Obj	nail	11
COR21	5030	Fe Obj		42
COR21	5032	Fe Obj	hobnails	27
All				1131

Table A2.11: Summary of other objects (weight in g).

Code	*Context*	*Type*	*Comment*	*Weight*
COR21	4008	Coal		11
COR21	5008	PBC		12
COR21	4034	Fe Conc		4
COR21	4043	Fe Conc		3
COR21	4013	Soil conc		23
COR21	4000	Stone		31

Roman material (187 fragments, 5458 g)

There was a large amount of Roman material found throughout the excavation. Some items were found in road structure [4032], but most of the material was collected from layers and fills. This indicates the material is the result of demolition/rebuilding phases. No complete examples were found. As commented before, the dating of the fabrics was taken from the Roman pottery identified within the same context.

The principal Roman forms were identified in the archaeological sequence. Bricks were the most common form with 24 fragments weighting 2437 g. The fact that many do not appear to be fresh would suggest they represent dumped and re-deposited material. Complete thicknesses range from 26 to 47 mm indicative of the smaller Roman brick forms, namely the bessalis, pedalis, and lydion. Bricks are made in all of the Roman fabrics identified, but type CAM2 dominated the brick assemblage.

The flanged roofing tiles are made of fabrics CAM2 and CAM3, totalling five fragments (479 g). Four of the fragments were found in Trench 5 with only one fragment from Trench 4 (4009). Only tegulae from the deposit [5007] had preserved squared-off types of early Roman flange. There were no large fragments from which any measurements of size could be taken.

Imbrex are well represented in the assemblage with 10 examples weighting 590 g. The fabrics identified are CAM2 and CAM3, the same fabrics used in the tegulae, suggesting that all the roofing material was made in both fabric types. The imbrices are also pretty typical in tapering slightly towards one end. It is possible, particularly with the more fragmentary pieces that curved ridge tiles are also represented, although imbrices would function just as well for this purpose. No full lengths were recorded but thickness range from 14 to 18 mm. The presence of roofing material suggests the buildings were constructed with ceramic building material from AD 90 onwards.

Horizontal elements in the form of small fragments of tile are poorly represented (15 fragments, 1030 g), but the majority of fragments are made of fabrics CAM2 and CAM3, suggesting that maybe some of these undiagnostic tiles are tegula with no preserved flange. Most of the fragments were collected from Trench 4 with a smaller quantity (four fragments) found in Trench 5. A fragment from layer (5034) had three digital lines (Type 64) preserved on the surface; these marks are usually associated with tile makers who prepared the surface in this manner for better adhesion of the wall plaster.

One box flue tile, with no marks preserved, was found in layer (5025). The fragment was made of fabric CAM2, dating AD 90–250. Flue tiles were used to transfer heat up the walls from beneath the floor and were used to line the interior of heated rooms, thereby enabling hot air to circulate through the walls from the hypocaust below. The presence of this fragment indicates the existence of a heated room nearby.

Post-medieval material (eight fragments, 169 g)

Post-medieval material is represented by bricks and roofing tiles. The roof tile assemblage consisted in one peg tile weighing 13 g made of local fabric CAM5. The other roofing tile identified was a fragment of pan tile from layer [5000]. This curved tile was introduced in England in 1630. The peg tile is well manufactured, with sharp edges and fine moulding sand, dating AD 1700–1900.

Bricks are presented by fabric CAM4 (six fragments, 28 g). Unfortunately, all the brick fragments appeared in a very abraded condition and not a single example have preserved any dimensions. The lack of measurements provided a wide range of date AD 1450–1900.

Unknown fabric and form (51 examples, 163 g)

High quantities of undiagnostic material were found in several contexts. The fragments were too small and abraded to identify form and fabric.

Fired Clay (299 examples, 2563 g)

There are large quantities of fired clay recovered from several contexts. Most of the fragments are abraded and small, which cannot be related to specific clay structures, however, it was not always easy to distinguish from thick sheets of fired clay. This material was found in dumped deposits, especially fills and layers, representing demolished remains of kilns, ovens, or hearths.

Three different fabrics were identified:

3102: general code, equivalent to London fabric including fired clay and daub.

Type 1: a very course clay, with frequent quartz and pebbles, 113 fragments, 896 g.

Type 2: very fine orange clay with occasional quartz inclusions and yellow silty lines, 24 fragments, 196 g.

Type 3: fine clay, with frequent yellow silty bands, marble aspect, 120 fragments, 1082 g.

Type 3 is the most abundant fabric, and the majority of the fragments were collected from layers (4028) and (5000). Fragments from layer (5003) had preserved wooden rod marks, although the fragments are in general too small to identify any surface. Type 1 is well-represented at this site, especially from different features from Trench 5, but mainly from layer (5000). Type 2 is a less common fabric, and it was found mainly in Trench 5.

Although recovered from fill (4025) of pit [4017], two fragments with iron fragments attached are probably related to a kiln for smelting iron. They are dark-grey, near black core, buff/pale-brown to grey surfaces, and with moderate organic impressions and sparse larger quartz grains. No marks are evident on the surviving fragments reported on here, although they are very incomplete, and none of the examples appears to have been exposed to high firing temperatures. There is little other evidence for iron work from the settlement, although this can be extremely ephemeral. Further work should seek to confirm how many slag fragments are present on site. This may help to determine if any particular activity can be identified, and if so, when and where on site this activity may have been focused.

In general, the three different types are related to unidentified fired clay fragments. The majority is too fragmentary to identify to form, with very few diagnostic features recorded, with the exception of two fragments from fill (5015). These probably originated from the clay lining of a cut, although could also represent collapsed fragments of walls or super-structure (Poole 2011). It is possible these derive from a clay plate (Lyne 2002), used as a portable oven or kiln furniture, often with pedestals to form a raised floor, but the pieces are too fragmentary to suggest anything further about the nature of the structure.

Type 3 was identified in the burnt clay assemblages from both COR19 and COR21. This fabric type shares the same silty micaceous matrix, indicating a shared common clay source, which includes an admixture of white silty clay giving a speckled and streaked appearance. The vegetal matter, however, was almost certainly additional temper added to help strengthen the clay and/or increase thermal resistance.

The burnt clay is predominantly in small, fragmentary, and featureless pieces. No identifiable withy or stave impressions from daub representing clay and timber structures were recorded and just a small number of fragments had slightly curved (either concave or convex) or flat surfaces. Some fragments are more likely to have a reduced dark grey or black core and oxidised margins, perhaps indicating they derive from objects or smaller structures that were exposed to a controlled heat. The remaining assemblage has more variable colouring, indicative of a more varied exposure to heat. The assemblages are all small in size with no particularly significant clusters in their distribution. When considered together with their condition, this could indicate the majority were re-deposited and have not been recovered from their primary location. The fragment of smithing hearth lining, is more diagnostic, likely relating to the secondary metalworking well-attested to on site.

Mortar (55 fragments, 179 g)

The mortar found throughout the site is present in a very fragmentary condition. One fragment of opus signinum was identified in layer (5000). Opus signinum is a very hard mortar, mixed with lime, chalk, and crushed CBM or pottery, and is used in many cases as waterproofing. The other fragments documented in layer (4039) and in the fill (5018]) was Opus caementicium, a very hard mortar, made of small and medium gravels and pebbles mixed with lime and chalk, some of them more than 4 cm in size. The rest of the mortar found had a white lime-based matrix with occasional quartz, but it could not be related to any dating as the fragments are quite small.

Stone (221 fragments, 8.505 kg)

The stone assemblage is mainly comprised of natural fragments, with no attached mortar observed and no worked stone was identified. Fourteen different lithotypes were identified, summarised in Table A2.12:

- Chalk clunch (fabric 3125; 47 fragments, 2663 g): A less durable creamy-grey coloured chalks was found in several contexts. This is a softer, friable chalk, which is not easily shaped into regular blocks. It has a low strength and weathers poorly, tending to absorb water and spall as a result of winter freezing. This chalk was used for course walls and foundations. All the fragments are very small, and no mortar has been attached.
- Slate (fabric 3115; 18 fragments, 64 g): Slate may have once been used as roofing stone for buildings or indeed as possible coursing levels in the wall core. In the absence of any definable nail holes, with the exception of a fragment from layer (4000), it is not possible to determine their function.
- Micaceous stone (fabric 3120a; 36 fragments, 266 g): This type of stone was collected from several contexts, but it is always present in small sized pieces. Probably these are natural fragments found within the local boulder clay. A fragment from layer (4000) had worked rounded arises and it could be related to a lid from a ceramic container. This fragment should be studied by a small find specialist. It is interesting to point out that a fragment from fill (4025) of Pit [4017] has residual iron attached, as did the fired clay found in the same context.
- Taynton stone (fabric 3120b; 1 fragment, 2467 g): This is a buff to white, coarse-grained ooidal limestone, typically cross-bedded and with abundant shell fragments.
- Chalk (fabric 3116; 59 examples, 1748 g): This type of stone was easy to cut, and could be shaped into uniform rectangular blocks, for use in regularly coursed walls or in the foundations.
- Gritt stone (fabric 3130; 25 fragments, 286 g): All the material recovered was in very small, fragmented pieces, so it is not possible to associate their use as natural stone or as querns.

Table A2.12: Quantity and weight of the different types of stone identified.

Lithotypes	Fabric code	Quantity	Weight (g)
Clunch	3125	47	2663
Slate	3115	18	64
Micaceous fine stone	3120a	36	266
Taynton	3120b	1	2467
Sarsen	3120c	2	261
Fine laminated sandstone	3121	1	12
Gritt stone	3130	25	286
Chalk	3116	59	1748
Quartzite	3137	1	6
Course aminated sandstone	3129	8	26
Course sandstone	3131	4	10
Oolitic limestone	3109	1	354
Ferruginous sandstone	3111	9	51
Niedermendig lava	3123	1	19

- Niedermendig lava (fabric 3123; 1 fragment, 19 g): Niedermendig lava stone used as quern, indicates the grinding of foodstuffs and inorganic materials. Niedermendig lavastone from the Rhineland is the most common quern stone material used in the Roman period and later.

Quartzite (fabric 3137), sandstone fine laminated (fabric 3121 and 3129), oolitic limestone (fabric 3129) coarse sandstone (fabric 3131), ferruginous sandstone (fabric 3111) and sarsen (fabric 3120c) are common stone easily found within the clay bulk as erratic stones. Sarsen stone occurs as large sandstone blocks up to several metres in length. The stone is a hard, silica-cemented quartz sandstone. Thus, sarsens were initially used in building, the fragment collected from the site are too small to identify their original function.

Distribution

The distribution can be broken down by context (Table A2.13) and trench (Table A2.14).

Table A2.13: Materials and fabrics by context.

Context	Fabric	Material	Quantity	Weight	Date range of material		Spot date
0	3125	Clunch fragment	2	79	UNC	UNC	UNC
4000	UNK; 3102a; 3102b; 3102c; CAM1; CAM2; CAM3; CAM4; 3130; 3120a 31216; 3121;3125; 3115; 3137; 3101	Unknown fabric and form; fired clay type 1, 2, 3, Roman tile and brick; post-medieval brick; Micaceous sandstone, coarse sandstone; chalk; fine laminated sandstone; clunch; slate, quartzite; white lime mortar	121	2654	90	1900	1700–1900
4001	3125	Clunch fragment	1	7	90	250	90–250
4001	3102	Fired clay type 1	1	5	90	250	90–250
4002	3129; 3116	Chalk; fine laminated sandstone	3	10	UNC	UNC	UNC
4003	3102	Fired clay type 3	1	11	90	250	90–250
4004	CAM1; CAM3; 3120a; 3120c;3116	Imbrex, Roman brick and tile; fired clay type 1 and 3;	23	562	90	250	120–250
4005	CAM2	Undiagnostic fragment	1	3	90	200	90–200
4006	CAM2; 3125; 3102 type 2	Undiagnostic fragment; fired clay; clunch fragment	3	30	90	200	90–200
4007	3131; 3102a; CAM3	Gritt stone; fired clay; undiagnostic form	13	67	120	250	120–250
4008	3109; 3102 type 3; CAM1; CAM2; CAM3; 3130;	Oolitic limestone; fired clay type 3; coarse sandstone; imbrex and roman brick	13	284	90	250	120–250
4009	3102; CAM2; 3130;3129;	Fired clay type 2; Roman brick and tegula; coarse sandstone; fine laminated sandstone	7	93	90	200	90–200
4010	3125	S	1	89	120	250	120–250
4010	3102	Fired clay	1	1	120	250	120–250
4010	3125; 3120; UNK	Clunch fragment; undiagnostic fabric and form	8	174	120	250	120–250
4012	CAM3	Undiagnostic form	3	1	120	250	120–250

(Continued)

Table A2.13: (Continued)

Context	Fabric	Material	Quantity	Weight	Date range of material		Spot date
4013	CAM1; CAM2; CAM3; 3120 type 2 and 3; 3116; unk	Fired clay type 1 and 3; Roman tile; undiagnostic form and fabric; chalk	18	26	90	250	120–250
4015	CAM2	Undiagnostic form	1	5	90	200	90–200
4017	CAM1	Roman brick	1	37	120	250	120–250
4018	3116; 3102 type 1; CAM3	Chalk; fired clay type 1; Imbrex	4	67	120	250	120–250
4020	3116; 3102`	Chalk; fired clay type 3	5	11	90	250	90–250
4022	3101; 3120; 3130`	White lime mortar; fired clay type 1; coarse sandstone	5	79	90	250	90–250
4023	CAM2	Roman brick	1	16	90	200	90–200
4024	UNK; 3102; CAM1	Unknown fabric and form, fired clay type.	3	23	120	250	120–250
4025	3102; CAM2; 3120a; UNK	Fired clay type 1; micaceous sandstone; unknown fabric and form; Roman brick	18	185	90	200	90–200
4026	3111; 3125; UNK	Ferruginous sandstone; clunch; unknown fabric and form	4	32	UNC	UNC	UNC
4027	UNK; 3125	Unknown fabric and form; clunch fragment	2	2	UNC	UNC	UNC
4028	3102; 3116	Fired clay type 3; chalk	32	519	90	250	90–250
4029	CAM1; 3102; 3116	Undiagnostic Roman form; fired clay type 2; chalk	4	24	120	250	120–250
4030	3125; 3102; 3116; CAM2, CAM3	Clunch; chalk; imbrex and Roman tile, fired clay type 1;	8	90	90	250	120–250
4032	CAM2	Imbrex	1	89	90	200	90–200
4034	3102; UNK	Fired clay type 3; unknown fabric and form	6	39	90	250	90–250
4035	CAM1; CAM2; CAM3; 3120type 2 and 3; 3116; unk	Imbrex and undiagnostic form	2	114	90	250	120–250
4039	3101R; 3102; CAM2	opus caementicium; fired clay type 3; Roman brick	4	25	90	200	90–200
5000	3130; 3116; 3115; 3125; 3120; 3111; 3123; 3129; UNK; CAM1; CAM2; COR; 2279	Coarse sandstone; chalk; slate; clunch; micaceous stone; ferruginous sandstone; Niedermendig lava quern stone; fine laminated sandstone; opus signinum; tegula; imbrex, Roman brick and tile; post-medieval pan tile; fired clay type 1, 2 and 3	281	2626	90	1850	1630–1850
5001	3101; 3115; 3130; 3102;	White lime mortar; fired clay type 1; coarse sandstone; slate	31	293	90	250	90–250
5002	CAM2; 3102`	Undiagnostic Roman form; fired clay type 1 and 2	11	36	90	200	90–200
5003	3102; CAM2; 3116; UNK; 3101	Fired clay type 1 and 3; undiagnostic Roman form; chalk	12	46	90	200	90–200
5007	3131; 3130; 3102; CAM3	Gritt stone; coarse sandstone; fired clay type 3; Roman brick	17	340	120	250	120–250
5010	UNK; 3102	Unknown fabric and form; fired clay type 3	14	24	90	250	90–250
5011	3102; CAM2	Fired clay type 2; undiagnostic Roman form	2	15	90	200	90–200
5012	3125; 3120b; 3102;	Clunch; sarsen stone; fired clay type 3	14	1741	90	250	90–250
5013	CAM2; CAM3	Roman tiles	2	108	120	250	120–250
5014	3120	Tayton stone; undiagnostic stone	3	2675	UNC	UNC	UNC

(Continued)

Table A2.13: Materials and fabrics by context. (Continued)

Context	Fabric	Material	Quantity	Weight	Date range of material		Spot date
5015	UNK; 3130; 3102	Unknown fabric and form; coarse sandstone; slab clay type 1	5	122	90	250	90–250
5017	3102	Fired clay	5	79	90	250	90–250
5018	UNK; 3120a; 3101R; CAM1; CAM2	Unknown fabric and form; Roman undiagnostic form; opus caementicium; micaceous sandstone	9	48	90	250	120–250
5020	3102; CAM2; CAM3	Fired clay type 1; unknown Roman form	7	34	90	250	120–250
5022	3102; CAM2; CAM3; UNK;	Fired clay type 1; tegula and Roman tile; unknown Roman fabric and form;	13	228	90	250	120–250
5023	UNK; 3102; CAM1; CAM2; CAM3; 3111; 3129	Fired clay type 1; tegula and Roman tile; unknown Roman fabric and form; ferruginous sandstone; fine laminated sandstone	8	30	90	250	120–250
5024	UNK	Unknown fabric and form	1	23	UNC	UNC	UNC
5025	CAM2; CAM3	Box flue tile; Roman brick and undiagnostic form	3	891	90	250	120–250
5026	3130; 3125; 3102; UNK; CAM3	Coarse sandstone; clunch; fired clay type 1, 2 and 3; imbrex and undiagnostic Roman form	19	97	90	250	120–250
5027	3102; CAM1; CAM2	Fired clay type 1 and 3; undiagnostic Roman forms	14	55	90	250	120–250
5028	CAM2; 3102	Fired clay and undiagnostic Roman form	2	15	90	200	90–200
5029	UNK; 3102	Unknown fabric and form; fired clay type 1	3	15	90	250	90–250
5030	3102' CAM2	Fired clay type 1; undiagnostic Roman form	3	6	90	200	90–200
5031	3102	Fired clay type 1 and 3	4	130	90	250	90–250
5032	CAM2; CAM4; 3102	Undiagnostic Roman form; post-medieval brick; fired clay	12	65	90	1900	1700–1900
5032	CAM5	Post-medieval peg tile	1	13	90	1900	1700–1900

Table A2.14: Comparative table between the material found in both trenches.

	Trench 4		Trench 5	
	Quantity	Weight	Quantity	Weight
Fired clay	110	1245	150	981
Ceramic building material	113	2401	79	1739
Stone	96	3307	124	4943
Total material including mortar	320	6956	405	8013

Trench 4

A large quantity of material was found in this trench, totalling 320 fragments weighing 6956 g. Most of the material was recovered from fills and layers. The assemblage from this trench was dominated by large quantities of Roman ceramic building material, amounting to 113 examples, followed by fired clay with 110 fragments, weighing 3307 g. Although the majority of the fired clay was found within different features, it probably represents pieces of oven superstructure. Fragments from (4025), are possibly part of a furnace, or the lining of a smithing hearth. The fragments had a similar orange body to the oven lining, although contains more sand and is more friable, likely due to intense heat exposure. The fragment changes to a buff colour towards the outer surface and has a burnt, aerated glassy outer margin and surface (dark-green/black in colour).

The ceramic building material comprised bricks and tiles in particular with a smaller number of tegula and imbrex. This material, found in layers and fills, was the result of dumping and the discard from demolished buildings. It is important to emphasise that CAM1 is only present in one fragment from layer (4000). Fabrics CAM2 and CAM3 were present in equal quantity.

The stone assemblage is represented by a majority of natural examples, with large quantities of the micaceous sandstone, chalk and clunch. The absence of mortar adhering to the stone fragments makes it impossible to determine if their presence is from a building/structure or from the geological substrate.

Trench 5

The material recovered from this trench is greater than that from Trench 4, and in greater density considering there are fewer contexts (11) with material than Trench 4 (16). The assemblage was collected mainly from fills and layers. Fired clay is the predominant material (150 fragments) although the weight is less than that in Trench 4, indicating that the fragments are smaller in size. The majority of the burnt clay recovered may be derived indirectly from oven features, including fragments of the structures themselves, but also fragments of a portable oven. Features of this type, and the accompanying kiln furniture, were used for a range of different domestic and industrial functions, from food preparation or cereal processing to salt and pottery production. Unfortunately, without associated assemblages it can be difficult to determine which function is represented.

Ceramic building material is almost half than Trench 4, but the fragments were bigger in size. CAM2 and CAM3 are the main fabrics with occasional CAM1 examples. One box flue tile was found in layer (5025) indicating the existence of a heated building nearby. The ceramic material is dominated by brick fragments and occasionally tegula and imbrex.

Stone is comprised mainly of undiagnostic examples, too small to identify to form, but probably mostly natural stones. The only diagnostic fragment is a very abraded piece from layer (5000) belonging to a quern made of Niedermendig lava. These querns are associated with food production and are indicative of settlement and domestic occupation. Lava quern is typically used from the 1st century AD onwards.

Discussion

The building material recovered from the excavation shows that the features uncovered dates to Roman period, with some later post-medieval occupation. The building material comprised the most common Roman forms: tiles, bricks, imbrex, and tegula with a single box flue tile suggesting the existence of a heated building nearby. Imbrex and tegula indicates the existence of ceramic building roofing in at least some of the buildings. The absence of any comparative ceramic building material study from Corbridge makes the dating of this material difficult, although it was compared with the Roman pottery, suggesting that the sites could be related to the early–mid-2nd century. Early Roman tile production was undertaken at both military and civilian tileries, but legionary tile production appears to have all but ceased during the early 3rd century (Warry 2010, 146). For the early period a model of centralised production is favoured, with production focused on York, although possibly including Catterick and another kiln beyond the town, but this refers specifically to production and distribution of legionary building material (Isserlin 2002, 524–525).

Fired clay is highly over-represented throughout all the archaeological sequence due to its small size and disaggregated condition. Big fragments and the ones with surfaces would suggest that the group, and broader related assemblage from nearby features, probably represents oven or kiln furniture. These may have lined the flues or base of an oven or hearth or acted as supports for an oven plate. The examples from site are well-fired and some demonstrate scorching.

The combination of fired clay forms identified would suggest that they are unlikely to be related to textile manufacture, but instead probably represent oven or kiln furniture. It remains possible that the pottery and clay objects are not directly related, with the latter originating from a hearth, oven, or furnace with another function. However, the condition of the assemblage, with multiple fragments from the same objects, would also suggest the material is unlikely to be re-deposited. However, due to the abraded nature of the pieces, there is little further work that can be done. The fragment of lining from a smithing hearth, is more diagnostic and likely relates to the secondary metalworking well-attested to on site.

The majority of the stone recovered derives directly from fills. Unfortunately, without associated assemblages it can be difficult to determine which function is represented, except for the lava quern stone.

Cat's Stairs: consolidation of collapsed fabric

Jane Harrison

The National Trust 2020 SMC application sought consent to dismantle and rebuild the collapsed section of the southern wall face, reinstate fill behind the face as necessary, and re-bed and augment the turf capping (NGR 375846 567697).

Following consultation with and agreement from Historic England, Northumberland National Park, and National Trust, the following conservation works were carried out by Heritage Consolidation in October 2020 adhering to the SMC working practices, with the Wall-CAP archaeologist Jane Harrison present to carry out the watching brief:

- The slumped stonework was dismantled until a stable course was reached;
- The curtain was rebuilt using agreed techniques, including tail-bedding as necessary; and
- The top was consolidated using the turf plug method: just over five metres of Wall were affected.

The Cat Stairs collapse was of a stretch of the Clayton Wall that had clearly been repaired relatively recently as

Terram was discovered in the wall core once the tumbled and loose stones were shifted. No undisturbed Roman courses were revealed and the only find was a 2012 one penny piece.

Port Carlisle: consolidation of collapsed fabric and insertion of new farm gate

Jane Harrison and Kathryn Murphy

Consolidation work on the surviving short lengths of stone curtain either side of the existing field gate were undertaken, and the relocation of that gate to the east, better to protect these rare survivals of standing Wall in the west. The work took place on 18–19 August 2021 and required two WallCAP team members, three craftspeople from *Heritage Consolidation* to do the Wall repairs, and three local contractors to insert the new gate and complete the re-fencing.

The *Heritage Consolidation* team removed all vegetation, consolidated the remains of the curtain Wall either side of the existing gate, and finished by turf capping the core with sods lifted from just south of the hedge line. A watching brief was maintained during the work. To the east of the gate, the vegetation removed included the mature hawthorn bushes and saplings of an overgrown hedge, which had rooted deep into the structural remains. To the west of the gate an overgrown and leaning hawthorn was cut down to prevent it pulling further on the *in-situ* facing stones when it collapsed. Some of the modern mortar used to repair the Wall west of the gate – almost certainly around the 1970s – was removed and appropriate lime mortar applied to tail bed strategic facing stones on both sides of the gate. Altogether just over 4 m of curtain Wall were consolidated.

The preparation work for consolidation fully revealed the poor state of the Wall in this location, especially to the east of the gate. On the west side up to three courses of the south face survived *in-situ* but the north side had completely collapsed with no facing stone remaining and little *in-situ* core. The situation was worse on the east side with only up to two courses of the south face still *in situ* and the north 'face' under the vegetation consisting only of piled up, loose core stones. This discrepancy in survival of the faces has been caused by the repeated flooding of the lower, northern field, with the shifting of light estuarine soils during inundations repeatedly undermining the curtain Wall remains. Once stripped of facing stone the destabilised core collapsed towards the north. Continuing attempts by those farming the land to improve drainage in the fields has also repeatedly disturbed the archaeology. Drains run alongside and through the Wall line. The destabilising of the Wall from the north was noted in excavation and was only too apparent during the consolidation work. Loose core stones scattered around the Wall remains were stacked up on the northern slope of what had been the core on each side of the gate to further protect the *in-situ* and re-bedded southern facing stones.

The intention had been to excavate a narrow north–south section through the gateway against apparently *in-situ* facing stones, to look for Turf Wall remnants and confirm the level of the foundation course. However, after a summer of heavy rains and further wear, the line and width of the north–south field drain punched through the gateway was much clearer, as was the extent of the disturbance caused by its insertion. The putative northern line of facing stones also appeared more likely to be undermined, slipped, and rotated stones. Despite earlier weeks of rain having washed more sediment from above and around the stones bedded in the gap, the ground was also extremely hard, and it was decided that attempting any excavation would cause more damage than was warranted by the likely outcome.

The old gate was wired shut across the gap, new wooden fencing posts erected 1 m north and south of the Wall remains and the whole area fenced off with a double strand of barbed wire. No further damage can now be inflicted by stock and machinery on the consolidated curtain Wall remnants or on any surviving archaeology in the gateway.

- *Consolidated section of Wall west of gateway*: 1.95 m east–west by 1.35 m wide (2.1 m wide including tumble re-piled to protect south face); max. 1.05 m high.
- Maximum width in gateway between line of *in-situ* south facing stones/foundation stones and line of northern facing stones (probably displaced): 1.75 m.
- *Consolidated section of Wall east of gateway*: 2.1 m east–west by 1.65 m wide; max. 1.1 m high. The field dyke is up to 3.5 m wide.
- *Measurements of south-facing stones revealed to east of gateway*
- Foundation course, moving west to east: 0.38 m long × 0.26 m wide (as seen); 0.32 m long × 0.23 m wide (as seen); 0.32 m long × 0.21 m wide (as seen);
- Next course up, *in-situ* stones from west: 0.52 m long × 0.31 m wide (as seen) by 0.18 m high (chock stones?); 0.21 m long × 0.25 m wide (as seen) by 0.17 m high.

The new gate was to be inserted to the east of the standing Wall lengths, in the location of PC21 Trench 1. This required the removal of a hedge bank over half-a-metre high, the wooden fence topping the bank and good deal of scrubby vegetation. A watching brief was maintained as a small digger was used to demolish the dyke. The 14 ft-wide gate and posts were to be inserted within the footprint of the agricultural building removed in the 1970s, which the excavations in April had investigated. The levelling of the bank was observed carefully; the material removed and examined as demolition progressed was in all respects similar to the disturbed layers recorded in the April excavation. There was one exception. At the far western edge of the opening being created for the new gate *c.* 4 m from the southeast corner of the field to the northeast), at field ground level and on the centre of the Wall line, a layer of modern-looking mortar sealed an uneven layer of core stones below. An area of *c.* 0.6 m^2 of the mortar was uncovered. The *Heritage Consolidation* team compared this mortar to that used, possibly in the 1970s, roughly to repair the Wall stub to the west of the old gate, and colour and composition appeared to match.

There was no need to remove the mortar patch or to disturb any possibly *in-situ* core stones below to erect the gate. Instead the rubbly end of field bank above, comprising re-used Wall core, was consolidated by *Heritage Consolidation* with lime mortar and an extra skim of lime mortar laid over the existing ground-level modern mortar. The modern mortar work may have been intended to create a firmer surface just west of the agricultural building or as foundations for a wall running from the dyke up to the west wall of the structure. Finally, the contractors used core stones from the demolished dyke to build a dry-stone cairn over the area. Any possible *in-situ* archaeology is now secure behind a barbed wire fence and beneath the dry-stone structure and mortar layers.

Postholes were dug for new metal gate posts in the higher field south of the Wall line, so that the gate opened to the south from the eastern post. This was the only positioning which allowed the gate to swing flat to the hedge. Below the field soil, excavation of the postholes encountered glacial tills, then at 0.6 m down from the field surface, mineral-stained sandstone was discovered. This bedrock material was discovered at the same depth in Trench 1 south of the Wall line and appears to be a relict estuary bank on the northern edge of which this stretch of the curtain Wall was built. This accounts for the relatively sinuous course of the curtain Wall as it tracks the bank.

Each of the new wooden fence posts pounded in south of the hedge bank encountered the same solid sandstone at a very similar depth. The change in vibration and effort needed by the fencing machine indicated when the rock was reached. The new posts required north of the dyke were easy to inset, being pushed through the silty deposits and glacial till seen in the excavation. Once all the posts were inserted and the concrete holding the gate posts in place had dried sufficiently the gate was hung and the fencing completed with a double line of barbed wire.

Steel Rigg: consolidation of collapsed fabric

Jane Harrison

The rebuilding of the collapsed section of the Wall in Peel Gap (NGR 375253 567534), the raising of a protective stone dyke, and the turf and stone reprofiling of sections of curtain top between Peel Gap and Steel Rigg was carried out by *Heritage Consolidation* in October and November 2020. The same parameters were followed in the work carried out in this area as had guided work at Cat Stairs.

After consultation with and agreement from Historic England, Northumberland National Park, and National Trust, the following conservation works were carried out by *Heritage Consolidation* in October and November 2020, with the WallCAP archaeologist Jane Harrison present to carry out the watching brief for the dismantling and rebuilding:

1. At the Peel Gap, west slope collapse: the slumped stonework was dismantled until a stable course was reached; the curtain was rebuilt using agreed techniques, including tail-bedding as necessary; and the top was consolidated using the turf plug method. Around 6 m of Wall were affected.
2. Stretches of curtain top were consolidated and reprofiled; some 70 m of the curtain were involved in total. The work at the gate into the Peel Bothy field also included repairing the ordinary stone dyke forming the southeastern side of the gate.
3. The stone field wall running north–south to Steel Rigg carpark was raised to deter people from climbing onto the end of the Wall from the road to take photos.

The collapsed section consisting of at least four courses of the south face of the Clayton Wall in the Peel Bothy Field was dismantled down to a secure foundation course of larger stones. Dismantling was needed of a further five stones of the course at the base of the collapse as they had slipped out and canted downwards as the wall bellied under the weight of the core and previous reprofiling. This course may have been surviving Roman fabric pushed out of position by the slump of Wall fabric.

Below the slipped course were four larger stones, exposed to a depth of *c.* 0.25 m. The length of the furthest west stone was not fully exposed but 0.5 m was visible, the next stone east was 0.62 m long, the next 0.47 m long and the furthest east, again not fully exposed, was 0.4 m long. These stones were completely secure and were larger than the majority of the stones used in the courses above. This course may well have been foundation and was almost certainly *in-situ* Roman construction. There appeared to be some contemporary mortar surviving at the back of the exposed stones, *c.* 0.15 m in from the faces.

The mortar had many inclusions including white and CBM-red coloured fragments and was an orangey pink colour on exposure. Silt had washed down from the wall above, but lenses of the mortar seemed to be relatively undisturbed, with the silt only on the surface. A sample of mortar was taken. The section was rebuilt up from the sound course of larger stones.

Turret 44b (Mucklebank), Walltown: consolidation of collapsed fabric

Jane Harrison

The conservation work to address issues at Mucklebank Turret was carried out by *Heritage Consolidation* in October 2020. The loose stonework at the remains of Turret 44b was consolidated and where necessary tail-bedded, and the top turfed using the method described below. Work focused on the SE corner (NGR: 3681409, 566703), which was where facing stones were tail-bedded.

Walltown Crags: reconditioning and consolidation of tumbled fabric

Jane Harrison

Issues lie with a short section of the Wall above Walltown quarry, where limited consolidation and capping works would address the management issues around actively collapsing fabric, consisting of misalignment and tumble of coursed facing stones, and tumble of expose core rubble.

Conservation work to the core along a 25 m stretch of Wall (NGR 367659.71, 566570.97) between the old fence line in the west (a 'safety indicator' to separate displayed remains of the curtain from Walltown Quarry East) and the site of excavation Trench 2 in November 2020. Within this area, any loose facing stones to either side of the Wall were reset, and if appropriate tail-bedded. Once the faces were deemed stable, clumps of turf were placed, in an apparently random and uneven manner, on top of the Wall curtain amongst the stones of the core. Where necessary, this turf was secured with short timber pegs. This newly introduced turf should merge into the Wall top as the grass grows, providing support for the facing stones and precluding further collapse. The turf was sourced as locally as possible, but from outside the scheduled area.

Bibliography

Alberti, M. and Mountain, K. (eds) 2022. *Hadrian's Wall: Exploring its Past to Protect its Future*. Oxford: Archaeopress.

Allason-Jones, L. and Bishop, M.C. 1988. *Excavations at Roman Corbridge: The Hoard*. London: English Heritage.

Allason-Jones, L. and McKay, B. 1985. *Coventina's Well: A Shrine on Hadrian's Wall*. Chesters: Trustees of the Clayton Collection.

Allen, D. 1988. Roman Glass from Corbridge. In M.C. Bishop and J.N. Dore, *Corbridge: Excavations of the Roman Fort and Town 1947–80*, 287–293. English Heritage Archaeological Report 8, London: Historic Buildings and Monuments Commission for England.

Allen, M.G. 2009. The re-identification of great bustard (*Otis tarda*) from Fishbourne Roman Palace, Chichester, West Sussex, as common crane (*Grus grus*). *Environmental Archaeology* 14: 180–186.

Austen, P.S. 1991. *Bewcastle and Old Penrith: A Roman Outpost Fort and a Frontier Vicus*. Kendal: Cumberland and Westmorland Antiquarian and Archaeological Society.

Baatz, D. 2000. *Der Romische Limes: Archäologische Ausflüge zwischen Rhein und Donau*. 3rd ed, Berlin: Gebr. Mann Verlag.

Bartlett, A.D.H. 1976. *Corbridge, Northumberland*. Unpublished report of the Ancient Monuments Laboratory Geophysics Section.

Bell, A. and Evans, J. 2002. Pottery from the CfA excavations. In P. Wilson, *Cataractonium Volume I*, 352–498. York: Council for British Archaeology.

Bennet, J. 1983. The examination of Turret 10A and the Wall and the Vallum at Throckley, Tyne and Wear, 1980. *Archaeologia Aeliana*, 5th series, 11: 40–43.

Bennet, J. and Turner, R. 1983. The Vallum at Wallhouses, Northumberland: excavations in 1980 and 1981. *Archaeologia Aeliana*, 5th series, 11: 61–78.

Betts, I. 1995. *Roman brick and tiles dating*. London: unpublished MoLAS guide.

Bidwell, P. 1999. *Hadrian's Wall 1989–1999*. Kendal: Society of Antiquaries of Newcastle on Tyne and Cumberland and Westmorland Antiquarian and Archaeological Society.

Bidwell, P. 2005. The systems of obstacles on Hadrian's Wall: Their extent, date and purpose. *Arbeia Journal* 8: 53–75.

Bidwell, P. 2010. A survey of the Anglo-Saxon crypt at Hexham and its reused Roman stonework. *Archaeologia Aeliana*, 5th series, 39: 53–145.

Bidwell, P. 2018. *Hadrian's Wall at Wallsend*. Newcastle: Arbeia Society and TWAM.

Bidwell, P. and Croom, A. 2002. The Roman pottery. In M. Snape and P. Bidwell, Excavations at Castle Garth, Newcastle upon Type, 1976–92 and 1995–6: the excavation of the Roman fort. *Archaeologia Aeliana*, 5th series, 31: 139–172.

Bidwell, P. and Croom, A. 2010. The supply and use of pottery on Hadrian's Wall in the 4th century AD. In R. Collins and L. Allason-Jones (eds) *Finds from the Frontier: Material Culture in the 4th-5th Centuries*, 20–37. York: Council for British Archaeology.

Bidwell, P. and Croom, A. 2018. The major coarse wares. In P. Bidwell, *Hadrian's Wall at Wallsend*, 199–204. South Shields: The Arbeia Society and TWAM.

Bidwell, P. and Holbrook, N. 1989. *Hadrian's Wall Bridges*. English Heritage Archaeological Report 9, London: English Heritage.

Biggins, J.A. and Taylor, D.J.A. 2007. The Roman Fort at Castlesteads, Cumbria: A Geophysical Survey of the Vicus. *Transactions of the Cumberland and Westmorland Antiquarian and Archaeological Society*, 3rd series, 7: 15–30.

Bird, J. 1986. Samian Ware. In L. Miller, J. Schofield and M. Rhodes, *The Roman Quay at St. Magnus House, London*. London and Middlesex Archaeological Society Special Paper 8: 139–185.

Birley, B. 2006. The Beads. In B. Birley and E. Greene, *The Roman Jewellery from Vindolanda*, 9–52. Greenhead: Vindolanda Trust.

Birley, E. 1959. Excavations at Corstopitum, 1906–1958, *Archaeologia Aeliana*, 4th series, 37: 1–31.

Birley, E. and Richmond, I.A. 1938. Excavations at Corbridge 1936–8. *Archaeologia Aeliana*, 4th series, 15: 243–294.

Bishop, M.C. 1994. *Corstopitum: An Edwardian Excavations*, London: English Heritage.

Bishop, M.C. and Dore, J.N. 1988. *Corbridge: Excavations of the Roman Fort and Town 1947–80*. English Heritage Archaeological Report 8, London: Historic Buildings and Monuments Commission for England.

Blair, R. 1895. *J. Collingwood Bruce's Handbook to the Roman Wall*. 4th edition, Newcastle: Society of Antiquaries of Newcastle on Tyne.

Brendel, O. 1941. The Corbridge lanx. *Journal of Roman Studies* 31: 100–127.

Breeze, D.J. 2006. *J. Collingwood Bruce's Handbook to the Roman Wall*. 14th edition, Newcastle: Society of Antiquaries of Newcastle on Tyne.

Breeze, D.J. 2009. Did Hadrian design Hadrian's Wall. *Archaeologia Aeliana*, 5th series, 38: 87–103.

Breeze, D.J. 2014. *Hadrian's Wall: A History of Archaeological Thought*. Kendal: Cumberland and Westmorland Antiquarian and Archaeological Society.

Breeze, D.J. 2015. The Vallum of Hadrian's Wall. *Archaeologia Aeliana*, 5th series, 44: 1–30.

Breeze, D.J. 2018. The building of Hadrian's Wall: A review of 50 years. *Archaeologia Aeliana*, 5th series, 47: 5–40.

Breeze, D.J. 2019. *Hadrian's Wall: A Study in Archaeological Exploration and Interpretation*. Oxford: Archaeopress.

Breeze, D.J. and Dobson, B. 1976. *Hadrian's Wall*. London: Palgrave.

Breeze, D.J., Hill, P. and Thiel, A. 2020. The Stones, the Core and the Offsets of Hadrian's Wall. *Archaeologia Aeliana*, 5th series, 49: 65–97.

Bulmer, W. 1955. Roman Glass Vessels in the Corstopitum Museum, Corbridge. *Archaeologia Aeliana*, 4th series, 33: 116–133.

Callender, M.H. 1949. Corbridge Amphora Stamps. *Archaeologia Aeliana*, 4th series, 27: 60–121.

Campbell, G., Moffett, L. and Straker, V. 2011. *Environmental Archaeology. A Guide to the Theory and Practice of Methods, from Sampling and Recovery to Post-excavation*. 2nd edition, Portsmouth: English Heritage.

Cappers, R.T.J., Bekker, R.M. and Jans, J.E.A. 2006. *Digital Seed Atlas of the Netherlands*. Eelde: Barkhuis Publishing.

Carlisle, D. 1794. Account of some Roman Antiquities lately discovered in Cumberland. *Archaeologia*, 11: 63–71.

Charlesworth, D. 1959. Roman glass in Northern Britain. *Archaeologia Aeliana,* 4th series, 37: 33–58.

Charlesworth, D. 1971. A group of vessels from the Commandant's House, Housesteads. *Journal of Glass Studies* 13: 34–37.

Chartered Institute for Archaeologists. 2021. *Toolkit for Specialist Reporting*. Available at https://www.archaeologists.net/reporting-toolkit (Accessed 20th February 2022).

Chenet, G. and Gaudron, G. 1955. *La Céramique sigillée d'Argonne des IIe et IIIe siècles*. *Gallia* Supplement 6, Paris.

Clayton, J. 1879. Discovery of a hoard of Roman coins on the Wall of Hadrian, in Northumberland. *Archaeologia Aeliana*, 2nd series, 8: 256–258.

Collingwood, R.G. 1922. Castlesteads. *Transactions of the Cumberland and Westmorland Antiquarian and Archaeological Society*, 2nd series, 22: 198–233.

Collins, R. 2012. *Hadrian's Wall and the End of Empire: The Roman Frontier in the 4th–5th Centuries*. New York: Routledge.

Collins, R. and Symonds, M. 2019. *Hadrian's Wall 2009–2019*. Kendal: Society of Antiquaries of Newcastle on Tyne and Cumberland and Westmorland Antiquarian and Archaeological Society.

Collins, R., Birley, B., Croom, A., Laskey, J., McIntosh, F., Padley, T., Parkin, A. and Price, E. 2020. *Living on the Edge of Empire: The Objects and People of Rome's Northern Frontier*. Barnsley: Pen and Sword.

Collins, R., Harrison, J., Kille, I., Murphy, K. and Shaw, K. 2023a. *Community Archaeology on Hadrian's Wall 2019–2022*. Oxford: Oxbow Books.

Collins, R., Kille, I. and O'Donnell, K. 2023b. *Fabric of the Frontier: Prospection, Use, and Re-Use of Stone from Hadrian's Wall*, Oxford: Oxbow Books.

Cool, H.E.M. 2004. *The Roman Cemetery at Brougham, Cumbria. Excavations 1966–67. Britannia* Monograph no. 21. London: Society for the Promotion of Roman Studies.

Cool, H.E.M. 2020. Vessel glass. In D.W. Fell, *Contact, Concord and Conquest. Britons and Romans at Scotch Corner*. NAA Monograph Series 5: 457–478.

Cool, H.E.M. and Price, J. 2002. Vessel glass from Catterick Bypass (Site 433). In P. Wilson, *Cataractonium: Roman Catterick and its Hinterland. Excavations and Research, 1958–1997, Part II*, 213–33. York: Council for British Archaeology.

Cool, H.E.M. and Price, J. 2008. The glass vessels. In H.E.M. Cool, *Roman Piercebridge*. York: Archaeology Data Service, Chapter 10. https://doi.org/10.5284/1000057.

Corder, P. 1937. A pair of fourth-century Romano-British pottery kilns near Crambeck. *The Antiquaries Journal* 17: 392–413.

Croom, A. 2016. The coarse wares. In A. Rushworth and A. Croom, *Segedunum: Excavations by Charles Daniels in the Roman Fort at Wallsend (1975–1984), Volume 2: The Finds*, 55–87. Oxford: Oxbow Books.

Daniels, C. 1959. The Roman Bath-house at Red House, Beaufront, nr. Corbridge. *Archaeologia Aeliana*, 4th series, 37: 164–166.

Daniels, C. 1989. *The Eleventh Pilgrimage of Hadrian's Wall*. Newcastle: Society of Antiquaries of Newcastle on Tyne.

Dearne, M.J. and Branigan, K. 1995. The use of coal in Roman Britain. *Antiquaries Journal* 75: 71–105.

Deru, X. and Feller, M. 2005. La Terre Sigillée moulée d'Argonne de la Cave 183 de L'agglomération gallo-romaine de 'Sarteaux' à Ville-de-Lûmes. *Archéologie de la Picardie et du Nord de la France, Revue du Nord* 87: 95–107.

Dore, J.N. 1998. Pottery production at Corbridge in the late 1st century. In J. Bird (ed.) *Form and Fabric: Studies in Rome's material pas in honour of B. R. Hartley*, 227–234. Oxford: Oxbow Books.

Eaton, T. 2000. *Plundering the Past: Roman Stonework in Medieval Britain*. Stroud: Tempus.

Fafinski, M. 2021. *Roman Infrastructure in Early Medieval Britain: The Adaptations of the Past in Text and Stone*. Amsterdam: Amsterdam University Press.

Foglia, A. 2014. Turrets as watchtowers: A GIS and source-based analysis of appearance and surveillance capabilities. *Archaeologia Aeliana*, 5th series, 43: 26–46.

Forster, R.H. and Knowles, W.H. 1910. Corstopitum: report on the excavations in 1909. *Archaeologia Aeliana*, 3rd series, 6: 205–272.

Forster, R.H. and Knowles, W.H. 1911. Corstopitum: report on the excavations in 1910. *Archaeologia Aeliana*, 3rd series, 7: 143–267.

Forster, R.H. and Knowles, W.H. 1912. Corstopitum: report on the excavations in 1911. *Archaeologia Aeliana*, 3rd series, 8: 137–263.

Forster, R.H. and Knowles, W.H. 1913. Corstopitum: report on the excavations in 1912. *Archaeologia Aeliana*, 3rd series, 10: 230–280.

Forster, R.H. and Knowles, W.H. 1914. Corstopitum: report on the excavations in 1913. *Archaeologia Aeliana*, 3rd series, 11: 279–310.

Forster, R.H. and Knowles, W.H. 1915. Corstopitum: report on the excavations in 1914. *Archaeologia Aeliana*, 3rd series, 12: 227–286.

Frain, T., McKelvey, J. and Bidwell, P. 2005. Excavations and watching briefs along the berm of Hadrian's Wall at Throckley, Newcastle upon Tyne, in 2001–2002. *Arbeia Journal* 8: 29–52.

Frodsham, P. 2016. *Hadrian's Wall World Heritage Site Heritage At Risk Survey*. Unpublished report.

Gerrard, J. 2012. The Native and Roman Pottery. In J. Proctor, *Faverdale, Darlington: Excavations at a major settlement in the northern frontier zone of Roman Britain.* Pre-Construct Archaeology Ltd. Monograph No. 15: 79–91.

Gillam, J.P. 1970. *Types of Roman Coarse Pottery Vessels in Northern Britain.* 3rd edition, Newcastle: Oriel Press.

Gillam, J.P. and Daniels, C.M. 1961. The Roman Mausoleum on Shorden Brae, Beaufront, Corbridge, Northumberland. *Archaeologia Aeliana*, 4th series, 39: 37–61.

Graafstal, E. 2012. Hadrian's haste: A priority programme for the Wall. *Archaeologia Aeliana*, 5th series, 41: 123–184.

Graafstal, E. 2018. What happened in the summer of AD 122? Hadrian on the British frontier – archaeology, epigraphy and historical agency. *Britannia* 49: 79–111.

Graafstal, E. 2020. Hadrian's Wall: the winding path of a Roman megaproject. *Archaeologia Aeliana*, 5th series, 49: 99–169.

Guido, M. 1978. *The Glass Beads of the Prehistoric and Roman Periods in Britain and Ireland.* London: Society of Antiquaries of London.

Guido, M. 1979. The glass beads. In G. Clarke, *The Roman Cemetery at Lankhills*, 292–300. Winchester: Winchester Studies 3.

Hall, A. and Huntley, J. 2007 *A Review of the Evidence for Macrofossil Plant Remains from Archaeological Deposits in Northern England.* Research Department Report Series No. 87-2007. London: English Heritage Publications.

Hansen, W.S, Daniels, C.M, Dore, J.N. and Gillam, J.P. 1979. The Agricolan supply base at Red House, Corbridge. *Archaeologia Aeliana*, 5th series, 7: 1–98.

Hartley, B.R. and Dickinson, B.M. 2008–12. *Names on Terra Sigillata. An Index of Makers' Stamps and Signatures on Gallo-Roman Terra Sigillata (Samian Ware).* London: Institute of Classical Studies.

Haverfield, F. 1914. Roman silver in Northumberland. *Journal of Roman Studies* 4: 1–12.

Hedley, W.P. 1937. The last days of Corstopitum and the Roman Wall – the coin evidence. *Archaeologia Aeliana*, 4th series, 14: 95–102.

Hill, P.R. 2004. *The Construction of Hadrian's Wall.* British Archaeological Report 375, Oxford: Archaeopress.

Hill, P.R. 2006. *The Construction of Hadrian's Wall.* Stroud: Tempus.

Hill, P.R. 2009. *Stonework assessment on the line of Hadrian's Wall at Cam Beck, NY 511639.* Unpublished report for English Heritage.

Hingley, R. 2012. *Hadrian's Wall: A Life*, Oxford: Oxford University Press.

Hird, L. 1997. The coarse pottery. In Wilmott 1997, 233–255.

Historic England. 1994. *Official list entry: Hillfort on Warden Hill.* Accessed at: https://historicengland.org.uk/listing/the-list/list-entry/1011421?section=official-list-entry. Accessed 04/08/2023.

Historic England. 2015. *Archaeometallurgy: Guidelines for best practice.* London: Historic England.

Hodgson, J. 1840. *History of Northumberland, Vol. 2, Part 3.* Newcastle.

Hodgson, N. 2008. The development of the Roman site at Corbridge from the first to third centuries AD. *Archaeologia Aeliana*, 5th series, 37: 47–92.

Hodgson, N. 2009. *Hadrian's Wall 1999–2009*, Kendal: Society of Antiquaries of Newcastle on Tyne and Cumberland and Westmorland Antiquarian and Archaeological Society.

Hodgson, N. 2010. Roman architectural fragments at Corbridge: A survey and study. *Arbeia Journal* 9: 1–42.

Hodgson, N. 2017. *Hadrian's Wall: Archaeology and History at the Limit of Rome's Empire.* Marlborough: Hale.

Howard-Davis, C., Leary, R. and Ward, M. 2017. Evaluation of Beckfoot Roman cemetery, 2006. *Transactions of the Cumberland & Westmoreland Antiquarian & Archaeological Society*, 3rd series, 17: 43–84.

Hudak, E. 2013. *Mortaria in Northern Britain: Rethinking Distribution in the Frontier Zone.* Newcastle University unpublished MLitt thesis.

Hunneysett, R. 2017. The consequences of 'priority milecastles'. In A. Parker (ed.) *Ad Vallum: Papers on the Roman Army and Frontiers in Celebration of Dr Brian Dobson*, 49–62. British Archaeological Report Series 631, Oxford: British Archaeological Reports.

Huntley, J. 1991. *Macrobotanical remains from the Roman fort of Banna (Birdoswld, Cumbria).* Portsmouth: AML Report New Series 104/91.

Huntley, J. 1997. Macrobotanical evidence from the *horrea*. In Wilmott 1997, 141–144.

Huntley, J. 2003. Appendix III: Vindolanda: analysis of environmental samples. 1998–2002 excavations. In A. Birley, *The Excavations of 2001–2002, Volume 1.* Hexham: Vindolanda Trust, 257–279.

Huntley, J. 2007. Vindolanda 2003–6: interim report on plant remains and charcoal from environmental samples. In A. Birley and J. Blake, *Vindolanda Excavations 2005–2006*, 205–215. Hexham: Vindolanda Trust.

Huntley, J. 2010. *A review of wood and charcoal recovered from archaeological sites in Northern England.* Research Department Report Series No. 68–2010, London: English Heritage.

Isings, C. 1957. *Roman Glass from Dated Finds.* Groningen: J.B. Wolters.

Isserlin, R.M.J. 2002. Brick and Tile Discussion. In P.R. Wilson *Cataractonium: Roman Catterick and its hinterland. Excavations and research, 1958–1997. Part 1.* CBA Research Report 128, Council for British Archaeology, 523–525.

Jobey, G. 1979. Palisaded enclosures, a Roman temporary camp and Roman gravel quarries on Bishop Rigg, Corbridge. *Archaeologia Aeliana*, 5th series, 7: 99–113.

King, A. 2005. Animal remains from temples in Roman Britain. *Britannia* 36: 329–369.

Kreiger, E. 2015. Watchtowers on the Upper German-Raetian *Limes*. In S. Matešić and C.S. Sommer (eds) *At the Edge of the Roman Empire: Tours along the Limes in Southern Germany*. Deutsche Limeskommission / Bayerisches Landesamt für Denkmalpflege, 38–39.

Lyne, M. 2002. The fired clay objects, in R. Taylor-Wilson, Excavation of a multi-period site at Laleham, 1997. *Surrey Archaeological Collections* 89: 159.

Martin-Kilcher, S. 1987. *Die Römischen Amphoren aus Augst und Kaiseraugst*. Forschungen in Augst 7:1, Allschwil: Gissler Druck AG.

McCarthy, M. 2005. Social dynamics on the Northern Frontier of Roman Britain. *Oxford Journal of Archaeology* 24.1: 47–71.

McCluskey, A. 2018. The 'functions' of Hadrian's Wall: A view from the trenches. In S. Sommer and S. Matešić (eds), *Limes XXIII: Proceedings of the 23rd International Congress of Roman Frontier Studies, Ingolstadt 2015*. Mainz: Bayerisches Landesamt f r Denkmalpflege, 159–163.

McCluskey, A. 2022. The present as epilogue: Urban conflict and the 'Corbridge destruction deposit'. In N. Hodgson and B. Griffiths (eds) *Roman Frontier Archaeology – in Britain and Beyond*, 277–286. Oxford: Archaeopress.

McDonnell, J.G. 1991. A model for the formation of smithing slag. *Materially Archeologicne* 26: 23–26.

McIntosh, F. 2019. *The Clayton Collection: An archaeological appraisal of a 19th century collection of Roman artefacts from Hadrian's Wall*. British Archaeological Report 616, Oxford: British Archaeological Reports.

Monaghan, J. 1987. *Upchurch and Thameside Roman pottery: ceramic typology for northern Kent, first to third centuries A.D.* British Archaeological Report 173, Oxford: British Archaeological Reports.

Morgan, T. and Bidwell, P. 2015. Rivers and streams cross by Hadrian's Wall and their possible surveillance at bridges and culverts. *Arbeia Journal* 10: 43–51.

O'Donnell, K.E.A. 2021. *The Quarries of Hadrian's Wall: Materials and Logistics of a Large-Scale Imperial Building Project*. Unpublished PhD thesis, University of Edinburgh. http://dx.doi.org/10.7488/era/1346.

Oswald, F. 1936–37. *Index of Figure Types on Terra Sigillata*. Liverpool: University Press.

Oxford Archaeology North (OAN). 2020. *King Arthur's Well, Hadrian's Wall, Northumberland: Archaeological evaluation report*. Unpublished Report.

PCRG, SGRP, MPRG. 2016. *A Standard for Pottery Studies in Archaeology*. Prehistoric Ceramics Research Group, Study Group for Roman Pottery, Medieval Pottery Research Group.

Perrin, J. 1999. Roman pottery from excavations at and near to the Roman small town of Durobrivae, Water Newton, Cambridgeshire, 1956–58. *Journal of Roman Pottery Studies* 8.

Petts, D. and Gerrard, C. 2006. *Shared Visions: The North-East Regional Research Framework for the Historic Environment*. Durham: Durham County Council.

Poole, C. 2011. Ceramic building material and fired clay. In E. Biddulph, R. Seager Smith and J. Schuster, *Settling the Ebbsfleet Valley: High Speed I Excavations at Springhead and Northfleet, Kent; The Late Iron Age, Roman, Saxon and Medieval Landscape – Volume 2: Late Iron Age to Roman Finds Reports*, 313–350. Oxford: Wessex Archaeology.

Poulter, J. 2009. *Surveying Roman Military Landscapes across Northern Britain*. British Archaeological Report Series 492, Oxford: Archaeopress.

Price, J. 1985. The Glass. In P. Bidwell, *The Roman Fort of Vindolanda*, 206–214. London: English Heritage.

Price, J. 1989. The Roman glass. In S.S. Frere and J.J. Wilkes, *Strageath: Excavations within the Roman Fort 1973–86*, 192–203. London: Society for the Promotion of Roman Studies.

Price, J. 1990. Roman vessel and window glass. In M.R. McCarthy, *A Roman, Anglian and Medieval Site at Blackfriars Street, Carlisle*, 163–179. Kendal: Cumberland and Westmorland Antiquarian and Archaeological Society.

Price, J. 2002. Two vessels from Llandovery, Carmarthenshire and Piercebridge County durham: a note on flavian and later Polychrome Mosaic Glass in Britain. In M. Aldhouse-Green and P. Webster (eds) *Artefacts and Archaeology: Aspects of the Celtic and Roman World*, 112–131. Cardiff: University of Wales Press.

Price, J. 2016. Roman glass and obsidian vessels. In C. Haselgrove, *Cartimandua's Capital? The late Iron Age royal site at Stanwick, North Yorkshire. Fieldwork and analysis 1981–2011*, 262–267. York: Council for British Archaeology.

Price, J. and Cottam, S. 1997. Roman glass. In Wilmott 1997, 341–355.

Price, J. and Cottam, S. 1998. *Romano-British Glass Vessels: A Handbook*. Practical Handbook in Archaeology 14. York: Council for British Archaeology.

Price, J. and Cottam, S. 2010. The Roman glass (I). In J. Zant, *The Southern Lanes, Carlisle: Publication of Unpublished Fascicules*, 238–259. Lancaster: Oxford Archaeology North.

Price, J. and Worrell, S. 2010. Roman glass. In I. Ferris, *The Beautiful Rooms are Empty: Excavations at Binchester Roman Fort, County Durham, 1976–81 and 1986–91*, 268–232. Durham: Durham County Council.

Richardson, B. 1986. The waterfront group: coarsewares and non-samian finewares. In L. Miller, J. Schofield and M. Rhodes, *The Roman Quay at St Magnus House, London*. London: Special Paper No. 8. of the London and Middlesex Archaeological Society: 106–138.

Richmond, I.A. 1943. Roman legionaries at Corbridge, their supply-base, temples and religious cults. *Archaeologia Aeliana*, 4th series, 21: 127–224.

Richmond, I.A. and Birley, E. 1940. Excavations at Corbridge, 1938–9. *Archaeologia Aeliana*, 4th series, 17: 85–115.

Richmond, I.A. and Gillam, J.P. 1950. Excavations on the Roman site at Corbridge 1946–1949. *Archaeologia Aeliana*, 4th series, 28: 152–201.

Richmond, I.A. and Gillam, J.P. 1952a. Further exploration of the Antonine fort at Corbridge. *Archaeologia Aeliana*, 4th series, 30: 239–266.

Richmond, I.A. and Gillam, J.P. 1952b. Milecastle 79 (Solway). *Transactions of the Cumberland and Westmorland Antiquarian and Archaeological Society*, 2nd series, 52: 17–40.

Richmond, I.A. and Gillam, J.P. 1953. Buildings of the first and second centuries north of the granaries at Corbridge. *Archaeologia Aeliana*, 4th series, 31: 205–253.

Richmond, I.A. and Gillam, J.P. 1955. Some excavations at Corbridge, 1952–1954. *Archaeologia Aeliana*, 4th series, 33: 218–252.

Richmond, I.A. and Hodgson, K.S. 1934. Excavations at Castlesteads. *Transactions of the Cumberland and Westmorland Antiquarian and Archaeological Society*, 2nd series, 34: 159–165.

Ricken, H. and Fischer, C. 1963. *Die Bilderschüsseln der römischen Töpfer von Rheinzabern (Tafelband)*. Bonn: Habelt.

Robinson, M. 2002. Domestic burnt offereins and sacrifices at Roman and pre-Roman Pompeii, Italy. *Vegetaion History and Archaeobotany* 11.1: 93–100.

Rogers, G.B. 1974. *Poteries Sigillées de la Gaule Centrale I: les motifs non figurés*. *Gallia* Supplement 28.

Rogers, G.B. 1999. *Poteries Sigillées de la Gaule Centrale II: les potiers*. Premier Cahier du Centre Archéologique de Lezoux.

Rushworth, A. and Croom, A. 2016. *Segedunum: Excavations by Charles Daniels in the Roman Fort at Wallsend (1976–1984)*. Oxford: Oxbow Books.

Serneels, V. and Perret, 2003. Quantification of smithing activities based on the investigation of slag and other material remains. In Associazione Italiana di Metallurgia (ed.) *Archaeometallurgy in Europe International Conference: 24–25–26 September 2003, Milan, Italy*, 469–478. Milano: Associazione Italiana di Metallurgia.

Simpson, F.G., Hodgson, K.S. and Richmond, I.A. 1934. New turret sites on the line of the turf wall, and the type of stone wall later associated with them. *Transactions of the Cumberland and Westmorland Antiquarian and Archaeological Society*, 2nd series, 34: 120–137.

Snape, M. and Bidwell, M. 2002. Excavations at Castle Garth, Newcastle upon Tyne, 1976–92 and 1995–6: The excavation of the Roman fort. *Archaeologia Aeliana*, 5th series, 31: 1–249.

Stace, C. 2019. *New Flora of the British Isles*. 3rd ed. Suffolk: C&M Floristics.

Stanfield, J.A. and Simpson, G. 1958. *Central Gaulish Potters*. Oxford: Oxford University Press.

Stevens, C.E. 1966. *The Building of Hadrian's Wall*. Kendal: Cumberland and Westmorland Antiquarian and Archaeological Society.

Stone, P. and Brough, D. (eds) 2014. *Managing, Using and Interpreting Hadrian's Wall*. New York: Springer.

Stuijts, I. 2006. Charcoal sampling sites and procedures: practical themes from Ireland. In A. Dufraisse (ed.) *Charcoal Analysis: New Analytical Tools and Methods for Archaeology*, 25–34. British Archaeological Reports International Series 1483. Oxford: Archaeopress.

Symonds, M. 2005. The construction order of the milecastles on Hadrian's Wall. *Archaeologia Aeliana*, 5th series, 34: 67–81.

Symonds, M. 2013. Gateways or garrisons? Designing, building and manning the milecastles, In R. Collins and M. Symonds (eds) *Breaking Down Boundaries: Hadrian's Wall in the 21st century*, 53–70. *Journal of Roman Archaeology* Supplementary Series 93, Portsmouth NJ: JRA.

Symonds, M. 2019a. Design and construction of the Wall. In Collins and Symonds 2019, 29–43.

Symonds, M. 2019b. The purpose of Hadrian's Wall: The Dorothy Charlesworth Lecture delivered at the Shakespeare Centre, Kendal on 6th November 2017. *Transactions of the Cumberland and Westmorland Antiquarian and Archaeological Society*, 3rd series, 19: 97–122.

Symonds, M. 2020. *Hadrian's Wall: Creating Division*. London: Bloomsbury.

Symonds, M. and Breeze, D.J. 2016. The building of Hadrian's Wall: A reconsideration. Part 2: The central sector. *Archaeologia Aeliana*, 5th series, 45: 1–16.

Symonds, M. and Mason, D. 2009. *Frontiers of Knowledge: A Research Framework for Hadrian's Wall, part of the Frontiers of the Roman Empire World Heritage Site*. Durham: Durham County Council.

Symonds, R.P. 1992. *Rhenish Wares: Fine Dark Coloured Pottery from Gaul and Germany*. Oxford: University Committee for Archaeology.

Tait, J. 1962. The Vallum at West Denton and Heddon on the Wall. *Archaeologia Aeliana*, 4th series, 40: 142–143.

Taylor, M. 2003. No Pane No Gain. The Roman Glassmakers article no.6 with update, published online at www.theglassmakers.co.uk/archiveromanglassmakers/articles.htm. Accessed: 01/11/21.

Thorpe, W.A. 1935. *English Glass*. 3rd edition, London: Library of British Art.

Tomber, R. and Dore, J. 1998. *The National Roman Fabric Reference Collection*. London: Museum of London Archaeology Service.

Tyne & Wear Museums. 2008–2009. *Hadrian's Wall Ceramic Database*. Accessed 01/10/21 at http://collectionsprojects.org.uk/archaeology/Ceramic%20Database/introduction.html.

University of Southampton. 2014. *Roman Amphorae: a digital resource* [data-set]. York: Archaeology Data Service. https://doi.org/10.5284/1028192

van der Veen, M. 1992. *Crop Husbandry Regimes: An Archaeobotanical Study of Farming in Northern England 1000 BC – AD 500*. Sheffield: J.R. Collis Publications.

Warry, P. 2010. Legionary Tile Production in Britain. *Britannia* 41: 127–147.

Waugh, D. 2020. A Corbridge School Remembered. *Corbridge Matters* 57.

Webster, P. 1996. *Roman Samian Pottery in Britain*. CBA Practical Handbook in Archaeology 13, York: Council for British Archaeology.

Welfare, H. and Swan, V. 1995. *Roman Camps in England: The Field Archaeology*. London: RCHME.

Whitworth, A. 2000. *Hadrian's Wall: Some Aspects of its Post-Roman Influence on the Landscape*. British Archaeological Report 296, Oxford: Archaeopress.

Whitworth, A. 2012. *Hadrian's Wall Through Time*. Stroud: Amberley.

Wilmott, T. 1997. *Birdoswald: Excavations of a Roman fort on Hadrian's Wall and its successor settlements 1987–92*. London: English Heritage.

Wilmott, T. 2009a. *Hadrian's Wall: Archaeological research by English Heritage 1976–2000*, London: English Heritage.

Wilmott, T. 2009b. The Hadrian's Wall Milecastles Project: 1999–2000. In Wilmott 2009a, 137–200.

Wilmott, T. forthcoming. *The Cemetery of the Hadrian's Wall fort of Birdoswald*. Cumberland & Westmorland Antiquarian and Archaeological Society Research Series, Kendal: CWAAS.

Wilmott, T. and Bennett, J. 2009. The linear elements of the Hadrian's Wall complex: four investigations, 1983–2000. In Wilmott 2009a, 72–136.

Woodside, R. and Crow, J. 1999. *Hadrian's Wall: A Historic Landscape*. Cirencester: National Trust.

Woodward, P. and Woodward, A. 2004. Dedicating the town: Urban foundation deposits in Roman Britain. *World Archaeology* 36.1: 68–86.

Woolliscroft, D.J. 1989. Signalling and the design of Hadrian's Wall. *Archaeologia Aeliana*, 5th series, 17: 5–19.

Young, C.J. 1977. *The Roman pottery industry of the Oxford region*. British Archaeological Report 43, Oxford: Archaeopress.

Zohary, D., Hopf, M. and Weiss, E. 2012. *Domestication of Plants in the Old World*. Oxford: Oxford University Press.

Index

Numbers in *italic* denote pages with figures, those in **bold** denote pages with tables.

agriculture, impact of 164–5
aims of study 10
anatomy of the wall 5–7
animal bones 210, **211–13**, 212–14
animal sacrifice/offering 112, 159
army, Roman 7
arrowhead 157, *157*

bangle *143*, 145
beads 137, *143*, 145
berm 5, *5*
Bishop Rigg 92
Black Carts 3, *5*, *10*
bolt or spike *81*, 83–4
bonding agents 55, 64, 71, 221
Bowness 3, *4*
bracket *151*, 153
bridgeworks 6, 86–7, *87*
Broad Wall 8
brooches/brooch pins 142–4, *143*
buckle 153–4, *153*
Buddle Street, Wallsend 55
building materials and fired clay 218–25
  ceramic building material 219–20
  discussion 225
  distribution 222, **222–4**, 224–5
  fired clay 220–1
  mortar 55, 64, 71, 221
  stone 221–2, **222**
building sequence 7–9, *8*
button 157, *158*

Cam Beck *see* Wall-crossing at Cam Beck
camps 7
?candlestick 149, *150*
Carlisle 90
Carvoran 5, *5*
casting waste *155*, 156
Castlesteads 6, *7*, *57*, 58
  see also Wall-crossing at Cam Beck
Cat Stairs *10*, 225–6
ceramic building material 219–20
ceramic objects
  counters *148*, 149
  crucible 154, *155*
  weight 154, *155*
charred plant remains 203–5, **206–9**, 210
chestnut shells 85
clamp or bracket *81*, 84
coins 141–2, *142*, 157, *158*
community archaeology project 2, *2*
consolidation work 225–8
copper alloy objects
  brooch or dress accessory frag. *143*, 144
  brooches and brooch pins 142–4, *143*
  button 157, *158*
  coins 142, *142*, 157, *158*
  dress accessory frag. *143*, 145
  earring *143*, 144
  finger ring *143*, 144
  jewellery chain link/ring *143*, 144
  mounts *81*, 82, *143*, 144, *151*, 153
  pins *143*, 144, 157, *158*
  scabbard slide 145, *146*
  school badge 157, *158*
  tweezers *143*, 145
  unidentified compound object *81*, 82
  unidentified other 156–7
Corbridge, survey and excavations *10*, 89–160, *89*
  animal bones 210, **211–13**, 212–14
  archaeological background 92–3
  artefacts 139–59
    analysis by trench and context 139, **140**
    catalogue
      coins 141–2, *142*
      dress accessories 142–5, *143*

eating and drinking 146–8, *147*
fittings 150, *150–1*, 152–3
leisure 148–9, *148*
lighting 149, *150*
medical/toiletry *143*, 145
militaria 145, *145*
modern artefacts 157–8, *158*
prehistoric flint 157, *157*
production 154, *155*, 156
trade and exchange 154, *154*
transport 153–4, *153*
unidentified 156–7
discussion by category 139–41
building materials and fired clay 218–25
ceramic building material 219–20
discussion 225
distribution 222, **222–4**, 224–5
fired clay 220–1
mortar 221
stone 221–2, **222**
bulk finds (nails/structural) **214–17**, **219**
charred plant remains and wood charcoal 204, 205, **207–9**
conclusions 163
discussion 159–60, *160*
excavations 94–5
geology and topography *89*, 90–2
geophysical surveys *91–2*, 93, 94
glass 135–8
metalworking debris 205, **215**, 218, **218**
pottery 121–35
assemblage 127–9, *131*
coarse and fine wares 124–35, **124–7**
distribution 129–35, **129–30**, *131–3*
Trench 4 130–2, *132–3*, 134
Trench 5 *132*, 134–5
functional composition 129, *131*
post-Roman pottery 135, **135**
Terra Sigillata and Samian Wares 121–2, *123*
site at Corchester Playing Field 93–4
Trench 1 *92*, 95–7, *96*
contexts 176
finds and dating 97
flagged surface 95
gully 96
levelling/ demolition spread 95
occupation surface 95
pit 96, *97*
road 95
roadside ditch 95
?yard surfaces 95
Trench 2, contexts 176
Trench 3 *92*, 97–8, *98*
burnt material 97
contexts 177
finds and dating 98
floors 97–8
levelling layer 97
stone layer 97
wall foundations 97
Trench 4 *96*, 98–113, *99*
contexts 177–86
discussion 112–13
Phase 1 99–103, *100–3*
finds and dating 102
levelling layer 102
road 99–102
yard area 102
Phase 2 *103*, 104–10, *105–6*
conduit 105–6, *106*
ditches *103*, 109
finds and dating 110
flagged surface 109
house wall 108–9
pits 109
road 104–5
roadside ditch 104
smithy *103*, 107–8, *107*
structure 105
yard surfaces 106–7
Phase 3 110–12
cremation burial pit 110–12, *111*
ditches 110
finds and dating 112
surfaces 110
Trench 5 *98*, 113–21, *114*
contexts 186–93
discussion 121
Phase 1, ground surface and wall 113, 115
Phase 2 115–19, *117*
domestic annex 119
finds and dating 119
floor layer 116, 118
hearth and surface 116
oven 118, *118*
strip building foundations 115–16, *115*
trough 118–19
Phase 3 *117*, 119–21
clay floor 119–20
domestic annex 120
finds and dating 121
pits 120, *120*
Corchester Playing Field 93–4
counters 148–9, *148*
cremation burial 110–12, *111*, 159
crucible 154, *155*
curtain
bedrock
at Port Carlisle 38
at Walltown Crags 46, 53, *53*
bonding agents
absence of 55

mortar at Cam Beck 64, 71
building sequence 8, *8*, 9
collapse and tumble layers
at Cam Beck *68*, *72*, 75–6
at Walltown Crags 46–8, *47*, 49, 51, *52*, 54, *54*
other sites 55
core material
at Cam Beck 64, *64*, 71, *72*
at Port Carlisle 38, 40
at Walltown Crags 48–9, *48*
definition *1*, 5, *5*
facing stones
at Cam Beck 72
at Port Carlisle 40, 41, *41*
at Walltown Crags *48*, 49, *50–1*, 51, 53, *53*, 55
foundations/footings
at Cam Beck 71, *72*
at Port Carlisle, possible 36, *37*
at Walltown Crags 46, *47*, 49, 53–4, *53–4*, 55
post-Roman collapse and re-use 164
re-used stone 9–10, 64, 88
robber trenches, at Cam Beck *68*, 76
spoil heaps, at Walltown Crags *47*, 48, 51–3, *52*
subsoil
at Port Carlisle 41, *41*
at Walltown Crags 51, *52*
curtain investigations
geophysical survey 24–32
Drumburgh 28–32, *28–31*, 162
Thirlwall 24–8, *25–7*
survey and excavation at Port Carlisle 33–42
archaeological background 34
excavation 37–42, *37–42*
geophysical surveys 34, *35*, 36
standing remains of the Wall 36–7, *36–7*
survey and excavation at Walltown Crags 43–55
archaeological background 43–5, *43–4*
discussion 53–5
excavation 45–53, *46–53*
see also Wall-crossing at Cam Beck

Denton 4, *5*
Dere Street 159
destruction deposit 160
dimensions 8, 9, 53–4, 58, 64
ditch, wall 5, *5*
Drumburgh *29*, 31, *31*
Port Carlisle *35*, 36, 37–8
ditches, other
Corbridge
other *103*, 109, 110
roadside 95, 104
Port Carlisle 41, *41–2*
Down Hill 5–6, *6*
dress accessory fragment *143*, 145
Drumburgh
curtain geophysical survey *10*, 28–32, *28–31*, 162
fort 28, *29*, 30

earring *143*, 144
escutcheon *147*, 148
Extra-narrow Wall 9

faience bead *143*, 145
faunal remains *see* animal bones
fieldwalking, at Cam Beck 76–7, *77*
finger ring *143*, 144
fired clay 220–1
fittings *81*, 84, *150–1*, 152, 153
flint *81*, 82, 157, *157*
forts 7, 8, *8*, *57*, 58
Castlesteads 6, 7, *57*, 58
Drumburgh 28, *29*, 30
frame *150*, 152
future work 165

gates 6
geology 58–9, *89*, 90–2, 164
geophysical surveys
Corbridge *91–2*, 94
curtain at Drumburgh 28–32, *28–31*, 162
curtain at Port Carlisle 34, *35*, 36
curtain at Thirlwall 24–8, *25–7*, 162
Vallum between Heddon and Throckley 14, *14–15*
Wall-crossing at Cam Beck 62, *63*
glaciofluvial deposits 59
glass objects
bangle *143*, 145
beads 137, *143*, 145
vessel fragments 135–8, 158, *158*
window glass 137

Hadrian 8
Hadrian's Wall Community Archaeology Project (WallCAP) 2, *2*
Hadrian's Wall, history of 1
Hadrian's Wall Research Framework 2
hammerscale 205
Heddon-on-the-Wall *see* Vallum investigations at Heddon-on-the-Wall
heritage-at-risk 2, 10, *10*
hillfort 92
hinge plate *151*, 152
hinge socket *151*, 152
history of Hadrian's Wall 1
hobnails *81*, 82, **146**, *146*, **219**

inscriptions
altars (RIB 1983, 1142) 88, 92
Hadrian (RIB 1736) 8
quarrying date (RIB 1009) 9
re-use of stone (RIB 1864) 10

Intermediate Wall 8, 58, 64
Iron Age settlements 92
iron objects
 bolt or spike *81*, 83–4
 bracket *151*, 153
 buckle 153–4, *153*
 clamp or bracket *81*, 84
 escutcheon *147*, 148
 fittings *81*, 84, *150–1*, 152, 153
 hinge plate *151*, 152
 hinge socket *151*, 152
 hobnails *81*, 82, **146**, *146*, **219**
 latches 158, *158*
 mounts *151*, 152, 153
 nails *81*, 83, 84, 159, **214–15**, **219**
 quartz pebbles 85
 stake 84, *84*
 tankard hoop *147*, 148
 terret *153*, 154
 unidentified modern ?plate 84
 unidentified other 156
 unidentified structural **215–17**
 vessel rim *147*, 148

jewellery chain link/ring *143*, 144

King Arthur's Well 44–5
Kirklinton Sandstone Formation 58–9

landscapes of the Wall corridor 3–5, *3–5*, 163–4
latches 158, *158*
lead objects
 ?candlestick 149, *150*
 casting waste *155*, 156
 counter/game piece *148*, 149
 fitting *150*, 152
 frame *150*, 152
 mount *150*, 152
 plugs/seals 146–7, *147*, *150*, 152
 shank 150, *150*
 slag *155*, 156
 spindlewhorls 154, *155*
 unidentified other 156
 washer *150*, 152
 weights 154, *154*
LiDAR data 24
 curtain at Drumburgh 28, *29*
 curtain at Port Carlisle 37, *38*
 curtain at Thirlwall 21, *23*, *25*
 curtain at Walltown Crags *43*
 Vallum between Heddon and Throckley 12, *13*

metalworking 159
 casting waste *155*, 156
 hammerscale 205
 slag/debris **215**, 218, **218**
 smithy at Corbridge *103*, 107–8, *107*
methods of research 10
Milecastle 39 6, *6*
Milecastle 45 (Walltown Nick) *43*, 44, *45*
Milecastle 57 *57*, 58
Milecastle 79 34, 37
milecastles 6, *6*
Military Way 6
mortar 55, 64, 71, 221
mounts
 copper alloy *81*, 82, *143*, 144, *151*, 153
 iron *151*, 152, 153
 lead *150*, 152
 silver 150, *150*
Mucklebank Turret (44b) *10*, *43*, 45, 228

nails *81*, 83, 84, 159, **214–15**, **219**
Narrow Wall 8, 53–4

objectives of study 10

Peel Gap 227
?pendant *81*, 82–3
pestle *147*, 148
pins *143*, 144, 157, *158*
placenames 6–7, 92
plant macrofossils *see* charred plant remains
plugs/seals 146–7, *147*, *150*, 152
Port Carlisle
 consolidation work 226–7
 curtain survey and excavation *10*, 33–42
  archaeological background 34
  conclusions 162
  contexts 194–6
  excavation 37–42, *37–42*
  geophysical surveys 34, *35*, 36
  standing remains of the Wall 36–7, *36–7*
pottery
 Corbridge, survey and excavations 121–35
  assemblage 127–9, *131*
  coarse and fine wares 124–35, **124–7**
  distribution 129–35, **129–30**, *131–3*
   Trench 4 130–2, *132–3*, 134
   Trench 5 *132*, 134–5
  functional composition 129, *131*
  post-Roman pottery 135, **135**
  Terra Sigillata and Samian Wares 121–2, *123*
 Wall-crossing at Cam Beck 78–9, **78–9**
prehistoric enclosure 26–7, *26–7*, 28

quartz pebbles 85

radiocarbon dates
 Cam Beck 69, 70, 74
 Corbridge
  conduit 106

cremation burial 111
hearth 116
pit 120
roadside ditch 104
surface 115
trough 119
Heddon-on-the-Wall 19, 161
RIB 1009 9
RIB 1142 92
RIB 1736 8
RIB 1864 10
RIB 1983 88
ridge and furrow
Corbridge *92*, 93, 94
Drumburgh *29*, 31, *31*, 32
roads 93, 159
robbing *see* curtain, re-used stone; curtain, robber trenches
Roman army 7

scabbard slide 145, *146*
scholarship, previous 1–2
school badge 157, *158*
Septimius Severus 9
settlement patterns 92, 164
shank 150, *150*
silver objects
coins 141, *142*
mount 150, *150*
slag *155*, 156, **215**, 218, **218**
smoothers *155*, 156
spindlewhorls 154, *155*
stake 84, *84*
Stanegate system 7
Steel Rigg *10*, 227
stone building materials 221–2, **222**
stone objects
?pendant *81*, 82–3
arrowhead 157, *157*
counters 148–9, *148*
drill, flint 157, *157*
flint flakes *81*, 82, 157, *157*
pestle *147*, 148
smoothers *155*, 156
whetstone 80, *81*
Stone Wall 5, 8–9, *8*
structure of the wall 5–7
Sycamore Gap 55

tankard hoop *147*, 148
tavern 159
terminology 5–7
terret *153*, 154
Thirlwall, curtain geophysical survey *10*, 24–8, *25–7*, 162
threats to the Wall 10
Throckley *see* Vallum investigations
topography
of Corbridge *89*, 90–2
of curtain at Thirlwall 24, 25–6, *26*
importance of 163
of Vallum between Heddon and Throckley 14, *15*
towers *66*, *68*, 72, 85, 86, *86–7*
towns *see* Carlisle; Corbridge
tumble layers *see* curtain, collapse and tumble layers
Turf Wall 5, 8, *8*
at Cam Beck 65, *68–9*, 85, *86*
at Drumburgh 32
Turrets 11a & 11b 12, 14
Turret 44b (Mucklebank) *10*, *43*, 45, 228
Turret 48b *6*
Turret 56b 32, *57*, 58, 62
turrets 6, *6*, 9
tweezers *143*, 145
Tyne-Solway isthmus 7
Tyneside 4

unidentified objects
copper alloy *81*, 82, 156–7
iron objects 156
iron ?plate 84
iron structural **215–17**
lead 156
urban defences 159–60

Vallum 5–6, *6*, 8, 12, 22–3, 33
Vallum investigations at Heddon-on-the-Wall *10*, 12–23
archaeological background 12, *13*, 14
artefacts 21
charred plant remains and wood charcoal 204, 205, **209**
conclusions 161, 164
discussion 21–3
excavation 16–21, *16–18*
north mound 20–1, *20–2*
south mound 21, *22*
Vallum ditch 19–20, *19–20*
geophysical and topographical surveys 14, *14–15*
vessel fragments
glass 135–8, 158, *158*
iron rim *147*, 148
tankard hoop *147*, 148

Wall-crossing at Cam Beck *2*, *10*, 56–88
archaeological background 57–8, *57*
artefacts 79–85
analysis by trench and context 80, **80**
catalogue *81*
agricultural 84
dress accessories 82–3
fittings 82
militaria 82
structural 83–4, *84*
tools 80

uncertain/other 82, 85
discussion by category 80
beck, course of 57, 59
charred plant remains **206**
charred plant remains and wood charcoal 204–5
conclusions 162–3
condition survey of Cam Beck Gorge 59–62
stonework associated with the weir 60–2, *61–2*, **201–3**
weir 59–60, *59–60*
excavation Trenches 1 & 3 64, *64*
contexts 166–7, 175
excavation Trench 2 *63*, 65–76, *66*
bridge tower *66*, *68*, 72, *87*
bridge tower robber trenches 71, 73
contexts 167–74
ramp or steps base 73, *87*
Stone Wall 71, *72*
Stone Wall robber trenches *68*, 76
Stone Wall tumble *68*, *72*, 75–6
Structure 2 and related deposits *72–5*, 73–5
subsoils 74, 76
Turf Wall and associated building (Structure 1) 65, *67–70*, 68–9
Turf Wall and Structure 1 demolition 69–71, *70*
weir stone? 75, *75*
fieldwalking 76–7, *77*
geology and subsoils 58–9
geophysical surveys 62, *63*
pottery 78–9, **78–9**
Wall sequence and discussion 85–8, *86–7*
Wall-mile 11 12, 14
Wall-mile 37 3, *4*
Wall-mile 44 44–5
Wall-miles 6–7
WallCAP 2, *2*
Wallsend 55
Walltown Crags
collapse of the curtain 164
consolidation work 228
curtain survey and excavation *1*, *10*, 43–55
archaeological background 43–5, *43–4*
conclusions 162
contexts 196–200
discussion 53–5
excavation 45–53, *46–53*
Warden Hill 92
washer *150*, 152
watchtowers 85
see also towers
weights 154, *154*, *155*
weir 59–60, *59–60*
whetstone 80, *81*
Willowford Farm 6, *6*
window glass 137
wood charcoal *see* charred plant remains
Written Rock of Gelt (RIB 1009) 9